THE SECOND CONSTITUTIONAL CONVENTION

How The American People Can Take Back Their Government

Richard Labunski

Marley and Beck Press
Versailles

Publisher's Cataloging-in-Publication
(*Provided by Quality Books, Inc.*)

Labunski, Richard E.
    The second constitutional convention: how the American people can take back their government / Richard Labunski. -- 1st ed.
    p. cm.
    Includes bibliographical references and index.
    LCCN: 99-69250
    ISBN: 0-9677498-7-5

    1. Constitutional law -- United States.
    2. United States -- Politics and government -- 1993-
    3. Constitutional conventions.   I. Title

KF4552.L33 2000   342.73'02
                 QB199-1938

Interior Design and composition by Publishing Professionals, New Port Richey, FL.

For Elisa

Acknowledgments

Several people have been extremely helpful during the preparation of this book, and I offer them my heartfelt thanks. My copy editor, Judith Margolis, who brought a legal background and strong editing skills to the project, worked conscientiously to improve the manuscript during its early stages. My colleague in the School of Journalism and Telecommunications at the University of Kentucky, Professor Karla Salmon Robinson, spent countless hours with a sharp eye and aggressive pen editing, praising and criticizing the manuscript, all of which significantly improved it. Her husband, Tony Robinson, who knows more about computers than any one person should, helped with many of the technology issues in the book. Mike Farrell, a teacher and Ph.D. student in the School, showed in every page the experience that comes from having been an accomplished newspaper editor for many years. Another colleague, Professor Maria Braden, was kind enough to read several early chapters and make useful suggestions.

I am grateful for the help of everyone named here, but nothing compares to what my wife, Elisa, has contributed to this project from the days when it was little more than my talking about what is wrong with our political system. She has read every word of the manuscript through multiple drafts. She has heard my ideas, offered her own, made suggestions for organizing the book, and helped in too many ways to list here. I dedicate this book to her with my love and gratitude.

Finally, I would like to acknowledge the contribution that a special person made to my career and interest in politics and law. I had the privilege of studying with the late Professor C. Herman Pritchett (1907–1995) while completing an M.A. and Ph.D. in political science at the University of California, Santa Barbara, from 1976–1979. He was the chairperson of my Ph.D. committee and my dissertation committee, and I was his teaching assistant for several years. Professor Pritchett was one of the leading constitutional scholars of his era, and through his writing and teaching, he inspired thousands of students at the University of Chicago and later at UCSB. His quiet and unassuming manner may have reflected his modesty, but it only added to the deep affection with which he was held by his students and colleagues. Professor Pritchett would probably not approve of a second constitutional convention, but I know he would have found the idea intriguing.

Author's Note

This book explains why the American people should hold a second constitutional convention and how they can organize it. A Second Convention Web site has been established to provide additional and updated information about this effort. The Web site also has links to important information about the Constitution, its Framers, and American legal history. The address is: <www.secondconvention.org>.

Article V, United States Constitution

The Congress, whenever two thirds of both houses shall deem it necessary, shall propose amendments to this Constitution, or, on the application of the Legislatures of two thirds of the several States, shall call a convention for proposing amendments, which, in either case, shall be valid to all intents and purposes, as part of this Constitution, when ratified by the Legislatures of three fourths of the several States, or by conventions in three fourths thereof, as the one or the other mode of ratification may be proposed by the Congress; provided that no amendment which may be made prior to the Year One thousand eight hundred and eight shall in any manner affect the first and fourth Clauses in the Ninth Section of the first Article; and that no State, without its consent, shall be deprived of its equal suffrage in the Senate.

Table of Contents

Part IV

Appendix

Foreword

by John Anderson
Member, U.S. House of Representatives (1960–1980)
Independent presidential candidate (1980)

𝕌his book has the potential to change our political system.

That is a bold statement, but if people read *The Second Constitutional Convention* and follow the plan outlined in it, politics in this country will never be the same.

With meticulous research and a lucid style that engages and challenges the reader, Professor Richard Labunski has provided overwhelming evidence that our political system is in trouble. He has also devised an unprecedented and controversial solution to make government more accountable.

Never before in the nation's history has money played such a pervasive role in politics. Candidates are raising staggering amounts and spending millions to stay in office. Much of that money comes from special interests that want something in return. With their campaign coffers overflowing with contributions, candidates inundate voters with political commercials, many of them attack ads that intentionally distort the opponent's record or background. Many Americans are understandably turned off by such tactics, and they show it by refusing to vote.

During the 20 years that I served in the U.S. House of Representatives, I saw all too often the influence that donors and money can have on Congress and its agenda. While running for president as an independent candidate against well-funded opponents, I discovered that candidates had to spend almost as much time raising money as talking about issues. The influence of money has grown dramatically since then.

Professor Labunski explains the complex system of "hard" and "soft" money contributions and recommends a solution in the form of an innovative amendment. If it ever becomes part of the Constitution, it will drastically alter the way elected officials are chosen.

But *The Second Constitutional Convention* does more than highlight campaign finance abuses. It also provides a blueprint for using Internet technology to organize a series of meetings leading to the calling of a convention. Professor Labunski explains in easy-to-understand terms how such technology works and how those interested in joining the effort to hold a convention can connect to the Internet. Although the Internet is already a communicative tool in politics, no one has suggested using the technology to arrange a constitutional convention.

This book combines the richness of academic scholarship with a detailed knowledge of contemporary politics. Professor Labunski examines the records of the Constitutional Convention of 1787 as the Framers debated how the Constitution should be amended. By choosing a system that makes it easy for a few legislators in a handful of states to defeat an amendment that most Americans want approved, the Framers all but guaranteed that the Constitution would become outdated. As Professor Labunski argues, relying only on the courts to keep the Constitution relevant will not solve the most challenging problems facing our political system.

The Second Constitutional Convention is as informative as it is stimulating. The proposed constitutional amendments should lead to vigorous debate. Some of them are probably going to be popular while others will generate strong opposition. Either way, they will encourage average citizens and scholars alike to consider how the Constitution could be changed.

The idea of a second convention will disturb a lot of people. After all, we have had only one such convention in our history. But whether one agrees with Professor Labunski, everyone who reads this book will think more seriously about the difficult issues we face in this new century.

Introduction

𝕯isappointment, disillusionment, and distrust are words that many Americans would use today to describe their feelings about politics and government. Probably at no time in our history have national and local political leaders and institutions been held in such low regard. Even with the strong economy of the last decade, when most people have never been better off, there is a deepening cynicism about politics. Voter turnout continues to decline as more people believe that elected officials are willing to sell their votes to anyone offering large campaign contributions.

The past few years have provided many reasons to be discouraged about politics. During the 1996 campaign, convicted felons were invited to the White House to meet President Clinton during fund-raising coffees, while major contributors purchased an evening in the Lincoln Bedroom. After the election, the nation was inundated with the sordid details of the president's sexual relationship with a young intern and accusations that he molested a former White House aide. When he lied about the sexual relationship before a federal grand jury and in a sworn deposition in a civil suit, the country was forced to endure a wrenching impeachment trial.

The scandals were not limited to inappropriate personal behavior. While the president was being impeached, independent counsels were investigating five current or former Clinton cabinet members. At the same time, close friends and associates of the president faced criminal prosecution and several served prison terms.

The White House should not get all of the blame for convincing the American people that something is seriously wrong with politics in this country. During the last half of the decade, Congress provided a textbook lesson in how partisanship and personal animosity toward the president can lead to stalemate and indecision. Congress did not merely fail to enact legislation dealing with urgent national problems such as health care; it continued to shamelessly waste the taxpayers' money. News stories about careless spending were in the media almost constantly: billion-dollar road improvement projects where there is no traffic; office buildings, day care centers and other facilities that cost millions to build, but were never completed or cannot be used; a $50 billion tax break for tobacco companies slipped quietly into a massive spending bill. The list could go on and on.

Such actions year after year should result in a substantial turnover among members of Congress as voters rise up in anger. But with the overwhelming advantages of incumbency — the ability to raise huge sums of money and name recognition from mailings and media appearances — few members of Congress are held accountable for their voting record or the quality of their work. In 2000, as in the last few decades, 95 percent of incumbents will probably be reelected. Perhaps no more than two dozen races for House seats — about five percent of the 435 up for election — will be competitive. In the remaining 95 percent of districts, incumbents will likely defeat underfunded challengers who never had much of a chance of winning.

No one should be surprised that voter turnout continues to decline as more citizens say they are not interested in politics. In 1996, half of the voting-age population did not bother to cast a ballot even though the country was electing a president. In the off-year congressional election in 1998, only about a third voted. Despite laws that have made it easy for anyone to register, and for those who could not get to a polling place to vote by mail, turnout continued to fall. The future looks bleak in this regard because the participation rate of young people age 18–24 is abysmal, with often no more than 30 percent voting. Without having learned the importance of voting from either parents or teachers, many will remain aloof and uninformed for the rest of their lives.

The 2000 presidential election may only add to frustration about politics. Even though there were many people inside and outside of government who had the potential to be successful presidents, campaign money — or the lack of it — forced the American people to again choose among only a few candidates. Months before the first caucus in Iowa and the first primary in New Hampshire, candidates with impressive experience and attributes dropped out of the race for the nomination because they could not raise anywhere near the amount of money donated to Republican Governor George W. Bush of Texas, and the personal fortune of businessman Steve Forbes. It is impossible to know how many Republicans, Democrats, and third-party candidates with innovative approaches to the nation's problems decided not to run because they could not raise enough money.

Explaining how America can be the world's most advanced democracy when so many of its citizens despise politics and public officials is not easy. Millions of people around the world who live under repressive governments — where they can only dream of free elections — would be appalled if they knew how indifferent Americans are about the right to choose their representatives. The failure of so many people to participate in the governance of their communities, states, and nation strikes at the heart of a democracy that depends on a well-informed and active electorate. Many Americans have, however, found a convenient excuse for their failure to learn about candidates and to vote. They say that by refusing to participate, they are "making a statement" about the sad state of contemporary politics that is, of course, always someone else's fault.

It is not hard to understand why some people are discouraged about politics. The way campaigns are financed is enough to demoralize anyone. As increasing amounts of money pour into campaigns, it becomes more difficult to run competitive races and almost impossible to defeat incumbents who raise money so easily. Incumbents quickly realize that if they want to stay in office, they are better off serving the interests of those who contributed to the last campaign and who will offer money for the next than worrying too much about what the folks back home think. Corporations, unions, political parties, and almost every group that wants something from the government know how to get around campaign finance laws. They support incumbents who understand how to show gratitude. Members of Congress and state legislators know their constituents rarely find out about the laws they quietly enact that bestow monetary benefits on donors. If the voters do hear about such laws, they are likely to forget the details when the incumbent unleashes an avalanche of television advertising during the campaign for reelection.

Contributors say they are merely supporting the best people to lead the country, but they often get a lot in return for their money. Their reward is access to the nation's most powerful legislators and other government officials. Donors meet public officials in committee meetings and in their offices, at parties and restaurants, and at such desirable places as ski lodges and Caribbean resorts. Contributors do not mind paying the cost of sending members of Congress and their families to warm-weather locales in the dead of winter because the special tax breaks, government contracts, and other benefits they get in return make it worth the investment. Meanwhile, advocates for underfunded but worthy public causes, who have not paid for such access, rarely get to see the representative or senator in a relaxed setting where they can tell them at length about legislation they support or oppose.

Being so beholden to special interests and ignoring the needs of constituents should be the fastest way out of office. But in this era in which candidates in contested House races may spend more than $2 million combined, and many millions of dollars are spent in Senate elections, incumbents are able to easily raise money from organizations that come under the jurisdiction of their committees and from other sources that give them a huge advantage in seeking reelection. Challengers will often barely acquire enough campaign funds to get their name out to the public and rarely get the chance to discuss the incumbent's voting record in detail. Incumbents can also easily raise thousands of dollars during nonelection years when no challengers are running. The larger the incumbent's campaign fund, the more likely potential challengers will be discouraged from entering the race. With money pouring into incumbents' coffers almost every day, it is not surprising that they almost always raise many times the amount their opponents do, and are almost always reelected.

The system works so well for those who benefit from it that there will be no serious campaign finance reform anytime soon. Despite the loathing that many citizens and even some elected officials have for a system that requires spending as much time raising money as legislating, there is little incentive for members of Congress to approve changes that make them more vulnerable to challengers. As long as voters do not hold them accountable, there is no reason for incumbents to restrict contributions that flow through a giant loophole in the campaign finance laws allowing any individual or organization to contribute *unlimited* sums of money to support or oppose candidates.

Congress has the authority, although obviously not the will, to reform campaign finance laws when it comes to contributions to candidates, parties, and independent groups. But it cannot do anything about how much can be spent in a campaign. That is because of *Buckley v. Valeo*, a pernicious 1976 Supreme Court decision that mistakenly concluded that expenditure limits violate the First Amendment. As a result of the Court's action, limiting expenditures would require a constitutional amendment or a reversal by the Court, neither of which is likely to happen in the near future. The absence of spending limits has a direct effect on contributions. Because candidates can spend as much money as they want, they will raise as much money as they can.

The political crisis has reached the point where drastic action is required. If the American people are going to make their government more responsive and accountable, they must change the way elected officials are chosen. They will not be able to bring about such fundamental change by trying to elect candidates who support reform in the hope they will defeat a few incumbents. Even if idealistic challengers were elected, many of them would find that being in office is more appealing than they had thought, and they would quickly become part of the same system they had promised to renovate.

Instead, the American people must begin the long process — one that would be unprecedented in the nation's history — of trying to organize a second constitutional convention. Although there have been political movements that required sacrifice over a long period of time to bring about reform, no individuals or organizations have ever seriously considered an undertaking such as the one recommended in this book.

The Constitution has been amended 27 times in its 212-year history. Congress proposed all of the amendments as provided under Article V, the section of the Constitution establishing procedures for the proposing and ratification of amendments. There is, however, another section of Article V — unknown to the average citizen — that requires Congress to call a constitutional convention if a sufficient number of state legislatures petition for it. The American people must dedicate themselves to forcing their elected officials to schedule such a convention if they are to reclaim their government from those who are no longer answerable through the ordinary processes of a representative democracy.

The Framers of the Constitution devoted relatively little time during the summer of 1787 to discussing how the great document should be amended and, in fact, hastily finalized the wording of Article V in the closing days of the Convention. As they did in many important sections of the Constitution, the Framers sought to create a system that would both respond to *and* resist the will of the people. They wanted to prevent frequent alteration of the Constitution and thus required supermajorities for the proposal and ratification of amendments. Unfortunately, the Framers miscalculated and not only made it too difficult to amend the Constitution, they failed to provide a method by which amendments could be initiated directly by the people.

There is great irony in the decision of the Framers not to allow the American people to directly propose amendments to the Constitution. The task of ratifying the new Constitution was given not to state legislatures, but to state conventions whose delegates would be chosen by the people and whose sole purpose would be to consider the Constitution. The Framers believed that if the new nation's founding charter was "ordained" by the people, it would have a legitimacy that would otherwise be lacking. But once the document was so ordained, the people would not be permitted to propose amendments to the new Constitution without first getting the approval of their representatives. Just as the Framers did not trust the people to directly elect the president or senators, and permitted the states to limit voting privileges to those who owned property and had other qualifications, they wanted to make it extremely difficult for anyone to tamper with the document they created in Philadelphia.

The text of the Constitution provides no evidence that the Framers anticipated the type of political crisis the country is facing at the beginning of the 21st Century. They expected that Congress, and especially the House — with election directly by citizens for two-year terms — would

implement the values and needs of the people in laws and policy decisions. Yet, as will be seen in various sections of this book, those members
of Congress who openly defy their constituents and brazenly serve the
narrow interests of contributors are not held accountable at the polls. Because those are the very individuals who have the sole authority to change
the system — through campaign finance reform and other initiatives —
but refuse to do so, the American people have no place to turn. The Constitution, as currently written, offers no solution. In fact, if the Supreme
Court was correct in *Buckley*, the Constitution impedes reform because it
does not permit laws regulating campaign expenditures, a crucial piece of
the campaign finance system that must be changed if elections are to be
more competitive and elected officials more accountable.

If the people use Article V to push for a constitutional convention,
they will not get help from their elected officials in Washington or their
state capitals in starting the process. Instead, the American people must
organize a series of meetings all over the country to generate publicity and
interest in their cause, and to develop petitions that can be taken to state
legislators to convince them to request a second convention.

Holding the meetings and writing petitions that will form the basis of
proposed constitutional amendments will be difficult enough. The next
phase — convincing state legislators to petition Congress — will be
daunting. Few people in this country can identify their member of the
U.S. House of Representatives and both of their state's U.S. senators. An
even smaller number know who their state legislators are and most know
nothing about their voting record. The challenge is to educate the public
and convince state legislators — many of whom will naturally be hesitant
to request a convention — that the only way the American people can take
back their government is for the legislators to courageously demand that
Congress call one.

This book proposes that through new communication technology
such as the Internet, and more traditional forms of mass media, the
American people can organize a series of meetings — beginning at the
congressional district or county level, then moving on to a state convention, and finally culminating in a national "preconvention" in Washington, D.C. — where petitions can be written to give to state legislators.
The petitions will propose a subject area for a constitutional amendment
and will ask legislators to forward them to Congress. There is no precedent in American history for citizens on their own to try to organize a
constitutional convention. Prior to the Internet, such an undertaking
would have been almost impossible.

The meetings proposed in this book are not authorized by any
governmental body and are thus a fulfillment of the highest principles of

democracy. The American people, not their elected officials, will decide how they will be conducted and what they will produce.

People who are part of the process will be able to communicate through a Second Convention Web site that provides information about activities in each state and links to important documents related to the Constitution and the founding of the nation. While citizens discuss and debate the issues and get involved in the various stages of the process, they can learn about the Constitution and the way it has been interpreted by the courts.

This book is divided into four sections. Part I explains why a second convention is necessary and includes a detailed discussion of abuses of the campaign finance system during the last few years. It also includes a review of the work of writers, commentators, and scholars who have recommended changes in the Constitution. The final chapter in Part I argues that the United States cannot continue to rely almost exclusively on the courts — with an occasional new amendment proposed by Congress — to keep a document written over two centuries ago relevant to today's complex society.

Part II offers specifics on how the three meetings — the congressional district/county meeting, state convention, and national preconvention — can be organized. An important section of Part II is devoted to how the Internet can facilitate the exchange of information that is essential to making the process work. There is also discussion of how the courts are likely to rule in cases that arise from efforts to hold the convention.

Part III is devoted to 10 proposed constitutional amendments. These amendments can be discussed at the initial meetings and eventually at a second convention. Those attending the meetings and convention will undoubtedly have other ideas on how the Constitution should be changed. The amendment chapters demonstrate how complex constitutional law and policy issues can be and how important it is to carefully consider the consequences of altering the Constitution.

The amendments considered in this book range from proposals that may enjoy substantial support — such as campaign finance reform and a crime victims' bill of rights — to more controversial amendments such as the repeal of the Second Amendment, which many people believe protects private ownership of guns.

Part IV is the final chapter. It considers whether the amendments proposed in this book satisfy the guidelines offered by an organization of former public officials and legal scholars who believe the Constitution should be altered only for extraordinary reasons. The chapter concludes by discussing what can be done if no convention is held.

This call for a second constitutional convention will generate strong opposition. Many people will think such an idea is not only naïve but dangerous. But no matter how the critics explain their position, there can be only one argument against holding such a convention: that the American people cannot be trusted to participate in a national discussion about the political health of their nation, and then use Article V to organize a second convention to propose amendments to the Constitution.

There is understandable concern that groups with extreme views would try to dominate the process and seize the opportunity to change the Constitution to the detriment of the great majority of citizens. On the few occasions when a second convention has been discussed, some people worried that such a gathering would be a "runaway" convention that, if given the opportunity, would repeal the Bill of Rights and other sections of the Constitution. The Framers in Philadelphia took care of that potential problem. As required by Article V, and as with amendments offered by Congress, any amendment proposed by a constitutional convention must be ratified by three-fourths of state legislatures or state conventions. This requirement ensures that there will be an opportunity during the long state-by-state ratification process to debate the proposed amendments. Even if the convention proposed radical amendments, they would not likely be approved by the states.

The concern that one side of the political spectrum or the other might try to misuse the process cannot justify discouraging the American people from undertaking this effort. At no point during the planning and holding of the meetings leading to the writing of the petitions, and the taking of those petitions to state legislators, can anyone argue that the endeavor is contrary to democratic principles.

People have the right to gather in their county or congressional district to discuss public issues with their fellow citizens. They can talk about a candidate they want to support or oppose, or how to reduce crime in their neighborhood. No one could argue that those attending such a meeting should not be allowed to talk about what is wrong with the Constitution and how it should be changed.

There also cannot be any dispute over whether people at the first meeting have the right to choose some of their fellow citizens to travel to the state capital to represent them in discussions with others around the state. When the statewide convention meets, the delegates cannot be criticized for identifying the sections of the Constitution most in need of revision and debating how those changes can be accomplished. Citizens already have the authority to choose their elected officials who run the government. They certainly have the right to discuss the Constitution.

Finally, the statewide meeting selects delegates to a national pre-convention. After thoroughly exploring how the Constitution should be amended, the national meeting in Washington will write petitions that go to state legislators. The First Amendment explicitly protects the right of the people to "petition the government for a redress of grievances." If 34 states approve and forward those petitions to Congress, Article V takes over.

Anyone contending that a second convention should not be held has to find a point in the process described here where the American people would have done something unlawful or wrong. The idea of a convention cannot be rejected simply because some may not like its possible outcome. Such an argument shows a fundamental misunderstanding of the role of the people in a self-governing society. It is, after all, *their* Constitution.

The delegates who attended the Philadelphia Convention, the courageous individuals who worked so hard to ensure the Constitution's ratification, the members of the First Congress who were persuaded by James Madison to approve the amendments that eventually became the Bill of Rights, all deserve the nation's enduring admiration and gratitude. But the Constitution does not belong to James Madison or others of his era. Today's generation is not forever bound by decisions made over two centuries ago. It must use the wisdom and experience that comes from more than 200 years of governing to make changes to the country's national charter that will strengthen democratic processes. The Constitution must not be altered casually and the amendments proposed by a second convention must be thoroughly debated. But the Constitution was never intended to endure forever without change, and it is in desperate need of repair.

The three meetings leading to the effort to convince state legislators to petition Congress for a second convention, and the convention itself, may never be held. It would be unrealistic for anyone to believe that as soon as people have access to this book and its related Web site, they will make immediate plans to hold the first meeting. If political cynicism has spread so deeply that millions of Americans have stopped learning about politics and do not care much about what their government does, they will not be committed to the long process of pressuring their leaders to hold a convention.

On the other hand, those who have become disengaged from civic affairs may find that participation at the meetings and through the Internet will revitalize their interest in politics and government. They may be inspired to take a direct role in revising their nation's founding document. They could join those who are politically active and want to participate in formulating the proposed amendments. If nothing else, perhaps those who had been turned off to politics will be so worried about others trying to change the Constitution, they will want to be involved just to prevent such an effort from succeeding.

Thomas Jefferson, who was in Paris during the Constitutional Convention, wrote many years later that the Constitution should be revised every generation or so, which based on Jefferson's formula for how long a certain percentage of the population would live, was around 20 years. Although some Founders, including Madison, did not believe that holding frequent conventions was a good idea, they probably would be surprised we have had only one federal constitutional convention in our entire history. With Jefferson's blessing, and with the help of modern communication technology, it is time for the nation to have its second convention.

Part 1

CHAPTER ONE

Why A Second Constitutional Convention is Needed

In the spring and summer of 1787, delegates from 12 of the 13 states traveled to Philadelphia to attend this nation's only federal constitutional convention. The Framers were some of the most distinguished citizens of the new republic including George Washington, Benjamin Franklin, and James Madison. Many of the 55 delegates had extensive political experience in colonial and state government. Forty-four were or had been members of the Continental Congress. Eight had signed the Declaration of Independence, while six penned their names to the Articles of Confederation. Thirty-five were lawyers or had legal training.

To say that the delegates faced formidable challenges would be a huge understatement. Just getting to the Convention over rugged dirt roads with bone-jarring holes was extremely difficult. Many of the roads were impassable in the rain, there were never enough bridges, ferries, or decent inns, and stage coaches were slow, uncomfortable, and dangerous. On the best routes with good weather, travelers might be able to go 50 miles in one day, but more often they were lucky to cover half that distance. Some of the 19 delegates who were selected by their state legislatures to attend the Convention chose instead to stay home because they could not endure weeks of traveling under such conditions.

The Convention was scheduled to meet at the State House in Philadelphia on May 14, 1787, but representatives from only two states — Virginia and Pennsylvania — were present on that day. It took until May 25 for a quorum to be formed. New Hampshire's delegates were the last to arrive, on July 23, two months after the Convention began its work. Although they faced additional weeks of arduous travel, some of the delegates attended the Convention for a period of time, went home to tend to business and personal affairs, and later returned. There were never 55 delegates in Philadelphia at the same time.

Not only was transportation prehistoric by today's standards, communication was also primitive. Although they met mostly as a group, the Convention divided the work among several committees that had responsibility for various sections of the new Constitution. However, without computers with word processing programs, there was no easy way to assemble the drafts of the committees into a complete document that could then be reviewed by the entire Convention. The Constitution runs some 7,500 words. Making copies of the work of the committees was onerous and time-consuming. Although the delegates agreed to keep their discussions and deliberations secret — which turned out to have been a significant factor in the Convention's success — they probably would have liked to consult with officials back home, but no telephones or e-mail were available.

Once at work at the State House in Philadelphia, the delegates made courageous decisions, but some of those judgments guaranteed that winning ratification of the new Constitution would be difficult. The first fundamental issue was resolved almost without discussion: Throw out the unworkable Articles of Confederation. The Articles, which had been adopted by the Second Continental Congress in 1777, but were not ratified until 1781, proved to be woefully inadequate for the task of creating a new republic. The confederation government — what there was of it — consisted of a weak, unicameral legislature in which each state, regardless of population, had one vote. There was no executive branch, no method by which to compel the states to pay the money they owed so the national government could carry out its functions, and most importantly, an unattainable requirement that all 13 states give their approval before the Articles could be amended.

There is substantial evidence indicating that many of the delegates chosen for the Philadelphia Convention knew in advance that the Articles had to be replaced and not simply revised. Still, that would probably have been a surprise to at least some members of Congress. In February 1787, after eight states appointed delegates to the meeting that would eventually be held in Philadelphia, Congress agreed to a convention for the "sole and express purpose of revising the Articles of Confederation." But even Congress recognized that many influential people believed the confederation government was not working. There had been an effort to hold a convention in Annapolis, Maryland, in September 1786, in order to deal with the problems of the Confederation, but only five states sent delegates. Until delegates began arriving in Philadelphia, there was understandable concern that this convention would also fail.

Madison and the other six members of the Virginia delegation arrived in Philadelphia on May 13th. That they were able to meet every day to develop the "Virginia Resolutions," also known as the "Virginia Plan," while waiting for a convention quorum to form is one of the most fortuitous events in the nation's history. The plan did not attempt to strengthen congressional powers or make other changes to save the beleaguered Articles of Confederation. The resolutions proposed a bold plan for a new central government that would be both *federal* — in that it would preserve the autonomy of the states and respond to their interests — and *national* — in that it would act directly against and derive its powers from the people and thus be supreme to the states in the constitutional hierarchy. One historian noted that in reaction to the Virginia Plan, "several delegates were rudely jolted by the daring scope of these 'preliminary propositions.'" Among the most controversial of the proposals was the sixth resolution dealing with the powers of the new national legislature. Madison insisted on the right of the new federal Congress to veto *all* laws passed by state legislatures that interfered with the national constitution. As presented by Governor Edmund Randolph of Virginia to the Convention on May 29, the resolution stated that the new federal legislature would be able to "negative all laws passed by the several States, contravening in the opinion of the National Legislature the articles of the Union."

Many historians credit Madison with being the "Father of the Constitution" partly based on his role in drafting the Virginia Plan. He never claimed to be *the* author of the Virginia Resolutions, and there are no surviving records from the daily meetings of the Virginia delegation to indicate how much of the document reflected his ideas. Madison was at the time considered Virginia's leading expert on federal issues, and all of the key provisions in the Virginia Resolutions were reflected in his preconvention writings. Although not all of the provisions in the Virginia Resolutions were adopted — the Convention rejected Madison's call for the veto power of Congress — the Resolutions did more than provide the basis for discussion by the delegates in the first weeks of the Convention. They did nothing less than lead them to abandon the confederation by offering a plan that would form the core of the new Constitution.

Throughout the summer, the Framers discussed, debated, and as would be expected, argued over the structure of the new government. Among the most difficult issues to be resolved were how large and small states would be represented in the new Congress; what powers the new legislative and executive branches would exercise; whether slavery would be permitted to continue in the South and be extended to new territories; and, in the final days of the Convention, whether the Constitution should have a bill of rights. Those issues were hard enough to work out in isolation, but the Framers knew that the wrong choice on any one of these difficult questions could disrupt the delicate balance that would become the primary feature of the new Constitution: a system of government that would respond to the wishes of the people, and at the same time, resist majority will when it was ill-conceived or shortsighted, or abridged the rights of numerical minorities.

Some of the Framers did not think much of the ability of the American people to govern themselves. Several made comments that no contemporary political figure would dare utter. Massachusetts' Elbridge Gerry said, "The evils we experience flow from the excess of democracy." Pennsylvania's Gouverneur Morris stated that "The people never act from reason alone . . . [but are the] dupes of those who have more knowledge." New York's Alexander Hamilton added that "the people seldom judge or determine right." But others, like Madison and George Mason of Virginia, and James Wilson and Benjamin Franklin of Pennsylvania, had more confidence in the people's ability to govern the new nation. Despite Morris's condescending statement, he and Wilson were apparently the only delegates who supported direct election of the president by the people.

As the summer wore on, the burdens of the work took their toll on the delegates. Some departed in disgust before the Convention ended. Others, like George Mason, the author of the Virginia Bill of Rights, stayed until the end but refused to sign the finished document, saying that he "would sooner chop off his right hand than put it to the Constitution as it now stands." He was especially distraught over the lack of a bill of rights, and he called for a new convention to create a constitution that would more explicitly protect civil liberties. Governor Randolph and Elbridge Gerry also refused to sign the Constitution, although Randolph later worked diligently on behalf of ratification and was influential in convincing the Virginia ratifying convention to approve the Constitution, which it did by a narrow margin.

Despite all the obstacles they had to overcome, and all the decisions that had to be made without knowing how they would affect the delicate distribution of power within the new government, and without being able to predict how the people would react to the new Constitution, the Framers produced a remarkable document. They created a complex system with enough checks and balances so that no branch of government could dominate the others. Each branch is viable and independent. The Framers were able to establish institutions of government that, with some notable exceptions in our history, have been able to respond to *and* resist the democratic impulses of the people. Although sometimes frustratingly vague, the Constitution has provided fundamental principles that have endured throughout the nation's history while allowing each generation some flexibility — through the court system and infrequent amendments — to shape it to reflect changing conditions.

But something has gone wrong. The Constitution is in need of serious repair. Even with its features that provide for self-correction when political institutions are unresponsive to the people, the Constitution can be stretched only so far. The problems are so extensive that neither judicial "amending" of the Constitution through decisions in individual cases, nor incremental changes brought about by an occasional constitutional amendment, will be enough to solve them.

Most disturbing is that the source of much of the trouble is the branch of government on which we most directly rely to implement the will of the people. The Framers envisioned, and they were mostly correct, that Congress would respond to the wishes of the people as expressed at the ballot box and through other means. If legislators refuse to adequately respond to the needs of their constituents and the interests of the country, they are supposed to be replaced by those who more accurately reflect the views and expectations of the people.

This system of representation was always complicated, and it never worked as well as school textbooks suggested. But in recent years, new and ominous developments have caused a breakdown in the process that is at the heart of a representative democracy. When elected officials know they can openly defy their constituents, without being held accountable, they can pursue policies that are in the interests of campaign contributors whether or not the people they are supposed to represent are well served in the process. When ordinary people who previously felt a part of governing the nation see how little is done for them, and how much is done for those who donate to campaigns and have access to lawmakers, they stop caring about politics and let someone else select who will govern. Even those who still vote often choose candidates only because they have a familiar name, or because they belong to a certain political party, without knowing much about the record of the incumbent or the promises of the challenger. Favors done for lobbyists and donors — which cost taxpayers millions of dollars and should be vigorously discussed during a campaign for reelection — are rarely examined because underfunded challengers cannot reach enough people to tell them what the incumbent has been doing. Media organizations also share much of the blame because they fail to adequately cover the activities and policies of public officials during their terms of office, and sometimes only mention their names at election time.

There is great irony in the ability of members of the House of Representatives to be reelected in overwhelming numbers despite often favoring their financial supporters over the people in whose name they govern. The Framers wanted the Senate to be insulated from the public so its members, drawn from the most affluent and educated, if not aristocratic elements of society, could do what they believed best for the country. With a six-year term and selection originally not by voters, but by state legislatures, senators would be able to provide a check on the democratic excesses of the "people's" branch, the House of Representatives, whose members are directly elected by the people and serve two-year terms. Today, the members of the House are almost always reelected and can pursue with near impunity the agenda of those who donate huge sums of money to them, or to parties and independent groups to be used on their behalf. Senators, with a slightly lower reelection rate, are somewhat less assured of lifetime tenure in Congress.

The processes and institutions provided for in the Constitution that would normally allow the American people to rise up in anger to reclaim their government are not working. Something more extreme is required. It is useless to continue to mutter vacuous platitudes urging the American people to vote out of office those who have figured out how to be both unanswerable *and* remain in power. The system is broken and the traditional tools the Constitution gave the people to fix the problems are inadequate to the task. There is nowhere for the people to turn. Congress will not respond to reasonable demands for reform, yet those members who openly defy their constituents get reelected anyway. The judicial branch cannot help because the Supreme Court determined that campaign expenditures are protected by the First Amendment and cannot be regulated. The president, who denounced the campaign finance system even while raising millions of dollars by trading access and favors, cannot act without Congress's approval. Since the Constitution does not provide the means by which our system of representative democracy can be restored, the American people must pursue an alternative, something that has not been attempted since the summer of 1787. Despite the risks and effort involved, this country must hold a second constitutional convention.

The delegates to a second convention could propose amendments that will give citizens a better chance of holding their elected officials accountable, and in the process, reduce the level of political cynicism that has infected the millions of people who do not care about public issues and do not vote. If the right amendments are proposed and ratified by the states, the Constitution will have been reinvigorated and adapted to the needs of an era where House and Senate races cost millions of dollars, and where the Supreme Court has narrowed the options for reform by legislation.

Successfully proposing and ratifying the amendments that emerge from a second convention will show that although the Framers made it very difficult for the people to change the Constitution through such extraordinary means, the system could, nevertheless, be described as having "worked" because the political crisis befalling the country would have been at least partially abated.

It may take years and the involvement of millions of people to organize a new convention. Those who stand to lose the privileges of elective office, and the lobbyists, contributors, and political friends who gain access to them with donations and flattery, will energetically fight efforts to change the Constitution. Every step in the process — from the meetings within each state, to the national preconvention — may be subject to intense media and public scrutiny, and pressure from special interests. The delegates to the new constitutional convention must have exceptional abilities and virtues because they will propose amendments that will fundamentally change a document many consider sacred, and they must do so without damaging the foundation on which our freedom and civil liberties rests.

The procedures the American people will have to follow to amend the Constitution are set forth in Article V. The Framers, exhausted as their work neared completion in September 1787, finished writing Article V in the closing days of the Convention. Perhaps because so many other key issues had to be resolved, or because they did not think it especially important, the delegates did not give the amending process the attention it deserved. During the struggle over ratification, the Framers learned just how important the amending issue was to gaining the approval of the ratifying conventions. The delegates were probably startled to see how much vigorous opposition there was to the new Constitution because it lacked a bill of rights, among other reasons. Many of those elected to the ratifying conventions demanded that in return for their approval, the First Congress would have to propose amendments that would explicitly protect civil liberties from encroachment by the new central government. If there had been no Article V process in the Constitution that allowed Congress to propose and the states to ratify amendments, the Constitution would not have been approved.

The American people should not have to go through the long and difficult process of organizing a second convention. They should have been able to count on their elected officials to make the changes required to restore the key elements of a representative democracy. But they have no choice. It is clear that comprehensive reform will not come from those who directly benefit from the system. The deep distrust and cynicism that the American people feel for their elected officials today is not misplaced.

There is plenty of evidence to suggest that without some drastic action by the people themselves, the situation will not change.

Distrust of and Cynicism about Public Officials

In July 1997, the *Washington Post* and ABC News conducted a poll asking Americans whether they opposed the way presidential and congressional campaigns are financed. Sixty-three percent said yes. They were also asked whether they thought the president or Congress was likely to substantively change the system by which campaigns are financed. The answer, given by 67 percent, was no. The American people had so little hope that elected officials will change the way federal campaigns are financed that they did not seem to give opposition to reform much weight when evaluating the president's performance. In 1998, President Clinton's approval ratings continued to be extremely high, especially considering the number of scandals swirling around the White House. The lawsuit brought by Paula Jones; the accusation that he molested former aide Kathleen Willey; the adultery committed with a young intern; close friends and associates being summoned by grand juries or heading to prison; cabinet members being investigated by independent counsels; all those events did not keep the American people from applauding the president's performance in office. In February 1998, according to another *Washington Post*/ABC News poll, the president's job approval rating stood at 67 percent.

The February 1998 poll made it clear that the president's high approval rating was directly related to the strong economy. While only 28 percent said the president "has high personal moral and ethical standards," 80 percent said he had done a good job on the economy. A substantial number of Americans also believed that their president had lied to them about having an affair with former intern Monica Lewinsky. On January 26, 1998, the president denied that he had an affair with the young woman. Yet two days later, when the poll was taken, 59 percent said they did not believe him.

Those responding to the poll also took the somewhat inconsistent position that simply having the sexual relationship with Lewinsky was not sufficient grounds for punishing the president, but if he lied about the affair, that was a more serious matter. Some people may not have considered that if he is guilty of the sexual relationship, he is also guilty of lying about it. Perhaps that ambivalence is reflected in a *New York Times*/CBS poll where 59 percent said it was "understandable [that] he would not tell the truth about his sex life."

The public appeared willing to separate a politician's private life from the job performance. In February 1998, 80 percent of those responding to a Harris poll were able to do just that by agreeing that "in judging Clinton, we should focus on how the country is doing and his policies, and not on his private life." Even when the president's personal behavior ceased to be purely private, as when he allegedly molested former aide Kathleen Willey in the president's private office in the White House, the American people were more interested in how he was doing his job and seemed willing to overlook personal shortcomings. Although the American people recognized that the president's behavior toward Willey constituted sexual harassment if it occurred — 63 percent responding to a CNN poll agreed it was harassment — the respondents gave the president a *personal* approval rating of 60 percent, and a 67 percent job approval rating. Perhaps more troubling — although open to various interpretations — is that 61 percent said that Willey's charges were not more serious than those made by other women.

The economy's strong performance through the mid-to-late 1990s had a lot to do with the public's forgiving attitude towards the president. With low unemployment, low interest rates, almost no inflation, a rising stock market, and generally healthy corporate profits, the American people have enjoyed a period of prosperity that may be unparalleled in the nation's history. When *Washington Post* reporters asked voters in three congressional districts around the country about the events in Washington, the voters cited the strong economy in the areas where they live and how well their own families were doing for their lack of interest in scandals involving the president and Congress. One person probably spoke for millions of Americans when he said, "Politics in Washington doesn't seem to affect me directly . . . It's all too remote. My job and the traffic and the kids swamp out national politics."

There is, however, a dark side to the willingness of the American people to tolerate serious transgressions on the part of their elected officials because the economic health of the nation is so good. There has been a fraying, if not breaking, of the trust that citizens must have for their leaders when things are not going so well. The economy will not keep humming along forever. There could be serious problems brought on — with little or no advance warning — by any number of events around the world or at home. A new crisis in Asia or Latin America, a sudden rise in interest rates and inflation, or any number of other events or issues could send shock waves throughout the global economy. When unemployment rises, and grocery bills and gas prices jump, and when Wall Street finally has a serious, prolonged bear market and the value of their stocks and mutual funds plummet, they will be looking for leadership from their government. If the American people believe that their leaders do not tell the truth, or that their elected officials do what is best for campaign contributors and not the citizens who put them in office, there will be little incentive to cooperate when those elected officials announce that austere measures are needed and call on citizens to make personal sacrifices to deal with the economic problems at hand.

When the president lies about his personal activities, when Congress and the president continue to be perceived as beholden to those whose money they take to get elected, the American people will not trust either of them to manage the economy and rescue the country from whatever crisis it is facing. There will be little confidence that public officials will tell the truth about how bad things really have become. It seems far-fetched in the bountiful and tranquil days of the late 1990s, but if the United States has a serious economic crisis — or commits troops to war, and Americans begin coming home in caskets — it will be crucial that the people believe not only that their elected officials know how best to protect the interests of the nation, but that they will be honest about the severity of the problems.

The president of the University of Oklahoma, David Boren, was for many years a respected U.S. Senator from Oklahoma. He knows Washington politics. He also comes into contact with young people almost every day. Boren told the *New York Times* after the Clinton scandals involving Jones, Willey, Lewinsky, and Whitewater, and the revelations involving campaign finance were widely circulated, that the level of distrust on the part of freshmen in his American government class was "deeply disturbing." He paraphrased his students' response to the scandals around the White House this way: "All politicians are crooks, very few of them tell the truth, few of them are faithful to their spouses, so why not have one who's smart and knows how to get things done?" The attitude of the students, according to Boren, is that "we really don't respect him, but what do you expect from a politician?" Boren worries about the day when this attitude interferes with solving the nation's problems: "In times of crisis, times of hardship . . . a level of trust between the American people and their Government, particularly their leader, is an essential element of what's needed in the country. We have passed from anger about what's going on in our political system to cynicism and alienation. And to me, cynicism and alienation are more frightening than anger."

Because there is only one president, and the scandals around President Clinton involved irresistibly salacious topics, it is understandable that much of the media coverage and public's attention were focused on the machinations in the White House. But the fascination with President Clinton's troubles should not have obscured the misbehavior and outright criminal activity of some members of Congress. The revelations during the late 1990s only added to the low regard people have for the legislative branch. Bad news from Congress dribbles in over time, and it often involves members who are unknown to the vast majority of the public. But there has been plenty of reason for the American people in recent years to think poorly of Congress.

For example, one of the most important officials in the government, Speaker of the House Newt Gingrich, was fined $300,000 by his colleagues in early 1997 for bringing discredit on the House by illegally funneling campaign contributions through tax-exempt foundations, and then providing false information to the House Ethics Committee about those activities. He decided to pay the fine himself, but he did so on favorable terms no ordinary citizen would ever get from a bank. In April 1997, Gingrich announced that he was borrowing the entire amount from former Senator and Republican presidential nominee Bob Dole. The loan was criticized by some Democrats because Gingrich would pay interest of 10 percent a year, but he would not have to make any payments in either interest or principal for eight years.

Gingrich was also criticized for a book deal he made with a publishing house owned by media mogul Rupert Murdoch, whose extensive holdings in broadcasting are regulated by federal officials and who wanted the speaker of the House to be an ally. Gingrich was to receive an advance of $4.5 million, many times what authors would receive for such a book if they were not an important government official. When there was an uproar about it, Gingrich returned the advance after the 1994 elections and agreed to wait for the royalties. As it turned out, the royalties amounted to a fraction of what he would have received as an advance, confirming the suspicion that the deal was a way for a major media company to funnel money to the speaker of the House without violating the law. Gingrich's predecessor as speaker, Jim Wright of Texas, also resigned because of an arrangement he made with a publisher that in effect required campaign contributors to buy copies of his book so money that would normally go into his campaigns would instead go directly to him.

Members of Congress must assume that either their constituents will not find out about some of their shady dealings, or that they will not care. Perhaps no one demonstrated more effectively in recent years how little shame some members of Congress have than Representative Jay C. Kim, a Republican member of the House from Southern California. In 1997, Kim pleaded guilty to accepting $250,000 in illegal contributions, including foreign donations. In March 1998, he was sentenced to one year of probation, a $5,000 fine, and for two months he would have to wear an electronic monitoring device to keep track of his movements. Such a light sentence with no jail time seemed remarkably lenient for what prosecutors called the largest case of campaign finance violations in U.S. history. The prosecutors themselves were criticized for allowing Kim to plead guilty rather than seeking felony convictions at trial. Because his crimes were all misdemeanors, Kim could continue to serve in Congress. The day after he was sentenced, Kim walked onto the House floor and cast votes on pending bills. When a few days later he began wearing his ankle bracelet, he became the first member of Congress to vote on the House floor while sporting an electronic monitoring device.

After his conviction and sentencing, many expected Kim to resign before his term ended in January 1999. Not only did Kim stay in office, he decided to run for a fifth term. Being convicted of a serious crime usually does not go over well with the folks back home, but Kim must have believed that his name recognition built up over four previous terms, and his steering of millions of dollars of federal money into public works projects in his district would be enough to win reelection. Speaker Gingrich, apparently not bothered by Kim's conviction, appointed the California congressman to the conference committee that was hammering out the details of a massive transportation bill. As the ranking member, Kim was able to direct millions of tax dollars in projects to his district, which includes parts of Los Angeles, San Bernadino, and Orange counties, in the hope that his constituents would appreciate the federal largesse and forgive him.

The judge, however, by refusing to postpone Kim's sentence, made campaigning for reelection difficult. Kim was not allowed to go back home until the 60 days of electronic monitoring was over, and that meant that he could not return to California before the June 2 primary. Although his campaign coordinator boasted that "the Congressman's spirits are high, and we're going to win this thing," the voters had something else in mind. In a four-person primary, Kim lost, coming in second. It is possible that if the judge had allowed Kim to return home to campaign, he would have been renominated and reelected.

These examples of serious misdeeds on the part of members of Congress may explain why the institution is held in such low regard by the public even while incumbents are overwhelmingly reelected. There are probably many reasons why voters send their own members back to Capitol Hill year after year. Challengers often lack name recognition compared to the incumbent; residents of the district may be afraid that if they do not send their legislator back to Washington, they will lose out on the seniority their member needs to direct federal money to the district or state; or those who are angry enough to vote against the incumbent stay home while many of those who think the system works well cast ballots.

The American people have been told for years in school and by commentators and scholars that under our system, the people are in charge. They are the governors, while those who are elected to office to carry out their wishes are the servants. The concept seems so appealing in theory, and consistent with the design of the Framers. But if that ideal ever actually described the relationship between the people and their leaders, it certainly does not apply in the 1990s.

The Corrosive Effect of Campaign Money on the Political Process

It is becoming clear that the American people cannot rely on the national legislative and executive branches to implement many of the policies they support, including reform of the campaign finance system. The people also cannot expect the judicial system — although it is independent precisely so it can identify and safeguard the enduring values of the Constitution — to fix the problems that permit elected branches of government to be unaccountable. For various reasons, judges cannot or will not make the changes that lead to greater accountability of elected officials. With no place to turn, the public becomes increasingly cynical.

This is not the only time in our history that efforts at reform have encountered powerful and well-financed interests that dominate the political system. In the late 19th and early 20th centuries, for example, the nation was plagued by corruption in government at all levels, control of the economy and politics by wealthy individuals and corporations, a Supreme Court determined to emasculate the 14th Amendment to protect businesses at the expense of individuals, voting irregularities, and other serious problems. Beginning with the Populist Movement in the late 19th century, and culminating with the reforms of the Progressive Era during the first two decades of the 20th century, the public was able to replace many of those in office who were the most corrupt and institute structural changes that addressed some of the major defects in the representative system. Although reforms took decades, the people were eventually able to reclaim their government from those who saw public service primarily as a way to acquire wealth and prestige.

What characterizes the current era is the contamination of the political process by campaign money and the growth of the electronic media. Much of the money raised in campaigns is needed to buy expensive television time. Except as a token gesture designed to get news coverage on a TV station or in a newspaper, no candidate for the House or Senate today will spend much time going door-to-door to meet voters to discuss issues.

That is a romanticized relic of the past. With an average of more than 600,000 constituents in a House district, and Senate candidates running in states with millions of people, those seeking election to Congress can only reach large numbers of voters through the mass media. They will get some news coverage that will reach alert citizens, but only through commercials can they completely control the content and image of their message.

In recent years, "hard" and "soft" money contributions — that go overwhelmingly to support those already in office — have so increased the advantages of incumbency that challengers who promise to work for reform cannot reach enough people to overcome the media blitz by their well-funded opponents. Voters are often forced to choose between incumbents with familiar names and challengers they do not know much about. When people see how little is done to address the problems they care about, and how much is accomplished for donors who talk to public officials in their offices, committee meetings, and at parties and resorts, they become demoralized and cynical, even mean-spirited about politics and government. It takes little effort today to find people who believe that all elected officials have been captured by monied interests.

Soft and hard money

Campaign finance is immensely complicated, and few average citizens understand the distinction between soft and hard money contributions. Nevertheless, the second constitutional convention must propose an amendment that recognizes the difference and sharply limits soft money contributions *and* how much is spent in campaigns.

"Soft" money refers to contributions — which are unlimited in size — made to political parties that are supposed to support "party-building" activities, but are almost always spent to help or oppose candidates for office. The law requires only that the money be spent "independently" of the candidates or their agents, a loophole that allows corporations, unions, and organized groups to give whatever money they want to support or oppose candidates as long as the expenditure is not directly coordinated by the candidate's campaign. In addition to soft money contributions and expenditures, millions are donated to and spent by so-called "independent groups" that run ads supporting and opposing candidates, often distorting the disfavored candidate's record. The ads can do anything short of directly saying vote for one candidate or the other.

"Hard" money donations, on the other hand, are given directly to candidates and are subject to the limits imposed by the 1974 amendments to the Federal Election Campaign Act of 1971. The 1974 Amendments were enacted by Congress after the Richard Nixon campaign raised over $60 million for his 1972 reelection — much of it practically extorted from businesses and other organizations — and after the Watergate scandal. Congress took four steps in the 1974 amendments to improve the campaign process by:

- Requiring disclosure of contributions and expenditures
- Limiting campaign contributions
- Limiting political expenditures
- Creating a system of public financing for presidential elections

Two years later, the Supreme Court eviscerated the heart of the reforms in its disastrous decision in *Buckley v. Valeo*. The Court upheld the disclosures and public financing provisions of the law, but it drew a line between limits on contributions and limits on expenditures. The Court approved limits on contributions made *directly* to candidates, the so-called "hard" money contributions, but struck down limits on expenditures by parties and independent organizations, thus allowing such groups to raise and spend as much "soft money" as they want.

The Court concluded that limits on direct contributions to candidates represented "only a marginal restriction upon the contributor's ability to engage in free communication," and therefore must yield to the greater interest in preventing the reality or appearance of improper influence by large campaign contributions. But the Court further determined that provisions of the law limiting expenditures by candidates or independent groups violated their First Amendment rights of free expression and association by curtailing access to expensive mass media, which the Court called "indispensable instruments of effective political speech."

As a result of *Buckley,* there are no limits on soft money contributions to so-called independent groups, and no limits on how much either independent groups or candidates can spend. Wealthy individuals have been able to spend millions of dollars of their own money to get elected. Political parties and other political organizations seek huge sums of soft money from individuals and corporations, which if given directly to the candidates, would violate the limit on contributions.

The rather stringent limits on hard money contributions encourage those wishing to purchase better access to elected officials to make large soft money donations. Individuals contributing hard money directly to federal candidates may give no more than $1,000 per candidate per campaign (the primary and general elections are considered separate campaigns) and up to $20,000 to all federal candidates in an election year. Political action committees (PACs) not associated with a political party may give no more than $5,000 per candidate per campaign in hard money.

There are, however, no limits on contributions to the national parties' House and Senate campaign committees.

In federal elections, corporations and unions are not permitted to contribute hard money directly to candidates. But any individual, business, union or group can make a soft money contribution to support or oppose candidates, and they do so with great vigor. According to Common Cause, a nonprofit political watchdog group, the political parties took in $262 million in soft money for the 1996 campaigns, three times the amount they received in 1992. Corporations and their executives were responsible for 93 percent of the Republican Party's $138 million and 74 percent of the Democrats' $128 million in soft money. Included in the list of biggest contributors to the Republicans was Philip Morris ($2.5 million) and RJR Nabisco ($1.14 million). For Democrats, their biggest supporters included the Communications Workers of America ($1.1 million) and the American Federation of State, County and Municipal Employees ($1 million).

Common Cause reported that during the first six months of 1999, the national political parties raised a record $53.6 million in soft money, a 75 percent increase in the amount they raised in the comparable period in 1995. The Republican and Democratic parties each raised $262 million in soft money for the 1996 elections, but that figure could easily double for the 2000 elections.

Many business executives resent having to donate so much money to the political parties in order to get access to public officials and have their views on legislation considered. In a survey published in *Business Week* in March 1997, 400 executives were asked if they wanted the law changed to eliminate soft money contributions, and 68 percent said yes. The same percentage also agreed with the statement that the "system is broken and is in need of fundamental reform." The executives said repeatedly that they were tired of endless appeals for donations.

If there is a serious revolt on the part of businesses that have long supplied a substantial portion of the money political parties desperately need, it may get the attention of lawmakers and inspire them to approve modest reform measures. But that seems unlikely in part because each side is afraid of ending or cutting back on contributions while their opponents refuse to do so. That would place whichever side held back at a disadvantage. As one Republican contributor observed, there would be opposition to an outright ban on soft money donations because "that would amount to unilateral disarmament for the GOP because unions would still be free to get out the vote for the Democrats." Another individual commented that "if everyone else is giving and we don't, our voice won't be heard."

Among the 400 executives answering the *Business Week* survey, 70 percent said they had contributed to the parties. Sixty-one percent said they would like greater freedom to make direct contributions to campaigns to gain access to politicians. Fifty-six percent favored requiring radio and TV stations to give candidates free air time. The *New York Times*, in an editorial commenting on the *Business Week* survey, called the process of soliciting soft money contributions from business executives a "shake down" and demanded that Congress change the system.

The executives who answered the *Business Week* survey complained about another aspect of soft money contributions that is frequently subject to abuse. Because soft money donations are not made directly to candidates, but instead are given to political parties for party-building activities, the money does not necessarily go to support or oppose candidates who are in a position to help the donor. In fact, the contributor may not know where the money is being spent. Some political parties have funneled soft money to state candidates while leading the donor to believe it went to support candidates for Congress. A lobbyist for a New Jersey company complained to *Business Week* that "you don't know if the money's being spent on cocktail parties and limousine rides or on ads that benefit statehouse candidates in Minnesota." One executive was quoted as saying the "whole process is out of control."

In the fall of 1999, some business executives tried to take more aggressive action by speaking out on campaign finance reform, only to learn how quickly they could anger powerful politicians. At least 20 members of the Committee for Economic Development — which includes executives of such corporations as General Motors, Xerox and Merck — endorsed a ban on unlimited campaign contributions. They soon found themselves the subject of an aggressive letter-writing campaign led by Senator Mitch McConnell (R-KY). McConnell accused the executives of trying to "eviscerate private sector participation in politics" by imposing "anti-business speech controls." He scribbled on the bottom of a letter he sent to one executive, "I hope you will resign from C.E.D." The senator apparently asked all 20 members of the group favoring reform to also resign. McConnell, who wrote the letters in his capacity as chairman of the National Republican Senatorial Committee, criticized the group for having a "radical campaign-finance agenda."

Many of these companies have important issues pending before Congress, but at least some of the C.E.D. executives refused to be intimidated. On October 3, 1999, they announced that the number of business executives favoring reform had swelled to 209 members since the McConnell letter. The president of the group said the letter had backfired; not one member had resigned, and there was renewed interest among executives around the country in reform efforts. McConnell "has been a tremendous help" in prompting more members to join, said the C.E.D. president.

The money moves around

Some donors get angry when they find out, as they sometimes do, that money donated for one purpose ends up somewhere else. William Jordan, a North Carolina doctor, is one such donor. In October 1996, he gave $50,000 to the National Republican Senatorial Committee (NRSC) because he wanted to help elect Republicans to the U.S. Senate. But the chairman of the NRSC, Senator Alfonse D'Amato (R-NY), thought he had a better use for Dr. Jordan's money and millions more from other contributors. Unknown to Dr. Jordan, D'Amato took the check and deposited it in an account called the "New York State Victory Committee." Dr. Jordan's money and the contributions of other unsuspecting donors thus ended up being used for a purpose they did not intend. The Victory Committee gave $1.9 million to Governor George Pataki's campaign fund and $300,000 to three Republican judicial candidates in New York state. Some months later it was revealed that NRSC money was also funneled to Republican candidates in New Jersey and Staten Island.

It gets worse. New York has strict limits on campaign contributions for candidates running for state office. For example, there is a limit of $28,000 that any individual can give to a candidate for governor. But because the money was — in the words of Charles Lewis, the director of the Center for Public Integrity — "laundered" through the D'Amato committee, it did not have to comply with the New York limits. According to the *New York Times*, the money laundering operation — all of it legal — even allowed executives from companies that are municipal bond underwriters, such as Goldman Sachs, to contribute to New York candidates when state law prohibits such donations. Ten executives of the financial firm donated $110,000 to the D'Amato committee. Most of the money went into a Republican "housekeeping" fund in New York. A $20,000 donation to the NRSC by Morgan Stanley & Company, also in the municipal finance business, ended up in the same housekeeping account.

One financial firm, Paine Webber, had specifically written its $30,000 check to a special Republican Senate "building" fund account. Building accounts are to be used only for general party activities and are not to be given to candidates, especially those running for local office. Paine Webber's money ended up being used to finance Republican party efforts in New York.

Senator D'Amato was unrepentant. He told the *New York Times* "there is nothing wrong with what I did . . . There was no intent to deceive. To suggest otherwise would be inappropriate and wrong." He admitted that few donors were told about the check transfers but said, "it's not necessary to tell people where their checks went . . . We don't have an obligation to tell people. Money is fungible." The day after the *New York Times* article appeared, D'Amato held a press conference to say again that the transferring of the checks was "proper and legal."

Probably few people who voted for or against D'Amato in his re-election bid in the fall of 1998 read the detailed articles in the *New York Times* and knew about the complicated shenanigans with the NRSC money. Even if Rep. Charles Schumer (D-NY), who defeated D'Amato, wanted to make an issue of it, campaign finance is tough to explain. But D'Amato's actions are a classic example of what is wrong with the campaign system. Few members of Congress were ever as accomplished at — and unashamed of — raising money from organizations with a direct interest in his work in Congress.

The amounts raised by D'Amato were legendary. By February of 1997, a year and a half before the election, he already had amassed a campaign war chest of $6.8 million. That was $4 million *more* than any other senator had raised for the next election. Not surprisingly, much of his money came from corporations with business before the two congressional committees D'Amato chaired: the Senate Banking Committee and the Urban Affairs Committee. The actions of those committees can mean millions in savings or costs for Wall Street, commercial banking, and the insurance industries. With nearly $7 million in hand 18 months before the election, D'Amato already had enough to blanket the state with television ads talking about what a good job he had done for New York. By June 1998, D'Amato had raised $17 million for his reelection campaign, the largest amount amassed by any senator.

Much of the money going to D'Amato also came from those under the jurisdiction of the Banking Committee. MNBA is one of the country's biggest issuers of credit cards. The company's PAC, its executives, and the executives' family members gave D'Amato more than $220,000. The company and its PAC also donated $170,000 to the New York Republican State Committee and $127,500 to the NRSC. What they got in return for their investment was D'Amato's insertion of an amendment into a bill that the company supported and which consumer groups strongly opposed. It would have allowed mortgage providers to pay fees to real estate agents for referring business to them. Consumer groups believed that changing the law would increase the cost of buying a home and present a situation that is ripe for abuse. The vice chairman of MNBA apparently believed that contributions of more than half a million dollars to D'Amato and the committees he controlled had nothing to do with getting favorable treatment on Capitol Hill. He told the *New York Times* "there is no connection between any campaign contributions and any piece of legislation. We support good government."

The financial services industry also supported good government by giving Schumer $2.3 million in his campaign against D'Amato. Schumer played a key role in October 1999, in helping the Senate reach an agreement with the White House to allow banks to sell stocks and insurance. It was a bill of immense importance to the industry, one that D'Amato had been unable to pass for four years when he was head of the Senate Banking Committee. Conglomerates in the banking business had been prevented from expanding the financial products they offered to include securities and insurance because of the Glass-Steagall Act enacted during the Great Depression, and other laws. The negotiations between the White House and Senator Phil Gramm (R-TX), the chairman of the Banking Committee, had dragged on for months. Schumer was proud of his work on the bill, and said he felt vindicated after suggestions during the campaign against D'Amato that New Yorkers should not replace a senator with many years of seniority with a freshman. Those who contributed to Schumer's campaign want a senator, whether D'Amato or Schumer, who will help with their agenda. How much seniority that person has is not always a decisive factor.

Seeing all that money flowing into campaign accounts when they know they cannot legally spend any of it on themselves must be frustrating for politicians. But Governor Pataki has found a way to add income to his $130,000 gubernatorial salary. In 1997 he moonlighted as a speaker, traveling to Ohio in March of that year to collect $15,000 for a talk to a charitable organization. He gave other speeches for $15,000 each in Illinois and New Jersey. Although he said he would give paid speeches only out of state, the governor addressed magazine publishers and cosmetics executives whose companies are regulated by his administration. Public interest groups were outraged and noted the potential for conflicts of interest in having a sitting governor paid to give speeches to organizations who do business in New York. After the press reported the story, Pataki agreed to inform reporters before he gave an out-of-state speech for money so they could cover it. When the governor spoke in Ohio, his staff notified reporters of the speech after he had already left on the trip and half an hour *after* the last flight of the day from Albany to Columbus had left. There was no time for statehouse reporters to get to the speech.

Voters stay away from the polls

Not surprisingly, voter turnout has generally declined as many citizens become discouraged about the way their elected officials raise money to stay in office, and serve the interests of campaign donors. Voter turnout in elections to choose members of the House or Senate — although somewhat better when a presidential race is on the ballot — is abysmal. In the 1994 off-year election to choose all members of the House and a third of the senate, 36 percent of eligible voters went to the polls. That figure, as awful as it was, was up from its all-time modern low of 33 percent in 1990. In 1992, for the first time in 20 years, more than 50 percent of eligible Americans voted in House races. Apparently, it took the excitement of a presidential election that year to boost the number of voters casting ballots. When no president is on the ballot, turnout drops by an average of 13 percentage points. In 1996, the turnout for the presidential election was about 49 percent, the lowest level for a presidential election since 1924. That compares with 55.1 percent of those 18 or older who voted in 1992 in the Clinton and Bush election, and the 62.8 percent who voted in 1960 Kennedy and Nixon race. In 1998, 36 percent of eligible Americans voted, the lowest percentage since 1942, and the lowest percentage outside the South since 1818.

The decline in voter turnout is especially appalling because so many additional citizens were registered to vote — with almost no effort on their part — through the National Voter Registration Act, which went into effect in 1995. The Act, known as the motor-voter law, helped more than five million voters sign up when they renewed their automobile registration or applied for a driver's license. Many of those who registered under the Act probably never voted before. Part of the reason may have been that it was too much trouble to register. But once registered, all they had to do was show up at the polls or request an absentee ballot, but many of them still did not participate. It is hard to understand why they would not be sufficiently motivated to vote in 1996, a presidential election year. Those who do not vote — whether they are disgusted with the process or just too lazy to follow media coverage of campaigns — have lost a sense of civic commitment and pride that should be ingrained in anyone who lives in a democratic society.

The damage to the political system that comes from so much money flowing into campaigns has been visible for many years in congressional races. Campaign contributions go to members based on their committee assignments, leadership positions, or mere incumbency. Money from PACs and political parties are given overwhelmingly to incumbents. Not surprisingly, incumbents outspend challengers, often in direct relation to how much money the challenger has raised. Because incumbents raise campaign funds so easily compared with their opponents, they often spend substantial sums preemptively to discourage potential challengers from entering the race. For example, the amount of money an incumbent member of the House would spend if the challenger spent nothing at all rose from $116,100 to $440,300 (in 1994 dollars) between 1972 and 1994. As a challenger raises money, the incumbent's expenditures substantially increase.

An incumbent has the advantages of easily raised campaign money, the ability to get pork-barrel projects for the district or state, enhanced name recognition through government-paid mailings and news media coverage, and staff to provide constituent service. Because so few incumbents who seek reelection are defeated — some obviously retire rather than face a close election — members of Congress soon learn that they do not have to make difficult decisions that offend the interests of large campaign contributors because on all but a few issues, not many people back home will care or remember. They also do not have to worry much about challengers who advocate reform of the system.

Typically, since the mid-1940s, more than 90 percent of House races include incumbents, and more than 90 percent of them win. In 1986, out of 393 House members seeking reelection, only eight were defeated, for a reelection rate of 98 percent. In 1988, out of 408 members seeking reelection, only seven lost, for a reelection rate of 98.3 percent. The reelection rate figure for 1990 was 96 percent; 1992, 88 percent; 1994, 90 percent. For senators, the rates were 85 percent in 1988; 97 percent in 1990 (when out of 32 incumbents, only one was defeated); 1992, 82 percent; and 1994, 92 percent. Even as incumbents are returned to office, Congress as an institution gets dismal approval ratings from the public. The percentage of Americans disapproving of Congress was nearly 70 percent in 1996, and was over 70 percent in 1992, and 1995.

It is important to note that there are some outstanding members of Congress — and have been throughout our history — whose integrity is beyond reproach, and who courageously represent the views of the people back home even when that means taking on powerful interests. Some are extremely hard-working and are trying to do good things in an environment that is designed to thwart progressive policies and reform. The public's generally negative view of the national legislature, which has to solve the difficult problems of a large, complex nation, may be partially undeserved. Nevertheless, there are too few in Congress with the determination to take action when it is the right thing to do and good for their constituents and the country even if that action jeopardizes their congressional careers. The bottom line is that those who contribute to campaigns still get access to elected officials and favors from the government because those officials know few, if any, people back home will catch on. Those policies often cost taxpayers millions of dollars. There is plenty of reason to be disillusioned with Congress.

Congressional Resistance to Reform: The Battle over Term Limits

Term limits are extremely popular with the public, but not with their elected representatives. It should come as no surprise that although there is overwhelming support among the electorate for limiting how many terms federal legislators can serve, Congress will not approve a constitutional amendment proposing such limits. Congressional term limits can only come about through a constitutional amendment because the Supreme Court in *U.S. Term Limits v. Thornton* in 1995 held that states could not impose such limits on federal officials. The qualifications for election to federal office are set out in the Constitution, and thus limiting how long someone can serve in Congress would require a federal constitutional amendment. Whatever one's opinion about term limits — and there are good arguments for and against — the people have shown overwhelming support for them. They have approved, often by substantial margins, term limits in 23 states for members of Congress and in 20 states for state legislators. Forty states impose term limits on their governors, while the 22nd Amendment imposes a two-term limit on the president.

The anger people feel toward their elected officials, and their commitment to winning the term limits fight, resulted in voters in nine states approving an extraordinary set of laws or amendments to their state constitutions in November 1996. Arkansas' constitutional amendment, for example, would have instructed the state's congressional delegation to support a federal constitutional amendment imposing term limits. But the voters did not trust their representatives to follow that instruction, so they went one step further. If any incumbent seeking reelection had failed to vote for a term limits amendment in the previous Congress, the Arkansas measure would have required that they be identified *on the ballot* at the next election with what could be called a "scarlet letter" label, stating that this candidate "Disregarded Voter Instruction On Term Limits." Arkansas voters approved the measure by a margin of 61 to 39 percent.

Arkansas voters were fortunate they even had the opportunity to express their views on the term limits amendment. Two weeks before election day, the Arkansas Supreme Court struck down the amendment as an unauthorized attempt to amend the federal Constitution, concluding that the Constitution can only be changed by the procedures established in Article V. The U.S. Supreme Court, acting on an urgent appeal by the state, granted a last-minute stay that allowed the vote on the measure to proceed even though its constitutionality remained unsettled. But although supporters of term limits won the initial battle when the voters overwhelmingly approved the amendment, the final result was not in their favor. In February 1997, the U.S. Supreme Court refused to hear their appeal; thus the Arkansas Supreme Court's decision striking down term limits stands. The U.S. Supreme Court's action had no legal effect in other states because when the Court refuses to grant certiorari — to agree to hear a case — it is not ruling on the substance of the issues raised in the appeal.

The Arkansas Supreme Court's decision to invalidate the term limits amendment was undoubtedly frustrating for the people of that state who worked so hard to get it on the ballot and approved. Massachusetts citizens must also have been disappointed when their state supreme court invalidated term limits in July 1997. But the anger of citizens in those two states was probably insignificant compared to what voters in California must have felt during the 11 months when their term limits initiative was in limbo after being invalidated by a federal court. Getting an initiative on the ballot in the country's most populous state is time-consuming and expensive, and requires the coordinated effort of hundreds of people statewide. In 1990, after years of frustration over the way legislators in California conducted themselves — who, nevertheless, were rarely defeated for reelection — voters approved a law that imposed lifetime term limits of six years in the state assembly and eight years in the state senate. Legislators could run for office in the other house after they reached the maximum number of years, and many of them were elected, but once they reached the limits imposed by the law, they could not run again for any seat in the state legislature.

The supporters of the law fought legislators in the California courts, and in 1991, the California Supreme Court upheld the measure and ruled that the lifetime ban was constitutional. The law had its intended effect. California was the only state whose legislature was entirely transformed by term limits, with no member of the legislature being elected prior to 1992, and even the most senior legislators forced to retire by 1998. Term limit supporters probably thought they had won a great victory.

But California's elected officials were not through. A former assemblyman had filed a lawsuit in federal court when term limits prevented him from seeking reelection. In April 1997, Judge Claudia Wilken of the federal district court in Oakland found that the California law's lifetime ban on legislators violated the federal Constitution. She wrote that "California's extreme version of term limits imposes a severe burden on the right of its citizens to vote for candidates of their choice." It was the first time that any court had struck down term limits for state legislators. Her ruling was initially upheld five months later by a three-judge panel of the U.S. Court of Appeals for the Ninth Circuit, but that panel's ruling was reversed by the full court of appeals — in an "en banc" proceeding, which is not often granted to the losing side in a case — a few months after the original panel upheld Judge Wilken's ruling. In March of 1998, the U.S. Supreme Court refused to hear the former assemblyman's appeal. Thus, the initiative approved by the voters imposing term limits was saved. If Judge Wilken's ruling had been upheld on appeal, California supporters of term limits would have had to rewrite the initiative and again go through the process of gathering hundreds of thousands of signatures to place a new measure on the ballot that did not impose a lifetime ban.

Congress saw how much support term limits enjoyed in the states. Everywhere they had been on the ballot they were approved, sometimes by large majorities. They knew that the term limits movement was inspired by the widespread belief that powerful interests dominate the agenda and outcome of issues before Congress, and that even candidates who promise reform, once they discover the appeal of being in office, get taken in by the attention of those with money to donate. There are few issues before the U.S. Congress on which the public has spoken more clearly than term limits. Despite the public's strong support, Congress not only refused to propose a constitutional amendment that could be considered by the states, it did so in a way that intentionally misled the voters so they would find it nearly impossible to know if their member of Congress supported or opposed term limits and whom to hold responsible.

Republicans seeking to win the House in the 1994 election, which they succeeded in doing, included term limits in the "Contract for America." Speaker Newt Gingrich promised the voters that term limits would be the House's first legislative business after the 1996 election when the Republicans were able to retain a majority in the House. A constitutional amendment was introduced in early 1997. But despite the "Contract for America" and the speaker's pledge, the congressional leadership had no intention of allowing Congress to propose an amendment that would limit the terms of its members.

They had a most creative — some would say sleazy — way of handling the debate and voting on the measure. The Republican leadership scheduled votes on several versions of a term limits bill with slightly different wording, knowing that none would get the necessary two-thirds majority. The advantage of scattering the votes was that members from districts where reelection was not assured could vote for term limits and tell their constituents they supported them, while the House leadership had carefully choreographed the voting so none of the measures would reach the necessary threshold.

The plan worked well. In mid-February 1997, the House debated 11 variations of a term limits amendment. The most popular one, which would have allowed six two-year terms in the House and two six-year terms in the Senate, was approved by a margin of 217-211, falling 69 votes short of the two-thirds required for a constitutional amendment. There were ten fewer votes for approval than there had been in 1995. Seven amendments that would have allowed just three two-year terms for the House were also defeated. The House members from the nine states where voters had passed initiatives requiring them to support that state's version of term limits and oppose all others dutifully carried out that duty, but they had nothing to worry about. None of those amendments got more than 87 votes. All the maneuvering made it very difficult for the average voter to know that when their lawmaker voted "yes" on term limits, it was not a sign of genuine support but was instead part of the leadership's plan to deceive the public.

Representative Bill McCollum, a Florida Republican and a strong supporter of a 12-year limit, said the "American people want us to pass a term-limits amendment. Seventy percent of them support it." Whether or not he is accurate as to the percentage approving of term limits, there is no doubt that a substantial number of voters believe that Congress will not enact comprehensive campaign finance reform or follow the wishes of the citizens on other issues, and that the only way to make Congress more responsive is to limit the number of years its members can serve. Yet Congress will not take action that so directly affects its members' ability to stay in office, and they know that few, if any, will suffer for this failure at the polls.

Congress may tinker with campaign finance laws if there is sufficient outcry, but it will not fundamentally change a system that gives incumbents an overwhelming advantage in elections. Although term limits deprive voters of the right to elect indefinitely those they want to represent them, such a drastic change may be the only way to restore the representative elements of the system. If Congress can so easily resist the voters' clearly expressed views on term limits, they can also ignore what is in the interests of their constituents when it comes to complicated issues that the public is not aware of or does not understand, but which are very important to campaign donors and lobbyists. Term limits will only become part of the Constitution if they are proposed by a second constitutional convention and ratified by three-quarters of the states.

The Clinton Reelection Campaign: Overflowing with Money

The campaign finance system involving Congress is bad enough. Contributors give millions to the parties and the parties spend most of it on congressional races while dispersing some of the money to local candidates around the country. But even after *Buckley* created the soft money loophole in the law, there were still strict limits on how much independent groups could spend in presidential campaigns. The Supreme Court soon took care of that. To further undermine efforts to limit the impact of money on campaigns, the Supreme Court decided almost a decade after *Buckley* that the Presidential Election Campaign Fund Act, which made it a criminal offense for independent "political committees" to spend more than $1,000 to further a presidential candidate's election if that candidate had accepted public financing, was a violation of the independent group's First Amendment rights. Essentially, the decision ensured that presidential campaigns would be subject to the same abuses as congressional races. In *Federal Election Commission (FEC) v. National Conservative Political Action Committee*, the Court allowed unlimited amounts to be donated to and spent by so-called "independent" groups on behalf of presidential candidates. That opened the door to the shocking excesses of the Clinton/ Gore reelection campaign in 1996.

After hearing about congressional scandals and the destructive influence of money on elections for years, it would be understandable if the American people were so jaded, if not numb, to the behavior of their elected officials that they were indifferent to the disturbing stories of how the Democratic National Committee (DNC) raised money for President Clinton's 1996 reelection effort. But no matter how cynical people may be about their public officials, any concerned citizen should be outraged at the methods used by the DNC and the Clinton/Gore Reelection Committee before and during the 1996 campaign. The way the Democratic Party, the president, and vice president raised money for the election was shameful and could only have added to public disgust about elected officials and the influence that campaign donors have over them.

In early 1997, there were numerous stories in the media about contributors who gave the DNC hundreds of thousands of dollars in soft money, and who were rewarded with unprecedented and unseemly access to the White House and president. There were so many examples that only a few need be discussed to show how the Democrats turned the White House into a fund-raising machine so that they could keep control of the presidency in 1996. The parade of unabashed favor-seekers included business executives whose industries are regulated by the government, convicted felons, disreputable characters whose backgrounds no one bothered to check in advance, and foreign visitors who helped obtain illegal contributions. That they were invited to the White House in expectation of large donations to the DNC showed, sadly, that the president and the Democratic Party willingly defiled the White House in an effort to raise money to stay in office. Almost no favor was too much or too inappropriate for potential donors.

An audience with those who regulate their business

Business executives have dreams about this kind of opportunity. You and your colleagues run some of the nation's largest banks and holding companies. You are taken to the Oval Office where you find the people in government whose decisions most affect your industry — who have been invited or summoned by the DNC — waiting to meet you: Secretary of Treasury Ron Rubin, his deputy John Hawke, and the best prize, Comptroller of the Currency Eugene Ludwig, the banking industry's top regulator. You get the opportunity, in front of the president, to enlighten them about why you should be able to expand into other businesses and why your banks should not be forced to bail out the savings and loan industry.

This was not a dream. It actually happened in May 1996. The DNC was hoping that the business executives would show their gratitude for this rare opportunity by making large contributions to the party. After news organizations forced the White House to turn over the lists of those who attended the meeting, President Clinton said it was a mistake to have donors and regulators at the same event.

The bankers who were in the Oval Office meeting may not have sufficiently demonstrated their gratitude through campaign contributions. A few months after the meeting, the Clinton Administration refused to endorse a plan to permit banks to enter all nonfinancial businesses, which the bankers had hoped would be the Administration's position. Instead, it was expected that the Treasury Department would support a bill making its way through the House that would allow banks to devote 25 percent of their business to nonfinancial enterprises. Perhaps larger campaign contributions would have increased that percentage.

Bankers and other business people are also keenly interested in federal bankruptcy law where millions of dollars are at stake. They want laws that put them ahead of other creditors when the assets of those declaring bankruptcy are distributed. In one of the most direct and brazen efforts to entice donors by offering them the chance to influence regulators and other public officials, veteran Democratic fund-raiser William Brandt — who described himself as a close friend of the president — told bankruptcy attorneys that if they attended a $10,000-a-plate dinner at his home in a Chicago suburb, they would be able to discuss policy with Brady Williamson. The president had just appointed Williamson, a bankruptcy lawyer, to lead a commission reviewing the nation's troubled bankruptcy system. The president and dozens of bankruptcy lawyers attended the event, which raised over a million dollars for the DNC.

The White House with rooms for rent

Some contributors and fund-raisers were invited to the White House dozens of time, enjoying access denied to ordinary citizens and even many members of Congress. The White House spared no expense in making sure the visitors had a good time. President Clinton personally approved a plan to reward large donors with overnight stays at the White House and other privileges. The strategy called for contributors to receive such perks as meals, coffees, and golf outings with the president, and the special treat of an overnight stay in the residential section of the White House. By February 1997, 938 guests had stayed overnight in the Lincoln Bedroom, the Queens Bedroom, or other bedrooms on the third floor of the White House. Many of them were personal friends of the Clintons or political figures, but many were individuals who contributed large sums to the re-election effort. The overnight stays were arranged by staff members with the knowledge of top officials. Even the president was actively involved. In his own handwriting, President Clinton wrote in a memo that he was "ready to start overnights right away," and suggested that those contributing $50,000 to $100,000 or more be considered. The president later denied that contributions had anything to do with invitations to the White House. He told a press conference in February 1997, that "the Lincoln Bedroom was never sold."

Demands on the president's time

The president helped raise money with such enthusiasm that the constant demand on his time began to cause problems. He made phone calls from the Oval Office to individuals who were identified by the DNC as potentially large donors. He was scheduled to appear at so many coffee events that some White House staff were concerned about him taking time away from official duties. But at least one White House staff member thought the president's running of the country was starting to interfere with fund-raising activities. Evelyn Lieberman, a White House aide, wrote to Chief of Staff Leon Panetta and Deputy Chief of Staff Harold Ickes on January 19, 1996, that White House staff who routinely meet with the President should take less of his time. According to Lieberman, during a period when fund-raising was "critical," White House staff should accept that "their briefings may be considerably truncated or eliminated" to make room for 27 additional coffees that were added to 13 dinners and 11 days of travel already scheduled for fund-raising and political activities.

At least one official at the DNC wanted donors to get more than just access to the president and a night in the White House. A memo written to a senior staff member of the DNC suggested that seats on Air Force I and II, private dinners at the White House, invitations to White House events, appointments to boards and commissions, and even coveted seats to the Kennedy Center be offered to contributors.

A "Rogue's Gallery" of White House visitors

With so many potential donors being rushed through the White House before and during the 1996 campaign, it was not surprising that the DNC did not screen of all them carefully. Several visitors had criminal records or shady backgrounds. For example, Jorge Cabrera, from Miami, contributed $20,000 to the Democratic Party. He had his picture taken with First Lady Hillary Rodham Clinton at a White House Christmas party in 1995, and was also photographed with Vice President Gore at a south Florida fund-raising event the previous November. Cabrera was first asked for a contribution by a prominent Democratic Party fund-raiser in a place where such requests are probably unusual: in the lobby of the Copacabana Hotel in Havana, Cuba. Cabrera is not someone you would expect to be welcomed at the White House. Three weeks after his visit there, he was charged with smuggling three tons of cocaine and 30 cases of Cuban cigars into the United States. He was later sentenced to 19 years in federal prison.

Another visitor to the White House would have been well-qualified to talk with the president about the criminal justice system. Eric Wynn, who was affiliated with a company that gave $25,000 to the Democratic Party, attended a White House coffee in December 1995. His White House visit, which included having his picture taken with the president, was five months *after* he was convicted of 13 counts of securities and wire fraud. While out on bail pending appeal, he was arrested three times within six months by New Jersey police on charges including assault, resisting arrest, and making threats. During his bail hearing, a witness used a photograph of Wynn and the president to help identify Wynn as the driver of a car who tried to run him down at a birthday party for Wynn's estranged wife.

Another frequent visitor was Roger Tamraz, the subject of an international warrant charging him with conspiracy and embezzling $200 million from a Lebanese investment company. While Interpol was looking for Tamraz around the world, he could have been found drinking coffee with the president. Tamraz does get credit for being among the most candid of the White House visitors. It had always been the White House position that invitations to coffees with the president and other social events had nothing to do with donations to the campaign. But Tamraz would not play along. He told Congress in September 1997, that he gave $300,000 to the DNC specifically for access to the president and other top officials. Tamraz wanted the government's support for a pipeline project in Central Asia. He attended a half-dozen social events at the White House and spoke briefly with the president about the project at a dinner. Although Tamraz never got the Administration's endorsement, he was able to boast abroad about his access to top U.S. officials. When asked by a member of the Senate Governmental Affairs Committee whether he got his money's worth for his large contributions, he said that in dealing with foreign leaders, such evidence of access "absolutely has some value." And he added, "I think next time I'll give $600,000."

Russ Barakat, the former Democratic chairman of Broward County, Florida, attended a White House coffee in April 1995. Five days after his visit, he was indicted on criminal charges. He was convicted a year later for filing a false tax return, and was sentenced to 21 months in prison. In December 1997, the U.S. Court of Appeals for the 11th Circuit overturned his sentence, but not his conviction.

One creative White House invitee tried to use his planned dinner with the president to keep from being locked up. A week before he was supposed to dine with President Clinton at a fund-raising event, Foutanga Dit Babani Sissoko, a West African philanthropist who Democratic Party officials thought would make a substantial contribution to the Party, was arrested in Europe on a U.S. warrant. He was charged with trying to smuggle two Vietnam-era military helicopters out of Miami to Africa and offering a $30,000 bribe to a U.S. Customs agent. After being extradited to Miami on the eve of the fund-raising dinner, he showed the invitation to a federal judge, asking that he be released from custody so he would not disappoint the president. Instead, the judge set bail at $20 million, an amount that lawyers in Miami said set a record for south Florida.

Several visitors had ties to industries that had a close relationship to the government of the People's Republic of China, raising the question of whether sensitive information was disclosed to a foreign nation. Among those who could have provided information about the China connection is John Huang. He worked for the Commerce Department, which gave him the opportunity to develop and enhance ties to the Chinese government. Huang was later appointed as the vice chairman of the DNC. China may have tried to influence more than the presidential election as allegations surfaced that it also funneled money to the campaign coffers of members of Congress, in violation of federal law. Vice President Al Gore, during a trip to China in March 1997, had to assure its leaders that an investigation into whether China tried to influence American elections would not affect Washington's relationship with the country.

Gore's efforts to reassure the Chinese did not stop media organizations from looking more deeply at their involvement in U.S. elections. It is illegal for foreign citizens to contribute to political campaigns in the United States. In the spring of 1998, there were news reports that the Chinese military had funneled $100,000 in contributions to the Democratic Party, and that such a contribution influenced the Clinton Administration's decision to allow the export of sensitive space technology to China. The *New York Times* reported that a Chinese military officer gave fundraiser Johnny Chung $300,000 to donate to the Democratic Party and told Chung that the money came from the intelligence agency of the Chinese military. Chung allegedly passed along $100,000 and kept the rest for himself. The Clinton Administration denied it had any knowledge of the source of Chung's contribution or that it affected the decision to make it easier for American companies to export communication satellite technology to China. Chinese officials also angrily denied the charges.

The U.S. Justice Department had opposed the decision to allow the American companies to export the technology. It was concerned that providing space expertise to China would enable that country to point long-range nuclear-tipped missiles more accurately at the United States. It also argued that allowing Loral Space & Communications to export the technology to China — a company that the Justice Department was investigating for previously sharing information with the Chinese in violation of federal law — would make prosecuting the company more difficult.

The money allegedly donated from the Chinese military was not the only incentive the White House had to approve the company's plans. The chairman of Loral, Bernard Schwartz, donated $100,000 to the Democratic Party four weeks before the export waiver application was approved in early July 1996, by President Clinton. The Republicans promised an investigation.

Lack of screening of foreign guests

The Democratic Party and the White House often did not want to be inconvenienced by having the National Security Council screen foreign visitors, a function the agency served in previous administrations. That allowed such people as Wang Jun to visit the White House for coffee with the President. Wang had been invited at the behest of Charlie Yah Lin Trie, a Clinton friend and fund-raiser from Arkansas. The White House later learned that Wang ran the Chinese government's weapons manufacturing and procuring agency, which, according to the *New York Times*, was involved in secret arms deals around the world. This highly unusual access, said one source, gave Wang the "appearance of being extraordinarily well-connected."

One visitor with entrepreneurial spirit knew how to make the most out of his time at the White House. Johnny Chung, the same fund-raiser involved in the controversy related to exporting satellite technology to China, donated $391,000 to the Democratic Party between 1994 and 1997, and visited the White House at least 50 times. After executives of a Chinese beer company gave Chung large sums of money to forward to the Democratic Party, one of the company's executives and several employees had their picture taken with the President and First Lady. Back in China, the photo was displayed in a window along with a beer bottle and mugs.

A donor with ties to China gave the First Lady's chief of staff a check for $50,000 *during a visit* to the White House, a possible violation of federal law prohibiting the soliciting or receiving of campaign funds on federal property. The White House's response was that the check was forwarded to the DNC, and therefore, there was no violation of law.

The president's friend

Despite the old expression that people should be judged by the company they keep, President Clinton cannot be held responsible for the wrongdoing of close friends. But when the president selects those individuals for high positions in the government, he is answerable to the American people when they see another example of a public official who should never have held high office. As those cases multiply over the years, they only add to the belief that many public officials are dishonest, but only rarely get caught.

President Clinton appointed longtime friend Webster Hubbell as associate attorney general, the number three position in the Justice Department, one of the most important jobs in the Executive Branch. Prior to his government service, Hubbell stole money from former law partners and clients. He was forced to resign from the Justice Department, then served almost 17 months in prison. He was later accused of other serious crimes. Because the Hubbells and Clintons had been friends for many years, it is hard to believe that President Clinton had no way of knowing that Hubbell was the type of person who might commit such acts. Although Hubbell apparently did not engage in wrongdoing related to his job at the Justice Department, the American people are entitled to a government that does not employ people with a propensity to commit such wrongdoing.

There were also disturbing reports that the president knew that his top aides were quietly helping Hubbell — who was in dire financial straits — to obtain more than $400,000 in consulting fees during the eight months between his resignation, guilty plea, and subsequent jail term. The money came from about a dozen businesses and groups, many of them with close ties to the president. The largest of the fees — $100,000 — was from the Riady family, longtime friends of the Clintons who control what the *New York Times* called "a vast financial empire based in Indonesia." There was speculation that the money was used to buy Hubbell's silence about Whitewater or other issues involving the Clintons.

In December 1994, Hubbell pleaded guilty to fraud charges stemming from the theft of almost $400,000 from the partners and clients in the law firm where he had worked in Little Rock and where Hillary Rodham Clinton had been a partner. It was not until three years later that many of the details about Hubbell's consulting work began to appear in the press. While the reports have not suggested that the president was directly involved in raising money for his friend, it appears that the president was at least informed of the efforts to help Hubbell. The aides involved in the effort to get work for Hubbell included Thomas McLarty, then White House Chief of Staff; Mickey Kantor, then U.S. Trade Representative; Erskine Bowles, who became White House Chief of Staff after McLarty stepped down; and Vernon Jordan, a Washington lawyer and close friend of the president. The *New York Times* reported that the president and First Lady had been informed of the efforts to help Hubbell and had given at least their tacit approval.

Some of the arrangements Hubbell had with clients would be the envy of consultants everywhere. The Los Angeles Department of Airports hired Hubbell — an audit later showed Hubbell was secretly hired by the president of the Airport Commission in violation of city procedures — to help convince the Department of Transportation to approve the transfer of $58 million from funds the airport controls to the city's general fund. The Commission's president apparently hired Hubbell because of his connections with federal agencies. For the over $8,000 a month that

Hubbell received, he had two five-minute telephone conversations with the general counsel of the Transportation Department, and some conversations with the person who had hired him. The decision to transfer the money was eventually approved although there is no indication Hubbell's involvement made a difference.

Hubbell had been hired for the airport money transfer based on the recommendation of a Los Angeles businessman and his wife, a former Small Business Administration official in the Clinton Administration who had known Hubbell in Washington. Hubbell was eventually paid $24,750 for the Los Angeles project. The city controller's office concluded in June 1997, that Hubbell had done little, if any, work for the money and that the city should try to get it back from him.

His legal troubles were far from over. In April 1998, Hubbell and his wife were charged in a 10-count indictment with conspiracy, tax evasion, and mail fraud. In June 1999, he pleaded guilty to a misdemeanor related to tax evasion as well as to an unrelated felony charge. The government had alleged that the Hubbells took steps to conceal their income and failed to pay taxes and penalties on more than $850,000 over the previous four years. Much of the income allegedly came from the lucrative consulting contracts the White House aides may have arranged for him. The indictment also charged two Arkansas advisers to the Hubbell family, an accountant and a lawyer, with helping the Hubbells to evade taxes.

There was some speculation that the indictment of Hubbell was a good sign for the Clintons because it suggested that Hubbell had been either unable or unwilling to provide incriminating information about the Clintons to Kenneth Starr, the Whitewater independent counsel. Hubbell was defiant in response to the latest indictment. He said, "I will not lie about the President" and insisted that he and his wife were innocent. In the meantime, Susan Hubbell kept her $66,000 a year job as a special assistant in the Interior Department.

Even a casual reader of newspapers or viewer of television newscasts knew that a former associate attorney general and close friend of the Clintons had spent time in federal prison, that he had been given hundreds of thousands of dollars in consulting fees when it was not clear what he did to earn the money, and that he and his wife and two advisers were later indicted for income tax evasion and other crimes. Ordinary people, who work hard for their salaries, and who do not have great connections and friends like the president, must think it is unfair when someone who does not play by the rules is rewarded. That the president allowed his top aides to be involved, even indirectly, in the raising of money for Hubbell from businesses and individuals with interests affected by Clinton administration decisions — even after he had been in prison and sullied the reputation of the Justice Department — must make voters think less of the president than they otherwise would. The fact that Hubbell and the others had been indicted, however, at least showed that the Justice Department was willing to aggressively investigate friends of the president. The judicial system also demonstrated that even people in influential positions sometimes get caught breaking the law and go to jail. But despite those factors, the Hubbell saga can only add to public cynicism about government.

The mixing of politics and the people's business

Just as staff members paid by the taxpayers are prohibited from working directly on campaigns when they are supposed to be doing the people's business, equipment that is paid for by the public and is intended for official government business is not supposed to be used for fundraising. That distinction seemed lost on the Clinton White House and DNC. In the White House was a computer database containing more than 350,000 names. Paid for by the taxpayers, the list was started by the White House to keep track of official visitors and supporters. Although the use of such data for political purposes is a violation of campaign laws, a large list like that is irresistible to those trying to raise millions of dollars for political campaigns. A White House spokesman told the *New York Times* that access to the database was strictly controlled, but a former finance chairman of the DNC said he used the list of names to make sure that major donors were rewarded for their generosity. It was also revealed that as many as 20 people working in the White House were being paid by the DNC. One of those staff members apparently had access to the White House computer database.

The vice president's role

Press reports of the fund-raising scandal initially concentrated on the role of staff in arranging coffees and other activities with the president, leading to the assumption that dedicated but misguided assistants organized such events while the president and vice president were preoccupied with the affairs of the nation. But the public soon learned that they were intimately involved and used their White House offices for fund-raising activities. Vice President Gore admitted that he directly solicited campaign contributions from his office in the White House. At a hastily called press conference, the vice president said he had consulted with counsel who told him that as long as the telephone calls were billed to the DNC — later amended by his office because the calls were actually

charged to the Clinton/Gore reelection committee — there was no violation of law. In a statement that only a seasoned politician could make with
a straight face, Gore said he had done nothing wrong, but would not do it
again. The public eventually learned that he had made at least 86 calls to
donors from his White House office. The contributors who heard directly
from the vice president were believed to be willing to give at least $25,000.
In denying that he had violated the Hatch Act, which forbids federal
employees from engaging in partisan fund-raising from federal buildings,
Gore told a press conference that "no controlling legal authority or
case" has ever concluded that what he did was wrong.

Vice President Gore should consider himself fortunate that Attorney General Janet Reno decided not to ask for an independent counsel to
investigate his role in fund-raising for the 1996 campaign. But the vice
president's fund-raising activities, including a bizarre appearance at a
Buddhist Temple in Los Angeles, hurt his otherwise pristine image. A
Wall Street Journal/NBC poll showed a steep slide in Gore's popularity
from July to September of 1997, with 57 percent of respondents saying
the scandal would affect his chances to be nominated and elected president. Republicans criticized the vice president, saying he should have
known the calls were improper and may have violated federal law. In his
first extensive interview on the subject, Gore refused to admit any mistakes on how he raised money, and blamed the Republicans for the
fund-raising controversy.

Giving money back

Despite the fund-raising frenzy during the 1996 congressional and
presidential reelection campaigns, the DNC was deeply in debt. It was
estimated that the party had as much as $14.4 million in red ink. Yet
because the source of some of the contributions could not be traced or
came from illegal sources, the DNC offered to give some of it back. In
the months following the 1996 presidential election, the Democratic
Party had a difficult time coming up with the $3 million in possibly illegal
and clearly improper contributions that it said it would return to donors.
That amount was many times greater than any party had ever returned.

Among contributions returned was $253,000 donated by the U.S.-
Thai Business Council because the DNC was unable to verify the origins
of the money. The Justice Department subpoenaed records of the Council after the FBI received reports that documents were being destroyed.
Dozens of members of Congress also returned contributions from those
associated with the campaign finance scandal.

The Republicans do it, too

The selling of the president's time during the 1996 campaign should not lead to the conclusion that only Democrats offer access to top officials. Although using the White House so brazenly as a forum for fundraising seems especially distasteful, the Democrats were not alone in raising money by selling time with important government officials. By giving at least $175,000 over four years to the Republican National Committee, more than 200 corporations and individuals were rewarded with invitations to meetings with top Republican leaders such as Senator Trent Lott (R-MS), the majority leader; Speaker Newt Gingrich (R-GA); and Rep. Robert Livingston (R-LA), the chairman of the House Appropriations Committee. One such event took place in February 1997, at the Breakers Hotel, an oceanfront luxury resort in Palm Beach, Florida. The donors were referred to as "Team 100" because their donations began at $100,000 each. According to Republican Party literature, a contribution of that size entitled them to be treated to the "fullest package of membership benefits of any political organization."

The Republicans' Team 100 Club could have been called the Team Million Club. Several corporations donated substantially more than the $100,000 entry fee. Amway Corporation gave the Republicans $2.9 million. The Philip Morris Companies gave $1.9 million, and RJR Nabisco gave $1 million. The Republicans actually outraised the Democrats in soft money during the 1995–1996 election cycle, raising $141.2 million, while the DNC raised $122.3 million. Those totals are nearly three times what they were four years earlier. As usual, a spokesperson for the Republican Party said — with a straight face — that the lawmakers were not going to the resort to meet with contributors because they made large donations. She said, "if I were a party leader, I would go anywhere in the country to get together with 200 people who have a real commitment to building the party."

The GOP also ran into problems with foreign donations. In May 1997, when the party returned $122,000 in contributions from a Hong Kong company, it was the first time that the Republican Party admitted to accepting foreign donations. Unfortunately for them, Republican leaders had denounced the Democrats and the White House for doing the same thing.

The Republican Party was also criticized for using nonprofit groups to funnel millions of dollars in donations to party candidates. Press reports indicated that the Republican Party worked closely with a nonprofit organization, Americans for Tax Reform, to elect Republicans. The tax group, which received more than $4 million from the party, used the money to support Republican congressional candidates in 150 districts. Federal election laws prohibit coordination of partisan activities between political parties and independent groups such as nonprofit organizations. Records show that as soon as the Republicans gave the $4.6 million "donation" to the tax group, the money was used to pay for a direct-mail campaign run by a former RNC official on behalf of Republican candidates.

The Republicans were also shown to have set up what appeared to be a bogus tax-exempt "issue development subsidiary" — called the National Policy Forum — through which the Party channeled millions in campaign contributions. The Forum, which was the brainchild of Haley Barbour, then the chairman of the Republican National Committee, began operations in 1993. The Forum spent $7 million, including $4.4 million in loans from the Republican Party, on Republican causes. In 1997, the Internal Revenue Service revoked the Forum's tax-exempt status because of its ties to the Republican Party. An official with Common Cause said the Forum was a "mechanism to evade campaign finance laws. . . . It is a front for the Republican National Committee that operates it as an arm of the party, but without being subject to the same rules."

The Republicans also took steps to make sure that GOP freshmen elected to the House of Representatives, who ran on a platform that they would reform the campaign finance system, would be cured of that idea. Republican leaders convinced the freshmen not to cooperate with Democrats who wanted to prohibit soft money contributions by arguing that their party would be hurt by such restrictions unless union support of Democrats was also limited.

For the 2000 election, Republicans substantially increased how much they expected major contributors to donate before being entitled to special privileges. In August 1999, the *New York Times* reported that Republicans had quietly formed a "Team $1 Million" group of elite contributors, with the goal that at least 100 individuals or organizations will make donations of $250,000 each year, or $1 million every four years. Among the many privileges the members of the elite club would enjoy would be private meetings with congressional leaders.

The governors come cheap

By comparison with Republican members of Congress, purchasing access to the nation's governors is relatively inexpensive. The National Governor's Association invited 100 big companies to contribute $12,000 a year to become a corporate "fellow." For the donation, which is funneled through a nonprofit entity called the "Center for Best Practices" — that allows the contribution to be tax deductible — the fellows get an array of benefits, according to a fact sheet from the governor's association. The association promises that executives and lobbyists from the corporations will be able to take part in the governors' plenary meetings, attend receptions with governors, and get briefings from the organization's leaders and staff. Contributors were also offered private work spaces and meeting areas at the association's annual gatherings, and an invitation to attend other events to help them "become better acquainted with governors' staffs and to share common interests."

The *New York Times* described a meeting in which lobbyists representing the corporate fellows were able to meet all day with the members of the association's national resources committee to discuss environmental issues, including the cleanup of toxic waste dumps. In the afternoon, when the director of the National Resources Defense Council, an environmental group, appeared before the committee, he was surprised to find himself facing not just the state environmental officials he had expected, but representatives of big corporations who had been lobbying against stringent air quality standards. Unlike the corporate officials, the environmentalists had not been invited to attend all day.

Association officials insisted that every meeting attended by the corporate fellows was open to anyone who wanted to show up. But, as explained by the newspaper, because the open meetings were not publicized, almost no one but corporate lobbyists ever attended.

The Thompson hearings

In June 1997, the Senate Governmental Affairs Committee began several months of hearings on campaign finance abuses. Chaired by Republican Senator Fred Thompson of Tennessee, the committee tried to look closely at how money was raised during the presidential and congressional elections of 1996 — especially donations made by foreign entities that would be illegal under federal law — to both the Democratic and Republican Parties. Despite Thompson's efforts to be fair, the Democrats on the panel criticized the hearings as a partisan attempt to embarrass them. The committee heard testimony from fund-raisers, contributors, and party officials. The senators found it frustrating that so many key individuals whom they wanted to question refused to testify. By the end of July, when the fourth week of hearings had concluded, the Republicans on the committee complained that at least 50 big-money donors and fundraisers in President Clinton's reelection campaign, whom the committee wanted to talk to under oath, had not testified. Those prospective witnesses either cited their Fifth Amendment right against self-incrimination, were out of the country, or did not testify for some other reason.

The committee was also frustrated by the response of politically active groups. More than two dozen nonprofit organizations told Thompson they considered the committee's subpoenas to be unconstitutional because they "pose a substantial threat to free speech, free association and privacy rights and the rights of other parties to have confidential communications with them." The groups included a cross section of the political spectrum including the Christian Coalition, the Sierra Club, and the National Right to Life Committee.

There were many instances of compelling and disturbing testimony before the committee, but the issues were extremely complicated and no single witness emerged as a symbol of the fund-raising scandal. The committee did hear evidence that foreign entities such as the Chinese government — and the government of Indonesia through the Lippo Group, an international financial holding company — tried to influence elections in this country. But the number of individuals involved was so large, and the complexity of the issues so great, it was difficult for the senators to follow the trail of donors and their contributions. It soon became clear that the television and reading audience was having a tough time following along as well.

At the beginning there was substantial news coverage of the hearings with CNN, MSNBC, and other networks carrying them live. But when it became clear that there would be none of the riveting testimony that characterized the Watergate hearings, television networks devoted less and less coverage to the work of the committee. Before long only C-SPAN provided significant coverage, but not live. It showed portions of the hearings late at night, as long as 12 hours after the testimony. Yet the hearings were important. As the *New York Times* noted in an editorial, the hearings had an educational value beyond the details of "last year's campaign shenanigans." The hearings showed that "American elections are so costly that it helps to think of fund-raising for them as a kind of arms race. The weapon perfected last year was . . . soft money."

At the same time that the Thompson hearings were going on in the Senate, House Republicans authorized an investigation into the campaign finance scandals by giving the Government Reform and Oversight Committee, chaired by Rep. Dan Burton (R-IN), the power to subpoena witnesses, thus forcing them to testify under oath. Democrats were outraged that the committee would be able to summon witnesses and take sworn testimony, and they called it a "witch hunt."

After adjourning during the end of Congress's summer vacation, the Thompson hearings resumed in the fall with Senator Thompson calling on the president to "step up to the plate" and help the committee get to the bottom of the fund-raising scandals. There was not much additional media interest in the hearings, but the public had heard enough in the preceding months to conclude the president did something wrong. In October, a *USA Today*/CNN/Gallup poll found that 25 percent believed the president had done something illegal, while an additional 36 percent thought he did something unethical but not illegal.

The Thompson committee did much to highlight some of the appalling methods used by the Democrats and Republicans to raise money for the 1996 campaigns. But the committee was unable to convince the American people that they should pay attention to the details — complex as they were — of the campaign fund-raising and spending abuses. The Burton committee had even less success. It got very little media coverage and was beset with even more partisan bickering than there had been on the Thompson committee.

The Thompson hearings did point out another aspect of the fund-raising scandal that Congress should have remedied immediately, but did not. The Federal Election Commission is charged with the responsibility of investigating potential violations of law when it comes to the raising and spending of money in federal elections. As the Thompson committee learned in September 1997, the FEC is woefully understaffed and cannot keep up with the numerous complaints it is asked to investigate. The FEC's general counsel told the committee that two-thirds of its cases are incomplete and that the commission has only two field investigators.

One positive aspect of the hearings may have been to energize the Justice Department to go after some of those who made illegal contributions. In October 1997, a Pennsylvania landfill company agreed to pay an $8 million fine — the highest penalty ever for a campaign-finance violation — in connection with a scheme to direct $129,000 in illegal campaign contributions to 10 political candidates. The biggest beneficiary of the scheme was the Dole Presidential campaign, which received $80,000. Former officials of the company and others faced multiple felony and misdemeanor counts.

In March 1998, Thomas Stewart, the owner of Food Services of America, one of the country's largest privately held companies, pleaded guilty to violating federal campaign finance laws and agreed to pay a $5 million penalty. Stewart admitted that he directed employees of his company to contribute to Republican candidates in Washington state and elsewhere in order to circumvent the legal limit on an individual's contribution to a federal candidate. This was not the first time Stewart was fined for violating campaign laws. In 1996, he paid $60,000 in fines for a local election violation.

In the same month, one of the most notorious figures associated with fund-raising for President Clinton's reelection campaign pleaded guilty to bank fraud, tax evasion, and conspiracy. Johnny Chung faced 37 years in prison and fines of more than $1 million when he was sentenced in July 1998, but because of his cooperation with the government, he was sentenced to probation.

The Public's Reaction and Responsibility

The almost daily disclosures of campaign improprieties did not, at first, affect the president's approval rating because the public said they expected no better of its politicians. A national poll conducted in mid-February 1997, found that 63 percent of respondents said they believed that President Clinton's behavior was typical of how the White House had been used by both parties, while 22 percent said it had been worse. In addition to the poll results, the *New York Times* asked residents of a state capital — Olympia, Washington — about their reaction to the fund-raising disclosures. Some respondents were quoted as saying all elected officials, both Republican and Democrat, raise money by selling access and other perquisites to donors with deep pockets. Others were more concerned that the campaign scandals distracted the federal government from more pressing problems. Still others did not find the news accounts of nefarious campaign activities to be worthy of their attention.

A Gallup Poll conducted after the 1996 presidential election found that 45 percent of the respondents were somewhat dissatisfied or very dissatisfied with the conduct of the presidential campaign and complained in particular about the barrage of political ads on television. Large majorities favored strict limits on the amount candidates can raise and spend. The Gallup organization found that part of the public's negative attitude about candidates and campaigns is the amount of money raised. In 1972, all candidates for Congress together spent a total of $77.3 million on their campaigns. In the 1996 races, congressional candidates spent an estimated $800 million while the presidential campaigns spent another $800 million. The public considers how money is raised and spent in the campaigns to be an important issue. Only 20 percent answering the Gallup poll said a candidate's campaign finances were *not* an important factor in deciding whom to vote for in the presidential election of 1996.

The public's initial reaction to the scandals of the late 1990s suggested that some people were already so inured to disclosures of abuse of the campaign system that they did not consider the misdeeds of the speaker of the House, the president and vice president, and the major parties, to be a big deal. They may believe that there is nothing they can do to change the system. Some of the president's supporters could shrug off the revelations by saying that the Democrats had to raise such large sums of money the way they did to keep up with the Republicans, and that is just the way the system works. Many citizens watch passively and conclude that the system is designed by and works well for those who directly benefit from it.

If people are so indifferent and cynical about politics that they will not make any effort to change the system, there will not be a second constitutional convention to address campaign finance reform and other issues. Especially during a time when the economy is doing well and there are few, if any, national issues that could be considered crises, it is easy for the American people to remain largely aloof from politics. If, however, people feel demeaned by a system so corrupted by money, and get angry and organized, momentum may build for revising the Constitution.

No single constitutional amendment is going to magically rid the campaign finance system of all its problems, and make elections more fair by giving challengers the opportunity to widely discuss their views on important issues and have a serious chance of winning. Whatever the language of the campaign finance amendment, those running for office and the narrow interests that support them will find a way to funnel money into campaigns. But certain changes — the overturning of *Buckley* that will allow limits on campaign expenditures; restriction on soft money contributions and money given to independent groups; the requirement that candidates for Congress raise half the money for their campaigns from their district or state — will have profound effects on the current system.

The American people have the right *and* the responsibility to govern their nation. In a large, complex society, direct democracy is obviously impossible and people must elect bright, energetic, and honorable leaders to carry out the policies the people support. Citizens need public officials who can also make decisions that are contrary to majority will when such judgments are in the best interests of the country. Once elected officials are chosen, however, the American people cannot assume that their work is done. The citizens are the direct descendants of those who approved the Constitution in the ratifying conventions. They have inherited powers and responsibilities under the Constitution. Although Americans enjoy rights that are the envy of people around the world, if they are going to live in a democratic society, there is one right they do not have: to do nothing. Although the contribution each person makes will vary, everyone has the responsibility to be part of the governing process.

With the campaign finance system the way it is, it is understandable that so many people do not want to fulfill the obligations of citizenship such as learning about candidates and voting. But their refusal to perform those duties can only excuse low voter turnout and ignorance about politics and government if there is no hope for reform. If there is a way to fix the system, the American people have an obligation to try. They may believe they have a good reason to be turned off to politics, yet there is no justification for refusing to help change the system when the means to do so are available.

Campaign finance reform is not an end itself, but the means to a more responsive system of representation. If the campaign finance constitutional amendment has positive effects, it will not merely curtail some of the worst abuses of the system by eliminating soft money contributions and restricting how much can be spent in campaigns. It will also increase the chance that candidates who will be more responsive to those who put them into office will win elections. Because of the urgent need for such a campaign finance amendment, and amendments dealing with other pressing issues, the American people must organize a second constitutional convention.

CHAPTER TWO

The Birth of Article V: Amending the Constitution

After more than 200 years of experience with the Constitution, it is clear that Article V — the only section of the nation's founding document that outlines the procedures for proposing and approving amendments — was poorly drafted, left many issues unresolved, and received insufficient attention from the delegates to the Convention of 1787. The delegates certainly had a lot of other important matters to resolve, and because of intense disagreements over the structure and powers of the new government, most of their efforts were directed towards dealing with those problems. But despite the Convention's overall success, the Framers failed to give the country adequate means by which the Constitution could be changed.

It is difficult to know everything about how the delegates arrived at the language that became Article V. The Convention met in secret, and guards were posted outside the doors of the State House in Philadelphia to prevent the curious from listening to the debates. The delegates strongly believed that they should be able to speak freely, float ideas, and criticize each other's proposals without worrying about the reaction of elected officials and the public. But that also meant that the nation has had to rely on the notes of the delegates themselves to know what went on behind closed doors that summer.

One of the first decisions the delegates made was to appoint a secretary, William Jackson of Philadelphia, to keep the official journal of the Convention. Jackson was an unfortunate choice because he did a poor job of taking notes and organizing the record. The delegates decided that the journal Jackson was preparing and "all the loose scraps of paper" left from the meeting would be delivered to the presiding officer of the Convention, George Washington, after the assembly adjourned. Later, in 1796 when Washington was president of the United States, he deposited the Journal written by Jackson and the other papers with the Department of State where they remained untouched until Congress approved a joint resolution in 1818 ordering them to be printed.

There are, however, serious questions about how accurately the official Journal represented the proceedings of the Convention. In 1818, President James Monroe requested his Secretary of State, John Quincy Adams, to take charge of the publication of the Journal. Adams soon learned that it would be no easy task. According to Adams, the papers were "no better than the daily minutes from which the regular journal ought to have been, but never was, made out." Adams tried to enlist the assistance of Jackson, but more than three decades had passed since the Convention and he could not provide much help. Jackson "looked over the papers, but he had no recollection of them which could remove the difficulties arising from their disorderly state, nor any papers to supply the deficiency of the missing papers." Most of Jackson's notes were a simple recording of motions and votes and included very little of the substance of the debates. By supplementing the Journal with the notes of several delegates, Adams was finally able to compile the record of the Convention in a form that was released to the public in 1819.

James Madison knew during the Philadelphia Convention that Jackson was planning to record the motions and votes, and little else. So with the approval of his fellow delegates, Madison agreed to act as an unofficial secretary of the Convention. His work turned out to be of tremendous importance because it is the most complete record of the proceedings, but the country had to wait a long time to see what Madison had written. His notes were not published until 1840, 53 years after the Convention and four years after Madison, the last surviving member of that famous gathering in Philadelphia's State House, had died.

Madison's reasons for not publishing his notes for so many years were partially based on his desire to spare the survivors of the Convention any political controversy in their old age and to keep the work of the delegates from becoming embroiled in the turmoil of current politics. But he may have had a monetary incentive for keeping his notes secret until his death. Madison, who died on June 28, 1836, left to his wife Dolley all his manuscripts, including his notes from the Convention. In his will, he recognized their value: "Considering the peculiarity and the magnitude of the occasion which produced the Convention at Philadelphia in 1787, the characters who composed it, the Constitution which resulted from their deliberations, its effects during a trial of so many years on the prosperity of the people living under it, and the interest it has inspired among the friends of free government, it is not an unreasonable inference that a careful and extended report of the proceedings and decisions of that body, which were with closed doors, by a member who was constant in his attendance, will be particularly gratifying to the people of the United States, and to all who take an interest in the progress of political science and the cause of liberty." In March 1837, Congress approved legislation purchasing from Dolley her husband's record of the Convention for $30,000. Congress purchased the rest of Madison's papers in 1848 for $20,000. She died in 1849.

If not for Madison's efforts, the nation would know relatively little about that historic meeting. He sat at the front of the assembly so he could face the delegates and hear all their comments and votes, and for three and a half months attended every day. While other delegates including Robert Yates of New York, Rufus King of Massachusetts, and James McHenry of Maryland also took notes at one time or another, none of their work compares in richness and breadth with Madison's records and observations.

But even Madison's notes cannot be considered completely accurate. It is known through his correspondence that after the Journal was published in 1819, he went over his own notes, perhaps for the first time in years. He looked for discrepancies between his records and those of the Journal and changed some of his recollections to conform with the information in the official record. These modifications are understandable because Madison was often occupied during the Convention with taking down the substance of the debate, so he may have had trouble keeping up with the motions and votes. He would thus consider the records as published in the Journal, which specifically recorded such votes, to be a helpful supplement.

Unfortunately, Madison did not simply add the votes from the Journal where he had not recorded them in his own notes. For reasons that historians do not completely understand, Madison changed his records of votes in the Convention so they would agree with the Journal. That action, taken so many years after the meeting in Philadelphia ended, sometimes affected the vote of a single state, or on other occasions, the votes of several states. The changes he made so many years later sometimes reversed his record of a vote taken by the Convention. His changing of his notes to reflect the work of Jackson and Adams would not be so much of a problem if the Journal itself was reliable. There are a number of occasions where Madison made corrections to his notes based on items in the Journal that were incorrect. Equally troubling is that in more than 50 instances, Madison changed quotes or statements from the debates that he had in his original records, or added comments to his recollections from the Journal.

The Debate over Article V

States began writing constitutions at the beginning of the Revolutionary War. Of the original 13 states, the constitutions of five of them contained no amending mechanism. Perhaps because they were written during a time of revolutionary fervor, the framers of those state constitutions may have believed that replacing a constitution rather than amending it provided the best way to institute a new government when, to paraphrase the Declaration of Independence, it became destructive of the people's rights. The remaining states allowed changes to their constitutions through one of three methods: legislative action; amendment by constitutional convention; or by a "council of censors," which would meet periodically to revise the constitution.

One of the great shortcomings of the Articles of Confederation was that they could only be amended after approval by Congress and ratification by *all* states. The smallest state, with a fraction of the nation's population, could veto any constitutional change supported by the overwhelming majority of the people. A month before the Articles became effective, Congress sent to the states an amendment permitting it to levy a duty of five percent ad valorem on all imports. All states approved the measure except for Rhode Island, which rejected the amendment in 1782. Thus, an important amendment that would have helped the new government to raise revenue was not adopted. Four years later, New York alone defeated a new revenue system by withholding its approval.

The first time the issue of amending the Constitution was raised at the Philadelphia Convention was four days after it began when Governor Randolph of Virginia presented the Virginia Plan. Resolution Number 13 of the plan stated that "provision ought to be made for the amendment of the Articles of Union whensoever it shall seem necessary." The resolution said nothing more about the amending provision except that the "assent of the National Legislature ought not to be required thereto." The delegates decided on June 5 to postpone a vote on Resolution 13, but not before briefly discussing the issue of amending the Constitution. According to Madison's notes, Charles Pinkney of South Carolina "doubted the propriety or necessity of it." Madison's notes do not make clear what "it" refers to in Pinkney's statement. He may have been talking about the section of Resolution 13 recommending that the new national Congress play no role in proposing or ratifying amendments, or he may have meant that no amending process of any kind should be included in the Constitution. It is likely that he meant the latter, for there were comments later in the summer by several delegates who believed that once the Constitution was finalized, it should not be altered. On the other hand, Elbridge Gerry of

Massachusetts favored a process for amending the Constitution, and said that the "novelty & difficulty of the experiment requires periodical revision." Gerry was later proved right in predicting that "the prospect of such a revision would also give intermediate stability to the Govt." He went on to say "nothing had yet happened in the States where this provision existed to prove its impropriety." After these comments about the amendment process, the delegates, who voted by state at the Convention, decided 7-3 to postpone further consideration of the issue.

On June 11, the delegates gave more detailed consideration to what would eventually become Article V. According to Madison's notes, "several members did not see the necessity of the (Resolution) at all, nor the propriety of making the consent of the Natl. Legisl. Unnecessary." However, George Mason observed that the new Constitution would certainly be "defective, as the Confederation has been found on trial to be." He suggested that "amendments therefore will be necessary, and it will be better to provide for them, in an easy regular and Constitutional way than to trust to chance and violence." Mason was especially concerned that if Congress had to give its approval for the Constitution to be changed, there was the danger that a too powerful legislature would not propose amendments even when the proposals enjoyed strong support: "It would be improper to require the consent of the Natl. Legislature, because they may abuse their power, and refuse their consent on that very account. The opportunity for such abuse, may be the fault of the Constitution calling for amendmt." The delegates unanimously approved the first part of Resolution 13, that an amending provision was to be included in the Constitution, but they postponed a decision on whether the national legislature should be involved in the process.

An important development in the history of Article V took place on July 26. It was on that day when the Convention voted to adjourn until August 6 so a "Committee of Detail" could "prepare and report a constitution comfortable" to the resolutions it had adopted during the first two months. The delegates had known for some time that a committee would need to draft specific language for the new Constitution that reflected the votes and debates of the Convention. During the first months of the Philadelphia meeting, the delegates had been urged to limit their discussion to "general principles" and to leave "precise and explicit" details to the committee that eventually would be appointed. Some of the most distinguished members of the Convention served on the Committee of Detail. It included John Rutledge of South Carolina as chair, who kept his four colleagues on the Committee focused on the task at hand with a minimum of controversy, and James Wilson of Pennsylvania, who took on the responsibility of putting the resolutions of the Convention into language that would be acceptable to the delegates, would win ratification in the state conventions, and would endure through the years. Because so many of the resolutions agreed to by the delegates in the first months of the Convention were general in nature, the Committee had substantial discretion when reducing them to specific constitutional provisions. That the Committee was able to do its job so well — by accurately reflecting the sentiments of the majority of the delegates as expressed in the resolutions, and at the same time, when there was little guidance, producing language that the delegates would mostly accept — was a significant factor in the Convention's overall success.

As found in the James Wilson papers in the Library of the Historical Society of Pennsylvania, the Committee discussed language that would become Article V early on in its work, but it was anything but "detailed": "Resolved That Provision ought to be made for the Amendment of the Articles of Union, whensoever it shall seem necessary." The Committee later refined and expanded the statement on amending the Constitution, and it resembled Article V for the first time. This is what it looked like as it appeared in Madison's notes: "(An alteration may be effected in the articles of union, on the application of two thirds nine <2/3d> of the state legislatures <by a Convention.>) <on appln. of 2/3ds of the State Legislatures to the Natl. Leg. they call a Convn. to revise or alter the Articles of Union>." In a later draft, the Committee established the procedure for calling a constitutional convention upon application by the states. Perhaps in reaction to Mason's statement about an oppressive Congress obstructing necessary constitutional reform, the Committee recommended that only a convention would be able to propose amendments: "This Constitution ought to be amended whenever such Amendment shall be necessary; and on the Application of the Legislatures of two thirds of the States in the Union, the Legislature of the United States shall call a Convention for that Purpose." The Committee kept the same language in a subsequent draft.

When the Convention returned on August 6, the Committee of Detail presented its report. According to Madison's notes, Article XIX stated that "On the application of the Legislatures of two thirds of the States in the Union, for an amendment of this Constitution, the Legislature of the United States shall call a Convention for that purpose."

On August 30, again according to Madison's notes, the Convention unanimously adopted the Committee of Detail's plan that did not permit Congress to propose amendments. Its only role would be to call a convention upon application from two-thirds of the states. Eventually Congress would have the authority to propose amendments, but not at this phase. The one comment Madison noted when the Convention adopted the

Committee of Detail's plan was Gouverneur Morris's of Pennsylvania, who "suggested that the Legislature should be left at liberty to call a Convention, whenever they please." He apparently did not argue the point energetically and his idea did not subsequently become part of the Constitution. Congress can only call a convention upon application by the states.

Article V Takes Shape

On September 10, 1787, only a week before the Constitution was signed and the Convention adjourned, the Framers gave serious consideration to the amending provision. It had been discussed sporadically during the summer, but time was running out and the delegates could not put off a decision much longer. Elbridge Gerry of Massachusetts moved to reconsider the article as written — that permitted amendment only by convention — out of concern that two-thirds of the states could force Congress to hold a convention, and then amend the Constitution in a way that harms the interests of the remaining states. He feared the possibility that a majority of states could "bind the Union to innovations that may subvert the State-Constitutions altogether." According to Madison's notes, "He asked whether this was a situation proper to be run into."

Alexander Hamilton seconded Gerry's motion. The brilliant New Yorker who had done so much to help bring about the Philadelphia Convention, played a major role in ratification by co-authoring the *Federalist Papers*, and later helped stabilize the new nation's economy as Secretary of the Treasury under President Washington, was a terrible disappointment at the Convention. He was away much of the summer and rarely participated enthusiastically when he attended in June and September. But when he spoke on September 10 about the need for Congress to be able to propose amendments, he convinced his colleagues and defined the process that the nation would use for the next two centuries when altering the Constitution.

Hamilton reminded the delegates of the unworkable system for amendments under the Articles of Confederation in which every state had to give its approval. He said that "an easy mode should be established for supplying defects which will probably appear in the new System." But he added that the proposal by the Committee of Detail, which had been approved by the Convention on August 30, "was not adequate" and he argued for permitting Congress to also propose amendments: "The State Legislatures will not apply for alterations but with a view to increase their own powers — The National Legislature will be the first to perceive and will be the most sensible to the necessity of amendments, and ought also to be empowered, whenever two-thirds of each branch should concur to call a Convention — There could be no danger in giving this power, as the people would finally decide in the case."

Hamilton's final phrase suggesting the people "would finally decide in the case" is difficult to interpret. He did not propose, and the Convention did not ultimately adopt, an amendment procedure that included a direct role for the people. He may have meant that because the people elected members of the House of Representatives, and the House had to give its approval before Congress could propose amendments, the public's views would be considered. Whatever the interpretation, the Framers had the opportunity, which they did not pursue, of having citizens either propose or approve amendments through a referendum or some other process.

At this point Madison raised an important question that the delegates were either too tired to resolve, or assumed that future generations would work out. Madison's notes say that he "remarked on the vagueness of the terms, 'call a Convention for the purpose.'" He said that phrase was "sufficient reason" for reconsidering the previously approved article. He also asked, "How was a Convention to be formed? by what rule decide? what force of its acts?"

The delegates then approved Gerry's motion to reconsider by a vote of 9-1, with one state's delegates evenly divided. Now that the Convention had agreed to reopen debate on the amending provision, it could decide some of the important issues that had been left unresolved. Roger Sherman of Connecticut wanted both the national legislature and the states to be involved in amending the Constitution. In addition to Congress calling a convention, he moved to add to the article the words "or the Legislature may propose amendments to the several States for their approbation, but no amendments shall be binding until consented to by the several States." Gerry seconded Sherman's motion.

If the delegates were going to give the states a role in approving amendments proposed by either Congress or a convention, they would have to decide what percentage of the states would have to give their assent. It was obvious, and needed no discussion, that a number less than unanimous would be required. The Framers knew all too well how difficult it had been for the Confederation Congress to change the Articles so the national government could collect revenue and take other appropriate actions. At the same time, the delegates also recognized that the new Constitution would be the fundamental law of the nation, and should not be amended by ordinary legislative means. Something between unanimity and a simple majority would be required.

James Wilson recommended that two-thirds of the several states be required to give their approval and Sherman seconded his motion. Today, that would be 34 states. Madison did not record any of the debate in his notes, but Wilson's motion failed when six states voted no, five states voted yes, and one state divided. When Wilson moved to change the required number to three-fourths of the states, the delegates agreed unanimously to adopt the plan.

At the time the Constitution was approved, the difference between two-thirds and three-quarters would have been one state. Today, with 50 states, the difference is four. It is impossible to know for certain why the Framers decided that two-thirds represented insufficient consensus while three-quarters was the appropriate threshold of approval for constitutional amendments. In the 1970s, the Equal Rights Amendment was approved by 35 states, but ultimately failed when it could not win ratification in three others. If 200 years earlier the delegates at the Philadelphia Convention had approved Wilson's original motion, the ERA would have become part of the Constitution.

The delegates were almost finished with Article V. After Wilson's motion requiring three-fourths approval of the states, Madison asked the delegates to postpone further discussion so they could consider his proposal allowing both Congress and the state legislatures to propose amendments. Except for the position of some phrases and substituting "Congress" for "Legislature of the U-S," Madison's proposal, which was seconded by Hamilton, eventually became the amending provision of Article V.

But time was running short. The delegates wanted to end their long summer of work and return home. The Convention would be over in a week and important issues, such as how the Constitution itself would be ratified, were still to be decided. In the final days, the delegates also had to contend with the strongly held belief of George Mason and others that a bill of rights had to be added to the Constitution before it was signed. There loomed the possibility that last-minute decisions made by fatigued delegates would create major problems.

With so many pending and complex questions to be resolved in such a short period, it was important for the Framers to complete what would become Article V, then move on. But a motion by John Rutledge of South Carolina threatened not only to prolong the debate over the amending provision, but to unravel many of the precarious compromises that the delegates had reached on other issues.

Rutledge said he could never approve of an amending provision "to give a power by which the articles relating to slaves might be altered by the States not interested in that property and prejudiced against it."

Madison and other delegates suddenly saw that Article V might become laden with proposals only indirectly related to the amending process. They were understandably distressed over the possibility that delegates who had been previously unsuccessful in getting what they wanted in the Constitution would see the debate over Article V as a chance for another shot at including provisions they considered important. To appease Rutledge and the slave states, the delegates agreed to include language that prevented amendments interfering with slavery for two decades by adding these words to what would become Article V: "provided that no amendments which may be made prior to the year 1808. shall in any manner affect the 4 & 5 sections of the VII article [sections relating to the migration or importation of slaves]."

Once the Rutledge addendum had been accepted, the delegates approved Madison's motion by a vote of 9-1, with one state divided. Article V was nearly complete, but not yet. Perhaps because they saw Rutledge and the Southern states get their way when trying to change Article V, the small states decided they would also attempt to add language to the proposed amendment. Suddenly, after being ignored for most of the summer, and with only days left before the planned adjournment, the small states saw Article V as an opportunity to revisit the major question of the relative powers of large and small states, and the states and the new national government.

In addition to the Committee of Detail, the delegates had appointed a Committee of Style. Made up of five members, the Committee was responsible for producing the final polished version of the Constitution. It began meeting on September 8, and approved the nearly complete Article V — which was then Article XIX — including Madison's language permitting Congress to propose amendments, and Rutledge's prohibition on interference with slavery. But two days before the Convention would end with the signing of the Constitution, the potential problem with Article V became apparent. Roger Sherman of Connecticut, probably expressing the apprehension of other delegates from small states, worried that the amending process would allow larger states to deprive their smaller brethren of representation in the Senate or their very existence. According to Madison's notes, "Mr. Sherman expressed his fears that three fourths of the States might be brought to do things fatal to particular States, as abolishing them altogether or depriving them of their equality in the Senate. He thought it reasonable that the proviso in favor of the States importing slaves should be extended so as to provide that no State should be affected in its internal police, or deprived of its equality in the Senate."

Sherman's proposal, especially coming so late in the Convention, must have been troubling to many of the delegates. What did he mean by "no State should be affected in its internal police?" "Police," as used in this context, did not refer to a modern day police force that deals with crime. The "police powers" of a state related to the health, welfare, and safety of citizens. Sherman appeared to be suggesting that the Constitution could not be amended in a way that interfered with the internal operations of a state. If that language had remained in Article V, it would have significantly altered the delicate balance between the states and the new central government that was carefully crafted over the long summer, and could have potentially led many of the delegates to refuse to sign the Constitution.

After Sherman offered his motion, George Mason sharply denounced the amendment provision. He thought the "plan of amending the Constitution exceptionable & dangerous." He criticized the procedure whereby Congress would be involved in both calling a convention and proposing amendments, arguing that "No amendments of the proper kind would ever be obtained by the people, if the Government should become oppressive." Madison's notes add that Mason "verily believed [this] would be the case." In the margin of his copy of the draft of the Constitution of September 12, Mason noted his anxiety about the people being excluded from the amendment process: "By this article Congress only have the power of proposing amendments at any future time to this constitution and should it prove ever so oppressive, the whole people of America can't make, or even propose alterations to it; a doctrine utterly subversive of the fundamental principles of the rights and liberties of the people."

At this point Madison raised an important issue which, unfortunately, the delegates either did not consider to be important enough or else they did not want to address it so close to the end of the Convention. Madison did not object to a convention for the purpose of amendments, but he was troubled by the "difficulties [that] might arise as to the form, the quorum &c. which in Constitutional regulations ought to be as much as possible avoided."

Roger Sherman tried again to include in what became Article V a declaration that no amendments would interfere with a state's "internal police" or "equal suffrage in the Senate." Madison argued against the first part of Sherman's motion. He saw the possibility that once Sherman's motion was approved, every state would want special protections included in Article V: "Begin with these special provisos, and every State will insist on them, for their boundaries, exports &c." The delegates took Madison's warning to heart as they defeated Sherman's motion 8-3. Not content to accept the decision of his fellow delegates, Sherman moved to eliminate Article V altogether. That motion was defeated 8-2, with one state divided.

Finally, Gouverneur Morris suggested the delegates include the language protecting the equal suffrage of the states in the Senate. Madison noted "this motion being dictated by the circulating murmurs of the small States was agreed to without debate, no one opposing it, or on the question, saying no." On September 15, 1787, two days before the end of the convention, the delegates completed Article V of the U.S. Constitution. If delegates from the small states had pledged not to sign the Constitution if Sherman's motion was defeated, or if the Northern states objected to the slave provisions, the debate over Article V could have continued indefinitely. Eventually, the Framers provided for two methods by which amendments can be proposed, and two methods for ratification. They protected slavery for a period of 20 years and any state from losing its representation in the Senate without its approval. What the Framers did not realize until they finished their work in Philadelphia was how important Article V would be to citizens of the country as they selected delegates to attend the ratifying conventions.

The Framers Had Many Options

The delegates to the Convention were primarily interested in creating a Constitution, and were much less concerned with providing a mechanism by which succeeding generations could adapt the Constitution to changing conditions. Considering its significance, however, the Framers devoted insufficient time to formulating the process by which the Constitution could be amended. There was general agreement that the Constitution had to include an amendment provision; only a few delegates suggested that once completed, the Constitution should never be changed. But the Framers, who finalized Article V only days before the end of the Convention, failed to provide answers to important questions surrounding the amendment process. The fact that the delegates, for example, provided so little guidance on how a second convention should be convened and conducted is probably one reason why the nation has never had one. The Framers did not expect Congress to be the only body that proposed amendments and they anticipated that conventions would be held at some point in the future. But instead of providing at least the outline of how such a convention should be organized, they apparently assumed that since they were able to conduct a successful convention in 1787, subsequent generations would be able to as well.

Even if the Framers had devoted more time to Article V, finding an appropriate process for changing the Constitution would not have been easy. They had to create the right balance between ordinary legislative majorities, that would be fairly easy to achieve, and nearly unanimous consensus that would be too difficult to obtain. Finding a middle ground would prove to be challenging. If the Constitution was too easy to modify, its legitimacy would be eroded by amendments proposed by whatever party or group was in power at the time, and it would no longer be a national charter establishing and preserving enduring values that would survive throughout later generations. If, on the other hand, the Constitution was too cumbersome and time-consuming to alter, and required an unrealistically high level of agreement approaching unanimity, it would quickly fall out of step with changing conditions and values. The resulting turmoil would put dangerous strains on the political system.

The sparse debate at the Convention of 1787 over Article V — which was mostly limited to a few comments about what role Congress should play, whether an amendment provision was necessary, and what percentage of states should be required to approve amendments — suggests that the delegates had few alternatives from which to choose in formulating the amending provision. But that was not the case. The Framers had numerous options that they did not explore, either because they did not have time, or because they considered the amending article of the Constitution to be substantially less important than other sections. Nevertheless, it is worthwhile to consider some of the procedures for amending the Constitution that the Framers did not debate, but that could be adopted by a second convention which must, as one of its highest priorities, amend Article V.

The individuals and institutions that could have been given a part or a more enhanced role in the amending process include:

- The president
- The vice president
- The Congress (either or both Houses)
- Federal conventions
- The Supreme Court
- State legislatures
- State conventions
- Governors
- The people as citizens of the United States or of their respective states
- Electors chosen by the people

The president

The president and vice president are the only nationally elected public officials in the nation. The Framers gave the executive branch powers that alarmed many of the delegates who had experienced the tyranny of George III and royal governors, and who knew that the people would be worried about whether the presidency could grow so strong as to threaten civil liberties. Despite the role the president plays in so many areas of public policy, the Framers decided that the president should be excluded from any involvement in the amendment process.

Article V does not mention the president, but another section of the Constitution could have been interpreted as requiring presidential approval of amendments. Article I, Section 7 of the Constitution requires that "Every Order, Resolution or Vote to which the Concurrence of the Senate and House of Representatives may be necessary . . . shall be presented to the President of the United States." The Framers discussed the president's power to sign or veto bills in the context of legislation, but nothing in the debates at the Convention suggested the Framers were thinking about the amendment process when they wrote that section of the Constitution. Eleven years after the Convention, the Supreme Court confirmed the view that the president's approval is not required for constitutional amendments.

The Court's eventual ruling that the president had no formal role to play in the amendment process began in 1793, when it decided the controversial case of *Chisholm v. Georgia*. The state of Georgia had purchased supplies from a merchant who lived in Charleston, South Carolina. When the merchant died, his executor sued Georgia in federal court to recover money owed his estate. The Supreme Court interpreted Article III of the Constitution, which extended judicial power to controversies "between a State and Citizens of another State," to mean that Georgia was subject to federal jurisdiction in such lawsuits. The *Chisholm* decision alarmed Anti-Federalists who had been assured during the debates over ratification that states would not be subject to such judicial interference.

Congress acted quickly. Using Article V for the first time since the Bill of Rights was ratified, Congress proposed the 11th Amendment to reverse the Supreme Court's *Chisholm* decision. It would be the first of only four occasions in the nation's history when the amendment process was successfully used to reverse a Supreme Court decision. The 11th Amendment explicitly stated that federal judicial authority would not extend to cases between a state and a citizen of another state. The Amendment became part of the Constitution on February 7, 1795. Three years later, when opponents of the 11th Amendment asserted that it had not been properly ratified because the president had not signed it as required under Article I, Section 7, the Supreme Court rejected that argument. In 1798, in *Hollingsworth v. Virginia*, the Court unanimously held that the presidential veto applied only to "ordinary cases of legislation" and that the president "has nothing to do with the proposition, or adoption, of amendments to the Constitution."

The Court found another reason to support the contention that the Framers did not intend to give the president a role in the amendment process. Because a two-thirds majority in both Houses is required to propose amendments *and* override presidential vetoes, it would make no sense to give the president the authority to veto proposed amendments, only to have those amendments returned to Congress so the veto could be overridden by the same margin. The Framers, the Court reasoned, could not have intended such an unnecessary step.

The Court had no practical choice in *Hollingsworth* but to decide the case the way it did. If the justices had concluded that the president must sign proposed amendments, the Bill of Rights could have been challenged as having been improperly forwarded to the states and thus potentially void. Even if the *Hollingsworth* decision applied such a rule to future cases only, it could have significantly changed the balance of power between the president and Congress. There would be nothing simple or automatic about returning a proposed amendment to Congress to override a presidential veto even though the original vote would have been by a two-thirds majority. If the vote was close, there would be intense lobbying on both sides, and it is possible that a proposed amendment that received sufficient majorities before the presidential veto would fall short when the amendment was returned to Congress.

Providing for such a presidential role in the amending process would have added an additional level to an already immensely difficult process. It is hard enough to get Congress to approve, and the states to ratify, constitutional amendments. If the president had a formal role, proposed amendments would be even less likely to win final approval.

That does not mean, of course, that the president cannot be involved in the amendment process at all. Article II, Section 3 of the Constitution grants the president power to "recommend" to Congress "such Measures as he shall judge necessary and expedient." And interestingly, on two occasions presidents have signed constitutional amendments before they were sent to the states for approval even though their signatures were not required. The president is always free to suggest and lobby for or against proposed amendments.

Just as Article V makes no mention of a presidential role in approving amendments before they are sent to the states, it is also silent on the role the president would play in the planning of a second convention. If a convention called under Article V had the support of the president, the Executive Branch could help with the organizing and convening of such a gathering. If petitions submitted by the states requesting a second convention approach the two-thirds threshold of 34, Congress will undoubtedly enact a statute that attempts to control the selection of delegates and the proceedings of the convention. The president will have to sign such a bill, and thus would likely be consulted about the procedures a convention would follow. The Framers apparently did not consider what the president's formal role should be if Congress ever calls a second convention.

The vice president

The vice president has so few official duties under the Constitution that it is understandable that some commentators would recommend that if the Constitution is ever revised, the position should be eliminated. Except for being available to assume the office of the president, the only substantive duty assigned to the vice president is to be president of the Senate and to break tie votes, a power exercised about 235 times in our history.

The Framers originally considered creating the position of president of the Senate and having that person assume the powers and duties of the president in case of removal, death, resignation, or disability. A committee of delegates later proposed that the vice president be available for that purpose, and also made him ex-officio president of the Senate. Late in the Convention, Elbridge Gerry and George Mason objected to this plan as an improper defiance of the principle of separation of powers. But Roger Sherman pointed out that "if the vice-President were not to be President of the Senate, he would be without employment."

The Framers likely created the vice presidency for the sake of the Electoral College, so two individuals — one who would be president, and one who could assume the presidency if necessary — could be elected at the same time. That system proved to be unworkable when Thomas Jefferson and Aaron Burr, running as presidential and vice presidential candidates, respectively, in 1800, both received 73 electoral votes. Under the original Constitution, the candidate with the most electoral votes became president, while the runner-up became vice president. The election thus had to be decided by the House of Representatives controlled by the lame-duck Federalists. The deadlock was still not broken after 35 votes, and it appeared that no president would be selected in time to take office on March 4, 1801. On February 17, Jefferson was finally elected president. The 12th Amendment, which was ratified on June 15, 1804, solved that problem by having electors vote separately for president and vice president.

Considering how little there is for the vice president to do under the Constitution, it is, perhaps, not surprising that the Framers did not assign any responsibility in the amendment process to the person holding that office. Because constitutional amendments must be approved by a two-thirds votes, there is not even the opportunity for the vice president to break a tie when the Senate considers an amendment. The Framers could have given the vice president some formal role in the amendment process either as vice president or as the president of the Senate. But as with the president, the Framers probably believed that the vice president should not be able to interfere with the changing of the Constitution.

The Congress (either or both Houses)

The Framers ultimately decided that if Congress proposed amendments for ratification — one of the two methods provided in Article V, and the only one ever used — both Houses would need to give their approval by a two-thirds majority. The Framers could have allowed amendments to be proposed by majorities smaller than two-thirds, but they clearly wanted the amendment process to be invoked only by a consensus greater than that required for ordinary legislation.

The Convention could also have given the responsibility of proposing amendments to one house of Congress only. There are a number of powers given to the Senate that are denied to the House, including approval of treaties, confirmation of high-level executive appointees and federal judges, and serving as the trial court for impeachment. The Framers expected the Senate, whose members were not elected directly by the people, and whom they assumed would be more protective of property and wealth, to resist ill-conceived policies supported by the majority of citizens and approved by the House.

Federal conventions

Some of the delegates to the Convention believed that the national legislature could become oppressive and entrenched, and would refuse to propose amendments despite widespread support for them. They recommended, and the Convention seriously considered, that Congress be given no role in the amendment process except for being required to call a convention when petitioned by a sufficient number of states. That proposal worried some delegates who believed that a numerical majority of states could conspire to petition Congress to hold a convention that would then curtail the rights of some states or eliminate them completely. The Framers decided to include both methods of amendment in Article V.

In the delegates' rush to complete the Constitution and adjourn, they neglected to provide any guidance as to how a second constitutional convention would be organized. There is substantial debate among constitutional scholars over whether Congress could limit the agenda of the convention to consideration of specific amendments, and whether the courts would have the authority to compel Congress to call a convention if it refused to do so.

The Supreme Court

The Supreme Court has no formal role in proposing or approving amendments, although it must interpret amendments once they become part of the Constitution. In debating the presidential veto, the Framers considered and then rejected a proposal that would have given the Supreme Court veto power over acts of Congress. The Framers, not unexpectedly, also denied the Supreme Court the authority to "veto" proposed constitutional amendments.

The Framers wanted to create institutions of government that would be accountable and responsive to the people, but would also resist their will when it was shortsighted or harmful to the nation's long-term interests. They created two government institutions that would be "insulated" from the people: the Senate, whose members would be chosen by state legislatures, and the federal courts, whose judges would receive lifetime tenure. The Framers also showed their distrust of the people by creating the Electoral College through which voters chose electors who would actually select the president.

Considering the features in the Constitution that were established to check the excesses of democracy, it would not have been entirely unexpected for the Framers to give the federal courts some formal role in the proposing and ratification of amendments. However, if they had given the Supreme Court such authority, it would have created many problems.

Any direct intervention by the Supreme Court in the amendment process would have raised troubling issues because amendments are sometimes specifically intended to reverse or curtail the Court's authority. At least four constitutional amendments have directly overturned decisions of the Supreme Court:

• The 11th Amendment reversed the 1793 decision in *Chisholm v. Georgia* that had permitted citizens of one state to sue the state government of another in federal court.

• The 14th Amendment reversed the disastrous 1857 decision in *Dred Scott v. Sandford* which held that slaves were not citizens of either the United States or their state, and therefore could not sue in the federal courts.

  • The 16th Amendment reversed the 1895 decision in *Pollock v. Farmers Loan & Trust Co.* that had invalidated the federal income tax.

  • The 26th Amendment partially modified the 1970 decision in *Oregon v. Mitchell* that had concluded that Congress could not force states to lower the voting age to 18 in nonfederal elections. The 26th Amendment was needed to create a uniform voting age in state and federal elections.

Considering the number of constitutional rulings the Court has handed down that were immensely unpopular, that number seems small and serves as another indication of how difficult it is to get a constitutional amendment approved. Even during the 1930s when the country was in the depths of the Depression and the Supreme Court invalidated major portions of the New Deal, President Franklin Roosevelt and his supporters in Congress did not pursue constitutional amendments as a way of reversing the Supreme Court decisions. FDR considered whether to recommend amendments during the period both before and after the 1936 election, when he enjoyed the largest electoral victory of any president. But he rejected the amendment option partly because no agreement could be reached within the Executive Branch as to the language of the amendments. The amendments would have to be drafted in broad terms because future developments could not be anticipated, and there was legitimate concern that the conservative Supreme Court would find the new amendments so broadly worded or vague, that it could continue to invalidate New Deal legislation. Perhaps most importantly, FDR realized that the amendment process would take too long. The economic crisis had to be dealt with immediately and could not wait several years for the proposed amendments to make their way through the states where there was always the possibility that state legislatures — dominated by conservatives opposed to the New Deal — would deny the amendments the necessary votes. Instead of going the amendment route, FDR proposed the ill-fated "court-packing" plan in 1937, which would have given him the chance to immediately appoint several justices, but which was strongly opposed by the country and Congress.

There is always the possibility of the Court ruling on amendments that would in some respects reverse its rulings or limit its power. There is some agreement among legal scholars that the Court must not be allowed to interfere with efforts by the elected branches of government to adopt amendments, and that its role should be limited to ruling on the procedures by which amendments are approved, but not their substance.

State legislatures

The final version of Article V gives the states a key role in both methods by which the Constitution can be amended. When Congress proposes amendments, they must be approved by three-quarters or 38 states. It is up to Congress to decide if the states ratify amendments through actions of the legislatures or by conventions elected by the people. If there is ever a convention called to propose amendments, two-thirds, or 34, of the state legislatures must petition Congress to call a convention, and any amendments proposed by that convention must subsequently be approved by three-quarters of the states.

Giving state legislatures such an important role in the amendment process may have helped the delegates at the Constitutional Convention find a balance between the states and the new central government, but it had significant consequences for the amendment process. Because 38 states must give their approval to changes in the Constitution, legislatures in 13 states can stop an amendment. Except for Nebraska, which has a unicameral legislature, all states must approve constitutional amendments by majorities in both houses. If one house of the legislature of those 13 states declines to ratify an amendment, it will not become part of the Constitution despite strong, nationwide support. No more than a few dozen individuals representing a fraction of the nation's population may hold the balance.

State legislative races often get substantially less media coverage than statewide elections such as those for governor and attorney general, and elections for federal office. Voters often know little about the record or behavior of the approximately 7,500 legislators who represent them in their state capitals. State legislatures can also be notoriously unrepresentative of their state's population. For example, in 1997 women held just 4 percent of legislative seats in Alabama, the lowest in the nation. In Kentucky, the next from the bottom, only 9.4 percent of legislators were women. The national average was 21.5 percent, although some state legislatures such as Washington state were almost evenly divided between men and women. Many legislators serve part-time, meet in formal sessions only every other year, and are paid low salaries. The 424 state legislators in New Hampshire who meet annually earn only $100 a year. Their California counterparts, on the other hand, are full-time and earn more than $50,000 annually. Although part-time legislatures may attract bright and dedicated public servants, and there is much appeal to the concept of the "citizen-legislator" who comes to the state capital a few months a year, then returns to the farm or small business or classroom, many people who would like to serve cannot because their jobs do not permit them to be away for several months at a time. Such a legislative environment does not always attract the most qualified people. Yet these individuals will decide whether an amendment proposed by Congress becomes part of the Constitution — unless Congress designates state conventions for ratifying amendments — or whether a second convention is held.

State conventions

In Article V, the Framers gave Congress the authority to choose whether the states ratify proposed amendments through their legislative body or state conventions. In only one case, when the 21st Amendment was proposed by Congress to repeal the 18th Amendment on the prohibition of alcohol, did Congress require states to ratify an amendment by convention. Congress was concerned that because many state legislatures were dominated by representatives from rural or "dry" districts, the 21st Amendment would not be ratified unless considered by specially elected state conventions. The Framers could have decided that constitutional amendments would always be ratified by state conventions. When they chose the method for ratifying the actual Constitution, they decided to bypass state legislatures and required that delegates to conventions approve the new document. All states allowed the people to directly elect those delegates.

The Framers may have anticipated more frequent amendments and believed that holding repeated conventions — with delegates having to campaign for election to those conventions — would be too cumbersome. More likely, they expected the states to continue to play a significant role in the new federal system, and therefore, wanted state legislatures to also play an important part in the ratification process.

Governors

The Framers gave no role to governors in the amendment process. They most likely considered it to be a legislative function, and just as the president should not be able to derail efforts to alter the Constitution, neither should governors. Governors are free to lobby their state legislatures and encourage citizens to contact their representatives when constitutional amendments are under consideration, but their role is informal.

The people as citizens of the United States or of their respective states

Article V does not provide a method by which the people can propose amendments directly on their own. The Framers may not have been motivated solely by a lack of confidence in the ability of the American people to rationally debate amendments to the Constitution. They may have believed that because transportation and communication systems were so primitive, it would be difficult for voters to get enough information to carefully examine amendments that may have made significant changes to the structure of government or their federal constitutional rights. If the Framers did not trust the American people to directly elect the president or their senators — acts that may be less complicated than proposing or approving constitutional amendments — they would not likely have looked favorably on an amendment process that gave citizens the ability to adopt amendments independent of their elected officials.

The Framers could have created a system by which proposed amendments would be submitted to a national or state-by-state referendum and require approval of those amendments by a majority or super-majority before they become part of the Constitution. Or the Framers could have allowed voters in individual states to consider amendments at the ballot, with their decision binding a representative to a national convention or assembly to ratify amendments.

The Constitution denies the people not only the right to propose amendments, but according to the Supreme Court, the right to ratify them as well. In *Hawke v. Smith* in 1920, the Court unanimously invalidated a provision of the Ohio Constitution that required federal constitutional amendments to be approved by voters before the state could certify it had sanctioned the amendment. The Court concluded that Article V imposes on state legislatures a federal function not derived from the people of the state, but from the Constitution. Since ratification of a proposed amendment is not an act of legislation, but an expression of assent of the state to the proposed amendment, Ohio could not delegate that responsibility to the voters.

Some scholars believe that the people, as citizens of their states, have the authority to amend the federal Constitution by means other than those outlined in Article V. Akhil Reed Amar, a professor at Yale Law School, made such an argument in a thoughtful and provocative 1988 article, "Philadelphia Revisited: Amending the Constitution Outside Article V." He insisted that because Article V does not say it is the *exclusive* method by which the Constitution is to be amended, the Framers intended for the people to be able to change the Constitution by referendum. He restated this thesis in a 1998 book, *For the People: What the Constitution Really Says About Your Rights.*

Although his ideas are more complex than summarized here, Amar believes the people are endowed with sovereignty as citizens of their states *and* as citizens of the United States. When the people approved the new federal Constitution, in the exercise of their national sovereignty, they agreed that the amendment process outlined in Article V would be the only method for changing the Constitution. However, the people retained their sovereignty as citizens of their states under their state constitutions, which were not nullified by the adoption of the federal Constitution. Therefore, even though the people agreed to be governed under a federal Constitution, they retained the right to offer and ratify amendments without depending on either Congress or a convention to propose them, or on state legislatures or state conventions to approve them.

Amar's thesis is interesting, but it would take an extraordinary effort to convince citizens, and most likely a substantial percentage of their representatives, that the people can change their Constitution by a procedure that is not explicitly outlined in Article V. So much time would be invested in making that argument and generating political support for it that debate over the substance of the amendments would be put off for many years if not indefinitely. Such a prolonged ordeal is unnecessary. Article V provides for a convention if a sufficient number of states petition for it. Once that convention has been organized, it will have the opportunity to propose a new Article V to allow the people a greater role in amending the Constitution. During such a convention and subsequent debate over ratification, there will be an opportunity to clarify many of the issues left unsettled by the Framers and by more than 200 years of experience with the Constitution.

Electors chosen by the people

The Framers could have created a system similar to the Electoral College to ratify amendments. Under the system by which presidents are chosen, "electors" gather after the election in their state capitals and cast ballots for presidential candidates. It is those electors, and not the people, who actually select the president. Under the law in some states, and customary in all of them, the elector is supposed to support whichever presidential candidate received the most votes of the people. However, on eight occasions electors have refused to vote for the candidate who won the popular vote and to whom they were pledged, with the last one being in 1988 when a Democratic elector gave her vote not to Michael

Dukakis who had won West Virginia, but to Lloyd Bentsen, the Democratic vice presidential candidate.

If the Framers had wanted, they could have created a similar system for approving constitutional amendments. Under such a system, voters would go to the polls in each state to approve or reject proposed amendments. After the election, electors would be chosen to attend a state convention or meeting at which they would be strongly encouraged, but not required, to approve or reject the amendment based on the popular vote. Presumably, if the voters made an unwise decision that would harm the interests of the country or interfere in some way with basic liberties, the electors would be free to act contrary to the results of the popular vote.

Such a system, of course, seems silly. If voters had the authority to approve or reject amendments at the polls, it would be unnecessary to take the additional step of sending electors to the state capital to confirm the voters' wisdom. But since that is exactly the system that the Framers created for election of the president, it would not have been inconceivable for them to establish a similar procedure for constitutional amendments.

The delegates to the Constitutional Convention had the option of creating an amendment system that, at least mathematically, would have offered dozens of potential proposal and ratification procedures. Their eventual decision to adopt two methods using only Congress and state legislatures or state conventions, and to reject the other possibilities, was based on the experience of their own states and the vicissitudes of the Convention.

Article V's Help in the Ratification Effort

As the debate over ratification of the new constitution moved to the states, the Anti-Federalists who opposed it — some of whom called for a second convention to immediately revise the work of the Philadelphia delegates — generated much support for their cause by criticizing the lack of a bill of rights and other characteristics of the new Constitution.

Madison strongly opposed a new convention. If the Anti-Federalists succeeded, he believed the new convention would damage the delicate balance struck by the delegates in Philadelphia. He wrote to a friend, "If an early convention cannot be parried, it is seriously to be feared that the system which has resisted so many direct attacks may be at last undermined by its enemies." It was a subject that concerned him throughout the battle over ratification. In *The Federalist No. 49*, Madison referred indirectly to the efforts to organize a new convention by arguing that "frequent appeals" for such a gathering would "in great measure deprive the government of that veneration which time bestows on everything, and without which perhaps the wisest and freest governments would not possess the requisite stability."

These and other statements are sometimes used by those who argue that Madison opposed a second convention under all circumstances. But what Madison strongly objected to was the organizing of a second convention even while the Constitution was being considered for ratification. Madison insisted that Congress, in a very short period of time, could propose amendments to protect civil liberties, and that a convention was not the most efficient way to bring about such changes. He worried about what a second convention would do: "Having witnessed the difficulties and dangers experienced by the First Convention, which assembled under every propitious circumstance, I should tremble for the result of a Second meeting in the present temper of America and under all the disadvantages I have mentioned." There is nothing in his writing to suggest that he believed a second convention should never be held.

There were certain "civil rights" that were enumerated in the Constitution such as a prohibition on bills of attainder (criminal prosecutions by a legislature), ex post facto laws (applying criminal laws retroactively), and providing for a jury trial on criminal charges. The original Constitution also established the privilege of the writ of habeas corpus (protecting against unlawful imprisonment or detention) except in cases of rebellion or invasion, and required that there be at least two witnesses before a defendant could be convicted of treason. But the lack of a bill of rights troubled some delegates and inspired Anti-Federalists to insist on a second convention to more explicitly protect procedural and substantive rights.

George Mason, among the most influential of the delegates at the Philadelphia Convention, refused to sign the Constitution because it failed to provide more explicit protection for civil liberties. He tried to persuade the delegates on September 12, a few days before adjournment, to create a bill of rights based on similar provisions set forth in state constitutions. Mason said he "wished the plan [the Constitution] had been prefaced with a Bill of Rights . . . It would give great quiet to the people; and with the aid of the State declarations, a bill might be prepared in a few hours." The Convention refused. Most of the delegates believed that the new central government did not have the authority to abridge personal rights and liberties, and therefore it was unnecessary to enumerate rights that the government could not infringe. Some maintained that the inclusion of some rights would necessarily imply the omission of others, and that the Constitution would thus be interpreted as granting the central government more power to interfere with the rights of the people than it rightly possessed. It is also likely that after almost four months, the Framers wanted to go home and did not want to undertake the difficult task of creating a bill of rights.

The Framers misjudged the fear that people had of the proposed Constitution. The Anti-Federalists were winning supporters by arguing that the new government would clearly be capable of depriving people of rights they had enjoyed under their state constitutions. The Federalists tried to calm fears by promising that if the Constitution was ratified, the First Congress would propose a bill of rights establishing in greater detail the procedural and substantive protections that the people would enjoy against encroachments on their liberty by the new government. They hoped to stall efforts to organize a new convention and increase the chances that the state ratification conventions would approve the Constitution.

State Ratifying Conventions

The Framers had chosen state constitutional conventions, whose delegates would be elected by the people, as the method for ratification out of fear that state legislatures would not approve a document that so significantly reduced their powers. Also to be considered was the more theoretical argument that the new government must derive its authority directly from the people who would elect representatives to a convention for the sole purpose of considering ratification of the new Constitution. On August 31, the Framers had agreed that nine of the 13 states would have to ratify the Constitution, as opposed to the unanimity required by the Articles of Confederation. Considering that Rhode Island did not send representatives to the Convention, it was highly unlikely that there would be unanimous agreement to the Constitution anyway.

There has been a debate lasting many years over whether the new Constitution enjoyed widespread support among the people. Some historians have argued that very few citizens voted in the elections to choose delegates to the state ratifying conventions, and thus the strong opposition to the new Constitution was not reflected in the ratification votes. Progressive-era historian Charles Beard, among others, claimed that either because of indifference, their isolated location away from towns or cities, or their lack of property qualifications, about three-fourths of male, white citizens 21 and older failed to vote in the elections for convention delegates. Beard cited research suggesting that no more than five percent of the population in general expressed an opinion on the Constitution by voting for delegates to the conventions. He argued that the voting was done chiefly by "a small minority of interested property holders."

Relatively few people may have voted for delegates to the conventions, but the delegates themselves held the key to whether the work of the Framers would be in vain. The Anti-Federalists were at a disadvantage arguing against the new Constitution because they were unable to offer a competing plan unless a second convention were held. Nevertheless, they mounted an effort — impressive for the time considering the state of transportation and communication systems — that came close to convincing enough delegates to vote against the new Constitution.

Patrick Henry of Virginia, an Anti-Federalist who had refused to be a delegate to the Constitutional Convention because he "smelt a rat," strongly opposed ratification. He did not believe the promises of the Federalists that the new amendments enumerating civil liberties would be proposed by Congress or ratified by the states. He objected to both the two-thirds requirement in Congress and the three-fourths threshold of state approval. Speaking of the latter requirement, he said that "to suppose that so large a number as three-fourths of the states will concur, is to suppose that they will possess genius, intelligence, and integrity, approaching to miraculous." He noted that four of the smallest states, which together contained one-tenth of the population of the United States, could prevent even widely supported amendments from being ratified.

Without Article V's amending process, the Federalists could not have promised a bill of rights. If they could not have assured the nation that the First Congress would offer such additional protections, the Constitution would not likely have been ratified by a sufficient number of states. In response to the Anti-Federalists, those supporting ratification maintained that the delegates had anticipated that changes would be necessary, and that Article V provided an orderly process by which to obtain amendments.

One of the great ironies of our constitutional history is that despite Henry's professed commitment to a bill of rights, he almost succeeded in denying James Madison a seat in the First Congress. That would have been a tragic outcome for without Madison's extraordinary efforts in the First Congress, there would have been no Bill of Rights. When Virginia's legislature met to select members to the new United States Senate, Henry persuaded the legislators to appoint two Anti-Federalists, Richard Henry Lee and William Grayson. Then, in an effort to deprive Madison of any elected position in the new Congress, he convinced the Virginia assembly to gerrymander the House district from which Madison would be seeking election by adding counties with heavy concentrations of Anti-Federalists to Madison's home base, Orange County. Henry also persuaded the highly-regarded James Monroe, later the nation's 5th President, to run against him. By campaigning energetically in the bitter cold winter of

December 1788, and January 1789, Madison was able to narrowly defeat Monroe by a margin of 336 votes out of 2,280 cast.

When James Madison, Alexander Hamilton, and John Jay wrote *The Federalist Papers* under the pseudonym of "Publius," they made frequent reference to the democratic nature of the amending process. The 85 *Federalist Papers* appeared in New York newspapers from October 1787 to May 1788. Although they were primarily intended to gain support in that key state for ratification, and must be viewed in that context, *The Federalist Papers* are considered by historians, political scientists, and judges to be the most authoritative interpretation of the meaning of the Constitution as envisioned by the Framers. They have been cited in hundreds of Supreme Court decisions, and judges often use them for guidance when ascertaining the original meaning of important provisions of the Constitution.

The amending mechanism is the subject of several of the most important commentaries in *The Federalist Papers*:

- Nos. 38 & 40 (defense of the new constitution).
- No. 43 (specific reference to the amending process).
- No. 49 (arguing against Thomas Jefferson's suggestion some years earlier that Virginia should adopt a new constitution that would make it much easier to call for a new convention, which the Federalists argued was unnecessary when Article V established a much better method for changing the constitution).
- No. 50 (arguing against a Council of Censors, which Pennsylvania used to "enforce" rather than "alter" the state constitution).
- No. 85 (in which Hamilton recognized that the new Constitution was not perfect, but argued that it is better to wait until it is ratified, then add amendments, rather than reject the Constitution).

The Federalists had made a commitment that if the new Constitution was ratified, they would use Article V to offer the nation a strong statement of protection of individual rights. It would take more than three years after the Constitution was ratified for the first 10 amendments to win final approval, but in the end, the Federalists were able to keep their promise.

The Amendments to the Constitution

One of the most remarkable features of our nation's history is how infrequently the Constitution has been changed. If the first 10 amendments are considered to be nearly a part of the original Constitution, then only 17 amendments in over 200 hundred years have made it through the long, difficult ratification process. There have been times in our history when more than half a century has passed with no constitutional amendment gaining sufficient approval by Congress and the states. Although there have been hundreds of serious proposals for constitutional amendments during the nation's history, the infrequency of constitutional amendments is testimony to how difficult it is to generate the national consensus needed to overcome the reluctance of many in Congress and the states to tamper with the Constitution, and the ability of organized interests to prevent approval of even widely supported measures. The Framers would probably be surprised at how few amendments have been added to the Constitution. Some of them would also be amazed that the Philadelphia Convention was the only one to be held, thus far.

Amendments inspired by petitions for a convention

Even when there is widespread support for constitutional change, Congress has often resisted. State legislators, reflecting the views of their constituents who were demanding reform, have sometimes become so frustrated with Congress's unwillingness to propose amendments that they forwarded numerous petitions requesting a second convention. At least four amendments were proposed by Congress and eventually ratified by the states only because Congress saw the possibility of enough petitions being submitted that it would have to call a convention. They include the 17th Amendment providing for the direct election of senators; the 21st Amendment repealing prohibition; the 22nd Amendment on presidential terms; and the 25th Amendment dealing with presidential disability and succession.

At first it did not appear that the states would make much use of Article V's petition process but eventually, over the course of the nation's history, over 400 petitions have been submitted by the states. In the first hundred years after the nation's founding, only 10 applications for a constitutional convention were submitted by states to Congress. Several of those petitions were offered shortly after the Constitution was ratified by states worried about the lack of a bill of rights. It would be another 40 years before petitions were next submitted, this time from several Southern states wanting to clarify the relationship between the states and the federal government in the wake of the nullification crisis in the 1830s. On the eve of the Civil War, several states — both free and slaveholding — petitioned Congress for a convention in an effort to prevent the nation from breaking apart.

From 1861 to 1893, no state applied to Congress for a convention, but by the time of the Progressive Era at the end of the 19th Century, a substantial number of petitions were submitted. Between 1893 and 1911, 30 states — just one short of the required two-thirds majority — filed a total of 73 petitions asking Congress to call a convention for proposing an amendment for direct election of senators. The House had tried for many years to convince the Senate to approve such an amendment, but because enough senators liked the old system, where they were appointed by state legislatures and did not have to face the voters, there had never been two-thirds support. Finally, with petitions for a second convention pouring into the capital, the Senate finally agreed to propose what would become the 17th Amendment.

After the Progressive Era, there was little effort made to call a second convention until the Depression. But there was at least one subject prior to the New Deal period that inspired petition activity. Between 1906 and 1916, 30 states requested a convention to propose an antipolygamy amendment, the catalyst for which was the admission of Utah as a state in 1896. No such amendment was ever approved by Congress and interest in calling a convention for proposing such an amendment quickly faded.

Several petitions were approved by states in the 1920s seeking to repeal the prohibition amendment, but efforts were primarily directed at convincing Congress to propose what would become the 21st Amendment. The Great Depression produced convention calls from several states to offer amendments specifically dealing with the financial crisis. After World War II, petitions were submitted related to the 16th Amendment and the federal government's ability to tax income. The financial burdens of the War had led to fears that the federal government would greatly increase taxes. Despite the substantial opposition to changing the 16th Amendment, 38 petitions reached Congress between 1939 and 1963 on this issue. However, a dozen of the states submitting petitions later rescinded them.

When Franklin Roosevelt broke with tradition and sought a third term in 1940, five states petitioned Congress to hold a convention to propose amendments limiting the president to two terms. Congress did not need much pushing from the states. It proposed its own amendment, the 22nd, which was ratified in 1951.

Other issues that inspired a few states to submit petitions included efforts to change the treaty-making process, and the utopian but clearly unrealistic goal of establishing a "global government," whose supporters later found some comfort in the establishment of the United Nations. Many more petitions were submitted by state legislatures in response to the activist rulings of the Supreme Court under Chief Justice Earl Warren.

States submitted petitions to reverse the 1954 school desegregation decision, *Brown v. Board of Education*, and the Court's reapportionment decisions including *Baker v. Carr* in 1962, and *Reynolds v. Sims* in 1964. By
1964, 28 states had petitioned Congress to call a convention to consider
amendments on reapportionment. Several states also sent petitions to
reverse the Warren Court's rulings on prayers in public schools such as
Engel v. Vitale in 1962, and *Abington School District v. Schempp* in 1963. In
the years since, states have sporadically called for amendments to change
the Electoral College, to propose amendments on presidential disability,
to overturn Supreme Court busing decisions, and to reverse the Court's
controversial 1973 abortion decision, *Roe v. Wade*. By 1983, 32 states had
submitted petitions to request a balanced budget amendment.

Six amendments were proposed by Congress but never ratified by
the states, including the original "First Amendment," that would have
greatly enlarged the House of Representatives. Many people incorrectly
assume that what we know today to be the First Amendment was intentionally put in that exalted position because members of the First Congress understood the importance of freedom of speech and press, and
freedom of religion. However, the First Congress placed such freedoms
third on the list when it approved the proposed Bill of Rights on September 28, 1789. The original "Second Amendment," requiring a general
election before congressional pay raises take effect, was ratified 203 years
after it was proposed by Congress. As with all of the proposed amendments in the Bill of Rights, the original Second Amendment did not have
a time limit by which the states had to act.

Another amendment that did not win approval by enough states
was proposed by the 11th Congress in 1810. It would have prohibited citizens from accepting any titles of nobility from a foreign entity without
the consent of Congress. A proposed amendment to protect slavery was
approved by Congress in 1861, but never ratified. Congress approved
an amendment in 1978 to give citizens of the District of Columbia full
representation in Congress, but that amendment was not ratified by a
sufficient number of states within the seven-year period.

An amendment that Congress approved and which should have
been immediately ratified by the states was the child labor amendment
proposed on June 2, 1926. The amendment was partly in response to an
exceptionally callous 1918 Supreme Court decision, *Hammer v. Dagenhart*, in which the Court held that Congress could not restrict the transportation in interstate commerce of goods produced by child labor. At
that time, very young children worked in shockingly dangerous conditions for long hours and terrible wages. Going into the workplace at such
young ages often kept children from receiving an education. Congress

had attempted to curtail the interstate transportation of goods produced by children as a way of improving working conditions and wages, and because state-by-state regulation was not practical. But the Supreme Court was concerned only with protecting the interests of business. In order to reach the conclusion that Congress could not interfere with such commerce, Justice William Day misquoted the Tenth Amendment and mangled American history and Supreme Court precedent going back to the 1819 decision in *McCullough v. Maryland*. The intentional misinterpretation of the Constitution in *Hammer* in order to protect corporations from federal regulation was finally corrected 23 years later when the Court specifically overruled *Hammer* in *United States v. Darby Lumber Company*. With the handing down of the *Darby* decision, there was little incentive to continue efforts to ratify the child labor amendment.

"Alterations" and "amendments" to the Constitution

When New Hampshire became the ninth state to ratify the Constitution in June 1788, the document written by the Philadelphia delegates officially became the new nation's founding charter. But even with successful ratification, there were numerous problems. During the debates in the ratifying conventions, several states had insisted that either the First Congress or a second convention correct problems in the new Constitution that they viewed as significant enough to require immediate attention. Those states were especially alarmed over the lack of a bill of rights in the Constitution. Efforts by George Mason and others to include an enumeration of such rights in the closing days of the Convention had been unsuccessful. Mason had warned his fellow delegates in Philadelphia that there would be substantial resistance to the new Constitution because of the absence of a detailed list of rights that would be protected from encroachment by the new central government.

Pennsylvania became the first state where Anti-Federalists made a serious effort to convince the delegates to the ratifying convention that a list of 15 "alterations" should be attached to their approval of the new Constitution. "Alterations" in this context usually meant changes in the structure or powers of the new federal government, while "amendments" generally referred to additional or more explicitly stated protection of civil rights and liberties, although some states used the terms interchangeably.

While the Pennsylvania Anti-Federalists were unsuccessful, it did not take long for another state convention to approve such amendments. On February 6, 1788, the Massachusetts convention became the first to adopt nine amendments and alterations and demand that Congress consider them in return for its ratification of the new Constitution. Several of the Massachusetts proposals were eventually reflected in the final Bill of Rights, but overall the nine amendments were hardly comprehensive and did little to comfort those worried about the potential of the new government to interfere with civil rights. They did not, for example, include protection of freedom of speech, press, assembly, or religion. There was no mention of the rights eventually guaranteed by the Fourth Amendment against illegal search and seizure, or the Fifth Amendment right against self-incrimination. In addition, the right to legal counsel, to confront witnesses, and to be compensated for property taken by the government, all eventually found in the Bill of Rights, were not mentioned in the nine Massachusetts amendments.

As in Pennsylvania, Maryland's convention rejected efforts by Anti-Federalists to include a list of 28 proposals for altering the Constitution. The delegates did, however, propose more amendments related to individual rights than the Massachusetts convention or the Pennsylvania Anti-Federalist minority. The South Carolina convention approved four changes, but none of them included protection of individual rights. South Carolina delegates knew that a bill of rights usually included a statement that "all men are born free and equal," and apparently a slave state like South Carolina did not want to go on record as having made such a declaration.

Several states with large Anti-Federalist constituencies looked as if they might not approve the new Constitution. The delegates to Virginia's ratifying convention had to accept 20 proposed alterations offered by Anti-Federalists in return for ratification. The proposed amendments were based on George Mason's 1776 Virginia Declaration of Rights. By its action, the Virginia ratifying convention became the first to recommend a complete bill of rights. Freedom of speech and press, which eventually became part of the First Amendment, were not the highest priorities of the delegates, however. The 15th amendment stated that the people have a right to peaceably assemble and petition their government, and the 16th said that the people have a right to "freedom of speech, and of writing and publishing their Sentiments."

In July, the New York convention called for 22 alterations and included an additional 23 "rights and explanations." The New York Federalists, in order to prevent the convention from approving a conditional ratification or an outright rejection of the new Constitution, had to accept demands that a letter be sent to state legislatures calling for a second federal convention to adopt amendments. Virginia had also adopted a call for a second convention. North Carolina added six of its own amendments during its ratifying convention, while Rhode Island, always independent and uncooperative, refused to approve the Constitution until after the new government had already begun operation and the First Congress started meeting. It is clear that if Article V had not been a part of the Constitution, and if there had been no amendment process to offer to Anti-Federalists — along with a promise that amendments would be immediately proposed — the Constitution would not have been ratified.

Despite such a commitment, the First Congress nearly failed to deliver a bill of rights to the states. If the Anti-Federalists had succeeded in keeping James Madison out of the First Congress, which they almost did, there would have been no bill of rights proposed in the first months of the new government. The failure to pass a bill of rights would have caused a serious constitutional crisis that could have imperiled the young nation. Madison's willingness to be flexible about the need for a bill of rights made a big difference in his campaign for the House. Although he was initially opposed to a bill of rights in the Constitution, Madison was persuaded to change his mind through his correspondence with Thomas Jefferson and because his supporters convinced him that he would not win the election without promising to add such a section to the Constitution.

Being elected to the House was only the first step in Madison's struggle to see a list of rights added to the Constitution. He had to work hard to convince his reluctant colleagues that they must fulfill their promise to the American people. On May 4, 1789, shortly after the First Congress convened, Madison informed the House that he would offer a series of procedural and substantive rights that would eventually become the first 10 amendments to the Constitution, and that they should prepare to devote substantial time during the summer to debating the proposed bill of rights. After reviewing many of the amendments offered by state ratifying conventions and the civil liberties provisions of state constitutions, and after reading extensively the works of political theorists who had developed ideas on how personal liberty should be protected, Madison offered the amendments to the House for the first time on June 8.

What he encountered must have surprised and disappointed him. The reaction of some of his colleagues ranged from indifference to hardened resistance, with many apparently holding the view that although approval of a bill of rights was important, there were far more pressing matters for the new Congress to consider. The bill of rights would have to wait. Apparently, too many House members did not seem to understand that ratification of the Constitution had been contingent upon the First Congress taking such action.

It took months of what must have been frustrating effort on Madison's part to convince the House that a promise had been made to the American people to propose a bill of rights, and that they must honor that commitment. Adding extra urgency to the work of the Congress were continued calls for a second convention. There was growing concern about what such a gathering would do especially if it was dominated by Anti-Federalists. Finally, after a summer of debate and struggle, and through Madison's extraordinary effort, the House approved 17 amendments and forwarded them to the Senate.

Although the House debate was extensively recorded, much less is known about the Senate's discussion of the amendments. At the time, the Senate conducted legislative business behind closed doors. It was not until February 20, 1794, during the second session of the Third Congress, that the Senate agreed to open the gallery doors during discussion of legislative business and voting on bills.

The Senate considered the 17 amendments proposed by the House from August 25 until it approved a modified version of them on September 9. The Senate combined some amendments, eliminated others, and sent back to the House a list of 12 amendments. Among the most unfortunate decisions made by the Senate was removal of the requirement that freedom of speech, press, and religion be protected from state authorities as well as the federal government. Madison considered this provision to be extremely important, yet the Senate did not want the Constitution to impose too many requirements on the states. The House debated the Senate version for three days beginning on September 21, and agreed to them on the 24th. The next day the Senate confirmed its support of the amendments as approved by the House and they were forwarded to the states. When the first and second amendments failed to receive sufficient support from the states, the third article moved up to become what we know today as the First Amendment.

Madison may have been the driving force behind getting the House to approve the Bill of Rights, but for all his intelligence and political savvy, he had recommended a way of amending the Constitution that could have seriously undermined their vitality and impact. Madison believed that the proposed amendments should be dispersed throughout the appropriate sections of the Constitution rather than be listed separately at the end of the document, as was eventually done. It took Roger Sherman — who had represented Connecticut at the Philadelphia Convention and was elected to the House in the First Congress, and who, ironically, was opposed to amending the Constitution — to convince Madison and some of his colleagues that the original Constitution should be preserved, and the amendments should be listed separately following the main document. Those who agreed with Sherman questioned whether it was right to change the original Constitution to which the Framers had affixed their names. They argued that it would not be the same document, yet it would still bear their signatures, thus creating a crisis of legitimacy that may have weakened the new government and the Constitution. Madison eventually agreed. If he had insisted on the original plan of dispersing the amendments throughout the Constitution, it is likely the Bill of Rights would not have been approved by the House. Even if approved and ratified, a bill of rights sprinkled throughout a long document would not command the same respect and reverence that the first ten amendments have enjoyed for most of our history.

Throughout the battle over ratification of the Constitution and continuing into the First Congress, there was disagreement over whether a bill of rights was necessary. Some argued that any list of proposed rights would necessarily overlook others, and thus the implication was that those unmentioned rights would not be protected. Others directly refuted that argument, claiming that just because the Constitution listed some rights did not mean that others would be unprotected. As long as state constitutions — many of which had their own provisions for protecting individual rights — remained viable, there was little danger that the federal government would exercise powers that interfered with fundamental liberties not explicitly mentioned in the Bill of Rights.

Although it took such fortuitous developments as the election of James Madison to the House, Roger Sherman's insistence that the amendments be placed at the end of the Constitution, and the absence of a second convention that could have upstaged the First Congress as it debated the new amendments, the Bill of Rights was eventually ratified by the necessary 11 states on December 15, 1791.

Although cherished by the nation, the Bill of Rights is more complex and has more shortcomings and problems than most people realize. The 10 amendments can be separated into four categories. The First Amendment covers freedom of speech, press, assembly, the right to petition government, and freedom of religion. The Second and Third Amendments deal with the right of the people to keep and bear arms and the quartering of soldiers in private homes. Both amendments have been the subject of relatively few court decisions. The Fourth through the Eighth Amendments are concerned primarily with procedural protections in criminal trials, but other issues are also included such as the prohibition on taking of private property for public use without just compensation. Finally, the Ninth and Tenth Amendments affirm the principle that although some rights are granted to the people in the Constitution, that does not mean that other rights are not retained by them or by the states.

The impact of the Bill of Rights and the special position that it has assumed in our constitutional system took some time to develop. There were severe limitations on the reach of the protections in the amendments.

First, for most of their history, they applied only to the states. About half the state constitutions had various provisions protecting such rights, and it was generally understood that the Bill of Rights would protect the American people from encroachment of their liberties only by the new central government. The Supreme Court, in the 1833 case *Barron v. Baltimore*, confirmed that the Bill of Rights did not apply to state authorities. That meant that until 1925, for example, the First Amendment could not be used to protect individuals from infringements of their right to free speech by state governments, and states vigorously prosecuted and imprisoned individuals with controversial views. It took until 1961 for the Supreme Court to hold that states could not use illegally seized evidence to prosecute criminal defendants in clear violation of the Fourth Amendment. Today, there are still several provisions in the Bill of Rights that do not apply to the states.

Second, the language of some of the first 10 amendments was so confining that courts have had to creatively interpret those provisions over the years in order to give them some meaningful role in the development of the nation's constitutional law. The First Amendment, for example, says "Congress shall make no law . . ." A literal reading would mean that the executive branch of the federal government including, for example, the FBI, could violate First Amendment rights with impunity since that amendment only mentions the legislative branch. Many problems would have been created if there were such a literal reading of many sections of the Constitution.

Third, the Bill of Rights protects individuals only from governmental bodies, or the actions of those closely associated with the government. A private entity cannot be accused of depriving an individual of the right of freedom of speech or press as guaranteed by the Constitution. That is why, for example, a private university cannot be sued for violating the First Amendment rights of faculty or students, while a public college is obligated to protect such rights and is subject to lawsuits for violations of them. Those who work for private employers must find an appropriate civil rights statute if they are to bring a lawsuit over deprivation of constitutional rights. In the famous *Civil Rights Cases*, the Supreme Court held more than a century ago that the words "no state shall deprive" in the 14th Amendment meant that only government or state actors could be held responsible for constitutional violations, not private individuals or organizations.

Finally, some of the most important phrases of the Bill of Rights are the most vague. The First Congress and the states that ratified the proposed amendments wanted the Constitution to contain broad statements of rights and responsibilities, while leaving to future generations the application of those principles to specific situations. The problem is that the Bill of Rights leaves many unanswered questions and requires judges to exercise substantial discretion when deciding cases based on those rights. As a result, the Constitution has sometimes been subject to widely varying interpretation of those provisions depending on the political predilections of the judges who decide constitutional cases.

After the Bill of Rights

The 11th Amendment, which was adopted in 1795, overturned the Supreme Court's 1793 ruling in *Chisholm v. Georgia* that had allowed federal courts to accept jurisdiction of lawsuits brought by a citizen of one state against the state government of another. The 12th Amendment, ratified in 1804, was intended to prevent the problem caused by the presidential election of 1800 when Thomas Jefferson and Aaron Burr, running as presidential and vice presidential candidates of the same party, received an equal number of electoral votes.

It would be 61 years before another amendment became part of the Constitution. The 13th, 14th, and 15th Amendments, known as the Reconstruction Amendments, were adopted as a result of the Civil War. The 13th, which abolished slavery, was ratified in 1865. The 14th, protecting the due process rights of individuals with regard to life, liberty or property from action by the states — among the most important provisions of the Constitution with ramifications far beyond protecting the rights of newly freed slaves — was ratified in 1868. When it appeared that the 14th Amendment would not secure the right to vote of the former slaves, the 15th Amendment — prohibiting the denial of the suffrage based on race — was adopted in 1870. Several Southern states did not give their approval to the Reconstruction Amendments voluntarily. Some states were under Reconstruction legislatures that clearly did not represent the views of most of the people. Congress overlooked numerous election irregularities by which legislators were chosen, and some states were readmitted to the Union only if they agreed to ratify the Reconstruction Amendments.

Despite the demand for reform during the Populist Era of the late 19th century, and the Progressive Era in the first quarter of the 20th century, no amendment was approved for 43 years. Finally, the 16th Amendment, ratified in 1913, reversed an 1895 Supreme Court decision, *Pollock v. Farmers' Loan & Trust Co.*, and allowed the federal government to impose a tax on incomes. Congress had levied a tax of 2 percent on incomes in excess of $4,000 the year before. The statute at issue in the *Pollock* case had been a great victory for progressive forces of the country, especially for the South and West over the industrial Northeast, where most of those with such incomes resided. But the tax did not survive for long, as the Court in the *Pollock* case held that it was a "direct" tax under Article I, Section 9, and was thus unconstitutional.

Today's overburdened taxpayer must wonder why the 16th Amendment was considered a reform measure. During the Progressive Era, wealthy corporations and individuals contributed a relatively small amount to the federal treasury, thus forcing the national government to depend on tariffs and excise taxes that did not generate sufficient revenue to carry out its functions.

The 17th Amendment, providing for direct election of senators, which had been a long time in coming, was ratified two months after the 16th, in 1913. By the time the 17th Amendment was adopted, half the state legislatures selected senators based on the popular vote of their citizens. But it took 125 years after the ratification of the Constitution for the people of the entire nation to be able to choose their senators, and thus tear down the barrier the Framers had erected to insulate the Senate from direct accountability.

The Senate's attempt to prevent a constitutional amendment providing for direct election of its members was an effort to protect an old system that had been fraught with problems. State legislatures often deadlocked on the selection of the two senators, and those precious seats were sometimes left vacant for long periods of time. Between 1891 and 1905, for example, the filling of no fewer than 45 Senate seats was delayed because legislatures could not decide on candidates. Fourteen seats remained empty for an entire legislative session or more. In the worst case, Delaware was represented by only one senator in three Congresses and none at all from 1901 until 1908.

Six years later, the controversial 18th Amendment prohibiting the sale or distribution of alcohol was ratified. In 1920, the right of women to vote throughout the nation was guaranteed in the 19th Amendment. It would be another 13 years before the 20th Amendment became part of the Constitution, which changed the dates on which Congress and the president took office to January 3rd and January 20th, respectively. The president previously took office in March, thus allowing too much time from November on for a lame-duck president to be in office. Because of the strange way the Constitution established congressional terms, until the 20th Amendment was approved, the Congress elected in November did not take office until the *following* December, thus giving the lame-duck Congress 13 months in office. The 20th Amendment also clarified certain issues with respect to presidential succession.

The 21st Amendment repealed the 18th — the only amendment that specifically repealed another — giving states the power to legalize the transportation, importation, or use of alcohol. The 22nd Amendment, ratified in 1951, limits a president to two terms in office. Support for the amendment was in response to Franklin Roosevelt having been elected to four terms, the only president to serve more than two.

The 23rd Amendment, adopted in 1961, gives residents of the District of Columbia the right to vote for president and three electoral votes. The 24th Amendment, which was ratified in 1964, prohibits the states from using a poll tax as a voting requirement in federal elections. Southern states had used the tax to discourage blacks from voting. The 25th Amendment, ratified in 1967, provides for the appointment of a vice president when that office becomes vacant, and also authorizes the vice president to act as president if the president is incapacitated. The 26th Amendment, which gives the right to vote to 18-year-olds in both state and federal elections, was adopted in 1971. It partially overturned a Supreme Court decision, *Oregon v. Mitchell*, holding that Congress could not force states to lower the voting age for nonfederal elections. Finally, the 27th Amendment, which became part of the Constitution in 1992, requires that if members of Congress want to raise their pay, the increase will not go into effect until after a general election.

Suggestions for Changing the Constitution: From the Creative to the Unusual

The long odds against an idea making it all the way through the amendment process has not stopped historians, political scientists, law professors, journalists, political figures and "visionaries" who are not easily characterized from recommending substantial revisions of the Constitution. Some of those proposals could generously be described as "creative," while others have some merit but are so unrealistic and impractical as to be worthy of relatively little discussion. Many of those suggesting changes to the Constitution were satisfied with contributing to the academic debate and public understanding of the defects in the document. Those efforts should be commended for there is much value in having the Constitution examined through scholarship and serious writing in the popular press, even if political forces have little interest in seeing those changes enacted in the short run.

Political scientist and constitutional scholar John Vile, whose numerous works on the amending process have provided invaluable insights into the history and operation of the amendment clauses of the Constitution, traced about 40 proposals to revise or significantly overhaul the Constitution from Reconstruction to the 1990s. Vile confined his 1991 book, *Rewriting the United States Constitution: An Examination of Proposals from Reconstruction to the Present*, to those plans that called for comprehensive alterations in the Constitution, and he did not consider the numerous suggestions for changes such as cleaning up language or minor structural adjustment. Vile traced the major proposals offered by an array of serious scholars and a few unusual ideas dreamed up by political activists and writers.

A few of the authors Vile discusses suggested that the revisions be enacted through a second constitutional convention, but those writers did not offer a plan to bring about such a convention. In fact, most of those whose works Vile examined did not concern themselves with how their proposals would generate the political support necessary to have a serious chance of becoming part of the Constitution. They simply wanted to add to our understanding of the creation, structure, and problems of the Constitution and the way that governmental entities have carried out their constitutional duties. They generally did not see their role as political activists who would work to bring about the modifications in the Constitution they considered desirable.

The proposals ranged from limited to comprehensive. Among the suggestions that would have important effects on our political system, but would not result in far-reaching change, were those requiring a majority vote of both houses of Congress for approval of treaties rather than a two-thirds vote of the Senate as now required by the Constitution. Other proposals included eliminating the office of vice president and substituting another method of presidential succession, and extending the terms of House members beyond two years so they would be better able to respond to a more general public interest rather than the demands of parochial constituencies.

More comprehensive and intriguing, but nevertheless unrealistic, reforms called for instituting a "cabinet" or British form of government. Many serious scholars, including a president of the United States in the years before he was elected, have argued energetically that the United States should adopt a parliamentary form of government. Features of such proposals have included allowing the president to dissolve Congress and call for new elections when it appeared that the legislative branch had failed to adequately represent the wishes of the people; and allowing members of the cabinet to serve in Congress, which is prohibited by Article I, Section 6. Modeled after the British system, where ministers are also members of the House of Commons, the expectation was that permitting cabinet members to serve in Congress would reduce some of the problems caused by separation of powers.

Some of the same scholars and writers proposing a British system also argued for extending terms of members of both houses of Congress on the theory that elected officials should enjoy sufficient insulation from the people to be able to legislate in the voters' long-term interest. There was also some sentiment for allowing members of Congress to be elected at large, or not require that they be from the district they represent, in order to free them from the obligation of funneling projects to the home district and being beholden to narrow district or state interests. It is unlikely, however, that such an idea would be seriously considered in this country.

These proposals are discussed here for several reasons. First, they demonstrate that serious people have given much thought to how the Constitution should be changed and what form of government the United States should have. Yet many of their ideas are so impractical that they would never be adopted and would not work well if they were. Second, many of the suggestions for change discussed below would drastically alter the structure of the federal government, and the relationship between the federal government and the states, and are thus significantly more radical than any of the amendments proposed in this book. One can argue that expecting the country to hold a second constitutional convention is unrealistic. However, recommending a campaign finance reform amendment or an amendment that abolishes the Electoral College should be treated more seriously than one proposing a parliamentary form of government or abolition of the states. Regardless of the likelihood of a second convention, it is established in Article V as an alternative method for proposing amendments.

Examples of Proposed Revisions
to the Constitution

Some ideas were both insightful and practical, although they were sometimes packaged with others that were unusual or even bizarre. Charles O'Conor (1804–1888) was a New York lawyer, a member of the New York state constitutional convention in 1846, later a U.S. attorney, and at one time a vice president of the "New-York Historical Society." He wrote in *The Nation* in 1877 that to reduce corruption and to cure other problems, state and national legislatures should be limited to passing general laws. He opposed legislation that benefited specific individuals or corporations. He also recommended that government be prohibited from coining money and issuing currency, and that tariffs and duties be abolished. O'Conor suggested that if taxpayers immediately paid for all government expenditures, the public would think more carefully about how its money is spent.

He believed that if the public had to pay for each governmental undertaking specifically, it would reduce the likelihood of war and foreign conquest, which can be expensive endeavors. Even with computers and other modern technology available today, but unknown in O'Conor's time, it is difficult to imagine a system by which the public could pay for even a limited number of expenditures of the federal government as they are made.

O'Conor also recommended that state and federal legislators be elected from multimember districts, a system that is similar to some European nations that have proportional representation in their legislative bodies. Many have suggested such a scheme for the United States as a way of electing numerical minorities or third-party candidates to office. For a brief time in their history, 24 American cities experimented with a plan called "preference voting" for electing members of city councils and other officials. Instead of choosing one candidate, voters ranked several candidates in order of preference. If their first-choice candidate did not receive a winning share of support, their vote was transferred to their second choice, and so on until a winner was declared. The idea was born in the Progressive Era to defeat political machines and open up the electoral process. It eventually withered away after World War II because it was cumbersome and costly, and because conservatives did not want individuals from fringe groups, such as socialists, to get elected. New York City used such a system from 1936–1949. Other large cities to try a preference voting plan were Sacramento (1920–1923) and Cincinnati (1924–1957). Cambridge, Massachusetts, may be the only city that still uses preference voting today.

Although some of O'Conor's ideas may be interesting, other proposals are more difficult to take seriously. He recommended that the president and governors not be elected. Rather, those positions should be filled "by lot every month from the representative body," by which he apparently meant Congress or state legislatures. He said that such a plan would "thus substantially extinguish . . . the great office of President." He also believed that the telegraph made the diplomatic corps unnecessary.

Albert Stickney (1839–1908), a Boston attorney, wrote in an 1879 book that the term system of elections led to a "convulsion of the whole nation," and he recommended that elected officials, including the president, serve indefinite terms during "good behavior" (the standard for continuing tenure of federal judges under Article III), and that they be paid well. His plan would allow the president to remain in office until removed by a two-thirds vote in Congress. He thought these reforms would put an end to the party system and would allow legislators to better serve the public. He also proposed the elimination of the office of vice president, that the presidential veto be abolished, and that all legislation require a two-thirds vote in Congress.

Among the most respectable political thinkers during the late 19th Century was Woodrow Wilson (1856–1924), later the 28th President of the United States. As a youth, Wilson was influenced by the English model of government. Among his best-known works was *Congressional Government*, which he published while a graduate student in political science in 1885. In addition to the more moderate step of allowing members of the cabinet to serve in Congress as official representatives of the administration — which would reduce some of the problems Wilson saw in governmental branches performing separate functions — he also suggested that the president select the cabinet from members of Congress of the majority party who would then support the party's platform. Wilson expected that a party system more akin to Britain's would reduce legislative support for special interests. Perhaps not surprisingly, by the time he became president in 1913, he had modified his views on congressional government.

Others supporting the British system included Henry Lockwood (1839–1902), a New York lawyer who argued in an 1884 book entitled *The Abolition of the Presidency* that the British had found the correct blending of the legislative and the executive branches. He said that the Senate should be abolished in part because he did not believe there were many advantages to a bicameral system. Lockwood also advocated abolition of the states and the division of the country into 13 equal parts. He also recommended the elimination of the presidency, to be replaced by an executive council chosen by Congress and headed by the secretary of state. The members of the council would have seats in Congress and could dissolve the legislature when the government was deadlocked on an important issue. Lockwood also argued against the courts being able to invalidate laws as unconstitutional and proposed to limit their power to interpreting the laws.

Cabinet government also appealed to Isaac Rice (1850–1915), a graduate of Columbia Law School and a librarian in the university's newly formed School of Political Science. In 1884, he wrote in *Century Magazine* that the Framers of the Constitution had misunderstood the advantages of the British system, and he called for a constitutional convention to propose changes such as making cabinet officers members of Congress, and designating one of them to perform a role similar to "prime minister," although he did not use that term. Rice also did not think much of judicial review, proposing instead to make the legislature "the sole and responsible judge of the constitutionality of its acts," and leaving the judiciary to "interpret" congressional will rather than "to control it."

Caspar Hopkins (1826–1893), a businessman and author, wrote in 1885 in *Overland Monthly* that after 100 years the Constitution had to be revised, and he recommended 10 constitutional amendments for doing so. Among his proposals was to change the presidential term to eight years, with the president having two or three vice presidents whose order of succession would be specified. Members of the House would serve six-year terms, while senators would serve terms of 10 years. He also had a strange idea of how to elect senators that was contrary to the movement to allow the people to directly elect senators. Hopkins said he recognized the "inevitable influence of wealth," and thus only the wealthy — those who paid taxes on $100,000 or more of income — should be allowed to vote for senators.

Judge Walter Clark (1846–1924), the chief justice of the North Carolina Supreme Court, delivered a speech that was later published as an article and as part of his papers. In his writings were some of the 20th century's first statements recommending substantial changes in the Constitution. Reflecting the views of the growing Progressive Movement, Clark argued that circumstances had changed since 1787, and that the Constitution must change as well. In addition to arguing for direct election of senators, he suggested that smaller states have only one senator and that larger ones get an additional senator for each million residents. He also advocated a single six-year term for the president. Perhaps surprisingly, because Clark was a judge, he denounced the lifetime tenure provided to federal judges under Article III and instead recommended that they be elected to fixed terms. Although controversial, Clark's views were shared by many people in the early 20th century who were exasperated by federal judges, especially those on the Supreme Court, who seemed determined to defeat progressive reform of the political and economic system. Clark criticized Supreme Court decisions for interfering with the will of the people and especially the Court's use of the 14th Amendment to protect businesses. He called for repeal or revision of the 14th amendment so future courts would not misinterpret it. Clark believed these changes would have to be made by a second constitutional convention.

Yandell Henderson (1873–1974), writing in and influenced by the Progressive Era, showed that one does not have to be an historian, lawyer, or political scientist to devise creative proposals for changing the Constitution. Henderson, a professor of physiology at Yale, was active in politics, running unsuccessfully for Congress as a member of the Progressive Party. In 1913, he wrote in the *Yale Review* that the United States should be governed by something akin to a board of directors with "the executive sitting in it and proposing measures to it." His second proposal, although probably supported by a substantial number of people, is impractical in a large, complex democratic society. He called for a system by which voters could overturn judicial decisions on constitutional issues presumably through a national referendum where the people would be able to revive laws struck down by the courts. Henderson believed that allowing the people to review constitutional decisions was preferable to creating new principles through the constitutional amendment process. He favored a constitutional convention to achieve these goals.

Shortly after World War I, William MacDonald (1863–1938), a former history professor at Brown University and later a writer for such publications as *The Nation*, argued in a 1922 book entitled, *A New Constitution for a New America*, that parliamentary government would be more "responsible." He suggested that fixed terms of office be replaced by maximum terms, making him perhaps one of the first serious thinkers to put forth what today might be called "term limits." In addition to selecting cabinet members from Congress, MacDonald preferred that the presidency be reduced to largely ceremonial functions, and that the government be instead headed by a premier. He would also vest the power to execute laws in the cabinet, eliminate the presidential veto, and provide for new elections when the presidency becomes vacant. MacDonald also wanted to enlarge the powers of Congress over such areas as education, marriage and divorce, and voting qualifications. He also believed that both houses of Congress should ratify treaties, and that the Bill of Rights should apply to the states.

For the judicial branch, MacDonald envisioned a much different system from what we have under the Constitution. Instead of federal judges being appointed by the president and confirmed by the Senate, then serving for life except in cases of impeachment and conviction, judges would be appointed by both the premier and the cabinet and could be removed at the request of Congress. According to MacDonald, this would ensure that judges would "interpret the Constitution and the laws in light of public opinion."

In the final section of his book, MacDonald reflected the dissatisfaction with government institutions shared by many during the Progressive Era, writing that the "Constitution is no longer adapted to our needs." To rectify the situation, he suggested a complete revision. Arguing that the country had learned during the century and a half since the Constitutional Convention that minority interests dominated the political process, he urged Congress to pass a resolution stating that it favored a second constitutional convention, and to then invite states to send petitions requesting one. If the states did not respond, MacDonald encouraged Congress to view Article V as nonexclusive and to call a convention on its own.

Charles Merriam (1874–1953), a respected political scientist at the University of Chicago, also saw advantages in a parliamentary system, but had little hope that one would be instituted. Even though such a system would not likely be adopted, he saw nothing wrong with members of the cabinet appearing before Congress or participating in congressional debates. Some reforms, he believed, could be implemented without formally changing the Constitution, but the most important ones would require amendments. Merriam wrote in a 1931 book that he wanted to invigorate the party system as a way of making government more responsive, and he identified several areas where the Constitution was at odds with an enhanced role for the parties. They included the requirement that no U.S. official can also be a member of Congress; that passage of a law requires both houses of Congress and the president to agree; that treaties are approved by a two-thirds vote of the Senate; and that Congress had been limited by the courts in its ability to regulate party primaries.

William Yandell Elliott (1896–1979), a highly respected Harvard political science professor, argued in a 1935 book that a constitutional convention was required to institute the many reforms he saw as necessary. Although some alterations could be made by piecemeal amendments such as giving the president the line-item veto, others would require more comprehensive changes. Because some of his proposals would affect Congress, Elliott believed it was especially important that the revisions be considered outside of the usual congressional amendment process.

Elliott's proposals included the creation of new regional governments made up of reorganized states; presidential power to dissolve the House of Representatives; changing House terms from two to four years; the nomination of presidential candidates by Congress; the creation of five-member districts for the House with proportional representation; approval of treaties by majority votes in both houses of Congress; and a provision for cabinet officers to serve in the Senate. Other proposals that Elliott advocated would change the workings of the judicial branch by requiring a two-thirds majority of the justices of the Supreme Court to invalidate a statute, and by allowing the justices to serve in an advisory capacity in selective cases. Elliott wanted to reduce the inefficiencies of government and deadlock among the branches, both of which he considered to be the result of dividing power among Congress, the executive, and the judiciary.

Although Elliott did not expect adoption of a parliamentary system, he thought that at least once during a term, a president should be able to force members of the House to stand for election. According to Elliott, if such an election favored Congress over the president, the president would resign and Congress would choose a successor. Among his more unusual ideas was to eliminate the states and instead create 12 regions that would elect members of Congress. The president would also appoint prominent individuals to the Senate. Representation in the House would continue to be based on population, but members would come from the new regions and not from existing states.

Another critic to suggest that the federal government was "dangerously inefficient" was journalist Henry Hazlitt (1894–1993). Writing during World War II, Hazlitt wanted to end what he viewed to be the stalemate brought about by the separation of the legislative and executive branches. Influenced by those who also demanded a parliamentary government, Hazlitt called for a premier who would be selected by Congress, in addition to the president. The premier would then appoint members of the cabinet. Hazlitt also suggested that senators be appointed, and that voters be able to rank their approval of candidates who were not their first choice. Both the premier and the new Congress would be subject to votes of no confidence, with provisions for new elections in such circumstances. Hazlitt's proposals also included eliminating the Electoral College; giving the president a line-item veto; providing for retirement of Supreme Court justices at age 70 or 75 and more flexible means of removing them; and abolishing the vice presidency.

Among Hazlitt's most interesting ideas was to change the amending process. He recommended that amendments become part of the Constitution when approved by majorities of both houses of Congress and when ratified by "a majority of the voters in a majority of the states." He also wanted to create a role for the states in proposing amendments without having to call a constitutional convention. He believed that the first step in constitutional reform was to change the amending process because it would "clear the way for later changes."

Hazlitt was not the only person in the 20th century to suggest altering the amendment process. In 1962, the National Legislative Conference of the Council of State Governments considered amendments that would strengthen the power of states in the federal system. More than 300 individuals from 47 states attended a meeting to consider such proposals. The group's report advocated a number of reforms including changing Article V so that if two-thirds of the states submitted identical language on petitions for new amendments, they would be forwarded to the states for ratification without any action by Congress. A second proposal sought to reverse the Supreme Court's 1962 landmark decision in *Baker v. Carr*, which for the first time permitted federal courts to hear claims related to state apportionment of their legislative districts. Subsequent decisions required states to form those districts to reflect population so that each resident was equally represented in the houses of the state legislature. Not surprisingly, the Council did not want the Supreme Court to tell the states how to draw their legislative districts.

The Council also called for the creation of a "Court of the Union" consisting of the chief justices of each state's highest court and requiring three-fourths present for a quorum. Upon receiving petitions from the legislatures of five states, the new court, by majority vote, would be able to reverse Supreme Court decisions. Once the court made its ruling, it could not be overturned except by constitutional amendment.

Ten years later, Leland Baldwin (1897–1981), an emeritus professor of history at the University of Pittsburgh, added his own perspective on constitutional change. Describing his proposal as a "modified version of the Cabinet or Parliamentary form," he suggested that the president and a unicameral Congress be given five-year terms with the president having the authority to dismiss Congress, while Congress would be able to oust the president. The president, though nominated in a convention, would be a member of Congress and its presiding officer and would be known as the "chief of the executive arm of Congress." Congress would have 200 regular members selected from multimember districts, while the vice presidency would be eliminated.

As if Baldwin's plan for combining the executive and legislative branches was not strange enough, his ideas for changing the judiciary were even more unusual. According to Baldwin, the judicial system would be headed by a Senate, whose 100 members would include 50 "Law-Senators" and 50 "Senators-at-Large" selected by the president and Congress from nominees submitted by the states. Senators would serve for life or until the age of 70, and would have the power to decide on the constitutionality of laws, and the authority to suspend presidential orders or congressional legislation for six months. He also called for changes in the amendment process. Perhaps anticipating criticism of his ideas as impractical and unrealistic, Baldwin wrote that he refused to "stand paralyzed before the basilisk of feasibility."

An academic with an impressive career provided among the most comprehensive alternatives to the Constitution. Rexford Tugwell (1891–1979) — former Columbia University economist, one-time member of Franklin Roosevelt's brain trust, Assistant Secretary of Agriculture, and governor of Puerto Rico — ended his career with the Center for the Study of Democratic Institutions in Santa Barbara, California. In his first six years there, Tugwell drafted 37 successive versions of the United States Constitution as he thought it should be. In his 1974 book, *The Emerging Constitution*, Tugwell published the 40th version and argued that the Constitution had fallen, in certain respects, into "irrelevance."

He believed that many of the problems were caused by the Framers having largely entrusted Congress with the amendment process. Because of the rigidity of the amendment system, the elected branches and the courts have had to fill in the gaps left by a largely unchanged Constitution. He argued that the Supreme Court had usurped power by altering the Constitution through judicial review. As part of the Roosevelt Administration, Tugwell knew well how the Supreme Court had succeeded in decimating many of the most important laws of the New Deal.

He believed the president had too many responsibilities and proposed that the person filling that office serve for a nine-year term with the possibility of being rejected by a vote of 60 percent or more of the electorate at the end of three years. The president would have two vice presidents, one for "internal" and the other for "general" affairs. In Congress, the House would get half its membership from those with national, rather than local, constituencies. Senators would be appointed for life by the president, the Principal Justice (who would head a changed Supreme Court), and the House of Representatives. Three new courts would take the place of the Supreme Court. Tugwell would have modified the Bill of Rights to exclude jury trials and the right to bear arms, but to include the right of privacy. He also suggested that every 25 years, corresponding to each new generation, there would be a referendum on the Constitution, and a Judicial Council to write a new one if the people desired. Despite Tugwell's diligent efforts, and the fact that his work sparked considerable discussion, there is no evidence that it generated practical results.

After the nation's governmental institutions survived the Watergate crisis and other wrongdoing in the Nixon Administration, there was much scholarly interest in changing the Constitution. Political scientist Charles Hardin (1908–1997), in a book published in 1974, proposed "party" government to reduce the abuse of presidential power that Watergate showed was possible. Hardin would have created a system where the president's party would always have a majority in Congress, and recommended allowing members of Congress to serve in the cabinet. Members of the House would nominate presidential candidates. The vice presidency would be eliminated and the House would select a replacement for a president who was disabled. As in Britain, Hardin proposed a strong opposition party, recommending that the defeated presidential candidate, or some other choice of the party, be the official opposition leader. Hardin was vague about how these proposals would be implemented. He suggested it would be better to allow some features of the new system to "develop by convention than to stipulate them in advance," but at other times seemed to believe they could be instituted through constitutional amendments proposed by Congress.

Henry Reuss, a Democratic member of the House of Representatives from Wisconsin during the Watergate years, recommended that Congress be able to pass, by a three-fifths vote, a resolution of no confidence in the president, which would then require a presidential election. He later modified his proposal and reintroduced it in Congress on August 15, 1974, a few days after Richard Nixon resigned from office, with the hopes that it would move the nation more toward the parliamentary model of government. According to Reuss, a no-confidence vote would result in a congressional as well as a presidential election.

Finally, a number of proposals emerged around the time of the Bicentennial Celebration of the Declaration of Independence. A group of scholars and politicians formed the Committee on the Constitutional System, from which several books developed. Donald Robinson, a Smith College political science professor, hoped for less separation between the executive and legislative branches. His specific reforms included an option for voters to choose a party slate, campaign finance limits, cabinet secretaries in Congress, and repeal of the two-term limit for the president. In addition, he was in favor of extending terms for House members to four years and for senators to eight.

James Sundquist, who had a distinguished political career and later was a senior fellow at the Brookings Institution, believed that American politics was irresponsible and unaccountable, and that those characteristics led to "stalemate, deadlock, and gridlock." He hoped for at least incremental steps toward more responsible government, including four-year terms for House members and eight-year Senate terms; allowing public officials to hold more than one office; and for a national referendum to break deadlocks. He recommended that the president and running mate be on a team ticket with members of the House and Senate so voters would be unable to split their votes. He also suggested that either the president or a majority of either house of Congress should be able to call special elections in which all members of the legislative and executive branches would be up for election.

The Limited Impact of the Plans to Revise the Constitution

The writers, historians, political scientists, and others who have creatively thought about the Constitution and the country's political problems over the years generally seemed content to merely describe defects or problems in our founding document and to recommend changes. It is difficult to know whether they would be disappointed that all the proposals discussed here have one characteristic in common: There is no evidence that a single recommendation has ever been adopted. Of course, it would not be expected that the publication of a book, magazine article, or the reprinting of speeches would suddenly result in a mass movement to change our current institutions to a cabinet form of government, or even change the length of terms of members of Congress. Some of the recommendations made by the commentators during the Progressive Era did eventually become part of the Constitution, but their writings probably had relatively little influence on elected officials as they debated and proposed amendments to the Constitution.

An argument can be made that the scholarly value of some of their research and writing transcended the lack of success in accomplishing any of the goals the authors recommended. Some of them painstakingly investigated and described the history and shortcomings of important provisions in the Constitution, and the fact that their suggestions for change were not adopted does not diminish the contribution their work makes to our understanding of the Constitution and the way it has been interpreted.

Some of their recommendations, however, would have required such a radical departure from the institutions created under the Constitution that the American people would never seriously have considered implementing them. It may be intellectually satisfying to write a book calling for the United States to adopt a British-like "cabinet" government, but there is no underlying support in this country for such a proposal. For a change that drastic to take place, huge majorities of people would not only have to be convinced that the governmental structure we have now is unworkable, they would need sophisticated knowledge of the British system in order to recognize its supposed advantages. Even widely supported policies dealing with relatively simple and straightforward issues have often failed to sustain sufficient momentum with the public to result in an amendment. More importantly, it is inconceivable that this country would adopt a foreign system of government as a solution to its problems.

Some of the authors discussed here recommended that states petition Congress for a constitutional convention, but few, if any, provided suggestions on how citizens or state governments would generate sufficient interest to see those proposals through the long and difficult amendment process. It is unrealistic to expect the American people to march through their state capitals to demand that their legislators petition Congress to hold a convention so that cabinet members can also serve in the national legislature. Not surprisingly, none of the proposals discussed here say anything about holding the series of meetings recommended in this book leading to the calling of a convention.

After reviewing the work of several dozen authors, Vile concludes that "extra-constitutional" methods are the best way to adapt the Constitution to changing conditions. He cites court decisions and actions by elected branches as not only the primary sources of constitutional change, but the superior method for keeping the Constitution evolving in a nation experiencing new political, social, and legal challenges. Vile correctly identifies the judicial system's vital role in "amending" the Constitution.

His faith in the ability of judges at all levels to adapt the law and Constitution to changing conditions is not totally misplaced. But the courts and elected branches of government are unable or unwilling to make the substantial revisions that are now required. The American people cannot rely on the president and Congress to propose needed reforms when those changes would make it more difficult to raise campaign money and more likely that incumbent members of Congress would be defeated. It is also a serious mistake to leave constitutional evolution solely in the hands of the courts. The judicial system has played an indispensable role in preserving the Constitution, but there are significant and urgent changes that only the American people can bring about through a second constitutional convention.

CHAPTER THREE

The Role of Courts in "Amending" the Constitution: Why A Second Convention Must Do What Judges Cannot

𝔉or more than 200 years, the Constitution has been primarily "amended" not through the procedures established in Article V, but through judicial decisions. On only 27 occasions — 17 of which occurred after the Bill of Rights was ratified in 1791 — has the Constitution been formally changed. Judges have had the principal responsibility of adapting the Constitution to the needs of a changing society. With some notable exceptions, they have generally been able to preserve the document's fundamental principles while keeping the Constitution from becoming so out of date that its very legitimacy is threatened.

Judges cannot, however, be the sole source of constitutional interpretation and evolution, aided by an occasional amendment. Because of the structure and political nature of the court system — especially the way cases come to and are decided by courts — judges cannot be expected to solve the problems created by an out-of-control campaign finance system and other challenges that must be addressed by a second constitutional convention. The judicial branch plays an indispensable role in preserving precious civil liberties against encroachment by government, in striking down laws that violate the Constitution, in interpreting statutes, and by settling other legal disputes. But judges cannot do more than make incremental changes in a system that cries out for more comprehensive reform.

It must be emphasized that judges exercise their powers by making decisions in *actual* cases. They cannot wander the political landscape looking for problems that need to be solved. They must wait for civil lawsuits or criminal cases to be brought to them. If a myriad of factors all work out, they may get an opportunity to settle the legal action in a way that has implications beyond the interests of the immediate parties and resolves important constitutional issues. There are, however, numerous obstacles that prevent the right cases from getting to the right courts at the right time and resulting in the best decisions. Without cases that include the appropriate litigants and facts, judges will make decisions that, at best, inadequately address important constitutional questions, or at worst, result in troublesome precedents that the courts and the country may be stuck with for years.

For the Constitution to evolve, judges must be able to accomplish the difficult task of deciding cases based on its fundamental principles while at the same time "modifying" the Constitution to keep up with changing values and conditions. They must be aware of how the nation has changed since the late 18th Century, yet still adhere to the standards embodied in a document written in that era. Judges cannot have an intractable political agenda that leads them either to blind obedience of what they believe to be the meaning of the words as intended by the Framers, or to unrestrained "rewriting" of the Constitution to suit their personal predilections. Finding the right balance is immensely difficult for even the most dedicated judges.

There is often an erroneous assumption — perhaps caused by too many law-related shows on television — that everyone in this country with an important legal issue to resolve can get to a courtroom. But unfortunately, that is not the case. Many litigants who could bring lawsuits that would raise important constitutional questions never sue because they lack the money or cannot find an attorney who will take their case on a contingency basis because the potential damage award is too small. Organizations like the ACLU and legal aid agencies can handle only a few cases at a time.

Even if the litigation makes it through the trial level, there may not be an appeal because there is no money to continue the case through the long and expensive appellate process. Whether a case is decided on appeal makes a substantial difference in its potential impact. If the case is not ultimately resolved by an appellate court, and the final decision in the case is at the trial court level, it will usually be of limited *precedential* value — that is, other courts will not likely apply the results of the case to ones they are deciding. The reasons are complex, but generally trial courts resolve factual disputes, while appellate judges review those decisions by applying principles of law. It is the application of principles of law — including the interpretation of constitutional provisions — rather than the settling of factual disputes, that courts use in subsequent cases. If the losing party could not appeal the trial court decision because of a lack of financial resources or some other reason, the courts will never have the opportunity to further develop the law on that issue by handing down an appellate decision that serves as precedent for future cases.

Cases may also not reach appellate courts when the party that would have raised the most compelling constitutional issues *wins* at the trial level, and therefore has no reason to appeal. Another scenario would be that the parties raise only some of the most important constitutional questions at the trial court level, and that has the effect of limiting the factual and legal issues that a higher court can review on appeal. Generally, an appellate court will only review issues that were raised by the litigants and addressed by the court below.

Even if the issues are present, and the losing party is able to raise those issues in an appeal, the appellate court may decline to review the case. Many appellate courts have the discretion to refuse to hear cases. Criminal defendants charged with serious crimes have the right to one appeal, and if they cannot afford an attorney, one will be provided for them. They may, for example, be able to appeal their conviction to a state court of appeals, but the state supreme court may to decline to hear their case. Litigants in civil cases, if they can afford the cost of the appeal, will generally be able to get to at least one appellate court, but any court above that — such as a state supreme court or the U.S. Supreme Court — has substantial discretion over its docket and turns down many cases.

Perhaps not surprisingly, the courts with the authority to decide cases with the widest potential impact are often the most difficult to reach. The higher the court within a state or the federal judicial system, the more likely their rulings will serve as precedents in subsequent cases. At the same time, however, they will generally hear the fewest cases. For example, a state supreme court's ruling applies throughout that state, and may influence the courts in other states, while a state court of appeals decision would have more limited impact. A U.S. Supreme Court decision is binding on every court in the nation, but it is extremely difficult to get the High Court to hear a case. Thus the courts that have the most authority to command adherence to their constitutional decisions are the ones with courthouse doors that are the most difficult to open.

Even when everything works out — litigants bring appeals in cases that have the facts necessary for a constitutional ruling, and the appellate court agrees to hear the case — there is still no certainty that the case will add much to our understanding of the Constitution. The appellate court may decline to rule broadly, and thus may base its decision on narrow grounds that answer few, if any, of the constitutional questions. In such a scenario, the decision is so closely tied to the facts of the case at hand that it provides no guidance to a judge in a future case on how that subsequent case should be resolved. Every case has different facts. Narrow rulings can often mean they are never applied to later cases, and thus do not add to development of constitutional principles.

Sometimes the reverse happens when a case with unusual or unrepresentative facts is decided by an appellate court, and the ruling by that court becomes the means by which a significant constitutional interpretation is announced. In that situation, the case may be difficult to apply to future cases because they are too factually dissimilar. However, if there are few relevant precedents in that area of the law, judges may be forced to apply the awkward precedent to the new cases, which then develop into their own set of principles that are applied to subsequent cases. It may take years for the new line of cases to be discredited or replaced even though they have taken the law in a direction that it would not have gone had the early cases presented more appropriate facts.

Judges know they occupy a special place in our system. They understand that because they are appointed for life in the case of federal judges — or appointed or elected for long terms, as they are in the states — they are not accountable to the people in the way that elected officials are, or at least, are supposed to be. In order to preserve the legitimacy of the courts — so people will respect and follow their decisions, even when they are unpopular — judges often try to exercise restraint by confining their rulings to the facts as presented to them. Judges do not want to be perceived as "robed legislators" who make policy decisions but are not electorally accountable. If such policy activism happened frequently, it would place intolerable strains on the vitality of the judicial system. Stated another way, judges generally want to interpret no more of the Constitution than is absolutely necessary to solve the factual dispute before them. If they went beyond that, there would be no reasonable limits to their powers. The personal and political views of the judge would be the only factors that mattered. In such a situation, citizens would feel that judges had abused the special independence they are granted in our system, and would feel no obligation to comply with judicial decisions that they do not like.

Judges try not to do too much too quickly that will arouse or alarm the nation in order to preserve the delicate legitimacy that courts possess — a legitimacy that reflects the widespread support among the American people for the authority of judges to make decisions relating to what the Constitution means, even when elected branches of government and substantial numbers of citizens disagree with those decisions. Courts do not have a standing army they can send out to enforce their decisions. They largely depend on voluntary compliance, without which they would not be able to function. Yet incremental interpretation, by its very nature, never permits a broad examination of the Constitution's fitness for dealing with difficult contemporary problems.

Judges view the Constitution in tiny fragments by deciding one case at a time. It is the nature of the judicial process that judges almost never get the opportunity to think about the nation's founding document as a whole when making decisions in individual cases. There are only rare occasions in which courts consider how interpretation of one provision of the Constitution would affect another section. Instead, a judge identifies the law as it has developed in cases that interpret statutory or constitutional text, then applies the law to the facts of the case before the court. Although the judge may also weigh such factors as the social needs of society, how the nation has reacted to such disputes in the past, and the extent to which the decision in the present case will add stability and predictability to the law, there is often limited opportunity to consider the Constitution's role in contemporary society.

The modern judicial system has characteristics that reflect the long struggle for its rightful place in the constitutional hierarchy. The evolutionary process has often been inconsistent and slow, and there were times in which political crises threatened to destroy the court's fragile legitimacy. The courts are a product of their history — perhaps more so than the legislative and executive branches — because of the enduring nature of the Constitution and the reliance on previously decided cases to shape the law. It is that history, and the court system it has created, that has resulted in a protection for civil liberties and other rights enjoyed by the people of no other nation.

The structure of the courts, the nature of the judicial process, even the way judges are selected — all of these factors lead to the conclusion that the courts cannot be the sole source of constitutional development. In order to understand why the people, not the courts, should be the source of comprehensive constitutional change, it is necessary to consider how the courts arrived at where they are today.

The Limitations of Article III

One of the most remarkable developments in our constitutional history is the Supreme Court's evolution from an institution few people took seriously to a coequal branch of government that eventually rivaled and at times has surpassed the scope of congressional and presidential powers. Compared to its stature today, the court system had, to say the least, humble beginnings in the Constitution and the early years of the nation. In its first decade, the Supreme Court issued a handful of significant decisions defining the powers of the new federal government, and established some procedural precedents that would be important later, but it showed few signs of its eventual strength within the national government. Compared with the detailed discussion of the structure and powers of Congress, and to a lesser extent the presidency, the Constitution devoted relatively little attention to the courts. Article III, Section 1 vested judicial power of the United States in "one supreme Court, and in such inferior Courts as the Congress may from time to time ordain and establish." Yet the Framers provided few clues as to what powers the federal courts would exercise in relation to the legislative and executive branches of government. They must have assumed that officials of the newly established government would work out the details.

What few decisions the Framers made about the court system gave a clear advantage to Congress in determining the structure and powers of the judicial branch. The Constitution established the Supreme Court, but *only* that Court. Under Article III, Congress had to create other federal courts and determine what cases they could consider. Under the Constitution, congressional power included the authority to:

• Establish and alter the number of justices who serve on the Supreme Court.

• Establish and alter the appellate jurisdiction of the Supreme Court. That far-reaching power theoretically gives Congress the authority to remove from the Court the discretion to review all but a few cases. The Constitution implies that the only cases Congress could not prevent the Supreme Court from hearing are those that the Court gets from its original jurisdiction. Those are cases, which are specifically assigned by the Constitution, that the Court hears directly without them having been appealed from a lower court.

• Manipulate the Supreme Court's calendar to prevent the Court from meeting to review federal statutes for their constitutionality.

• Establish, alter, or abolish *all* federal courts below the Supreme Court level.

• Withdraw *all* cases dealing with almost any legal issue from the lower federal courts if Congress did not like the way the judges were ruling.

• Grant or withhold jurisdiction of the lower federal courts to hear certain civil suits between citizens of different states — the so-called "diversity" jurisdiction — by setting a minimum dollar amount that must be at issue before the federal courts can hear the case.

As long as the president signed the legislation or there were enough votes to override a presidential veto, there was little that Congress could *not* do to the new federal court system. The Constitution prohibited Congress from lowering the salaries of federal judges or removing them from office except by impeachment and conviction. Yet it is difficult to overstate how much the newly created court system was subject to congressional whim in the years before the American people recognized the indispensable role of a strong, independent judicial branch in a democratic system. The support of the American people eventually discouraged potentially devastating incursions into judicial autonomy by the elected branches when the courts were still vulnerable to such interference. Although Congress still has the authority to exercise all of the above-stated powers, it would likely find strong resistance among the courts and the people if it attempted, for example, to change the number of justices who serve on the Supreme Court, or to remove cases from its appellate jurisdiction or that of the lower federal courts, which would have the effect of limiting the cases the Supreme Court could review. The Senate does, however, make ample use of its discretion to delay or deny the confirmation of nominees to the federal courts.

Whatever Congress's potential stranglehold on the court system in the early years, and the difficult road the courts had to travel to become a viable branch of the federal government, there is no disputing today that the courts in this country are immensely powerful. The more than 800 federal judges who serve pursuant to Article III of the Constitution, appointed by the president and confirmed by the Senate, serve for life and can only be removed by impeachment and conviction. The Constitution states that federal judges shall "hold their Offices during good Behaviour," a phrase that did not explicitly require lifetime tenure. But ever since the first member of the Supreme Court was confirmed in 1789, "good Behaviour" has been interpreted to mean that federal judges may remain in office until they die, resign, or are impeached and convicted.

Besides the nine members of the Supreme Court, there are approximately 180 judges on the various U.S. courts of appeals, and about 650 U.S. district court judges. There are also federal judges who do not serve under Article III and do not have lifetime tenure. Non-Article III judges include administrative law judges (ALJ) who are assigned to administrative agencies but are under the control of the Merit Systems Protection Board. ALJs review disputes between the agency and a party subject to agency action. Their decisions can be reviewed at higher levels in the agency and almost always by courts, but their conclusions are often left intact by the reviewing authorities.

Article III judges are not chosen or confirmed by the people, and are not electorally responsible to them. Because federal judges are not democratically chosen and answerable to the voters, their powers must be strictly confined to prevent interference with decisions more properly made by the popularly elected branches of government. Yet, despite the self-restraint that is an essential element of the legitimacy of the judicial branch, judges exercise sweeping powers. A *single* judge sitting in any federal court can declare a duly enacted law passed by Congress and signed by the president to be unconstitutional. That same judge can issue an order immediately preventing the implementation of that law, and it may be months or even years before the decision is reviewed by an appellate court.

This power of the judiciary raises difficult issues. A democratic society succeeds only when the desires of the people are implemented through laws passed by the legislature and carried out by administrators in the executive branch. The people must be able to hold accountable and vote out of office those who fail to conscientiously represent those values. The federal courts, staffed by judges who never have to stand for election, are not supposed to interfere with the implementation of the people's wishes except when laws or regulations clearly violate a provision of the Constitution. Judges cannot invalidate laws just because they disapprove of them. Courts should only strike down laws when required by the Constitution. Determining where the line should be drawn has always been difficult because judges have substantial discretion and authority to declare acts of Congress or any legislative body to be a violation of the nation's fundamental law as expressed in the Constitution.

The public is sometimes understandably angry when federal judges exercise that authority and frustrate the will of millions of people as expressed at the polls. For example, on December 23, 1996, less than a month after California voters, by a margin of 54–46 percent, approved Proposition 209 — a ballot initiative to end preferences based on race and gender in hiring or contracting by public agencies, and for admission to public colleges and universities — Judge Thelton E. Henderson of the U.S. District Court for the Northern District of California issued an injunction prohibiting the implementation of the law. Judge Henderson wrote that there was a "strong possibility" that the measure was unconstitutional. The U.S. Court of Appeals for the Ninth Circuit overturned the judge's order, and sharply criticized his action: "A system which permits one judge to block with the stroke of a pen what 4,736,180 state residents voted to enact as law tests the integrity of our constitutional democracy."

Federal judges have issued orders that required them to oversee the management of school systems, prisons, and other public agencies when they believe that the Constitution is being violated. They have ordered cities and states to integrate schools and neighborhoods, to fund programs, to build housing in locations not favored by local governing bodies, and have taken other actions that government entities opposed. Although such orders were often needed to remedy past discrimination and other problems, they required courts to "manage" major activities of school districts and other public agencies in order to supervise compliance with the remedies the court was seeking. Several decades may have passed before the judge returned complete control to those elected or chosen to run them. The public is sometimes incensed when federal judges — whom they cannot directly influence and cannot vote out of office — supervise their school district.

Despite the strains that such court decisions place on the political system, the powers that courts exercise are as indispensable as they are awesome. Although democratically elected branches of government play an important role in preserving the procedural and substantive rights established by the Constitution, they are fully capable of depriving those with insufficient political clout or numbers in the population of rights enjoyed by more affluent or better-connected citizens. Only the courts can ultimately protect the civil liberties of unpopular individuals and groups or those accused of crimes by vigorously applying the Constitution even in the face of overwhelming opposition.

The challenge is for courts to know when to aggressively apply the Constitution and when to defer to the elected branches so they can reflect the values of those who elected them to office. If federal judges over an extended period of time insist on an interpretation of the Constitution that is seriously out of step with the current thinking of the country, or they use their exalted positions for the primary purpose of implementing their personal political agendas, they will be in a constant struggle for acceptance of their authority to make unpopular decisions. That acceptance, which is far more fragile than many recognize and which rests to a large degree on psychological grounds, would be imperiled if judges were constantly perceived as using cases to impose their personal views of the Constitution. Recognizing that their powers must be exercised with discretion, courts have developed a complex system by which they limit what cases they will consider and the scope of their decisions. It is because of those limits, and other factors, that courts cannot be the sole source of constitutional evolution.

The struggle for legitimacy

The Framers expected that federal judges would perform the traditional function of the judiciary by settling lawsuits between adverse parties and dealing with criminal cases, but they apparently did not give a lot of thought to the role that the judicial system would play within the federal hierarchy. The Constitution provided little support to the judicial system and, at least on paper, created a branch of government that appeared likely to be forever subservient to the elected branches. Alexander Hamilton, in No. 78 of *The Federalist*, argued for an independent judiciary, but he was quick to assure the American people that the new federal courts would be unable to interfere with the rights they had secured in the Constitution and which they had previously enjoyed under their state constitutions. He described a court system that did not seem to have much of a future when he wrote that "as from the natural feebleness of the judiciary, it is in continual jeopardy of being overpowered, awed, or influenced by its co-ordinate branches."

Hamilton's remarks must be considered in the context in which they were written. He was speaking to those who could potentially be delegates to the New York ratifying convention and was trying to convince them that the federal courts, even though its judges would have lifetime tenure, would not be strong enough to interfere with personal rights. While Hamilton emphasized the harm the new federal judiciary would be pre-vented from inflicting, Thomas Jefferson believed that the courts would be an indispensable source of protection for such rights. In a letter written to James Madison on March 15, 1789, in which he noted the absence of a bill of rights in the new Constitution, Jefferson wrote: "In the arguments in favor of a declaration of rights, you omit one which has great weight with me, the legal check which it puts into the hands of the judiciary. This is a body, which if rendered independent, and kept strictly to their own department merits great confidence for their learning and integrity."

Hamilton's observations about the weakness of the federal court system were initially accurate, as the Supreme Court's early years suggested it would never amount to anything special. The Court was supposed to meet for the first time in New York in 1790, but only three of the justices appointed by President Washington showed up. The original justices were all Federalists, and the Court quickly developed a partisan tone. Service on the Court was considered so unimportant that the first chief justice, John Jay, spent one year in England on a diplomatic mission and ran twice for governor of New York while on the bench. After he was elected in his second try for governor, he resigned as chief justice. John Rutledge, another original member of the Court, did not attend any of its sessions during its first two years. Rutledge was appointed chief justice to succeed Jay, but served only four months before the Senate refused to confirm him. The dual service of some of the early justices also reflected the close ties that the colonial courts had to the executive branch.

The next chief justice, Oliver Ellsworth, served four years and resigned in 1800. James Wilson, another member of the original Court, narrowly avoided being imprisoned for debt while serving on the Court. Samuel Chase, appointed by Washington in 1795 and who served until 1811, was a rabid Federalist who prevented the Court from holding one of its sessions in 1800 because he was away campaigning for President John Adams. When the Jeffersonians came to power, Chase was impeached but escaped conviction in the Senate. Chase's acquittal has been viewed as an important step in establishing the independence of the judiciary.

The Court's lack of prestige in the early years was also demonstrated by how willing Congress was to change — for unabashedly partisan purposes — the number of justices who served on the Court. Up until the Civil War, Congress reduced or enlarged the size of the Court on several occasions in an effort to curtail or enhance a particular president's opportunity to make appointments. The Supreme Court began with six members, but was reduced to five by the lame-duck Federalists in Congress in an effort to avoid tie votes and to give incoming President Jefferson one less vacancy to fill. As new circuits were added, Congress increased the number of justices. A seventh member was added in 1807, and two more in 1837. A tenth justice was added for a tenth circuit in 1864. Congress's disputes with President Andrew Johnson led it to adopt an act in 1866 reducing the number to seven, although there were actually no fewer than eight members at any one time. In 1869, with Johnson gone from office, Congress again increased the Court to nine justices, and the number has not been changed since then.

Years later, the American people expressed strong resistance to further tampering with the size of the Court, even when it was proposed by one of the nation's most popular presidents. Franklin Roosevelt, having been reelected in 1936 by the largest margin in American history, could not convince Congress or the American people to allow him to appoint one member of the Supreme Court for every justice over the age of 70, and to increase the Court's number to a maximum limit of 15. Having served in office since 1933 with no vacancies opening up on the Supreme Court, FDR believed that Congress must increase the size of the Court in an effort to save major components of the New Deal that had been ravaged by conservatives on the Court. Despite FDR's popularity and the continuing hard times of the Depression, there was strong opposition to his "court-packing" plan and it was defeated in Congress.

The Supreme Court did issue some important opinions in its first decade, including several that strongly supported federal authority against the states. But because of the nature of the jurisdiction of state and federal courts, and how difficult and expensive it was to reach the remote locations where the circuit courts were sitting and from which appeals were taken, the Supreme Court heard relatively few cases during its first decade. During the 12-year period from 1789 to 1801, for example, the Supreme Court heard only three cases appealed from state courts.

The Court continued to hear few cases and showed little evidence of its eventual powerful status until President John Adams, a month before he left office 1801, appointed his Secretary of State, John Marshall, as chief justice. It was one of those special times in American history when the right person was appointed to a key position at an auspicious moment. For the next 35 years, Marshall dominated the Supreme Court and did more than any individual to establish its place within the constitutional system. He is often cited as the most influential justice ever to serve on the Supreme Court. Legal scholar Bernard Schwartz has Marshall at the top of his list of the ten greatest Supreme Court justices. Schwartz quoted Oliver Wendell Holmes, a Supreme Court justice from 1902 to 1932, as saying that "if American law were to be represented by a single figure, skeptic and worshipper alike would agree that the figure could be one alone, and that one, John Marshall." Others agreed with Schwartz. Justice Benjamin Cardozo said this about Marshall: "He gave the constitution of the United States the impress of his own mind; and the form of our constitutional law is what it is, because he moulded it while it was still plastic and malleable in the fire of his own intense convictions."

Marshall's ability to elucidate the general and often vague provisions of the new Constitution in a way that created and enhanced the Court's power entitles him to be considered among the greatest leaders of the nation.

The Threat of Congressional Retaliation in the Early Years

Throughout the Court's first decades, the possibility remained that Congress would exercise the authority granted to it by the Constitution that would seriously undermine judicial autonomy. If Congress had taken such action frequently, it would have kept the Supreme Court and lower federal courts forever subordinate to the legislative and executive branches. Trusting Congress to create a federal judiciary with appropriate powers, the Framers wanted the legislative branch to have broad discretion to establish and refine the structure and jurisdiction of the federal courts. Among the tools that Article III gave Congress was the authority to establish and alter the *appellate* jurisdiction of the Supreme Court and lower federal courts. The Supreme Court primarily hears cases on appeal that have previously been considered by other courts; thus the great majority of cases come to the Court through its appellate jurisdiction.

The Constitution does provide for a narrow range of cases that can be heard in the Court's *original* jurisdiction, where cases come first to the Supreme Court without having been heard by lower courts. Those are cases in which a state is a party, and those affecting ambassadors, public ministers, and consuls. The grant of original jurisdiction comes directly from Article III, Section 2 of the Constitution and requires no legislation from Congress to make it effective. Thus even if it wanted, Congress could not interfere with the Court's ability to review cases in its original jurisdiction, but the Court hears few such cases.

The First Congress knew that one of the most urgent laws it had to pass was a judiciary act that would establish and define the jurisdiction of a federal court system below the Supreme Court. Congress did so in the Judiciary Act of 1789. For lower federal courts to have jurisdiction of a case or controversy, it must be one that the Constitution has defined as within the judicial power of the United States, and an act of Congress must have conferred jurisdiction over such cases in the courts. For example, the Constitution extends federal judicial authority over controversies between citizens of different states, known as "diversity of citizenship" jurisdiction. But Congress has given the federal courts jurisdiction of such cases only if the amount in controversy exceeds $50,000. In 1988, Congress amended the law to raise the jurisdictional amount from $10,000 to $50,000, a move that is partially responsible for the reduction in the number of lawsuits brought in the federal courts between 1988 and 1993. Diversity cases, which are only in federal court because the parties are residents of different states, add significantly to the caseload of federal judges. The increase in the threshold dollar amount was a compromise between those who wanted to abolish diversity jurisdiction and those who wanted to maintain the rights of litigants to choose between state and federal courts. Some litigants feel that state courts will favor their own citizens and thus, they want to sue in federal court. Congress is considering raising the minimum amount in controversy to $75,000 and other actions to force more cases into state as opposed to federal courts.

By giving Congress control of the Supreme Court's appellate jurisdiction, the Constitution handed the legislature a formidable weapon. If Congress, for example, wanted to eliminate Supreme Court review of all cases related to such controversial issues as abortion, prayer in public schools, or the rights of criminal defendants, the Constitution strongly implies that it has the authority to do so. Several times in our history Congress has tampered with the appellate jurisdiction of the Supreme Court to keep it from invalidating clearly unconstitutional laws. In 1868, the period immediately following the Civil War, Congress removed the Supreme Court's authority to hear appeals under an important law passed the previous year. That law gave federal judges the power to grant a petition of habeas corpus to any person being held in violation of the federal Constitution or laws, and provided for appeal to the Supreme Court in such cases. Congress feared that the Supreme Court would use a case brought under the statute to interfere with military rule in the Southern states. In *Ex Parte McCardle*, the Supreme Court reluctantly concluded that it could not hear the case because Congress had withdrawn its jurisdiction to decide the appeal. The Court noted that "without jurisdiction the court cannot proceed at all in any cause. Jurisdiction is power to declare the law, and when it ceases to exist, the only function remaining to the court is that of announcing the fact and dismissing the cause."

Shortly after ratification of the Constitution, the Supreme Court had an opportunity to consider whether Congress did, in fact, have the power to curtail the Court's appellate jurisdiction. However, once it recognized that Congress had legislated on the subject of the Court's appellate jurisdiction in the Judiciary Act of 1789, the Court concluded in its 1796 decision in *Wiscart v. D'Auchy* that without a statute prescribing a rule for appellate proceedings, the Court could not assume jurisdiction.

Although Congress has periodically considered legislation over the last half century that would remove certain types of cases from the Supreme Court's appellate jurisdiction, none has passed. While it is possible that Congress could still try to remove a class of cases from the Court's appellate docket, such action would likely alarm the American people who have long recognized the role of federal judges in our constitutional system even while they disagree with particular decisions. In addition, the Supreme Court itself would likely find sections in the Constitution outside of Article III that would allow it to invalidate congressional efforts to keep the Court from reviewing cases on certain issues. Among other grounds, it may find that a statute taking away such authority would be contrary to the principle of separation of powers.

The justices go on the road

In establishing the federal courts, Congress created a plan that imposed nearly intolerable burdens on the justices of the Supreme Court. The transportation system in the late 18th century was prehistoric by today's standards, yet that did not stop Congress from requiring justices to travel several months of the year to preside over local courts. The scheme Congress developed had the effect — whether intended or not — of inhibiting the Court's development.

Congress created the federal court system in the Judiciary Act of 1789, one of the first laws it enacted. The law was the result of a lengthy debate during the summer of 1789 between the Federalists who wanted a strong and complete system of federal courts, and the Anti-Federalists who attempted to limit the power of judges. The law created trial courts, known as "district" courts, in every state. It also established three circuit courts for the eastern, middle, and southern sections of the country. Instead of providing for additional federal judges for the circuit courts, Congress decided that justices of the Supreme Court, along with the district judge in whose district the circuit court was sitting, should preside over those courts. With the flimsy justification that the justices should be aware of local judicial controversies and issues, Congress required the six justices of the Supreme Court to spend months each year traveling to distant cities and rural areas to hear cases in the circuit courts.

In "riding circuit" as it was known, the justices had to endure long trips in uncomfortable coaches on sometimes impassable roads. Justices would spend as many as 19 hours a day traveling. The image of a Supreme Court justice, after enduring hours of a jarring ride, being required to help lift a coach out of the mud, contradicts the usual picture of a learned and scholarly judge sitting on a bench dispensing justice. Despite bitter complaints of the justices and constant threats to resign, Congress relented only somewhat in 1793 by reducing to one the number of circuit trips each year. With relatively little time spent in the nation's capital, and with the justices often sick and exhausted by the time they returned, it was difficult for the Court's members to work together to elevate its status to those of other branches of government. There were individuals who probably declined appointment to the court because they did not want to subject themselves to the ordeal of riding circuit.

There was another serious problem with the new court system. By having Supreme Court justices on the circuit courts, there was always the possibility that they would hear the case again if it were appealed to the High Court. Under such circumstances, the justices would not only have "prejudged" the case when it was in the circuit court, the justices would be reviewing their own decisions in the cases.

The lame-duck Federalist Congress temporarily ended circuit riding with the passage of the Judiciary Act of 1801. But the primary purpose of the law was to create new federal judgeships that could be filled by President Adams and confirmed by the Federalist Congress in the final days of the Adams administration. When the Republicans took office, Congress repealed the Act, replaced it with a new judiciary act in 1802, and sent the justices of the Supreme Court back on the road. Under the 1802 law, there were six circuits, composed of one Supreme Court justice and one district judge. It was not until after the Civil War, in 1869, that the circuit-riding responsibilities of the justices were greatly reduced. The justices were not freed completely of these onerous burdens until the Circuit Court of Appeals Act of 1891.

The Origins of Judicial Review

The Constitution did not give the Supreme Court the one tool it very much needed to rise above Hamilton's dour description of the judicial system created by the Framers: The power to declare acts of Congress or state legislatures to be unconstitutional. In what was one of the most important developments in the nation's history, the Supreme Court found a way to establish that authority on its own in a case that presented the right factual situation to a justice who knew how to accomplish what the Framers had declined to explicitly provide.

There had been much discussion by the delegates at the Constitutional Convention about whether the Supreme Court should have such power, and whether it should include the authority to review both federal and state laws. But despite the efforts of the delegates to draft specific language about court review of legislative acts, the Constitution is silent on whether the courts could invalidate laws duly enacted by the elected branches of government.

It is unthinkable today that the Supreme Court and other courts would not have the power of "judicial review." Without it, there would be intolerable strains on the political system, with the most dire threats to civil liberties. Imagine a scenario where Congress passed, and the president signed, a law that clearly violated the Constitution, and the only remedy was for the people to replace the miscreant officials at the next election with new leaders who would immediately repeal the offensive law. If such a law, for example, seriously inhibited the exercise of First Amendment rights of free speech or press, and the courts were powerless to invalidate it, the communication process by which people learn what their government officials are doing would be severely hampered. In such a situation there would be the strong possibility that those responsible for such unconstitutional acts would remain in office because voters would have insufficient information about their actions.

Through the efforts of extraordinary jurists who ascended to the Supreme Court at the right time in our history, there is now firmly established the power of federal and state judges to strike down laws passed by any legislature, from Congress to the lowliest city council, if that law violates the U.S. Constitution and has been challenged in a lawsuit or other appropriate legal action. Judges also have the authority to invalidate executive actions ranging from the president's taking over the steel industry during wartime, to a mayor's refusal to allow a public building to be used for peaceful assemblies. Whether judges have always used that power wisely has been debated for as long as this nation has had a court system. But it has been settled for nearly two centuries that courts can invalidate the actions of the elected branches of government.

The delegates to the Constitutional Convention debated, and eventually rejected, several plans that would have called for review by the Supreme Court of acts of Congress. One plan, advanced by James Madison, seems out of place today considering the nation's long commitment to separation of powers. The delegates considered a proposal by Madison and James Wilson to establish a council composed of the president and a "convenient number" of members of the national judiciary that would have veto power over congressional legislation. Such a plan, which required members of the Supreme Court to collaborate with the president in deciding whether to veto legislation, would have created serious problems. Among the arguments against giving Supreme Court justices a role in the veto process was that they would already be on record as disapproving congressional legislation before any appeals arising from that law came to the full Court for review in an actual case, thus creating the impression that the justices could not approach the case with open minds when it came before the Court. There was also the understandable concern that such a plan would violate the principle of separation of powers by which the branches of the federal government exercise authority within their domain, and also have institutional controls known as "checks and balances" over certain activities of the other branches.

Despite the misgivings expressed by some delegates, Madison argued that such a council was necessary because the president needed both control and support, and allowing judges to participate in the vetoing of legislation would enhance both. He told the delegates that the "Executive Magistrate would be envied & assailed by disappointed competitors: His firmness therefore would need support. .... An association of the Judges in his revisionary [veto] function would both double the advantage and diminish the danger. It would also enable the Judiciary Department the better to defend itself against Legislative encroachments." The delegates rejected this form of "judicial review" in favor of a purely executive veto of congressional legislation by a vote of 11-3.

Once the initial proposal was defeated, delegates who believed that members of the Supreme Court should participate in the veto process offered a new, rather creative plan for involving the judiciary in reviewing congressional legislation, but one that presented as many problems as the rejected "veto council." Under the second plan introduced by Madison on August 15, all bills passed by Congress would go to the president and the entire Supreme Court. If either the president or a majority of the members of the Court objected, Congress would have to repass the bill by a two-thirds vote in each House before it would have the force of law. If both the president *and* the Court objected to the bill, Congress would have to repass it by a three-fifths vote. Some delegates strongly objected to judges participating in legislative business. Charles Pinckney of South Carolina said it will "involve them in parties, and give a previous tincture to their opinions." John Francis Mercer of Maryland wanted the delegates to go even further in limiting the role of the courts. He opposed the judiciary reviewing legislation either upon passage *or* when a case is later brought to the Court, telling the delegates that "laws ought to be well and cautiously made, and then to be uncontrollable." The delegates defeated this proposal on the same day by a vote of 8-3.

No additional effort was made at the Convention to give the Supreme Court explicit powers to review congressional legislation. The absence of such efforts did not mean the delegates opposed judicial review, but without specific language in the Constitution, the issue was left unsettled. Constitutional scholars who have studied the debates at the Convention have reached conflicting conclusions about whether the Framers intended for courts to have the power of judicial review. There was some discussion of the issue in the ratifying conventions, with the subject often raised by those delegates who had attended the Constitutional Convention. Some scholars have focused not on the Philadelphia Convention, but instead on Hamilton's statements in No. 78 of *The Federalist*, in which he strongly argued for the right of courts to strike down legislation that conflicts with the Constitution. In describing the judiciary as the branch which is the "least dangerous to the political rights of the Constitution," Hamilton argued that a "limited Constitution" can be "preserved in practice no other way than through the medium of courts of justice, whose duty it must be to declare all acts contrary to the manifest tenor of the Constitution void."

And he added, such authority does not "by any means suppose a superiority of the judicial to the legislative power. . . . It only supposes that the power of the people is superior to both."

In a 1989 book, Chief Justice William Rehnquist wrote that the Framers of the Constitution "wanted the judges to be independent of the president and of Congress, but in all probability they also wanted the federal courts to be able to pass on whether or not legislation enacted by Congress was consistent with the limitations of the United States Constitution."

The Court assumes the power of judicial review: Marbury v. Madison *(1803)*

Although the Supreme Court had asserted the right of judicial review in previous cases, it was not until the famous case of *Marbury v. Madison* that the Court removed any doubt that it had the power to invalidate an act of Congress. The case involved four of the most important political figures of the time — John Adams, Thomas Jefferson, John Marshall, and James Madison — and one person who would have remained unknown in history had his commission been delivered before a midnight deadline.

The Federalists had suffered a stunning defeat by Thomas Jefferson and the Republicans in November 1800. In the final days of his administration, President Adams appointed as many Federalists as he could to judgeships and other positions while the lame-duck Federalist Congress confirmed them. Adams frantically attempted to complete the paperwork to appoint what became derisively known as "midnight judges" in the days leading up to Jefferson's inauguration on March 4, 1801. Among his appointments were 42 new justices of the peace for the District of Columbia. In the confusion of getting the paperwork to John Marshall — who despite being chief justice was still acting as Secretary of State in the final months of the administration, and who had to affix the great seal of the United States for them to be effective — some commissions were not delivered on time.

One of those who would have been a justice of the peace was William Marbury. He believed he was entitled to his commission, and sought relief in the Supreme Court. In December 1801, Marbury petitioned the Court for an order, known as a "writ of mandamus," that would require the new Secretary of State, James Madison, to deliver Marbury's commission. Such a writ is a court order requiring an executive branch official to perform an official duty that the official is obligated to carry out.

The Supreme Court agreed to hear the case, which angered the new Republican Congress, and new legislators were quick to find a way to retaliate. The Constitution appeared to give Congress the power to set the dates on which the Supreme Court would be able to meet. Upon learning that the Supreme Court would hear the *Marbury* case, it immediately passed a law preventing the Court from meeting for 14 months. As a result, it was not until 1803, when the Court was finally able to resume its work, that it heard arguments in the case.

Chief Justice John Marshall faced a terrible dilemma. He knew that if the Court ordered Madison to deliver Marbury's commission, he would ignore the order, thus exposing the Supreme Court as powerless to enforce its decisions. On the other hand, if Marshall found that Marbury was not entitled to his commission, the Jeffersonians would claim victory and the Court would be viewed as too timid to defy the party that controlled the Congress and the presidency. Either outcome would have been potentially disastrous for a court attempting to establish itself as an independent and coequal branch of government. At this early stage in the Court's history, having a president or secretary of state openly defy an order from the Court, with the Court having no means by which it could enforce such a decision, would demonstrate that the elected branches of government can simply ignore judicial orders they did not like.

Marshall ingeniously found a third alternative that avoided the immediate crisis while at the same time enormously enhancing the Court's prestige. Writing for a unanimous Court, which handed down its decision in *Marbury v. Madison* on February 24, 1803, Marshall concluded that Madison had wrongfully withheld Marbury's commission and that he was entitled to it. Marshall also determined that the laws of the nation provided a remedy for the right that Madison had violated. But as to the crucial issue, Marshall decided that the Supreme Court could not order the commission to be delivered to Marbury. The reason was that the federal statute that Marbury hoped the Supreme Court would use to get him his commission was unconstitutional. It would be the first time the Supreme Court had so boldly struck down an act of Congress.

The law that the Supreme Court held to be unconstitutional was Section 13 of the Judiciary Act of 1789, which provided that "The Supreme Court . . . shall have power to issue . . . writs of mandamus, in cases warranted by the principles and usages of law, to any courts appointed or persons holding office, under the authority of the United States." Marbury did not file his petition in a lower federal court and then ask the Supreme Court to review his case in its appellate jurisdiction. Instead, he went directly to the Supreme Court, thus seeking relief through the Court's original jurisdiction.

Marshall found that Section 13 of the Act had enlarged the Supreme Court's original jurisdiction by giving it the right to issue writs of mandamus, a power that is not listed in the Constitution as part of the Court's original jurisdiction. Section 13 was therefore contrary to Article III, Section 2, and thus unconstitutional. Marshall relied on Hamilton's arguments in No. 78 of *The Federalist* in stating that "a legislative act, contrary to the constitution, is not law." He further noted that the justices of the Supreme Court take an oath to support the Constitution, and it would be immoral for them to allow a law to be implemented that violates the document they have been sworn to uphold. Marshall left no doubt that the Supreme Court had the right to invalidate legislation that conflicts with the Constitution: "It is emphatically the province and duty of the judicial department to say what the law is."

The genius of *Marbury* is that the Supreme Court invalidated a federal statute because it offered the Court powers that the Court said it could not exercise. At the same time that the Court was asserting the authority to hold unconstitutional an act of the national legislature, it declined to accept an augmentation of its own powers. That gave the impression that the Court was not looking for a way to enhance its own authority or prestige.

Such a strategy, although solving the immediate problem, has not convinced some scholars that Marshall was required to reach the conclusion he did. There is much to the argument that Marshall was merely looking for a creative way to get out of the crisis facing the Court and to preserve its limited prestige. Section 13, it could be argued, did not unconstitutionally enlarge the original jurisdiction of the Court. Nevertheless, Marshall was able to clearly establish the power of judicial review of congressional legislation by deftly concluding that the Supreme Court could not accept the authority that Congress had offered it. Marbury was entitled to his commission, which Madison should have delivered, the Court concluded. But because he could not ask the Supreme Court to issue an order requiring Madison to do so, Marbury would have to seek such a remedy elsewhere.

Having established the authority to declare an act of Congress to be unconstitutional, the Supreme Court was in no hurry to use it. After *Marbury*, no act of Congress was invalidated until the Missouri Compromise, which had already been repealed, was voided in the disastrous *Dred Scott v. Sandford* decision in 1857. The Court did extend its power of judicial review to state actions in its 1810 decision in *Fletcher v. Peck*, where it held that a state legislature could not constitutionally rescind land grants to individuals who had purchased the land in good faith; in its 1816 decision in *Martin v. Hunter's Lessee*, in which the Court asserted the right to review a decision of a state court over land ownership; and in its 1821 decision in *Cohens v. Virginia* in which the Court reviewed a state criminal conviction.

Years after the Court invalidated a second congressional act in *Dred Scott*, it began to declare acts of Congress to be unconstitutional more frequently. From 1865 to 1970, the Supreme Court held 84 acts of Congress to be unconstitutional in whole or in part. During the New Deal, the conservative Court handed down decisions holding 12 acts of Congress in 1935 and 1936 to be contrary to the Constitution. By 1994, the Supreme Court had declared at least 128 acts of Congress to be unconstitutional in whole or in part.

Where Judges Find the Law

If the primary responsibility for "amending" the Constitution has been assumed by the courts, it is important to identify and understand the sources of the law on which judges rely for settling actual lawsuits and thus establishing precedents for future cases. Unfortunately, as with so many aspects of a complex society, there is no easily discernible source to which judges can turn to discover the law. There is, moreover, no formula that shows judges how they can consistently apply the law to similar cases. What is simply referred to as the "law" is a complex collection of statutes, administrative regulations, state and federal constitutional text, and the principles that emerge from previous cases. The law also includes the moral precepts of the community which, although not universally shared or always clearly articulated, nevertheless permeate both philosophical discussions of the law and the actual work of judges.

Although identifying the "law" to apply to the facts in a lawsuit or criminal action is rarely a simple process, it is but a first step to the more difficult challenge that judges face, namely, deciding how the various elements of the law are to be *viewed*. Even the most common judicial action — interpreting the act of a legislative body and applying that interpretation to the facts of the case — involves complex decisions that require a judge to weigh numerous factors. The judge first begins with the actual text of the statute. But even that step requires active interpretation and the exercise of judicial discretion. City councils, state legislatures, and Congress often write laws in general terms. Those statutes are the products of legislative compromise. The law's final language may be the result of haste, fatigue, ignorance, campaign contributions, political pressure, or the political views of a committee chair, as much as the product of thoughtful and reasoned debate. Within legislatures it is easier to form a majority to approve pending legislation when it is stated in general terms. Legislators know they can let courts decide the specifics in the context of individual cases, and therefore, they do not have to keep debating detailed language that may unravel carefully nurtured legislative majorities.

The legislature cannot anticipate all of the factual situations that may arise under a law. That requires the judge to decide whether the actions at issue in the lawsuit or criminal action are even covered by the statute. The judge may take a narrow view that unless the legislature specifically indicated that the statute covers such activities as those before the court, it does not apply. Or the judge may take a more expansive or "activist" approach by finding that although the legislature did not address the issues before the court specifically, the judge has a sense of what the legislature would have concluded had it anticipated those issues. The legislative history of the bill — in committee reports, debates in committees and on the floor of the respective houses — will sometimes provide insight into the expectations of the legislators. But with no fixed principles and often conflicting legislative evidence to guide the decision, the judge is left with substantial discretion in these matters.

Having gathered the basic implements — the text of the statute, the facts of the case at hand, conclusions about the applicability of the statute to the actions of the litigants before the court, and the law as it has emerged in previous cases — the judge must then mix all those elements together to determine how the present case will be decided, and the basis for that decision. It is the reason for the decision, what is known in the law as the *ratio decidendi*, that will serve as precedent for future cases. Judges look to previously decided cases as an essential element of determining what the "law" is that should be applied to the case before them. This is the essence of the "common law" — thousands of court decisions from hundreds of jurisdictions around the country contribute to the judge-made law that evolves gradually over time. The case law developed by judges helps fill in the gaps left by the general language of a statute or constitutional provision and is an essential part of the judge's work. As Cardozo observed, "It is true that codes and statutes do not render the judge superfluous, nor his work perfunctory and mechanical. There are gaps to be filled. There are doubts and ambiguities to be cleared. There are hardships and wrongs to be mitigated if not avoided."

The common law's great virtues are also its vices. Because it is developed through case-by-case adjudication over a period of time, the common law can be adapted to changing conditions and needs of the nation. Judges are appointed from the population and are likely to have some knowledge of the changing priorities of society. They can apply those emerging values as they decide specific cases. Yet even though judges may not be the most qualified to assess current trends in society — if, for example, before and after they are appointed to the bench they enjoy a lifestyle that sharply limits their contact with and understanding of those from other social or economic classes, or they were appointed so many years ago that they are part of a previous generation that does not understand contemporary problems — that function is an important and essential part of their work. Cardozo observed many years ago that judges may not always be able to assess the current thinking of society: "You may say that there is no assurance that judges will interpret the *mores* of their day more wisely and truly than other men. I am not disposed to deny this, but in my view it is quite beside the point. The point is rather that this power of interpretation must be lodged somewhere, and the custom of the constitution has lodged it in the judges. If they are to fulfill their function as judges, it could hardly be lodged elsewhere."

If judges are going to *make* law — which they must do despite the rhetoric of so-called "strict constructionists" who argue that good judges only apply and do not create the law — it is essential that underlying principles be in force that give the law some stability and predictability. Those characteristics become imbued in the common law through the principle of *stare decisis*, by which judges determine the law as established in previous cases, and then apply those standards to the case before them. If there was no principle of *stare decisis*, every case could be decided on an ad hoc basis and no one would know society's rules in advance. The political philosophy or personal prejudice of the judges would always transcend the precedents established in previous cases. Chaos would reign as each case would require a painstaking effort to gather and carefully weigh all the facts and apply some standard of the law to them. Despite all the time and effort this would entail, there would be nothing to stop the judge in the next case from reaching the opposite conclusion even though it presented similar facts and legal issues.

Judges must exercise this discretion with care. Because there are so many cases available on which to base the current case, each with slightly different factual situations, judges can — if they wanted — *first* determine how the case should come out, and *then* find appropriate precedents to support that conclusion. Judges are human and subject to personal frailties, but if the American people suspected judges did that very often, the judicial system would enjoy much less respect.

The development of the law is further complicated by the structure of the court system. Not all cases or precedents are created equal. The rulings of certain courts constitute *mandatory* authority for other courts. For example, a U.S. district court — the trial court level in the federal system — may find that a relevant case has been decided by the court of appeals circuit in which that trial court is located. Under such circumstances, the trial court judge must follow the precedent handed down by the court of appeals. If there is no such precedent, the district court judge is likely to look at the decisions of courts of appeals in other circuits or other federal district courts around the country for guidance on how to decide the case. The same situation would be true for a state trial court. If the state supreme court has ruled in a case that is directly relevant to the case at hand — what lawyers refer to as being "on point" — the trial court must follow the state supreme court's ruling.

There are several problems with this process. Judges often have many precedents from which to choose, and can frequently "distinguish" the case before them from precedents even if they are from courts with binding authority. "Distinguishing" a case means that the judge in the case being decided (Case "B") finds that the facts are sufficiently different from a previous case (Case "A"), that the judge deciding Case "B" does not have to apply the principles of Case "A." Put another way, even if the U.S. Supreme Court has handed down a constitutional decision, that does not mean it will be followed. If a judge determines that the Supreme Court's decision is not controlling because the facts are different, the judge is largely freed of the obligation to apply the Supreme Court's precedent, and can instead adopt the rulings of whatever court seems the most persuasive.

This process by which the common law is developed — one case at a time — is agonizingly slow. It does allow the law to adapt to changing social, economic, and political conditions, but often over an extended period of time. Even when change is more urgently needed, the common law by its very nature will often evolve at a glacial pace. Although this steady, slow pace preserves its stability and prevents the chaos of a more ad hoc system, it often means that society has to wait a long time for the law to catch up with changing conditions and values.

When there is sufficient demand for more immediate change, legislatures will sometimes pass statutes to do what courts either have declined to do or have been unable to accomplish because the right cases have not been available. However, if the legislature is going to modify the common law as it has been developed by judges, it must say so explicitly in the statute or else the courts will assume that the legislature did not intend to disrupt the evolutionary process of the common law and will strike it down.

The lack of deference to legislatures

Judicial development of the law is further circumscribed by a legal principle too often neglected by some judges. Theoretically, statutes passed by legislative bodies are higher in the constitutional hierarchy than the common law that emerges from cases. The legislature is made up of officials directly elected by the people, and it is expected that the representatives will ascertain and implement the desires of the people of their state or district. If legislators misunderstand those wishes, then ideally they will be replaced in office in the next election by those who better perceive the desires of the voters. Yet judges often assert that legislators either did not anticipate the factual situation presented by the case before the court, or that they made the wrong decision. Activist judges in such circumstances may be less than candid about how they arrive at their conclusions. Rarely will judges explicitly proclaim that they do not like what the legislature has done and are now fixing it. Instead, they select from any number of previous cases or general principles based on lofty constitutional phrases such as "due process of law" or "equal protection of the law," and assert that the standards that have developed from those cases compel them to reach a conclusion that is contrary to what the statute appeared to require. They may go through the motions of actually beginning their analysis with the text of the statute or Constitution, but they quickly seek out friendly precedents that, remarkably, tend to bolster their ultimate conclusion.

Judges are sometimes justified in not waiting until a legislative body takes action — even in the absence of specific phrases in the Constitution — when an exercise of moral leadership is required. Such was the case in *Brown v. Board of Education* in 1954 when the Court began the process of dismantling state-mandated segregation. Congress would not likely have acted for years. With Southern senators in key committee positions, Congress was clearly unable to do what the Supreme Court felt it was both compelled to by the Constitution and was fully justified in doing. Courts were obligated to protect the rights of criminal defendants that legislatures would likely never have done on their own. But there is often a price to pay when the courts, and not the elected branches, are out front on an issue. When judges make unpopular decisions, the complaint is heard that the judiciary — unaccountable and often unresponsive — exercises too much power and that something needs to be done to curtail that power.

"Oracles" of the law

Throughout our history, judges have had substantial discretion in deciding cases, many of which have had far-reaching consequences. No legal system could function properly if judges were forced to follow a list of rules that removed from them any ability to make decisions based on the circumstances of a particular case. On the other hand, judges cannot appear to be imposing their own views and prejudices on the litigants and the nation whenever they want. It is important that judges apply identifiable legal principles that have been developed from other cases, from statutes, and the text of the Constitution, while at the same time adapting the law to changing values. Citizens will have little respect for the judicial branch if they believe that the factor that always matters most in how cases are decided is the judge's personal beliefs.

To encourage such respect and the development of a stable system of laws, a philosophy of jurisprudence — inspired by 18th century English jurist Sir William Blackstone — emerged over many years that suggested that the law consisted of fixed and immutable principles, and that a judge's role was limited to simply discovering and announcing the law. It did not matter, the theory goes, whether the judge was conservative or liberal, or appointed by a Republican or a Democrat. Instead, the judge's responsibility was to identify the law as it was enunciated in previous cases and to "mechanically" apply those standards to the present case. Such a theory characterized the judge as an "oracle" of the law — someone who discovers and then announces the law by applying principles of logic — rather than someone who "makes" law by considering social and political factors. In practice, such a theory would prevent a judge from deciding in advance how a case should come out based on personal bias and then justifying the outcome by searching for relevant precedents.

This theory of the limited role of judges, it can be argued, is consistent with democratic philosophy, which maintains that elected branches of government should be the place where society's values are identified and debated, and where electorally responsible public officials write the rules by which society is to be governed. It is antidemocratic, and creates crises of legitimacy, the argument would continue, for "robed legislators" who, in the case of federal judges, are appointed for life, to create law when citizens have no direct opportunity to influence those decisions by voting them out of office.

The theory sounds wonderful. Presidents and governors and legislators would only have to appoint or confirm bright and energetic people to the bench. Judges appointed in such an idealistic environment, regardless of their background, upbringing, experience, political affiliations, and personal qualities, would be able to find principles of law either in nature or through cases decided by other courts over time, and apply them to the legal disputes before them. They would add nothing to and take nothing away from the law, but would simply apply principles of deduction to determine the appropriate rule, and then decide the current case based on that rule.

The theory is, however, more than unrealistic. For many years it prevented judges, law school professors, and legal writers from viewing the law as it really was, and how it actually affected people, rather than as a mathematical formula that could just as well be implemented by machines as by judges. Throughout the first 100 years of this nation's history, the Blackstonian view of jurisprudence dominated legal training and the practice of law, and still today partially obscures the function that judges actually serve.

This nation may have defeated the British in the Revolutionary War, but ironically, it warmly embraced many of the characteristics of the British common law, including the Blackstonian principle of jurisprudence. For a century after the Constitution was ratified, the nation was still being told that the law had almost everything to do with science or logic and almost nothing to do with the views of individual judges or the problems of real people. At the end of the 19th century, a group of judges and scholars rebelled against the Blackstonian theory and became part of a movement known as the school of "sociological jurisprudence," which challenged the prevailing theory that judges are confined to merely discovering and applying the law.

Oliver Wendell Holmes had the opportunity before and during his service on the Court to develop and disseminate the principles of the sociological jurisprudence movement. In his 1881 book, *The Common Law*, one of the most important works ever published on American law, Holmes challenged the theory that judges had little or no role to play in the development of the law. In one of the book's most famous passages, Holmes wrote: "The life of the law has not been logic; it has been experience. The felt necessities of the time, the prevalent moral and political theories, intuitions of public policy, avowed or unconscious, even the prejudices which judges share with their fellow-men, have had a good deal more to do than the syllogism in determining the rules by which men should be governed."

Another respected member of the movement was Benjamin Cardozo, who for many years was the chief judge of New York's highest court, and from 1932–1938 was an associate justice of the Supreme Court. He helped demystify the judicial process by candidly asserting that judges are real people who look at the same constitutional text and previously decided cases and come to reasonable, but different conclusions. His influential essay, *The Nature of the Judicial Process*, was one of many works of the era that showed the crucial role that judges play as individuals in shaping the law. He recognized that custom, history, philosophy, and other factors played a significant role in the judicial process: "My analysis of the judicial process comes then to this, and little more: logic, and history, and custom, and utility, and the accepted standards of right conduct, are the forces which singly or in combination shape the progress of the law. Which of these forces shall dominate in any case must depend largely upon the comparative importance or value of the social interests that will be thereby promoted or impaired."

Some legal scholars found the challenge that Holmes, Cardozo, and others made to the "declaratory" theory of law to be too timid. Beginning in the 1920s, these individuals — called "legal realists" — broke from the sociological jurisprudence school. The "realists," who were mostly law professors but also included political scientists, philosophers, economists, and psychologists, argued that legal study should concentrate on judicial decisions and their effects. They believed that judges, with all their biases and imperfections, play a central role in shaping the law. They also argued that because the law does not take place in a vacuum, but develops within a complex social and political system, other social sciences must play a stronger role in describing and influencing the role of courts and law in this country.

It has been clear for a long time that the views of individual judges do matter. A case raising important issues under the Bill of Rights, for example, is likely to find Justice Clarence Thomas and Justice John Paul Stevens, to choose two members of the current Supreme Court, on opposite sides. It does not disparage the judicial process to recognize that one is an extremely conservative justice who almost always supports the government over the rights of the individual, while the other is much more moderate and likely to favor the individual. If judges were machines who merely ascertain and apply the laws, Justices Thomas and Stevens would almost always be on the same side.

How Judges Look at the Law

The great majority of the work of all judges is to interpret statutes, administrative regulations, and other texts. A much smaller number of cases directly involve the Constitution. Yet when judges apply a provision of the Constitution to a case, they are exercising powers enjoyed by no other officials. Any interpretation of the Constitution is immediately placed at the top of the legal hierarchy. The Constitution is the supreme law of the nation, and its provisions can be used to invalidate any statute passed by state or federal legislative bodies — from a city council in a small town, to a state legislature, to Congress — as well as almost any administrative actions taken by mayors, governors, and even the president. Any provision of a state constitution, even if approved by the legislature and voters of that state, can be declared invalid by a judge who finds it conflicts with the federal Constitution.

The Constitution has often been described as a "living" document, which grows and adapts as the nation faces new challenges. Conservatives have never been comfortable with such a description and disagree with the suggestion that each generation can "revise" the Constitution to serve its needs. To conservatives, the Constitution is not like a statute or administrative regulation. It is the nation's fundamental law and the values it embodies must endure throughout the generations. Such a view would hold that judges should not be able to scour the Constitution and its amendments — which often use general language open to wide-ranging interpretation — to find words to justify their view of what the Constitution *ought* to mean. The misuse of the Constitution, conservatives would argue, is then further compounded by the same activist judges who, after yanking a section out of its historical context, then select previously decided cases that support their interpretation of the Constitution. That only adds to the body of law that develops on a foundation that may have been unsound to begin with.

Conservatives often urge judges to determine the "original meaning" of the text of the Constitution, and to then make a reasonable effort to apply that meaning to contemporary cases. People holding such a view believe the primary motivation of judges must be to grant legislatures — as democratically elected branches of government — the discretion to do what they want as the representatives of the people. Judges should only interfere when legislative action clearly violates a specific provision of the Constitution as it was understood at the time the document was adopted.

The more liberal position supports judicial "activists" who see the Constitution as an invitation to aggressively review the action of legislatures and executive officials to determine if they conflict with any of the "aspirational" and other eloquent phrases of the Constitution and its amendments. Such judicial activists believe that the Constitution must be adapted to changing conditions, and they see their role as accomplishing goals that legislatures and the people do not support or cannot bring about through legislative means, but which nevertheless, in their view, would be good for the country. They also understandably believe that judges have a special obligation to protect unpopular individuals whose rights to free speech, a fair trial, and other essential liberties could otherwise be trampled by legislative bodies.

The elusiveness of "Original Intent"

When it comes to constitutional interpretation, judges may feel compelled to look for the "intent" of the Framers, or the original meaning of the words, to provide guidance as to how the Constitution should be applied today. Some judges and legal commentators believe that if the meaning of the phrases of the Constitution at the time they were written and ratified can be discovered, those meanings must be the decisive factor in current disputes. Their reason is that the Constitution is an enduring statement of fundamental principles that cannot be altered through ordinary legislative means by transient majorities impatient for immediate change. Original intent proponents argue that only extraordinary developments leading to near-unanimous consensus should result in the alteration of the nation's founding document.

Unfortunately for those who believe in this mode of interpreting the Constitution, it is impossible to establish the original intent of the Framers and their contemporaries. James Madison's notes tell us much about what was said inside the State House in Philadelphia in the summer of 1787, but they do not reveal what the drafters of the Constitution *intended* by the phrases that were the subject of much debate and compromise and which were eventually included in the Constitution. The fact that a single delegate, or even several delegates, made a statement as to the meaning of language that the Convention considered does not necessarily mean that the statement reflected the view of the assembly.

Discovering original intent in the next phase of the process of ratification is even more elusive. Voters in the various states elected delegates to ratifying conventions. Although voters in a number of states seemed to have been sharply divided over whether the proposed Constitution should be approved, suggesting that they had at least some knowledge of the details of the new document, they most likely did not have a deep understanding of the complexities of the Constitution. Furthermore, Charles Beard and other scholars have argued that very few citizens actually voted for delegates to the convention. As a result, those elections cannot be used to make general conclusions about the intent of those who participated in that stage of the ratification process.

It is equally difficult to ascertain the intent of the delegates to the ratifying conventions. The conventions not only debated the proposed Constitution, several of them recommended a substantial number of amendments to fix what many considered to be a serious shortcoming in the proposed document — the absence of a bill of rights. With several state conventions keeping no official records, and a number of states holding more than one convention, it is impossible to accurately describe the intent of the delegates.

Finally, even as eloquent a source of commentary on the Constitution as *The Federalist* cannot be considered the definitive word on the intent of the Framers. Although two of the three authors, James Madison and Alexander Hamilton, were delegates to the Constitutional

Convention — with Hamilton absent for much of the summer — *The Federalist* was written for the specific purpose of persuading the population of New York and the delegates to that state's convention to support the new Constitution. Although *The Federalist* provides much insight into the thinking of those who attended the Philadelphia Convention, it is not an authoritative summary of their interpretation of the various provisions of the new Constitution.

Activism spans the ideological spectrum

It is easy to trust judges to make decisions when one approves of the outcome. Unfortunately, there have been periods in our history in which the Supreme Court and other courts were dangerously out of touch with the needs of the country. The efforts of the conservative majority of the Supreme Court during the 1930s to dismantle the New Deal at a time of extreme national crisis are but one example of judges being unwilling to put aside their personal views and allow the Constitution to reflect the changing needs of the country. Such activism was not, as it was argued by the Court in the 1930s, a virtuous defense of enduring principles of the Constitution in the face of a liberal president and a desperate, irrational nation. The Court's activism in the 1930s was, instead, an unabashed effort to treat the Constitution as a majority of the justices' personal medium for their pro-business, pro-state rights, anti-regulation, and anti-integration philosophies. They proved, as have others, that judges can be as activist as conservatives as they are as liberals.

The conservatives on the Supreme Court in the 1930s, known derisively as the "Four Horsemen," demonstrated how a determined Court could use the Constitution to advance almost any political philosophy. The conservatives were Justices Willis Van Devanter, appointed by President William Howard Taft, who served on the Supreme Court from 1910–1937; James McReynolds, appointed by President Woodrow Wilson, who served on the Court from 1914–1941; George Sutherland, appointed by President Warren Harding, who served from 1922–1938; and Pierce Butler, also appointed by Harding, who served from 1922–1939. The "pliable" colleague was Justice Owen Roberts, appointed by President Herbert Hoover, and who served from 1930–1945. Chief Justice Charles Evans Hughes, who was appointed chief justice in 1930 by President Hoover, and who served until 1941, was finally able in 1937 to convince Roberts to join the majority to uphold progressive statutes. With the first of nine appointments that FDR eventually got to make to the Supreme Court — eight associate justices and the elevation of Justice Harlan F. Stone to chief justice — the constitutional crisis eventually passed.

By far the most reprehensible of the group was McReynolds, who clearly deserves recognition as the worst justice to ever serve on the Court, and who is a permanent black mark on Woodrow Wilson's presidency. McReynolds was not only openly anti-Semitic and racist, he was determined to foist his personal prejudices and philosophy upon the nation no matter what the damage to the Court or the country. In one of the kinder comments about McReynolds, Chief Justice William Howard Taft wrote that he was "fuller of prejudice than any man I have ever known."

Two views of the Constitution

Supreme Court Justice Antonin Scalia, appointed by President Reagan in 1986, is intelligent and hard-working. He also seems never to doubt his ability to analyze complex legal issues and arrive at the correct conclusions, occasionally belittling those who disagree with him in the process. Although his judicial philosophy defies easy description, he is among the most conservative justices to have served on the Court in recent years.

A former judge of the U.S. Court of Appeals for the District of Columbia and a law professor, Scalia's judicial philosophy is complex and multifaceted, and it is sometimes difficult to predict how he will vote in a particular case. He displays occasional flashes of what some might consider liberalism, although he would resent such a characterization. Scalia voted with the majority in the two flag-burning cases — *Texas v. Johnson* in 1989 and *United States v. Eichman* in 1990 — in which the Supreme Court held that two laws punishing desecration of the flag violated the First Amendment. The *Johnson* case was decided by a 5-4 vote; thus Scalia's decision to strike down the Texas law was decisive. In response to *Johnson*, Congress passed the Flag Protection Act of 1989, subjecting anyone who mutilates a flag to a fine and imprisonment. In *Eichman*, the Supreme Court overturned two convictions under that law by the narrow margin of 5-4, with Scalia again joining the majority.

Scalia's decisions in the flag-burning cases should not lead to the conclusion that he is often willing to side with individuals against the government. Instead, he consistently votes to uphold the authority of the state at the expense of individual rights, sometimes displaying callousness towards those who are not affluent and well-connected, yet who still have legitimate claims to make under the Constitution. In the 1992 case *Hudson v. McMillian*, Scalia joined the dissent of Justice Clarence Thomas which found that a Louisiana prison inmate who was beaten by guards while handcuffed and shackled — the guard's supervisor watched the whole time, telling the guards only "not to have too much fun" — could

not invoke the Eighth Amendment's prohibition against cruel and unusual punishment because the inmate's injuries, which included facial
swelling, bruises, loosened teeth, and a cracked dental plate, were not
sufficiently serious. Only Thomas and Scalia dissented. In *Harmelin v.
Michigan*, also in 1992, Scalia upheld a life sentence without the possibility
of parole for a first-time cocaine possession conviction, concluding that it
did not violate the Eighth Amendment. The defendant argued that because the sentence was mandatory under Michigan law, it was cruel and
unusual punishment in that it prohibited the judge from considering
"mitigating factors." Scalia held that such mandatory sentences may be
cruel, but they are "not unusual in the constitutional sense."

When Scalia was nominated for the Court, Anthony Lewis, a respected
New York Times columnist and astute observer of the Supreme Court, was
less concerned than others about Scalia's conservative credentials. "Yes,
Judge Scalia is certainly a conservative; there is every reason for concern
about his position on such questions as free speech and people's right of
access to the courts." But, Lewis added, "As far as an outsider can tell,
he is not a judge who willfully distorts precedent and hides difficulties in
order to reach a predetermined result." But four years later, Lewis was not
so tolerant of Scalia's judicial philosophy, stating, "No one is more radical
in the desire to wipe out precedents that he considers ill founded."

In his opinions and speeches, Scalia has energetically engaged lawyers, judges, law students, and legal commentators in a debate over how
judges should do their jobs and how the Constitution should be interpreted. Among Scalia's many contributions to the discussion of the role of
courts in the United States is his 1997 book, *A Matter of Interpretation: Federal Courts and the Law*, which consists of a short essay by Scalia, followed
by comments and criticisms of his essay by five academics, some of them
leading constitutional scholars. Scalia then responds to them. Scalia raises
provocative questions over whether a democratic system is well served by
judges who routinely substitute their judgment and interpretation of the
Constitution for those of the elected branches of government. He argues
that judges too often decide what the Constitution *ought* to mean based
on their own views, and then search for precedents and specific language
in the Constitution to support their activist predilections. He calls for
deference to the elected branches of government and a restrained role for
judges.

Scalia describes himself as a "textualist" and strongly rejects the
implication that he is searching for the "original intent" of the Framers
of the Constitution when determining how a case should be decided. To
Scalia, the "intent" of the Framers is as irrelevant and most likely undis-
coverable as is "legislative intent" when courts are interpreting statutes.

What matters is what the statute says, Scalia explains, not what certain members of Congress entered into the *Congressional Record* or a committee report. Much of Scalia's essay criticizes judges who do not feel obligated to follow the dictates of the legislature as enacted in statutes, but instead ignore the clear intent of the statute by searching among previously decided cases — cases that were resolved by judges who also likely failed to give legislatures sufficient deference — for the outcome the judge is seeking. According to Scalia, when judges are not committed to following the will of the people as expressed through the laws enacted by their representatives, but instead decide on their own what the people want, there is a deterioration of the underlying principles essential to a democratic society.

Scalia concentrates initially on statutory interpretation because the overwhelming majority of work that judges do is to interpret "texts" such as statutes of state legislatures and Congress, and regulations of state and federal administrative agencies. In the Supreme Court, for example, Scalia estimates that no more than a "fifth of the issues we confront are constitutional issues." He adds that if criminal law cases are excluded, "probably less than a twentieth" of the cases are constitutional in nature. Much of the rest of the Court's work involves interpreting statutes and regulations.

In regard to judicial interpretation of the Constitution, Scalia maintains that because the Constitution is no ordinary text, it is especially troublesome in a democratic system when judges show the same lack of deference to constitutional provisions that they do to statutes. The reason, he argues, is that the Constitution is the supreme law of the nation, and thus any application of its provisions overrules all statutes, regulations, and any court decision. All laws passed by democratic branches of government, or approved directly by the people, may be nullified by a judicial decision holding that such a law conflicts with the Constitution.

To Scalia, the Constitution did not take from the legislature the "power of changing rights" and give it to the courts. Unlike ordinary laws that can be altered by legislatures after courts have identified their shortcomings, the Constitution cannot be changed easily. It was established by the people as the fundamental law of the nation and was created to endure throughout the generations. Scalia strongly believes that the Constitution is not a blank slate on which each generation can write its views on what the Constitution means. He rejects the idea of a "living Constitution" that grows and changes from age to age to meet the needs of an evolving society. Legislatures, he says, through the process of elections, reflect the changing values of the people. Scalia argues that judges misunderstand and misapply the Constitution when they treat its provisions as mere guidance for the solutions they most favor, rather than recognizing that the words of the Constitution are the controlling standards to be applied to the case.

Scalia's philosophy differs markedly from traditional conservatives who look to what the Framers had in mind when they wrote the various provisions of the Constitution. He instead argues that constitutional interpretation must center on the original *meaning*, not *intent*, of the phrase or clause. The great challenge for judges, therefore, is to apply that meaning to current conditions as presented in the cases they decide. This view is different from the approach of those interested in "original intent," which explores the debates and writings of the Framers, the debates in the ratifying conventions, and such commentaries as *The Federalist*. To Scalia, it is the meaning of the words — as they were understood in the latter part of the 18th century — that should control interpretation of the Constitution today.

Scalia cites several examples, but one clearly illustrates how his philosophy leads to a limited role for modern-day judges. The Eighth Amendment, which prohibits cruel and unusual punishment, has been interpreted by such justices as William Brennan, Thurgood Marshall, Harry Blackmun, and at one time by a Court majority, to mean that the death penalty is unconstitutional. Scalia cannot understand how those justices determined that the Eighth Amendment leads to such a conclusion. The Framers did not abolish capital punishment in the Constitution. In fact, the death penalty was in existence at the time of its ratification. The First Congress not only did not abolish capital punishment, it acknowledged the death penalty's existence in the Fifth Amendment by requiring "that no person shall be held to answer for a capital crime . . . unless on a . . . indictment of a Grand Jury." Therefore, in Scalia's view, use of the death penalty is "explicitly contemplated in the Constitution" and judges must accept that interpretation until the Constitution is formally amended. If the Constitution is "living" and available for each generation to reinterpret, Scalia continues, it would be up to each judge to decide whether the Eighth Amendment prohibits the death penalty with no appropriate standards to guide them. In Scalia's opinion, judges do not have that option. The original Constitution recognizes the death penalty, and if state legislatures and Congress believe it is the right punishment for certain crimes, judges have no right to interfere.

Scalia also cites the 19th Amendment, granting women the right to vote in all elections, as an example of how judges from a previous era were more respectful of the original meaning of the Constitution. The 14th Amendment, prohibiting the states from denying "equal protection of the laws," has been part of the Constitution since 1868. Although "equal protection" would seem to prohibit the government from excluding individuals on the basis of gender from being able to vote, those who wrote the 14th Amendment clearly did not intend to include women in the franchise. Thus, the equal protection clause was not a shorthand phrase for extending such a privilege.

Scalia's point is that if the 14th Amendment was supposed to extend the suffrage to women, it would have said so explicitly. He observes that no judge in the years after the ratification of the amendment decided that equal protection actually meant that women should be granted the right to vote. Instead, it took the 19th Amendment, which was ratified in 1920, to grant such a fundamental right to women. He noted that "seventy-five years ago, we believed firmly enough in a rock-solid, unchanging Constitution that we felt it necessary to adopt the Nineteenth Amendment to give women the vote."

Today's judges, Scalia believes, would not show such restraint. If a modern judge had to decide a case invoking the equal protection clause to extend the franchise, that judge would "amend" the Constitution by holding that the equal protection clause prohibits the exclusion of women from voting. Scalia believes the modern-day judge, so willing to create constitutional law, would be unwilling to stand against public opinion and require that the change be made only through legislation or formal amendment of the Constitution.

Scalia's analysis sounds good in theory, but it breaks down when he attempts to apply the original meaning of the Constitution to contemporary problems. The Framers of the First Amendment, for example, could not have anticipated an era of radio and television broadcasting, cable, satellites, computers, and digital technology. Scalia offers little insight into how the First Amendment, which became part of the Constitution more than two centuries ago, would apply to such technological advances. He observed that the "Court must follow the trajectory of the First Amendment, so to speak, to determine what it requires — and assuredly that enterprise is not entirely cut-and-dried but requires the exercise of judgment." Nevertheless, Scalia argues that judges must determine what the words of the First Amendment meant in 1791, then apply those standards to modern communications issues.

A stark example of how the Scalia philosophy would apply to First Amendment cases came in a documentary broadcast on PBS in 1996 entitled "Mr. Justice Brennan." Justice William J. Brennan Jr., who died on July 24, 1997, at the age of 91, served on the Supreme Court for almost 34 years. The author of more than 1,300 opinions, Brennan was widely regarded as one of the most influential justices in the history of the Court, and one of its towering figures of the 20th century. Among Brennan's most important and eloquent opinions was in *New York Times v. Sullivan* in 1964.

In *Sullivan*, the Supreme Court reversed a $500,000 judgment against the *New York Times* in a lawsuit filed by an elected city commissioner in Montgomery, Alabama. L.B. Sullivan sued the newspaper over minor errors in a full-page advertisement paid for by members of the clergy and black entertainers to protest the way civil rights activists were being treated by Southern authorities. The ad did not mention Sullivan by name, but because his duties included supervision of the police — and there was criticism of the police in the ad — Sullivan convinced a jury and the appellate courts of Alabama that his reputation had been damaged. The jury awarded the full amount he sought.

The Supreme Court unanimously reversed the decision of the Alabama courts, greatly extending the First Amendment protection given to news organizations covering the activities of public officials. Brennan's exceptional opinion, which contains phrases that have become the poetry of First Amendment jurisprudence, established a standard that is extremely difficult for public officials to overcome in seeking damages for libel, thus giving news organizations substantial "breathing space" in which to make errors without having to worry about devastating libel suits. The Court created a test that required a public official to show that the publisher "recklessly disregarded" the truth. In other words, the Court required that those who hold public office could only win damages when publishers have serious doubts as to whether their statements are false, but disseminate the information anyway. This standard, known as "actual malice," is remarkably forgiving of even serious journalistic transgressions. But to Brennan and the Supreme Court, it was necessary if this nation was to have an independent, vigorous press to keep the American people informed about their government's actions.

In the documentary, Justice Scalia criticized the *Sullivan* decision and implied that if he had been on the Court when the case was decided, he may have dissented. To Scalia, this was the key question: "Was there in 1791 liability for libeling a public official even when you did not consciously libel him or were not recklessly saying something that you didn't know whether it was true or false? The answer is clearly there was liability and for me, that's the answer to the case. So as a matter of constitutional interpretation, of course it [*Sullivan*] went too far."

The most forceful rejoinder to Scalia's judicial philosophy included in *A Matter of Interpretation* was that of Laurence Tribe, a professor at Harvard Law School and a leading constitutional scholar. Tribe argues that judges should not look to the original meaning of the words of the Constitution — the approach favored by Scalia — but to what the words actually say. He maintains that the Constitution is a mix of specific instructions — such as how to elect members of Congress and the president — and broad statements of principle, such as the equal protection clause of the 14th Amendment. He cites *Brown v. Board of Education*, the Supreme Court's landmark case on racial discrimination, to show that it is the "aspiration" of the words of the Constitution that matters, not their original meaning.

Tribe recognizes that in attempting to establish the civil rights of newly freed slaves, the Congress that wrote the 14th Amendment clearly did not intend to integrate American society. They understood that such a dramatic change would not come about overnight through the adoption of a constitutional amendment. In fact, Congress had to coerce Southern states to ratify the 14th Amendment by making readmission to the Union contingent upon such approval. Without such heavy-handed tactics, the 14th Amendment would likely not have been approved by three-quarters of the states.

In striking down segregated schools in *Brown*, the Supreme Court concentrated not on the original meaning of the 14th Amendment as intended by the members of Congress who wrote it, but on the words "equal protection of the law" themselves. To Tribe, the *Brown* decision correctly interprets "what the Fourteenth Amendment says (and *always* said) even though it may well defy what the amendment's authors and ratifiers expected the amendment to do." Tribe believes that the original meaning of the 14th Amendment and other "aspirational" provisions of the Constitution are not fixed for all time.

Tribe also criticizes Scalia's approach to the First Amendment, but argues that even Scalia has been more flexible in his actual Supreme Court opinions compared to the essay in his book. Tribe noted that regardless of what Scalia "has *said* in these lectures about his understanding of the First Amendment as freezing a fixed set of rights into constitutional ice in accord with a supposed original meaning of that provision, he has recognized that constitutional principles may evolve over time." Thus, Scalia, despite what he has written in his book, has not actually interpreted the First Amendment and other provisions of the Constitution as a "mere codification of the memories" of those who wrote the Constitution and their ideas as to what rights they believed they were securing in the late 18th century.

In his response Scalia criticized Tribe for misunderstanding his use of original meaning, and he disagreed with Tribe's suggestion that "aspirational" provisions of the Constitution that state general principles authorize succeeding generations to rewrite the Constitution. Scalia argues that the Constitution is a "practical and pragmatic charter of government," with "concrete and specific dispositions." He further disagreed with Tribe's suggestion that when the Framers intermingled more abstract principles with specific structural provisions, they were inviting future judges to apply whatever standards they believe current society requires. Instead, Scalia argued that the "context suggests that the abstract and general terms, like the concrete and particular ones, are meant to nail down current rights, rather than aspire after future ones."

This summary of Scalia's and Tribe's constitutional philosophies does not adequately describe the complexity and subtlety of their arguments. It does, however, raise the important question of whether the American people should continue to rely so heavily on courts for constitutional development. Judges, and the legal commentators who often influence them, have sharply divergent views about how the Constitution should be interpreted. Just the examples cited here — Scalia's more narrow focus on the original meaning of the constitutional phrase, contrasted with Tribe's broad focus on the aspirational characteristics of the Constitution — demonstrate how intelligent people who have studied law for a long time can come to differing conclusions on how the Constitution should be interpreted. In Scalia's book, he and Tribe had the opportunity to pick the cases they wanted in order to make their points. When judges hear cases that come before their courts, they are often stuck with factual scenarios that make interpreting the Constitution's 18th century phrases extremely difficult. By allowing courts to largely control constitutional change, the American people must hope that the right judge with the appropriate judicial philosophy — and one untainted by narrow political considerations — will find a case with representative facts and arrive at the best conclusions. There is a lot at stake and a lot that can go wrong.

Yet, the seemingly appealing alternative of relying on democratically elected branches of government to not only implement political change, but to also bear the major responsibility for preserving and enhancing individual rights, is often impractical in practice. Besides being dominated by interests that are often hostile to the constitutional claims of unpopular individuals and causes, there are strict limits on how much legislative bodies can do to preserve constitutional rights. The Supreme Court said as much in June 1997, when it struck down the Religious Freedom Restoration Act of 1993 in *City of Boerne v. Flores*. In that case, the Court held that Congress cannot give the practice of religion more freedom than the Court itself found to be constitutionally required without violating the principle of separation of powers and interfering with the autonomy of states to pass laws that may incidentally affect religious practice. Justice Anthony Kennedy, writing the majority opinion, concluded that Section 5 of the 14th Amendment, which gave Congress the power to enforce that amendment's provisions, did not authorize Congress to pass "legislation which alters the meaning of the Free Exercise Clause . . .

Congress does not enforce a constitutional right by changing what the right is. It has been given the power 'to enforce,' not the power to determine what constitutes a constitutional violation."

How Federal Judges Are Selected

The Constitution says simply that the president appoints federal judges subject to confirmation by the Senate. The process is, however, substantially more complicated than that. When appointing a judge to a U.S. district court, which will always be located in one state, a president must seriously consider the recommendation of a senator from that state, especially if the senator is in the president's party. A longtime practice known as "senatorial courtesy" gives a senator almost total veto power over appointments of judges to the district courts. The hometown senator expresses disapproval to the Senate Judiciary Committee. If the committee gets the word, the chairman usually refuses to hold hearings on the nominee and the appointment is dead. A president obviously wants to avoid such a confrontation by clearing nominees in advance with key members of the Senate. One former assistant attorney general noted the Senate's power over these appointments: "The Constitution is backwards. Article II, Section 2 should read 'The senators shall nominate, and by and with the consent of the President, shall appoint.'" If neither senator is from the president's party, the senator from the party from the nearest neighboring state will be consulted.

Occasionally, the nomination of a federal judge reaches the full Senate despite the objections of the state's senator, but that does not mean the nominee will be confirmed. In October of 1999, the Senate rejected a nominee for a federal district court in Missouri by a vote of 54-45, with all Republicans — except for one who was absent — opposing the nomination and all Democrats supporting it. Ronnie White, a justice of the Missouri Supreme Court, was accused of being soft on crime, an accusation not supported by his record. Senator John Ashcroft (R-MO) accused White of being "pro-criminal" and that he had "a tremendous bent toward criminal activity." All Ashcroft had to do to stop the confirmation of White was to tell his colleagues he opposed him. Ashcroft, who is up for reelection in 2000, apparently believed opposing the nomination and appearing to be tough on crime will go over well with voters. That "senatorial courtesy" still survives is shown by the fact that even moderate Republicans, some of whom voted for White in committee, voted against him on the floor of the Senate.

The president has somewhat greater flexibility in making appointments to the federal courts of appeals. Each court has jurisdiction over more than one state, thus no individual senator can dominate the process. However, senators often believe that each state covered by a court of appeals circuit should be equally represented, and when a judge from one state leaves the bench, the senator who represents that state is likely to be actively involved in choosing a successor.

Because of the national scope of Supreme Court appointments, the president enjoys somewhat greater independence from individual senators in making the selection. There are, however, numerous constraints on a president's ability to select justices of the High Court. The nomination of a Supreme Court justice is among the president's most important and visible duties. The choice will be affected by the current makeup of the Court — everything from its racial and gender composition, to the judicial philosophy of its members — and by politics in the country at large. Sometimes that process has positive outcomes. President Eisenhower, for example, just before his reelection in November 1956, selected William Brennan, who was then a member of the New Jersey Supreme Court, because he was Roman Catholic and a Democrat. Eisenhower told his attorney general, Herbert Brownell, that the appointee must be a Catholic and that party affiliation did not matter; he wanted the appointment to be made on a bipartisan basis. Both Eisenhower and Brownell understood that appointing a Democrat would likely help broaden Eisenhower's support in the upcoming election.

Although there are many outstanding individuals who are appointed to the federal courts, the process by which federal judges are chosen gives the American people much reason to be cautious about allowing courts nearly complete control over constitutional change. The process is plagued by political machinations. Because of the active involvement of senators and well-organized special interest groups, a nominee to a federal judgeship — especially at the district court and circuit court of appeals levels — is as likely to be chosen because of the right connections to important senators or by having made contributions to the party as for a distinguished career in the law.

Among President Reagan's long list of undistinguished appointees to the federal bench, Daniel Manion, a former Indiana legislator, stands out as appallingly unqualified. His nomination to the U.S. Court of Appeals for the Seventh Circuit in 1986 generated opposition from public interest groups, deans of law schools, and the highly unusual public opposition by an incumbent member of the Seventh Circuit. The deans of 40 law schools wrote to the Senate, complaining that Manion lacked "scholarship, legal acumen, professional achievement, wisdom, fidelity to the law and commitment to our Constitution." The deans were especially concerned that Manion had never served as chief counsel in a federal trial nor dealt with any of the constitutional issues faced by an appeals court judge. Senator Edward Kennedy (D-MA) said that Manion was "the least qualified appellate nominee submitted to the United States Senate by any President of either party since I have been in the Senate."

The Senate confirmed Manion by a vote of 50-49, but it was certainly not that august body's finest moment. Illustrating the political nature of the confirmation process, Senator Slade Gorton (R-WA) cast the deciding vote for Manion, despite serious concerns about his qualifications. He gave Manion his vote only so that the Reagan administration would advance his nomination of William Dwyer — whose qualifications were considered to be outstanding by all those who knew his record — to be a federal district court judge in Seattle. If Gorton had not agreed to vote for Manion, who should never have been considered much less confirmed for a lifetime position on the court of appeals, the Reagan administration would not have followed through with its appointment of Dwyer.

A few years later, Senator Gorton was again involved in judicial appointment intrigue. Apparently, he helped engineer a bipartisan deal whereby Republicans would get an appointment they wanted to the U.S. Court of Appeals for the Ninth Circuit — the conservative chief justice of the Washington State supreme court, Barbara Durham — and in return, Senate Republicans agreed to confirm the appointment of a Berkeley law professor to the same appellate bench. Professor William Fletcher was considered by many Republicans to be too liberal, and for three years they had refused to act on President Clinton's nomination of Fletcher.

Such wheeling and dealing and trade-offs when choosing lifetime federal judges demonstrate how susceptible the process is to political considerations and how it may not produce the best nominees. In striking the deal with Senator Gorton, the Clinton administration said it would never have considered Barbara Durham for appointment if her nomination to the court of appeals were not required to unblock the appointment of Professor Fletcher.

In recent years, the appointment system has begun to deteriorate to the point where serious questions should be raised about whether it can continue in its present form. With the Senate controlled by the Republicans, President Clinton has found it almost impossible to select nominees he favors, and to see those nominees confirmed within a reasonable time. As of August 1997, there were 101 unfilled federal judgeships, nearly 12 percent of the federal judiciary. The chief judge of the U.S. Court of Appeals for the Ninth Circuit — which covers nine western states and two Pacific territories, and on which nine of the 28 judgeships were vacant —

had to cancel oral arguments for 600 cases from January to August of 1997 because of the lack of judges. Even a court covering a smaller area — the Sixth Circuit, which hears appeals from Michigan, Ohio, and Kentucky, and where three of 16 judgeships were vacant — had to cancel oral arguments for 60 cases. The delays create hardships for litigants who must wait years for their cases or appeals to be decided. An appeal to the Ninth Circuit, for example, can take more than three years with the backlog in addition to all the years it initially took to get to trial in a U.S. district court.

In January 1998, there were still 85 vacant positions in the federal courts. In his end-of-the-year report, delivered on January 1, 1998, Chief Justice Rehnquist criticized the Senate for not acting quickly enough on judicial appointments. Stating that "vacancies cannot remain at such high levels indefinitely without eroding the quality of justice," Rehnquist urged the Senate to act on appointments — by either voting up or down — after a reasonable period of time. He believed that inaction on the nominations, causing them to linger for long periods of time before the Senate, had resulted in so many vacancies that the situation imperiled the federal judicial system. He noted that on the U.S. Court of Appeals for the Ninth Circuit, one-third of the seats were vacant as of the time he prepared his report.

In response, the chairman of the Judiciary Committee, Senator Orrin Hatch (R-UT), defended the Senate's performance on judicial nominees and said that the courts themselves were partly to blame for their heavy caseloads. He disagreed with the assertion that the courts were overburdened because of a large number of judicial vacancies

The Senate Republicans claimed that President Clinton's nominees were too liberal and senators had to scrutinize them before approving their lifetime appointment. Even allowing for a close look at the nominees, the Senate took a long time to make decisions about judicial appointments. During the nine-month period from January to August of 1997, the Senate approved only nine Clinton nominees to the federal bench. Most of the rest of the nominations languished in the Senate Judiciary Committee where Republicans believed they could be delayed indefinitely.

Some Republican senators did not want to take any chances that the current system would permit too many Clinton appointees to squeak through. They considered, but narrowly rejected, two plans by which the Senate could practically have halted all confirmation proceedings of Clinton appointees that they considered to be too moderate or liberal. The two proposals were debated by the Republican Conference — consisting of all Senate Republicans — and thus could have been implemented informally without a vote on the Senate floor. One plan, sponsored by Senator Phil Gramm (R-TX), would have given a small group of senators the power to block appointments to the federal courts of appeals. Under the Gramm proposal, if a majority of Republican senators from the states in the circuit objected to a Clinton nominee, the Republican majority would have been obliged to kill the nomination. As mentioned earlier, a similar practice is already in effect for appointments to the federal district court. A second proposal, by Senator Gorton of Washington, would have required the Republican majority to reject judicial nominees whose philosophies had not been approved by the Republicans.

Senator Orrin Hatch also had his own ideas on how to change the process. He said he wanted to consider ending the longtime role of the American Bar Association in advising the Senate about the qualifications of candidates for the federal bench. Presidents since Eisenhower have relied on the ABA to help screen judicial candidates, but conservatives have argued in recent years that the organization is little more than a liberal lobbying group. In its defense, the ABA has long maintained that it makes recommendations based on qualifications and not politics.

Meanwhile, a group of House conservatives began to draw up a list of "activist" judges who should be impeached. The House Republican Whip, Tom DeLay (R-TX), believed that impeaching such judges was not as drastic an action as some of the decisions those judges were making, arguing that "They have thrown out the Constitution to advance their own political views." Although such efforts did not succeed, it is troubling that some members of Congress believe that "liberal" decisions constitute "high crimes and misdemeanors," the standard required by the Constitution for impeachment of federal officers.

Ironically, President Clinton's appointees, such as Supreme Court Justices Ruth Bader Ginsburg and Stephen Breyer, have been more moderate than some of the judges appointed by his Democratic predecessors. On some occasions, the president's opponents have been quick to oppose his nominees only to learn later their charges were unfounded. For instance, Republicans had to back off from their criticism of a nominee to the federal district court in Los Angeles when it was revealed that Margaret M. Morrow had a distinguished reputation as a widely respected corporate lawyer. She had served as president of the city and the state bar associations, and her appointment to the federal bench generated strong support from some of the state's most conservative business and political leaders. It was a setback for a Republican effort to gather information on Clinton appointees called the "Judicial Selection Monitoring Project," which had denounced the appointment of Morrow. The news also took the wind out of several senators who had said they would oppose her nomination based on the recommendation of the monitoring project.

It is always difficult to predict how someone will deal with the variety of cases that come before the federal courts, and Republican senators who instinctively try to derail Clinton appointments to the federal bench are wrong in assuming his nominees are all liberal activists. For example, predictions that a federal district court judge in Boston appointed by President Clinton — and confirmed by the Senate in 1993 — would be an unrepentant liberal on the bench have turned out to be untrue. Nancy Gertner was a self-described "radical" lawyer early in her career and had represented plaintiffs in several sex discrimination lawsuits. But a review of her record after three years on the bench revealed that she was anything but radical. According to Harvard Law professor Laurence Tribe, "the fact that even someone with as clear an ideological vision as Nancy Gertner can become a moderate federal judge underscores the bizarre character of the Senate's current resistance [to approving Clinton nominees]." Judge Gertner has conscientiously upheld the law as established by the court of appeals, while sometimes discreetly criticizing precedents she has to follow, but disagrees with, in footnotes.

There is no doubt that nominations to the federal judiciary ought to be carefully reviewed. Once confirmed, federal judges may serve for decades and will almost certainly be on the bench beyond the term of the person who appointed them. With increasing life spans and healthier lifestyles, some federal judges may serve well into their nineties.

If judges do not voluntarily retire or die in office, they cannot be removed except by impeachment and conviction, which has happened only a few times in our history. Those federal judges who have been impeached are almost always removed from office not for their rulings or judicial ideology, but because they were accused or convicted of crimes. Since 1789, the U.S. House has initiated impeachment proceedings against 13 federal judges, although an equal number of judges resigned before formal action was taken against them. Of those cases where the House voted to impeach, only seven resulted in conviction. In October 1989, the Senate convicted Judge Alcee Hastings on eight of 17 charges brought in impeachment proceedings against him. Hastings, a Jimmy Carter appointee and the first African-American federal judge to serve in Florida, had been acquitted of charges he accepted a bribe. But the House and Senate must have believed that Judge Hastings had committed the crimes, and he was removed from office. Ironically, after being forced from the federal bench, Hastings was elected to the U.S. House of Representatives where he currently serves with some of the same colleagues who voted for his impeachment. Two weeks after the Senate removed Hastings, it convicted Judge Walter Nixon on two of three impeachment charges, the last federal judge to be removed from office.

Considering how many judges have served on the federal bench in the past two centuries, seven convictions are a very small number. In 1980, a law entitled "The Judicial Councils Reform and Judicial Conduct and Disability Act" went into effect, giving federal judges the authority to remove the caseload of disabled or incompetent colleagues, while allowing judges in such a situation to continue to receive their salaries. Only Congress can remove an Article III federal judge from office.

Although there is one formal procedure for selecting federal judges — the president appoints and the Senate confirms the nominee — there are several different methods by which state judges are chosen. For selection of judges to the highest courts, 11 states use partisan elections; judges in four states are chosen by the legislature; 13 states hold nonpartisan elections; governors in eight states appoint members of the highest court; and 14 states use the "Missouri Plan," where governors appoint judges based on the recommendations of a select committee. Under the Missouri Plan, after the judge has been in office for a year or so, the voters are given the opportunity to retain or oust the appointed judge. It is important to note that in states that hold elections, the governor almost always appoints a judge when there is a vacancy prior to the end of a term, and frequently that appointee has no challengers or only token opposition in the forthcoming election. State judges do not enjoy the lifetime tenure of those who serve on the federal bench, so it may be more difficult for judges who must face reelection or reconfirmation to make unpopular decisions. With so many interested parties involved, the selection and retention of state judges is subject to even more political intrigue, corruption, and partisanship than appointments to the federal bench. Moreover, because of judicial codes of ethics, candidates for judgeships may not discuss substantive issues — how they would rule, for example, in abortion or other controversial cases — so the public is left with little or no information about those seeking election to the bench. Once on the bench, either by original election or appointment by the governor, a judge is likely to serve for many years.

Limits on Judicial Decisionmaking

One of the most important features of our legal system is that courts decide actual disputes between individuals who bring or defend lawsuits, or between the government and persons accused of crimes. Article III, Section 2, states that the judicial power of the United States shall extend to "cases and controversies," a principle that is followed, with few exceptions, by state courts as well. In deciding actual disputes between parties with adverse legal interests, the Supreme Court, for example, is performing dual roles, the first of which is essential for the second: It is deciding actual cases, and if they raise constitutional issues, it uses the facts of those cases to determine what the Constitution means.

When the Supreme Court hears a case, it is deciding a legal dispute just like any other court in the nation. There are two parties, both of which claim some right under the common law, statute, provision of the federal Constitution, or some combination of the three. The Supreme Court decides which side has the better legal argument and rules in favor of that party. But in deciding actual cases where constitutional issues are at stake, the courts are doing more than settling a dispute. In *applying* a provision of a state or federal constitution to the lawsuit, the courts are also *interpreting* that provision. The interpretation becomes part of the body of law to be applied to future cases presenting similar circumstances.

Many constraints prevent courts from hearing cases that settle important constitutional issues. Among the most obvious and important is that courts must wait for cases to be brought to them. They cannot seek out cases that they think will provide an opportunity to interpret the Constitution or establish other important principles. Courts are further limited by the general requirement that they base their decisions on the *facts* of the cases they hear. Courts will also generally resist reviewing issues that were not considered by the lower courts below. Thus, if a party did not raise certain key legal issues at the trial court level, appellate judges will often refuse to consider those issues on appeal.

These two characteristics of judicial process — that courts must wait for cases to be brought to them, and that they must limit their decisions to the facts presented in those cases — significantly inhibit the ability of courts to make comprehensive changes in the Constitution. The political and legal systems have a difficult time accepting action by unelected, lifetime-tenured federal judges who bring fundamental changes to the Constitution too quickly. The changes brought about by courts must be gradual and incremental and must be accomplished through the settling of legal disputes between adverse parties. Because of the nature of the legal system, courts do not always get the opportunity to decide a case with appropriate facts, and that can lead to the wrong conclusions about what the Constitution means.

Cases courts will not decide

From the earliest days of the Republic, the requirement that courts decide actual cases and controversies has meant that the Supreme Court will not serve an advisory function by informing the president or Congress in advance what the law would be on a hypothetical set of facts. President Washington found in 1793 that the Supreme Court would not offer an advisory opinion on a proposed treaty and the Court's unwillingness to offer such an opinion has been followed ever since, and with good reason. If there is no actual dispute, the Supreme Court would not have the benefit of arguments of opposing counsel, which are often extremely helpful in elucidating the relevant facts of a case and the appropriate law to be applied. Even if the Supreme Court issued an opinion in advance as to what the law means, it would not be binding on an actual case raising the same issues if one should come before the Court. Offering advisory opinions would likely embroil the Court in frequent political disputes and would diminish its independence and prestige. Despite all the arguments against advisory opinions, supreme courts in several states are required to issue such opinions at the request of the governor or state legislature.

Adherence to the principle that a lawsuit must be between parties with adverse legal interests also means that courts will not hear so-called "friendly suits." If the interests of the parties are not adverse, then there will be little incentive for all of the relevant facts to be disclosed in the legal arguments.

Courts also do not hear "test cases" that are largely engineered for the purpose of obtaining a ruling on disputed constitutional issues. Public interest groups often look for cases that can be used to obtain a favorable constitutional ruling. Test cases must meet all the requirements of a valid case or controversy, but if the Supreme Court believes the case is "staged" simply for the purpose of obtaining the Court's opinion, the Court may decline to accept the case.

Despite this principle, courts occasionally hear such cases. One of the most famous examples was *Pollock v. Farmers' Loan and Trust Co.*, in which a conservative Supreme Court declared the income tax unconstitutional in 1895. Lawyers in New York arranged for Charles Pollock, a resident of Massachusetts who held stock in the New York Farmers' Loan and Trust Company, to sue the company's directors to block their payment of the income tax. The same lawyers also arranged for another attorney to defend the bank. Although both plaintiffs and defendants desired the same outcome, and therefore the case was not a dispute between adverse parties and should have been dismissed, the Supreme Court used it to strike down the modest tax that would have required the wealthiest Americans to pay more of the cost of the national government.

A significant issue for a court in deciding whether to accept a case is whether the party bringing the action has legal "standing" to sue. Many cases raising important issues are never heard by courts because the plaintiffs are denied the opportunity to pursue the case. The legal rules related to standing are complicated and have been developed over many years. Generally, in order to bring a lawsuit, an individual must have a personal interest in the case as opposed to one that the plaintiff shares with all other citizens generally. This requirement is why "taxpayer" lawsuits challenging government action are almost never successful. In addition, plaintiffs bringing environmental lawsuits have often found they cannot get past the standing requirement. Courts also require that the interest the person is defending is a legally protected interest or right, which is immediately threatened by government action.

The personal interests in a case that plaintiffs must usually demonstrate are often financial. They cannot bring a lawsuit challenging a government policy or expenditure simply because they disapprove of it. As the Supreme Court observed in 1923, the party who challenges the constitutionality of a federal statute must be able to show "not only that the statute is invalid but that he has sustained some direct injury as a result of its enforcement, and not merely that he suffers in some indefinite way in common with people generally." Although the Supreme Court has occasionally relaxed its view on standing to allow lawsuits by some individuals whose interests are indirect, it has mostly adhered to the principle that the plaintiff must show some direct interest or injury before being allowed to sue.

Waiting for cases that never come

States and federal courts are inundated with lawsuits and criminal actions. More than 250,000 cases are filed in federal courts every year. That is a small number compared to the estimated 100 million lawsuits filed in the courts of the 50 states and the District of Columbia. Although some of those deal with relatively minor matters, about 12 million cases of importance are filed each year in state and federal trial courts. In recent decades, prosecutions of drug laws and other criminal statutes have clogged the courts. For the 12-month period ending September 30, 1993, almost 50,000 criminal cases were begun in the federal district courts, up more than 30 percent over the previous ten years. Criminal cases take priority because of a defendant's right to a speedy trial, but the majority of cases filed in federal district courts are civil in nature. In 1993, almost 230,000 such cases were begun in federal court, representing 83 percent of the case load. Once cases have been decided or disposed of in the federal district court, they may be appealed to the next level. In 1993, more than 50,000 cases were before one of the U.S. appellate courts.

At the same time that lower federal courts have been overrun with cases, the Supreme Court has been steadily decreasing the number of cases it accepts for review. When the Supreme Court closes its doors to all but a few litigants, it leaves many urgent constitutional issues unsettled. More than 7,000 cases are appealed to the Supreme Court each year, but it reviews fewer than 2 percent. While in the 1980s the Court wrote opinions in about 150 cases annually, in recent years, it has handed down written opinions in fewer than 90 cases each year, the lowest number in several decades. In the term that ended in June 1999, the Court decided 75 cases.

The low number of cases reviewed by the Supreme Court creates a lot of problems because there are urgent issues that only the nation's highest court can settle. It is not unusual for two courts of appeals to come to opposite conclusions on important constitutional questions. Especially when those decisions interpret fundamental rights such as those guaranteed by the First Amendment, it is essential that conflicting interpretations of the Constitution or important statutes by lower courts not be left hanging. Generally, the First Amendment should not mean one thing in one state or jurisdiction, and something else in another. Oftentimes, lower courts will not broadly apply constitutional principles in the absence of Supreme Court guidance. With fewer cases accepted for review, it is even less likely than in the past that the Supreme Court will hear a case with the factual issues necessary to solve difficult constitutional problems.

Courts try to avoid making decisions based on the Constitution

Even if a case raising important constitutional issues overcomes all the procedural and substantive obstacles and makes it to the Supreme Court, and the Court decides the case on the merits, the Court's opinion may provide little if any guidance as to what the Constitution means in that area of the law. The Supreme Court, and the lower courts to a lesser degree, make a substantial effort to *avoid* basing their decisions on the Constitution. If the case requires constitutional interpretation, the courts try to invoke as little of the Constitution as possible. There are several reasons for this. The Supreme Court, in particular, has long recognized that once it bases its decision specifically on a provision of the Constitution, that ruling can only be reversed or modified by a subsequent case decided by the Supreme Court — and it may take years for one to come along — or by a constitutional amendment, which is very difficult to enact.

The opportunity to avoid a constitutional decision often arises when the Court is interpreting a statute. It will make every effort to determine whether the facts in the case are covered by the statute and avoid deciding whether the law — in all circumstances or as applied to this case —

violates the Constitution. The Court believes that if it misreads the statute or the intent of the legislature, that misinterpretation can be corrected by the legislature passing a new law. But if the Court invokes a section of the Constitution to settle the matter, that interpretation cannot be reversed by the legislature.

If, for example, the Court is deciding whether an antidiscrimination statute applies to a certain group when the law does not say so specifically, and the Court wrongly decides that such a group is excluded, the legislature can pass a new law specifically identifying that group as included in the statute. Such a new law would effectively reverse the Supreme Court's decision because the Court based its ruling on statutory grounds.

If, instead, the Court concluded that the 14th Amendment's equal protection clause requires the extension of such rights to the group, and that is not what Congress intended, the legislature cannot correct the Supreme Court's mistake because a new statute cannot reverse the Supreme Court's holding that the 14th Amendment confers certain rights. Only the Court itself — and it may take years before the Court reconsiders — or a constitutional amendment can do that. In the meantime, the state and federal courts, and the American people, must abide by the decision.

No court review of a "constitutionally suspect" amendment

There are numerous examples that would serve to illustrate the principle that many cases raising important constitutional issues are never heard by the Supreme Court. Several factors determine whether a case is appealed to the Court, and whether four justices — which by tradition is the number who must agree to hear a case — accept a given case for review. Considering the subject of this book, it seems appropriate to use as an example one that deals with a constitutional amendment. The 27th Amendment, on congressional pay raises, became part of the Constitution in 1992. It was, however, ratified by a process that a court, if it had the opportunity, would likely have ruled to be unconstitutional. Yet because no one brought a lawsuit challenging the ratification process, it remains a part of the Constitution. The 27th Amendment serves as a continuing reminder of the issues the Framers left unresolved in Article V, and which could be addressed by amendments proposed by a second constitutional convention.

The First Congress in 1789 was concerned about whether it should set its own salary. Along with the Bill of Rights and the original "first amendment" — which would have limited congressional districts to 50,000 constituents, compared with today's average of nearly 600,000 — it proposed an amendment, listed second, requiring that there be a general election to choose a new Congress before a pay raise can go into effect. Interestingly, Congress did not include an expiration period by which the 12 amendments had to be ratified.

An insufficient number of states approved the original first and second amendments when they ratified the Bill of Rights. But because there was no expiration date, the states could theoretically approve the pay-raise amendment at any time. In the 1980s, anger over congressional salaries ignited an organized effort to ratify the original second amendment. Finally, in May 1992, 203 years after it was proposed by Congress, the "second amendment" became the 27th Amendment to the Constitution.

If a court had the opportunity, it would likely have concluded that the ratification process for the 27th Amendment was unconstitutional. In a number of cases earlier in this century, the Supreme Court struggled with the question of whether Congress alone has the authority to determine how long an amendment can be before the states. Although the Supreme Court originally held that a constitutional amendment must be ratified within a reasonable time after it was proposed so that the conditions that led to the amendment will not have significantly changed, it later decided that determining a period for ratification is largely a "political question" to be decided by Congress. Nevertheless, the Court expressed concern over whether an amendment could linger before the states for an extended period of time, thus making it "no longer responsive to the conception which inspired it."

Even if the Supreme Court deferred to Congress on the length of a ratification period — whether, for example, it should be seven years or 10 years — it would not likely have allowed an amendment to remain before the states for over 200 years. If the 27th amendment was still alive two centuries after it was first proposed, then so are other amendments that were unratified and had no expiration date. Not surprisingly, Congress worried that voters would be outraged if it refused to certify that the amendment had been properly approved. The House by a vote of 414-3 and the Senate by a margin of 99-0 declared the 27th Amendment properly adopted. Always creative, Congress found a way around the 27th Amendment by enacting a law that provides for automatic cost-of-living adjustments (COLAs) unless majorities in both houses vote to reject the pay increase.

The Supreme Court will never get the opportunity to review the process by which the 27th Amendment was approved, and provide guidance for the future about acceptable amendment procedures. Because only members of Congress would have "standing" to bring a lawsuit challenging the 27th Amendment, and no member of Congress concerned about a political future would dare initiate such a court challenge, no lawsuit was brought. With no case pending, courts, including the Supreme Court, cannot expose the irony of having an amendment of the Constitution added by a process that was most likely unconstitutional.

When the Wrong Case Makes It to the Supreme Court

When the Supreme Court agrees to hear a case, at least four justices have determined that it raises important legal issues on which lower courts need some guidance. Rarely do the justices explain why they have accepted some cases for review but turned down thousands of others. A principle that the Court tries to follow is that the case accepted for review should not be "fact-specific," meaning that although the litigation is of great interest to the parties, the Court would be doing little more than deciding a legal dispute if it ruled in the case. Instead, the Supreme Court prefers to hear cases that have broader implications, including settling legal questions on which two or more courts of appeals have reached opposite conclusions, or cases that require the interpretation of important provisions of the Constitution or federal statutes. Because it only handles 100 or fewer cases a year, the Court cannot settle all of the nation's legal problems. It must carefully choose the appropriate cases in which to announce legal principles that lower courts can apply to subsequent cases.

As with all courts, the Supreme Court must accept the factual circumstances of the case as it finds them, and must generally confine its opinion to answering the questions raised by those facts. It is not unusual for a case heard by the Supreme Court or another court to present factual circumstances that do not permit the Court to settle important legal issues. This characteristic of the law is especially frustrating when many years pass before another case comes along to answer some of the lingering questions. When a ruling is made in a case with an unusual factual situation, a troublesome precedent may be created that is subsequently applied to future cases that *do* have representative facts. If the right case had been considered by the court originally, the precedent would have been considerably more helpful to lower courts deciding similar cases. Instead the opposite becomes true; the lower courts must struggle to apply the principles laid down in the unusual case even if the facts before them seem rather dissimilar to the case decided by the higher court. Although this is difficult to follow in the abstract, and examples will show how it works in actual cases, the implications of this process for constitutional interpretation are profound.

The First Amendment loses

In an important First Amendment case, *Branzburg v. Hayes* in 1972, to choose one of many potential examples, the Supreme Court held that journalists have no constitutional right to keep the names of sources confidential. Although the practice of protecting the identity of sources has probably been on the decline in recent years, there are many important stories that cannot be reported any other way. The Watergate scandal, covered initially by Bob Woodward and Carl Bernstein in the *Washington Post*, is among the best examples of stories in which unidentified sources were essential. Without sources whose identities could be protected, it would have been very difficult to expose the coverup that reached the highest levels of the executive branch.

In recent years the public has been frustrated with the techniques journalists have sometimes used to gather information. A North Carolina jury, which awarded the Food Lion grocery store chain $5.5 million — later reduced to $315,000 by the judge — against ABC Television in 1997 for a report the network aired about allegedly unsanitary conditions at the store, was probably speaking for millions of their fellow citizens. The jury did not rule that the report itself was inaccurate; instead it assessed penalties against ABC for the methods the network used to report the story. Despite the public's impatience with undercover methods, there are extremely important stories that can only be covered using confidential sources, and some journalistic techniques where the reporters are not fully candid with the subject of the story.

Journalists have argued for years that the First Amendment safeguards not only the dissemination of information, but also newsgathering. They have maintained that without a First Amendment right to seek out information, the right to publish or broadcast would be severely inhibited. They have also argued that sources with sensitive information that the public needs to know will not talk to reporters if the publication of their name would lead to the loss of their job, or in extreme cases, physical danger to them or their families. The Supreme Court took up the important question of source confidentiality in *Branzburg v. Hayes*, and handed down its ruling in 1972.

If journalists could have selected a case to go to the Supreme Court to resolve the issue of whether they have to reveal the names of sources, *Branzburg* would have been among the last they would have chosen because it had the worst possible facts for testing this key constitutional question. In *Branzburg*, a newspaper reporter did a series of stories for the *Louisville Courier-Journal* in which he described the activities of drug dealers in his area. In gathering information for the story, Branzburg *saw* his sources committing a crime by manufacturing hashish from marijuana. The newspaper carried a picture of the sources' hands actually making the drug.

The fact that Branzburg was not just someone who reported on a crime, but was also a witness to it, made his case clearly unrepresentative of the overwhelming majority of situations where reporters decline to reveal the names of sources. Reporters are usually told about criminal activities or get information about them in documents. Rarely are they witnesses to a crime. Despite the unusual circumstances, these are the facts that the Supreme Court had to deal with when reviewing the case. Not surprisingly, the Court concluded that reporters had an obligation, just like any other citizen, to testify before a grand jury about crimes they witnessed. The Court thus concluded that the First Amendment did not extend a constitutional privilege to journalists to keep the names of sources confidential.

Justices of the Supreme Court, and other judges, cannot hand down decisions that have the force of law on any topic they choose. The legitimacy of our legal system is based on the principle that judges will confine themselves to deciding actual disputes and limit their decisions to the facts of the case. In *Branzburg*, the Supreme Court did not believe that it had the discretion to decide whether a reporter is entitled to protect the names of sources in some circumstances. It was confined to deciding whether a reporter who witnessed a crime had the same duty as other citizens to testify before a grand jury. The difference is extremely important and worth emphasizing. Because the Court is composed of judges with lifetime tenure who are not electorally responsible, it will exercise self-restraint so it does not make decisions that should be left to the elected branches of government. That includes not trying to use individual cases as a vehicle for solving any constitutional problem as long as it is at least indirectly related to the dispute before them. The Court maintains its legitimacy because it generally confines itself to the facts of the cases as presented.

In *Branzburg*, the Court, in an opinion in which the justices divided 5-4, concluded that the reporter had no First Amendment right to refuse to testify about the criminal activity he witnessed. Some lower courts have recognized the unusual nature of the case, and have found creative ways to extend a First Amendment privilege to source confidentiality despite *Branzburg*. But that also causes problems when lower courts refuse to apply Supreme Court decisions with which they disagree because the highest court in the nation is supposed to be able to establish national standards. In the almost three decades since *Branzburg*, the Supreme Court has never reconsidered the issues raised by the case by reviewing one that more accurately portrays the circumstances under which reporters claim source confidentiality. More than a few reporters have spent time in jail on contempt charges for refusing to identify the names of sources. *Branzburg* undermined their argument that the Constitution recognizes such a privilege.

Varying constitutional standards

When the Supreme Court provides relatively little guidance because it reviews so few cases, appellate courts must exercise greater discretion in deciding difficult legal disputes. That alone results in substantial variance among courts around the country as they grapple with constitutional issues. But in addition, it is inevitable that some of the cases appellate courts will be deciding will have unrepresentative facts. The combination of lack of guidance from the Supreme Court and the likelihood that appellate courts will be forced to review such cases means that key constitutional rights become subject to jurisdiction-by-jurisdiction interpretation. The First Amendment right to free expression, the Fifth Amendment protection against self-incrimination, the Sixth Amendment right to a fair trial, and the 14th Amendment's guarantee of equal protection may mean one thing in one state or federal court, and something different in another.

For example, the U.S. Court of Appeals for the Fifth Circuit Court, which has jurisdiction over Texas, Louisiana, and Mississippi, invalidated the University of Texas Law School's dual-admission system by which minority students were judged separately and were admitted with lower grades and test scores than those of some whites who were rejected for admission. Because the Texas admission program considered minority and non-minority students as separate groups, it was unlike almost every other law school admission program in the country. The court in *Hopwood v. Texas*, reacting to what it considered to be a clear violation of the rights of non-minority applicants, went beyond simply declaring the dual system to be a violation of the 14th Amendment. It also held that any consideration of race, even as part of a single admission process weighing many factors, was unconstitutional. The Supreme Court refused to hear the school's appeal. Justice Ruth Bader Ginsburg took the unusual step of explaining that the Court could not hear the case because the University of Texas had already changed its admission policy, and thus justices could not review the old policy. She wrote, "We must await a final judgment on a program genuinely in controversy before addressing the important question raised in this petition." The implication is that had the University of Texas Law School not changed its admissions policy, the Supreme Court would have been able to hear the case. It is another example of how the actions of a litigant can prevent courts from considering cases that present important issues.

The Fifth Circuit's decision in *Hopwood* means that in those three states, the 14th Amendment does not permit race to be a factor in admission decisions. According to the U.S. Court of Appeals for the Ninth Circuit, which has jurisdiction over western states, the 14th Amendment also prohibits such an admission policy. But until other courts of appeals follow *Hopwood*, or until the Supreme Court issues a ruling dealing with affirmative action at universities, the 14th Amendment, as it applies to admissions policies, will vary significantly across the country. Although it is expected in a large, complex society that judges will reach differing conclusions on similar legal questions, jurisdictional differences present many problems when important constitutional rights are at stake.

When Judges Go beyond the Facts

Generally by the time an appellate court hears a case, a trial court below — with either a judge and a jury or just a judge — has developed a factual record to which the appellate tribunal must apply the law. Appellate court judges do not hear from witnesses or review evidence as do trial courts. Except for certain cases like those involving the First Amendment, they do not reexamine evidence or facts in the case and do not second-guess the decision of juries. Appellate courts decide whether there was a significant error in the *application of the law* and usually do not reverse lower court decisions unless there has been a clear abuse of discretion by the trial judge or the decision was clearly erroneous.

Theoretically, any statements made in judicial opinions that are beyond what is required by the facts are *dicta* and not binding on future courts. As with other aspects of the law, however, determining what is the principle of the case, or the *ratio decidendi*, and what is *dictum* is not often easy. It is not uncommon for *dicta* in one case to become the primary legal principle in a subsequent one.

A famous example of *dicta* in a Supreme Court decision occurred in *Near v. Minnesota* in 1931. In *Near*, one of the most important First Amendment decisions ever handed down by the Supreme Court, the justices, divided 5-4, held that an injunction issued by a judge against a Minneapolis weekly newspaper to keep it from publishing was an unconstitutional prior restraint. The *Saturday Press* was clearly anti-Semitic, and made what appeared to be reckless and unfounded charges against elected officials and prominent citizens. In the course of explaining why the First Amendment did not permit a prior restraint order against the press in this case, Chief Justice Charles Evans Hughes expressed the opinion that the government would be able to prevent news organizations from publishing information under some circumstances. He cited as examples information related to the "sailing dates of transports or the number and location of troops" during a war; the decency standards of a community that could be upheld by enjoining "obscene publications"; and the preventing of speech that is the equivalent to "incitements to acts of violence" and that encourages the "overthrow by force of orderly government."

Hughes's exceptions are clearly *dicta*. Not only were they not necessary to deciding the case, they "created" more law than the facts permitted. The judge ordered Near's newspaper to cease publication because of his attacks on public officials. Near did not reveal the location of troop movements, his publication was not obscene, and he did not incite acts of violence or the overthrow of the government. Once the Supreme Court departs from applying the law as required by the facts, it is doing more than judicial legislating. It is giving judges who decide future cases relevant to prior restraint of the press something they dearly covet: the discretion to decide cases the way they see fit. If Hughes had simply stopped with the principle that the First Amendment does not permit the enjoining of newspapers that criticize public officials, lower courts would have had no choice but to apply that standard to subsequent cases. But by providing a list of possible exceptions to the prior restraint rule, the justices invited courts deciding future cases to feast on the smorgasbord of *dicta* either by choosing one of the Hughes examples, or creating one of their own.

What happened after *Near* is also instructive. Hughes had actually been quite restrained in that case by listing so few exceptions to the prior restraint rule. There are many people today who dislike media organizations and could think of a dozen or more circumstances under which they should be prevented from disseminating information. Once the "exceptions" to the rule were unleashed in *Near*, however, they were available to any court at any level to apply to future cases. But just as those judges supportive of freedom of speech and press could use the Hughes list because of what it *lacks*, so could those who rule against the First Amendment use the list for what it *includes*.

Four decades after *Near*, in 1971, the Supreme Court had to determine in *New York Times v. United States* whether injunctions issued against the *New York Times* preventing them from continuing to publish the Pentagon Papers — an historical study about U.S. involvement in Vietnam — were unconstitutional prior restraints. The Court overturned the injunctions against the newspapers.

Justice William Brennan, in his concurring opinion, treated the Hughes *dicta* in *Near* as if they were the authoritative statements of the law as handed down by the Supreme Court. Brennan believed that the circumstances surrounding the publication of the Pentagon Papers did not fall into one of the categories listed by Hughes in *Near*. Chief Justice Warren Burger, in dissent, replied that "there are other exceptions, some of which Chief Justice Hughes mentioned by way of example in *Near*," where prior restraint is permissible. He would have included the Pentagon Papers case as an example of when the press should be prevented from publishing.

The Hughes exceptions in *Near* did not prevent the *New York Times* from winning the Pentagon Papers case. But eight years later, the exceptions Hughes had outlined almost half a century before came alive and were used to justify a court order preventing a magazine from publishing an article about how easy it was to build a hydrogen bomb. In *United States v. Progressive* in 1979, Judge Robert Warren, of the federal district court of the Western district of Wisconsin, issued an order prohibiting *Progressive* magazine from publishing the article even though the information came from public sources. Warren completed the transformation of Hughes's exceptions from *dicta* to an authoritative statement of the law by writing that "In *Near v. Minnesota*, the Supreme Court specifically recognized an extremely narrow area, involving national security, in which interference with First Amendment rights might be tolerated and a prior restraint on publication might be appropriate." And this is how Warren applied the *dicta* from *Near*: "This Court concludes that publication of the technical information on the hydrogen bomb contained in the article is analogous to publication of troop movements or locations in time of war and falls into the extremely narrow exception to the rule against prior restraint." The judge understood how serious the decision was to issue such an order against the press, and recognized that the injunction "constitute[d] the first instance of a prior restraint against a publication in this fashion in the history of this Country." But he concluded that the government had met its heavy burden. What began as *dicta* in 1931 thus became *ratio decidendi* in 1979. The exceptions Hughes outlined so many years ago have become one of the constitutional standards by which exceptions to the prior restraint rule are to be judged.

Self-Restraint Taken to the Extreme

Few sections of the Constitution are more important than those protecting freedom of speech and the press. There must be an independent and vigorous press in this country to report on the activities of public officials and individuals who play a significant role in public affairs. There also has to be substantial protection for news organizations when reporting on private individuals even when errors are made that harm the reputation of such persons. Although such protection will be less than that provided to news organizations when discussing public officials and public figures, there must be sufficient breathing space for journalists to make mistakes when covering the activities of private persons. Balancing the First Amendment right of the media to cover the news with the right to protect one's reputation and privacy has always been difficult for the courts.

The last case discussed in this chapter is considered in some detail. It is an example of how factual issues in a case and the way that the trial develops can deprive the Supreme Court of the opportunity — as it turns out, its *only* opportunity — to resolve an important constitutional issue. Although the point has been made previously that courts are limited to the cases that are brought to them, and that they cannot develop the law beyond that which is necessary to settle the legal disputes raised by the facts, this case makes the point even more firmly. It demonstrates how certain issues may only be presented once in a great many years, and when a court misses the opportunity to decide the issue, it may remain unresolved indefinitely.

Cantrell v. Forest City Publishing Co., decided by the Supreme Court in 1974, is typical of constitutional cases in that it cannot be discussed in isolation. Other cases decided before *Cantrell* had a direct impact on its outcome, and examining the *Cantrell* case in relation to those precedents serves as an example of how complicated the law can be, and how courts frequently cannot solve compelling constitutional problems.

To understand the *Cantrell* case, it is necessary to keep in mind these three Supreme Court cases, which are discussed throughout this section:

• *New York Times v. Sullivan*, a 1964 *libel* suit in which the Court held that a public official must prove "reckless disregard for the truth" — known as the "actual malice" standard — before being able to collect damages against a news organization for defamation. It is a very difficult standard to meet.

• *Time, Inc. v. Hill*, a 1967 *invasion of privacy* case in which the Court applied the "actual malice" standard to a plaintiff in a false-light privacy lawsuit involving a matter of public interest.

• *Gertz v. Welch*, a case decided in 1974 a few months before *Cantrell*, in which the Court held that *libel* plaintiffs who are private persons do not have to prove actual malice, and it allowed the states — within some limits — to determine what standards would apply. It was expected that *Gertz* would directly affect the outcome of *Cantrell*.

A family death and a news reporter's irresponsible behavior

Margaret Mae Cantrell became a part of constitutional law through a family tragedy. Her husband Melvin, a coal miner, was killed in the collapse of the Ohio River Bridge in Point Pleasant, West Virginia, in December 1967. Joseph Eszterhas, a reporter for the Cleveland *Plain-Dealer*, a newspaper owned by Forest City Publishing, wrote an article about the Cantrell family shortly after Melvin Cantrell's death. Five months later, Eszterhas returned to the Cantrell home with a photographer to do a follow-up story on how Margaret and her four children were managing in the months since the accident.

The newspaper published an article, with pictures of the children, which stressed the family's dire situation. The article gave the impression that the family was living in poverty, in dirty and dilapidated conditions, and that the children were wearing old, ill-fitting clothes. At no time during the reporter and photographer's visit was Margaret Cantrell at home; they talked to the children only. Yet the article included the following statement, which strongly suggested that the reporter had interviewed, or had at least seen, Mrs. Cantrell: "Margaret Cantrell will talk neither about what happened nor about how they are doing. She wears the same mask of non-expression she wore at the funeral. She is a proud woman. Her world has changed. She says that after it happened, the people in town offered to help them out with money and they refused to take it."

Mrs. Cantrell convinces the jury and the Supreme Court

Margaret Cantrell sued the newspaper for "false light" invasion of privacy. False light generally means that a news organization has created "publicity that places the plaintiff in a false light in the public eye." She argued that the newspaper misrepresented the family situation; that although they were going through difficult times, the children were well cared for and the family was not living in the impoverished conditions suggested by the article. The jury found in favor of her, concluding that the newspaper had presented them in a false light and thereby had made them objects of pity and ridicule and caused them to suffer outrage, mental distress, shame, and humiliation. The jury awarded $60,000 in damages.

The newspaper appealed to the U.S. Court of Appeals for the Sixth Circuit, which reversed the jury's decision and sided with the newspaper. But the Supreme Court, by an 8-1 vote, reversed the court of appeals decision and reinstated the jury's award. Having settled the dispute between Mrs. Cantrell and the *Plain-Dealer* in her favor, the Supreme Court then had to interpret the First Amendment in light of the facts presented in *Cantrell* so that courts in future cases would know what the First Amendment says about false-light invasion-of-privacy disputes. Deciding that Mrs. Cantrell had been wronged by the newspaper was easy for the Supreme Court. Applying the First Amendment to the facts of *Cantrell*, however, was not.

Mrs. Cantrell had to sue for invasion of privacy

It is important to recognize that Mrs. Cantrell could not sue the newspaper for libel because she did not allege that the article harmed her reputation, and thus the Supreme Court did not have the opportunity to clarify how defamation law would apply to someone like her. The newspaper did not suggest that she was a bad person or had done bad things such as neglecting the children, statements that would be potentially damaging to her reputation. She was suing for the humiliation and personal suffering that the article caused her by falsely suggesting that the family was in dire circumstances. It was the mental anguish for which she was seeking compensation, not for damage to her standing in the community.

Although *Cantrell* was not a libel case, her status as a private person, defined in such cases, was important. Mrs. Cantrell was a private person under First Amendment standards developed in libel cases. The issue of whether an individual suing a news organization is a private person, or is instead a public figure or public official, is highly significant because it drastically affects what that individual has to prove to win a lawsuit. If Mrs. Cantrell had been able to sue for libel, she would have probably won by showing that the reporters and editors had acted *negligently* by not checking carefully the accuracy of the information they published. Considering the grossly irresponsible behavior of the reporter in this case, it would have been easy for Mrs. Cantrell to demonstrate negligence.

She also would most likely have won a much higher award from the jury. Libel suits often result in substantial damages because juries believe that more money is required to compensate for damage to one's reputation, which depending on the nature of the publication or broadcast, may never be properly restored. Juries in these cases often find that a large award is necessary to vindicate the plaintiff's reputation and send a message to other news organizations not to commit the same transgressions. False-light privacy suits, on the other hand, compensate for humiliation and anguish as a result of a report that is most likely not damaging to one's reputation. It is more difficult to measure such harm, and thus juries may conclude that a smaller award is sufficient to compensate plaintiffs for the mental anguish they suffered from being falsely portrayed in the media.

The judge in her case decides what standards to apply

The trial judge in Mrs. Cantrell's case decided that a previous invasion-of-privacy Supreme Court decision, *Time, Inc. v. Hill*, in 1967, would control the legal standards to be applied in her lawsuit. *Hill*, which was a false-light case like *Cantrell*, involved a New York family that sued *Life Magazine* because of an article it published about the family's ordeal at the hands of escaped convicts. The *Hill* case was one of several in the 1960s in which the Supreme Court extended substantial protection to news organizations in libel and other First Amendment areas to discuss issues of public interest, and *Hill* gave the Court the opportunity to broaden that protection to news organizations defending false-light lawsuits.

What the Supreme Court did in 1967 in *Hill* directly affected the decision in *Cantrell* seven years later. The New York courts in *Hill* had allowed the family to win its lawsuit by showing that *Life Magazine* had "negligently" published false information about the family's ordeal. But the Supreme Court, consistent with its commitment to protecting the First Amendment, reversed the trial court and instead imposed a much more difficult burden on those suing news organizations for false light. The Court held that plaintiffs like the Hills had to demonstrate that the magazine had acted with "reckless disregard for the truth," or actual malice as it is often called. Actual malice is one of the most difficult legal hurdles to overcome. To win an actual malice lawsuit, a plaintiff must demonstrate with "convincing clarity" that the journalists entertained serious doubts as to the truthfulness of their report, but published it anyway. The failure to investigate, without more culpability, does not constitute actual malice unless there was such overwhelming evidence available which the reporter intentionally ignored that would have refuted allegations made in the publication. Under those circumstances, the Supreme Court has concluded that the "purposeful avoidance of the truth" can lead to a finding of actual malice. However, this "avoidance" is very difficult to prove.

The Supreme Court had established in several key decisions beginning with *New York Times v. Sullivan* that in order to give journalists sufficient "breathing space" in which they can make mistakes without having to defend costly lawsuits, those who are public figures or public officials must prove actual malice in order to recover damages. It tentatively came to the same conclusion as to private persons involved in matters of public interest in a 1971 case. But a few months before the Supreme Court handed down *Cantrell*, the Court decided in *Gertz v. Welch* that private persons who sue media organizations for libel should not have to prove actual malice. Instead, the Court allowed the states to choose the appropriate standard of liability within some limits, and the majority of states selected negligence — a much easier burden for plaintiffs to overcome than the one for actual malice.

Gertz had thus settled the issue for libel plaintiffs so it was reasonable to expect that *Cantrell* would settle the issue for false-light invasion-of-privacy suits because they are a close cousin of libel. There are legal differences between the two, but it is possible to bring claims of both false light and libel based on the same factual issues. *Cantrell* provided the opportunity — and as it turned out, the *only* chance — for the Supreme Court to apply the standard that it adopted for private persons suing for libel to private persons suing for false light.

The Supreme Court finds in her favor but fails to resolve the constitutional issues

The Court did not settle the important legal issues in the *Cantrell* case. The reason the justices failed to do so says a lot about how the facts of a case can prevent courts from interpreting important provisions of the Constitution, in this case the First Amendment. The reason the Supreme Court did not settle the issue is that it concluded that the reporter's action in giving the false impression that he had talked to or seen Mrs. Cantrell constituted actual malice; that he had portrayed the Cantrells in a false light through "knowing or reckless untruth." Thus, the key fact of *Cantrell*, that the newspaper reporter acted not merely negligently, but maliciously, prevented the Supreme Court from applying the *Gertz* standard to false-light plaintiffs.

In other words, if Mrs. Cantrell had been unable to prove actual malice — which is always difficult — and instead proved only negligence, the Supreme Court would have been able to say that as a result of *Gertz*, false-light plaintiffs only have to prove the same standard as private person libel plaintiffs, which in most states is negligence. But because the Supreme Court cannot on its own "rewrite" the law unless the specific facts in the case are present that allow it to do so, the issues remain unsettled a quarter of a century after *Cantrell* and show no sign of being decided anytime soon.

Why the Court's refusal to settle the issues matters

The failure of the Court to decide this issue in *Cantrell* is significant. A democratic society depends on courts to develop relatively clear standards so that other courts and the American people will know what the rules are they must follow. Especially when First Amendment interests are at stake, journalists and those who believe they have been harmed by irresponsible reporting must know in advance what protections are granted to the press and what remedies are available to those suing a media organization. This nation will not have a healthy press system if journalists do not know what behavior will lead to potentially damaging lawsuits. In addition, those harmed by journalistic errors must know before they commit thousands of dollars and years of their lives to lawsuits whether they are likely to be successful.

The Court's unwillingness in *Cantrell* to clarify the law has done more than confuse media organizations and those considering a lawsuit against them. In the aftermath of *Cantrell*, states and lower federal courts are all over the place on how they apply false-light privacy standards. Some states hold that because *Cantrell* did not change *Hill* by applying *Gertz* to false-light plaintiffs, such plaintiffs must prove actual malice even if they are private persons. That discourages anyone who is a private person from suing for invasion of privacy, and instead forces them to sue for libel if the facts permit, which likely increases the cost of litigation and the potential for huge damage awards. It is an example of how the law appears to have little to do with common sense. A private person suing for false light has to prove malice; the same private person suing for libel has to demonstrate only negligence. There is no reasonable explanation for requiring different standards.

It is hard to criticize the courts that have stuck with the actual malice standard from *Hill*. They maintain that the Supreme Court "consciously abstained" from confronting the issue in *Cantrell*, and it is therefore the duty of the lower courts to "follow the mandate" of the Supreme Court's previous decision in *Hill* until modified. But other courts have come to the opposite conclusion. They believe that the Supreme Court, if it had been presented with the opportunity in *Cantrell*, would have made it easier for private persons to win such invasion-of-privacy cases. They have decided on their own to apply the more relaxed standards.

That leaves privacy plaintiffs and news organizations subject to widely varying interpretations by state and lower federal courts. A private person bringing a false-light claim against a news organization in California, Colorado, Oklahoma, Illinois, or Pennsylvania, for example, must prove actual malice and might as well either bring a libel action or not bother suing because the chances of success are so low. If, on the other hand, the lawsuit is brought in the District of Columbia, Kansas, Michigan, West Virginia, or New York, one can win a false-light action by proving something less than actual malice, usually negligence.

Especially in an era of national news organizations, the First Amendment should not mean one thing in one state, and something different in another. The Supreme Court has made it easy for a plaintiff in a libel action to bring the lawsuit in almost any court where the publication or broadcast was disseminated so plaintiffs often have the option of looking for the forum that is most hostile to First Amendment interests, where juries are most likely to award staggering sums of money to those suing news organizations. Although the law should be developed at the state as well as the federal level, the Constitution is this country's national charter and should not be subject to widely varying interpretations based on the decisions in a few lawsuits.

The Supreme Court missed its only chance

The Supreme Court's conclusions in *Cantrell* say a lot about how the facts of a case can prevent the Court from answering important constitutional questions. The irony is that *Cantrell* actually presented the Court with the opportunity to settle the issue; it either did not want to move beyond a narrow holding in this area of First Amendment law, or did not recognize that it had the chance to do so. The clearest evidence that the Court had the discretion to decide what private person false-light plaintiffs would need to prove is that in proving actual malice, Mrs. Cantrell *also* demonstrated negligence. Because Mrs. Cantrell showed the newspaper had been negligent, the Supreme Court could have decided whether negligence would be the appropriate standard for false-light plaintiffs. Instead, it concluded that this case "presents no occasion to consider whether a State may constitutionally apply a more relaxed standard of liability for a publisher or broadcaster of false statements injurious to a private individual under a false-light theory of invasion of privacy, or whether the constitutional standard announced in *Time, Inc. v. Hill* applies to all false-light cases."

In the quarter of a century since *Cantrell*, the Supreme Court has not had an opportunity to answer the questions left hanging by that decision. It may be decades before another case presenting just the right facts comes along. In the meantime, there are no national standards interpreting the First Amendment on these issues. *Cantrell* is not unusual; there are many cases decided by the courts where the facts get in the way. It is another example of why the American people should not have to wait indefinitely for important constitutional changes to be made by the courts.

For the judicial branch to serve its indispensable function within a complicated political and legal environment, it must be able to create certain standards that preserve its independence and legitimacy. Many of those standards permit judges to be creative in advancing the law and shaping it to reflect changing conditions. But many of the self-imposed rules and procedures — which have developed over a long period of

time and which judges believe are necessary for the courts to function —
significantly limit the scope and pace of constitutional change. The American people cannot wait while the courts make incremental modifications
to the Constitution one case at a time over many years. They must take
bolder and more comprehensive action by holding a second convention
to recommend amendments that will help restore democratic principles
and make government more accountable.

Part II

CHAPTER FOUR

The Road to Amending the Constitution: The Local and Statewide Meetings, and the National "Preconvention"

The American people should not have to undertake the long and difficult task of trying to organize a second constitutional convention. Public officials should have responded by now to repeated demands that the campaign finance system be changed to make elections more competitive and to make their officials more accountable. Because the electoral system itself is broken, and politicians have been able to ignore the calls for change and still remain in office by raising so much campaign money, the Constitution as currently written provides no workable solution. The courts cannot be expected to comprehensively change the system because of the nature of the political and legal environment in which they function. As this situation continues year after year, cynicism about politics grows while voter turnout declines.

Those who want to be part of the effort to organize a second convention would be naïve if they did not feel intimidated by what is ahead for them. No precedent exists in American history for such an undertaking. In order to have any chance of making this effort successful, they will have to understand the way Internet technology and traditional mass media organizations work. They will also need to know how to use them to find fellow citizens in their congressional district and state, and later around the country, who want to join this endeavor. They will have to work tirelessly throughout the entire process to generate publicity for their cause. After the petitions are written, those who have taken on this task will have to coordinate the massive campaign to convince state legislators to forward those petitions to Congress. All of this could take many years and involve thousands of people around the country. Organizing any cause in a country as large and diverse as the United States is incredibly challenging. Just convincing people who have been turned off to politics to pay attention to the issues raised here will be difficult.

The Constitution lays out the formal rules: Two-thirds (34) of state legislatures must approve petitions requesting a convention, and then forward the petitions to Congress. Congress is then required to call a convention to propose amendments. In order to become part of the Constitution, those amendments then must be approved by either state legislatures or state conventions. The formal requirements the Constitution establishes in Article V are actually the second phase of a complex process that involves multiple steps. If the first phase — organizing the three meetings discussed in this book — is not successful, there will never be a second, and the effort to bring about a convention will be over.

The opposition to organizing a second convention will come from many quarters. Public officials — if they have to comment at all on the effort rather than just ignore it — will denounce such a plan. They will argue that the Constitution and the electoral system work well, and that voters can always elect challengers to office. The lobbyists, unions, businesses, and other organizations that contribute to campaigns will vigorously oppose anything that could threaten their stranglehold on politics. The financial communities representing investors would worry about the effect of a convention on the stock market and other sectors of the economy. Groups from both sides of the ideological spectrum will worry that a "runaway" convention would seize the opportunity to propose ultra-liberal or ultra-conservative amendments. Some might even go so far as to say that just having the three initial meetings is not healthy for a democracy because it is part of a process that could lead to the calling of a convention. Legal scholars will argue that the Constitution should be changed for only the most urgent of reasons, and moreover, even many issues of transcendent importance should not be solved by constitutional amendment but must be addressed by legislation.

Some organizations criticize members of Congress when they introduce constitutional amendments on various subjects; they certainly would not be enthusiastic about a constitutional convention. Such a group formed in Washington, D.C. in late 1997. "Citizens for the Constitution" opposes what it considers to be efforts to degrade the nation's founding document by the proposing of too many constitutional amendments.

Originally funded in part by the Twentieth Century Foundation, the group includes several distinguished former members of Congress, presidential advisers, U.S. attorneys general, federal judges, and legal scholars. The organization stated that its purpose was to call attention to the "adverse effects of fast-paced 'constitutional tinkering.'" In a brochure, the group claimed that between January 1997, and March 1998, more than 100 constitutional amendments had been introduced, and it argued that Congress was "rushing to dilute our defining document." Citizens for the Constitution did not specify when it would be appropriate to amend the Constitution, although two years later the group wrote guidelines that sought to establish such standards.

Organized groups with foundation money and the names of distinguished individuals on the letterhead will not be the only ones to oppose this undertaking. A lot of ordinary citizens will wonder why anybody would care enough to even try to organize such a convention. When average citizens are contacted initially, it may be before there is any publicity about a second convention — publicity which could give the cause some initial legitimacy or at least arouse interest — and before individuals have given any thought to how the Constitution should be altered and what part they might play in recommending changes. When they are contacted by "activists" who want to get the process going, the reaction of most people will be that they are too busy with their daily lives and besides, it is not going to change the system anyway. It will be difficult to overcome that attitude.

The Peace Conference

In the history of the United States, there has never been an assembly of ordinary citizens or even elected officials who have met to debate the Constitution and write petitions that can be considered by state legislatures to request an Article V constitutional convention. Perhaps the only similar gathering in American history took place on the eve of the Civil War when an extraordinary, but ultimately unsuccessful, "peace conference" convened in Washington to try to stop the impending outbreak of the war. Dissatisfied with congressional efforts to prevent the secession of Southern states and the onset of hostilities, the Virginia legislature in early 1861 called for a conference of the states. Kentucky, New Jersey, Indiana, Illinois, and Ohio responded to Virginia's request by asking Congress to call an Article V convention. Recognizing that it would take too long for two-thirds of the states to petition Congress to hold a convention, 21 states accepted Virginia's invitation and sent 132 delegates to the gathering that began in Washington's Willard Hotel on February 4, 1861. With former President John Tyler presiding, the Peace Conference met for three weeks and produced a package of complex constitutional amendments both protecting slavery where it existed and limiting its expansion into new territories. The proposed amendments were defeated in the U.S. Senate and never came to a vote in the House.

The Peace Conference of 1861 was probably doomed from the start. On the day it convened, the seven secessionist states were meeting in Montgomery, Alabama, to draw up a constitution for the Confederacy. None of those states sent representatives to Washington. The delegates not only had to deal with the meeting in the South, but also with indifference on the part of some Northern and Western states. Only about two-thirds of the states of the whole Union were represented at the Willard Hotel. California, Oregon, Texas, and Arkansas did not send delegates. Michigan, Wisconsin, and Minnesota also declined to participate. A joint resolution by the Michigan legislature declared that "concession and compromise are not to be entertained or offered to traitors."

Although the peace conference was not an officially sanctioned meeting recognized in a federal statute or the U.S. Constitution, its delegates were selected by state officials, thus giving it a legitimacy that a gathering of ordinary citizens in a current-day national preconvention is not likely to have. Some peace conference delegates were appointed by governors, others by state legislatures. All of them held official credentials certified by administrative authorities in their states. In Ohio, the General Assembly, despite serious reservations about the value of such a conference, authorized its governor to select delegates with the consent of the Senate. Some states selected prominent officials such as former senators and ministers, and others who had been active in political parties and public office. Several state legislatures complicated the work of the conference by sending delegates with specific instructions not to compromise on certain issues related to the expansion of slavery, and to submit any proposals to the legislature before the delegation would be authorized to give its approval.

The Peace Conference of 1861 took place in an atmosphere of crisis, with the United States on the verge of breaking apart and the first battles of the Civil War only a few months away. Considering the urgency of the issues and the limited time available, it was important that the delegates to the peace conference have the authority to speak and vote on behalf of their states without having to defer every important issue until they had consulted with officials back home. If the peace conference delegates had not been chosen by state officials, their meeting would have been little more than an assembly of concerned citizens that Congress and the rest of the country could have treated as having never taken place.

But no crisis of such proportion faces those who would participate today in the various phases leading to a national preconvention in Washington, D.C. The preconvention can do its work — discuss the Constitution, write petitions that will be presented to state legislatures, and generate public interest in the reforms set forth in the petitions — without the delegates being appointed by public officials. What the preconvention loses in legitimacy by not having its delegates selected by governors or state legislators, it gains by allowing delegates the freedom to exercise independent judgment without being directly instructed or manipulated by powerful political entities. The absence of official approval of the preconvention will give delegates the chance to make tough choices that political figures representing entrenched interests would be afraid to seriously consider. There will be a time and place for an assembly that formally represents the people and the officials of each state when an actual constitutional convention is held as provided by Article V. The preconvention, and its predecessor meetings, on the other hand, are to be organized and controlled not by government officials, but by ordinary citizens.

Although Congress cannot interfere with the preconvention, there is no doubt that it will try to control every aspect of an actual constitutional convention. As the number of states approving petitions begins to approach the required 34, Congress will take one of several actions: It will attempt to preempt the convention by proposing legislation — as opposed to constitutional amendments — that at least superficially addresses the issues raised in the petitions. If that effort does not slow or stop additional legislatures from forwarding petitions, Congress may propose constitutional amendments that relate to the issues raised in the petitions with the expectation that the efforts to win ratification by three-fourths of the states will fail. And finally, if the drive for petitioning Congress to call a convention persists despite congressional efforts to pass legislation or propose amendments, Congress will enact a comprehensive bill that will outline every aspect of the constitutional convention process from the selection of delegates, to the procedures the convention must follow, to the way the proposed amendments will be presented to the states. Basically, ordinary citizens will only be able to control the process until the preconvention has ended and petitions are presented to state legislatures. After that, elected officials will take over.

The national preconvention, to be held in Washington, D.C., is an indispensable step in the long process of persuading states to petition Congress to call a constitutional convention. Some would argue that a preconvention would be a colossal waste of time and money, if it can be pulled off at all. It may take years, beginning with the initial meetings at the congressional district or county level, with a subsequent convention in each state capital, to get to the point of holding a national convention. It could be argued that citizens have neither the interest nor the capacity to sustain such a movement over what may be a long period of time. Instead, citizens should spend their precious time and money directly asking their state legislators to petition Congress to call a convention. If state legislators ignore such pleas — which they surely will — it can be said that at least an effort was made. Despite the simplicity of such a plan, there would be no incentives for state legislators to pay attention to the request for petitions, much less forward them to Congress. A longer term strategy, which generates news coverage and other forms of attention, has a better chance of being successful.

Despite the financial and personal resources that would have to be committed to such a cause, a national preconvention would not be a frivolous political exercise. A preconvention, with participants selected by a fair process that allows even those without political connections to be chosen to represent their states, would galvanize the nation's attention and be the best vehicle for generating the momentum necessary to persuade suspicious state legislators that a second constitutional convention should be held. As the meetings at the congressional district and county level create news coverage, increasingly larger news organizations with nationwide circulation will take notice. As one state after another holds a convention in its capital city and prepares to send delegates to the national convention, the purpose of the national preconvention will become widely known. The media coverage of a national preconvention will be intense if not frenzied. That coverage may have as much impact on state legislators as their later face-to-face meetings with pro-convention constituents. Although state conventions and the national preconvention in Washington, D.C. can and must be held without the approval of state legislators or other state officials, it is to attract their interest and to educate them about the need for constitutional revisions that is the primary purpose of the preconvention.

Not surprisingly, Article V makes no mention of a preconvention. The Framers of the Constitution did not contemplate such a gathering and would probably have considered it an unnecessary prelude to the convention method that they created in Article V. The preconvention's lack of constitutional legitimacy is, however, one of its virtues. It is difficult to underestimate the importance of citizens being able to meet without having to first gain approval from their governor, state legislature, or Congress. Ordinary citizens, activists, political veterans, people from various organizations and all walks of life, can compete for the right to be a delegate to a national convention to be held in the nation's capital that discusses the future of the Constitution. Those who attend the convention will have substantial autonomy over its agenda and deliberations — but must also cope with the inevitable chaos — and select capable leaders who will help steer the meeting through the numerous challenges it will encounter. There will always be the danger that having finally made it to a national preconvention, the delegates will be unable to conduct themselves in a way that results in a coherent set of proposed petitions that can be taken to state legislators. Regardless of its final outcome, trying to hold such a meeting, unprecedented in this nation's history, would reflect the highest values of a democratic society.

The National Issues Convention

One other historic gathering provides important lessons for those who will organize efforts to hold a second constitutional convention. A distinguished political scientist at the University of Texas, James S. Fishkin, organized an extraordinary meeting that brought 460 people to a "National Issues Convention" (NIC) in Austin, Texas, in January 1996. The weekend-long meeting gave attendees the opportunity to learn about important policy issues related to the economy, America's role in the world, and the current state of the American family, and to express informed opinions about how those policy issues should be resolved. Fishkin had helped organize a similar and successful effort in Great Britain, where 300 people participated in a convention in Manchester in April 1994.

The meeting in Austin presented a much greater challenge than the meeting in England. Not only is the United States more populous than Great Britain, its population is also spread out over a vast geographical area. Fishkin contracted with a respected polling organization to select the attendees from a scientifically chosen random sample. The 460 people who eventually came to Austin accurately represented, with a few exceptions, not only the larger group of 914 respondents who were invited to the gathering, but also the general population of the United States. For example, the weekend group had slightly more people from the West, fewer attendees over the age of 70, and fewer people who had only a high school education as compared with both the original group selected by the polling organization or the country as a whole.

There was much publicity surrounding the meeting. PBS became an active partner in promoting efforts to recruit attendees and to generate media coverage. PBS's Newshour anchor Jim Lehrer served as host for the event. Other news organizations, such as *Parade Magazine*, publicized the convention. By the time the convention was held, there was substantial interest in the meeting.

The convention proved that ordinary citizens would go to a city far away from their homes to meet with others from around the country to discuss important issues and to recommend to public officials policy preferences in dealing with those issues. Fishkin's delegates were provided with expenses including plane fare, hotel, and meals to attend the convention; such incentives may or may not be available to those who attend a preconvention as part of an effort to amend the Constitution. Even though the expenses of the attendees' were paid, going to a convention in a distant city is a substantial undertaking for many people. Bad weather in various parts of the country just before the weekend made traveling to Austin all the more difficult. Nevertheless, the NIC showed that people cared enough about politics and the direction of their country to participate in the experiment.

The participants filled out a questionnaire exploring their views on various issues related to the three policy areas. Those responses were compared with surveys they had previously completed when selected for the Austin meeting, and a questionnaire that they filled out as the meeting was ending. During the weekend, attendees were able to confer with each other and to learn about issues from experts. They spent time with experts such as leading political figures, and had an opportunity to talk with those experts in small groups about policy options.

The surveys from the end of the meeting clearly demonstrated that the 460 people learned a lot. Those questionnaires showed a much higher level of sophistication about complex policy issues as compared with the answers given off the top of their heads when a pollster contacted them before the meeting. The process of providing citizens with information with which to form opinions on policy issues, and allowing them to confer with each other before expressing that opinion, is what Fishkin called "deliberative polling." Not only did a substantial number of attendees change their attitude about the policy issues as compared to their responses to the questionnaire as the weekend began, they also later became more politically active in their communities and states after their experience.

The Long Road to a Second Constitutional Convention

The effort to amend the Constitution by an Article V convention will involve at least six stages (the list does not include the court battles that would likely begin once the preconvention has completed its work):

1)   The first meeting, which will last one day, at the congressional district or county level, where revisions to the Constitution will be discussed and delegates to the state convention will be selected.

2) The state convention, which will take place over several days, in the state capital, where proposed petitions will be refined and delegates to the national preconvention will be chosen.

3) The preconvention in Washington, D.C., which could last a week or more, where petitions will be written and strategies for persuading state legislatures to approve them will be considered.

4) The campaign after the preconvention to convince state legislatures to petition Congress to hold an Article V constitutional convention.

5) The calling of a constitutional convention by Congress upon receiving petitions from two-thirds of the states.

6) The effort to convince three-fourths of state legislatures or state conventions — depending on which method Congress has selected — to ratify the new constitutional amendments.

It is difficult to conceive of a more arduous challenge than for ordinary citizens operating independently of their government to organize a series of meetings culminating in a national convention to propose amendments to the Constitution. Every decision about how to organize such an undertaking may be criticized as inadequate in one respect or another. Even as the first words are spoken or written about the procedures that will be followed, a jaundiced eye will be cast on what outcomes the process will likely create. If groups with a narrow and divisive agenda dominate the process from the first meeting, the petitions written by the national preconvention will not attract broad support. Without such support, there will be little chance that state legislators will seriously consider forwarding the petitions to Congress. If, on the other hand, the process encourages participation by those with a broader perspective and the proposed petitions attract widespread support, there is a greater chance that state legislatures will approve those petitions and Congress will be forced to call a second convention. Media coverage of the meetings and the issues will be a crucial factor in determining whether there will be a constitutional convention.

Because such an effort is unprecedented, there is little guidance from the past on how to avoid mistakes that will thwart such an undertaking. There are probably many plans by which delegates could be selected and procedures for the convention established. Nevertheless, certain principles should guide the deliberations of those organizing the meetings and the conventions.

Among the most compelling of those principles are access and inclusiveness. The process will begin at the local level in either a congressional district or county, depending on the state's population. Ideally, even those who long ago decided that government and politics are unresponsive will try to convince their fellow citizens that the Constitution should be revised, and that some of the people they encounter at the first meeting should represent them at the state convention. By beginning the process at the local level, there is at least the chance that everyone — both well-to-do and those from lower economic groups — will be able to offer their opinions about the Constitution and the political health of the nation.

The state convention may well require a greater expenditure of funds by attendees for such items as travel and a few nights in a hotel in the capital city. Although more affluent individuals will be able to more easily afford to pay those expenses, persons of limited financial means should still be considered as delegates to the state convention. What is needed is a commitment at the local level to raise funds to defray the cost of attending the state convention. Lack of money should not prevent anyone from being considered for delegate to the state or national meetings.

The individuals attending the first meeting and the subsequent conventions should recognize the diverse nature of the population of that district or county and be sensitive to the interests of those with varying backgrounds. But no delegate should be chosen on the basis of race, gender, ethnicity, or other similar factors. All persons attending the first meeting should have the opportunity to offer their credentials to the rest of the group. Those who will do the best job at the state convention should be selected.

The Congressional district/county meeting

Deciding where to hold the first meeting requires striking a delicate balance. People should be able to attend the initial meeting close to home so that travel time or the lack of a vehicle does not discourage them from participating. However, if the meetings are too local, there will be too many of them with too few participants at each one. If there are a small number of people at the first meeting, it will be more difficult to generate media coverage.

An argument could be made that the first meeting should be at the county level. Counties are clearly defined legal entities with which almost everyone identifies. Most people are able to reach their county seat fairly easily, although some may have to travel an hour or more to reach the far end of their county. The problem is that some states have so many counties that organizing meetings in them would be an overwhelmingly difficult task. In Kentucky, for example, there are 120 counties. Expecting people to gather in their county seats all over the state to discuss the Constitution and choose individuals to send to the state capital seem unrealistic. In the states where there are only a few congressional districts and people would have to travel great distances to attend, it is appropriate to have the initial meeting at the county level. Everywhere else, the first gathering should be at the congressional district level.

By holding the first meeting based on the boundaries of a congressional district, there is a greater chance that people will actually show up. With more than 500,000 residents in an average congressional district, there is a good chance that people discouraged about politics and interested in discussing and revising the Constitution will come to the meeting. Some congressional districts are geographically huge, and some individuals may be prevented from attending because they cannot get from one end of the district to a central location within it. But most people who would be interested in such an event will have access to transportation to travel to the location of the meeting. The trade-off for having the meeting far away from some people is the substantially larger population in the congressional district from which to draw participants. It is extremely important that there be a good turnout at the first meeting, with news coverage helping to spread the word that an effort to amend the Constitution is underway.

An additional advantage to congressional district level meetings is that unlike counties, which may vary considerably in size, congressional districts — with some variation between states with the fewest residents and the rest of the states — are approximately the same size in terms of population. If the meetings were held at the county level and each county had the same number of representatives at the statewide convention, residents of the more populous counties would argue that they are at a disadvantage compared with the counties with fewer people.

Perhaps as importantly, because a meeting at the congressional district level covers a larger geographical area than would a county meeting, there are likely to be more media organizations located nearby to cover the event. A congressional district will usually be in the circulation area of more radio and television stations and newspapers than a county. There are exceptions, as some rural congressional districts have few media outlets. But because a congressional district probably has several population centers which at least have newspapers and radio stations — and may have a TV station not far away — there is a greater chance that a reporter would not have to travel as far for the congressional district as opposed to the county meeting. Press coverage must remain a high priority for those planning each phase of the process. It is a critical element in building interest in the work of the state conventions, and later for the national preconvention.

As with so many political issues, nothing related to this process will be simple. There are states that have only one or two congressional districts. If the process described above is followed in those states, there will be a very small statewide convention. For those states with fewer than five congressional districts, the initial meetings should be at the county level even if there are many counties within the state and they vary significantly in terms of population.

Expert advice

Constitutional issues can be immensely complicated, and for lay citizens, somewhat intimidating. Those organizing the initial meeting should consider inviting several constitutional law experts — law or political science professors from a local university, or attorneys who have handled constitutional cases — who can help guide the group as it undertakes an examination of the Constitution and a discussion of the petitions. The law experts can explain how various provisions of the Constitution have been interpreted by summarizing some of the major cases decided by the Supreme Court. The experts can also discuss what changes in public policy have traditionally been considered through ordinary legislation, and which areas have been constitutional in nature. The experts should help attendees at the first meeting decide what issues should be discussed by the delegates they send to the statewide convention. It is important to remember that the people attending the meeting must be able to run it. The experts are there to help facilitate discussion and inform individuals about how the Constitution has been interpreted, not to dominate the deliberations of the group.

When James Fishkin planned the NIC, he had to decide which model to follow: whether the attendees should meet first with each other in small groups to formulate questions and issues, which would then be supplemented by the information presented by the experts who appeared throughout the weekend, or whether the attendees would "absorb" information from the experts and then discuss that information among themselves. Fishkin favored the more activist model of deliberative polling, and both the British and U.S. meetings were conducted in that manner.

Unlike the NIC in Austin where attendees answered questions about their views on policy related matters, those attending these congressional district meetings will have a more difficult task because most of them will know relatively little about the way the Constitution works or has been interpreted. It is probably worthwhile to have the law experts appear relatively early in the meeting so that information disseminated by the experts can be used in the discussion. On the other hand, at the statewide convention, which will last several days, it may be appropriate to have more discussion among delegates before they hear from experts. If the attendees have the benefit of articulate and knowledgeable experts at the congressional district meeting, they likely will be better prepared for discussing the key issues with fellow delegates before they meet with the experts at the statewide convention.

There is precedent in many states for holding meetings at the congressional level. States that have used caucuses instead of presidential primaries to choose delegates to the parties' national nominating conventions often meet initially at the congressional district level to choose delegates to the state convention. The state convention then selects delegates to the national convention. A meeting at the congressional district level to begin the process of amending the Constitution will not, of course, have many of the advantages of a presidential caucus. Party officials publicize and organize presidential caucuses in conformity with party rules and state law. Once the caucus has begun, there are detailed procedures that must be followed in selecting delegates to the next phase of the presidential caucus process. The presidential caucuses have not always been quiet affairs, but there would likely be less confusion and disagreement at such a gathering as compared with a meeting as part of the process to change the Constitution. The delegates to a constitutional meeting will not have policies established in party rules and state law to guide their deliberations. They will largely have to decide on their own how their meetings will be conducted.

Individuals who have been politically active will probably take the lead in organizing the first meeting. Someone will have to solicit funds or pay for a hotel meeting room, a convention center room, or facilities at a library or church in a city that is centrally located in the congressional district. A meeting room could cost as little as one hundred or up to several hundred dollars depending on where it is located and if food or beverages will be served. It will probably not be difficult to find someone who will step forward to put up the money for renting a hotel conference room or some other facility.

Publicizing the meeting

Press coverage informing people that a meeting will be held in the congressional district for the purpose of discussing amendments to the Constitution is an indispensable part of the long-term success of the effort to call a second convention. The same individuals who find an appropriate location and pay for the meeting room will have to develop a comprehensive plan so that news organizations around the congressional district and the state will know that such a meeting is going to be held. Because there will be only one gathering at the congressional district/county level, it is essential that anyone interested in attending be informed in advance.

To accommodate as many people as possible, the meeting should be held on a Saturday, beginning no later than 9 A.M. There will be a morning and afternoon session. Depending on the number of people attending and the contentiousness of the issues, the meeting may last into the evening.

Those who organize the district/county level meetings must recognize that people gathering to discuss the way their country is governed is newsworthy, and that reporters will be interested if approached in a way that accommodates their needs. Press releases outlining the purpose, date, and location of the district/county meeting must be sent to every news organization within the area and to large news organizations around the state. Organizers must call news editors to make sure they are aware of the importance of this event. In addition, events that are visually interesting must be held in advance of the meetings so that television stations can cover them. These events can vary from marches and demonstrations to bringing in a figure of statewide or national prominence to address groups interested in attending the district or state convention. If the events are offered when there are few other stories to cover — weekends, for example, are an excellent time for such events — and they are visual in nature, television reporters will be there. A demonstration drumming up interest in an upcoming meeting of citizens to change the Constitution — and later, the meeting itself — are likely to be sufficiently interesting and unusual to attract the attention of print and broadcast journalists.

The meeting itself is likely to get news coverage. Many TV reporters are always looking for stories that can be covered in a short period of time — where video can be shot and people can be interviewed in one location — so the reporter will have time to edit the piece for the newscast or go on to a different story. The TV reporter will appreciate the fact that the district/county meeting begins early in the day, rather than later in the afternoon closer to the time of the newscast.

The more difficult challenge is to get news coverage before the meeting so that a lot of people will know about it and attend. Having more people there will not only create a more interesting meeting, journalists will probably take it more seriously. Those people who have assumed the responsibility of organizing the initial meeting must find creative ways to get reporters to do stories — which will help publicize the meeting — in advance so people will know about it beforehand rather than afterward when it is too late to have participated. If assignment editors or producers at TV stations, reporters at radio stations, and editors at newspapers are told that a meeting is going to be held as part of the process of people amending the Constitution, there is likely to be interest. If some prominent individuals or those with some legitimacy in the community get involved early on, it may be easier to get the word out through the traditional mass media that the meeting is going to be held.

It has to work the first time, because if reporters go to a meeting in a congressional district or county and find no more than a dozen people sitting around talking about the Constitution and the plan to hold a second convention, little news coverage will result. They may offer a brief mention in the newspaper or a short TV news report, but if a subsequent meeting is held with more people, reporters are not likely to return. The nature of the news business — especially television — is such that reporters often move on after covering a story. Unless there is something significantly different about a previously covered story, reporters generally believe that the audience will be bored if it sees or reads about it a second time.

Using "new" technology to generate interest

News coverage by magazines, newspapers, radio and television stations of the congressional district or county meeting, and the state and national conventions, will be an essential part of generating interest in the cause, but in the early stages, it may be less important than the communication that takes place through newer forms of communication technology. A fully operational Second Convention Web site would allow individuals within each state or congressional district — who would otherwise never speak or write to each other — to discuss everything from how the Constitution should be changed to where the congressional district or county meeting should be held. People with access to computers in homes, libraries, schools or at work would be able to interact with individuals in their own state and across the country about how to pursue the goal of holding a second constitutional convention.

The Web site will provide comprehensive information on how to organize the meetings leading to a convention. It will also keep people informed of developments around the country. If a congressional district meeting is held in one state, for example, the minutes of the meeting could be posted on the Web site so citizens in any other part of the country would learn how many people attended, what they discussed, how they chose delegates to the statewide convention, and what amendments they are recommending. Participants could use digital cameras to record the proceedings, and post the pictures to the Web site. A newspaper might run such a picture even if no reporter attended the meeting. As the information from around the country is uploaded to the site, people will learn more about the Constitution, and how to better conduct the meetings leading to the national preconvention. The Web site will also permit people to exchange e-mail addresses or leave messages on a "bulletin board" or "newsgroup" so they can contact each other directly.

The Second Convention Web site will, however, be much more than a bulletin board or e-mail exchange service, or a place to read the minutes from meetings. It will provide links to a rich array of documents, photographs, and paintings maintained by governmental entities and private institutions that provide important and interesting information about the Constitution and our legal system. Web sites are currently available, with more coming online all the time, that make history come alive. Pictures and biographical information about the Framers and depictions of original documents, such as the Constitution and the Bill of Rights, are available with a few clicks of the mouse. Finding such documents and pictures through the Second Convention Web site will be comparatively easy for people who are otherwise unfamiliar with Web browsers and usually intimidated by computer technology.

Individuals who have never read anything about the debates at the Philadelphia Constitutional Convention — or who have never seen the great paintings that line the walls of the U.S. Capitol or are housed in the collection of the Library of Congress — may gain a greater appreciation for the nation's founding and history, and a deeper understanding of how much is at stake in the effort to amend the Constitution. The technology is available today that makes it possible for two people who live thousands of miles apart — and who will never meet face to face — to access through their computers the same passage from one of the *Federalist* papers, or Madison's notes from the Constitutional Convention, or Jefferson's letter to Madison outlining the importance of the federal judiciary in protecting individual rights. Those people can then discuss with each other, or anyone else who cares to leave or retrieve bulletin board messages, what the Framers really intended by the words they included in the Constitution.

Making such technology available and easily accessible, however, presents many challenges. Although the Internet has been used by political activists and others to raise money for campaigns and to reach prospective voters, there has never been an effort similar to organizing a national constitutional preconvention that relies so much on cyberspace technology. An initial Second Convention Web site — the address is listed in the author's note at the front of this book — will begin the process. It will offer information about the three meetings, excerpts of the book including the list of proposed amendments, and links to historical and contemporary information about the Constitution and government.

If no organization or individual will underwrite the cost of a single "national" Web site, there may be individuals who will create the sites used to organize the meetings in their state. Considering how important a second convention — or just the organizing of meetings in a handful of states — would be to the self-governing process of the nation and the potential interest in this unprecedented effort, it is not inconceivable that a foundation or generous individual would find this endeavor to be worth supporting.

Whoever maintains the site must be strongly committed to the principle of access and robust debate. Although some limits may have to be imposed if the function of the site itself is impaired by those determined to prevent it from operating, individuals must be able to have their say on the Constitution, the second convention, and proposed amendments, without being censored. Although there is no legal obligation to open the site to all viewpoints, it would be hypocritical to encourage the American people to engage in a debate about their nation and the Constitution, then exclude from the site views that are controversial or upsetting. To the extent that the site is moderated, care must be taken to limit material that is potentially libelous or obscene, or violates an individual's right to privacy, but the Second Convention site should be a forum where a wide range of views can be exchanged.

Conducting the Congressional District/County Meeting

Once the district/county meeting has been publicized through brief notices or full-length articles in the newspaper, or in a radio or TV news report, at least several dozen people are likely to show up. In congressional districts that have energetic political activists and interested news reporters who give the pending meeting coverage, as many as several hundred people may crowd into the hotel meeting room. A few dozen or few hundred people are obviously a fraction of the six hundred thousand residents who live in a congressional district, but political movements often begin slowly and take time to develop. The district/county meeting is but the first step in a long process.

The number present at the initial meeting likely will determine how difficult it is for the group to accomplish its goals. It is possible that the more people attending — especially if some of them need to be heard on every subject — the longer it will take to discuss the Constitution, consider amendments, and choose delegates to the statewide convention. Those at the meeting must be patient and cooperative as the group undertakes its first important decision, selecting someone to serve as chairperson. People interested in the position should get five minutes each to explain why they have the necessary background, experience, and temperament to do the job. Those who volunteer should understand that, depending on the size and demeanor of the group, chairing the meeting might be a difficult job. The selection of the chairperson should be by secret ballot.

Once the chairperson is chosen, a motion to adopt *Roberts Rules of Order* as the official rules of the meeting should be introduced. Unlike public bodies, which are often required to follow *Robert's Rules* by statute or regulation, an "extra-governmental" body is under no obligation to conduct itself by such procedures. *Robert's Rules* have been used for many years and are essential if there is to be an orderly discussion of the issues and votes on motions before the body.

The chairperson should appoint a secretary to take minutes of the meeting. The most important task of the secretary during the meeting is to write down the exact words of proposed motions so the group can hear them read back before a vote is taken. The secretary will also serve an important function after the meeting has ended by writing up the minutes, which will then be made available through the Second Convention Web site. The minutes can also be mailed to news organizations along with a press release describing the event.

The secretary should understand that if all significant statements are included in the minutes verbatim, they will be too long. Moreover, some individuals will hesitate to speak candidly because they know their comments will be widely distributed through the Web site or news organizations. The secretary should recognize that the important debates and decisions of the group can be reflected in the minutes without necessarily including every statement that may be potentially embarrassing or troublesome to those who made it. There is an important precedent for "cleaning up" words that are uttered in the passions of the moment. James Madison's notes were the most comprehensive made at the Constitutional Convention, without which little would be known about the debates and decisions of the Framers at the Philadelphia Convention. Madison decided that in order to avoid embarrassing any of those who attended the Convention, he would not permit his notes to be published while any of the delegates were alive. Ironically, Madison outlived all of the other 54 delegates to the Convention. While in retirement in Montpelier from 1821 until his death in 1836, Madison went over his notes of the Convention and his correspondence on important issues and made some changes before he would permit them to be published. One author described Madison's changes as those he believed were "justified in the name of historical accuracy" or in the case of his correspondence, to "avoid offense to the living."

Once the group has chosen a chairperson, a secretary, and has adopted *Roberts Rules of Order*, it is ready to undertake its primary tasks. The attendees face two difficult challenges. First, they must discuss how the Constitution should be changed, which will require knowledge of the Constitution itself and how it has been interpreted by the courts, the elected branches of government, as well as the people, over the years. Those who attend the meeting will also have to recognize what changes are appropriate at the constitutional level, and which should be implemented by ordinary legislative means. And second, the group must select delegates to attend a statewide convention. At the statewide convention, possible constitutional amendments will be discussed in more detail, and delegates will be selected to attend the national preconvention in Washington, D.C.

To avoid having the initial meeting stall over specific details and degenerate into endless arguments, it is important for those attending to identify areas of the Constitution that need to be altered without getting bogged down in the wording of the new amendments. That more difficult task will be partially undertaken by the national preconvention and finished by a constitutional convention called by Congress. The district/county meeting will have plenty to do without trying to write the proposed amendments. For example, attendees at the first meeting may agree, after reading Chapter Seven of this book, that the law related to congressional campaigns must be changed at the constitutional level because Congress is unable or unwilling to provide true reform by legislation, and because of the Supreme Court's *Buckley v. Valeo* decision in 1976. The group may conclude that the amendment to be proposed by the second convention should require that all congressional candidates raise half the money for the campaign from the congressional district or state depending on whether the race is for the House or Senate. If the attendees support such a plan, they should have the opportunity to send a delegate to the state convention who shares that view without having to write an amendment that implements the change. In the same vein, if the group strongly supports term limits at the congressional level, which can only be accomplished by constitutional amendment, it should vote for a delegate who also supports term limits.

Instead of spending and most assuredly wasting time trying to write the proposed amendments, there should be a spirited discussion of the problems to be addressed by such amendments, and general ideas should be offered about how those amendments would implement the desired change. But it would be time-consuming and difficult for individuals at the congressional district or county level to do more than identify the general areas — such as campaign finance reform, term limits, and the

Electoral College, to name a few — and actually try to write the language of proposed amendments.

There will, undoubtedly, be some dispute about the accuracy of the minutes after they are published. The district/county meeting will be held only one time. It will then disband, and sometime later, the minutes will appear. Some individuals may disagree with the accuracy or interpretation of the statements in the minutes. The Web site should include a section where those who attended the meeting, but disagree with the recollections of the secretary or the way the minutes reflect the debate, would have the chance to offer a rebuttal.

Who should be the delegates to the state convention?

The congressional district/county meeting will have accomplished a lot — and surprised its critics — if it does three things: convenes in the first place, identifies the areas of the Constitution most in need of renovation, and selects delegates to the statewide convention. The last of these tasks is essential if the process is to move forward. Those selecting delegates to the state convention should choose individuals who are knowledgeable about public issues, and who are also articulate and assertive enough to express their views while interacting with others who share those characteristics. The delegates to the state convention must approach their task in the spirit of tolerance for people who may hold differing views or may not be as knowledgeable about constitutional issues as they are. The statewide delegates must be good listeners who are not so argumentative or difficult that they are likely to disrupt the work of the meeting.

No matter how many attend the district/county meeting, and how impressive the attributes of those selected for the state convention, it will be argued that both groups are unrepresentative of the population of the congressional district, county, or state because they are "self-selected," meaning that they were not drawn from a random sample and do not necessarily reflect the social, economic, and racial characteristics of the jurisdiction. Not only do they not accurately represent the makeup of the district or state, they were not selected by voters to attend the initial meeting; they just showed up. For the statewide convention, delegates were selected by fellow citizens who were at the first meeting, not by the voters.

Such a criticism is accurate but unavoidable. The only response can be that anyone who wants to attend the initial meeting can do so. No one is excluded because of social, economic, religious, racial, or gender characteristics. The meeting's time and location will be publicized in local media, and there will be information about the pending meeting available through the Second Convention Web site. Assuming there is sufficient news coverage of the upcoming meeting at the local level, individuals who are interested in shaping the direction of their country have a responsibility to be informed and to attend. Those who are so disconnected from politics that they do not follow news events through a newspaper or television, and thus do not hear about the meeting, or do not make the effort to attend if they learn about it, cannot say later that the group at the district/county level and the state convention did not adequately represent their interests.

The one restriction that seems appropriate is that in order for someone to vote at the district/county meeting and to be eligible to be a delegate to the state convention, that person must be a registered voter in that district or county. Individuals younger than 18 can certainly attend and participate during the local meeting, but only those old enough to legally vote for public officials and ballot measures should be permitted to vote at the initial meeting. No other requirement should be imposed on who can vote at the initial meeting or on who can serve as a delegate to the state convention.

How many delegates should there be?

The statewide convention, which should be held no more than three months after the district/county meeting, should have no more than 52 delegates, which is the number of congressional districts in California, the nation's most populous state. The first constitutional convention in Philadelphia managed with 55 members, no more than 41 of who were there at the same time. The country obviously did not have 250 million people then; but the convention size must not be so large as to prevent the group from accomplishing its goals. In states with large populations, that will obviously mean there will only be one delegate from each congressional district, while in states with fewer congressional districts, there will be more delegates from each one. In those states with four or fewer congressional districts, which must hold the initial meeting at the county level, the number of delegates from each county will vary significantly from state to state. The overriding goal must be numerical fairness *within* the state. The fact that a California congressional district will send one delegate to its statewide convention while a congressional district in Kentucky — a state with six congressional districts — could send as many as eight delegates from each district, does not necessarily prevent the state convention from being broadly representative of the people of the state as a whole.

The district/county meeting and the statewide convention must also choose alternates who can attend if a delegate cannot. In states with few congressional districts, and thus many delegates to the statewide convention from each one, there will be individuals who were selected but cannot attend. By having as many alternates as delegates, there is a greater chance that a sufficient number will attend the various meetings.

Discussion of the constitutional amendments

How each district/county meeting will be conducted will vary significantly depending on how many people attend, their knowledge of the Constitution, their commitment to the effort to work toward a second convention, and their willingness to compromise on important issues. Some meetings will probably run smoothly because an appropriate number of people attend, and they are willing to learn about the issues and make reasonable choices that advance the process. Other meetings will be more chaotic: Too many people attend; the chairperson may favor one side over another; or the group may be dominated by those with narrow interests who are unwilling to be flexible on key issues. Regardless of how peaceful and deliberative or disorganized the meetings are, they will be an unprecedented and important lesson in democracy.

The chairperson at the district/county meeting should solicit comments from the group about what parts of the Constitution need to be amended, and in general terms, how those goals will be accomplished. As discussed previously, the actual implementation of the changes in the form of a constitutional amendment should not be decided by the district meeting. Instead, the group should identify those areas that need change and make general statements about how those changes could be accomplished.

Many of the people who attend the meetings probably will not know much about constitutional law and policy issues. They may have been out of school a long time and may feel unprepared to discuss with their fellow citizens how the Constitution should be amended. To alleviate that problem to some extent, the Second Convention Web site will identify and describe books and other materials that provide information about constitutional history in an accessible and engaging manner. The Web site should also include links to government and university sites that offer informative videos, pictures, and documents that provide a shorthand education about the Constitution. Before the first meeting, those most interested in participating fully at the initial gathering and in being considered for selection to the state convention should read at least one or more of the books identified in the site as the most informative and understandable. Among many potential examples, two books provide a brief yet comprehensive introduction to the constitutional system. They are *The Meaning of the Constitution* by Angela Roddey Holder and John Thomas Roddey Holder, and *A Companion to the United States Constitution and Its Amendments* by John Vile. Both books offer a brief introduction to constitutional history, then discuss each important provision of the Constitution by describing its original purpose and how it has been interpreted over the past 200 years. People who buy these or related materials — especially if they contain a copy of the complete Constitution — should bring them to the meeting.

There will be many important constitutional issues for the group to discuss, and there may be substantial disagreement on many of those issues. Some issues on which the country is bitterly divided should be avoided. That point may seem inconsistent with the overriding principle governing these meetings, namely that ordinary citizens, without having to seek approval of their elected officials, may gather to discuss the future of their Constitution and nation. Moreover, the principles of free speech would suggest that all subjects be on the table for consideration. Nevertheless, some issues such as abortion — which a quarter of a century after *Roe v. Wade* continues to divide the nation, and about which each side feels great passion, and where there is no clear basis for compromise — cannot be resolved by a constitutional amendment. There is not nearly enough consensus in the country to lead to the adoption of an amendment either to extend or restrict the right to abortion. Trying to resolve such a contentious issue may lead to prolonged and ultimately fruitless debates that prevent the district/county meetings and state conventions from considering amendments on which there is sufficient agreement.

The district/county meeting would obviously not attract many people if its sole purpose is to choose delegates to the state convention. There must be the opportunity for a wide-ranging discussion of what sections of the Constitution need to be changed, and some consideration of how those changes would be addressed by constitutional amendments. There is, however, a risk that the meeting will become stalemated over language for proposed amendments even though it has been strongly suggested here that the writing of them be avoided. If the meeting adjourns before the delegates to the state convention have been selected, the process itself will be severely hampered. Even if there is not much agreement on the substantive issues, those attending the meeting must select state convention delegates from among those who heard the discussion at the first meeting, and the selected delegates must make a reasonable effort to convey to fellow delegates at the state capital the tone and substance of the discussion at the local level.

It is important that only those who attend the district/county meeting be eligible for selection to the state convention. That would also mean that only those who attended the first meeting *and* the statewide meeting could be considered for the national preconvention. Political activists and officeholders may take notice of the district/county meeting only after it has taken place, especially if there was little news coverage in advance. Once those individuals realize that the state convention is going to be held, they may want to serve as delegates, and may try to use their political clout to displace ordinary citizens who were selected for the statewide meeting, but lack political influence. At the district/county meeting, everyone has a chance to be chosen to attend the next stage in the process. If elected officials or party officials attend the initial meeting, it may be tempting to pick them because of the attention and legitimacy their participation would generate. But it is up to the attendees at the district/county meeting to decide who will represent them at the state convention. Those who did not bother to attend the first meeting, but who later claim great interest in the effort to amend the Constitution, should not be able to use political influence to seek appointment to the state convention at the expense of a person who cared enough about the Constitution and the future of the country to go to the first meeting.

Records of the district/county meeting

The chairperson of the meeting should solicit discussion of the current constitutional or policy problems that are to be addressed by the proposed constitutional amendments. They should be listed on a large blackboard or overhead projector. The next step is to identify those sections of the Constitution most relevant to those issues. The resource materials, such as books and Web sites, as well as the presentation by the constitutional law expert, will provide assistance as the group learns how those constitutional provisions have been interpreted in the past. That task will not be easy because many sections of the Constitution are not self-explanatory. Only by understanding how courts have interpreted those provisions can one fully appreciate the complexity of many of the phrases in the Constitution. An example is campaign finance reform. The language of the First Amendment does not reveal why the Supreme Court found that limits on federal campaign expenditures are unconstitutional, while contributions to candidates can be restricted. One must understand *Buckley v. Valeo* — a long, complicated opinion — before proposing a constitutional amendment to reverse that troublesome decision. Even when a section of the Constitution appears to be directly relevant to issues under discussion at the district/county meeting, there will often be conflicting and inconsistent judicial interpretations of that provision which prevent even the most accomplished legal scholar from stating definitively what that section of the Constitution means. Finally, the chairperson should identify the specific goals that constitutional amendments — which are eventually proposed by an actual Article V convention — should accomplish.

The more comprehensive the records of the meeting, the better. It will be difficult to know in advance how important those documents will become during later stages of the constitutional convention process. Courts may want to examine them in canvassing the records of the local, statewide, and national meetings and conventions. People of other states who have not yet held their district/county meeting may find it helpful to know how their fellow citizens conducted themselves at such a meeting and what was accomplished. The Web site will be the repository of a grass-roots effort to change the direction of the nation, and the progress of such an effort can be followed around the country — or even in other nations — in a way that previous communication technology would not have permitted.

The selection of the delegates to the state convention

After the group has finished its initial task of identifying those sections of the Constitution that must be changed, and debating how to accomplish such change, the chairperson should entertain nominations for delegates to the state convention. Individuals can nominate themselves. Selecting the right people to attend the statewide meeting is probably as important as the discussion of the constitutional amendments at the district/county meeting. If articulate and thoughtful individuals are chosen, the state convention could attract much attention and significantly advance efforts to persuade state legislatures to petition Congress to call a second constitutional convention. If, on the other hand, the delegates to the state convention lack those and other important attributes, the meeting is likely to be ridiculed as a useless exercise.

Each nominee should be given 10 minutes to explain why he or she should be considered as a delegate to the state convention. It is important that the selection of delegates take place after the group's debate over what sections of the Constitution need to be amended because delegate candidates must comment on the discussion they heard and the extent to which they share the group's attitude toward constitutional change.

Delegates to the state convention will also be charged with the important task of selecting those who will attend the preconvention in Washington, D.C. Candidates wanting to be delegates to the state convention should talk about what characteristics they would look for in national delegates. Because all those attending the statewide conventions would likely want to be considered for the national gathering, it would not be surprising if the characteristics and background identified as important by the candidates for delegate to the state convention mirrored their own qualifications.

If delegates are selected who will have a difficult time attending the state convention because of lack of money, the group should make an effort to raise funds to help pay the cost of travel to the state convention for the delegates chosen. No one should be prevented from participating for lack of financial resources. Depending on the size of the state and the distance between the delegate's home and the state capital, it probably would cost at least a few hundred dollars for someone to attend a convention lasting two or three days in the state capital.

The State Convention

In an ideal world, the district/county meetings would all take place on the same Saturday. Considering what a mammoth task it is to organize such meetings all over a state, however, it is unlikely that the initial meetings will all be held on the same day. Nevertheless, an effort should be made to hold the convention in the state capital no later than 30–60 days after the district/county meetings have been completed.

The agenda for the state convention will motivate, inspire, and alarm large numbers of people, including some who probably are not politically active. Some people may want to attend as a spectator because of concern about fellow citizens trying to tamper with the revered Constitution, and those visitors may want to make sure that delegates hear their views before deciding what to do. Some will be so alarmed by such a gathering that they will make an effort to stop the statewide convention from doing anything, arguing that fundamental rights would be jeopardized by the organizing of a second constitutional convention. Others will see the state convention as an outlet for their frustration about politics and elected officials, and will eagerly join the debates over how best to bring about campaign reform and other changes. Still others will enjoy the hoopla and drama of an event that could potentially be a media spectacle, attracting the attention of major news organizations.

The delegates will have two major responsibilities. First, they must create a document that identifies those sections of the Constitution most in need of revision, and agree to general language that will likely bring about the changes they believe are necessary. And second, they must select the two individuals who will represent the state at the national preconvention to be held in Washington, D.C. It is likely that most of those attending the statewide meeting will want to be considered as delegates to the national preconvention.

Accomplishing those tasks will be extremely difficult. Fifty or so individuals from around the state, most of whom do not know each other and who may represent ideologies across the spectrum, must develop a consensus on what sections of the Constitution are most in need of modification and what amendments would bring about those changes.

If any 50 people met for two days in their state capital and accomplished those two goals, it would be a remarkable event. Such a feat would silence critics who will argue that the American people on their own are incapable of conducting a civilized dialogue on such a controversial matter as amending their Constitution. More importantly, it will also mean that a national preconvention is likely to be held.

Preparation for the state convention

There will be little time at the state convention for detailed discussion of constitutional problems and proposed amendments. If, for example, 50 delegates attend the state convention and each one talked for ten minutes, it would take more than eight hours for everyone to be heard. To allow maximum time for substantive discussion, the work of the district/county meetings must be available to the statewide delegates prior to the convention. That will give the statewide convention a starting point based on the discussions held and the decisions made at the previous stage.

Such communication can be facilitated through the national Web site or statewide Web page. Each district/county meeting will have prepared a document that describes the sections of the Constitution that the attendees believe are most in need of revision and general suggestions on how to make those changes. Prior to the statewide convention, each district or county chairperson will have selected someone who will be responsible for sending the documents to a central location where they can be scanned and placed on the Web site. The statewide delegates will have the opportunity to read the documents prepared not only by district/county meetings in their state, but by those in other states as well. If practical considerations prevent the loading of those documents onto the Web site, the documents created by the district/county meetings can still be mailed to the statewide delegates prior to the convention.

The state convention begins

On the first day of the state convention, which will probably last two to three days, delegates must select a convention chair and a secretary who will take minutes and keep other records of the convention. The convention should also formally adopt *Robert's Rules of Order*. Not every delegate will be able to speak at length on the issues before the convention, and the chairperson must be aggressive in limiting comments to the essential issues before the body. At the same time, it is important for delegates to have the opportunity to describe the debate at the district/county meetings and to relay the sentiments of those who attended the initial meetings that led to the statewide convention.

The convention will have to decide how much time should be devoted to hearing presentations from experts who will be on hand to help throughout its deliberations. Some delegates will have come from district/county meetings where university professors or lawyers helped provide an overview of the major provisions of the Constitution. All delegates should have read as much as they can about constitutional law between the time they were selected by the initial meeting and the statewide convention. There will not be enough time at the meeting in the state capital for long presentations on the Constitution by experts. It may be best if the experts are available to consult with the delegates as they complete their work over the weekend, but they should not make formal presentations.

Once subject areas of the Constitution to be considered for amendment are designated, they should be divided into several sections with each being assigned to a committee of three to six delegates. The delegates on the same committee should be from different areas of the state. The committees, which will probably need at least several hours to complete their work, will develop a portion of what will be the overall record of the state convention. Each committee will specifically list the problems that need to be addressed by amendment, the relevant section of the Constitution, and the goals any proposed amendments would seek to accomplish. Computers will aid significantly in the process of combining the work of the various committees.

There are likely to be some issues on which there is immediate agreement, while on others there will be no consensus, and thus nothing on that issue will be in the committee's report beyond noting that agreement could not be reached. The committees and eventually the entire state convention should not try to write the actual language of the proposed amendments. With limited time, and perhaps limited consensus, it is important for the state convention delegates to move the process along to the next phase without getting bogged down in the details of the language of the specific amendments. The state convention can venture beyond the work of the district/county meeting by actually drafting general language that should be considered by the national preconvention for inclusion in the proposed amendments, but it would be a mistake to ask the state convention to write the specific words of the proposed amendments.

The process of deliberation and compromise will be an extremely fragile one as ordinary citizens — almost every one of them doing something like this for the first time — struggle to accomplish the goals cited previously. The state convention must be able to complete its identification of the constitutional issues subject to amendment and select delegates if there is going to be a national preconvention. Without a preconvention, which would get substantial news coverage and continue the momentum begun by the two previous phases, there will be little chance that state legislators will petition Congress to request a constitutional convention.

In the afternoon of the first day, the full body should reconvene and each committee should report on its findings. The delegates will then vote to accept the recommendations of the committees, reject their suggestions, or attempt to modify them. If no agreement develops over a reasonable period of time, the convention should move on to the next committee's report. Even under the best of circumstances, the committee reports and the votes on them by the full convention will take the rest of the day.

On the second day, the delegates should put together a draft of a document that represents the consensus of the convention. The secretary or others designated by the chairperson will be responsible for completing the report of the convention, a process that may take several weeks. The report should accurately reflect the deliberations and decisions of the convention. The state convention will have adjourned before the report is completed, so there will not be a formal vote designating the report as being officially approved by the convention. But a draft report will have been reviewed by the delegates on the second day, and those responsible for preparing the final report must make a reasonable effort to accurately reflect the work of the convention in the final report.

Once the final document is prepared, it will be posted on the state and national Web sites. Those who attended the state convention will have the opportunity to add comments to the end of the report indicating where they believe it failed to accurately and fairly portray the work of the convention. The report itself, however, cannot be amended because the state convention will have adjourned. Those reading the comments on the Web site will have to decide for themselves who has the better argument or appears to remember more precisely what was said or done at the convention. But arguments over the accuracy of the final report cannot impede the progress toward a national preconvention.

By being posted on the Web site, the report will be available for anyone to see in the months before the national preconvention. The report should also be sent to news organizations within the state and region, accompanied by summaries or press releases that make it easy for busy reporters to do stories on the work of the state convention. Creating the report of the convention, placing it on the Web site, and distributing it to news organizations and other interested parties, will obviously cost money. Financial support from foundations, public interest groups, or private individuals will have to be raised to ensure the distribution of the report which is necessary to help create and maintain the momentum that will lead to a closely watched, well-covered, and lively national preconvention. Although the report of the state conventions will be available on the Web site and elsewhere, the delegates to the national preconvention should take copies of the report with them to Washington, D.C.

Debating the Constitution

Because time is limited, it is important for delegates at the statewide convention to have some document on which to base the initial discussion. Delegates cannot simply walk into a meeting room in their state capital and begin from scratch. There will have to be some plan. They could begin with the amendments listed in the final section of this book, remembering that their role is to identify the sections of the Constitution most in need of amendment, and adopting general language suggesting how those changes could be implemented, but not trying to write the amendments. If delegates have read some of the recommended books and other materials, they may have thought enough about the issues to have developed a list of their own. It would be useful for such materials to be distributed to the delegates before the convention.

James Madison and his fellow delegates from Virginia understood how important it is to begin with a plan. In May of 1787, Madison, Governor Edmund Randolph, and other members of the Virginia delegation arrived in Philadelphia a week before the Convention was to begin. By the time the other delegates arrived and a quorum was in place, the delegates had before them what became known as the "Virginia Plan," which formed the basis on which the debate was centered during much of the Convention. Among the plan's most important contributions was to lead the delegates to the conclusion that it would not be sufficient to merely revise the Articles of Confederation. Many of the major provisions of the Virginia Plan were eventually included in the final version of the Constitution.

It would be arrogant for modern authors to suggest that their review of the Constitution and recommendations of appropriate amendments is comparable to the Virginia Plan introduced at the beginning of the Constitutional Convention, and that suggestion is not being made here. One's passion for the subject and earnest belief that a second constitutional convention should be convened are no substitutes for the brilliant mind and remarkable accomplishments of James Madison. But if this book merely identified the methods by which a second convention could be convened and included no suggestions for the amendments that such a convention should produce, it would have missed an opportunity to persuade readers that serious defects in the Constitution need to be corrected and that the extraordinary effort involved in convening a second convention is worthwhile.

Selection of delegates to the national preconvention in Washington, D.C.

No matter how populous the state, each should send only two delegates to the national preconvention. The largest states would understandably argue that they are unfairly underrepresented, and some may refuse to participate. The same argument can be made about the U.S. Senate. But unlike Congress, there is no "House" in the constitutional convention that can represent the states by population.

There are several reasons why each state can send only two delegates. First and foremost, it is unwieldy to have more than 100 delegates attend a convention where so much needs to be accomplished in such a short time. Any more than 100 delegates would make a difficult task all but impossible. The preconvention may take several weeks, and if there were more than 100 delegates, their work could take months or, what is more likely, never be finished. Another reason to limit each delegation to two members is that it will be costly for delegates to attend the preconvention. If individuals of modest means are selected by their state conventions, there will need to be a fund-raising effort to provide enough money for them to travel to Washington and stay in a hotel for what may be several weeks. Although the money could come from foundations or other nonprofit organizations within the state, funds for the delegates to attend the preconvention should not come from the state's taxpayers or special interests such as political action committees. It is important that the source of the funding reflect the fact that the delegates are representing the citizens of the state.

Those selected to attend the preconvention must have been delegates to the statewide convention and have been chosen by the delegates to that convention to go to Washington. Limiting the national delegates to the pool of statewide delegates is something about which rational people could disagree. A prominent individual — even one who would enhance the visibility of the national convention and who would bring good ideas and a cooperative disposition to the assembly — cannot be selected if that person did not attend a district/county meeting, and later, a state convention. The main reason for requiring service in the two previous meetings is to encourage participation from the earliest stages by those people who would make good delegates to the national convention. If those delegates can only be selected from among the members of the state convention, and delegates to the state convention are chosen from among those who attended the district/county meeting, people with a strong background and appropriate temperament will have to be involved from the first stages. If they are well-known, their participation in the district/county meeting and state convention will enhance the news coverage and interest in those gatherings.

Such a rule also encourages attendance at the statewide convention because the delegates know that two of the people who attend that meeting in the state capital will be chosen to go on to the next phase. Requiring those who want to be delegates to the national convention to attend the previous meetings is also consistent with the democratic principle that anyone can participate. Individuals do not have to be prominent in their communities or hold public office to convince their fellow citizens that they would do a good job representing them at the subsequent conventions. Considering the resentment some people have for elected officials, those attending the district/county meeting and state convention would probably appreciate the opportunity to see someone other than the usual officeholder or political activist represent them.

The state convention itself can develop rules by which it selects the delegates to the D.C. convention. Nominations will be accepted, then all candidates should be given time to describe their background and experience. Because the delegates will be selected toward the end of the second day, the nominees should describe their view of how the discussion should proceed about proposed changes to the Constitution.

All voting should be done by secret ballot. Depending on how many delegates want to be considered for the national convention, there may need to be several ballots. If a large number of candidates are running, the initial speeches should be limited to a few minutes and cover background and experience. Those who make it to a shorter list after the first vote, perhaps ten delegates, can then address the convention on such issues as their views of the proposed changes to the Constitution and how they would seek to implement those views at the national convention. The list of ten should be narrowed to the top four vote-getters in a second ballot. The four finalists, for a fixed period of time, will then answer questions posed by the delegates. Finally, the four should stand for election. The two individuals who receive the most votes shall be the delegates, while the person in third place will be the alternate to the delegate receiving the most votes, and the person in last place will be the alternate for the other delegate. The alternates can attend the national convention and consult with the state's two delegates, but they may not directly participate in the convention's activities. The state convention delegates should only select individuals who they are confident will attend the national convention.

The National Preconvention

It would be ideal if all state conventions could be held within a reasonably short time span, such as in the same month. But states are fiercely independent and it is likely to be difficult to persuade 50 different states to hold their district/county meetings, or the statewide conventions, at around the same time.

The national convention should not be delayed while the country waits for the final states to organize their conventions. After a reasonable period of time — perhaps three months after the majority of states have finished their state conventions — the national convention should convene in Washington, D.C.

Some will oppose holding the convention in Washington on both practical and symbolic grounds. The nation's capital is not centrally located, and thus it is more expensive for delegates to come from the Western sections of the country. There is a possibility, or it may be perceived as such by others, that the national preconvention would be dominated by Eastern interests — and especially powerful interests in Washington, D.C. — because fewer delegates from the Midwest and West may make the trip. Some people may argue that because the federal government is the source of many of the problems that citizens are trying to correct by working for a constitutional convention, it is inappropriate to hold it in that location. A more neutral location in the center of the country, it could be argued, would be easier to travel to and would show the nation's elected officials and lobbyists that there are people beyond the Beltway who want to shape the direction of the country.

Despite such arguments, it is necessary to hold the convention in Washington for several reasons. First, the preconvention must be the subject of massive media coverage if state legislators are to feel the pressure to petition Congress to call a constitutional convention under Article V.

Unless the nation is able to follow closely the deliberations and accomplishments of the preconvention, and people become both interested in and alarmed by its activities, there will not be sufficient momentum leading to efforts to persuade state legislatures to petition Congress for a second convention, or efforts to defeat state legislators who refuse to approve such petitions. News organizations have large staffs and substantial technical capabilities already based in Washington. It would be much less expensive for them to cover the convention there, rather than move the necessary personnel and equipment to a more central location.

Second, it is possible that prominent political figures will lend their support to the goals of the preconvention. By having it in Washington, D.C., those individuals may find it more convenient to appear at the preconvention than they would if it was halfway across the country.

And third, adding additional amendments to the U.S. Constitution is a serious and complicated undertaking. It should stimulate a national debate that requires citizens of this country to think about their future and the future of the Constitution. Washington, D.C. is the symbolic as well as the actual capital of the nation. It is appropriate that a meeting to help determine the country's future be held there.

After the delegates arrive

The 100 delegates and 100 alternates to the national preconvention should be prepared for a long stay as their work may take several weeks. The group will not be writing the Constitution from scratch — a task that took the delegates to the Philadelphia convention about four months — but will instead be considering probably fewer than ten amendments. Unlike the delegates in 1787, who often returned home during the Convention to tend to personal business and to consult with political figures, the delegates to the preconvention should stay in Washington until their work is finished. If the convention looks like it will last more than several weeks, a recess as long as a few days or a week may be appropriate, but the momentum of the convention should not be disrupted for long.

Paying for the convention

The convention will be expensive. Private or foundation sources should have been provided to those delegates who needed financial help to attend. But that will only help defray the costs of travel, hotel, and meal expenses. Conducting the convention itself will be very costly.

The appropriate facility will have to be found. Although there will only be 100 delegates on the "floor" of the convention, there may be several hundred news people who want to cover it. Each news organization should be charged a reasonable fee for press facilities provided for them — as is a common practice — and for access to the convention, with that money being used to defray expenses.

It is not unrealistic to believe that wealthy individuals, or well-endowed foundations, will underwrite the costs of the convention. Some foundations may well see the cost of such a convention, perhaps $100,000 or more, as a small price to raise the visibility of the foundation and to sponsor a forum that is unprecedented in American history.

Whether the convention should be funded in part by corporate money raises more complicated issues. It clearly commercializes and cheapens the convention if the lunch on a given day is sponsored by a major corporation or lobbying organization, which prominently features signs around the banquet room and includes handouts on every table. The convention should probably be paid for only by contributions from individuals or foundations that are not seeking anything except enhanced visibility, and supplemented by fees paid by news organizations. The convention organizers should probably not accept corporate money at the same time they are recommending changes to stop abuses of the campaign finance system.

The work of the preconvention

The challenges facing this gathering of citizens are formidable. The delegates must, in a period of a week or two, arrive at a consensus as to what sections of the Constitution need to be amended, and they must lay the groundwork for the delegates to the Article V convention who will propose specific constitutional amendments to be submitted to the states for ratification.

It could be argued that the best that one could hope for in a meeting of 100 individuals from all around the country would be general agreement on what provisions of the Constitution need to be changed. Expecting such an assembly to take the additional step of developing general or specific language as to how those concerns should be addressed is probably unrealistic.

The preconvention, of course, will be conducted without the benefit of detailed rules provided by political parties or statutes. It will also be the last stage in the process where Congress does not control the proceedings. Because the preconvention is a gathering of citizens outside the formal institutions of government, Congress cannot — even if it wanted to — establish rules and policies that the preconvention must follow. Those attending the convention will determine how the group will conduct its business.

After the preconvention has ended, an effort must be undertaken to convince state legislatures to formally petition Congress to hold an Article V convention. If the number of states requesting such a convention begins to approach two-thirds, Congress will almost certainly enact legislation that governs every aspect of the convention from selection of delegates to the process by which proposed amendments are discussed and approved. That the preconvention does not have to follow procedures established by Congress or other governmental bodies may be a blessing or a curse. If the preconvention is unable to organize or discipline itself, and the gathering is little more than endless debate and argument, punctuated by occasional shouting matches and rowdy demonstrations, little of value will have been produced that could be brought to state legislators. If that happens, many will argue that the meeting was a waste of time, if not dangerous to the country's political institutions. In such a scenario, it could be argued that if there had been binding rules and procedures established by a governmental body that the delegates had to follow, the delegates to the preconvention may have been able to complete their work.

On the other hand, the preconvention will have the opportunity, if it can make the best use of it, to engage in a dialogue about the future of the country that is in the best tradition of a self-governing democracy. A group of citizens will be able to gather in their nation's capital to discuss and propose changes to the Constitution without having to obtain their government's permission and without limiting themselves to topics approved by Congress or other governmental entities. They will serve as a symbolic, if not literal, reminder that the people are sovereign in this nation and that government officials serve as their agents. In some respects the gathering of the preconvention will be less "extra-legal" than the Philadelphia Convention of 1787, which was organized for the purpose of revising the Articles of Confederation but instead created a new Constitution. The preconvention has no such restrictive mandate, and is, in fact, exercising the right of assembly and the right to petition the government that are clearly protected by the First Amendment and should be regularly exercised by citizens. It can be further argued that in organizing the preconvention with the goal of submitting proposals for amendments to state legislatures, delegates are acting within the general precepts of Article V.

The more limited role of the preconvention — identifying those sections of the Constitution in need of revision, and writing general petition language that can be submitted to state legislatures — may be all that is possible. Regardless of how detailed the proposals are that emerge from the preconvention, it is essential that the delegates agree on *identical* language for the petitions that state legislatures will use to ask Congress to convene an Article V convention. Congress will strongly resist calling such a convention, and it will especially dislike proposals for constitutional amendments that alter the way members of Congress are elected and how long they can serve. There will undoubtedly be a court challenge brought by members of Congress or political activists that may delay the meeting of a convention for some time. One of the grounds that Congress has used in the past to resist calling a convention is that the petitions do not all request that the same subject area or amendment be addressed. If states do not submit identical petitions, Congress will try to persuade the courts to block an Article V convention by arguing that the constitutional requirement that two-thirds of states request a convention will not have been satisfied. There is a greater likelihood that the courts will order Congress to hold a convention if the states' petitions use the same language.

Writing text for the petitions that can be taken home to legislatures in every state is, therefore, the most important task of the preconvention. Convincing state legislatures around the country to forward those petitions without alteration will require a nationwide effort — facilitated by new communication technology — that would have been nearly impossible in the pre-Internet days.

The petitions

Article V requires that states petition Congress to call a constitutional convention. The Framers apparently never discussed what forms the petitions must take, and so not surprisingly, the hundreds of petitions requesting a convention throughout our history have varied widely. Some called specifically for a constitutional convention to consider certain amendments, while others made more general statements about defects in the Constitution without requesting a convention or indicating what type of amendment should be considered to address the problem.

In the early 1960s, the Supreme Court handed down a series of landmark decisions declaring malapportioned state legislative and congressional districts to be unconstitutional. Beginning with *Baker v. Carr* in 1962 (dealing with state legislative districts), and continuing with *Wesberry v. Sanders* in 1964 (involving congressional districts), and *Reynolds v. Sims* in 1964 (applying the 14th Amendment's equal protection clause to legislative reapportionment), the Court developed a strong commitment to the principle of "one person, one vote." Not surprisingly, many state legislators who benefited from the malapportioned districts that heavily favored rural over urban interests were up in arms over the Court's decisions. Predictably, the legislators argued that the federal government was impermissibly intruding into state affairs in clear violation of the Constitution. But their real objection was that reapportioning state legislatures and congressional districts to more accurately reflect the populations within them would likely mean the loss of their previously safe seats.

After the reapportionment decisions, many states demanded that Congress propose a constitutional amendment to reverse the Supreme Court's rulings. In August 1965, the Senate responded to those demands by voting on a long-debated constitutional amendment introduced by Senate Republican minority leader Everett Dirksen of Illinois. Although the Senate approved the amendment 57 to 39, it failed to win the two-thirds vote required for passage. Dirksen did not give up and persuaded the Senate to reconsider on April 20, 1966. His proposed amendment suffered the same fate, being approved by a vote of only 55 to 38, well short of the two-thirds threshold.

Dirksen had been encouraged by efforts of the Council of State Governments, which had attempted to persuade Congress to reverse *Baker v. Carr* since 1963. He asked every state legislature that had not already done so to adopt a resolution calling for a constitutional convention. Over the next few years, although it was not widely known by the public, state legislatures began approving petitions and forwarding them to Congress. At times it appeared that Congress did not know what to do with the petitions. They were often published in the *Congressional Record*, filed with the House and Senate judiciary committees, and then largely ignored. The *New York Times*, in a March 1967, front-page article, startled the nation by reporting that with the recent approval of petitions in four states, 32 states had requested a constitutional convention to reverse the apportionment decisions, only two short of the 34 required.

There is much reason to doubt that the campaign to call a convention was "nearing success" as indicated by the *New York Times*. Five petitions asked for something other than the Dirksen amendment, and two states never officially sent their petitions to Congress. Senator William Proxmire (D-WI) argued that since 26 of the 32 petitions came from malapportioned state legislatures, their petitions were invalid. Senator Joseph Tydings (D-MD) observed that the petitions had not been submitted simultaneously and they requested different types of amendments. Senator Dirksen responded that all the petitions had to do was to call for the convening of a constitutional convention to propose amendments to deal with the apportionment of state legislatures. They did not have to be identical or submitted simultaneously, according to Dirksen.

Senator Sam Ervin (D-NC), considered by his colleagues to be extremely knowledgeable about constitutional issues, was alarmed over the possibility of a convention being called that would not limit itself to dealing with the apportionment decisions. In August 1967, he introduced the Federal Constitutional Convention Act, which among other things, required that two-thirds of the states had to submit uniform petitions within a four-year period before Congress had to call a constitutional convention. Among the most important provisions of the bill was the requirement that the constitutional convention could not propose amendments that differed significantly from those stated in the call for the convention. It also required that the state petitions deal with the same subject in order to be counted among the two-thirds. The Ervin bill was never brought to a vote in the Senate. Although he introduced later versions that won Senate approval, they eventually died in the House Judiciary Committee.

In 1985, Senators Orrin Hatch (R-UT), Strom Thurmond (R-SC), and Dennis DeConcini (D-AZ), introduced a bill to establish procedures for a constitutional convention. The bill was inspired by efforts on the part of state legislatures to petition Congress to call a constitutional convention to consider a balanced budget amendment. In March 1983, Missouri became the 32nd state to request a convention for the purpose of proposing such an amendment, two short of the number needed. Although several states came close to approving such petitions, no more than 32 states have filed them with Congress. Section 2(a) of the Hatch-Thurmond-DeConcini bill provided in part that the "legislature of the state . . . shall adopt a resolution . . . stating in substance, that the legislature requests the calling of a convention for the purpose of proposing one or more specific amendments to the Constitution . . . and stating the subject matter of the amendment or amendments to be proposed." Although approved by the Senate Judiciary Committee, the bill never made it to the Senate floor.

Most of the amendments that have been submitted to Congress over the years have dealt with a single subject area. That will not be the situation when the preconvention proposed in this book meets in Washington. The preconvention will recommend perhaps a dozen or more subject areas for amendments in petitions to state legislatures with the hope that they will be forwarded to Congress in the form of a call for a convention. Because there will be only one Article V convention, state legislatures cannot request that a convention be called on each subject. Instead, states must request that Congress call a single convention to consider multiple issues.

The debate over the petitions will be an important part of the records of the preconvention that will likely be considered by the courts that hear the cases challenging the constitutionality of the petitions and the calls for a convention. Although the debate at the preconvention can be wide-ranging, eventually the delegates must agree on common language. The more general the language, the more likely there will be agreement. However, if the language of the proposed amendments or areas of the Constitution identified as needing revision is *too* general, the courts may conclude that the petition requirements under Article V were not satisfied.

More than 25 years ago the American Bar Association appointed a committee to study the issues raised by an Article V constitutional convention. The "Special Constitutional Convention Study Committee," which issued its report in 1973, did not think it likely that a sufficient number of states would petition Congress to hold a convention, and that therefore, one would not be convened. But the committee did conclude that Congress should not resist calling a convention because the petitions coming from the state legislatures were not identical. The committee stated that such standards "would be improper since they would tend to make resort to the convention process exceedingly difficult in view of the problems that would be encountered in obtaining identically worded applications from thirty-four states." The ABA committee further cautioned Congress against exercising "a policy-making role in determining whether or not to call a convention," suggesting that once a sufficient number of petitions are received, Congress should call a convention even if it opposed such an idea.

On the question of what form the petitions must take, the ABA committee concluded that at a minimum, the petition "must contain a request to Congress to call a national convention that would have the authority to propose an amendment to the Constitution." An application that "simply expressed a state's opinion on a given problem or requested Congress itself to propose an amendment would not be sufficient for purposes under Article V." On the other hand, the petitions cannot overly restrict the convention's deliberative function by calling for an assembly that would only be able to vote yes or no on an amendment provided by the states. The ABA committee concluded that the convention must have the discretion to evaluate amendment proposals and to adopt language it deems appropriate for submission to the states.

Although the ABA special committee found that it would be improper for states to attempt to restrict the ability of a convention to debate and determine the exact wording of an amendment, it concluded that the states may propose specific language for the amendment because the convention itself would still be free to decide on its final form. The committee reiterated in this context that the petitions do not have to be identical and do not have to deal with a single subject matter.

States seeking the calling of a convention will thus have a difficult balancing act to perform. If the petitions are too general, Congress will seize upon that characteristic to argue that the requirements under Article

V have not been met and no convention need be called. If the petitions are too specific — in that they not only identify the sections of the Constitution in need of repair, but demand specific language for the proposed amendment — Congress will claim that the deliberative function of the convention that is contemplated by Article V will have been abrogated and thus no convention can be held. These and other issues that the federal courts will have to eventually sort out will be further complicated by whatever legislation Congress passes outlining the procedures for the convention as the number of petitions calling for such a gathering begins to approach 34.

The timing of the petitions

The prospect of an Article V convention has generated much scholarly interest over the years. More than half a century ago, law professor Lester Orfield recognized the difficulty of using the petition process to persuade Congress to call a convention. Orfield considered whether Congress could be forced by the courts to call a convention if it refused to do so. Unlike some who have argued that the petitions must be identical, Orfield instead maintained that even if the petitions do not call for the same amendments, Congress must call a convention anyway because a sufficient number of states have indicated a need for constitutional change. Rather than be concerned about the states' request for different amendments, Orfield argued that "the better view would seem to be that the ground of the applications would be immaterial, and that a demand by two-thirds of the states would conclusively show a widespread desire for constitutional changes." Congress has never adopted the approach of accepting petitions regardless of their subject matter. It is unlikely that either Congress or the courts would do so today.

Orfield also raised the important issue of when the petitions have to be forwarded to Congress to count toward the two-thirds total. He argued that the petitions must be relatively simultaneous, adding that it would be unreasonable for a request made by one state legislature to be counted with one made many years later in determining whether a sufficient number of states had petitioned Congress. Orfield suggested that the "maximum life of a request should not be more than a generation." He also considered whether an appropriate analogy was the "length of time allowed for the ratification of amendments by the state legislatures." The problem of the timing would be largely solved if state conventions could be held within a reasonable time of each other, perhaps a few months, and the preconvention could be organized within a short time after most of the state conventions were over. Then an organized effort to persuade state legislatures to submit petitions to Congress could begin as soon as the preconvention ended. Not every state will likely send delegates to the preconvention, but efforts to persuade state legislatures to forward petitions should move forward in those states as well as the ones that were represented at the convention.

In states where legislatures meet infrequently — sometimes every other year — governors may have to call the legislature into special session if the petition for a constitutional convention is to be considered in a timely manner. Those working to convince state legislatures to petition Congress will know fairly soon whether there is any chance of success. If there is little or no interest on the part of legislators and the voters have not made a substantial effort to persuade them to take action, or in a subsequent election have not replaced those opposed to a convention with those who support it, another year or two is not likely to make much difference.

A middle ground

The last section of this book provides specific language that could be considered for new constitutional amendments. It is obvious, however, that no single person or small group will be able to write a perfect amendment that identifies a constitutional defect and is guaranteed to solve the problem. Revising the Constitution requires a national debate in which even individuals not usually involved in politics take part. The proposed language for amendments in this book is meant as a starting point to stimulate a discussion and show how complex and far-reaching the effects can be of even seemingly minor constitutional changes. Despite the specificity of language provided here, the petitions that emerge from the preconvention cannot include proposed amendments. The final wording of the amendments will be written by delegates to an Article V convention. The preconvention must be content with the more limited steps of:

• Identifying the *problems* that will be addressed by constitutional amendments. Those attending the preconvention have substantial discretion to discuss not only those issues that are fundamental or structural in nature and have traditionally been the subject of constitutional change, but also policy issues that are normally dealt with through ordinary legislative means. Some policy issues, such as campaign finance reform, cannot be solved through legislative means because of intractable shortcomings in the political system and must be included in proposed constitutional amendments.

• Identifying the specific *sections* of the Constitution that will be considered for revisions based on the discussion of the issues as described in the previous paragraph. Staying with the earlier example, campaign finance reform will require revision of Article I of the Constitution, and possibly the First Amendment. The preconvention will link the constitutional or policy issue with a specific provision in the Constitution.

• And finally, suggesting *in general terms* language that may be appropriate for the new amendments. This language will provide guidance to state legislatures when they formulate their petitions, and to the constitutional convention when it writes the words of the proposed amendments. This will be the most difficult task of the preconvention and cannot be allowed to derail the entire process. If the convention can accomplish the first two steps, and only has general discussions of the third, that would still be quite an accomplishment.

The work of the preconvention — identifying the constitutional and policy issues, specifying the sections of the Constitution that will be modified, and writing general language that will be helpful to those eventually writing the amendments — will provide a detailed and informative record that can be widely circulated and debated as the campaign to convince state legislatures to submit petitions to Congress begins. But although the more detailed record of the preconvention will be an important part of the national debate over changes to the Constitution, there must be a simple, straightforward document that can be given to state legislators, which they can use to petition Congress.

The petitions cannot be so general that they allow the delegates to an Article V convention to wander the constitutional landscape to propose amendments on almost any subject. Instead, the petitions must signal what areas of the Constitution the convention should consider modifying and what solutions it should explore that would address those issues. The petitions must provide enough information that the nation will know what the Article V convention will be debating, while at the same time allowing the convention the discretion that courts will almost certainly agree it must have under Article V.

In trying to find that balance, the preconvention should consider petitions that look like this:

1) The legislature of the state of _____, being composed of the duly elected representatives of the people thereof, formally request that the United States Congress call a constitutional convention under Article V of the United States Constitution so that the convention can consider, and in its discretion, propose an amendment or amendments modifying Article I by addressing the subject of the raising and spending of campaign money in federal elections. This petition was approved by both houses of this legislature in accordance with its established rules and procedures.

2) The legislature of _____ further formally requests that Congress call a constitutional convention under Article V of the United States Constitution to consider, and in its discretion, propose an amendment or amendments modifying the Twelfth Amendment by addressing the subject of whether the Electoral College should be modified or abolished.

3) The legislature of _____ further formally requests that Congress call a constitutional convention under Article V of the United States Constitution to consider, and in its discretion, propose an amendment or amendments modifying Article V by addressing the subject of how constitutional amendments are proposed and ratified.

Even the sample petition above may be seen as too general by federal judges who will review the cases challenging this process as inconsistent with the requirements under Article V. But demanding any more specificity would likely prevent the state convention and national preconvention from successfully completing their important tasks in the amendment process. Furthermore, when states have petitioned Congress in the past for a convention to consider such amendments as those related to apportionment of legislative districts, a balanced budget, and other proposed amendments, they have recognized that the delegates to the constitutional convention will determine the specific language of the amendments. The preconvention and those who support its work will only have to convince state legislatures to forward a similarly general petition to Congress. If anything, the preconvention may create petitions — and the records that accompany them — that are more detailed than some petitions submitted in the past by legislatures, and thus may be less vulnerable to judicial challenge.

The petitions and news coverage

As has been stressed several times, an essential element of the success of the effort to persuade Congress to call a constitutional convention will be the breadth and nature of news coverage. Those attending the congressional district/county meeting, and the delegates to the state convention and national preconvention, must shape their agenda and activities in a way that accommodates the needs of the news media. If a serious effort to amend the Constitution through this process gets underway, there will be plenty of news coverage. However, it will be much more difficult to generate interest among news organizations at the earliest stages of the process.

The challenge for those who participate in the three meetings leading to an Article V convention is to produce records of those meetings and petitions that are specific enough to interest reporters, but general enough to keep the process from being derailed by endless debate when delegates cannot agree on more detailed language. The more general the petitions as they make their way through the various stages, the less likely that they will be covered by the media. Comparing these two statements, it is easy to see which one would likely get more news coverage:

A convention should be called to consider a proposed amendment to modify the section of the Constitution related to the election of members of Congress.

A convention should be called to consider a proposed amendment to require that those seeking election to Congress raise one half of all campaign funds from their home district or state.

The latter is more easily explained in a newspaper headline or on the evening news and is more likely to be remembered by a reader or viewer. If those attending the three meetings can only agree that campaign finance reform is a worthwhile goal, as suggested by the first statement, but cannot agree on specific action as represented in the second statement, they will have missed the chance to create a better headline in the newspaper or story on television.

Despite the compelling need for media coverage, those attending the district/county meeting, and later the state convention and preconvention, must resist the temptation to write headline-grabbing specific statements that may get a lot of press but will ultimately prevent the consensus necessary to advance to the next phase. Those involved in this long process must understand and accommodate the needs of news people, but they must do so without compromising the overall goals.

This may sound more manipulative than it is or should be. The need for comprehensive news coverage must not be allowed to dictate the work and results of those attending meetings during various stages of the process. It is easy to understand how delegates could get carried away as they try desperately to get news organizations to write stories and do broadcast news reports about their activities. Delegates should not, however, decide how the Constitution should be amended based on what language would result in the most headlines. On the other hand, those responsible for moving the process through the various stages must recognize that print and broadcast reporters and editors have certain substantive interests and technical needs, and they must be accommodated if there is going to be enough media attention, especially in the earliest stages.

To those attending the meetings and the reporters who are asked to cover them, the idea of persuading Congress through state legislatures to hold the first Article V convention in the nation's history will seem like a difficult, if not impossible goal, a long way down a difficult road. The process followed must overcome the natural reaction of many reporters that this idea is far-fetched, and that there are more important stories to cover.

After the Preconvention

Much of the most difficult work will come after the preconvention has ended. If there is a petition endorsed by a majority of delegates that identifies problems that must be addressed by a constitutional convention, those petitions must be forwarded to every state legislator in the country. A grass-roots, well-organized campaign to convince those legislators to approve petitions to Congress must be undertaken.

Delegates to the preconvention will have to play a leadership role in motivating their fellow citizens to persuade state legislators to petition Congress to hold a convention. If the past is any indication, getting legislators to take such petitions seriously will be a challenge. Even when states have approved petitions in the past — and hundreds have been forwarded to Congress throughout our history — many state legislators have given them scant attention and have often treated them haphazardly.

In 1979, the public interest organization Common Cause analyzed petitions forwarded to Congress by state legislatures seeking a constitutional convention to propose an amendment mandating a balanced budget. Its report stated that "most of the calls for a constitutional convention have passed in legislatures without hearings at which the public could testify and sometimes without even being referred to committees." It further noted that out of the first 21 state petitions for a balanced budget amendment, "in only six states were committee reports issued explaining the proposed action; hearings where the public was allowed to testify were held in only six legislatures; in two states no committees considered the petitions before they were passed by the two bodies of the legislature."

The report also noted that petition resolutions are sometimes prepared by individuals or groups outside the legislature with a strong interest in the issues raised by the petition. One such group, the National Taxpayers Union, prepared a petition on the balanced budget amendment that was approved by several legislatures with little, if any, debate. In the state of Maryland, for example, the petition asking Congress to call a convention to deal with the reapportionment of state legislatures was apparently slipped into a bill — with almost no one watching — that became law. Although it was eventually discovered, the legislative session ended before the petition amendment in the law could be repealed.

In contrast to the superficial treatment of petitions by some state legislatures was California's experience with the balanced budget amendment. Governor Jerry Brown, in his second inaugural address in 1979, called on the state legislature to add California to the growing list — numbering around 30 — of those states requesting a convention. The state legislature's Ways and Means Committee held extensive hearings on the amendment and convention process, the first state legislative body to do so. After testimony from 15 witnesses, including Governor Brown, Senator Sam Ervin, and leading constitutional scholars such as Laurence Tribe and Charles Black, the panel rejected the application for a petition.

As opposition to holding a convention mounted nationwide, President Jimmy Carter appointed a nine-member White House task force to counter the drive in the state legislatures to approve petitions. Members of Congress also took a closer look at the petitions. Eventually, Senators Birch Bayh (D-IN) and Alan Cranston (D-CA) announced that only 14 to 16 petitions were "in good order." The rest were either out of date or improperly required specific language for the proposed amendment, while others suffered from such defects as having not been signed by the proper state official. The effort to reach the required 34 states eventually stalled, despite strong support for a balanced budget amendment on the part of the public and Carter's successor, President Ronald Reagan. Reagan threatened to begin a campaign to persuade two more states to file petitions for a convention if Congress did not propose a balanced budget amendment. But even that threat did not convince either the final two states to approve petitions or Congress to propose a constitutional amendment.

The campaigns in the states

A national preconvention will generate a torrent of media coverage. It will have been the first time in our history that citizens from all around the nation gathered for the specific purpose of discussing amendments to the Constitution, and wrote petitions that could be presented to state legislatures so they could request Congress to call an Article V convention. With all of the media attention, including a fair amount of highly visible commentary by political pundits, those who try to persuade state legislators to approve petitions to Congress will not have to start from scratch by explaining what they are seeking. Many state legislators will be familiar with the proposed petitions and will probably understand the serious nature of the issues at stake.

Despite the fact that state legislators enjoy many of the advantages of incumbency of their congressional counterparts, including easy access to campaign contributions from organized interests and a high rate of reelection, they often come from small enough districts in terms of population that energetic challengers have a legitimate chance of winning. A candidate who favors petitioning Congress to call a constitutional convention may have a real shot at capturing a state legislative seat where the same person would be hopelessly outspent if running for Congress against an incumbent.

The number of legislators per population varies widely. In New Hampshire, for example, where there are the fewest citizens per legislator, there are 369 state legislators for every million residents. That means that each of the 400 members of the New Hampshire House has about 2,800 residents in a district. In California, where there are the most residents per legislator, there are four legislators for every million people; thus each of the 80 House members has about 375,000 residents in a district. The average for the nation is 28 legislators per million population. If each of those 28 legislators represented distinct districts, there would be a little over 35,000 residents per legislative district. Based on just the numbers, and not on local political characteristics, it is probably easier to defeat an incumbent in New Hampshire than California because a challenger would be able to shake the hand and talk to almost every voter in the district. In California, the challenger would have a difficult time raising enough money to buy media time to overcome the incumbent's name recognition.

The overall numbers do not, however, tell the whole story. In many states, House and Senate members represent the same district; thus the population per district is much higher than it would be if representatives and senators were selected from different areas. In the Washington State legislature, for example, the two House members and one senator represent the same district with an average of about 110,000 residents. If each representative and senator came from distinct districts, there would be about a third of that number of constituents in each district. A challenger can have direct contact with a substantial percentage of potential voters in a district with only 30,000 residents. A far smaller percentage can be contacted in a district with over 100,000 people. These figures contrast with congressional districts which, it is estimated, will average about 632,000 residents by the year 2000.

In some states, there is a high turnover rate among state legislators due to either retirements or incumbents being defeated for reelection. *Congressional Quarterly* analyzed the results of state legislative elections in 1995 and 1996 and found that Maine had the largest percentage of new legislators (42 percent), followed by California (40 percent), South Dakota (36 percent), Arizona (34 percent), and Oregon (32 percent).

Some states had high rates, such as California, because of term-limits laws and not because incumbents were defeated. Among the states with the lowest percentage of new legislators were Alabama (0 percent), Maryland (0 percent), Delaware (6 percent), Connecticut (11 percent), and Wisconsin (11 percent). The average for all 50 states was 20 percent.

Many voters do not know the name of their state representative or state senator, and even if they do, they probably know little about their voting record. State legislators often do not enjoy the widespread name recognition that comes from television advertising, an important factor that helps incumbents in congressional races to overpower challengers who can afford few, if any, commercials. Much of the money a state legislator would spend on television would be wasted because the ad would be seen by so many viewers who live outside the district. Therefore, a challenger for a state legislative seat who knocks on the doors of those with a record of voting regularly and who carefully targets households for direct mail may be able to defeat an incumbent who has been in office many years.

Concerted efforts will be needed to convince recalcitrant state legislators that if they do not join the push for a constitutional convention, they will face defeat at the polls. If the preconvention has articulated subject areas for proposed amendments which most Americans can endorse, and the challenger supports a second convention, it will be difficult for an incumbent to oppose approving the petitions even if that person believes that an Article V convention is a bad idea. Legislators who refuse to approve the petitions must be convinced that such a position will inspire a swarm of dedicated campaign workers and financial contributors to help a challenger in the next election. It is also important that those legislators who courageously support the petition effort get the assistance of hard-working volunteers who help with campaigning and contributions.

It must be stated again that the long process described in this chapter — beginning with the first discussions among concerned citizens in living rooms and through the Internet, leading to the congressional district/county meeting, the state convention, and finally, the national preconvention — will be extraordinarily difficult to accomplish. It is hard to overestimate how many obstacles will stand in the way; how long even the most conscientious and dedicated citizens will have to work to bring about even the first steps; how much money it will take to keep the process going. Yet, considering what is at stake — an unprecedented effort on the part of the American people to make significant changes in their Constitution, and reclaim their government — such efforts have to be seen as worth undertaking. Even if the endeavor is ultimately unsuccessful, there is much to learn from going through the process. Those who come away with increased political knowledge and a record of activism will be available to work for reform another day.

CHAPTER FIVE

The Internet, Politics, and the Constitution

It is difficult to fully comprehend, much less describe, the impact computers have had on communication in the late 20th century and the potential of computer and Internet technology to change the nature of politics and government in this nation. Someone sitting down today at a computer purchased for less than $1,000, or provided by a library, school, or employer, can do things that could not have been imagined a decade ago. Buying and selling almost every conceivable item using a computer connected to a telephone line is now easy. Online sales have reached billions of dollars a year, and the growth rate is phenomenal. Online auctions such as those run by eBay and Yahoo! sell millions of items, ranging in cost from a few dollars to several hundred thousand. Almost every major retail business has a Web site that is responsible for a growing percentage of sales. Many businesses sell only through the Internet and have made a fortune doing so. As more commercial sites provide secure technology that makes it more difficult for intruders to obtain credit card information, and as the public feels more comfortable with purchasing a product after seeing only a written description, picture, or brief video of it, Internet sales will continue to grow.

Computer users will never run out of people with whom to interact. An e-mail message can be written and delivered within minutes across the country, with a response sometimes coming moments afterward. If that individual had written a letter, it would have taken days to arrive at the destination and several more for a response, and would have cost the price of a stamp. A lot of people who use e-mail would never have written the letter in the first place. No typewriter or printer, no envelope or stamp, and no trip to the post office are necessary to compose and send e-mail. Moreover, what one sends by e-mail is not limited to written text. E-mail can include attached "documents," such as reports, newspaper articles, graphics, pictures, drawings, or even short video or audio clips. But as convenient as e-mail is, there is a downside: Millions of Americans are inundated with e-mail and spend hours each working day responding to electronic messages, some of which would not have been sent if it was not so easy and quick to do so. E-mail can also be impersonal and provide an easy way to say things that should have been communicated in person or by a written letter. In addition, e-mail is not always private, and there is always a chance that an employer, colleague, or stranger will get access to sensitive or controversial messages.

E-mail is not the only way to communicate by computer. "News-groups" — which are strangely named, because they do not have much to do with news — are forums where computer users view text, pictures or video, or upload that material for others to see. The estimated 15,000 newsgroups are arranged by subject, and not surprisingly, information is available on almost any area of interest. Although there are several ways of finding newsgroups, a Web site, "DejaNews" (www.dejanews.com), which searches over 54 million newsgroup articles, is the most popular. Generally, newsgroup messages are not directed toward individuals but are for all those who are interested in the subject. A substantial number of newsgroups include sexual material, some of it shockingly graphic. Many newsgroups, however, provide a forum for discussing worthwhile subjects such as politics and journalism, and hobbies such as movies and books. Those who see a newsgroup message have the opportunity to communicate directly with the individual who posted the message through e-mail. Such a system allows people with shared interests to find each other, something they could never have done in an era of more primitive communication technology.

In addition to newsgroups, many computer users subscribe to "lists." Just as if they were on a mailing list, those belonging to lists or listservs — which are also organized by subject — get periodic messages from either other subscribers, or if the rules permit, from those outside the list who have information of interest to the list's members. Some are "moderated" where a list manager checks to see if the message is appropriate before it is sent to all subscribers. Those who attempt to post messages that are off the subject, try to sell a product or service, or use libelous or sexually explicit speech, may find themselves suspended or dropped from the list. List managers with a tendency to censor the messages of nonconformist members have sometimes excluded messages that are directly related to the subject of the list, but challenge conventional thinking. When those lists are maintained by public universities, for example, they may be considered a "public forum" for First Amendment purposes, and thus the exclusion of those ideas raises important constitutional issues.

As with all forms of new communication technology, lists can be too much of a good thing. Those who belong to lists with a large number of active members soon find their e-mail "inboxes" overflowing with messages that they do not have time to read. There are more than 85,000 lists which are best found through "The Liszt" (www.liszt.com). A computer user only needs an e-mail program to participate.

Another method by which people can find each other and communicate over the Internet is the "chat room." Although requiring somewhat more sophisticated technology on the part of the individuals hosting chat rooms, they are an easy way for the computer user to have "real time" communication with strangers located almost anywhere in the country or the world. For people planning political activities, such real time exchange of information may be useful.

A more sophisticated forum for communicating by computer, which is becoming increasingly accessible to even those with limited technical skills, is the World Wide Web. Until a few years ago, creating a Web site required knowledge of HTML — hypertext markup language — and fairly sophisticated skills. Creating such sites was time-consuming and frustrating, with problems ranging from computers having insufficient random-access memory (RAM) to hold all the necessary graphics and word processing programs at the same time, to finding a server that would store the Web site inexpensively. Software now exists that takes a computer user through the steps necessary to create a simple site. Server space is inexpensive and widely available from businesses specializing in providing these services and from online companies such as America Online and Prodigy.

With a Web site, almost anyone can become a "media outlet" and reach a potentially large audience. In the old days, only those who owned newspapers, magazines, or broadcasting stations could disseminate information quickly to a substantial number of people. Today's cyberspace-era communicators can comment on any subject ranging from impeachment of the president to favorite recipes; "report" news stories as if they were journalists; sell almost any product; offer documents, graphics and video; and find individuals with common interests who are scattered all over the country or around the world who previously would have been impossible to locate. The challenge is to get people to discover your site. Among the millions of sites on the Web are many that are almost never visited except by those who created them.

At the same time that Internet technology has developed, powerful word processing programs and inexpensive printers have made it significantly easier to write and distribute letters, commentaries, essays, and reports. Although the invention of word processing programs has not necessarily resulted in a correspondingly higher level of public discourse, today's technology makes the lonely pamphleteer whose political statements were set to type on a primitive printing press, and who then relied largely on newspapers delivered by horseback to spread the information, seem like a prehistoric relic.

The growth of the Internet has been extraordinary in recent years. In 1981, the Internet linked fewer than 300 computers, mostly operated by scientists at labs and other university facilities. By 1989, about 90,000 computers were directly linked. Those figures are not to be confused with private individuals who connect to the Internet mostly through modems. It is estimated that in 1995, there were 30 million Internet users around the world, while by 1999, there were at least 70 million Americans who use Internet technology. There may be 200 million Internet users around the world at the beginning of the 21st century.

The U.S. Commerce Department noted that it took the Internet four years to reach an audience of 50 million people, compared with 13 years for television and 38 years for radio. In cities such as Washington, D.C. and San Francisco, it is estimated that more than 40 percent of homes have Internet access. A study in June of 1998 by the Pew Research Center found that 20 percent of American adults go online at least once a week for news, up from 6 percent only two years before.

Development of the Internet

Many people assume, incorrectly, that the Internet is a tangible entity under the direct control of a group of talented managers. Unfortunately, things are not so simple in the cyberspace world. The Internet is not managed; in fact it is barely subject to even indirect control. No government or private entity administers the Internet, although both government and private companies have been involved in the assigning of Internet addresses, known as domain names. It exists and functions because hundreds of thousands of separate operators of computers and computer networks use common protocols — which allow different computers to communicate with each other — to exchange information. The lack of direct control over the Internet creates many potential problems including the overloading of its capacity, its vulnerability to small glitches leading to widespread failures, and its susceptibility to sabotage and intrusion by hackers and others.

The Internet has been appropriately described as a "network of networks." It is a huge network that interconnects a large number of smaller groups of linked computer networks. Some of them are closed, and thus not linked to other computers or networks. But many of them are linked to other networks, which are connected to still more. This permits every computer to communicate with computers on any other network in the system. It allows someone to send an e-mail across the country in a matter of minutes. An e-mail, or a picture, or a downloaded Web site —which is broken up into "packets" and "reassembled" by the receiving computer — could take one of several dozen different routes to its destination. When computers along the way get busy, the time it takes for the receiving computer to get all the information increases. Besides textual messages, pictures, and recorded video, the Internet can also carry live audio or video. Although the audio and video quality are still primitive compared to a radio signal or television picture, people located on different sides of the world can see and hear each other through computers connected to the Internet.

The Internet began in 1969 as an experimental project of the Advanced Research Project Agency, and was called ARPANET. This network linked computers and computer networks owned by the military, defense contractors, and university laboratories conducting defense-related research. The network later allowed researchers across the country access through what were considered then to be powerful supercomputers located at a few universities and laboratories. As this original network evolved far beyond just a few scientists at universities or defense specialists in military facilities to include educational institutions, corporations, and people all around the world, the ARPANET eventually came to be known as the "Internet."

Individuals have several ways of connecting to the Internet. One can use a computer or computer terminal that is directly, and usually permanently, connected to a computer network. The other common method is through a personal computer with a modem that is used to connect over a telephone line to a larger computer or computer network that is directly or indirectly connected to the Internet. Many universities provide computers with direct access to the Internet for students in such facilities as the library and in computer labs, and for professors in their offices and sometimes in their classrooms. The advantage of a direct connection is almost always greater bandwidth and thus speed of transmission. An Ethernet line, for example, which many universities provide to faculty in their offices and students in computer labs, carry information at a speed many times faster than a telephone line. Especially when downloading pictures, speed makes a substantial difference. A Web site that loads slowly and is often disrupted by normal fluctuations in the quality of the telephone connection will not be visited as often or as long as one with faster loading words and images. Many businesses also link the computers on their premises and at other locations to a local network, which in turn provides direct and speedy access to the Internet.

Those who do not have access to university computer facilities or a personal computer with a modem are at a disadvantage, but can still get at least limited access to Internet resources. Various cities provide "free-nets" or community networks that offer citizens a local link to the Internet. Although free-nets can be accessed from a personal computer and modem, computers with free-net access are also found in libraries, educational institutions, nonprofit community groups, or in community buildings. Some cities, businesses, and airports have "cyber cafes" where customers can use computers to access the Internet for a small hourly fee.

The millions of people with personal computers and a modem can contract with an Internet service company for access to the Internet, but many get such access through one of the major online providers such as America Online or Prodigy. Getting access to the Internet this way has improved greatly over the past few years.

The Internet and Politics

The impact of new communication technology on politics is growing, but has yet to reach its potential. Beginning mostly during the early 1990s, candidates for public office began to use e-mail and Web sites to provide information about their candidacy and positions, and to solicit contributions. During the same period organized groups created sites to distribute information, recruit new members, and raise money. Although many candidates used Web sites in the 1996 and 1998 elections to reach potential supporters, by the year 2000, almost every candidate for major state and federal office had one. The advantages include the low cost, the substantial amount of information about a candidate or issues that can be offered directly by the site or by linking to another site, and the positive impression that a sophisticated site makes on the voter. Because Web sites are so inexpensive to create compared to the cost of many traditional campaign activities, it is easy to develop a site that looks good and thus sends the message that the candidate should be taken seriously. The most well-funded organization or political party's site will not necessarily be more functional or dazzling than the site of a struggling campaign.

A University of California, Santa Barbara, political science professor surveyed 1,021 adults in February 1998, and concluded that an increasing number of adults are turning to the Internet for political information. His survey found that 46 percent of adults nationwide have access to the Internet, and the number who had sought political information through such means had about doubled since a similar survey was conducted before the elections in November 1996. In 1998, the survey found that 17 percent of the respondents used the Internet to express political views, to browse for political information or get in touch with elected officials or candidates. Of those 17 percent, it was estimated that seven percent were actively engaged in the political process in one way or another. Some candidates for public office published newsletters by e-mail that informed potential contributors and voters about the candidate's platform and campaign events. Political aides in several statewide campaigns reported that several thousand people subscribed to the newsletters.

When Governor Jeb Bush (R-Florida) was running for that office in 1998, his campaign had a Web site that was the envy of many other politicians. Whereas most Internet sites created by politicians cost less than $5,000 dollars, his cost closer to $25,000. Information was updated daily on the site by aides who accompanied him on campaign appearances around the state, taking pictures with digital cameras, which were then posted to the campaign's Web site. The campaign made every effort to let voters know where they could find the site by including the address in letterhead and in campaign commercials. Despite the apparent success of the Bush Web site, some analysts believe that at least for now, too few people use Web sites, newsgroups, and other Internet resources to download and exchange political information. One political consultant, whose clients have included U.S. senators, said "as a tool of political communication, the Internet today is of marginal value, but increasing value."

In 1996, both major political parties and all the presidential candidates established elaborate home pages on the Web, which typically offered photos, position papers, news releases, and even video clips from speeches. The official campaign sites, however, were greatly outnumbered by unofficial sites that variously supported, discussed, criticized, or simply made fun of the candidates. One of the most difficult challenges for the voter was to distinguish the serious sites from the unofficial ones that looked authentic. For example, a site devoted to Pat Buchanan's campaign for president looked like the real thing, except when one looked closely and saw a swastika rather than 50 white stars on the flag in the background.

Many of the sites used to parody or criticize some 1996 presidential candidates such as Bob Dole, Phil Gramm, and others were created by individuals who made use of inexpensive and easy-to-use software that permitted the creation of sites the *New York Times* described as "lively." Once established on the Web, the sites created by amateurs that did not attract much traffic could cost as little as $25 a month to keep on a server, while the more elaborate sites that generated a lot of traffic would cost many times that amount, as much as several thousand dollars a month. Interestingly, many of the unofficial sites were created well before the campaigns of the presidential candidates got around to creating the official ones. Until the Dole campaign put up its site in the summer of 1995, the only place on the Internet for Dole supporters was the "Unofficial Bob Dole Home Page" created by a graduate student at the University of Pennsylvania. An MIT graduate student created a site called "The Information Headquarters for the Republican Primary" before the Republican National Committee set up its elaborate site.

Many of the unofficial, and for that matter, official sites, had too few visitors for them to have had a substantial impact on the outcome of the elections in 1996. But a growing number of campaign strategists believe the Internet is likely to become a genuinely important political tool by the 2000 presidential election. They also expect the soliciting of campaign funds through Internet sites to increase. For example, in the 1998 election, Senator Barbara Boxer (D-Calif) raised $25,000 online, a tiny amount compared to the total of $20 million that she raised during the campaign. But it was enough money to pay for the campaign's Web site and the campaign's banner ads on other sites. A survey done in October 1998, which sought information from 133 candidates, including 68 Senate candidates and 65 for open seats in the House, found that 20 percent of those candidates were getting contributions directly through secure online transactions. Overall, 72 percent of the campaigns solicited money on their sites.

Another candidate who made use of the Web and who may not have won without it was Jesse Ventura, the Reform Party candidate who was elected governor of Minnesota in 1998. Ventura's campaign site, which was set up for $600, included a lively mix of position papers, biographical information, and statements about the Reform Party. It was intended, its founder said, to produce "money, volunteers and votes." The remarkable results demonstrated the potential of the Web in politics. The campaign raised more than one-third of its $600,000 in donations and loans through the Web site. The site gave Ventura a chance to respond within hours to charges that he supported legalizing prostitution, which were untrue. In the final days of the campaign, the Web site was used to publicize the location of rallies as the candidate drove from town to town, with the result that people who saw the information on the Internet turned out to see him in substantial numbers.

Interestingly, the site that helped elect the governor was later used to pay off his campaign debts when Ventura sold action figures of himself on the Web site. The public seemed interested in not only buying the figures, but also in following his progress in office. By early 1999, the site received an average of 3,823 visits a day. "Jesse Net," Ventura's e-mail list, had 3,000 subscribers at election time and 6,000 by March of 1999. Ventura planned to communicate with voters directly through the Web site, unfiltered by media or spokespeople.

While the Web helped Ventura and was apparently a positive influence on the campaign, Web sites used in political campaigns can create problems. In Philadelphia, two top campaign aides to a Democratic candidate for mayor admitted that they had created a phony Web site to disrupt the campaign of a Democratic rival. John White, the rival candidate, did not have a Web site, yet the site developed by a Cambridge, Massachusetts, Web designer at the request of Dwight Evans's campaign workers looked like the real thing. On the site was posted a racially insensitive remark about black and Latino voters that was attributed to White. The quote had him saying, "the black and the brown, if we unite, we're going to control this city." White actually did make such a statement, but it was taken out of context. What he meant to say, according to press reports, was that minorities should participate in the political process. After the creation of the phony page became known, the Evans campaign aides resigned and apologized for "harming" the White campaign. One White adviser called it a "cybersmear."

The 2000 presidential campaign

All of the major presidential candidates in the 2000 race had a Web presence, and some of them had innovative and increasingly useful sites for raising money and finding supporters. With an estimated 67 million Americans online, up from 7.5 million in 1995, Web sites are becoming an important part of political campaigns. The sites encourage people to donate money and to find others who might be interested in supporting the campaign. For those who want to volunteer their time, or just want to be on the mailing list, it takes only a few moments to fill in the blanks on a form that is then e-mailed back to the campaign. Democratic presidential candidate Bill Bradley's campaign, for example, sent e-mail to 5,000 supporters in the Northeast encouraging them to take part in a weeklong canvass in New Hampshire during the summer of 1999. These sites — which can do so many things — were created for a small amount of money compared to traditional media advertising.

Republican Texas Governor George W. Bush posted everything from his baby pictures to information about his positions on major issues on his Web site. During the seven months prior to October 1999, the Bush campaign spent $57,000 on its Web site. Governor Bush also became the first presidential candidate to make updated lists of campaign donors available online. Bradley's site brought in about $7,000 a day in the fall of 1999, and received 5,000 visits each day, probably more people than he would see in person in a full day of campaigning. The campaign estimates that Bradley's site had received half a million visits between December 1998, and October 1999. Bradley promoted his site — which included everything from cookie recipes to positions on major issues — by displaying the address on every lectern he used and at every other opportunity.

Vice President Al Gore's campaign, recognizing that their candidate is closely identified with the cyberspace era, created an elaborate site with substantial amounts of information about the candidate and his positions. Gore's site gave people the opportunity to interact with the candidate through electronic town halls, where citizens asked questions on any subject. Businessman Steve Forbes invited visitors who paid $10 each to see live video of a fundraising event in New York that cost $10,000 each for those who attended in person.

Although people have to make a decision to visit a Web site — which is obviously different from passively encountering a radio or television ad — studies indicate that once they do so, they may pay more attention to the candidate's message than they would through other media. One study indicated that people spent an average of eight minutes at a candidate's Web site, compared with the 45 seconds of voter attention given to campaigns when people are contacted by telephone and 30 seconds through a television commercial.

Some analysts predict that the Internet will initially be a decisive factor in a campaign on a smaller scale, where a few hundred or perhaps a few thousand votes make the difference. Those same analysts predicted that probably the first time the Internet will make a substantial impact at the national level will be in the 2004 presidential election. By then, high-speed Internet access will be available to millions of Americans, and it will be much easier for everyone to go online.

Another development in the fall of 1999 encouraged use of the Web in campaigns. The Federal Election Commission ruled that Web sites created by supporters who are independent of the candidates will be considered volunteer activities and not contributions to the campaigns. That means that the cost of creating or maintaining the sites does not count toward the amount that can be legally donated to a campaign. Even when the volunteer site provides links to the candidate's site, the FEC held that such activities are volunteer in nature.

The FEC's action came in response to questions from the Bush campaign about the status of such sites. What the Bush campaign did not ask, and what the FEC for now did not answer, is how sites that specifically encourage visitors to vote for or against a candidate will be characterized. The FEC has ruled in the past that organizations that make such statements must register as a political action committee if they spend at least $250. The FEC will have to address at some point the issue raised by an individual spending large sums of money on a Web site who then encourages people to vote for or against specific candidates. The FEC was not as concerned about volunteers setting up their own sites or sending e-mail on behalf of candidates.

Not surprisingly, political parties also want to use the Internet to find ways to identify and energize supporters. In November 1999, the Republican National Committee announced that it would begin offering subscriptions in January to a "family friendly" Internet service — family friendly because it will filter out sexually explicit material — that would deliver the party's messages directly to supporters and help raise money. The new site will act as an Internet service provider — like AOL, for example — and as a closed system providing information about Republican politics. Its large contributors will get the service for free, while others will pay a fee of $19.95 a month, about standard for access to the Internet. The party will receive a small portion of the monthly fee, but more importantly, the new service will allow it to send messages to the party faithful whenever they connect to the site. A spokesman said that "when Al Gore double-speaks on his record . . . we'll get our response in their [subscribers to the site] hands the same minute as it reaches a state party chairman."

A simple Web site created by a single supporter of a presidential candidate may not get a lot of attention, but any site that provides useful information in an easily accessible form will get the attention of policymakers. A lobbyist for a large communication firm found that if he gathered information on satellite technology and regulation, for example, and let key staff members on Capitol Hill know of the existence of the site, he would be able to inform and lobby at the same time. The former congressional aide who created the site recalled how difficult it was to research dozens of issues and keep track of their status on the Hill and in regulatory agencies. Such "Internet lobbying" sites may have a small audience — 200 people in the case of the communication site — but they are among the most important to staff members on the Hill when it comes to communications issues. A policy advisor for a senator said the site is a "great resource." The idea is certain to grow as other organizations, which cannot afford a large presence on Capitol Hill, try to provide useful information to busy staff members, but in a way that both persuades and informs.

Other individuals seeking to use the Internet to reach and influence elected officials have created controversy. Former presidential adviser in the Clinton administration, Dick Morris, created a site that went online in October 1999. It asked visitors to vote "yes" or "no" on issues featured on his site, which then converted the votes into thousands of e-mail messages that were sent to elected officials. Morris said that his site had sent 82,000 e-mail messages to the White House within a week. Morris's critics argued that the visitors, not Morris, should be choosing the issues on which to comment. Moreover, they were concerned about thousands of e-mail messages being forwarded to the White House and elsewhere obscuring correspondence from individuals. Morris charged that the White House programmed its computer to block messages from Morris's site, or at least limited how many came in each day. A staff member said the Web servers in the White House automatically limit how many messages can come from the same location to deter the practice of "mail bombing," a technique used by hackers to cripple Web servers.

The Harvard Study

Researcher Elaine Ciulla Kamarck conducted a study that looked at the use of the Internet by candidates running for federal office in 1998. As of June 20, 1998, there were 34 U.S. Senate races and 36 governor's races. Twenty-nine U.S. senators and 25 governors were running for reelection. In addition, there were a number of independent and third-party candidates running for office. Her study used the first 20 days of June as a "snapshot" of use of the Internet by candidates.

Among the 153 active candidates for U.S. Senate, 44 or 29 percent had Web sites. Among the 267 active candidates for governor, 117 or 44 percent had Web sites. Kamarck speculated that because races for governor had a tendency to be more competitive, candidates for that office would be more likely to use the Internet because they would not want to leave any media source untapped. The study further examined whether incumbents or challengers were more likely to use the Internet to campaign or raise money, and found that challengers were far more likely to have Web sites. Kamarck believed that many incumbents were in noncompetitive races and did not need to bother with new media technology. In addition, the incumbents may have felt they had sufficient visibility through their official, government Web sites even though they could not raise money or recruit volunteers through those as they could through a campaign site. The study further found that the third-party candidates who used Web sites did not seem to have benefited significantly from them.

Kamarck was surprised to find that relatively few Web sites directly asked for campaign contributions. Of those that did ask for money, most provided a mailing address where a contribution could be sent. A few of the more sophisticated sites provided supporters with the opportunity to submit a credit card number and make a contribution electronically. The study found that most content on the sites centered on biographical information of the candidate and positions on issues. Many of the sites contained a photo of the candidate and the family, and a biography. Many sites also included copies of speeches or position statements. The study also found that very few of the sites had "interactive" characteristics, meaning there was some way for visitors of the site to convey information to the campaign and a way for the campaign to respond. At least a few sites provided voters with the chance to ask candidates direct questions by e-mail to which they would respond.

Political information on the Internet down the road

The Internet has the potential to profoundly alter the nature of politics and government in this country. At some point in the not-too-distant future, millions of Americans will seek detailed information about candidates and their positions through Web sites and other forms of Internet technology, and will exchange views about the records or promises of elected officials and candidates through e-mails, lists, and other methods. Although it seems unlikely that elections will actually be conducted through computers located at polling places, libraries, or other public places any time soon, there is no doubt that the use of computers to interact with public officials and those seeking elective office will greatly increase.

At the same time that candidates have used the Internet to get their message out and to provide much more detail about their records or plans, public interest groups and news organizations have created sites that provide more objective and detailed information about candidates. Those sites will continue to develop as voters look beyond the limited information provided in a campaign ad or in brief broadcast news reports.

During various elections in the 1990s, including two presidential elections and off-year congressional elections, relatively few Americans accessed the Web sites created by candidates or public interest groups. Millions may have done so, but in terms of percentages of total users or voters, their numbers were still small. It is likely that many more people came across political information while visiting one or more of the many sites developed by news organizations. As the Internet continues to grow, it is indisputable that new media technology will play a significantly greater role in the way Americans choose elected officials and influence public policy decisions.

One can imagine a system — which is not yet in place but may be within a few years — in which a broad range of information about candidates and elected officials would be *easily* available through the Internet: It's early in the 21st century, and a conscientious citizen wants to learn about those seeking public office. Such a citizen could sit at a desktop computer — or perhaps, use a hand-held computer that will allow Internet searches, e-mail to be written and sent, and that will also double as a cellular telephone — and with a few keystrokes and clicks of the mouse, the computer offers a wide range of political information. For example, Web sites would provide pictures and detailed information about the candidates running for the U.S. House of Representatives. Assuming for the moment that there are candidates from the major parties only, the screen would be divided into two sides, with the respective candidate's picture on each. Underneath are links to pictures, video clips of the candidate answering questions or talking before groups in the district, and links to other sources of information provided by the candidates. The video clips are especially important. Because congressional districts average more than 500,000 residents, many voters never see a congressional candidate in person, or if they do, there is not much time to talk. People want to know that their representative is articulate and can communicate through new technology in an era in which such skills are so important. Although there is always a chance that the more photogenic but less qualified candidate will benefit from such a format, the public is likely to recognize sincerity when they see it, and the more charismatic candidate will not necessarily win.

Additional links provide detailed written statements about the candidates' positions on the important issues facing the country and the district, and information about the candidates' record and background. At the bottom of the page are links to news organizations that have done detailed, objective, research about the candidates. The site explains how the incumbent representative has voted on issues, how many votes that representative has missed, and comments from insiders who talk candidly about the quality of the work of the House member, something that is rarely provided to the public at large.

Additional links take the voter to the Web sites of public interest groups that have done a detailed analysis of the record of the incumbent or the qualifications of the challenger, and have provided that information in a visually interesting format. Among the most important information the public interest group will offer is related to campaign contributions. A voter can often find out a lot about a candidate by seeing which organizations and individuals are contributing money to the campaign. Although many public interest groups will present information from their perspective and may emphasize the candidate's support for positions favored by the organization and overstate the shortcomings of the disfavored candidate, information from such sites nevertheless can be extremely useful.

There is already substantial information, usually in the form of news coverage, about high-profile races including those for president and U.S. Senate, and to a lesser extent for U.S. House, but voters usually face a serious lack of good information about candidates running for many state offices. A system in the future that provided comprehensive information would take voters to sites offering detailed information about candidates running for state legislature, statewide office, and for judicial posts. In many states, where legislative districts have relatively few residents, or where legislators are part-time, it is very difficult to learn much about the record and promises of candidates seeking those important but lower-profile offices. Ideally, Web sites would provide that information so the public will know more about the voting record of the incumbent or the qualifications of the challenger.

Millions of voters go to the polls every election to choose state trial court and appellate court judges without knowing anything about the candidates. This voter ignorance is one of the great failures of the political system in this country. Incumbent judges are almost always reelected because their names have been in the newspaper or on television a few times. Only occasionally does a judge's controversial action result in sufficient news coverage to motivate citizens to work for or against that judge's reelection. In many states, lawyers can contribute huge sums of money to the campaigns of judges who will hear their cases at the trial court and appellate levels. Web sites providing information about how the incumbent judge has ruled in important cases, including what kind of sentences the judge has handed down, and who has contributed to that judge's campaign, would greatly enhance the knowledge the average voter has of those seeking such offices. Ideally, comments from lawyers and others able to see the incumbent judges at work would offer a detailed perspective on the performance of the judge. As the system works now, the public elects judges to do work that is crucial to a democratic society while knowing almost nothing about them. It seems likely, however, that it will be many years before such information about judges will be available online, if ever.

Gathering such detailed information about candidates for Congress or state legislature, or for judicial positions, and posting that information on Web sites would take a tremendous amount of work by those who undertake such projects. The expense of doing such sites may have to be paid by foundations or other organizations. It is unlikely that there will be enough commercial value or civic commitment for the private sector to pay for them.

The Internet will only be able to fulfill its potential for providing such important information if those who create and disseminate it are granted substantial First Amendment protection to closely examine, and sometimes sharply criticize, the record and promises of those seeking public office. In the course of such discussion, incorrect or inaccurate statements will inevitably be made. Even seasoned journalists, whose work is often reviewed by layers of editors, and sometimes the news organization's lawyer, make errors that lead to legal trouble such as libel suits. When those who do not have the experience of traditional journalists, or an ethical commitment to fairness and accuracy, become their own "media outlet" and share their assessment of those seeking public office with a potentially large audience, there is an almost endless potential for legal problems. Those mistakes will range from innocent error where the writer honestly believed the statements were true, to the statements of those who intentionally and recklessly lied about someone's record or background. What is even more troublesome is that the public is going to have an increasingly difficult time identifying what information has been carefully gathered and written, and which statements are unfair, inaccurate, and unreliable. As more lawsuits based on information disseminated through the Internet go to court, judges and litigants will face the challenge of developing First Amendment standards that are appropriate for an era of rapidly changing technology.

Increased Potential for Libel and Privacy Suits

The First Amendment has been a part of the Constitution since 1791. For more than a century and a half, libel suits were mostly the province of the states. State court judges and federal judges applying state law were generally free to develop standards to balance the right of freedom of expression with the right of individuals to be compensated for harm to their reputation. Those standards overwhelmingly favored plaintiffs suing news organizations and represented an appalling insensitivity to the protections guaranteed by the First Amendment. For the most part, if a news organization published inaccurate information about an identifiable individual, which damaged that person's reputation, the newspaper or other media outlet lost the lawsuit. It did not matter whether the mistake was innocent error, or whether the publisher or reporter genuinely believed the statements were truthful. The juries in these cases were free to impose huge damage awards.

Despite the harm that such lawsuits created for the First Amendment, for a long time there was little effort made to stop judges determined to favor the rights of plaintiffs at the expense of those attempting to keep the public informed. State judges did not have to bother much with interference from their legislatures, which largely confined themselves to the limited role of defining what is considered defamatory material — what harms someone's reputation — and some procedural issues related to the filing of lawsuits such as whether the statute of limitations had expired. Those same judges also did not have to worry about the U.S. Supreme Court imposing standards that more fully protected First Amendment rights. The Court did not hand down its first major libel case until 1964, and it took until 1974 for the Court to develop most of what are today's complex libel standards.

By the 1980s, the Supreme Court had become heavily involved in deciding the circumstances under which those whose reputation had been harmed by irresponsible reporting would be compensated. The Court left substantial discretion to the states to develop rules related to *private* persons in such lawsuits, and those standards often favored plaintiffs. At the same time, the Court imposed national constitutional principles for discussion of public officials and public figures that were significantly more protective of the First Amendment than were the old state standards in the pre-1964 era. As litigants in the cyberspace era bring lawsuits arising from disputes involving new communication technology, courts will have to decide whether traditional First Amendment standards that mostly developed in cases involving newspapers, magazines, radio, and TV stations will apply to cases involving the Internet and other forms of new media technology. The danger is that the judges may decide the new cases without feeling an obligation to apply the standards that vigorously protected traditional media organizations. When new cases seem to present issues that are materially different from those previously decided, judges may believe they have a clean slate on which to write freedom of speech and press standards for new communication technology. As if that is not troubling enough, once the new precedents are established, judges who believe current standards are overly solicitous of the press may try to apply the new principles to cases involving *traditional* media, and thus undermine the special status of the First Amendment that took so long to establish.

In recent decades, courts have granted media organizations substantial protection from libel suits not because they think reporters are all virtuous, but because they know the press plays an indispensable role in facilitating the exchange of information necessary to the functioning of a democratic society. Judges have sometimes gritted their teeth and extended First Amendment protection to even outrageous behavior by irresponsible journalists for fear of chilling the fragile rights of free expression. Courts also recognized a more subtle justification for tolerating serious transgressions on the part of traditional journalists. Journalism is an identifiable craft, which although lacking detailed ethical principles, nevertheless generally follows certain standards of fairness and accuracy. It is generally believed that reporters for legitimate news organizations make an effort to check the accuracy of their news stories before broadcasting or publishing them. This is not to suggest that all journalists are conscientious and all false statements that damage someone's reputation are the result of innocent error. But journalists have generally been granted the "breathing space" the Supreme Court said they needed in order to encourage "uninhibited, wide-open" debate on public issues.

Libel suits in the cyberspace era will present procedural and substantive questions that are different from those usually present in traditional libel actions against news organizations. Just finding out who made the original statement may be difficult. When messages that raise potential legal problems are disseminated through a computer service, the plaintiff is likely to sue the company. The online company is an appealing defendant not only because it can be identified, but also because it is more likely than the average computer user to have the assets or insurance to pay a libel judgment.

One of the more difficult decisions courts have had to make is whether online services, newsgroup operators, list sponsors, and others who oversee cyberspace messages are "publishers" under traditional First Amendment standards. Publishers are responsible for the information they disseminate, and may be liable for defamatory and other harmful statements. If, however, courts conclude that online services are more like vendors or bookstore owners, or "distributors" of communication, they will not be responsible for the content of messages they carry. The financial success of new media technology and the extent to which it enjoys First Amendment rights may be directly affected by the courts' decisions on this issue.

The early cases suggested that judges have generally reached the conclusion that Congress intended to grant immunity to Internet service providers for content that passes through their facilities, but which they did not create. Section 230 of the Telecommunications Act of 1996 included language that appears to provide a broad exemption for online services. In *Zeran v. America Online*, the U.S. Court of Appeals for the

Fourth Circuit ruled in 1997 that Congress wanted to protect Internet service providers such as AOL from liability for statements created by third parties. The conclusion reached by the Fourth Circuit in *Zeran* and a federal district court in Washington, D.C., in a case involving cyberspace communicator Matt Drudge, may have accurately reflected what Congress intended, but it is arguable whether Congress should immunize Internet service providers from liability even when they have the opportunity to review in advance what is written by others and carried on their systems.

The early cases establish immunity

One of the first lawsuits against the user of an online service was one brought by Medaphone, a medical equipment company, against Peter DeNigris of Babylon, New York. DeNigris, the 42-year-old administrator of the Suffolk County Board of Elections, allegedly posted critical comments about the company's financial health on "Money Talk," a bulletin board run by Prodigy, an online service provider. After DeNigris's messages were posted on the bulletin board — which investors used to "swap tips and assess stocks" — the company's stock began to drop. The company sued DeNigris for $40 million but did not sue Prodigy. In December 1993, Medaphone settled for one dollar in damages, and DeNigris proclaimed that "freedom of speech prevailed." The company may have settled because the cost of litigation would have been substantially greater than the compensation available from a public employee earning a modest salary.

The next time Prodigy was not so lucky. In October 1994, an unknown Prodigy user posted a message, potentially seen by millions of computer users, that Stratton Oakmont, a brokerage firm, and two of its officers, had committed criminal and fraudulent acts in connection with an initial public offering of stock. When the firm filed a $200 million libel suit against the computer service, Prodigy responded that it could not be held responsible for the comments of its users because it was not a traditional publisher. The company argued that because millions of messages are posted every day on its bulletin boards and other services, it was impossible to monitor them.

In May 1995, Justice Stuart Ain in Mineola, New York, held that Prodigy could be sued as a publisher, a decision that startled free speech advocates and the online computer industry. Justice Ain concluded that because Prodigy had advertised itself as family-oriented, its subscribers assumed that the company maintained some control over the messages posted to its bulletin boards. He recognized that Prodigy had well over

2 million subscribers, and that "Money Talk" was one of the most widely read financial computer "bulletin boards" where people could discuss financial news, swap stock tips, and talk about other issues. But the justice found that when Prodigy boasted that it "exercised editorial control" over the content of messages on its bulletin boards, and thus tried to distinguish itself from competitors who did not provide such a service, it was "expressly likening itself to a newspaper." He did not consider it significant that the company had rescinded, before the lawsuit, its implied commitment to monitor messages when it saw how difficult it would be to review so many messages passing through its facilities.

In its defense to the lawsuit by Stratton Oakmont, Prodigy relied heavily on *Cubby Inc. v. CompuServe, Inc.* where the defendant — a computer network providing subscribers with various electronic publications and related online sites, including a forum devoted to journalism — was sued over statements made about the plaintiff, an electronic newsletter. The court in *Cubby* found that CompuServe had no opportunity to review the contents of the publication at issue before it was uploaded into CompuServe's computers. The company had hired a different company, Cameron Communications, to control the contents of the Journalism Forum. The court held that "a computerized data base is the functional equivalent of a more traditional news vendor" and should not be held liable any more than would a "public library, book store or newsstand." Justice Ain declined to apply such a principle to *Stratton Oakmont*, concluding instead that Prodigy had created an editorial staff that had the ability to "continually monitor incoming transmissions" and because they did censor some notes, they were responsible for the content of messages posted on the Money Talk bulletin board.

In October 1995, Stratton Oakmont dropped its lawsuit in return for an apology from Prodigy. Even though the lawsuit was settled, Justice Ain had the opportunity to reverse his previous ruling that Prodigy was a publisher and that online services that carry bulletin boards could be sued for the messages posted by those who use the service. In December 1995, he refused to reconsider his decision, stating that "there is a real need for some precedent" in the area of online liability. Justice Ain may have wanted to establish a precedent for future courts as they develop law related to online services, but the impact of his ruling was far different. It convinced Congress that online providers should have immunity from lawsuits arising from content they did not control.

If Prodigy had been forced to go to trial in the *Stratton Oakmont* case, it would have had a difficult time persuading the jury to apply traditional libel standards. The company may have had little choice but to argue that the statements made by the unknown author were substantially true and thus constitutionally protected. The anonymous writer told the readers of the bulletin board that after the Securities and Exchange Commission (SEC) investigated the firm's "fraudulent and deceptive sales practices," the company and its officers paid a substantial fine. However, because the company and its officers acknowledged no wrongdoing in settling the SEC complaint, they argued that the message posted on the bulletin board was false and defamatory.

The difference in interpretation was rather technical, and if in fact the company did not admit that it did anything wrong when it paid the fine, the misleading statement by the anonymous commentator was incorrect. Yet it was an error that even an experienced reporter could have made. Prodigy would have been without the usual defense in such a suit that the writer may have been wrong about the company's settlement with the SEC, but there was no level of "fault" beyond innocent error. Under Supreme Court libel standards, it is not enough to show that the published statement was false and injured someone's reputation. There has to be some type of negligence on the part of the publisher. Prodigy, however, could not have made that argument because it did not know anything about the credentials and commitment to accuracy of the anonymous writer. It had no idea how carefully that person had checked out the facts before posting the message. Juries, which are often unsympathetic to the claims of experienced journalists who carefully prepare their stories, would probably not have been very understanding.

Other online computer companies have also been involved in legal disputes. The owner of a Caribbean resort and his scuba diving instructor filed a petition for discovery against AOL to force the company to reveal the identity of a user known only as "Jenny TRR." The person using that name posted a message on a bulletin board devoted to scuba diving, complaining that while visiting the Carib Inn and getting diving lessons, the instructor used drugs and was "stoned." The writer did not name the instructor, but provided enough description so that he could easily be identified. The owner of the resort posted a message on the same bulletin board that the allegation was untrue, and asked "Jenny" to admit that "she" lied about the incident. When she did not come forward, the resort owner and diving instructor filed a motion in Cook County Court in Chicago to compel AOL to reveal her name.

The owner of the Carib Inn, Bruce Bowker, had good reason to complain about the message that "Jenny" posted and to think something was odd about the whole incident. In an industry newsletter published on the Internet, Bowker stated that a former employee, who had been fired in 1990, admitted to using the name "Jenny TRR" to try to injure the reputation of the Inn and its owners by posting negative messages on the

Internet. According to Bowker, the former employee confessed that he "knowingly, intentionally, and falsely" attacked the Carib Inn's reputation. Bowker listed other false "screen names" that the employee had used to try to damage the Carib Inn and when he impersonated a Florida law enforcement official and an FBI agent.

The "new" communicators

Peter DeNigris, who made critical comments about the medical company; the unknown Prodigy user who criticized the brokerage firm; and the former employee who used the name "Jenny TRR" to try to damage the Carib Inn, were not journalists. Yet they and the online services that carried their messages would like to use the legal protections granted to traditional media organizations. When they made their online statements, it is unlikely they talked with trusted sources, searched public records, sought a comment from those they were allegedly defaming, had the story reviewed by several levels of editors, or took other steps which responsible journalists often follow. Instead, they had opinions about alleged wrongdoing or the financial health of several businesses, or tried to retaliate against a former employer, and they disseminated that information to a potentially large audience.

It is only a short step from individuals making extemporaneous comments at their computer to "covering" events and people and then writing "stories" for the modern-day equivalent of newspapers or TV newscasts. Those "reporters," who may have little training or experience, are not to be confused with serious journalists who have made the move from traditional news organizations to companies that publish magazines, newsletters, and other materials on the Internet. Those individuals make an effort to bring established journalistic tools and principles to the new media outlet and to publish information that is fair and accurate. It is the new "cyberspace-era" communicators who have a powerful new medium at their disposal who pose the most serious threat to the First Amendment and the legitimacy of traditional journalism.

Those individuals, often working alone at a computer at home, go to the Internet determined to share with the world their thoughts on a broad range of issues often without making a minimal effort to be thorough, fair, and accurate. The recipient of the information provided by these commentators may have a hard time evaluating the accuracy of the statements. When anyone with a computer can operate a "media" outlet, a public skeptical about the work and motives of traditional journalists will become even more cynical when it cannot judge the credibility of the speaker or publisher. The coming of cyberspace "journalists" may create severe problems of public perception and lead to much litigation. At the same time, it would be a shame if the full potential of the Internet does not develop because of those who use it irresponsibly.

The troubling case of Blumenthal v. Drudge

Among the best known and most controversial of the cyberspace-era communicators is Matt Drudge. Drudge provided news reports and commentaries about government officials and other issues on his own Web site. When his work later attracted some coverage from traditional news organizations, Drudge entered into a contract with AOL, thus making his column available to millions of AOL subscribers. He was also later hired by Fox News, a nationwide cable news service and appeared periodically on C-SPAN.

Drudge was one of the first people to report that Monica Lewinsky had kept a dress with DNA evidence of her sexual relationship with President Clinton. He was, apparently, among the few to initially report on an aspect of the story involving a cigar — an especially tawdry and controversial aspect of the sordid tale. Despite doubts on the part of many who heard the story as to whether the cigar tale was true — and there were some who criticized Drudge for reporting it regardless of its accuracy — the tale of the cigar eventually became fodder for late-night talk shows and jokes on radio stations all over the country.

Drudge was known to be controversial, and in fact made a substantial effort to call attention to his stories that were the most salacious and scandalous. But on August 10, 1997, Drudge went too far. On that day, he posted to his Internet site a story about Sidney Blumenthal, an assistant to President Clinton, who occupied one of the most important positions in the White House. In the story, Drudge alleged that Blumenthal "has a spousal abuse past" that Republicans could use for leverage in dealing with the White House and in criticizing Democrats. According to the *Drudge Report*, court records showed that Blumenthal had been violent against his wife, yet the Democrats were covering up the story and hoping that it would never become public. Drudge suggested that Republicans stood ready to expose Blumenthal if they needed, and concluded by saying, "there goes the budget deal honeymoon." Drudge's report was published the day before Blumenthal assumed his new duties at the White House. The sources of the story were unnamed "GOP operatives."

Drudge is emblematic of many purveyors of information in the new media environment. Considering the importance of his revelations — whether about Blumenthal or Lewinsky — and the attention that those revelations received, it is disturbing that Drudge has so few journalistic credentials. In 1995, Drudge created an electronic publication called the *Drudge Report*, which the federal district court in the Blumenthal case described as "a gossip column focusing on gossip from Hollywood and Washington, D.C." Drudge's base of operations for his media adventures was an office in his Los Angeles apartment. Computer users visiting Drudge's site on the Internet could click on a link that took them to the most recently published edition of his report. The site also contained links to other online news publications and news articles.

Drudge also developed a list of regular readers or subscribers to whom he e-mailed each new edition of the *Drudge Report*. By March 1995, the Drudge Report had 1,000 e-mail subscribers. In the Blumenthal lawsuit against Drudge and AOL, the plaintiffs alleged that by 1997, Drudge had 85,000 subscribers to his e-mail service. In late 1996, Drudge entered into a six-month licensing agreement with the publisher of *Wired*, giving the magazine the right to display Drudge's column in its new electronic Internet publication. Not long afterward, in the spring of 1997, Drudge entered into a written contract with AOL, making the *Drudge Report* available to all AOL subscribers for a period of one year during which time Drudge was to receive a monthly "royalty payment" of $3,000. According to the court, when Drudge wrote the Blumenthal piece that led to the libel suit, the payment from AOL was his only source of income. In addition to submitting his work to AOL, Drudge continued to distribute the material via e-mail and his own Web site.

Having a contract with AOL greatly increased the likelihood that large numbers of people would see Drudge's work. AOL had over 9 million subscribers at the time Blumenthal sued him. On Sunday evening, August 10, 1997, while presumably sitting in his Los Angeles apartment, Drudge wrote the piece about Sidney and Jacqueline Blumenthal, posted it on his Web site, sent it to his e-mail subscribers, and forwarded it to AOL, which made it available to its customers. Perhaps in keeping with the lightning-fast transmission of information, the next day Drudge received a letter from the Blumenthals' counsel. After receiving the note, Drudge retracted the story alleging spousal abuse in a special edition of the *Drudge Report* posted on his Web site and e-mailed the story with the retraction to his subscribers. At 2:00 A.M. on Tuesday, August 12, 1997, Drudge e-mailed the retraction to AOL, which posted it on its computers. Drudge later publicly apologized to the Blumenthals. Apparently the sources of the allegation against Blumenthal had misinformed Drudge, who went with the story without sufficient confirmation from reliable sources. Drudge later admitted that this was "a case of using me to broadcast dirty laundry," and he added, "I think I've been had." The apology was not enough for the Blumenthals. They filed a $30 million libel suit against Drudge and AOL in federal district court in Washington, D.C.

Blumenthal had good reason to believe that Drudge had seriously damaged his reputation, and he wanted not only Drudge but also AOL to compensate him for the harm he suffered. But although Blumenthal could sue Drudge, he was not able to pursue his lawsuit against AOL because of the Telecommunications Act of 1996. Congress included Section 230 of the Act partially in response to Justice Ain's decision in the *Stratton Oakmont* case and effectively granted immunity to companies providing interactive computer services from being sued for material disseminated by them, but created by others. Congress appeared to decide that such providers could not be treated like newspaper or magazine publishers, or over-the-air broadcast licensees who are responsible for the content they disseminate. Instead, Congress believed that the Internet would best develop in an environment in which online providers would not fear lawsuits over content that passed through their facilities, but which they had no part in creating. Congress thus established in Section 230 what courts have concluded was immunity from such lawsuits: "No provider or user of an interactive computer service shall be treated as the publisher or speaker of any information provided by another information content provider." Congress did not attempt to distinguish between "publisher" liability and notice-based "distributor" liability where there is an opportunity to review potentially controversial material in advance. As the U.S. Court of Appeals for the Fourth Circuit noted in *Zeran*, "if computer service providers were subject to distributor liability, they would face potential liability each time they receive notice of a potentially defamatory statement — from any party, concerning any message." Congress apparently believed that such notice-based liability "would deter service providers from regulating the dissemination of offensive material over their own services" by confronting them with "ceaseless choices of suppressing controversial speech or sustaining prohibitive liability." In other words, in the Fourth Circuit's view, Congress did not want to discourage providers from doing some checking of messages before they are distributed just because they are unable to screen all communication.

The statute goes on to define the term "information content provider" as "any person or entity that is responsible, in whole or in part, for the creation or development of information provided through the Internet or any other interactive computer service." The court noted that whether or not the *Washington Post* or some other newspaper would have done what AOL did — publish Drudge's story without doing anything to edit, verify, or even read it, knowing that the information provided by Drudge was often controversial — was irrelevant. According to the court,

Congress chose, wisely or not, to provide such an exemption to Internet content providers.

Although Congress does not always speak clearly — and in this case, the words "information content" provider seem redundant, as if there is some substantive difference between information and content — the court concluded that Matt Drudge was an "information content provider" and thus AOL must be dismissed from the lawsuit. In granting summary judgment to AOL, the court further determined that Drudge was not an employee or agent of AOL despite the contract between them, and thus AOL could not be held responsible for the harm done by the *Drudge Report*.

The Blumenthal court was not the first to interpret Section 230. In *Zeran*, the Fourth Circuit granted summary judgment to AOL in a suit brought by a Seattle resident who had been listed in a fraudulent advertisement as selling T-shirts with tasteless expressions related to the Oklahoma City bombing. Zeran had nothing to do with the ad and no T-shirts were created or actually offered for sale. The statements in the ad inflamed Oklahoma City residents when they learned about the ad from two morning radio hosts who broadcast Zeran's Seattle telephone number and encouraged listeners to call him. The court held that even if Congress had not provided immunity for Internet service providers, they should not be liable for defamatory material posted by others, which the provider had no role in developing.

Although the federal district court deciding the Blumenthal case had dropped AOL from the lawsuit, it still had to determine whether Drudge also should be dismissed from the lawsuit, a decision that had potentially wide-ranging implications for the development of the Internet. The court concluded that it had personal jurisdiction over Drudge even though he was a California resident and had limited contacts with the District of Columbia, and thus he would remain as a defendant. A court in a distant location cannot automatically assert jurisdiction over a defendant in a case just because a plaintiff names that defendant in a lawsuit filed in that locale. The court must have personal and subject matter jurisdiction before it has the authority to consider a lawsuit.

The court's decision that it had personal jurisdiction over Drudge — primarily because the Web site was accessible from Washington, D.C., and because of its "interactive" features — suggests that anyone who disseminates information over the Internet may have to defend a lawsuit in the home jurisdiction of the plaintiff. That differs significantly from the more traditional lawsuits where the plaintiff has no choice but to sue the defendant in the jurisdiction in which the defendant or the defendant's business is located. In deciding whether it had personal jurisdiction over

Drudge, the court had to consider whether Drudge "regularly does or solicits business in the District of Columbia," or whether he "derives substantial revenue from goods used or consumed or services rendered in the District," or "engages in any other persistent course of conduct here."

Drudge argued that he had not specifically targeted persons in the District of Columbia for readership, largely because of the "non-geographic nature of communicating via the Internet." He also claimed that his travels to Washington, D.C. were not sufficient to establish a persistent course of conduct there. The court concluded, nevertheless, that Drudge had sufficient contacts with Washington, D.C. to warrant exercise of personal jurisdiction. In reviewing decisions by other federal courts, the judge found that the exercise of personal jurisdiction was contingent upon the Web site involving more than the maintenance of a home page; it must also allow computer users to interact directly with the Web site on some level. Although Drudge argued that his Web site was passive, the court found that Drudge's site was sufficiently interactive to permit personal jurisdiction. It allowed computer users, including D.C. residents, to directly e-mail Drudge, thus permitting an exchange of information between the computer user and Drudge's host computer. In addition, visitors to Drudge's site could request a subscription to Drudge's newsletter by leaving their e-mail address. To the court, "the constant exchange of information and direct communication that District of Columbia Internet users are able to have with Drudge's host computer via his web site is the epitome of web site interactivity."

The judge's interpretation of Section 230 and the dropping of AOL from the lawsuit may have been consistent with Congress's interest in protecting Internet companies from liability for messages they did not originate and presumably cannot control. But that decision seems odd in light of the facts of Drudge. It is one thing to argue that AOL is not responsible for monitoring the huge number of messages that pass through its facilities every day; it is something else to assert that it did not have the staff available to read Drudge's copy before it was posted on the AOL site even though Drudge was under contract. If someone with journalistic credentials at AOL had seen Drudge's story and asked the questions that a newspaper editor or broadcast news director would have asked, AOL would never have posted that edition of the *Drudge Report*. AOL would have been spared the negative publicity that Drudge's irresponsible statements generated for the company and for the Internet as a medium of communication. For Sidney Blumenthal, the court's decision to dismiss AOL from the lawsuit must have been frustrating because AOL has "deep pockets" and almost certainly has libel insurance coverage. Drudge, by comparison, probably has limited assets despite his recent success and may not have a libel insurance policy that would help pay a large judgment. The Blumenthals vowed to appeal the decision to drop AOL from the lawsuit.

Other issues

Cyberspace technology has other characteristics that will potentially lead to more litigation and rewriting of First Amendment law. For example, an original article or commentary is often stored for a significantly longer time, and in a more accessible form, than has been the case with traditional news organizations. A broadcast journalist or newspaper editor used to know within a reasonable time if something they aired or published would lead to a libel or invasion-of-privacy lawsuit. Now, with the original information being saved in computer databases and being available worldwide years after the original news story appeared, the likelihood that someone will be harmed by inaccurate information is greatly increased.

In addition, computer databases contain a huge amount of supplementary material — information that was not printed or broadcast — that no one in the newsroom had a chance to carefully review, but which may contain defamatory and false statements that are now preserved for posterity. Years after the news story — which may have been carefully checked — was broadcast or published, the supplementary material will be available for wide dissemination. Considering the nearly permanent nature of potentially harmful statements, and the fact that a potential plaintiff did not know until years after the initial news report that defamatory supplementary material was being stored, courts may be more willing to relax traditional statute-of-limitations standards.

The sheer volume of stored material may result in more lawsuits. Traditional print and broadcast media organizations have always been faced with space and time limitations. Although journalists spend their careers frustrated about how little space there is in the newspaper or time in the newscast for their reports, they recognize that the more limited the news material disseminated to the public, the more likely that the content will have been closely monitored by editors who spot potential legal problems. With new media technology, it is easy for editors to make available in the organization's Web site voluminous amounts of material that they did not have the opportunity to review but which could include defamatory information. Such information may consist of not only printed communication, but also of pictures, graphics, and video. Judges and juries are unlikely to be sympathetic to defense arguments that the journalists could not closely monitor the extra material available through their companies' Web sites, but could only examine what appeared in the newcast or newspaper. Faced with such lawsuits, journalists may be inclined not to store the additional material. That would waste one of the great attributes of digital technology, namely the capacity to store a huge amount of information in a relatively small space and make it easily accessible.

Organizations that store information on computers not only have to worry about data that are archived and accessible for years, but they also need to be concerned about information they thought they had successfully removed from their computers. Companies and law enforcement agencies have developed technology that retrieves messages that had been "deleted" from a hard disk, but are still retrievable from the hard drive for plaintiffs to use in lawsuits. When an executive lost her job at a West Coast company, she was told that the organization was cutting back in a tough economy. She hired a computer firm that found a disparaging message written by her supervisor preserved on the hard disk even though it had been deleted. According to news reports, the company settled her lawsuit for $250,000 within hours after the message was discovered.

The Many Challenges Ahead

New media technology raises numerous legal, policy, and social issues that have yet to be fully discussed, much less settled. Among the most difficult issues is how to control access to sexually explicit materials by children. Children, from kindergartners to teenagers, understandably love exploring the Internet. If they are fortunate enough to have a computer in their bedroom, they may spend hours playing the latest video games or surfing the Internet to learn about subjects and to see pictures that their parents want to keep away from them. Harried parents, who are often at work or doing something else while their children are in front of the computer, may have a difficult time monitoring their discoveries very carefully.

In reaction to this problem, software companies have created an array of programs that filter out potentially harmful information. Although such programs may be effective under certain circumstances, they are a cumbersome method of controlling child access to controversial Internet sites. Some of the best-known filtering programs do more than eliminate access to sites with graphic material. Because they use some of the same words as the more sexually oriented sites, Web pages that offer important information on sexually transmitted diseases, or pregnancy, or many other helpful topics, will also be blocked. One solution has been to require verification of age through a credit card for access to certain sites. That may prevent many children from accessing controversial sites, but it also discourages adults from viewing that material because they do not know if the manager of the site will misuse the credit card information.

Libraries especially have been struggling in recent years to find an appropriate balance between unrestricted access to materials — a creed to which many libraries appropriately subscribe and which is recommended by the American Library Association — and preventing children from viewing text and pictures they are not mature enough to understand. Some libraries have chosen to use filtering software programs that prevent children *and* adults from visiting sites with certain words. In November 1998, a federal district court in Loudoun County, Virginia, issued an injunction requiring the library to remove such filtering devices on the grounds that they prevented adults from viewing constitutionally protected material. Other libraries continue to use such software, perhaps hoping that no judge or administrative authority will have the opportunity to apply the legal standard adopted by the Virginia court.

Some libraries have chosen a middle ground. They have one or more computers for children, with filtering software, and other computers for adults without such software. Other libraries have decided not to use filtering software, but have adopted a different approach. They place computers in a section of the library where there is a lot of patron traffic, or near the circulation or reference desk, on the theory that someone who wants to look at controversial material would worry that someone who knows the patron will see what they are viewing. An unmarried teenager or adult might be hesitant to check material about pregnancy, or be nervous about looking at sites about sexually transmitted diseases, if they thought someone was looking over his or her shoulder. Even the viewing of political sites may be controversial if a patron is visiting Web pages of a candidate or party disfavored by family members or a majority of citizens in the town. Just as a library patron is entitled to complete privacy when it comes to checking out books, the patron should not have to use a computer terminal whose screen is visible to other patrons or library staff.

Parents have even more to worry about than their children looking at sexually graphic material on the Internet. Pedophiles all over the country use the Internet, especially chat rooms, to persuade children to meet them in person. Parents are sometimes horrified to learn that their children have been exchanging e-mail or conversing in chat rooms with such dangerous people for an extended period of time. Only later, when law enforcement authorities are involved, do some parents find out that their child had corresponded with adults who were trying to lure them into potentially life-threatening situations.

The Supreme Court gets involved

The Supreme Court of the United States made it more difficult to control sexual material on the Internet in 1997 when it struck down the Communications Decency Act, a section of the Telecommunications Act of 1996. Two provisions of the CDA sought to protect minors from harmful material on the Internet by criminalizing the "knowing" transmission of obscene or "indecent" messages to any recipient under the age of 18. Another section of the statute prohibited the "knowing" sending or displaying to a person under 18 any message "that, in context, depicts or describes, in terms patently offensive as measured by contemporary community standards, sexual or excretory activities or organs." Those responsible for providing such material could assert as a defense to criminal prosecution that they took "good faith . . . effective actions" to restrict access by minors to the prohibited communications.

A three-judge federal court in Philadelphia had struck down the CDA a year earlier on the grounds that "indecency" was too vague a term to withstand First Amendment scrutiny. The Supreme Court agreed that the CDA violated the First Amendment but for additional reasons. The Court concluded that the law was unconstitutional because:

- it did not allow parents to consent to their children's use of restricted materials;
- it failed to provide any definition of "indecent" and omitted any requirement that "indecent" material lack socially redeeming value;
- it did not limit its restrictions to certain times of the day;
- it applies to a medium that, unlike traditional over-the-air broadcasting, is entitled to full First Amendment protection;
- it is a "content-based blanket restriction on speech."

After thoroughly reviewing many of the Court's major First Amendment cases, the justices concluded that the CDA lacked the careful wording that the First Amendment requires when a statute regulates the content of speech. Although the Court recognized the government's interest in protecting children from potentially harmful material, it could not suppress material that adults have a constitutional right to send and receive.

An argument could be made that restricting sexually explicit material on the Internet, which Congress tried to do in the CDA but which the Supreme Court held violated the First Amendment, would have little effect on the Internet's value in facilitating political discussion. Under such a narrow view, one could aggressively limit access to such material and still allow the American people the opportunity to use new media technology for a full discussion of political and governmental issues. After all, it often appears that a line can be drawn between speech that enhances our capacity for self-governance and speech that is meant to be sexually provocative with little apparent social value. However, the First Amendment has historically prevented government from making such a distinction unless the sexual material is legally obscene under the standards created in *Miller v. California* and other obscenity cases. The First Amendment recognizes that speech related to self-government may take many forms, including fiction, art, and such controversial symbolic speech as the burning of an American flag. Our society would be much less free if only material with political content enjoyed First Amendment protection. Thus, the extent to which sexual material is restricted on the Internet will affect how new media technology provides a forum for the exchange of ideas essential to governing a complex society in the 21st century. As distasteful as many of the images are that can be downloaded from the Internet by children and adults, it is essential that there be substantial protection of even sexual material in order to protect the free exchange of ideas. As overburdened as parents are juggling work, children, and household duties, they must bear most of the responsibility for monitoring the activities of their children and raising them so they know how to react when they find material they are not mature enough to handle.

Hate and extremist groups

Our commitment to First Amendment principles is severely tested when it comes to the Internet sites of organizations and groups that espouse hate against individuals because of their race, religion, or political views. Such communication is even more troublesome when it encourages violence. White supremacist groups have found the Web to be an inexpensive place to reach many more people than they would have in the days of handing out pamphlets or sending a circular to a small mailing list, or publishing a limited-circulation newspaper. Today, there are Internet sites that support the separation of races and often use extreme language that may inspire lawlessness on the part of followers prone to commit violent acts.

On February 2, 1999, a jury in Portland, Oregon, had the difficult task of deciding whether a Web site known as "The Nuremberg Files," created by a group opposed to abortion, exceeded First Amendment protection by inciting violence against those who work in abortion clinics. The Web site featured detailed information about doctors who perform abortions including their pictures, home addresses, license-plate numbers, names of their spouses and children, and other information. In recent years, at least seven people working at abortion clinics around the country have been killed, and there have been more than 250 clinic bombings and incidents of arson. Planned Parenthood and a group of doctors sued the 12 individuals and two organizations that created or maintained the site under federal racketeering statutes and the Freedom of Access to Clinic Entrances Act of 1994, which makes it illegal to use "force or threat of force" against anyone seeking or providing an abortion. A federal jury awarded the plaintiffs $107 million after apparently concluding that the defendants did more than oppose abortion. They went beyond the protections offered by the First Amendment by encouraging action against doctors and others who work for organizations providing abortion services.

The Supreme Court and lower federal and state courts had struggled for years with the issue of where energetic advocacy of a viewpoint ended and criminal activity began. The Supreme Court's first major effort to balance First Amendment rights with national security interests was a failure. The Court created the misnamed "clear and present danger" test — misnamed because the Court upheld the convictions and long prison sentences of dissidents when the danger they posed was neither obvious nor imminent — in *Schenck v. United States* in 1919. The clear and present danger test rarely kept anyone out of jail and was a powerful tool to punish unpopular speech. It was consistently used to uphold the convictions of those who opposed U.S. involvement in World War I; who criticized U.S. efforts to stop the Bolshevik Revolution; and who advocated the overthrow of the government yet did not commit or incite anyone else to commit unlawful acts.

The clear and present danger test was used so perniciously to suppress what was clearly constitutionally protected speech that when the Supreme Court temporarily modified the test in 1951 to permit the government to prosecute officers of the Communist Party, it did so by holding that as long as the "evil" to be prevented was serious — and no one could argue that the overthrow of the government was not serious — individuals who believed that a new government was needed could be prosecuted for merely belonging to an organization that advocated such a policy. It was not until 1957 that the Court began to recognize the difference between the "advocacy of abstract ideas" and the incitement of lawless acts. Finally, in 1969, the Court extended First Amendment protection to such expression unless the speakers or publishers intended to provoke lawless behavior, and someone who heard or read the words took action based on the statements.

With today's technology, such controversial speech can be widely and inexpensively disseminated. A Web site, especially one that gets some attention from traditional news organizations that publicize its existence, may be visited by hundreds or thousands of people who are influenced by what they see on the site. The jury in Portland evidently believed that people who would otherwise not know how to locate abortion doctors, or their families, or their home addresses, could easily find that information on the Web site. The standards that have served the First Amendment so well in recent decades by protecting even speech that is distasteful, upsetting, and sometimes dangerous, will be tested in the Internet era. It is possible that because of the potential for wide dissemination of such controversial information, judges will redraw the line so government can prosecute those espousing such ideas online earlier than they could have been prosecuted had they used old media technology.

Courts will have to sort out these and many other issues. In the meantime, and for the foreseeable future, the Internet will continue to develop largely unmanaged, and with few, if any, individuals in a position to control the content that passes through its networks or the behavior of those downloading the information through their computers. The First Amendment, which was proposed by the First Congress and ratified by the states before there were any modern media technologies, will have to be adapted to the changing conditions without losing the very substantial protections it has offered most forms of expression. How those decisions are made, and the outcomes, will have profound effects on the future of the country.

A profile of Internet users

The Internet's remarkable growth is reflected in the number of Americans who are increasingly turning to online sources for news and information. The Pew Research Center for the People and the Press conducted a survey in June 1998, and found that 25 percent of respondents said they had checked an online source of news the day before. Sixty percent said they got news the day before from television, 47 percent from newspapers, and 29 percent from magazines. The percentage of adults who get news online at least once a week rose from 4 percent in 1995 to 20 percent in 1998. Men are more likely to use online resources for news. Fifteen percent of all women and 25 percent of all men go online to get news at least once a week. Among the most popular sites are those that provide local and national weather information.

The percentages get even larger when education is considered as a factor. Some 35 percent of college graduates get news from the Internet at least once a week. That number rises to 47 percent when considering college graduates under the age of 30. When there is a breaking news story, such as the shootings inside the U.S. Capitol in July 1998, the number of people who turn to Internet sources for information rises significantly.

CNN's Web site went from 25 to 100 percent capacity five minutes after the gunfire erupted. Other Internet news sources such as MSNBC saw a similar surge in traffic.

It is estimated that by the year 2000, more than 50 million people in the United States will subscribe to an online service that allows them to get access to the Internet. Several factors suggest that although the growth of the Internet has been remarkable, it will eventually plateau or rise more slowly as most of the people who are inclined to use Internet resources would have already signed on. However, as new technical improvements make it easier to use the Internet, a significant number of people may sign on in the next decade or so.

A controversy developed in the fall of 1998 about the mental health or social skills of those who spend a lot of time surfing the Internet. A study conducted at Carnegie-Mellon University and published in *The American Psychologist* monitored the computer habits of 73 families in the Pittsburgh area. Computer companies contributed $1.5 million toward the cost of providing the families with computers, modems, and dedicated phone lines for one to two years. Family members were given psychological tests for loneliness, stress, and depression at the start of the experiment and again at the end, and in the interim researchers tracked how much time they spent reading and sending e-mail, talking in chat groups, or looking at Web sites. The researchers concluded that spending as little as one hour a week on the Internet was associated with statistically significant increases in depression, loneliness, and loss of friendships. The authors of the study probably alarmed some parents when they urged them to take computers out of their children's bedrooms and to move them to common family rooms.

Some critics challenged the methods the researchers used and argued that although the results may tell us something about the 73 families, they cannot be generalized to a larger population of Internet users. Among the flaws cited were the lack of a control group and a random selection of subjects, two standard features of most scientifically conducted studies. The researchers defended their lack of scientific rigor, arguing that it was difficult to keep the control group involved because there was no financial incentive for them. They also claimed that a random sample could not be used because they wanted to see how groups that already had social connections to each other would change during the course of the study.

An executive with AOL, which did not participate in the study, said he could not believe that people would find the Internet less than "a very positive, uplifting thing in their lives." He noted that AOL's 13 million customers, of whom 11.5 million are in the United States — about half the American households connected to the Internet — generate 34 million e-mail messages a day and 290 million "instant messages," which are real time exchanges between users who are logged on at the same time. Millions are accessing Web sites that provide valuable information on an array of subjects. The AOL executive suggested that computer users not only get to interact with others through the Internet, but also enjoy ample opportunities to learn new and useful information.

Getting Access to the Internet

Those planning to use Internet technology to organize meetings and exchange information related to a second constitutional convention may encounter individuals who are not part of the Internet world, but want to be. Compared to just a few years ago, it is easy to get access to the Internet. Internet access is available on computers at many libraries and other public institutions, as well as at work and school. However, the advantages of being able to download information about the second convention and discuss various issues related to it from home make it worth the effort to establish Internet service there.

Someone obviously needs to acquire a computer to get started, or a box that uses a TV as a computer monitor. Some companies now market computers for less than $1,000 that will do an adequate job of connecting to Internet resources. If the computer is that inexpensive, its micropro-cessor may not be very fast, it will probably have limited random access memory (RAM) which will slow down its operation, and the hard disk may not have much storage space. Even if the modem speed is at 28.8 or 56.6 kps (kilobytes per second), images from the Internet will download relatively slowly, and when there is a lot of traffic, this process will test the patience of the computer user. New methods of delivery are becoming increasingly available that will greatly improve the speed of transmission and the quality of text, images and video transferred over the Internet.

There are several features the computer should have including a CD-ROM drive, and if it is within the budget, a DVD drive that will run both DVDs and CDs. So many programs come on CDs, and increasingly, DVDs, as opposed to an old-fashioned floppy disk, that anyone without a CD drive will be at a disadvantage. A DVD disk, which looks like a CD-ROM, can hold a tremendous amount of information, as much as 17 gigabytes if both sides are used. Many DVDs hold the equivalent amount of information as four to six CDs.

Once a computer has been purchased and the operating system has been installed — by the user if it has not already been done at the factory — it is time to connect to the Internet. Some computers come with information already installed on the hard drive on how to establish an account and get access to an Internet Service Provider (ISP). If someone uses Windows 98 as the operating system, the computer will come with what is called a "Connection Wizard," which will take both the novice and the more experienced user through the steps of signing up with an ISP.

Another path to the Internet that has great advantages and is used by millions of people is to connect through Internet service provider AOL. It is easy to obtain the software for AOL because it is sent by mail to millions of households for free without being requested, or is available for free at office supply stores. When you sign up, you get several hours of free use. If you are not on AOL's mailing list, you can call the company's 800-number and someone will send the software. You can also download the software from the Internet, but it takes a long time.

Many computers come with AOL already on the hard drive. With a few clicks of the mouse and keyboard, the AOL software can be installed and you are ready to begin getting access to the Internet. The great advantage of AOL is that once you enter your area code, it will give you a choice of telephone numbers where you can connect by a local call. If you highlight one of the numbers and tell the computer to start, it will dial that number and take you through the steps to sign up. You will be asked for a credit card number — which you can provide without worrying that someone will misuse it — and other information. You will then be connected to the huge AOL computers in Virginia and will pay only the equivalent of a local phone call when you are connected.

Some who are not computer savvy or have no experience with the Internet may find all of this confusing. If that is the case, one should hire a consultant — and it can be done for relatively little money — to help the new user pick the right computer and establish an Internet account. There is no reason today for someone who has enough money to buy the hardware and the few programs necessary to get online not to be connected to the rest of the world by computer. Anyone interested in participating in the debate over a second convention, and who has the economic resources, should be able to access the Internet and join the discussion over the future of the country.

Some strongly argue that just as with telephone service, the government should adopt policies that provide universal access to the Internet. If people are going to increasingly communicate with each other and their elected officials by computer, it is important that the "have-nots" be included. Some have suggested a government program such as "computer stamps" modeled after the food stamps program to provide financial subsidies or incentives for families to purchase computers and Internet accounts. Such a program seems grandiose and would probably be prohibitively expensive.

Some negative consequences are possible from encouraging everyone to get access to computers. First of all, the Internet is already congested. If someone is online during times of high traffic, downloading e-mail or getting access to Web sites can be agonizingly slow. Second, many people intentionally choose a lifestyle that is "noninteractive." After a long day at work, they want to read the newspaper or watch TV. They do not want to have to deal with other people on the Internet, or use browsers to search for news and information on a particular subject. Even if a government program gets them a computer and they learn to use it, they will not necessarily become a "Netizen" who spends time on the computer trying to impact local and national policy issues. There have to be financial or intellectual rewards that come from using a computer that outweigh the cost of acquiring the equipment and software, and the challenge of finding and using Web sites.

Becoming a "Media Outlet"

Something is fundamentally democratic about the potential for millions of people in the United States — and ultimately the world — to be able to share their views on almost any subject with anyone who pays attention. For much of the nation's history, mass media outlets were controlled by owners who strongly supported business interests and made a concerted effort to prevent controversial views from being widely disseminated. Even today, national newspapers such as the *New York Times* and *Wall Street Journal*, the major networks, CNN, and other cable news organizations, are highly influential in setting the public agenda and certain subjects — such as those that reflect negatively on the business interests of those organizations — rarely receive much space in the newspaper or time on the air.

The time is not terribly far away in which millions of people will rely less on networks and major news organizations and will communicate more directly with each other through Web sites, newsgroups, lists, and other Internet resources, and will do so in enough numbers to have a major impact on the outcome of elections and policies that governments at all levels pursue. The use of a computer to disseminate ideas does not automatically mean a higher level of political discussion. But if people have the incentive and technical capacity for expressing their thoughts on public issues, and know that they can reach a potentially large audience, they will do so in increasing numbers. The technology will make it too easy to communicate with large numbers of fellow citizens for many people to resist the intrinsic rewards of self-expression.

If computers become easier to use, and if people believe there is information and commentary on issues they care about that they do not get from mainstream news organizations, cyberspace communicators will become more prominent and influential. The initial phase of discussing political issues — including complaining about public officials, suggesting legislation, and arguing about public policy issues — already exists online. The next phase, where people use the Internet to organize activities that seek to directly influence legislators and government at all levels, is just beginning. It is probably true that in 2000, too few people still use the Internet to seek out fellow citizens to engage in political activity for that effort to have a broad impact on American politics. Internet communication on specific issues has already helped interested citizens to organize and influence their elected officials. But in national elections, and in individual congressional districts and states, the impact of cyberspace communication has probably been limited. That will begin to change in the early part of the 21st Century. Many more people are computer savvy. They are connected to the Internet in increasing numbers and are learning how to sort through the huge number of Web sites and newsgroups to find information about candidates and issues, and to use e-mail to discuss those issues with their fellow citizens.

At the same time that the Internet has grown dramatically, so has skepticism — even cynicism — about politics and government. Although the two developments evolved largely independent of each other, their relationship will become increasingly important over the next decade. Millions of Americans take seriously their responsibility as citizens and are still committed to learning about the positions of those who are running for public office. They vote regularly, despite their anger and disgust about politics. Many of those people also believe that media coverage of campaigns — even with some improvement in recent years — remains superficial, ignores important issues, is occasionally biased, and is overly focused on the "horse race" rather than the key issues. There is also little information about what officials do after the campaigning is over and they must govern. Those citizens may find the "unfiltered" information from Internet resources to be increasingly important.

A serious question is whether it is fair to ask the American people — whose knowledge and skills in using new communication technology are still developing — to undertake such a major effort. Some would argue that although the technology is in place to permit such an exchange of ideas and the organizing of a vast number of people around the country, most citizens do not have sufficiently sophisticated computer skills and the political experience to accept such a challenging task. Perhaps some years from now, it could be argued, when a majority of American homes have computers and more people know how to navigate the Internet, such an effort should be seriously discussed.

Despite the merit of such argument, the time is now to use such technology for the purpose of calling a convention. Political cynicism about politics and government is dangerously high and seems to be increasing. Many people express suspicion and hostility toward elected officials and those who seek public office that something drastic must be done. An effort to organize meetings within a congressional district or county, then a statewide convention, and eventually a national preconvention in the nation's capital, would obviously be a grand experiment. Nothing like it has ever been tried in the history of the country and it will require a coordinated effort on the part of dedicated citizens scattered all over the nation. Many of those citizens not only do not know each other, they probably have never given any thought to using the Internet to organize a political movement, much less considered the idea of a second convention for the purpose of proposing amendments to the Constitution. The odds against a second convention being held are overwhelming. It will be opposed by well-meaning people who consider the idea too risky, and by those in political power who will fight any effort to enact serious campaign reform and other changes. But the technology is available and should be used for this noble purpose. There is much to be learned about our capacity for self-government by going through the effort, whether a second convention is ever held.

Too Much Democracy?

Some thoughtful people believe that in some respects, modern communication technology does not enhance participatory democracy, but inhibits it. Larry Grossman, a former president of NBC News and PBS, argued in a 1995 book, *The Electronic Republic*, that elected officials are so inundated with feedback from constituents — which comes to them through computer networks and more traditional communication such as telephone calls, letters, faxes, and telegrams — they are often unwilling to make unpopular decisions. Grossman wrote his book before the Internet made e-mail communication accessible to millions of people who inundate congressional offices with messages, but his general argument is that when elected officials are bombarded with correspondence from the folks back home, they are reluctant to make difficult policy choices that are unpopular in the short term, but may be in the best long-term interests of the country.

The principle that "too much" feedback from constituents can be harmful to the long-term interests of a democracy raises serious issues, but it is not directly analogous to revising the Constitution. The Constitution derives its authority directly from the people, and thus the people have a right, limited only by the procedures established in the document itself, to review the fitness of the Constitution and determine whether it needs to be modified to reflect changing conditions and values.

The Framers in Philadelphia specifically decided that the nation's founding document would be ratified through state conventions whose delegates would be elected by the people. They believed passionately that the legitimacy of the new Constitution depended on direct support of the people as expressed through representatives at the ratifying conventions. When the people consented to the creation of the nation's founding document, they specifically approved a plan of government that established elected branches of government charged with the responsibility of carrying out the will of the citizenry. An indispensable element of such a representative system is the ability of the people to learn what their elected officials have done on their behalf, and what promises those seeking elective office have made. The problem is not that elected officials are discouraged from making difficult decisions because the "will" of the people is expressed too completely, or in inconveniently large numbers. The problem is that individuals and organizations that contribute money to the campaigns of elected officials are granted access and favorable treatment, and yet those officials have figured out how to be unaccountable to the people they represent.

The Constitution, on the other hand, is not subject to ordinary legislative modification and must embody enduring values that do not necessarily change during every generation. Yet the 21st Century descendants of those who approved the founding document by sending representatives to the ratifying conventions are not forever bound by decisions made more than 200 years ago. If that were the case, we would never be able to make changes based on the wisdom that has come from more than two centuries of experience of governing a complex democratic society.

It would be in keeping with the principles established in the Constitution to recognize that if the people have the opportunity to share their views about the nation's founding document and whether it should be renovated at the start of the 21st Century, they would be acting in their capacity as "governors" whose views must be accommodated. The Framers could not have anticipated modern communication technology that makes it easy for constituents to flood Capitol Hill, the White House, and state legislative offices with messages by telephone and traditional mail, and now through electronic messages. They certainly had no way of knowing that millions of people would someday download thousands of Web sites that provide potentially important political and governmental information. But if the nation is committed to self-governance, the people must be permitted to take the next step: To engage in a national debate about their Constitution and to try to organize meetings that lead to the calling of a second convention.

The Constitution includes sections that prove the Framers were worried about the potential of electoral majorities to make short-sighted decisions that imperil the rights of numerical minorities. The Framers dealt with that by creating institutions of government that are able to both resist and respond to the will of the people. They also established a difficult and cumbersome process for amending the Constitution that prevents hasty decisions. They did not, however, create mechanisms — nor have any evolved — that permit government officials to ignore political communication by the people, including criticism of the Constitution, because there are too many citizens sending too many messages. The argument that too much democracy is bad for the country is untenable in a society in which sovereignty is retained by the people.

There is much to the criticism that a national debate over changing the Constitution conducted using Internet technology will be "undemocratic" because it will leave out people who lack computer skills and access. But it is likely many of those people would not have participated anyway. For the millions who stay at home on election day, registering to vote and getting to the polls are either too much trouble, or they are so cynical about politics and government that they are making a "statement" by not learning about public issues and participating in elections. Relatively few people go to the trouble of writing their members of Congress or calling a congressional office. A substantial number of people do not know the name of the person who represents them in the U.S. House of Representatives, and many cannot identify the two senators from their state. One survey revealed that only 11 percent of respondents could remember how their House member voted on any issue during the preceding two years. The number of people who work in campaigns or contribute financially to a candidate is also low.

Mark Edmundson, a professor of English at the University of Virginia, argued in 1997 that Americans are unprepared for a direct democracy where millions of people would use Internet technology to influence government decisions and elections. He believes that because so many Americans cannot read well, and because many people are ignorant of major events and issues in our history, self-government exercised through new media technology is beyond the capacity of the American people: "We Americans couldn't handle it. We don't read enough, don't think enough. We're much too undereducated to make our country into what we frequently claim it already is, a true democracy." According to Edmundson, in order for direct democracy to work in the Internet era of the future, everyone would have to be "deeply versed" in American and international history; everyone would have to write effectively and speak well; and everyone would have to be well-versed in the law, beginning with study in high school and continuing through the university level. In his opinion, too many people do not even have the skills to become part of the process. Edmundson believes that Americans could be divided into two classes: the wired and the tired. The wired are online, affluent, educated, and informed, while the tired are working class, may hold more than one job, and have a much lower economic status. If America is going to become a nation in which everyone has the opportunity to directly participate in politics and government, according to Edmundson, the country needs to make the educational changes to make it work.

Professor Edmundson may be accurate in describing the lack of knowledge of American history and institutions on the part of the American people, but everyone in this country — whether well-educated or not, whether well-informed about politics and government or not — gets the same voting privilege. The new technology can and should be used to elevate public discourse. It should allow those who previously felt left out or those who are too cynical to participate to share their views with a substantial number of their fellow citizens. Planning a second convention will provide an important test of the new technology's potential to enhance the capacity of the American people to govern their nation.

CHAPTER SIX

The Legal Consequences of a Second Convention: The Role of the Elected Branches and the Courts

Congress has proposed 33 constitutional amendments since the nation's founding, but not surprisingly, none of those amendments has been designed to limit congressional power. The Framers at the Philadelphia Convention were understandably reluctant to give Congress the sole authority to initiate or approve amendments. If the legislative branch abused its power in a way that could only be remedied by a constitutional amendment — and Congress refused to propose such an amendment — there could be a serious constitutional crisis. Such a crisis would be especially difficult to overcome if what Congress was doing interfered with the electoral process or the exchange of information necessary to inform voters of the nature of the abuse. It is for that and other reasons that the Philadelphia Convention provided a potential check on the use of such power by including the convention method of proposing amendments in Article V.

The Framers were also concerned about state legislatures blocking reforms that advanced the nation's interests. Thus, Article V gives Congress the discretion to choose between two methods of ratifying proposed amendments: They can either be approved by state legislatures, or by state conventions consisting of delegates elected by the people. The latter method has been used only one time.

Although no second constitutional convention has ever been held, the threat of such a convention led Congress on several occasions to approve amendments that would likely not have won — at least for a long time, if ever — the two-thirds support in each house. Among the best examples was the 17th Amendment, which provides for direct election of senators. Despite having been approved by the House on numerous occasions, and enjoying overwhelming support in the country, the Senate stubbornly refused to forward such an amendment to the states. It was not until some 30 states — one short of the two-thirds needed — petitioned Congress between 1893 and 1911 for a convention to propose direct election that the Senate finally went along. On May 13, 1912, the Senate, rather than face the strong possibility of a convention, approved the direct election amendment that easily obtained approval from three-quarters of the states.

If the meetings discussed in Chapter Four were held, and a serious effort were undertaken to persuade state legislatures to forward petitions to Congress to hold a second convention, Congress would try to be involved in almost every phase of the process. It could not interfere during the organizing of the initial meetings — the congressional district/county meeting, the state convention, and the national preconvention — because those gatherings are clearly "extra-governmental" and are thus not subject to congressional control. Congress cannot tell citizens who want to meet in their local districts, their state capitals, and in Washington, D.C., how the delegates to those meetings are to be selected and what they can discuss. However, once the petitions written at the preconvention are brought to state legislators and they begin to petition Congress to call a second convention, Article V will kick in and Congress will aggressively intervene to try to control the process.

How successful Congress will be in regulating the selection of delegates, the agenda of the second convention, and the procedures used to ratify amendments proposed by the convention, may be largely determined by the federal courts. There will assuredly be lawsuits arising from almost every phase, perhaps even before petitions are taken to state legislatures. For example, if a statewide convention is not representative of the state's racial, ethnic, or gender population, it is possible that litigation will be brought arguing that if the state convention uses public facilities, it must abide by federal statutes prohibiting discrimination based on race and gender. However, litigation is much more likely to arise as soon as a few states petition Congress to call a convention.

The Supreme Court has handed down relatively few decisions related to the process by which constitutional amendments are proposed and approved. It has answered some important questions and sketched the outlines of congressional power to control the amendment process, but many issues remain unresolved. Moreover, few of the decisions provide much guidance as to how Article V should be interpreted and applied to a second convention. Among the many issues Congress and the courts will have to settle are:

• Can Congress set the qualifications and method of selection of the delegates to the convention?

• Can Congress limit the agenda of the second convention to one or two amendments? Or does the Constitution require that it be a general convention with the authority to propose amendments on any subject?

• Can Congress enact a law that requires congressional approval of any amendments proposed by the convention before they can be forwarded to the states?

• Can Congress pass a statute that requires congressional "promulgation" or endorsement of any amendments *after* they are approved by the states, but before the secretary of state can certify that they have been ratified and are part of the Constitution?

• Can Congress declare that certain sections of the Constitution are so essential to the functioning of a democratic society that they are unamendable?

• Can Congress find the petitions forwarded by state legislatures to be too specific or too general, and thus conclude that the petition requirement under Article V is not met?

• Can Congress decide that the amendments proposed by the convention varied too significantly from the petitions that led to the calling of the convention, and thus refuse to forward them to the states for ratification?

Court Involvement in the Amendment Process

The first time the Supreme Court decided a case related to the process for proposing and ratifying constitutional amendments was in *Hollingsworth v. Virginia* in 1798. As discussed in Chapter Two, the Court held that despite some conflicting language in the Constitution, the president had no formal role in the amendment process. The president's approval was not required to approve amendments and forward them to the states, and was not needed at the end of the ratification process. Opponents of the 11th Amendment, which prohibits the federal courts from hearing lawsuits between a state and a citizen of another state, had argued that Article I, Section 7 — which required that "every order, resolution, or vote to which the concurrence of the Senate and House of Representatives may be necessary (except on a question of adjournment) shall be presented to the

President of the United States" — meant the president had to sign the amendment. In *Hollingsworth*, the Court responded that the presidential veto applied "only to the ordinary cases of legislation" and that the president "has nothing to do with the proposition, or adoption, of amendments to the Constitution." The Court recognized that because proposed amendments required two-thirds approval of each house — the same margin that would be necessary to override a veto if the president rejected a proposed amendment — the Constitution did not require that amendments disapproved by the president be resubmitted to Congress for a second vote requiring the same majority. Thus, the 11th Amendment had been properly added to the Constitution without the president's involvement.

It was many years before the Supreme Court again considered cases involving the amendment process. In *Hawke v. Smith* in 1920, the Court had to decide whether the states could require that voters approve a constitutional amendment before state ratification of the amendment could be completed. In November 1918, Ohio amended its constitution to require that any federal constitutional amendment be submitted to voters for a referendum after it had been approved by the state legislature.

The Supreme Court concluded in *Hawke* that when Congress designated state legislatures to ratify amendments, that ratification cannot be subject to popular referendum. The Court found that state legislatures voting on proposed amendments were performing a *federal* rather than a legislative function, and thus because Article V limited ratification of amendments to two methods — by state legislatures or by conventions — it did not permit a referendum process within the states. The Framers could have chosen a different method, the Court observed, including permitting or requiring a vote of the people before amendments became part of the Constitution. But according to the Court, the language of Article V is "plain and admits no doubt in its interpretation." The Court noted that "any other view might lead to endless confusion in the manner of ratification of federal amendments."

Later in the same year, the Supreme Court had to deal with seven cases, known as the *National Prohibition Cases*, where it had to decide several issues related to the amendment process. Among the most important judgments made by the Court was that Article V required two-thirds approval of those present in each house of Congress, not the entire membership, to propose constitutional amendments. A decision to the contrary would have made it even more difficult to secure congressional approval of amendments.

It was not long before the Supreme Court again considered a case involving the constitutional amendment process. Congress had adopted the National Prohibition Act, also known as the Volstead Act, to implement the 18th Amendment. In *Dillon v. Gloss*, decided by the Court in 1921, the petitioner, charged with transporting intoxicating liquor in violation of the Act, argued that the seven-year ratification period that Congress had included in the proposed amendment was too long a time period for the amendment to have been properly ratified. The Court, recognizing that Article V did not specify a ratification period, found that the proposing and ratification of amendments are "not unrelated acts, but as succeeding steps in a single endeavor, the natural inference" was that "they are not to be widely separated in time." Although ratification must be, in the words of the Court, "sufficiently contemporaneous" with the proposing of an amendment, and that "a long series of years would not do," it concluded that the seven-year span that Congress had established for the 18th Amendment was reasonable. The Court noted that Article V speaks in general terms and that it is up to Congress to deal with "subsidiary matters of detail as the public interests and changing conditions may require."

The Court in *Dillon* implied that four pending amendments that had been proposed by Congress without ratification deadlines — two in 1789, one in 1810, and one in 1861 — could not be ratified so many years after they were proposed. The idea that amendments could be slowly ratified by states over a period of many years was, in the words of the Court, "quite untenable." If this view had prevailed or been tested in court, the 27th Amendment dealing with congressional pay raises, an amendment that had lingered before the states for 203 years before being ratified in 1992, might not have become part of the Constitution. The justices apparently rethought their position in *Dillon* when they later decided that the courts should not interfere with congressional discretion to determine the ratification period for constitutional amendments.

A year after *Dillon*, the Court had to contend with Maryland public officials who refused to accept that women were entitled to vote in all elections upon the ratification of the 19th Amendment in 1920. Maryland, whose constitution limited the suffrage to men, had declined to ratify the amendment. State officials argued that by so greatly enlarging the national electorate with the inclusion of women — and applying the new amendment to those states that had not ratified it — Congress had destroyed the state's political autonomy and thus exceeded the amending power. In *Leser v. Garnett* in 1922, the Court answered that the 15th Amendment, which extended voting privileges to blacks and which Maryland also had not ratified, was properly adopted and if the 15th Amendment was certified as a valid addition to the Constitution, so was the 19th Amendment.

Maryland officials also argued that several states had ratified the 19th Amendment in violation of their state constitutions, and thus the ratification was improper. Referring to *Hawke v. Smith*, the Supreme Court responded that legislatures ratifying constitutional amendments were performing a federal function derived from the U.S. Constitution, and it "transcends any limitations sought to be imposed by the people of a State." The final argument made by Maryland officials was that the legislatures of two states, Tennessee and West Virginia, had violated their own rules of legislative procedure in ratifying the amendment. The Court concluded that when the U.S. secretary of state certified that the proposed amendment had been ratified by a sufficient number of states, it became part of the Constitution.

Finally, in *U.S. v. Sprague* in 1931, the Court unanimously rejected a challenge to the procedures used to ratify the 18th Amendment. Opponents of the prohibition amendment argued that the 10th Amendment required that whenever a change in the Constitution restricts the right of the people, the amendment can only be ratified using the convention process. The Court held that Article V was "clear in statement and in meaning" and contains "no ambiguity" when it assigns the responsibility of choosing the method of ratification to Congress. Ironically, the 18th Amendment was repealed by the 21st Amendment when Congress used — for the only time in our history — the convention method of ratification.

The Troublesome *Coleman* Decision and the "Promulgation" Process

By its action in *Dillon*, the Supreme Court strongly suggested that the issue of how long a proposed amendment can be pending before the states is a "justiciable" question, meaning that the courts had the jurisdiction and competence to review it. In *Dillon*, the Court held that a seven-year ratification period was reasonable, although the Court majority indicated that a significantly longer time would probably not be acceptable.

In *Coleman v. Miller*, decided in 1939, the Supreme Court not only ruled that such an issue is within the discretion of Congress — and thus the courts should stay out — it also added a phase to the ratification process that is not found in Article V, but which is potentially devastating to efforts to amend the Constitution through a second convention process. Unless this aspect of *Coleman* is reconsidered, or Congress agrees not to withhold the certification of amendments that have been properly proposed and ratified, there will be no constitutional amendments implementing campaign finance reform, term limits, or any other amendment of which a majority of members of Congress disapprove.

Coleman involved a lawsuit brought by Kansas legislators challenging the constitutionality of the state's ratification of the child labor amendment. At issue was whether the lieutenant governor had the right to cast the deciding vote in the state senate. Those bringing the lawsuit also argued that the 13-year period between the amendment's proposal and the ratification by Kansas was unreasonable. The Supreme Court was evenly divided on the issue of whether the lieutenant governor could cast the deciding vote, and thus expressed no opinion on that question. The Kansas Supreme Court had approved the participation of the lieutenant governor.

Chief Justice Charles Evans Hughes, writing for the U.S. Supreme Court majority, did not directly overrule *Dillon v. Gloss*, but the Court did hold that the issue of how quickly proposed amendments have to be ratified, and the effect on the ratification process of rejection of the amendments by some states, were "political questions" for Congress to decide. The "political question" doctrine in constitutional law is extremely important because the courts will not interfere with decisions they believe should be made by the elected branches of government. The doctrine gives Congress and the Executive Branch substantial discretion over policy issues even when they raise serious constitutional questions.

If the Court in *Coleman* had said that Congress determines whether an amendment pending for more than a decade is still properly ratified when the three-quarters threshold is finally reached, that would have given Congress formal authority to block some amendments that had been pending a long time. But the Court did not stop there. Instead, it also gave Congress a powerful tool that could potentially thwart efforts to enact amendments that Congress does not like.

When the 14th Amendment was ratified, Congress had to deal with the difficult question of whether states that had previously rejected the amendment could be counted among those later ratifying it when newly elected state legislatures gave their approval. Several Southern states had rejected the 14th Amendment when it was first proposed. When new legislatures were chosen under the direction of Congress — elections that history has clearly demonstrated were thoroughly corrupt and did not represent the will of the majority — they approved the 14th Amendment in the very states where a short time before it had been rejected. In addition, two states, Ohio and New Jersey, previously approved the amendment, but then subsequently voted to rescind their ratification.

Congress wanted to make sure that there would not be a lingering dispute over whether the 14th Amendment had become part of the Constitution. On July 9, 1868, Congress adopted a resolution requesting the secretary of state to communicate "a list of States of the Union whose legislatures have ratified" the amendment. On July 20, the Secretary reported to Congress that if the Southern states that had approved the amendment after first rejecting it were counted, and if Ohio and New Jersey were not permitted to rescind their ratification, then three-quarters of the states had endorsed the amendment. The next day, Congress adopted a concurrent resolution that declared the 14th Amendment to be part of the Constitution and that it should be "duly promulgated as such by the Secretary of State."

This was the only time in the history of the amendment process that Congress took action to "promulgate" an amendment. Congress apparently did not give the matter much thought. There was no discussion on the floor of either house about whether Congress had the authority to determine whether an amendment had been properly ratified. The resolution proclaiming ratification was accompanied by little debate and was adopted by a voice vote in the Senate. The Supreme Court in *Coleman* could have interpreted such an action as nothing more than congressional recognition that a sufficient number of states had ratified the 14th Amendment. Instead, the Court suggested that congressional promulgation of an amendment that had gone through the long proposal and ratification process was necessary before an amendment could be considered part of the Constitution:

> We think that in accordance with this historic precedent [the promulgation of the 14th Amendment] the question of the efficacy of ratifications by state legislatures, in light of previous rejection or attempted withdrawal, should be regarded as a political question pertaining to the political departments, with the ultimate authority in the Congress in the exercise of its control over the promulgation of the adoption of the amendment.

Later in the opinion, the Court referred again to the promulgation process by saying that it is up to Congress to determine when the "time arrives for promulgation of the adoption of the amendment." Three members of the Court, Justices Owen Roberts, Felix Frankfurter and William Douglas, joined Justice Hugo Black's concurrence in *Coleman* by asserting that "undivided control of [the amending process] has been given by [Article V] exclusively and completely to Congress."

Walter Dellinger, a former U.S. solicitor general and currently a professor of law at Duke University, called *Coleman* a "venerable" case, but one that is "profoundly wrong." Dellinger argued that neither the language of Article V nor the process by which amendments have been ratified suggests that Congress alone determines whether amendments have been properly adopted. Grover Rees III, a law professor at the University of Texas, also criticized *Coleman* by stating that it was "a very bad decision when handed down, and the Court almost certainly would decide it differently today."

As Dellinger and Rees recognize, much of *Coleman* centers on the question of whether states ought to be able to rescind previously approved amendments, and the effect of such rescission efforts on whether a sufficient number of states have ratified an amendment. The Court in *Coleman* held that such a decision is clearly political in nature and should be left to Congress. But *Coleman* also approves a promulgation process as a step that must be followed before an amendment has been formally adopted when such a process is neither established by Article V's language nor is in keeping with the goals of the Framers.

As noted by Dellinger, if the Framers in Philadelphia had wanted to give Congress the authority to approve or disapprove amendments as the final step, they could have included such language in Article V: "A proposed amendment that has been ratified by the legislatures of three-fourths of the states shall become valid as part of this Constitution when accepted and promulgated by both houses of Congress." Or, Dellinger wrote, the burden might have been reversed: "An amendment shall be valid as part of this Constitution when ratified by three-fourths of the states unless it is rejected by a majority of both houses of Congress within one year of ratification."

Giving Congress so much control over the amendment process, which *Coleman* appears to do, is difficult to square with the intent of the Framers in creating the convention method of proposing amendments. The Framers were understandably concerned that if amendments were necessary to modify congressional power, it would be difficult to convince Congress to propose them. The convention process, although never used, was designed to allow people — through their elected representatives at the state level — to propose amendments without having to seek congressional approval.

If, for example, a sufficient number of state legislatures petition Congress for a convention, a convention is held that proposes amendments related to campaign finance reform, term limits, shortening the terms of senators, and other amendments that Congress would strongly resist, and those amendments make it through the difficult process of ratification by the states, it would be clearly contrary to the wishes of the Framers if — in the final hour — Congress were to withhold its approval by refusing to "promulgate" the amendments. Although an argument could perhaps be made that Congress should have the right to certify an amendment if it had proposed the amendment in the first place, it is dangerous and contrary to the expectations of the Framers to permit such a role for Congress in regard to amendments that came from a convention.

The Court in *Coleman* also failed to distinguish that case from *Hollingsworth v. Virginia, Hawke I, Hawke II,* the *National Prohibition*

Cases, Dillon v. Gloss, and *United States v. Sprague,* where the Court had previously ruled on issues related to the ratification process without being worried about whether they were violating the "political question" doctrine by interfering with congressional authority to decide whether an amendment was properly approved.

Congress has the discretion, if it chooses to exercise it, to pass a resolution declaring that an amendment has been properly ratified. But such a declaration is neither required by Article V, nor should it be determinative of the question of whether the amendment becomes part of the Constitution. It should also not prevent the Supreme Court from reviewing congressional refusal to promulgate an amendment after it has been approved by a sufficient number of states.

The very use of the word "promulgate" by Congress in its resolution approving the 14th Amendment, and the adoption of the term in *Coleman,* suggests that the Court in *Coleman* gave Congress authority it does not have under Article V. According to *Black's Law Dictionary,* "promulgate" is defined as "to publish; to announce officially; to make public as important or obligatory. The formal act of announcing a statute or rule of court." The definition does not suggest that promulgation gives Congress authority to substantively review the procedures used to approve an amendment. Instead, if Congress enjoys the right of promulgation, it is limited to waiting for the ratification process to run its course, and then announce that the process has been completed. If Congress fails to make that announcement, the amendment still becomes part of the Constitution if it has been approved by three-quarters of the states.

Even if there is agreement that Congress's role should be limited, the courts would still be required to settle arguments over the amendment process, and that creates a different set of problems. There is always the danger that the courts would try to prevent the adoption of amendments that limit judicial power or overturn court decisions. At least four amendments that became part of the Constitution sought to reverse or at least modify court rulings. If the Supreme Court, for example, had to sort out disputes related to the time limit for amendments or whether states could rescind their approval, it could use those disputes to invalidate amendments that the Court considered threatening to its powers. Justice Lewis Powell made this point in *Goldwater v. Carter* in 1979 when he wrote approvingly of *Coleman.* But most amendments have not attempted to reverse Supreme Court decisions and there is nothing in the Court's history to suggest that it would use the opportunity of reviewing a procedural issue to obstruct efforts to amend the Constitution. Furthermore, when it had the chance to invalidate an amendment that reversed one of the Court's decisions — in *Hollingsworth* when it reviewed the 11th Amendment, an amendment that directly overruled the Court's decision in *Chisholm* — it concluded that the amendment had been properly ratified.

Professor Laurence Tribe of Harvard Law School disagrees with Dellinger's argument that the courts should be able to play an active role in the amendment process. Tribe recognizes that the Supreme Court would have to intervene if Congress, for example, claimed that a constitutional amendment had been ratified when an insufficient number of states had given their approval. Tribe also acknowledged that there are many other circumstances under which judicial review of the amendment process would be appropriate. But Tribe argues that there are few, if any, rules that would govern court involvement in the proposing and ratification of amendments. He is especially concerned about the Court interfering with amendments that overturn Supreme Court decisions or restrict judicial power.

Tribe admits that the case for judicial review is stronger if the convention method is used to propose amendments. If states petition for a convention because of congressional inaction, "there will be a special cause to fear legislative sabotage, and the courts should then be much less deferential to procedural determinations made by Congress." But Tribe also strenuously opposes the calling of a second convention absent "compelling circumstances," until Article V is amended to "clarify the process of amendment by convention." Testifying before a committee of the California legislature when the state was considering joining the call for a convention to propose a balanced budget amendment, he argued that the Constitution embodies fundamental law and will lose respect if it is "cluttered with regulatory specifics."

In his brief response, Dellinger criticized Tribe's view that Congress has substantial discretion to decide issues related to amendments and that the courts should largely refrain from being involved in the process. In rejecting the idea that Congress should have the authority to decide when to promulgate amendments, Dellinger stated that "the important goal of having relatively clear rules for ascertaining whether the Constitution has been validly amended is poorly served by such an ad hoc and politicized process for resolving Article V disputes."

After Coleman

Although the Supreme Court has not directly ruled on issues related to the amendment process since *Coleman*, several lower courts have handed down decisions. In *Dyer v. Blair* in 1975, the U.S. District Court for the Northern District of Illinois upheld some of the state's requirements for ratification of federal constitutional amendments, but invalidated others. The state constitution required a three-fifths vote of the state legislature to ratify an amendment. Several members of the legislature sued after they failed to gain the necessary votes to approve the Equal Rights Amendment. Judge John Paul Stevens, who was then on the U.S. Court of Appeals for the Seventh Circuit but was later that year appointed to the Supreme Court, wrote for the special three-judge panel that despite *Coleman*, the issue of whether Illinois could require a supermajority to ratify amendments was not a "political question." Stevens concluded that although Article V does not require an extraordinary majority in state legislatures, it also does not prohibit states from adopting such a majority.

However, Stevens struck down another aspect of the Illinois process. The state constitution required that an election of a new legislature precede a vote on a federal constitutional amendment. Stevens decided that such a state constitutional provision would inhibit state legislatures from exercising federal power — as when ratifying proposed amendments to the U.S. Constitution — and was thus not permitted under Article V.

In *Idaho v. Freeman*, a federal district court in 1981 had to decide the difficult question of whether Congress, by a *majority* vote in each House, could extend the ratification period for the ERA. When Congress originally proposed the ERA in 1972, it included a seven-year time limit for ratification in the proposing clause of the resolution, but not in the amendment's text. In 1978, President Carter signed a resolution extending the period of ratification until June 30, 1982. The next year Idaho and Arizona, along with certain members of their legislatures, sued for a declaratory judgment that the time extension was unconstitutional, that Congress was required to extend the deadline by a two-thirds vote in each house, and that Idaho had validly rescinded its ratification of the proposed amendment.

Judge Marion Callister upheld all three of the states' arguments. Citing *Dyer v. Blair*, Judge Callister discussed at length whether the issues presented in the case were political questions and thus should not be resolved by courts. After reviewing the criteria established by the Supreme Court in *Baker v. Carr* in 1962 for deciding whether issues were political questions, Callister concluded that those criteria were not present in this case. He also found that Congress, in dealing with the 14th Amendment in 1868, had not decided the status of rescission votes. The judge further held that, although Congress is not required to set a ratification deadline, once it does so it must abide by it. Thus, the extension of the ratification deadline for the ERA was unconstitutional. If Congress wanted to extend the deadline legally, it would have to do so with a two-thirds vote in each house as required by Article V. Judge Callister's opinion, which included much discussion of the history of the amendment process, nevertheless was of limited duration and impact. His ruling was stayed by the U.S.

Supreme Court and eventually became "moot" when a sufficient number of states failed to approve the ERA within the extended time period.

Congressional Interference

Those who support a second constitutional convention have more to fear from congressional involvement in the process than the judiciary's because it is Congress that has refused to seriously consider campaign finance reform, term limits, and other changes that enjoy widespread support in the country. Although it is possible that the Supreme Court would view some amendments proposed by a second convention with sufficient alarm that the justices would use challenges to the process to stop legitimate efforts to amend the Constitution, it seems unlikely that the Court would do so.

If, for example, a proposed constitutional amendment sought to reverse *Buckley v. Valeo* — the Court's decision in 1976 which held that campaign expenditures are protected by the First Amendment and are thus not subject to regulation — the Supreme Court would not see such an amendment as a limitation of its power to decide cases. Most of the justices would probably regard such an amendment as an appropriate use of Article V and the sovereignty exercised by the people. However, if an amendment to change the lifetime tenure of judges were to be proposed, it is likely the justices would more closely scrutinize the process by which the amendment was initiated and ratified. But that does not mean that the justices would want to or be able to stop approval of the amendment.

If, as suggested in *Coleman*, Congress has the authority to approve amendments at the end of the process through some type of promulgation procedure — without which the amendments could not be certified as properly ratified — it is entirely possible that Congress would use such power, then react as it usually does when it clearly and brazenly defies its constituents. Incumbents would raise more money from more organizations with interests before Congress and overwhelm underfunded and lesser-known challengers. Those running for reelection, if they have to answer at all for their decision to withhold final approval of a duly passed amendment, would simply argue that there were defects in the way the second convention's delegates were selected or the way the convention conducted its business, or the way the proposed amendments were submitted to or ratified by the states. Thus, they would claim that they are protecting the Constitution and saving the country by refusing to give their approval to an amendment by withholding promulgation at the final stage. Those who go through the long process of organizing a second convention to propose amendments, and who lobby state legislatures all over the country to see them ratified, should take their chances with the Supreme Court and not Congress.

Statutory Efforts in the Past
to Control the Process

Congress has never enacted a law related to a second convention. Several bills have been introduced going back to the 1960s, and some have been seriously considered by either a House or Senate committee, but at no time has such legislation come close to passing. If the meetings described in this book are held and petitions are taken to state legislators who are urged to forward those petitions to Congress, and some states ask Congress to call a convention, Congress will quickly pass a law to try to control the process. Such legislation will probably be based on bills that have been introduced in the past. If those are any indication, it is likely that Congress will dominate the process and leave few decisions to the people trying to organize the convention.

Among the most prominent of the members of Congress who have thought about procedures for a constitutional convention was the late Sam Ervin, a Democratic senator from North Carolina. Ervin became a household name when he chaired the Senate Watergate Committee that investigated the wrongdoing of the Nixon Administration and the Committee to Reelect the President. The Watergate hearings, which were carried live on television for months in 1973 and 1974, eventually led to Nixon's resignation.

In 1967, Ervin introduced the Federal Constitutional Convention Act. He and Republican Senator Everett Dirksen of Illinois were trying to organize a convention to repeal the Supreme Court's reapportionment decisions. The Ervin bill passed the Senate in 1971 and 1973, but the House did not act on it. In 1979, Senator Orrin Hatch (R-UT) introduced the Constitutional Convention Implementation Act, which was the most comprehensive bill considered by Congress on how a convention would be called and the procedures that the convention would follow. Hatch's bill, S. 40, was approved by the Senate Judiciary Committee on September 10, 1985, but did not pass the Senate. The House has never approved a bill related to a second convention.

Both Ervin and Hatch believed that Congress has the power to adopt such legislation under the necessary and proper clause. That clause — Article I, Section 8 — gives Congress authority to pass legislation on numerous subjects that are not explicitly enumerated in the Constitution.

Both senators also believed that it was better to pass legislation related to a second convention that could apply to any issue or proposed amendment, rather than enact a bill in the middle of a heated debate that may be seen as favoring one side. The Ervin bill originally proposed that applications for a convention be valid for seven years, but he subsequently reduced that period to four years. The Hatch bill provided a convention-application period of no longer than seven years. Section 5(a) of S. 40 gave states the discretion to include in their petitions instructions that the petition was to remain effective for less than a period of seven years. Although Section 5(b) of the bill allowed a state to rescind its application, it would not be permitted to do so once the two-thirds threshold has been met.

S. 40 authorized the states to petition for a convention by adopting a resolution stating that the legislature "requests the calling of a convention for the purpose of proposing one or more specific amendments to the Constitution of the United States and stating the subject matter of the amendment or amendments to be proposed." The legislation did not say how specific the petitions must be. However, the petitions must find a middle ground between being so specific that the second convention's delegates would have insufficient discretion to debate and write proposed amendments, and being so general that courts will rule that the requirements of Article V have not been met.

A revised version of the Ervin bill and the Hatch bill followed the model of the Electoral College in giving each state votes equal to its total number of U.S. senators and representatives and allowed for majority rule. S. 40 required that two delegates from each state be elected on an at-large basis and one delegate be elected from each congressional district in the manner provided by state law. Current U.S. senators or representatives, or anyone holding "an office of trust or profit under the United States," would be prohibited from serving as a delegate.

Both the Ervin and Hatch bills would have permitted Congress to specify, based on the state petitions, the general subject matter of the convention. Section 10 of S. 40 stated that "no convention called under this Act may propose any amendment or amendments of a subject matter different from that stated in the concurrent resolution calling the convention." This provision would be a potentially serious roadblock to reforms that Congress opposes. The courts would then have to decide whether Congress can limit the convention to certain subjects. That is one reason it is especially important that the petitions approved by state legislatures and forwarded to Congress calling a convention be identical or as similar as possible. S. 40 also gave Congress the right to refuse to forward the proposed amendments to the states if, in its view, they vary from the subjects in the original petitions. Section 11(b)(ii) stated that Congress will not direct the Administrator of General Services to forward the proposed amendment to the states if "such proposed amendment relates to or includes subject matter which differs from or was not included in the subject matter named or described in the concurrent resolution of the Congress by which the convention was called."

Although Congress wants to be able to control the process both before and after a convention is held, S. 40 did not provide for a "promulgation" phase after the states have ratified the amendments. Despite the Supreme Court's decision in *Coleman* approving such a procedure, Section 12(a) of S. 40 required that any amendment approved by three-fourths of the states be recognized as part of the Constitution. Once three-fourths have ratified, the Administrator of General Services shall issue a "proclamation that the amendment is a part of the Constitution of the United States." Finally, S. 40 permitted any state "aggrieved by any determination or finding" as part of the convention process to bring an action in the U.S. Supreme Court. This provision would appear to undo some of the potential damage of *Coleman*, which strongly suggested that questions related to a second convention were not to be considered by the courts.

Questions for the Courts

It is not difficult to imagine that from the moment delegates to the preconvention write petitions that are brought to state legislatures all over the country, and as soon as the first states approve such petitions and forward them to Congress, there will be litigation challenging almost every aspect of the process. Because nothing like this has ever been undertaken in the history of the country, many issues will have to be settled by the courts, or the courts will have to rule that the issues are political questions that they should leave to the elected branches of government.

Those who want to stop the process may not even wait until the initial three meetings are over before rushing to courthouses all over the country. But it is difficult to see how the courts could intervene during that phase. The organizing of the three meetings clearly implicates rights protected by the First Amendment including freedom of speech, right to petition government, right to peaceably assemble, and the implied right of freedom of association. The three meetings are "extra-governmental" and neither Congress nor the states should be able to interfere with the right of people to gather in their congressional districts or counties, and later in their state capitals and the nation's capital, to discuss how the

Constitution should be revised. Although someone may file a lawsuit to try to stop the first meetings, there appears to be no reasonable basis on which the courts can interfere at the initial phase.

That situation will change as soon as the petitions that come from the preconvention are considered by state legislatures. At that point the process becomes "governmental" and is undertaken pursuant to procedures established in Article V. Thus, the first lawsuit is likely to be filed over the language of the petitions. The plaintiffs, who will not want state legislatures to have the chance to forward the petitions to Congress, will argue either that the petitions are too general, and thus do not satisfy the requirements under Article V, or that they are too specific, and thus inappropriately limit the discretion of the second convention. If there is much variance in the language of the petitions, the plaintiffs seeking to stop the process will argue that Congress need not respond to such a call because too many of the state petitions ask for the convention to consider different subjects or proposed amendments. This presents a serious danger to the whole effort that will require extraordinary cooperation among the individuals and groups involved. Getting delegates to the national preconvention to agree on the language of the petitions will be difficult enough. Convincing 34 state legislatures to approve the same language and forward the petitions to Congress will be a huge task. Nevertheless, in order to get past the first set of lawsuits, the petitions need to be relatively uniform and neither too general nor too specific.

The next set of lawsuits will likely be based on whatever legislation Congress has approved to establish the selection of delegates and the conduct of the convention. If Congress seeks to monopolize the entire process, including limit the convention's agenda to subjects that Congress approves, litigation will argue that it cannot exercise so much control over convention procedures. The case will be made that the Framers in Philadelphia intentionally provided in Article V a mechanism by which Congress can be bypassed so that when changes in the Constitution are necessary that Congress opposes, there will be some opportunity to bring about those reforms. Article V still gives Congress the authority to decide whether proposed amendments will be ratified by state legislatures or state conventions, but nothing in Article V gives Congress the right to prevent the alternate method of amending the Constitution from being used successfully. Other lawsuits will argue that Congress has no authority to limit the subjects considered by the convention, while the response will be that Article V is silent on whether Congress must call a general convention.

Once the numerous lawsuits related to congressional authority to establish convention procedures have been resolved and the convention is actually held, litigation will challenge the way the convention conducted its business. Some will argue that the proposed amendments should have been ratified by a two-thirds vote, the threshold required for amendments to be proposed by Congress. Others will insist that if the Framers intended to require two-thirds approval in a convention, they would have said so. The Framers could speak with clarity and specificity when they wanted to, it will be argued. They did not establish such a requirement in Article V, and none should be inferred from the absence of such language.

If the statute Congress enacts requires congressional approval of amendments before they can be forwarded to the states for ratification, and Congress refuses to forward some or all of the amendments agreed to by the convention, a lawsuit will seek to force Congress to release the amendments by declaring that section of the statute to be unconstitutional. There will also likely be litigation over whether the delegates chosen were representative of the population of the state or nation; whether voting should have been by states at the convention, as done in Philadelphia in 1787, or by individual delegates; and whether the convention violated open meetings laws by holding private sessions, or open records laws by keeping some documents away from the press and public until the convention had ended.

After the convention ends, if Congress has decided that state legislatures should ratify the proposed amendments, there may be lawsuits over how long the period of ratification should be — was the time period established by the convention or Congress, for example? — and whether states that approve the amendments can later rescind that vote; whether states can require that such amendments be approved by a supermajority in the legislature, and other issues. If Congress instead chooses state conventions for ratification, there will be lawsuits over how the delegates are selected. It may make a big difference, for example, whether delegates are elected from smaller districts as opposed to running statewide for delegate positions to the convention. At-large elections may well limit the representation of certain groups at the convention unless some type of proportional voting is used. If district elections are to be held, the question of what district is appropriate — the county, a congressional district, or some other political unit — must be addressed.

Decisions will have to be made about the campaigns for delegates to the ratifying convention. Will there be public financing of campaigns so those who cannot afford to pay for the campaign themselves, or who are not well-connected politically, will have a chance of winning? Because there may be a large number of candidates, will candidates run by party and will there be a primary? Or will it be a nonpartisan race with finalists having to face voters again in a runoff election?

These and many other questions about using the convention method to amend the Constitution will have to be answered with little guidance from the nation's history. Article V provides no instruction on how a second convention is to be conducted. Because there has never been a second convention, we cannot look to the past to help avoid mistakes that could be terribly costly to the process. Those involved have to believe that not only is the goal of seeing amendments become part of the Constitution important, the exercise of going through the process is likely to tell us a lot about our capacity for self-government. Regardless of the ultimate outcome of this endeavor, the process will provide useful experience for future efforts to use new communication technology to influence governmental decisions.

Part III

CHAPTER SEVEN

Amendment "A": Campaign Finance Reform

The Petition

𝕿he legislature of the state of _____, comprising the duly elected representatives of the people thereof, formally request that the United States Congress call a constitutional convention under Article V of the United States Constitution so that the convention can consider, and in its discretion, propose an amendment or amendments addressing the subject of the raising and spending of campaign money in federal, state, and local elections. This petition was approved by both houses of this legislature in accordance with its established rules and procedures.

Amendment "A"

Section 1. Regulation of contributions and expenditures in election campaigns at the federal, state, and local level shall not be construed by any court as violating the First Amendment to the United States Constitution.

Section 2. Candidates for Senator or Representative in Congress shall be required to raise half of all funds spent in the campaign from persons, groups, or organizations residing within or based in that State or House district, respectively. The legislatures of the several states and Congress shall have the power to enforce this provision by appropriate legislation. An administrative agency within each state will monitor compliance with this provision and widely disseminate its findings through traditional mass media and advanced forms of communication technology.

Section 3. For elections for Congress, president, and vice president, Congress will impose a limit on campaign expenditures by determining an appropriate dollar amount per registered voter, an amount that will change only to reflect an increase in population or an increase in inflation as measured by accepted government indexes. Expenditures made independently of the candidate or the candidate's campaign will be covered by this limit.

Section 4. For state and local elections, the legislatures of the several states will impose a limit on campaign expenditures by determining an appropriate dollar amount per registered voter, an amount that will increase only to reflect an increase in population or inflation as measured by accepted government indexes. Expenditures made independently of the candidate or the candidate's campaign will be covered by this limit.

Section 5. Congress shall adequately fund the Federal Election Commission, or another federal agency, so that it can carry out statutory responsibilities to monitor compliance with federal campaign and election laws and to widely distribute its findings through traditional mass media and advanced forms of communication technology.

Section 6. All states shall be required to create and adequately fund a state administrative agency that monitors compliance with state campaign and election laws and distributes its findings through traditional mass media and advanced forms of communication technology.

Section 7. Both Congress and the legislatures of the several states shall require comprehensive disclosure of campaign contributions and expenditures of candidates throughout the campaign, and shall provide such information to the American people through traditional mass media and advanced forms of communication technology.

Section 8. Congress and every state shall study a plan by which elections are publicly financed and shall widely report the results of such studies no more than two years after ratification of this amendment.

Section 9. This amendment shall be in effect immediately upon its ratification.

Section 10. This amendment shall be inoperable unless ratified as an amendment to the United States Constitution within seven years from the date of its submission.

Section 11. Ratification of this amendment shall take place by conventions in each state whose delegates will be popularly elected.

Cleaning Up the Campaign Finance Mess

Every year millions of school children in the United States read in their textbooks and hear their teachers say that we live in a free society based on democratic principles, and that our system of politics and government is the envy of the world. We learn that the American people are the sovereign, and are thus the "governors," while our elected officials are the "servants." Under such a theory, the people retain ultimate authority and delegate only a portion of that authority to their public servants. The key to the system is the freedom to elect those who represent us in government. The right to choose our leaders in open elections is precious and enjoyed by relatively few people around the world. We are taught to appreciate that freedom as we learn about people who live under repressive regimes or governments where such a right does not exist.

In order for our democratic system of representation to work, we are told, the American people must be able to choose leaders who understand our views and who will make decisions based on what is in our best interests. If elected officials do not adequately represent those views in the laws they pass and the numerous other decisions they make, we have the ability to replace them with those who will more conscientiously try to carry out our wishes.

Certain assumptions must be made about the way elections and campaigns work if this nation is truly going to be a democratic society. Some of these assumptions are explicitly stated in textbooks, by teachers or our parents, while others we learn more indirectly. They include these essential principles:

• Citizens are interested and informed about politics and government and are eager to participate by voting. For many, just being knowledgeable and casting a ballot is not enough. They will also make donations to candidates or work in their campaigns.

• People will read newspapers and magazines, watch television news reports, listen to radio broadcasts, and explore Internet sites so they will be well informed about those they will choose to represent them. Voters will discuss political issues with their families, friends, and colleagues. They will attend debates or other political events and make an effort to meet candidates in person.

• All candidates have the opportunity to present their ideas and qualifications to the voters no matter how poorly their campaigns are financed, and no matter how controversial their ideas. Even if those ideas challenge the prevailing attitude on important issues, they will be heard by potential voters who will rationally consider their value.

• When deciding whether to return an incumbent for another term, voters will remember the votes taken over the past two or four or six years. They also will know how much or how little those incumbents have worked on their constituents' behalf and whether they have the temperament, commitment to important principles, and intelligence to carry out the difficult duties of an elected official.

• Once the election is over, citizens will follow the activities of government and will seek to influence policy decisions by writing letters, sending e-mail, and organizing groups that try to persuade government officials to consider their views. The information gathered through this process helps prepare voters for the next election.

These assumptions sound great. What could be better in a free society than enthusiastic, informed voters poring over political information, debating issues with friends and family, and when possible, with candidates, then making a rational choice about who will represent them in government? Unfortunately, those descriptions do not even come close to portraying the way politics and government work in the United States as we approach the end of the century. The following statements are, unfortunately, much more accurate:

• A substantial number of American adults are appallingly uninformed about politics, American history, and the way government works. Many do not follow campaigns closely and do not learn much, if anything, about candidates' qualifications or positions even when there is plenty of interesting and accessible news coverage.

• A depressingly small number of citizens vote, even though it has never been easier to register and to cast a ballot. In 1996, presidential election turnout was the lowest in 70 years despite millions of Americans being registered in recent years without any effort on their part when getting or renewing a driver's license.

• Many who do vote know little about the candidates' record or promises, but vote for them because their name is vaguely familiar or appealing.

• Relatively few elections are competitive, and thus there is often no real choice for voters. Many districts are drawn so that only one party has a reasonable chance of winning.

• The advantages of incumbency are overwhelming, and not surprisingly, incumbents almost always win. Many challengers, even those who are well qualified and have good ideas, often cannot raise enough money to be seriously competitive when facing an incumbent who has been gathering money from the moment the previous election ended.

• Even when incumbents have no serious challenger, they still raise huge sums of money to make sure there is no opponent with a good chance to win next time.

• Election campaigns are incredibly expensive and the costs escalate each year. Incumbents and those challengers who dare to make the race spend too much of their time raising campaign funds and not enough time legislating or concentrating on issues. Potential candidates who do not want to devote so much of their energy to asking people for money often do not run.

• Once in office, incumbents know they are unlikely to lose no matter what their positions on the issues. They soon find out it is better to pay more attention to the interests of those keeping them in office with large campaign contributions than those they represent back home. There are relatively few issues that will be so visible or controversial that elected officials feel they must follow the wishes of a majority of their constituents.

• Those who contribute substantial sums to help elect favored candidates or keep them in office get a lot in return for their money including access to legislators, special legislation, government contracts, and a commitment from members to stop legislation harmful to their interests from being enacted.

• Millions of dollars are spent on attack ads that intentionally distort an opponent's record or promises. The public gets confused and discouraged and eventually stops paying attention and learning about candidates and issues.

• Campaign finance laws at the federal level, as they have been interpreted by the courts, permit *unlimited* indirect contributions to candidates and permit candidates and parties to spend *unlimited* sums of money in the campaign. State campaign finance laws have met with limited success if the goals are making elections more competitive and giving voters more choices of candidates to consider.

• The Supreme Court gutted many of the most important provisions of the federal law that was amended in the wake of the Watergate scandal to clean up federal elections. The Court's 1976 decision in *Buckley v. Valeo* has contributed greatly to the level of cynicism and disgust about politics and government and is a huge impediment to reform.

• The amount of money spent on campaigns has tripled since *Buckley*. The increase in campaign spending has not, however, meant a corresponding increase in available information or knowledge and interest in politics. Many more people today appear to be turned off to politics and not interested in voting than in the recent past.

• Many incumbents who benefit from the current system success-fully resist efforts to enact campaign finance reform, despite overwhelm-ing public support for it, yet are reelected anyway.

• Wealthy individuals can often buy elections by spending huge sums of their own money that challengers cannot begin to match. Not surprisingly, a disproportionate percentage of members of the U.S. House and Senate are millionaires.

No single constitutional amendment will make the reality of elections in this country more like the mythical description taught in schools. The issues are too complex. One of the clear lessons from efforts to enact campaign finance reform at the federal and state level is that such measures often lead to unintended consequences. There is also the serious question of how to enact reform without trampling on the First Amendment rights of candidates, and the right of groups and individuals independent of the candidates to discuss issues in the campaign. Protection of political speech has long been considered a core value of the First Amendment. Any changes to the Constitution related to campaign finance reform will undoubtedly cause some bad side effects. But the amendment proposed in this chapter attempts to address some of the most serious flaws in the system, ones that elected officials will not enact because it will make them more vulnerable to defeat at the polls.

Overturning *Buckley*

The Watergate scandal involved more than a break-in at the head-quarters of the Democratic National Committee and a coordinated effort extending to the Oval Office to cover up the crime. Part of the Watergate story was the uncontrolled contributions by individuals and corporations to President Nixon's reelection campaign in 1972. Single contributions were as high as several million dollars. The Nixon campaign received con-tributions of over $50,000 from each of 142 individuals. The campaign also collected $750,000 in illegal donations from 12 corporations. People who wanted to be considered for ambassadorships and other positions knew that if they made large enough contributions, their chances of appoint-ment were greatly increased. The overall campaign raised more than $60 million to defeat Senator George McGovern (D-SD), who never had much of a chance of beating Nixon. There was also evidence that some contributions were extorted from individuals and corporations who wor-ried about retaliation if they did not support the reelection effort. At the same time that the public was inundated with reports about contributions to the president's campaign and thousands of dollars in cash being stored in White House safes, there were also news stories about huge contributions, by individuals and corporations, to congressional campaigns.

In response to the public outcry about the money scandal, especially the appearance of "quid pro quo" corruption — which suggested that contributions bought the allegiance of grateful elected officials — Congress amended the Federal Election Campaign Act of 1971. Several important changes were made to the Act in 1974 to limit contributions and expenditures, and to enhance disclosure requirements. It is important at the outset to recognize a distinction between *contributions* to a campaign (directly to a candidate or to "independent" groups or political parties) and *expenditures* (money spent by the campaign or by independent groups or parties). The Supreme Court interpreted the Constitution in a way that treats contributions differently from expenditures.

In the 1974 amendments, Congress imposed four different types of contribution limits, most involving money given directly to a candidate's campaign. The Supreme Court ultimately upheld all of them in *Buckley*, and they remain in force (they are sometimes referred to as "hard money" contributions):

• Congress limited the amount that an individual could give a candidate for federal office to $1,000 per election ($1,000 for the primary, $1,000 for the general election).

• Congress permitted political action committees (PACs) to contribute $5,000 per election. A PAC is a fund created by a corporation, labor union, or political organization to which individuals "voluntarily" contribute to advance the interests of the organization. The law requires, for example, that in the case of corporations, a PAC must only raise money from individuals who freely contribute to it. The money cannot come from the assets of the corporation. Whether employees of corporations are always able to say no to management requests to give money to the political action committee is another matter.

• Congress limited how much could be contributed to the national political parties. Individuals were limited to $20,000 per year, and PACs to $15,000.

• Finally, Congress imposed an aggregate cap of $25,000 per year on the amount that an individual could contribute to all federal candidates, PACs, and national parties.

An essential element of the reforms of 1974 were the limits on the amount of money a campaign could spend. The invalidation of these limits by the Supreme Court has had a profound impact on contributions *and* expenditures. These are the limits on spending that Congress approved in 1974 but that the Court struck down in *Buckley*, leaving in their wake the "soft-money" loophole:

• For presidential campaigns, Congress imposed a spending limit of $10 million for the primaries and $20 million for the general election.

• Senate campaign limits varied, depending on the state's voting-age population. A candidate could spend no more than eight cents per voter for the primary, and 12 cents for the general election. House campaigns were limited to $70,000 for a primary election and another $70,000 for a general election.

• Congress also limited how much of a candidate's personal wealth could be spent on a campaign. The limits were $50,000 for presidential candidates, $35,000 for Senate candidates, and $25,000 for House candidates.

• Perhaps most surprising was the strict limit on how much could be spent independently by groups or individuals to support a federal candidate. Congress set that amount at $1,000 per election.

With the same speed with which it approved the 1971 Act, Congress enacted the 1974 amendments without including some findings that may have kept the Supreme Court from invalidating so many of its provisions. Congress rushed to pass the amendments without providing detailed findings of fact, predictions of beneficial effect, or statements in the legislation of the purposes that it would fulfill. In the important book *Buckley Stops Here*, a group of lawyers, legal scholars, and representatives of public interest groups describe how the changes to the law were a recipe for judicial disaster:

> Take a very complicated, highly nuanced area in which Congress has scarcely ever legislated. Be sure it is a field involving critically important issues — like the very health of our democracy. Impose upon it a complex tangle of regulations infused with ambiguity. Authorize an expedited review. Dump the whole mess on the courts just as a critical deadline for resolution of its validity approaches. Make sure there is no time to develop a factual record. Make sure there is no time to assess the facts through time-tested adversarial devices of discovery, deposition, expert testimony, cross-examination, and full briefing. . . . Mix these ingredients together, and, presto, you have an unmitigated disaster that looks a lot like *Buckley*.

Congress permitted opponents of the law to challenge it without it having gone into effect and before its impact could be seen in the 1976 elections. The case raced through the appellate process and reached the Supreme Court for oral argument in November 1975, less than 13 months after the law was enacted. The Court handed down the decision on January 30, 1976. Perhaps in keeping with the importance of the subjects it covers, the *Buckley* opinion is incredibly long and complicated. It runs

294 pages, with 232 footnotes. The splintered Court issued five separate opinions. Its unsigned lead opinion upheld the contribution limits (to candidates and to parties) and invalidated all the restrictions on spending (whether by a candidate, party, or independent group).

The Supreme Court was badly divided on the key issues. With eight justices participating (Justice John Paul Stevens recused himself), only three accepted the lead opinion's rationale in full (Justices William Brennan, Potter Stewart, and Lewis Powell). Contribution limits were approved by six justices, with only Chief Justice Warren Burger and Justice Harry Blackmun dissenting. Spending limits were invalidated by seven justices, with only Justice Byron White dissenting, joined by Justice Thurgood Marshall on the narrow issue of a candidate's personal expenditures. The slimmest majority of all was reserved for the issue that has become the biggest problem in the wake of *Buckley*. Four justices (Brennan, Stewart, Powell, and Rehnquist), accepted the argument that the First Amendment makes a distinction between contributions and expenditures. A fifth justice, Marshall, accepted the distinction in principle, but believed that a candidate's personal spending should be treated as a self-directed contribution. Justice Marshall later repudiated the belief that such a distinction can be drawn. Three justices (Burger, Blackmun, and White) flatly rejected the notion that contributions and expenditures were different for First Amendment purposes.

The Court did uphold the presidential public financing system under which major party candidates receive large sums of public money (about $65 million in the 1996 election) in return for a promise to forgo their own general election fundraising. The Court's reasoning was that the expenditure limits were voluntary because no presidential candidate had to accept public financing. Even if a presidential campaign accepts such financing, however, there is nothing in the current law that prevents the national parties or independent groups from raising millions of dollars of soft money to spend on the presidential election, money that is in addition to what the taxpayers provide as part of the public financing system. If this soft-money loophole were closed and a presidential candidate were actually limited to the amounts designated under the public financing system, that part of the process might work fairly well.

By striking down limits on campaign expenditures on First Amendment grounds, the Court permitted the creation of several loopholes that have seriously damaged the election process. *Buckley* upheld contribution limits, but only as they pertain to "hard money" contributions that are given directly to the candidate's campaign. The elimination of expenditure limits for both the campaign and independent groups has meant that corporations, unions, and wealthy individuals who want access, government contracts, help with passing or defeating legislation, and other rewards, know they can donate whatever they want as long as it is not given directly to a campaign. Such contributions are permitted even though it has been against the law for corporations to contribute directly to campaigns since 1907, and for unions to do so since 1947. (Many states permit direct contributions by corporations and unions to state candidates). *Buckley* and the campaign laws also allow so-called independent groups and political parties to make unlimited expenditures as long as those efforts are not coordinated with the candidate's campaign.

By basing *Buckley* on constitutional as opposed to statutory grounds, the Court made it all but impossible for Congress to enact serious campaign finance reform until the Court itself reconsiders the decision. When the Supreme Court bases a decision on a provision of the Constitution, it can only be formally reversed by the Court itself or by a constitutional amendment. Under the supremacy clause of Article VI, the Constitution is superior to all other laws. Thus Congress, even if it were inclined to do so — which it is not — could not pass an expenditure limit.

The Court's belief that contribution limits will cut down on potential corruption — at the same time that it allows unlimited expenditures by candidates or on their behalf — is naive to say the least. A politician can be beholden to those who "independently" raise and spend hundreds of thousands of dollars in support of the campaign without those supporters contributing any money directly to the candidate. The candidate almost always knows what groups and individuals have generously donated to the campaign, whether those contributions are made directly through hard money or indirectly through soft money. The same is true with groups and individuals who make "independent" expenditures. The notion that the electoral system is more likely to be free of actual or perceived corruption by laws that only limit direct contributions is absurd.

Buckley has haunted this country for a quarter of a century. Although the Court has had several opportunities to reconsider the principles of *Buckley*, it has declined to revisit the key issues and it seems generally unconcerned about the damage to our political system that the decision has caused. As recently as 1996, the Court not only refused to limit or overturn *Buckley*, it expanded some of its key principles. In *Colorado Republican Federal Campaign Committee v. Federal Election Commission*, the Court rejected efforts of the commission to limit how much Republicans could spend to attack a likely Democratic candidate for the U.S. Senate even before the Republican nominee was chosen. The FEC had argued that the Federal Election Campaign Act, which imposed a dollar limit upon political party expenditures "in connection with the general election campaign" of a congressional candidate, prevented the Colorado group from exceeding the limits. The lower courts and the Supreme Court held that as long as the expenditure is made by a group without coordination with any candidate, it is not subject to the spending limit.

The division of the justices in *Colorado Republican* demonstrated that although some of them have doubts about *Buckley's* continuing validity, there is nowhere near a majority ready to overturn the 1976 decision. Three justices, without invitation from the parties, rejected *Buckley's* distinction between contributions and expenditures. Justice Stevens, joined by Justice Ruth Bader Ginsburg, said that both contributions and expenditures can be regulated. On the other side of the trio was Justice Clarence Thomas, who emphatically stated that neither contributions nor expenditures can be regulated. Such a breakdown of votes suggests that no more than two justices currently believe that the amount of money candidates and groups spend in campaigns can be limited. The three justices who wrote the lead opinion (Stephen Breyer, Sandra Day O'Connor, and David Souter), suggested that the *Colorado* case was not the right vehicle for reconsidering *Buckley* because the parties had not briefed the Court on those complex issues.

Several other cases in recent years have provided an opportunity for the Court to reconsider *Buckley* in light of all the problems it has caused, but in each case the Court declined to grant certiorari, and thus *Buckley* remains in force. In November 1998, the Court declined to hear cases from Ohio and Arkansas that could have provided the opportunity to limit or modify *Buckley*. In the Ohio case, *Cincinnati v. Kruse*, a 1995 city ordinance had placed a cap on city council election spending of three times a council member's annual salary, or a limit of about $140,000. The U.S. District Court and the U.S. Court of Appeals for the Sixth Circuit declared the limit unconstitutional under *Buckley*. The National Voting Rights Institute, a Boston-based advocacy group working to change election laws, handled the legal defense of the ordinance for the city. It argued that enough time had passed since the *Buckley* ruling for the Court to see the problems that the decision had caused. The attorneys general of 26 states joined the group's petition, which stated in part that "A ruling forever closing the door to the lessons of governmental experience with unlimited campaign spending runs contrary to the constitutional responsibilities of this Court."

In the Arkansas case, which the Court also refused to hear, voters in a 1996 referendum set a low contribution limit as part of an overhaul of the state's campaign laws. The law provided for a $50 income tax credit for political donations, and contribution limits were reduced from $1,000 to $300 for statewide offices and from $1,000 to $100 for judicial candidates. The U.S. Court of Appeals for the Eighth Circuit struck down the limits as being "too low to allow meaningful participation in protected speech and association." The appellate court noted that *Buckley* had upheld limits of $1,000 on contributions to federal campaigns, but it concluded that the $100 and $300 limits were different "not just in degree but in kind" from the $1,000 limits.

The Court Keeps Contribution Limits

The Supreme Court appeared indifferent to the damage done by *Buckley* by its refusal to hear the Ohio and Arkansas cases, but it showed some concern about the negative effects of money on the campaign finance system in *Nixon v. Shrink Missouri Government PAC*, decided January 24, 2000. In this important case, the Court upheld, by a vote of 6-3, a Missouri law imposing a *contribution* limit of $1,000 on candidates for state office. The organization, Shrink Missouri, wanted to contribute more than the limit to a candidate for the Republican nomination for Missouri state auditor in 1998. The group and the candidate claimed the law violated their First and Fourteenth Amendment rights.

Although the case had nothing to do with soft money or with campaign *expenditures*, if the Court had invalidated the Missouri law, the federal limits for hard money contributions — which are $1,000 for candidates in the primary and $1,000 in the general election — would also likely have been voided. Thirty-five states have limits on campaign contributions. If the Supreme Court had rejected the Missouri law, there would be no contribution limits *and* no expenditure limits. Independent groups and parties would still have been able to raise and spend huge sums of money; but in addition, candidates could have directly accepted donations above $1,000.

In the *Nixon* case, the U.S. Court of Appeals for the Eighth Circuit, based in St. Louis, concluded that although the $1,000 figure may have been appropriate for 1976 — when *Buckley* was decided — that amount has been so eroded by inflation 20 years later as to stand in the way of "meaningful participation in protected political speech and association." In the view of the appellate court, the limits were "so small that they run afoul of the Constitution by unnecessarily restricting protected First Amendment freedoms." The appellate court found that $1,000 in 1976 was the equivalent of $400 in 1998.

Justice David Souter, in his opinion for the Court, said the key issue was not any fixed dollar amount, but whether a contribution limit was so low "as to render political association ineffective, drive the sound of a candidate's voice below the level of notice, and render contributions pointless." The Court held that Missouri's $1,000 limit met this test without violating the First Amendment. A concurring opinion by Justice Stephen Breyer, and joined by Justice Ruth Bader Ginsburg, recommends deferring to the "political judgment" of the states as long as they permit meaningful participation in the election process. Antonin Scalia and Clarence Thomas held that Missouri's limits were "patently unconstitutional," and that *Buckley* should be overruled.

Although several justices in recent campaign finance cases have indicated a desire to reconsider *Buckley* — either by permitting limits on both contributions and expenditures, or by eliminating restrictions on contributions — the Missouri case makes it clear that no majority currently exists for overturning *Buckley* and more directly involving the Court in campaign finance issues.

The Court may have may felt compelled to review the Missouri law because the U.S. Court of Appeals for the Sixth Circuit, based in Cincinnati, had come to the opposite conclusion in upholding a $1,000 contribution limit in a 1997 case originating in Kentucky. Because the Sixth and Eighth Circuits were divided on this important issue, the Court may have wanted to clarify the law by rejecting the $1,000 limit outright or recommending that it be adjusted for inflation. Another explanation may be that the Court's conservative justices saw an opportunity to complete the work of *Buckley* by getting rid of contribution limits all together.

Although the Court agreed to decide the *Nixon* case, it turned down review of a companion case from Missouri that sought to directly challenge the continuing validity of *Buckley*. *Bray v. Shrink Missouri Government PAC* was filed by a member of the Missouri House of Representatives, who asked the Court to decide "whether the analytic structure undergirding *Buckley v. Valeo* has become so confused and unwieldy as to call for reconsideration of the relationship between the First Amendment and content-neutral efforts to regulate the financing of political campaigns."

The Supreme Court provided further evidence that it is not likely to overturn *Buckley* in a case decided in January 1999. By a 6-3 vote, the Court overturned a Colorado law that sought to regulate the process of getting initiatives on the ballot. The law required that people who circulate petitions be registered Colorado voters, that they wear badges identifying themselves by name, and that sponsoring organizations employing paid petition circulators include in monthly and final reports the name, address, and compensation of each worker. In her majority opinion, Justice Ginsburg emphasized the strong protection that the First Amendment grants to political speech. She said the Court must be "vigilant" in guarding against "undue hindrances to political conversations and the exchange of ideas."

The Money Pours in for Incumbents

Although Congress cannot overturn *Buckley*'s holding that campaign expenditures violate the First Amendment, it has the authority, consistent with the Constitution, to eliminate the soft-money loophole that has led to so many problems. Soft money is contributed by the millions to political parties and so-called independent groups. Corporations, wealthy individuals, and unions know they can ignore the hard-money contribution limits imposed by federal law by giving the donation to parties and campaign organizations that will spend the money on behalf of the candidate. In addition, the soft-money loophole allows those groups to spend unlimited sums as long as they pretend that the money is being spent without coordinating the campaign activity with the candidates.

There is overwhelming support among Americans for eliminating the soft-money loophole and making other changes in campaign finance laws, but Congress knows that as long as huge contributions pour in and they can spend whatever they want to remain in office, they do not have to listen to the urgent call for reform. As Senator Mitch McConnell (R-KY) has said on several occasions, "No one in the history of American politics has ever won or lost a campaign on this issue." As explained in Chapter One, Senator McConnell threatened to filibuster the McCain-Feingold bill to reform campaign spending in the fall of 1999. Proponents lacked the votes in the Senate to stop him if he and other opponents of reform began a filibuster.

Senator McConnell was also in charge in 1998 of the Republican Party committee that decided how much money GOP Senate candidates would receive. His ability to dole out funds from a $75 million account gave him substantial influence over many Senate races around the country. A conservative member of the U.S. House, Linda Smith — a Republican challenging incumbent Senator Patty Murray (D-WA), who would normally get McConnell's enthusiastic support — found out how perilous it is to oppose him. Because Smith supported campaign finance reform during the campaign, McConnell refused to provide her with more than a token amount of money, while candidates in other states who kept quiet about reform were rewarded by McConnell with large contributions. McConnell also spent over $1 million on television commercials in Wisconsin in an effort to defeat Senator Russell Feingold (D-WI), the co-sponsor of McCain-Feingold. Feingold, who imposed unusual restrictions on his own campaign in order to show his commitment to reform, barely won reelection. McConnell had more success in his home state of Kentucky where he helped defeat Rep. Scotty Baesler (D-KY) in a tight race with Rep. Jim Bunning (R-KY) for the Senate. Baesler had also made campaign finance reform an important part of his campaign. Bunning said he agreed with McConnell that campaign finance laws should remain intact. He took that position despite a survey conducted by a major Kentucky newspaper the previous year showing that 80 percent of those responding believed that the law should be changed to limit campaign expenditures.

It should come as little surprise that members of Congress are in no hurry to change the system that works so well for them. During the 1990s, for example, House incumbents have outspent challengers by a huge margin. Eighty-two percent of House incumbents in 1992 raised at least $200,000 more than their challengers, and 30 percent raised at least $500,000 more than their opponents. In 1998, in about 60 percent of the races for the House, one candidate — almost always the incumbent — outspent the opponent by 10 to 1 or more. In the 21 months leading up to the November 1998 election, House incumbents raised an average of $625,000 — more than four times the amount raised by the average challenger.

The trend in the 1990s clearly showed that the congressional candidate who raises the most money is most likely to win. In 94 percent of the Senate races and 95 percent of the House races in 1998, the candidate who spent the most money won. Those figures are up from earlier in the 1990s. In 1992, 89 percent of the House candidates with the most money won, as did 86 percent for the Senate. In 1994, 88 percent of candidates for the House and 86 percent of the Senate candidates who spent the most money won their election. The percentages increased again in 1996 when 92 percent of the House races and 88 percent of the Senate races were won by the candidate spending the most money.

The impact on the races is clear. In more than 60 House districts in 1998, incumbents had a 10-to-1 money advantage. More incumbents were reelected — 98 percent — than at any time in the past decade, one of the highest rates in this century. In 1998, the average House incumbent raised $733,731 compared to $184,357 for the average challenger. In the Senate, incumbents raised a total of $156 million compared with the $65 million raised by challengers. Political action committee donations went overwhelmingly to Senate incumbents, totaling $37 million, while challengers got just under $4 million.

A challenger who finds a House or Senate incumbent raising money almost every day since the last election two or six years ago faces an almost impossible task of getting access to enough money to be a viable candidate. Reducing the amount that can be spent in campaigns would give some additional advantages to challengers and make elections more competitive.

Congressional opposition to reform

Despite how well the system works for incumbents and for powerful interest groups who invest in candidates, some members of the House and Senate are committed to enacting at least modest reforms. In August 1998, a remarkable event happened. Overcoming strong opposition from the Republican leadership that had fought to keep the bill off the floor, the U.S. House of Representatives approved Shays-Meehan (named after its co-sponsors, Christopher Shays, a Republican from Connecticut, and Martin Meehan, a Democrat from Massachusetts), a bill that would change the campaign finance system, by a vote of 237-186. A second vote later in the week gave the bill even stronger support when it passed 252-179. Shays-Meehan, which was never approved in the Senate — in part because of Senator McConnell's threatened filibuster — would have effectively banned the unlimited, unregulated soft-money donations to the political parties that led to abuses in the 1996 presidential campaign and in congressional campaigns over the past decade or more. The bill would have also banned "issue advocacy" commercials, which attack or support candidates, by groups independent of the campaign in the 60 days before an election.

The Republican leadership had done almost everything it could to keep the measure from coming to a vote. After trying to block it from reaching the House floor, Speaker Newt Gingrich and other Republican leaders tried to bury it by requiring that the House debate an astounding 258 amendments before the bill would have a final vote. The decision to allow such prolonged debate was highly unusual, but the Republican leaders pushed it through with a vote of 221-189. It eventually took almost ten weeks of on-and-off debate to consider all the amendments. When Democratic supporters of the bill complained about the procedure, Majority Whip Tom DeLay (R-TX) responded, "now the so-called reformers are complaining . . . because the debate will be too open for their taste." The *New York Times* called it "death by amendment." Although Republican leaders eventually lost the battle to keep Shays-Meehan off the floor of the House, they openly expressed pleasure over the dim prospects that the bill had in the Senate, and congratulated themselves for delaying the House vote until after the Senate had left for its August recess.

Despite the urging of major newspapers, and no doubt many of their constituents, senators never voted on Shays-Meehan. When it returned from its August recess, the Senate voted 52 to 48 to cut off debate and vote on the legislation, eight votes short of the 60 needed to end a threatened filibuster. The vote was the same as in February 1998 when the Senate last voted on campaign finance reform. Senator John McCain (R-AZ), a co-sponsor of the Senate bill proposing campaign finance reform, believed that as the Senate became more involved in pending impeachment proceedings against the president, there was less interest in changing campaign finance laws. "Everyone's diverted... All the oxygen has been sucked out of the room by this firestorm [the pending impeachment]," observed McCain. As with Shays-Meehan, McCain-Feingold would have banned unlimited donations to political parties and would have curbed the practice of independent groups running ads praising or attacking candidates. Those senators who opposed the bill said they were protecting the First Amendment right of free speech of those who want to support candidates.

Although no campaign finance measures were approved by both the House and Senate in 1998, they were revived in 1999. Once again, the Republican leadership in the House — this time in the form of new speaker Dennis Hastert (R-IL) — made it as difficult as possible for Shays-Meehan or other reform measures to be considered by the full House. Congressman Shays had received assurances from Rep. Bob Livingston (R-LA), who was expected to be the next speaker, that the campaign reform bill would not face such formidable obstacles as it did in 1998. But when Livingston withdrew from consideration as speaker and resigned from Congress because of ethical problems, the Illinois congressman became speaker.

In February 1999, Christopher Shays and Martin Meehan reintroduced their campaign finance reform bill in the House. Speaker Hastert kept the bill in committee for months, arguing that the House had more important matters to consider before taking up campaign finance issues. After it appeared that the Speaker was in no hurry to see the legislation appear on the House floor, an effort was started to collect signatures on a discharge petition, a rarely used procedural device that forces a bill from committee and permits a vote on the floor. A majority of House members must sign the discharge petition for it to be in effect. Because Republicans were the majority party, at least some GOP members had to agree to sign. That was however, a step they clearly did not want to take. The Republican leadership made it clear they did not want Shays-Meehan to be considered.

If a Republican House member defied the leadership on this issue, there were numerous ways for the leadership to retaliate. Republicans who signed the discharge petition would likely find bills they sponsored tied up in committee and kept from the House floor. Perhaps rebellious members would be denied a position on a committee they would like, or worse, be put on a committee that has nothing to do with their district, as when members from urban districts are put on agriculture committees. Even Rep. Shays, who shook the hand of each Democratic member as they lined up to sign the discharge petition, had not signed it himself. Although 30 Republicans co-sponsored the bill, as of the end of April 1999, not a single one had dared to defy the House leadership by signing the discharge petition.

Even after House Republicans met with Speaker Hastert in May 1999, and pleaded with him to allow Shays-Meehan to advance, he would not make a commitment to act earlier than September. In a statement issued later, the Speaker said he had "serious concerns about certain definitions of reform that unduly regulate free speech and that unfairly discriminate against certain political parties." That could be translated to say that until the voters catch on, or care enough, there is no reason to change the system.

Reform at the State Level

Despite the limitations imposed by *Buckley* and the unwillingness of Congress to enact campaign finance reform for federal elections, states have experimented with various methods for improving the system by which candidates for state elective office raise and spend money. Not surprisingly, these efforts have met with mixed success. About two-thirds of the states have enacted major campaign finance laws in the last 20 years. More than a third have changed their laws since 1990. In the years immediately after the Watergate scandal, nearly all states required candidates to report contributions and expenditures. Twenty-nine states required candidates to list all contributors who gave more than a minimum amount, while 17 states also required that expenditures be itemized.

While most states had disclosure requirements, only 22 states imposed limits on campaign contributions by 1980 despite the Supreme Court's upholding of such requirements in *Buckley* four years before, and most of those laws affected only large donations. Even fewer states, 16, restricted contributions by political action committees. Nine limited direct contributions from the parties to candidates. Sixteen states had public funding programs for parties or candidates in 1980.

As the cost of campaigns at the statewide level and for state legislature continued to rise, states began imposing limits on how much could be spent in a campaign. For example, after adjusting for inflation, the average spending by gubernatorial candidates increased 44 percent between the four-year periods 1977–1980 and 1989–1992. State spending in legislative races also increased sharply. After adjusting for inflation, total campaign expenditures in Kansas House elections grew by 66 percent between 1982 and 1992. In Kentucky House elections, the average amount spent jumped 45 percent between 1981 and 1992. And in Maine Senate elections, the increase was 292 percent over the same period.

States reacted to the sharp increase in campaigns by imposing additional requirements. Most added or strengthened reporting requirements so voters would know what individuals and organizations were making contributions to a candidate's campaign. Some states passed more restrictive contribution limits. Those states that limited contributions to very small amounts — of around $100 — later saw those laws overturned by courts that found that the limits unconstitutionally interfered with free speech. In applying the standards from *Buckley*, those courts held that in order for such limits to be justified, the state would have to demonstrate a compelling government interest.

Other states in the last decade have created public funding programs. The number of states with some public financing for candidates or parties grew from four in 1974 to 19 in 1984. Since 1994, three new states have adopted or expanded such programs. It is, however, becoming increasingly difficult for states to find the money to fund candidates as citizens seem less interested in committing tax dollars for that purpose. Almost all states with public financing systems rely on an income tax checkoff system, yet the number of taxpayers participating has been declining in recent years. Evidence also suggests that although public financing may help a challenger get going in a campaign, it does not overcome the tremendous advantages of incumbency.

Despite state efforts to increase the fairness and competitive nature of elections, there have been lots of problems. Too many states fail to make available to the public in usable form the information that candidates provide about campaign contributions or expenditures. A few states now make such information available on the Internet, but in too many places in this country citizens who want to know more about contributions or expenditures than they read in the newspaper must travel to the county clerk's or secretary of state's office and sift through paperwork.

In addition, the agencies created by states to oversee compliance with the complicated campaign laws are woefully underfunded and are not always staffed by the most sophisticated employees. Some state legislators have quieted public outcry over campaign funding abuses by enacting what appear to be effective laws, but then they deprive oversight agencies of enough resources to do the job required by the statute.

If the goals of campaign finance reform are to restore accountability, limit the direct financial relationship between contributors and candidates or incumbents, promote competition, and increase public participation in elections, the experience of the states has been mixed. Efforts at the state level have shown how difficult it is to convince legislators and governors to support reform and how hard it is for the changes to achieve the desired goals. It has been relatively easy for contributors, political parties, and candidates to find ways around the regulations. In many cases, they find some other legal way of collecting and spending money in campaigns that do not look much different from how it was done before the reforms were enacted. Despite all the reform efforts, most campaign contributions still go overwhelmingly to incumbents who are almost always reelected.

The New Amendment

No single constitutional amendment will fix all the problems associated with campaign finance. The system is too complex and provides too many opportunities for those determined to get around the limits to find a way to do so. But what is also clear is that the American people cannot rely on the ordinary processes of a representative democracy if they hope for comprehensive changes in the way money is raised and spent in campaigns.

The clearest evidence that electing people to office who promise to make changes will not work is what happened to the freshmen class of 1996 in the U.S. House. Shortly after they took office in January 1997, freshmen Republicans — many of whom had promised to do something about campaign finance, and who were elected at least in part because of that commitment — formed a freshmen task force to promote a bill ending soft-money contributions. They sided with Democrats who were also working on reform efforts.

It did not take long for the Republican leadership to convince the freshmen that if they wanted to advance their careers in the House or see any of the bills they sponsored acted on by committees, they would have to abandon such plans. House freshmen are vulnerable to such persuasion, especially early in their House tenure. Congressional leaders can do a lot to help or hurt their careers. The leaders told the freshman that even though they had run on a platform that included campaign finance reform, ending soft-money contributions would hurt the Republican Party. Behind closed doors, the leaders probably told the freshmen that by the time they run for reelection, they will have hundreds of thousands of dollars in their campaign coffers given by groups whose interests come under the jurisdiction of their committees. The leaders certainly told the freshmen that if the usual happens, their challengers — if there even are serious challengers when they run again — will not have enough money to tell very many voters about the earlier promises left unfulfilled.

The amendment outlined at the beginning of this chapter will address some of the major defects in the current campaign finance system. Section 1 is intended to reverse *Buckley* by amending the Constitution so that the First Amendment is not an impediment to limits on contributions and expenditures. In an effort to reduce the influence of political action committees and wealthy donors, corporations, and unions, Section 2 requires that every Senate candidate and every House candidate raise half their campaign funds from within their state or district, respectively. Currently, Senate and House incumbents raise hundreds of thousands, and sometimes millions of dollars, from interests who are under the jurisdiction of their committees. Those groups give donations without the slightest concern for how good a job the member of Congress does representing the citizens of the state or district. They only care that the member is reelected and will continue to support the priorities of the organization. By requiring that half of the funds be raised close to home, Section 2 would force incumbents and challengers to have more contact with individuals and groups within the state. That may reduce some of the advantages of incumbency and make elections more competitive.

Section 2 would also require states to establish administrative agencies to monitor campaign activities and to report that information to the public. The phrase "advanced forms of communication technology" in Section 2 means that such information should be available through the Internet or in the future, through whatever advanced technology has developed. It is essential that information on contributions and expenditures, and how well candidates are complying with campaign laws, be made available to the public in a timely manner and in an accessible form.

Other sections of Amendment "A" would require Congress and state legislatures to set limits on how much money can be spent in campaigns. If the costs can be reduced or at least prevented from rising more sharply, more qualified challengers may be willing to run. Other portions of the amendment require Congress to adequately fund the Federal Election Commission — which is seriously underfunded now — so that it can carry out its duty to monitor election activities and to report on them to the public. Finally, the amendment requires that Congress and the states study public financing of campaigns and produce a report within two years of the ratification of the amendment. If such plans would improve the campaign system, they should be adopted throughout the country and the public should support them with their tax dollars.

Some of the sections of the amendment may seem redundant. It is, however, important to remember that when courts interpret constitutional language — and this amendment will be the subject of much litigation if it ever becomes part of the Constitution — they look carefully at every word and phrase, and if there is any doubt about what the amendment is trying to accomplish, there is a chance it will be narrowly interpreted and made largely irrelevant. That has happened to many provisions of the Constitution. It is necessary, therefore, to have some overlap to make it clear to those who bring lawsuits and the judges who hear them that the new amendment seeks to overhaul the campaign system.

Campaign finance reform is urgently needed. If it is successfully implemented and makes federal and state elections more competitive — and elected officials more responsive to those they represent — it will restore some of the basic principles of a democratic society that seem to have been lost in recent years as campaign money has negatively affected the political process. If serious reform is not enacted, cynicism and anger on the part of so many people toward their government will only get worse, with serious ramifications for the country.

CHAPTER EIGHT

Amendment "B":
The Equal Rights Amendment

The Petition

The legislature of the state of_____, being comprised of the duly elected representatives of the people thereof, formally request that the United States Congress call a constitutional convention under Article V of the United States Constitution so that the convention can consider, and in its discretion, propose an amendment or amendments addressing the subject of equal rights based on gender. This petition was approved by both houses of this legislature in accordance with its established rules and procedures.

Amendment "B"

Section 1. Equality of rights under the law shall not be denied or abridged by the United States or by any state on account of sex.

Section 2. The Congress shall enforce, by appropriate legislation, the provisions of this amendment.

Section 3. This amendment shall not be construed to invalidate legislation, administrative regulations, or other acts of Congress or the states that have benign effects on the economic or political status of women.

Section 4. When federal and state courts review legislation, administrative acts, regulations, and other actions by government or those acting under color of law, they shall apply the highest level of judicial scrutiny.

Section 5. The interstate commerce clause of Article I, Section 8, shall not be construed by any federal or state court as inhibiting congressional authority to enact laws related to gender-motivated violence.

Section 6. This amendment shall be in effect immediately upon its ratification.

Section 7. This amendment shall be inoperable unless ratified as an amendment to the United States Constitution within seven years from the date of its submission.

Section 8. Ratification of this amendment shall take place by conventions in each state whose delegates will be popularly elected.

The Struggle for Equal Rights

The treatment of women during much of this nation's history has been a national disgrace. Although there may be historical reasons dating back to the dawn of civilization for why women have been deprived of economic and political rights, and often human dignity, there is no excuse for a country founded on principles of equality and democracy to have treated half its population so poorly for so long. Some of the indignities to which women were subjected seem outdated to us now, but they were formally enacted into statute and enforced by judges applying common law principles. Such restrictions were further imposed informally by fathers, husbands, civic leaders and others who believed that women were incapable of thinking clearly or learning about politics or playing a role in the nation's governance.

It is a feature of every child's education to learn that women could not vote in all elections until the ratification of the 19th Amendment in 1920. What is perhaps less known is that under laws in effect during much of our history, a woman, at the moment of marriage, became merely an appendage of her husband and "civilly dead." Married women were subject to the common law doctrine of "coverture" and the associated legal fiction of "marital unity." As English legal commentator William Blackstone explained in 1765, "The very being or legal existence of the woman is suspended during the marriage, or at least is incorporated and consolidated into that of the husband; under whose wing, protection and cover, she performs everything." The common law thus rendered women incapable of exercising basic rights of citizenship, including the right to hold, sell, and will property, and the right to make legally binding agreements.

A divorced woman, for example, almost always was denied custody of her children. Only a husband could bring a lawsuit on his wife's behalf;

she could not sue on her own. A married woman could keep money she earned only if her husband made a gift of the money to her. With some exceptions, all property brought into the marriage belonged to the husband, which discouraged women from seeking divorces. Although a woman could establish a trust to protect her children's inheritance, the "unity" doctrine led to the husband being appointed trustee, and thus he could spend the assets as he pleased.

It became essential for women to obtain the right to vote so they could elect representatives who would dismantle the common law and statutory restrictions on their economic, political, and personal rights. Just how important it had become for women to be able to vote was demonstrated by a decision of the U.S. Supreme Court in 1873. During the Civil War, feminist leaders had suspended their efforts for women's rights to help in the war effort, including being energetically involved in the abolitionist and temperance movements. After they helped bring the war to a successful conclusion, they were stunned to learn what Congress would do to them in the 14th Amendment. Not only did it become clear that the equal protection clause in Section 1 of the 14th Amendment would not apply to women, Congress inserted into Section 2 a provision that explicitly identified "male inhabitants" of each state and "male citizens" when it created a formula by which states would be punished for failure to enfranchise newly freed slaves. The previously gender-neutral language of the Constitution was now tainted with an explicit statement that blacks, but not women, would be protected by the 14th amendment. Women would have to wait a century — even long after they had won the right to vote — before the 14th Amendment was interpreted as applying to them.

Women had been crusading for civil and political rights since early in the 19th century. They knew that if they were ever to be granted full rights of citizenship, they would have to organize politically. In 1848, a group of 250 courageous women and some male supporters — led by 32-year-old Elizabeth Cady Stanton — met in upstate New York and wrote the Seneca Falls Declaration of Rights and Sentiments. Although controversial at the time for its seemingly strident tone, the declaration denounced the treatment of women as second-class citizens, and demanded their political emancipation.

Despite the Seneca Falls meeting and other efforts, it soon became clear that the enjoyment of civil rights by women was still many years away. No government institution better represented the Dark Ages of women's rights than the U.S. Supreme Court. In *Bradwell v. Illinois* in 1873, the Court had to decide the constitutionality of an Illinois statute that permitted only men to practice law. Myra Bradwell, who had studied law with her attorney husband, was the co-founder and publisher of *The Chicago Legal News*, the leading midwestern legal publication. In 1868, she graduated from law school and passed the Illinois bar exam. When Illinois denied Bradwell a license to practice law because of her gender, she asserted that the 14th Amendment — which had been ratified in 1868 — invalidated laws excluding women from the bar. The Court rejected her arguments, holding instead that the right to practice law was not a privilege of national citizenship, and was therefore not protected by the 14th Amendment. Justice Joseph Bradley, only a day before in the famous *Slaughterhouse Cases*, had written in dissent that "a law which prohibits a large class of citizens from adopting a lawful [employment] deprives them of liberty as well as property without due process of law." If Bradley had been consistent, he would have concluded that Illinois could not deprive Bradwell of her right to practice law. But instead, in a concurring opinion famous for its Neanderthal-like sentiment, Bradley said this about women in *Bradwell*:

> The natural and proper timidity and delicacy which belongs to the female sex evidently unfits it for many of the occupations of civil life. The constitution of the family organization, which is founded in the divine ordinance, as well as in the nature of things, indicates the domestic sphere as that which properly belongs to the domain and functions of womanhood. The harmony, not to say identity, of interests and views which belong or should belong to the family institution, is repugnant to the idea of a woman adopting a distinct and independent career from that of her husband . . .
>
> It is true that many women are unmarried and not affected by any of the duties, complications, and incapacities arising out of the married state but these are exceptions to the general rule. The paramount destiny and mission of woman are to fulfill the noble and benign offices of wife and mother. This is the law of the Creator. And the rules of civil society must be adapted to the general constitution of things, and cannot be based on exceptional cases.

Two years later in *Minor v. Happersett*, the Court acknowledged that women were "persons" and "citizens" within the meaning of the 14th Amendment, but held that the right to vote was not a privilege of U.S. citizenship. The Court concluded that the Framers of the Constitution had never intended to extend the suffrage to women, and in its very narrow reading of the 14th Amendment's due process and equal protection clauses, the Court found that the states, not the federal government, should decide who can vote. It appeared that the words "all men are created equal" in the Declaration of Independence a century earlier were to be read literally.

After the Civil War, women continued to struggle to obtain the right to vote. As more women began working outside the home, efforts to improve working conditions and to organize unions helped energize women around the country. The working conditions of women were often deplorable. In the garment industry, for example, by 1900, more than 600,000 women worked as long as 16 hours a day, six days a week, often in sweatshops notorious for their dangerous and inhumane conditions.

With the emergence of two organizations — the National American Women Suffrage Association (NAWSA) in 1890, and the Women's Trade Union League (WTUL) in 1903, an organization that lobbied for protective labor laws — and after women again contributed greatly to the country's war effort during the First World War, they began to make progress toward gaining political rights. The membership of NAWSA increased from 13,150 in 1893 to over 2 million in 1917. Suffragists worked tirelessly around the country within party organizations and legislatures to push for the right to vote. Dozens of women were imprisoned or fined for attempting to vote, but the momentum toward political rights could not be stopped. Wyoming was admitted to the union with full suffrage in 1890. Colorado granted women the right to vote in 1893, followed by Idaho and Utah three years later, and Washington in 1910. California approved a referendum granting the right in 1911, and Arizona, Kansas, and Oregon did so in 1912. But the nine Western states were the only success stories. In 1915, states such as Massachusetts, New Jersey, New York, and Pennsylvania all rejected referenda that would have extended the right to vote to women.

The struggle to win adoption of the 19th Amendment giving women the suffrage throughout the country and in all elections was long and involved. The assumption that men in the United States had simply come to the conclusion that the time was right to grant women this basic right of citizenship does not accurately reflect how much resistance there was to the 19th Amendment, how much sacrifice it took on the part of women all over the country to see it enacted, and how close it came to failure. If not for a single Tennessee House member who resisted intense pressure to vote against the amendment, it may have been many more years before women all over the country could vote.

The 19th Amendment Is Finally Approved

World War I may have given women the decisive boost they needed to finally see the 19th Amendment become part of the Constitution. President Woodrow Wilson, who for years had callously disregarded the pleas of women as they demonstrated outside the White House, and who believed that women had no proper role to play in government, publicly recognized the contribution of women to the war effort shortly after the United States entered the War in the spring of 1917. In May of that year, Wilson encouraged the U.S. House to establish a committee on women's suffrage. He also endorsed a New York state suffrage amendment for which NAWSA was campaigning. The approval of the amendment in that state represented the first victory for suffrage in the Northeast. Two years earlier, only 42 percent of New York voters had favored granting the ballot to women.

Wilson took further steps to help passage of the 19th Amendment. He issued a public statement on January 10, 1918, "frankly and earnestly" advising House members to support the amendment "as an act of right and justice." While Democrats were divided largely along regional lines — with Southern members strongly opposed to women's suffrage — Republicans were largely supportive, both in state legislatures and at the congressional level. Wilson's effort may have made the difference when the House, with two votes to spare, approved the amendment by a vote of 274-136.

Senate resistance continued, however. Southern senators were still angry about passage of the 14th and 15th amendments — even though half a century had passed — and they resisted federal intrusion into state autonomy, including the right to decide the qualifications of voters. President Wilson then took a step that was unprecedented in the history of amendment politics. With only 30 minutes notice, Wilson appeared in the Senate chamber, accompanied by his cabinet, to urge passage of the amendment. He argued that after having made women partners in the war effort, the nation needed to enfranchise them to demonstrate its commitment to democracy. The senators, resentful of what they considered to be a breach of protocol and senatorial tradition, voted to reject the amendment the day after Wilson's visit.

At the next election a month later, women were determined to help defeat those senators who had opposed them. Four senators who appeared the most vulnerable were targeted. Republican John Weeks of Massachusetts and Democrat Willard Saulsbury of Delaware were both defeated. The other two were reelected, but by narrow margins. Despite those developments, the Senate was still reluctant to give women the right to vote. On February 10, 1919, the Senate again rejected the amendment. The margin of defeat was a single vote. When Congress convened for a special session a few months later, the House again approved the amendment on May 21, 1919, this time by a wider margin. After parliamentary maneuvering that for a time looked like it would prevent the Senate from voting at all on the amendment, it was approved on June 4, 1919, by a vote of 56 to 25, sending it on to the states for ratification.

Although ratification came quickly in several states, momentum slowed as Southern states refused to approve the amendment. Opponents needed only one house in each of 13 state legislatures to reject the amendment for it to be defeated. Women's organizations worked tirelessly around the country to generate support for ratification. Some governors who opposed granting the suffrage to women refused to convene their legislatures. In other states, the amendment was defeated by a wide margin. Republicans, who had supported women's rights for longer and more energetically than Democrats, appeared to be satisfied that so many Democratically controlled legislatures were defeating the amendment. They believed that women would eventually gain the right to vote and they would show their gratitude for Republican support, which they apparently did in 1920 with the election victory of Warren Harding.

By midsummer in 1920, only Tennessee had not voted on the amendment. At the urging of President Wilson, the governor called the legislature into special session. Supporters and opponents descended on Nashville. The state Senate approved the amendment after a brief debate, but the state House was going to be a problem. After protracted parliamentary maneuvers and efforts by the speaker, who opposed the amendment, to keep it from coming to a vote, the youngest member of the House, a Republican, kept a promise made to his suffragist mother that he would ignore the preferences of his rural east Tennessee district if his support was needed to approve the amendment. The governor certified that ratification had taken place and the 19th Amendment was thus ratified on August 18, 1920, in time for women to vote nationwide in the presidential election of 1920.

The Equal Rights Amendment

The Equal Rights Amendment was first introduced in Congress in 1923, but it failed to receive the two-thirds vote needed in each house. Many women in the 1920s and in the decades that followed saw the ERA as the constitutional equivalent for women of the equal protection clause of the 14th Amendment which guaranteed racial equality. But others thought it was a waste of time to push for an abstractly worded amendment to the Constitution, arguing instead that what was needed were specific reforms enacted by Congress addressing working conditions, minimum wage, women's health, child labor, and other issues. Some efforts in that direction paid off. In 1961, President Kennedy created the

Commission on the Status of Women. Congress passed the Equal Pay Act in 1963, which required the Department of Labor to examine whether there were pay disparities based on gender. A year later, Congress enacted the Civil Rights Act, which included the important Title VII that prohibits sex discrimination in employment.

Despite division over whether to concentrate on a constitutional amendment or ordinary legislation, the ERA enjoyed enough support to be introduced in every Congress until it was finally proposed to the states in 1972. The amendment was approved in the House by an overwhelming margin of 354 to 24, and by an 84 to 8 vote in the Senate. Expecting easy ratification, neither of the amendment's floor leaders in Congress objected to the seven-year time limit. But ERA supporters underestimated the ability of those opposed to the amendment to mobilize support in the states. The anti-ERA forces, led by Phyllis Schlafly and Senator Sam Ervin (D-NC), who had led the Senate opposition, framed the issue as removing the ability of legislatures and courts to approve legislation that *protected* women.

The opposition organization, STOP ERA, was an acronym for Stop Taking Our Privileges. It argued that an amendment to the Constitution that eliminated gender distinctions would require the invalidation of laws that recognized gender differences and would thus subject women to hardships they had long ago overcome. Even with support from Presidents Nixon, Ford and Carter, as well as early momentum when 15 states ratified within a year and a half, the federal ERA failed to get the necessary state support. When Congress realized that the seven-year time limit would expire without approval of the amendment, it took the unprecedented and controversial step in 1977 of extending the ratification period until 1982, just over ten years from the time of its proposal. It did so by a *majority* vote and not two-thirds, on the basis that extending an amendment was an ordinary congressional act. Extending the deadline by less than two-thirds only added to the controversy. On June 30, 1982, the extension expired and the ERA was dead. It had enjoyed substantial support among the American people, but not enough to overcome the resistance of state legislatures. If the ERA is ever proposed again by Congress or a second convention, ratification should be by popularly elected conventions — where its support among the people would likely be more accurately reflected — than in state legislatures.

Why the Federal Era Is Still Needed

Since the defeat of the ERA, women have made substantial strides in attaining political and civil rights. But despite the enforcement of Title VII and other statutes such as those prohibiting sexual harassment in the workplace and in schools, and the general change in attitude toward women at work and at home, there are good reasons for supporting a revised ERA. Many federal and state judges remain reluctant to interpret either statutes or the equal protection clause of the 14th Amendment in a way that sufficiently elevates the legal status of women.

When courts review federal or state statutes, administrative regulations, or other actions taken by government or those acting on behalf of government to see if they have a discriminatory impact on women, they apply only "midlevel" or intermediate scrutiny. That standard offers significantly less protection than the "strict scrutiny" that is applied to cases involving racial discrimination. Women not only are treated differently from racial minorities when challenging classifications based on gender, they are sometimes treated less favorably than noncitizens who challenge laws based on their alien status.

Since the mid-20th century, classifications based on race have been inherently "suspect" under the 14th Amendment. This means that when a statute, regulation, or administrative rule makes a distinction between racial groups — or even has a negative effect on racial minorities — courts look very closely at the statute or regulation and almost always invalidate the classification. That aggressive posture is different from the usual deference that a court is expected to extend to the legislative branch of government.

Such judicial deference is set aside when statutes or actions involve racial groups. Laws that showed any signs of *intent* to discriminate on the basis of race — such as laws in the Southern states passed after the Civil War — have been automatically subject to the courts' closest examination, "strict scrutiny," for about half a century. In recent decades, any laws that had a negative *impact* on racial minorities have also been subject to the strict scrutiny standard. In order for a statute to survive such a close evaluation — which it rarely does — the government must show three things:

- that there is a compelling (not just important or substantial) need for the law;
- that there is a direct relationship between the law and the goals sought; and
- that the law uses the least restrictive means of obtaining that goal.

If any of the three elements is not met, the law is invalidated as unconstitutional.

Because of the nation's history of slavery, Jim Crow laws, and oppressive racial discrimination, strict scrutiny has been appropriately applied in the equal protection context in race-related cases for many years. But women do not enjoy the same status. Even as late as 1948, when the Supreme Court should have long emerged from the Jurassic period of women's rights, it held that a Michigan law that prohibited a woman from working as a bartender unless she was the wife or daughter of a male owner did not violate the equal protection clause of the 14th Amendment. Justice Felix Frankfurter wrote that the "Constitution does not require the legislatures to reflect sociological insight, or shifting social standards, any more than it requires them to keep abreast of the latest scientific standards." In 1961, the Court upheld as "rational" a jury selection system in Florida that excluded women who did not affirmatively indicate a desire to serve. Justice John Harlan wrote for the Court that a "woman is still regarded as the center of home and family life. We cannot say that it is constitutionally impermissible for a State, acting in pursuit of the general welfare, to conclude that a woman should be relieved from the civic duty of jury service unless she herself determines that such service is consistent with her own special responsibilities."

It was not until 1971 that the Supreme Court for the first time invalidated a gender classification under the equal protection clause of the 14th Amendment. An Idaho statute required that when it came to deciding who would administer the estate of someone who died without leaving a will, and both a man and woman were eligible, the man would be chosen. The state said this would eliminate an area of controversy when two or more persons, otherwise equally entitled, sought to administer an estate. In Reed v. Reed, the Court held that this preference violated the equal protection clause. Chief Justice Warren Burger, writing for the Court, maintained that a gender classification of this type was "the very kind of arbitrary legislative choice forbidden by the Equal Protection Clause."

Although it did not say so explicitly, the Court appeared in Reed to apply the lowest level of scrutiny — rational basis — to the statute. The question the justices ask in such cases is whether there is any rational basis for the legislature's action. If there is, the courts will not invalidate the statute. As long as there is some reasonable relationship between the statute and the goals sought — in this case, to make it easier for probate courts to decide who should administer estates when there is no will — courts should defer to legislatures. Interestingly, in Reed, even under the rational basis standard where maximum deference is given to legislative acts, the Court apparently found that there was no reasonable relationship between the statute and the objective sought to be advanced by the statute.

If the standard for gender discrimination had been left as rational basis, that would have been dangerous for women's rights even though the outcome in *Reed* was supportive of women. But two years later, the Court changed the standard it would use to review gender-based legislation to an intermediate level, somewhere between rational basis and strict scrutiny. Unfortunately, the Court has largely left such review at midlevel scrutiny when it should have elevated the legal status of women to a heightened standard of review.

In *Frontiero v. Richardson* in 1973, the Supreme Court overturned a grossly unfair statute governing the way men and women in the armed services were treated. Under the law, a male member of the uniformed services could automatically claim his spouse as a dependent, thereby receiving a higher housing allowance and medical benefits. However, a female member of the uniformed services could claim comparable benefits only if she demonstrated that her spouse was in fact dependent on her for over half his support. Eight members of the Court agreed that this distinction violated the equal protection clause. Unfortunately for women, only four justices decided that classifications based on sex are inherently suspect and, like racial classifications, should be subject to strict scrutiny.

Writing for the four justices, Justice William Brennan observed that "there can be no doubt that our Nation has had a long and unfortunate history of sex discrimination. . . . Our statute books gradually became laden with gross, stereotyped distinctions between the sexes and indeed, throughout much of the 19th century the position of women in our society was, in many respects, comparable to that of blacks under the pre-Civil War slave codes." And Justice Brennan added, "It is true, of course, that the position of women in America has improved markedly in recent decades. Nevertheless, it can hardly be doubted that, in part because of the high visibility of the sex characteristic, women still face pervasive, although at times more subtle, discrimination in our educational institutions, in the job market and, perhaps most conspicuously in the political arena." Justice Brennan also believed that the approval of the equal rights amendment by Congress suggested that the legislature had decided that "classifications based upon sex are inherently invidious." The government argued in *Frontiero* that the different treatment of men and women served the purpose of administrative convenience. However, Justice Brennan held that when subject to close scrutiny, administrative convenience hardly justifies treating men and women differently in this regard.

Justice Lewis Powell, as he did so many times in his distinguished career on the Supreme Court, held the decisive vote. Powell would not join Brennan and the three other justices to form a majority that would have designated women as a suspect classification entitled to maximum judicial scrutiny. Instead, he believed that it was unnecessary to reach that conclusion in order to invalidate the statute. In addition, Powell noted that the ERA had been proposed by Congress and was under review by the states. If the ERA were ratified, he said it would resolve the issue. But he cautioned against reaching that conclusion in advance of ratification: "By acting prematurely and unnecessarily," the Court would have "assumed a decisional responsibility at the very time when state legislatures, functioning within the traditional democratic process, are debating the proposed Amendment."

If Justice Powell, or another member of the Court, had joined Brennan's opinion, government actions that have a disparate impact on women would be subject to the highest level of review. As it stands now, however, instead of requiring strict scrutiny, women are stuck with an intermediate standard. The Court outlined this midlevel of review in *Craig v. Boren* in 1976, and subsequent cases. For government actions that disparately impact women to be found constitutional, the government interest must be important, but not necessarily compelling, which would be required under strict scrutiny. Also, under the midlevel standard, the law or rule must be substantially related to the achievement of its objectives, but the government does not have to show a direct relationship between the goals and the methods used to obtain them, which it would have to do under the higher level of review. This means it is easier for the government to justify statutes with discriminatory impact on women than it is for blacks, and under some circumstances, aliens and children whose parents are not married.

The standards apply to men, too

So far, the cases discussed here could lead to the conclusion that the issues always involve statutes that disadvantage women. However, midlevel scrutiny applies to all *gender* classifications, and sometimes laws subject to such review have their greatest impact on men. In *Craig*, the Court invalidated an Oklahoma law that allowed 18-year-old women to purchase 3.2% beer, while not permitting men to buy such beer until age 21. The Court, by applying a midlevel analysis, found that the gender-based difference constituted a denial to males 18–20 years of age of their equal protection rights under the 14th Amendment. It will be recalled that in the *Reed* decision five years earlier, the goals of reducing the workload on probate courts and avoiding "intrafamily controversy" were not sufficiently important to sustain the use of gender in deciding who would administer estates. Applying a midlevel standard, the Court found in *Craig* that the objectives Oklahoma sought — namely, to reduce the number of young people cited for driving under the influence of alcohol — did not justify treating men and women differently. The Court accepted Oklahoma's claim that many more men that age were cited for drunken driving and involved in accidents than women. But the Court concluded that the difference could not be used to justify distinguishing between the sexes without violating the equal protection clause.

Similarly, in *Mississippi University for Women v. Hogan* in 1982, the Court required an all-female nursing program at a public university to admit a male who had been rejected solely because of gender. He wanted to attend the nursing program closest to his home. In a 5-4 decision, Justice Sandra Day O'Connor, in her first opinion for the Court, applied the intermediate scrutiny test from *Craig*. The state had argued that its "important interest" was that the policy of not admitting men to the program compensated for discrimination against women. Justice O'Connor concluded that the exclusion of men did nothing to compensate for discriminatory barriers faced by women. Furthermore, the state failed to show that the policy "substantially furthered" the alleged objective since men were permitted to attend classes as auditors. The dissenters argued that there were other co-educational nursing programs within the state that Hogan could have attended, and they worried the majority opinion would lead to the banning of women-only state colleges. The Court decided, however, that the school's interest in maintaining an all-female nursing program did not justify the violation of Hogan's equal protection rights. The Court further noted that "excluding males from admission to the School of Nursing tends to perpetuate the stereotyped view of nursing as an exclusively woman's job."

Court approved gender differences

Despite the decisions in *Craig* and *Mississippi University*, the Supreme Court has upheld classifications based on gender when the statute has a direct relationship to an important government interest. In *Kahn v. Shevin* in 1974, the Court approved a Florida statute providing a property tax exemption for widows but not widowers. The Court held that the distinction was justified by the greater financial difficulty confronting a single woman. The Court noted, "Whether from overt discrimination or from the socialization process of a male-dominated culture, the job market is inhospitable to the woman seeking any but the lowest paid jobs."

In *Schlesinger v. Ballard* in 1975, the Court sustained a federal statute granting women in the Navy a longer period than men in which to achieve mandatory promotion. The Court reasoned that this distinction, unlike those disapproved in *Frontiero* and *Reed*, was not based on "archaic and overbroad generalizations." Rather, it reflected the "demonstrable fact that male and female line officers in the Navy are not similarly situated with respect to opportunities for professional service." Since women were precluded from participating in combat and most sea duty, they would "not generally have compiled records of seagoing service comparable to those of male lieutenants."

In *Rostker v. Goldberg* in 1981, another case involving the military, the Court approved the federal statute that required men, but not women, to register for the draft. Congress had debated whether to require draft registration by women as well as men when it resumed registration in 1980, but after lengthy consideration, declined to require women to sign up. On July 18, 1980, three days before the new draft registration was to begin, a three-judge district court held that this gender-based classification was unconstitutional and enjoined the government from proceeding with the plan.

The Supreme Court, by a vote of 6-3, decided that the courts must generally defer to the decisions of Congress when it comes to national security matters. It recognized that Congress had thoroughly debated the issue and had concluded that since registration could lead to the drafting of individuals who could be sent into combat, and women were precluded from combat roles, it was acceptable for Congress to require registration of men only. It further concluded that the test of "heightened scrutiny" articulated in *Craig* — by which the Court meant midlevel analysis — was satisfied because military flexibility was an important government goal. The Court noted that although women occupied noncombat positions in the military, they are substantially smaller in number. It further found that it was reasonable for Congress to conclude that requiring all women 18 to 21 to register was not an appropriate way to fill those noncombat positions. The Court majority did not consider whether excluding women from combat roles violated the Constitution.

The Court has also permitted distinctions based on gender on the theory that women need some protections in the law that need not be extended to men. In *Michael M. v. Sonoma County Court* in 1981, the Supreme Court, by a 5-4 decision, upheld a California statutory rape law that provided for punishment for the male, but not the female, when both of them were under the age of 18. In that case, the 17-year-old man was prosecuted while the 16-year-old woman was not. After reviewing the standards it had previously applied in cases involving gender-based classifications, the Court stated that although it had not concluded that gender classifications are inherently suspect — and they therefore do not automatically trigger the strict scrutiny standard — it had applied more than the minimum level rationality test in the previous cases. The Court noted that in *Reed*, it upheld a gender-based classification when it had a "fair and substantial relationship" to legitimate state ends, while in *Craig*, the Court restated the test to require the classification to bear a "substantial relationship" to "important government objectives."

In the *Michael M.* case, the Court upheld the statute on the grounds that the state had legitimate reasons for making a distinction between men and women. The Court observed, "We need not be medical doctors to discern that young men and women are not similarly situated with respect to the problems and the risks of sexual intercourse. Only women may become pregnant, and they suffer disproportionately the profound physical, emotional, and psychological consequences of sexual activity. The statute at issue here protects women from sexual intercourse at an age when those consequences are particularly severe."

The Court was willing to defer to California's decision to punish only the male, but not the female. "We cannot say that a gender-neutral statute would be as effective. The State persuasively contends that a gender-neutral statute would frustrate its interest in effective enforcement. Its view is that a female is surely less likely to report violations of the statute if she herself would be subject to criminal prosecution." The Court concluded that the important government interest of reducing teen pregnancy was "substantially furthered" by the statute.

Applying the equal protection clause to private discrimination

It is not well understood by the American people that the Constitution applies only to the government and not to private entities. For example, professors and students at a public university are entitled to the explicit protections provided by the First Amendment's freedom of speech clause, and the 14th Amendment's due process clause, while those at private universities are not. Only laws passed by legislative bodies — statutes passed in pursuance of the goals stated in the constitutional provisions — are binding on private entities. In other words, a private employer is forbidden from discriminating against women or racial minorities not because of the 14th Amendment — which applies only to government or those working so closely with government that they are considered "state actors" — but because of the civil rights laws passed by Congress and state legislatures.

Although federal courts, and to a lesser extent state courts, have made substantial progress in recent years in reducing discrimination against women and unfair gender-based classifications — even without a federal equal rights amendment — less progress has been made in the private sector. "Equal pay for equal work," which sounds great in theory, continues to be an elusive goal. Women still earn substantially less than men for performing similar tasks. There are also many occupations —

many of them low-paying — which are almost always filled by women. Although sexual harassment laws have sometimes been vigorously enforced, it remains extremely difficult for many victims of such behavior to bring successful lawsuits, especially against private employers.

Section 2 of Amendment "B" seeks to extend constitutional protection to women in the private sector. It states that "Congress shall enforce, by appropriate legislation, the provisions of this amendment." This proactive language is different from the more passive language found in some amendments to the U.S. Constitution. For example, the 13th Amendment, abolishing slavery, states in Section 2 that Congress "shall have power to enforce this article by appropriate legislation." Section 5 of the 14th Amendment states that "The Congress shall have power to enforce, by appropriate legislation, the provisions of this article." The 15th Amendment has a similar provision in Section 2. So do most of the Amendments ratified since 1961.

In order for Congress to regulate the actions of nongovernmental entities, it must pass legislation to enforce the constitutional amendment. But there is nothing in existing amendments that says Congress is *required* to pass such laws. The Constitution, in many respects, is not self-executing. Until Congress enacts legislation that enforces the goals stated in the amendments — whether specific or general — the words of that section of the Constitution remain largely symbolic.

Amendment B's "shall execute" language requires Congress to enact laws to carry out its provisions. Section 2 does not merely permit Congress to enforce the amendment by legislation. It mandates that Congress enact legislation that will apply to both government and nongovernmental entities. Without strong legislation to enforce the new Equal Rights Amendment, the protections it guarantees to women will apply mostly in the public sector, and much less so to private entities.

Violence Against Women

For centuries, women have been vulnerable to the violent proclivities of men. Husbands, boyfriends, strangers, and stalkers have taken advantage of the physical differences between men and women, and the attitude that women are the property of men, to beat, maim, intimidate, harass and, not infrequently, kill women. Laws have often provided little or no protection for women who are physically and emotionally abused by the men in their lives. Until recently, there were no laws against stalking; thus women often had to wait until a violent act was committed against them before they could seek police protection.

In 1994, Congress passed the Violence Against Women Act (VAWA) that had been introduced by Senator Joseph Biden (D-DE) in 1990. Congress held hearings and debated the bill for years before final approval. The Act sought to create a federal right to be free from violence motivated by gender. In explaining why such a law was necessary, Congress relied on a variety of statistics including:

• Approximately 4 million women are battered by their husbands or partners in America each year.

• 95 percent of domestic violence victims are women.

• 35 percent of women visiting hospital emergency rooms have injuries due to domestic violence.

• Domestic violence alone costs employers between $3 billion and $5 billion annually due to absenteeism.

• Almost half of rape victims lose their jobs or are forced to quit in the aftermath of the crime.

• Problems of domestic violence transcend the abilities of state law enforcement agencies because of their interstate nature.

The Act has several key provisions:

• It created a federal civil cause of action against a person who commits a crime of violence motivated by gender. Prior to the VAWA, few, if any, federal statutes permitted women to sue those who committed violent acts against them.

• It provided that a victim may recover compensatory and punitive damages, injunctive, and declaratory relief against the liable party.

• It defined a crime of violence as an "act or series of acts that would constitute a felony" under state or federal law.

• It provided $1.6 billion over six years for grants to support law enforcement and prosecution efforts to reduce violent crime against women, education and prevention programs, battered women's shelters, and community programs on domestic violence.

Before the VAWA was enacted, concern existed that such a statute would greatly enlarge the number of lawsuits in the already-crowded federal courts. Chief Justice William Rehnquist predicted it would embroil the federal courts in a "whole host of domestic relations disputes." However, five years after it was passed, the federal courts have issued an average of fewer than 10 decisions a year regarding the law.

In March 1999, the Act ran smack up against the Constitution. When the Framers created the Constitution in 1787, they recognized the importance of the continued viability of state governments, and provided for them in the document they wrote. In the absence of specific constitutional language to the contrary, Congress does not have the authority to legislate on subjects that are within the domain of the states. It frequently must rely on the commerce clause of Article I, Section 8, which authorizes Congress to "regulate commerce . . . among the several States." Since the 1930s — when the Supreme Court invalidated major New Deal laws on interstate commerce grounds — federal courts have been much more willing to uphold federal laws even when they appear to have little to do with interstate commerce. Only in recent years have the Supreme Court and lower federal courts struck down federal statutes on the grounds that there was no interstate commerce involved.

An example of the Supreme Court drawing the line was *United States v. Lopez* in 1995. By a 5-4 decision, the Court struck down a federal statute passed in 1990 known as the Gun-Free School Zones Act. The Act made it a federal offense to possess a firearm in a school zone. Congress relied on the authority of the commerce clause to justify passage of the legislation as a way of stemming the rising tide of gun-related incidents in public schools. In one of the few cases since the 1930s to strike down a federal law on interstate commerce grounds, the Court held that Congress had violated the right of the states by trying to legislate control over public schools. Chief Justice Rehnquist criticized the argument that when a high school senior brings a gun to school, it involves interstate commerce. Rehnquist held that given the theories advanced by the federal government in this case, "it is difficult to perceive any limitation on federal power, even in areas such as criminal law enforcement or education where States historically had been sovereign. Thus, if we were to accept the Government's arguments, we are hard-pressed to posit any activity by an individual that Congress is without power to regulate."

In March 1999, the U.S. Court of Appeals for the Fourth Circuit in Richmond, Virginia, struck down on interstate commerce grounds the section of the Violence Against Women Act creating a cause of action. The court, dividing 7-4, concluded that a Virginia Tech student could not bring a federal lawsuit against two men who allegedly sexually assaulted her, and the university for the way it handled her complaint. She claimed violation of Title IX of the Civil Rights Act, and the VAWA. The district judge had dismissed the Title IX claim and found the VAWA unconstitutional. A three-judge panel of the Fourth Circuit had reversed that decision, but the full court of appeals overturned the panel's decision.

The court of appeals rejected the two grounds the government had used to support the law. The Fourth Circuit found that the law did not substantially affect interstate commerce: "The statute does not regulate the manufacture, transport or sale of goods, the provision of services, or any other sort of commercial transaction. Rather, it regulates violent crime motivated by gender animus. Not only is such conduct clearly not commercial, it is not even economic in any meaningful sense."

The government had also argued that it had the authority to pass the law under Section 5 of the 14th Amendment, which gave Congress authority to enforce the provisions of the amendment such as the equal protection clause. The Fourth Circuit found that the VAWA regulated only private conduct, not government action, and thus cannot be limited by the Constitution. Since congressional findings leading up to the passage of the law did not find intentional discrimination by state and local officials, the Act cannot be upheld as a proper exercise of congressional authority under the 14th Amendment.

A constitutional amendment can resurrect the cause of action in cases falling under laws such as the VAWA, but it cannot directly impact private behavior. It can, however, authorize or require Congress to enact legislation that provides a cause of action in cases involving private, nongovernmental violence against women. Such an amendment would reverse the Fourth Circuit and the Supreme Court if it should uphold the lower court decision in the VAWA case.

Why an ERA Is Still Needed

There can be no question that women have made great strides in the past few decades. In a report for the Roper Center for Public Opinion Research, Elizabeth Fox-Genovese, a professor of history and women's studies at Emory University, reviewed some of the progress made by women in recent years:

> Most Americans have come to view equality between women and men as a matter of elementary justice — even as a moral norm — and to view vestiges of inequality between them as injustices. . . . Women's gains during these two decades ['60s and '70s] touched — and often revolutionized — virtually every aspect of American life. In quick succession women secured the right to legal abortion, no fault divorce, credit in their own names, equal pay for equal work, and membership in a variety of institutions. . . . The most striking aspect of this equality is the rapidity with which it has occurred and the ease with which the American public has accepted it. It would be difficult to find a group of working people in all of history that has improved its position as dramatically or in as short a period of time as American women have during the past two or three decades.

Although Professor Fox-Genovese identifies elsewhere in her report areas where women have not attained full economic rights, the description she paints of the status of women in the late 20th century is generally positive. A reasonable argument could be made that the effort to add the

ERA to the federal Constitution in the 1970s and early 1980s, although technically a failure, helped to energize women and persuade the country that the time had come to afford women political and economic rights.

Progress has clearly been made on certain fronts, such as the number of women who serve in government. The lower house of Nevada, for example, historically a rather conservative state, boasts the largest percentage of women in the country. In a state that repeatedly rejected the ERA in the 1970s, 43 percent of the 42 assembly members are women. Arizona, which is number two, has 40 percent women in its House of Representatives, and all five of its top statewide elected officials are women. Because only five of the 21 state senators in Nevada are women, it ranks second to Washington in total female legislative representation. Many states, however, have relatively few women legislators.

In 1976, the National Commission on the Observance of International Women's Year issued a report entitled ". . . *To Form A More Perfect Union . . ." Justice for American Women*. The report identified a number of reasons the ERA, pending at the time, should be approved. Several of those reasons are no longer necessary because of the progress women have made in recent years, but some still provide support for the addition to the Constitution of an equal rights amendment. The authors wrote that the ERA is needed:

• To enshrine in the Constitution the moral value judgment that sex discrimination is wrong;

• To ensure that all States and the Federal Government review and revise their laws and official practices to eliminate discrimination based on sex;

• To ensure that such laws are never again enacted by governments, including labor laws restricting women's job opportunities;

• To give constitutional sanction to the principle (ignored in most family law) that the homemaker's role in marriage has economic value that entitles one to full partnership under the law.

The impact of a new federal ERA would be impossible to predict. It should require Congress and state legislatures to review laws that continue to inappropriately distinguish the rights of women from men. A new amendment should inspire legislative bodies to enact legislation that reaches private behavior that is beyond the direct reach of the Constitution. It should allow laws, regulations, and practices that have benign effects on women to survive unless those laws discriminate against others based on immutable characteristics. Perhaps most importantly, a new amendment will require the Supreme Court to apply its highest level of review of legislation for laws making gender-based distinctions or having a discriminatory impact on women. Although one could argue that women have been able to assume positions of power and responsibility in government and business more successfully than racial minorities, considering what women have been through during the history of this nation, they deserve the highest level of judicial review.

If nothing else, a federal ERA will finally add what was missing to the statement in the Declaration of Independence in 1776 that "all men are created equal." Even if the ERA's impact is largely symbolic because of the progress women have made, it would be an important statement to make and should be part of the Constitution.

CHAPTER NINE

Amendment "C": A Crime Victims' Bill of Rights Amendment

The Petition

The legislature of the state of _____, being comprised of the duly elected representatives of the people thereof, formally request that the United States Congress call a constitutional convention under Article V of the United States Constitution so that the convention can consider, and in its discretion, propose an amendment or amendments addressing the subject of the rights of victims of crime. This petition was approved by both houses of this legislature in accordance with its established rules and procedures.

Amendment "C"

Section 1. All victims of crimes shall enjoy certain rights that shall be enforceable by federal and state courts including the right to be present in all public proceedings to determine release from custody, acceptance of a plea agreement, or a sentence; the right to be informed of and to offer written or oral testimony at parole hearings; the right to reasonable notice of release or escape from custody of the defendant; and the right to compensation for crimes in amounts fixed by federal and state law.

Section 2. All victims of federal and state crimes shall enjoy a civil right of action in federal and state courts, respectively, against those convicted of the criminal offense.

Section 3. In cases where conduct of prosecutors or judges or other public officials results in gratuitous harm to the crime victim, and where the conduct of such officials is reckless or malicious, the crime victim shall have a right of action against federal or state authorities. In such cases, state sovereign immunity, prosecutorial immunity, and judicial immunity cannot be asserted as a defense to such a lawsuit.

Section 4. The testimony of victims at proceedings before the trial, at the trial itself, at post-trial hearings, and parole hearings, shall be considered by federal and state courts, as well as federal and state administrative bodies, when making decisions as to the disposition of a criminal trial and parole.

Section 5. Congress and the states shall have the power to implement and enforce this amendment by appropriate legislation.

Section 6. This amendment shall be in effect 180 days after its ratification.

Section 7. This amendment shall be inoperable unless ratified as an amendment to the United States Constitution within seven years from the date of its submission.

Section 8. Ratification of this amendment shall take place by conventions in each state whose delegates will be popularly elected.

The Constitutionally Based Rights of Criminal Defendants

One of the characteristics of the Constitution that has helped make this nation among the most advanced democratic societies is the protection afforded to those charged with criminal offenses. The provisions of the Bill of Rights and sections of state constitutions that provide procedural rights to those who are at risk of losing their liberty or life are indispensable in a civilized country.

For much of our history, however, treatment of many criminal defendants was barbaric and should have been the cause of national shame. Torture and other forms of coercion were routinely used to extract confessions, which courts then willingly admitted into evidence. It took until 1936 for the Supreme Court to finally decide that police officials could not beat suspects until they confessed and use the so-called confessions at trial. Amazingly, in the 1936 case, *Brown v. Mississippi*, the state courts permitted the convictions of three black tenant farmers accused of murdering a white planter even though prosecution witnesses freely admitted that the defendants had been badly beaten until they said they committed the crime. The confessions were admitted into evidence, and the defendants were convicted by a jury and sentenced to death. The Mississippi Supreme Court affirmed their convictions.

The U.S. Supreme Court — which had the chance to review the case only because courageous individuals raised the money to bring the appeal — decided that the due process clause of the 14th Amendment was violated when criminal suspects were brutalized until they confessed. It is not difficult to imagine that the coercion of confessions had taken place throughout much of the 19th and early 20th centuries, and that it continued even after the *Brown* decision.

Just to make sure the Supreme Court would not be perceived as too concerned about the rights of criminal defendants, the Court reminded the country in *Brown* that the self-incrimination clause of the Fifth Amendment did not apply to the states. The Court thus narrowed its ruling by concluding that when defendants are beaten until they confess, those confessions cannot be used in court without violating their 14th Amendment rights. The country would have to wait another 30 years before the protection against self-incrimination provided by the Fifth Amendment would be extended to defendants in state prosecutions.

The nation's courts were also in no hurry to make the Sixth Amendment right to counsel available to most criminal defendants. For many years, states could convict defendants of serious crimes and sentence them to long prison terms without providing an attorney. Only when Alabama shocked the nation in 1931 by permitting a death sentence against nine black youths accused of raping two white women on a train near Scottsboro, Alabama — when the defendants were not provided an attorney — did the Supreme Court reluctantly agree that the Constitution would not permit defendants to be put to death without the assistance of counsel. Two of the most conservative justices ever to serve on the Court dissented from the decision to reverse their convictions.

Speaking for the Court in the Scottsboro case, Justice George Sutherland held the convictions of the black youths must be reversed under the due process clause of the 14th Amendment. The Court did not rule, however, that the Sixth Amendment right to counsel applied to proceedings in state courts. It would take until the Court's 1963 decision in *Gideon v. Wainright* to reach that conclusion. Despite what appeared to be a humane result in the Scottsboro case, the Court did its best to limit the scope of the decision. It held, in effect, that the 14th Amendment could be invoked only when it can be shown that an unfair trial resulted from the lack of counsel. The Court apparently believed that the burden of demonstrating potential unfairness should be the responsibility of the accused.

Many other examples would make the point. Until 1964, if police broke down the door of a residence and illegally seized evidence, that evidence could still be used in state courts in violation of the Fourth Amendment because that Amendment applied only to prosecution by federal authorities. The federal government had been prohibited from using illegally obtained evidence since 1914. But it was decades before the rule excluding such evidence protected defendants in state prosecutions.

Among the most appalling examples of how meaningless the Constitution was for many criminal defendants was the case of Frank Palko. He was convicted of second-degree murder in Connecticut and sentenced to life in prison. Under state law in effect at the time, if an error in the trial was prejudicial to the prosecution, the state had the right to appeal the conviction, which is what the prosecutors did. After a second trial, Palko was convicted of first-degree murder and sentenced to death. He appealed his conviction to the U.S. Supreme Court on the grounds that the double jeopardy clause of the Fifth Amendment prevented the state from trying him a second time for the same offense in order to obtain a harsher sentence. In 1937, the Supreme Court ruled in *Palko v. Connecticut* that the Fifth Amendment could not be invoked by Palko because he was tried in state court. Justice Benjamin Cardozo, writing for the majority, decided that the right to be free from a state repeatedly trying a defendant until it obtained the desired conviction was not "implicit in the concept of ordered liberty," meaning that protection from double jeopardy was not a fundamental freedom guaranteed by the Constitution. In 1969, the Supreme Court reversed *Palko* and found that the ban on double jeopardy "represents a fundamental ideal in our constitutional heritage" and that it was binding on the states through the 14th Amendment.

The Warren Court (1953–1969) substantially enhanced the procedural rights granted to those accused of crimes. Many police officers and prosecutors have argued that the complex rules related to when they can search suspects, seize evidence, and use confessions in court has greatly complicated their jobs. In *Brewer v. Williams* in 1977, for example, the Supreme Court would not allow the confession of a man accused of murdering a 10-year-old girl. When arrested, Williams was given Miranda warnings about his right to remain silent and to have an attorney. His attorney advised him not to talk to police, and Williams agreed. While transporting Williams to jail in another city, a police officer commented that the girl's body had not been found. "I wish we could stop and locate the body," the officer said, "because this little girl's parents are entitled to give her a Christian burial." Williams then agreed to show the police where the body was located. The Supreme Court ruled that the officer's remarks were "subtle coercion" because he took advantage of Williams's mental illness and religious beliefs, and thus the confession could not be used in court.

No Constitutional Protection for Crime Victims

The debate still continues over whether the decisions of the Warren Court granted criminal suspects and defendants too much protection, and thus interfere with police and prosecutorial efforts to combat crime. There is also debate over whether the Burger (1969–1986) and Rehnquist (1986–) Courts have moved the pendulum to a more moderate position between the rights of defendants and society's interest in punishing criminal behavior. There can be no argument, however, that protection for those accused of crimes is constitutionally grounded, while the rights of crime victims are not. This disparity has sometimes meant that crime victims and their families are not only excluded from participating in efforts to bring the perpetrator to justice, they are not even allowed to observe the proceedings. A federal constitutional amendment is needed to extend constitutionally based rights to those who suffer as a result of criminal activity.

More than 30 states have included victims' rights amendments in their constitutions. As would be expected, they vary substantially. Some are detailed and lay out specific procedures that prosecutors and judges must follow to facilitate meaningful participation by crime victims, while others are short, general, and largely ignored. The U.S. Department of Justice has concluded that the state amendments, and related federal and state statutes recognizing the rights of victims, are inadequate and will remain so until a federal constitutional amendment is approved. As Attorney General Janet Reno has observed: "Efforts to secure victims' rights through means other than a constitutional amendment have proved less than fully adequate. Victims' rights advocates have sought reforms at the State level for 20 years. . . . However, these efforts have failed to fully safeguard victims' rights. These significant State efforts simply are not consistent, comprehensive, or authoritative enough to safeguard victims' rights."

Ellen Greenlee, president of National Legal Aid, put it more bluntly in testimony before the House Judiciary Committee in 1996. She said state victims' amendments "so far have been treated as mere statements of principle that victims ought to be included and consulted more by prosecutors and courts. A state constitution is far. . . . easier to ignore than the federal one."

Ignoring provisions in state constitutions is apparently widespread. A 1998 report from the National Institute of Justice found that even in the several states identified as giving "strong protection" to victims' rights, fewer than 60 percent of the victims were notified of the sentencing hearing and fewer than 40 percent were notified of the pretrial release of the defendant.

There is not only a lack of uniformity among states when it comes to the treatment of crime victims, the federal Constitution does not recognize that they have rights at all. No federal constitutional rights are granted to crime victims to do the following:

• To attend the preliminary hearing or trial of the accused. Judges often will rule that if someone is going to be a witness in the case, that person cannot hear the testimony of other witnesses. The concern is that the crime victim will shape his or her testimony based on what is said by other witnesses.

• To testify during the sentencing phase or at a parole hearing. Many states do not permit victim impact statements to be introduced when the judge is making a sentencing decision or when the parole board is considering release of the prisoner.

• To be informed about various stages in the process that can stretch for months or years.

• To be consulted before a plea bargain is approved by the court.

• To be informed that the defendant is out on bail or has been released from prison.

• To be compensated for monetary loss as a result of the crime, although both the federal government and many states have victim compensation programs.

• To bring a civil action against the prosecutors or judges whose sometimes egregious behavior results in serious, unnecessary harm to the crime victim.

Not only does the U.S. Constitution fail to recognize the interests of crime victims, the legal profession has also been slow to respond to demands that victims be afforded certain procedural and substantive rights. A typical law student can go through an entire three years of study without meeting a crime victim, or ever analyzing issues from the victim's perspective. Almost the entire focus in criminal law and criminal procedure classes is on the prosecutor's and defendant's interests. A typical criminal law textbook barely mentions victims' rights issues or organizations.

Efforts to Enact a Constitutional Amendment

Several national organizations are energetic advocates for the rights of crime victims. They lobby Congress and state legislatures, provide services for victims, and conduct programs for criminal justice agencies, mental health professionals, lawyers, and others involved with crime and its impact on society and individuals. Among their most difficult challenges has been the promotion of a federal constitutional amendment to recognize and protect the rights of crime victims and their families.

Among the largest of such organizations is the National Organization for Victim Assistance (NOVA). Founded in 1975, NOVA says it is the oldest group of its kind in the worldwide victims' movement. Its literature suggests a substantial growth in victim assistance programs in the past few decades. According to NOVA, in 1980 there were 27 victim compensation programs in the United States. By 1998, there were 50 state programs and one in the District of Columbia. NOVA lobbied for a law, passed in the wake of the Oklahoma City bombing, that authorized the use of federal funds to serve the needs of victims of terrorism and mass violence.

The group further notes that in 1980, only a few jurisdictions took into consideration the impact of the crime on the victim when determining the offender's sentence. By 1998, almost every state allowed victim input at sentencing as well as parole hearings, although there is evidence that many of the programs have not been implemented successfully. Two decades ago, few state constitutions had provisions recognizing victims' rights. Today, more than 30 have such amendments.

Another large and active organization is the National Center for Victims of Crime (NCVC). In addition to lobbying states to amend their constitutions to recognize victims' rights, NCVC has actively tried to persuade Congress to propose a federal constitutional amendment. Among the reasons why no federal amendment has been successful are the difficulty of writing one to deal with the numerous issues involved, and because NOVA and NCVC cannot agree on what such an amendment should do and how it should be written.

A group of senior staff members at NOVA formed a new organization in the mid-1990s to specifically push for a federal constitutional amendment. The National Victims' Constitutional Amendment Network (NVCAN), based in Denver, supported the amendment sponsored by Senator Jon Kyl (R-AZ) in April 1998. When the amendment was originally introduced in 1996, the NCVC supported it. But because the amendment did not attract sufficient support in Congress to win two-thirds approval in each house, it was modified and reintroduced in 1998.

The Kyl amendment has five sections. It requires that "each victim of a crime of violence" be notified of and permitted to attend all public proceedings related to the crime. Victims would have the right to be heard if present, or to submit written statements when the offender is being considered for release, when there is an acceptance of a negotiated plea, or when a sentence is being decided. The rights the offender has at a nonpublic parole hearing would also be extended to the victims of the crime. The amendment further requires reasonable notice of a release or escape from custody; consideration for the interest of the victim in a trial "free from unreasonable delay"; an order requiring the convicted defendant to make restitution to the victim; and notice of the rights established in the amendment.

Section 2 limits legal "standing" — in this context, the right to assert the protections in the amendment — to the crime victim or his or her representative. It also seeks to maintain the traditional discretion granted to prosecutors and courts. It specifically excludes the right to challenge the decision whether to charge someone with a crime; to overturn a sentence of a negotiated plea; to obtain a stay of the trial; or to compel a new trial. It also denies a cause of action for damages against the United States, a state, a political subdivision of a state, or a public official, based on the rights granted in the amendment.

There is understandable concern that giving crime victims an active role in criminal prosecutions could overwhelm an already heavily burdened system. The Kyl amendment seeks a balance between the efficient running of the criminal justice system and the rights of victims to be able to meaningfully participate in a matter in which they have a compelling interest. In order to find that balance, the amendment's sponsors chose to limit the application of the amendment to certain crime victims and to further limit their participation in the process.

After the Kyl amendment was introduced in 1998, NCVC withdrew its support. The organization disagreed with the amendment being limited to victims of violent crimes. It argued that there is "no principled reason to deny any victim of crime constitutional rights to participate in the criminal justice system." NCVC specifically asserted that victims of nonviolent offenses have as much right to see justice done in their cases and to be included in the process as victims of violent offenses. Two years earlier, when the amendment was first introduced in Congress, NCVC had reluctantly agreed to language limiting the scope of the amendment to "crimes of violence and other crimes as defined by Congress." At the time, NCVC called that compromise a "major" concession on its part. But when that section was changed to limit the amendment to the victims of violent crimes only — without giving Congress the discretion to add additional crimes that would be covered — NCVC would not go along. NCVC worried that crimes such as statutory rape, burglary, child molestation, drunken driving, and emotional abuse in the context of domestic violence might not be considered "violent" crimes and would thus not be covered by the amendment. The organization rejected the argument that including all crime victims in the amendment would place intolerable burdens on the criminal justice system.

Among the most controversial of NCVC's objections to the proposed amendment was the group's contention that crime victims should be able to force the courts to reopen proceedings if they had been improperly excluded. Victims who were not notified of sentencing or plea agreement hearings, and were not given an opportunity to attend or speak at such proceedings, would not have any remedy for the violation of their rights unless they could demand rehearings. Under the Kyl amendment, victims who were excluded from the trial or were not properly notified would not be able to appeal the court's ruling. NCVC claimed the new language would "effectively eliminate a meaningful remedy for some of the most important of the victims' rights." The group argued that since offenders who are denied important procedural rights are entitled to seek a new hearing, the crime victim should have the same right.

The organization argued that the Kyl amendment was so complicated and difficult to interpret that it harmed the chances of winning congressional approval. It further maintained that because only some victims were covered, it would not attract sufficient public support.

The group's pessimism about the prospects of congressional approval may be well-founded. During the current Congress (1999–2000), no amendment has been introduced in the House. The current version has one-third fewer co-sponsors in the Senate as it had in 1996. NCVC believes that compromises on the language of the amendment have made approval even less likely.

Academic and Legal Arguments

Law professors and other academics have considered for some years whether the federal Constitution should be amended to recognize victims' rights. Those opposed to such an amendment generally argue that it is unnecessary or would cause significant problems for the criminal justice system. Some believe, for example, that only government officials should be in charge of criminal prosecutions and that allowing crime victims who are not part of the system to play a constitutionally mandated role would create additional burdens that the system cannot tolerate. They also argue that if victims' rights are to be more fully recognized, it should be done by ordinary legislation and not by constitutional amendment. Changing the Constitution, they argue, would make it much more difficult to adapt to changing conditions and problems that arise after the amendment is approved.

Additional arguments include the assertion that victim impact statements harm the rights of defendants. There is concern that juries, and even judges, could be persuaded by emotional stories of crime victims and their families and, therefore, less likely to follow their duties as established under the law. Courts are also worried that if crime victims have a constitutionally guaranteed right to attend preliminary hearings, trials, and other proceedings, the victims' testimony will be influenced by that of other witnesses. The federal constitutional amendment pending in the Senate would allow exclusion of such witnesses only when necessary to achieve a "compelling interest."

There is the legitimate problem of whether involving victims at each phase of the proceedings will further strain the legal system's resources and cause even greater delays. As it is now, the defendant's right to a speedy trial under the Sixth Amendment is often violated. If the proceedings had to wait until crime victims were properly notified and could be present to participate or until written statements were submitted, additional delays would result.

A federal constitutional amendment would also raise serious questions of implementation. Would the state have to pay to transport crime victims from distant cities — or even from other states — so they would be able to participate in the trial or some other phase of the process? Criminal prosecutions already clog the courts and strain the financial resources of the criminal justice system. If such an amendment were passed, Congress and state legislatures might have to spend millions in transportation, food, and lodging costs to make sure that crime victims who cannot pay their own way could still participate or be represented. In addition, debate would continue over whether only victims of violent crimes should be covered by a constitutional amendment or whether it should include any crime victim.

Those opposed to a federal constitutional amendment also argue that principles of federalism require that the states have substantial autonomy over the prosecution of state crimes. If a federal amendment were approved, states would have to abide by its requirements and would thus give up some of the independence they have long enjoyed.

Professor Paul Cassell of the University of Utah College of Law energetically answered each of these arguments in his testimony in favor of a federal constitutional amendment before the Senate Judiciary Committee on March 24, 1999. He contended that such an amendment would not harm the defendant's rights. He cited the testimony before a House committee of Professor Laurence Tribe of the Harvard Law School. Tribe stated that the proposed amendment is "a carefully crafted measure, adding victims' rights that can coexist side by side with the defendant's." Professor Cassell further cited a study indicating that there is "virtually no evidence that the victim's participation is at the defendant's expense." The study analyzed data from 36 states and found that victim impact statements resulted in only a negligible effect on sentence type and length.

In some respects, citing the statistics from that study seems inconsistent with the argument in favor of an amendment. A constitutional amendment guaranteeing victims the right to speak or submit written statements prior to sentencing would not interfere with the defendant's rights, the argument goes, because they are generally ineffective. If they have little impact on prosecutors and judges, one could ask why should they be included in a constitutional amendment. The appropriate response is that first, such a study may not accurately reflect the use and impact of such involvement by crime victims. Judges are probably hesitant to admit that they increased the punishment given to the offender because of an emotional statement offered by a crime victim. In addition, the option to participate should be given to the crime victim regardless of whether it is likely to be persuasive to the court. If that person chooses to make a statement or participate in some other way, it may help to alleviate some of the anger and sorrow associated with being a crime victim or the family member of a victim. Even if victim participation slows down the process, and even if the impact on prosecutors and judges is limited, it may be therapeutic for victims and will serve as a reminder to the offender and the community that behind the cold statistics are real people whose lives can be disrupted or devastated by criminal activity.

Professor Cassell also rejected the idea that giving victims the option to be heard will overwhelm the system. Many implementation issues would have to be settled, such as who will be responsible for notifying the victim and making sure that person has the opportunity to address the court or submit written statements. But those challenges can be overcome without the criminal justice system grinding to a halt. He further disagreed with the argument that the statements of survivors during the sentencing phase of a death penalty case are often so emotional that they are "prejudicial and inflammatory." Cassell believes that the jury should have a full understanding of a murder's harmful effects on the victim's families and friends. The jury is entitled, in Cassell's words, to a "full picture of the murder's consequences."

Cassell also rejected the often-made argument that the presence of the crime victim in the courtroom, especially when that person will be a witness in the case, is prejudicial to the defendant. He contended that judges would still have the discretion in unusual circumstances to exclude prospective witnesses, who are also the victims of the crime, from the courtroom. Such a situation would arise when there are multiple victims who are all eyewitnesses to the same event and who thus might tailor their testimony if allowed to observe the trial together.

The Oklahoma City Bombing Case

As an example of why a federal constitutional amendment protecting victims' rights is necessary, Professor Cassell cited the way victims and family members were treated after the bombing of the federal building in Oklahoma City. During a pre-trial hearing, the judge ruled that anyone who wanted to provide victim impact testimony at sentencing could not observe any proceeding in the case. The victims and their families were outraged. In order to have the opportunity at the sentencing phase — after the guilt of the defendants had already been determined — to tell the judge and community what impact the bombing had on their lives, they had to give up the right to attend any of the trial's proceedings. The judge based his decision on Rule 615 of the Federal Rules of Evidence, the so-called "rule on witnesses." Victims and their families had one hour to decide whether to watch the hearing or maintain their eligibility to speak or submit written statements at the sentencing phase.

When 35 victims and survivors reminded the judge in a motion that a federal statute guarantees victims the right "to be present at all public court proceedings, unless the court determines that testimony by the victim would be materially affected if the victim heard other testimony at trial," the judge scheduled a hearing. After the hearing, he concluded that victims present during court proceedings would not be able to separate the "experience of trial" from "the experience of loss from the conduct in question," and thus they would have to choose between attending the trial and related hearings, and testifying during the sentencing phase.

With the support of the Department of Justice, the victims appealed the judge's decision to the U.S. Court of Appeals for the Tenth Circuit. The appeals court rejected — without oral argument — the claims of the victims on jurisdictional grounds. The court decided that the victims lacked "standing" because they had no "legally protected interest" to be present at trial and thus had suffered no "injury in fact" from their exclusion.

The victims were not finished. With the support of the Oklahoma Attorney General's office, they convinced Congress to enact a law to prevent victims from having to choose between testifying at sentencing and attending the trial. The Victims' Rights Clarification Act of 1997 was passed by overwhelming margins in the House and Senate. Armed with the new law, the victims petitioned the judge to rescind his previous order. Remarkably, even after the victims were able to persuade Congress to move so quickly in enacting the new law, the judge would not reconsider. He refused to hold a hearing on the issue and concluded that the constitutional issues raised by the new law were "premature." The Oklahoma City families were stuck with having to choose between attending the trial or seeing it on closed circuit television, or testifying at the sentencing phase.

The New Amendment

Seeking a constitutional amendment to recognize the rights of crime victims would be more popular than trying to further protect the rights of criminal defendants. Crime victims and their families are sometimes motivated after a criminal act has affected them or their communities to organize politically and to lobby for laws granting them the right to participate in the legal process. Criminal defendants, although they enjoy the benefits of specific provisions in the Bill of Rights, do not have much influence in the halls of Congress or state legislatures.

How well a democratic society functions is determined in part by how we treat those suspected of criminal activity. The procedural rights developed and extended during the Warren Court years, and in some decisions by the Burger and Rehnquist Courts, must honor the country's commitment to fairness. The rights enumerated in the Fourth, Fifth, Sixth, and Eighth Amendments, as applied to the states through the due process clause of the 14th Amendment, must be vigilantly protected by courts even in the face of strong opposition on the part of many people. While continuing to recognize the nation's long commitment to due process and the protection of the rights of criminal defendants, a way must be found to also protect the rights of crime victims.

Amendment "C," outlined at the beginning of this chapter, incorporates many of the principles in the Kyl amendment. But the amendment here goes beyond the one being considered by Congress in several respects. Section 3 of Amendment "C" is probably the most controversial provision. Currently, states enjoy substantial protection against lawsuits because of a misreading of the 11th Amendment. The error has been compounded repeatedly by a Supreme Court more interested in consistency than fairness.

The principle of state sovereign immunity has meant that many people injured by the actions of state officials cannot sue state governments, but must sue public officials as individuals. In addition, judges enjoy absolute immunity from lawsuits over wrongdoing arising from their official duties. Although judges can, for example, be sued for sexual harassment of employees and other actions that fall outside their judicial responsibilities, almost any other behavior, no matter how appalling, cannot be the subject of a civil action.

Section 3 would permit lawsuits against the state and against judges in those rare cases when the actions of prosecutors and judges are shocking and egregious, and result in substantial harm to crime victims. Judges should not be subject to legal action for misdeeds related to their official duties for many compelling reasons. However, when judges act with such recklessness that they needlessly endanger the safety of crime victims who have already suffered, and who are depending on the courts to protect them and their families, a limited right to sue should be available. An example would be a situation where there is substantial evidence that a criminal suspect would harm victims or witnesses if given the opportunity, and the offender is released from custody before trial or after a conviction but before beginning a prison sentence. If the prosecutor or judge treats such a situation with indifference because there are too many cases on the docket or because they are too busy to pay close attention, and harm comes to victims and witnesses, there must be legal recourse.

Permitting lawsuits against judges would create a lot of problems. The state or county or other jurisdiction — thus the taxpayers — will have to pay for the judge's defense and for any damages awarded by a jury. Whatever time a judge spends in court as a defendant in a civil suit or at an arbitration hearing would obviously take time away from judicial duties. It is also true that subjecting judges to lawsuits could discourage them from making decisions they believe to be consistent with the law, but which may lead to litigation. Permitting such actions against judges may also diminish respect for the judiciary by exposing accusations of wrongdoing of the courts, as well as affect the judge's career by making reelection more difficult. But despite all the potential negative consequences, judges should not enjoy absolute immunity for actions so reckless that the community cannot permit them to go unpunished. It is not enough that some states have judicial oversight panels that occasionally sanction irresponsible judicial behavior. A process should exist by which those who have already suffered as a crime victim, and suffer again needlessly because of the actions of prosecutors or judges, can be compensated.

CHAPTER TEN

Amendment "D": Congressional Term Limits

Amendment "E": Reducing Senate Terms

Amendment "F": Changing the Majority Required for Approval of Treaties

The Petition

The legislature of the state of _____, being comprised of the duly elected representatives of the people thereof, formally request that the United States Congress call a constitutional convention under Article V of the United States Constitution so that the convention can consider, and in its discretion, propose an amendment or amendments addressing the subject of congressional term limits, Senate terms, and the majority required for approval of treaties in the Senate. This petition was approved by both houses of this legislature in accordance with its established rules and procedures.

Amendment "D": Congressional Term Limits

Section 1. Members of the House of Representatives shall serve no more than eight years, or four two-year terms. Once a representative has completed the eight years of service, that person shall forever be ineligible to serve as a member of the House. The eight years do not have to be consecutive as long as the person serves no more than eight years in total.

Section 2. Members of the Senate shall serve no more than 12 years, or two six-year terms. Once a senator has completed the 12 years of service, that person shall forever be ineligible to serve as a member of the Senate. The 12 years of service do not have to be consecutive as long as the person serves no more than 12 years in total.

Section 3. If the length of Senate terms is ever reduced from six years to four, Section 2 of this amendment shall be interpreted to reflect that change. Under those circumstances, the maximum number of years allowed in the Senate shall still be 12; however, that period shall include three four-year terms.

Section 4. This amendment shall be implemented for current representatives through the following procedure: The eight-year limit shall begin for all current House members after the next general election beginning with the convening of the next Congress.

Section 5. This amendment shall be implemented for current senators through the following procedure: Senators, who at the time of this amendment's effective date are in the first three years of their first Senate term, shall be eligible for reelection to two additional terms. Senators who at the time of this amendment's effective date are in the last three years of their first Senate term, shall be eligible for reelection to one additional term. Senators who are in their second term or beyond shall not be eligible for reelection.

Section 6. No later than 180 days after this amendment has been ratified, a Senatorial Election Commission shall be appointed. It shall be composed of 11 members with six members chosen by the president (including the chair) and five by the Senate. No more than six members of the commission shall be from the same political party. Six members shall constitute a quorum. The commission shall determine the best method for maintaining staggered Senate terms during the implementation of this amendment. No more than one-third of the Senate shall be elected at any given time, with one-third elected in subsequent elections. The staggered-term process must be implemented during the years immediately after ratification of this amendment so that the system is in place no later than 14 years after its effective date. The Commission shall finish its work within one year of being appointed and shall be abolished when its work is completed.

Section 7. This amendment shall be in effect 30 days after its ratification.

Section 8. This amendment shall be inoperable unless ratified as an amendment to the United States Constitution within seven years from the date of its submission.

Section 9. Ratification of this amendment shall take place by conventions in each state whose delegates will be popularly elected.

Congressional Term Limits

If serious campaign finance reform is approved either by statute or constitutional amendment — both of which seem unlikely anytime soon — and federal elections become significantly more competitive, congressional term limits may not be necessary. But unless the appropriate laws and regulations are enacted to reduce the influence of money on elections and improve the chances of challengers, term limits may be required to make elected officials more accountable to those they represent.

Term limits should not, of course, be necessary at all. Voters have the ability to limit terms every two years for members of the House and every six years for those serving in the Senate. That voters do not often use that power by defeating incumbents, even when Congress as an institution is held in such low regard, is due to a number of factors. The advantages of incumbency — free news coverage; taxpayer-funded mailings to the district or state that keep the incumbent's name before the public; the ability to acquire huge sums of campaign money from PACs and other interest groups based merely on the representative or senator's committee assignments; and the opportunity to offer constituent service — discourage challengers and almost always lead to the defeat of those who run.

The support of term limits is one of the great paradoxes of American politics. Voters think Congress as an institution does a lousy job. There is too much partisanship, members are too close to special interests, and, after a while, those who serve in Congress often have a difficult time understanding the lives of ordinary people. Yet, at the same time that voters reelect their House members — and to a somewhat lesser extent, their senators — in overwhelming numbers, they also strongly support term limits. In the 20 or so states where terms limits for state legislators or members of Congress have appeared on the ballot, the voters have almost always approved them by substantial margins. In Florida and Wyoming in 1992, ballot measures limiting state legislative and congressional terms were approved by 77 percent of the voters. Arizona and Missouri voters gave their approval by 74 percent. It is difficult to find any issue on which three-quarters of the American people agree. During the last decade, voters in 23 states approved limits for members of Congress, while an even larger number imposed limits on state lawmakers. Forty states impose term limits on their governors.

Arkansas voters approved in 1992 with a 60 percent majority a constitutional amendment that applied term limits to three groups: elected officials in the executive branch, members of the state legislature, and the Arkansas congressional delegation. The amendment restricted its representatives in the U.S. House to three two-year terms and those in the U.S. Senate to two six-year terms. The amendment provided that those who exceeded these limits would not be certified to be on the ballot, although those who had already reached the maximum could run as a write-in candidate. Sponsors of the amendment argued that the states, not the federal government, had the authority to determine issues related to elections, and that their amendment did not establish an additional qualification, but instead was a ballot-access measure of the type authorized by the Constitution.

In 1995, the Supreme Court, in a 5-4 decision, *U.S. Term Limits v. Thornton*, held that the Arkansas measure was unconstitutional as it related to members of Congress. According to the Court, the Constitution establishes in Article I only three qualifications for service in Congress: age, citizenship, and residence. The state constitutional amendment, the Court decided, unconstitutionally added another qualification based on how long someone had already served in Congress.

Justice John Paul Stevens, writing the majority opinion, concluded that the Framers intended for the nation to have a uniform national legislature and that states were prohibited from establishing their own qualifications for congressional service. The Arkansas amendment was an effort to circumvent the requirements of the Constitution. Stevens noted that the Articles of Confederation had a provision limiting service in the Continental Congress. Even James Madison had to leave Congress and return to Virginia in 1783 when he served the maximum time allowed under the Articles. But, according to Stevens, since the Framers in Philadelphia did not impose term limits on Congress, they were implicitly rejected. Stevens concluded that, "Permitting individual states to formulate diverse qualifications for their representatives . . . would result in a patchwork of state qualifications, undermining the uniformity and the national character that the framers envisioned and sought to insure."

During the Constitutional Convention, the Framers rejected term limits apparently because they did not want to restrict the ability of the people to choose members of the House and state legislators to choose senators, and because they assumed that because of the hardship of serving in Congress — including the unpleasant and often dangerous travel required in the late 18th century — members would not want to serve very long. They also recognized the advantages of having experienced legislators. To have constant turnover in Congress would make it more difficult for that body to deal with the complex problems facing the nation. The Framers also believed that having to face reelection was a strong incentive for House incumbents to conscientiously represent the interests of the people and Senate incumbents the interests of the state.

Arguments For and Against Term Limits

Since the 22nd Amendment limiting the president to two terms was approved in 1951, there has been recurring discussion about whether Congress should also be subject to term limits. Those who support limiting the terms of members of Congress argue that increasing turnover would allow consideration of fresh ideas, and that if "citizen-legislators" went to Capitol Hill for a fixed period of time, rather than the career politicians who may serve for decades, they would be more likely to understand and care about the needs and interests of their constituents.

Shortly after being elected, members of Congress learn that they can almost always stay for an indefinite period of time if they raise enough campaign money to overwhelm prospective challengers. That money comes easily from lobbyists and various interests who expect that in return for their donations, the member of Congress will, at a minimum, be more accessible to them than they are to ordinary voters. Moreover, those who donate to campaigns also require that serious consideration be given to their opinions supporting or opposing legislation. Imposing a fixed number of terms may be the only way to break the grip that most incumbents have on their seats and increase competition.

Opponents of term limits argue that at election time voters can remove from office any member of Congress. If voters are disappointed with the voting record or performance of the incumbent, they can replace that person through the orderly process established in the Constitution. Furthermore, the nation faces complex problems, and experience in Congress is essential if House and Senate members are to monitor the activities of the huge federal bureaucracy and understand how best to allocate precious resources. Opponents of term limits argue that inexperienced legislators, lacking the expertise that develops over a long period of time by sitting on the same committee and by working on Capitol Hill, would be even more dependent on bureaucrats, lobbyists, and congressional staff for information and advice on how to legislate.

Even those members of Congress who strongly supported term limits while running for election — and may have won their races in part because of that position — have apparently decided that it is more enjoyable to be in Congress than they expected. Of course, they do not explain it that way. Instead, they say that they did not realize how important experience and seniority are on Capitol Hill. But they apparently figure as long as they are there and want to stay, they will find out if the advantages of incumbency are enough to overcome the disapproval of voters who expected them to keep their word.

The most notable member of this group is George Nethercutt, a Republican member of the House from eastern Washington State. In 1994, in his first race for public office, he beat Tom Foley, then the speaker of the House, in a district that Foley had represented for 30 years. No speaker had been defeated for reelection since the Civil War. Foley's defeat was partially due to his opposition to term limits. He helped file the lawsuit in the Washington courts that led to the overturning of term limits on Congress. Nethercutt told voters in the Fifth District that he would serve no more than three terms. But in 1999, he appeared ready to run for reelection. As for his pledge to serve only three terms, Nethercutt offered this: "I know what I said and I wish I hadn't said it . . . I have lived and learned." One of Nethercutt's constituents interviewed by the New York Times perhaps spoke for many people when referring to the congressman's commitment: "Maybe he should be held accountable. The man made a pledge."

Nethercutt is not alone. Fifty-eight members of Congress have set a limit on their time in office. At least 10 have pledges that come due in the fall of 2000. Of those 10, all but one of them Republicans, at least four are wavering on their commitments. With only a six-person majority in the House, Republicans are reluctant for any of their incumbents to voluntarily give up their seats and increase the chances of a Democratic victory. The one Democrat in the group, Martin Meehan of Massachusetts — the co-sponsor of the leading campaign finance reform bill in the House — was described as leaning toward running despite his pledge to step down. He said he made a mistake in promising to limit himself to four terms.

In an editorial in April 1999, the New York Times argued that representatives who make such a pledge should stick to their word. The paper noted that voters probably chose Nethercutt because of his term limits commitment. "If they had wanted seniority, they would have stuck with Mr. Foley." The editorial board also recognized that because he represents a safe Democratic district, Meehan would probably be reelected anyway. But although the newspaper has argued against term limits, it believes that "people who run for office should be accountable for what they say."

A Term Limit Amendment

Most states that have term limits for state legislators restrict house members to either three or four two-year terms. Two states, Oklahoma and Utah, allow house members to serve for six two-year terms. The limit for senators in most states is eight years, either two four-year or four two-year terms. The Arkansas amendment struck down by the Supreme Court in *Thornton* permitted only six years for house members and eight years for senators.

Amendment "D" provides for a maximum of eight years' service in the House of Representatives and 12 years in the U.S. Senate. If Amendment "E," discussed below, ever becomes part of the Constitution and Senate terms are reduced from six to four years, then Amendment "D" should probably limit Senate service to the same period of 12 years, or three four-year terms in office.

Designing the right formula to attain the desired goals of increasing competition in federal legislative elections and responsiveness to the public is incredibly challenging. The experience of a number of states demonstrates how creative elected officials can be in responding to term limits. In those states where house members are limited to six or eight years in office, the house member will run for the state Senate either during his or her last year in the House, or in the election before. The state senator, recognizing that the eight-year limit is approaching, will often run for a secondary statewide office such as lieutenant governor or state treasurer, or, depending on how the term limits law is written, for the House. If the term limits law allows someone to run again for the House or Senate after sitting out a term or two, that person is likely to regain that seat when the new person has to vacate it. In short, many of the same people with the same close connections to special interests will change office, but will ultimately still be in charge. With each new office they seek, they will often be able to use the money they stashed away from previous campaigns — when they had little chance of losing — to spend on the new race, thus scaring away challengers or defeating those who run.

It is much more difficult to switch back and forth between the U.S. House and U.S. Senate than it is to do so between the counterparts at the state level. State legislative House and Senate districts are smaller and thus the large campaign coffers that "incumbents" begin with after serving in the other House provide a substantial advantage. In addition, less is known about the voting record of state legislative incumbents, so name recognition from previous service is a substantial advantage. On the national level, a U.S. House seat does not automatically lead to victory in a Senate race. An open Senate seat often attracts competitive candidates, and there would be more such elections if Senate service were limited to 12 years.

Among all the options, it is probably best to create a lifetime ban on additional service in each house once service within that house has reached the limit. For example, once someone has served in the U.S. House for eight years, that person cannot serve in the House again. The same limit would hold in the Senate. The amendment would not prevent switching from one house to another. There is less danger that the same individuals will move from one body to the other because, unlike in state races, voters will often have access to a sufficient amount of information about federal candidates that will allow them to make rational judgments about whether someone who has been in the House is entitled to go to the Senate, and whether the reverse is true.

The amendment has to establish an orderly process during the transition to term limits. It should not be imposed on members during their current terms, and probably should allow some time for the people and their elected officials to prepare for the change. But once everyone in Congress comes under the term limits requirements imposed by the new constitutional amendment, there should be significant changes in the way Congress conducts itself.

Amendment "E": Reducing Senate Terms

Section 1. Terms for United States Senators shall be four years.

Section 2. This amendment shall be implemented for current senators through the following procedure: Senators, who at the time of this amendment's effective date are in the first three years of their Senate term, shall stand for election in their fourth year of service. Thereafter, their terms shall be four years. Senators who at the time of this amendment's effective date are in the last three years of their Senate term, will be able to finish their term and will stand for election in the sixth year. Thereafter, their terms shall be four years.

Section 3. No later than 180 days after this amendment has been ratified, a Senatorial Election Commission shall be appointed. It shall be composed of 11 members with six members chosen by the president (including the chair) and five by the Senate. No more than six members of the commission shall be from the same political party. Six members shall constitute a quorum. The commission shall determine the best method for maintaining staggered Senate terms during the implementation period of this amendment. No more than one-third of the Senate shall be elected at any given time, with one-third elected in subsequent elections. The staggered-term process must be implemented during the years immediately following ratification of this amendment so that the system is in place no more than 10 years after its effective date. The commission shall finish its work within one year of being appointed and shall be abolished when its work is completed.

Section 4. If a term limits amendment becomes part of the Constitution, the commission identified in Section 3 of this amendment shall implement a staggered term plan while implementing both this amendment and a term limits amendment.

Section 5. This amendment shall be in effect 30 days after its ratification.

Section 6. This amendment shall be inoperable unless ratified as an amendment to the United States Constitution within seven years from the date of its submission.

Section 7. Ratification of this amendment shall take place by conventions in each state whose delegates will be popularly elected.

Shortening Senate Terms

The Framers in Philadelphia strongly believed that the popularly elected House had the potential to demonstrate the worst aspects of democracy. They wanted the second branch of Congress to be able to stop the House if it acted irrationally. Although there was constant discussion in the years leading up to the Convention and behind the closed doors of Independence Hall about the people being the sovereign, it was clear that many of those creating the new Constitution did not want the people to have too direct a role in running the new government. The indirect election of the president by the Electoral College, the failure to require universal suffrage, the decisions to give the election of senators to state legislators and to provide insulation from popular pressures by giving them a six-year term, are but a few examples of provisions of the Constitution that demonstrate concern on the part of the delegates about the excesses of democracy.

Some of those attending the Constitutional Convention, including James Madison, thought that Senate terms should be longer than six years. There was also discussion at the Constitutional Convention about making the terms of House members four years instead of two. The argument was that elected officials must be able to make difficult decisions without always being required to follow the momentary whim of the people, who can often be short-sighted or poorly informed. At a minimum, learned and dispassionate representatives would be able to put aside short-term gain and make decisions that are better for the long-term health of the country. Although there was agreement that the House would be directly elected by the people so that it would be more accountable to them, the Senate was to be more insulated and thus its members would have longer terms and would be chosen by state legislatures.

In the modern era of communication technology, people can know much more about the voting record and behavior of their elected officials than has been the case in the past. With traditional and cable television networks, newspaper and news magazines, Web sites devoted to news and information, and a seemingly endless number of political Web sites created by candidates, interest groups, and concerned and angry citizens, plenty of political information exists for those interested.

However, one aspect of human nature has not been changed by the great advances in communication technology. The human memory capacity has not been radically enhanced, and except when it comes to those things that matter the most to us, it is easy to forget events and issues that took place four or six years before. Today, it is difficult for average voters — for whom political information is usually not considered urgent news — to remember how their U.S. senator voted several years earlier. Even if a citizen remembers something about a vote taken some years ago, that recollection is likely to be pushed aside when the incumbent senator spends millions on advertising to create the right image.

A challenger may try desperately to remind the public about a vote the incumbent cast earlier in the term that was, for example, excessively solicitous of special interests or was out of step with the views of the majority in the state. But there are always easy ways for the incumbent to deflect such criticism. The senator could argue that there were little-publicized aspects of the bill that were good or bad, depending on which way he or she voted. The incumbent senator could assert that the challenger is distorting the record. The incumbent could also argue that the controversial vote was a matter of principle, hoping that many people will admire an exercise of principle even when disagreeing with the actual vote. The senator could also just ignore the challenger. Except for face-to-face confrontations, it is almost always possible for the incumbent to respond to criticism of a previous vote that the senator is not running a negative campaign — as if that really answers the criticism. If the charge is made during a debate when ignoring it is more difficult, the senator can simply say that tough decisions on difficult issues have to be made, and the challenger does not have experience making those tough choices. Moreover, the senator will often be able to point to votes taken on different bills that seem to refute the charge that the incumbent is a pawn of special interests.

Congressional Intransigence

Over the years, at least 200 proposals for constitutional amendments have been introduced in Congress to alter House or Senate terms. Proposals have ranged from calling for yearly election of House members to requiring terms of three, four, or six years. Similarly, 13 proposals were introduced to shorten the terms of senators to three or four years or to raise them to eight years. The most common proposal has been to lengthen the terms of members of the House to four years. The argument for such an idea is that House members would be able to spend more time on legislative duties and less time fundraising and campaigning.

It is unlikely that Congress would propose a constitutional amendment to alter the terms of its members. If a proposed amendment were to lengthen House or Senate terms, there would be an outcry from the public that members of Congress wanted to be even less accountable to the citizens than they are under the current system. There would be the risk of a great public uprising that would result in the defeat of many incumbents. Even if longer terms were tied to a term limits constitutional amendment, it is hard to imagine Congress approving such a plan and the public supporting it. At the same time, Congress is not going to reduce the length of House terms and it seems unlikely to consider shortening Senate terms.

The six-year Senate term allows incumbents to raise money for reelection from the first day in office. Senators can vote the way lobbyists want them to during the first five years with the public back home knowing little — and perhaps caring little — about the voting record. Meanwhile, the money pours into campaign coffers, often at the rate of thousands of dollars a day, even while there is no challenger in sight.

Then, as the sixth year approaches, the candidate for reelection must be more careful, and cast a few votes that make it look like the senator has had a moderate voting record all along. The special interests that have invested heavily in the senator know how the game is played, and will forgive some votes they do not like during the months leading up to the election. Those interests, after all, do not want their hard work and money to go down the drain with the defeat of the incumbent. How well the senator represents the views of the people back home only matters if there is danger of the incumbent losing the election. After the election is over, there will be another five years for the reelected senator to show gratitude for the support of the lobbyists and contributors. On occasion, a pending bill or confirmation decision is the subject of heavy news coverage and many people will remember how their senator voted. But there are not very many of those issues during a six-year term.

It is difficult to predict the impact on our political system of changing Senate terms to four years. Having half the senate, instead of a third, stand for election every two years means that there could be a larger turn-over in senators if the public decides to get interested in politics again and takes action by voting against incumbents. Ideally, if terms for senators were four years, the public would have a greater opportunity to keep track of the senator's record and the chance to exercise a knowledgeable vote on election day. There are plenty of arguments against a shorter term, including that there would be more time spent fund-raising, and less on legislating, and that the fund-raising would have to begin earlier. But there is also the possibility that challengers would have a better chance of winning because there would be two fewer years in which the incumbent could raise campaign funds, and two fewer years of voting decisions which the public has to learn about to make an informed decision at the polls.

Amendment "F": Changing the Majority Required for Approval of Treaties

Section 1. The Senate shall ratify treaties by a majority of those present.

Section 2. This amendment shall be in effect 30 days after its ratification.

Section 3. This amendment shall be inoperable unless ratified as an amendment to the United States Constitution within seven years from the date of its submission.

Section 4. Ratification of this amendment shall take place by conventions in each State whose delegates will be popularly elected.

Reducing the Majority Required to
Approve Treaties

Article II, Section 2, of the Constitution provides that the president "shall have Power, by and with the Advice and Consent of the Senate, to make Treaties, provided two-thirds of the Senators present concur." Note that the language does not actually give the Senate the power of ratification. The Constitution appears to give the president that authority. However, the president cannot approve a treaty without the endorsement of the Senate.

During the nation's history, there have been numerous clashes between the president and Congress over treaties, with sometimes serious consequences for the country. Sometimes, every branch of government wants to be involved. The Constitution discusses only the role of the president and the Senate in the treaty process, but that did not stop the House from insisting on a role in the earliest years of the nation. The House threatened to withhold its approval to provide funding to carry out the Jay Treaty, an agreement between the United States and Great Britain debated in 1794–1795 to resolve violations of the Treaty of Paris after the American Revolution. President Washington sent the Senate-ratified treaty to both Houses of Congress with the expectation that they would appropriate money to cover the expenses of implementing the new agreement. Instead of going along, the House insisted on knowing more about the way the treaty negotiations were conducted. Its leadership demanded to see documents and correspondence that would provide more information about the treaty and that would subject it to additional discussion during the appropriations process. After a debate that lasted over a month, the House still insisted that as part of its responsibility to appropriate money, it had a right to review the treaty and how it was negotiated. President Washington, however, refused to turn over the documents. When public pressure mounted, the House gave up the fight and appropriated the money.

The Senate has often been difficult about approving treaties. President Woodrow Wilson's failure to win Senate approval of the Treaty of Versailles after World War I, because it contained an agreement binding the United States to the proposed League of Nations, launched calls for changing the process for approval of treaties. Some commentators suggested in the 1920s that treaties be approved by a majority vote in the Senate. Others called for a majority vote in each House of Congress. At the end of World War II, when there was increased concern about the president's ability to conduct foreign affairs and conclude treaties, the House approved a constitutional amendment to enable a majority of both houses to ratify treaties. The Senate, however, did not go along.

The Senate rarely turns down treaties outright. It has done so only 19 times since 1789. More often, the Senate attaches reservations to a treaty, amends it, or simply postpones action. In most recent years, presidents have bypassed the Senate's formal power over treaties by concluding "executive agreements" with foreign countries. Of the approximately 13,000 U.S. international accords signed between 1946 and 1992, more than 12,000 were executive agreements. Such agreements are enforceable under international law, which considers a "treaty" to be any binding agreement among nations. Many, but not all, such arrangements are eventually approved by Congress. In 1993, the North American Free Trade Agreement was approved by a majority vote in both Houses under such an arrangement. This agreement, and others in the past, have been described as a constitutional change outside the procedures provided in Article V.

If the prospects for Senate approval were improved by reducing the majority required, a president would probably be more inclined to consult with and include the Senate before committing the nation to international agreements. The Framers obviously wanted at least the upper House of Congress to share with the president the authority to bind the nation to important agreements with other countries. By requiring a supermajority for approval of treaties, the Framers instead forced the president to try to minimize Congress's role. Changing the vote required to a majority in the Senate should result in greater consultation with Congress on the part of the president, and would be more consistent with the goals sought by the Framers.

CHAPTER ELEVEN

Amendment "G":
Abolition of the Electoral College

The Petition

The legislature of the state of _____, being comprised of the duly elected representatives of the people thereof, formally request that the United States Congress call a constitutional convention under Article V of the United States Constitution so that the convention can consider, and in its discretion, propose an amendment or amendments addressing the subjects of direct election of the president and abolition of the Electoral College. This petition was approved by both houses of this legislature in accordance with its established rules and procedures.

Amendment "G": Direct Election of the President; Abolition of the Electoral College; Modifying the Method for Choosing the President When No Candidate Receives a Majority

Section 1. The president of the United States shall be elected by the direct vote of the people. The Electoral College is abolished.

Section 2. There shall be one general election for president to be held on the first Saturday following the first Monday in November every fourth year.

Section 3. The names of all candidates who meet residency and age requirements under this Constitution, and who are qualified to appear on the ballot in individual states, shall appear on the ballots in the several states. States will have substantial authority to determine who is entitled to appear on the ballot. However, no state shall unfairly prevent candidates from any party from appearing on the ballot.

Section 4. When casting a ballot, voters will have the option of designating their first, second, and third choices. Voters cannot cast more than one ballot for the same candidate. A candidate must win 40 percent of the first-choice votes to be elected president after the initial calculation. If two candidates win 40 percent of the vote, the candidate with the most votes wins the election. If no candidate wins 40 percent after the initial calculation, the second-choice votes will be allocated to the two candidates finishing with the largest number of votes. Only two candidates will be eligible to be elected president at this point. If allocation of the second-choice votes results in one of the two candidates reaching the 40 percent threshold, that person is elected president. If both candidates reach 40 percent, the candidate with the most votes wins the election. If the second stage does not result in a candidate receiving 40 percent, all third-choice votes shall be added to the totals of the two candidates. If this results in one of the two candidates reaching 40 percent, that person is elected president. If both candidates reach 40 percent, the candidate with the most votes wins the election.

Section 5. If, after the third stage where third-choice votes are assigned, no candidate has attained 40 percent, the election shall be decided by members of both Houses of the new Congress, with members voting as individuals. They will choose between the two candidates. A majority vote of those present in each House is required to select a president. If no candidate is selected by Congress prior to five days before the scheduled inauguration of the president, the Senate shall choose one of its members to be acting president. A new presidential election will be held no later than the first Saturday following the first Monday in March. The election shall follow the procedures outlined above. The inauguration of the president shall take place immediately.

Section 6. During all phases of the allocation of votes described in Sections 4 and 5 above, the 40 percent threshold will be based on the total number of first-choice votes cast for all candidates in the election.

Section 7. This amendment shall be in effect 30 days after its ratification.

Section 8. This amendment shall be inoperable unless ratified as an amendment to the United States Constitution within seven years from the date of its submission.

Section 9. Ratification of this amendment shall take place by conventions in each State whose delegates will be popularly elected.

Direct Election of the President

It is election night in November. Millions of people are following the returns on radio and television, through Web sites, and at campaign headquarters around the country. As the votes are counted in the most important race of all, the presidential election, it becomes clear that one candidate will have several million more votes than the closest challenger. Almost everyone assumes the person with the most votes will be the next President of the United States. But then news reports inform us that the candidate who came in *second* will move into the White House in January. The Electoral College — the complicated and archaic system by which we select the president — has given the victory to the runner-up.

Such an outcome would be a shock to a majority of Americans. Understandably, there would be concern about how much support the new president would have when that person was not the people's first choice. Next to the image of the president-elect on magazine covers, network newscasts, and Internet sites, would be the faces of Benjamin Harrison and Grover Cleveland — the presidential candidates in 1888 — the last time the nation saw a presidential candidate with fewer popular votes win the election. Demands for a constitutional amendment to prevent another such occurrence would lead to a national discussion of how the president should be elected.

The Electoral College — which one legal scholar describes as a "constitutional accident waiting to happen" — can create these problems and more. As if it is not bad enough that the method by which electoral votes are allocated allows a second-place finisher to win the election, the Electoral College can inflict even more damage to a political system that depends so heavily on popular support. In the past few years, third parties and their candidates seem to be gaining more acceptance. The governor of Minnesota is from the Reform Party. A Green Party candidate is a member of the California legislature. There are other elected officials around the country — such as U.S. Rep. Bernie Sanders, an Independent member from Vermont — who do not come from one of the major parties. Although it is highly unlikely that a candidate who is not a Republican or Democrat will be elected president any time soon, there is the possibility that a popular third-party candidate will win enough electoral votes to prevent either of the two major party candidates from getting a majority. If that were to happen, the Constitution requires that the House of Representatives select the president.

The Framers may have thought they were being creative by giving Congress a role in presidential selection, but allowing the House to choose the president from among the top three candidates in the Electoral College

— changed from five by the 12th Amendment — is a recipe for disaster. The Constitution says that the House votes by states, with each state getting one vote. It makes no sense today — or in 1787 for that matter — for states with the fewest people to have the same vote as California or Texas. House members representing only a small portion of the nation's citizens may be in a position to choose the president. To further complicate matters, under the current system, all the political machinations — the compromises, backroom deals, trades for votes on pending legislation, exchanges of votes for high-level appointments in the new administration — have to be accomplished in a very short period of time. The new Congress convenes on January 3. The new president is inaugurated on January 20. If congressional delegations were closely divided by party — a delegation consists of the members of the House from one state — it is possible that no presidential candidate would receive the votes of a majority of the delegations within the allotted 17 days.

A presidential election has been thrown into the House twice in the nation's history: first, in 1800, when Thomas Jefferson and Aaron Burr each received 73 electoral votes. The likelihood of another tie vote was greatly diminished by the 12th Amendment, which was ratified in 1804 in part to prevent another such occurrence. The second time was in 1824, when a partisan and divided House chose John Quincy Adams over Andrew Jackson. Jackson had won not only the popular vote, but the electoral vote as well. But because two other candidates won 78 electoral votes between them, Jackson was deprived of a majority. When Henry Clay, who had the fewest electoral votes, threw his support to Adams — he later became Adams's secretary of state — Jackson was deprived of the office that was rightfully his. He had to wait another four years before being elected president.

Several times in recent history there have been close calls when it looked as if no candidate would win a majority of electoral votes. In 1948, the States Rights Party bolted from the Democratic Party to protest Truman's support for civil rights and nominated South Carolina Governor Strom Thurmond for president. Running as a "Dixiecrat," as the states-rights segregationists were called, Thurmond won four states and 39 electoral votes. With Thurmond's success, the switching of as few as 25,472 votes in Ohio and California — out of the 6.7 million votes cast in those states — would have deprived Harry Truman of a majority in the Electoral College and the election would have been decided by the House. Again in 1960, a shift of only a few thousand votes in key states could have deprived both John Kennedy and Richard Nixon of a majority of electoral votes because of the 15 electoral votes committed to Senator Harry F. Byrd of Virginia. In 1968, George Wallace won five states and 46 electoral votes. A shift of relatively few votes between Richard Nixon and Hubert Humphrey would have sent the election to the House.

Probably few Americans understand the main features of the Electoral College. They probably do not know — or do not remember between elections — that they do not vote directly for a presidential candidate. They choose electors — whose names do not appear on the ballot in three-fourths of the states — who gather in their state capitals in December to cast ballots for president. Those ballots are then sent to Washington where they are opened and counted before a joint session of Congress. The integrity of the system depends on electors casting their ballot for the presidential candidate who won the popular vote in that state. But sometimes electors have refused to abide by their pledge. Perhaps more troubling is that in the latter half of the 20th Century, there was a concerted effort to maintain the independence of the electors to give some states a larger role in picking the president in a closely divided election. That would mean that no matter how the state's citizens voted, the elector would be free to choose any presidential candidate. The turmoil that would result if a few independent electors held the decisive votes and demanded political favors in return for selecting a certain candidate would have long-lasting consequences for the country.

If there should ever be a dispute over the validity of the votes cast by electors, it is possible that this nation could see a repeat of some aspects of the most scandalous presidential election in American history. In 1876, there was no doubt Democrat Samuel Tilden had more popular votes than Republican Rutherford Hayes. Tilden received approximately a quarter of a million more votes than Hayes, about 4,300,000 to 4,036,000. Tilden also had 184 undisputed electoral votes to Hayes's 165. Unfortunately for Tilden, his 184 votes were one short of the majority needed. Twenty electoral votes — seven in South Carolina, eight in Louisiana, four in Florida, and one of Oregon's three — were in dispute. Tilden needed only one of them, but Republican officials claimed their candidate was entitled to all the disputed votes. Rival sets of ballots were sent to Washington from those states amid charges of fraud and violence. Congress had to decide which ballots were valid.

To complicate matters, the Republicans controlled the Senate while Democrats had a majority in the House. The 12th Amendment states that the president of the Senate should open the ballot certificates, but does not say who should do the counting or what votes should be counted. If the president of the Senate decided which votes were valid, Hayes would win. If the election were decided by the House, Tilden would be elected. After weeks of acrimonious debate, Congress agreed to set up an Electoral Commission composed of five members of the House, five senators, and five members of the Supreme Court. The commission, infected with partisanship and charges of bribery, voted 8-7 to award all the disputed votes to Hayes. The struggle over the outcome of the election had lasted from November 8, 1876, until March 2, 1877. Finally, on March 2, two days before inauguration of the new president, the president of the Senate announced that Hayes had been elected.

The method used to settle the dispute between Hayes and Tilden is not mentioned in the Constitution and demonstrates how many potential problems there are with the Electoral College system. Congress tried to prevent a similar dispute from plaguing future presidential elections by enacting a law in 1877, which provided that any dispute over appointment of electors was to be conclusively settled by the state itself if it did so at least six days before the meeting of the electors. If a state failed to perform this function and its electoral votes remained in dispute, they would not be counted unless both Houses of Congress agreed. Unfortunately, such a statute would not prevent lawsuits in state and federal courts arguing that there was a defect in the procedure by which electors were chosen or pledged. In a close election, the outcome of such litigation could determine who is elected president.

Average citizens also do not understand the impact of the winner-take-all system on the way campaigns are conducted. If a presidential candidate wins California by one vote, that candidate gets all of the electoral votes. The allocation of votes under such a system means that a presidential candidate in the year 2000 could lose 39 states by huge margins and still be elected if he or she won 11 of the most populous states. Because of this system, there is little incentive for presidential candidates to travel to sparsely populated states. No candidate is going to spend much time in Nevada when California, Texas, New York, and other states have so many more electoral votes to offer. In addition, many of the smaller states almost always vote for the same party — Vermont has given its three electoral votes to Republican presidential candidates in all but two elections since 1860 — so there is little reason for presidential candidates to spend time or money there.

There is also a psychological factor at play that may add to cynicism about politics. The votes that go to the losing candidate count for nothing, even if the margin is tiny, because the winner captures all of the electoral votes. In a state that traditionally votes for one party, there is not only little incentive for candidates to campaign in the state, there is little inducement for voters of the minority party to go to the polls if they know their presidential vote will be wasted. Some people will only vote if there is a presidential race on the ballot, and will not vote in off-year elections even when important congressional and state positions are to be decided. This attitude created a lot of problems for Democrats running for Congress in the western part of the country in November 1980. Jimmy Carter conceded defeat to Ronald Reagan early in the evening Eastern Standard Time when polls were still open for several hours in the West. Many people believe that after Carter issued a statement congratulating Reagan, many Democratic voters in California and other Western states stayed home because they knew the presidential election was over. They should have voted anyway because the decision as to who represents them in the U.S. House and Senate, and in state offices, is extremely important. But some Democratic members of the House and Senate, who lost their seats by a small margin, believed that this factor was the key to their defeat.

Why the Framers Chose the Electoral College

The Framers in Philadelphia debated at length how the president should be chosen. Some believed that Congress should elect the president because its members would be better informed and would choose a more qualified candidate than would the people. The Framers recognized that given the primitive transportation and communication systems of the time, citizens might not know much about the candidates and thus may not make the best choice. Others at the Convention argued that the people should be able to directly elect the president. Some delegates wanted to retain a role for the states in keeping with the federal nature of the new Constitution, and thus allow states to determine how presidential electors are selected. They also gave the House an important role if no candidate receives a majority in the Electoral College.

The delegates ultimately decided on a process that involved Congress, the states, and indirectly, the people. States would have discretion to choose electors by any method they wanted with the exception that electors could not hold federal office. Some Framers thought the system was close to a direct election by the people because the electors would be morally obligated to reflect the vote of the people in their state. Congress would not select the president but would play a key role whenever there was a tie — later changed by the 12th Amendment — or when a candidate failed to receive a majority of the electoral vote.

With the development of political parties in the 1790s, it became clear that the Framer's plan was in trouble. Under the original Constitution, electors were to cast two ballots. The person with the largest number of electoral votes became president, while the person having the next highest vote count became vice president. Such a scheme may have seemed appealing when being discussed at the Convention, but it was terrible in practice. The Framers probably envisioned the two leaders of major parties — or "factions" as Madison called them in *Federalist No. 10* — coming together to run the country. But the effect in 1796 was to force a president to have a vice president from a different party. John Adams received the most number of electoral votes. Because Jefferson came in second, he became vice president even though he had been Adams's foe in the election. Unless the president died in office, or the vice president played an active role as head of the Senate, when the two officeholders came from different parties there would be nothing for a vice president to do.

The situation got worse in 1800 when Thomas Jefferson and Aaron Burr received an equal number of electoral votes. As the candidates for president and vice president of the same party, they were supported by all the party's electors. But under Article II, there was no separate designation of votes for the two offices. When they each got 73 electoral votes, the election moved to the House of Representatives where there were weeks of intrigue, deal making, and charges of corruption. Only when Alexander Hamilton reluctantly agreed to give his support to Jefferson — he despised Burr and was later killed by him in a duel — did Jefferson win the election in the House in February 1801. The 12th Amendment fixed some of the major defects in the presidential selection system by having electors choose the president and vice president separately.

Despite the problems that the Electoral College has caused during the nation's history, many would argue that it has worked fairly well. Generally, competent individuals have been elected to the nation's highest office. The electoral vote margin — which often is much larger than the percentage of popular vote — gives the impression that the new president enjoys strong support in the country, and that may help in governing. Furthermore, no president has been chosen by the House since 1824, and no president was elected with fewer popular votes than his opponent since 1888. Those favoring strong major parties believe the Electoral College supports that system because third parties rarely attract enough votes to win states. Finally, although more than a dozen presidents have been elected with less than 50 percent of the popular vote, only three were supported by fewer than 45 percent of the voters. Thus, for all its faults, some would argue, the system should not be changed.

The New Amendment

That the system has worked fairly well does not mean there may not be serious problems down the road. Because of Ross Perot's success in the 1992 and 1996 presidential elections, the Reform Party candidate in 2000 will have at least $12 million in federal money to spend on the campaign. Several well-known and respected individuals, some with significant political experience, are thinking about seeking the Reform Party nomination. If voters want to show the Republicans and Democrats how unhappy they are with politics as usual, it is possible that a third-party candidate could win enough electoral votes to deny any candidate a majority. Regardless of how well a third-party candidate does, there remains the possibility that a president will be elected with fewer popular votes than the opponent.

At least 850 proposals have been introduced in Congress to end the Electoral College system and replace it with one of several alternatives. By far the most popular plan is one calling for direct election. Most of the plans have suggested a runoff election if no candidate receives 40 percent or more of the vote. The U.S. Chamber of Commerce and the American Bar Association supported such an idea in the 1960s. In 1969, the House adopted a direct election proposal by a margin of 338-70, but the supporters in the Senate twice failed to get enough votes to overcome threatened filibusters.

In a nation this large, conducting a presidential election is extremely expensive. If there were to be direct election of the president, and the winner has to receive at least 40 percent of the vote, a runoff election may be needed. Besides the millions of dollars it would cost to hold such an election, having a second election would mean a new campaign between the two top candidates. That would be on top of the year and a half of campaigning that took place before the first election. The advantage of the system described in Amendment "G" is that there would be one campaign, and the "runoff" would take place at the same time as the general election.

In the precomputer era, allocating second- and third-choice votes to candidates would have been complicated and susceptible to fraud. Now, the technology is available to allow the calculation to be made almost instantly. Computers within each state would send information to a computer at a federal agency that includes how many first-, second-, and third-choice votes each candidate received. The computer in the nation's capitol would be programmed to know that if no candidate receives 40 percent of the total, the second- and third-choice votes are to be allocated as described in the proposed amendment. There would be plenty of time for the states and federal government to rehearse this process so it would work well on election night. There would also be the opportunity to make the system as secure as possible so that no one could interfere with the flow of information between the states and Washington, D.C. These things are never as simple as they sound, but it cannot be that complicated for the states and federal government to figure out which of two remaining candidates should be elected president on the basis of second- and third-choice votes. Even if there had to be a national recount because there was evidence of mistakes or fraud, states have experience conducting recounts. The states and federal government should be able to ensure a fair — and technologically advanced — election process.

Changing the Nature of Campaigns

Although there have been some strong third-party candidates in presidential elections — such as Theodore Roosevelt as the Bull Moose Party candidate in 1912 — most third-party candidates receive relatively few votes. Ross Perot's almost 19 percent of the vote in the presidential election in 1992 surprised many and energized the Reform Party. But four years later, Perot was able to attract less than 9 percent. Even if many voters feel that the traditional parties are not responsive to their interests, they are often hesitant to choose a third-party candidate for fear of wasting their vote.

In a presidential election system where first-, second-, and third-choice votes are awarded, there is more incentive for candidates from third parties to campaign energetically and for people to vote for them. A third-party candidate could make a more respectable showing than would be possible under the current system, and thus demonstrate that the party is viable and its views on important issues should be taken seriously.

As the campaign progresses, a third-party presidential candidate could appeal specifically for second-choice votes by urging people to send a message to Washington and the nation. The candidate would not be able to "keep" those votes unless the candidate was one of the top two finishers on election night. But the public will still know on a state-by-state and nationwide basis how many second- and third-choice votes that party received. If, for example, in a dozen states the Republican candidate won the most number of votes, but when the first-, second-, and third-choice votes were distributed, the third-party candidate received more votes than the Democratic candidate, that would send a strong message to the major parties. The message would be that they should pay some attention to the views of the leadership and the members of that party. This new visibility would help energize the third party and would bring closer the day when third-party candidates are elected to Congress and eventually the White House. In the short run, more third-party candidates would be invited to debates with major party candidates running for state offices and Congress, and that would increase the viability of those parties. The advantage of a presidential election system that allocates second- and third-choice votes is that the American people can choose the nominee from the Republican or Democratic party for president while demonstrating quantifiable support for a third party.

Disputes and Other Changes

If direct election became the method by which the president is selected, and several presidential candidates received roughly equal vote totals, it is possible that none of the candidates would receive 40 percent of the total even after the second- and third-choice votes were assigned. It is also possible that there will be disputes about the fairness of the voting process and the allocation of votes that will prevent a clear winner from being inaugurated by January 20.

Amendment "G" provides that if no candidate attains 40 percent of the total, the president will be chosen by the new Congress that was sworn in on January 3. Instead of voting by state in the House, the voting will be by member. The Senate will also vote by member, although as with any action taken by the Senate, the states with the smallest population would have a disproportionate role in selecting the president. But that is the situation whenever the Senate takes any votes. A majority of both Houses is required for the candidate to be elected.

If Congress were deadlocked by January 15, five days before the scheduled inauguration of the new president, the Senate would choose one of its members to be acting president. That acting president would serve until another presidential election was held in March.

The process gives Congress very little time, but unless the country is willing to have the president selected by the old, lame-duck Congress, or change the date when the new president takes office, there is no way to increase the number of days to make this important decision. Congress should not base its action on which party has the majority in each House. Instead, it should examine the voting results from November and try to make the choice that reflects the wishes of the people.

Amendment "G" also makes one other significant change. It requires that voting for president — and presumably other general elections such as off-year congressional elections — take place on Saturday. The idea is that more people may be able to vote on a Saturday than on a Tuesday. As with other events on weekends, some people with certain religious practices will not be able to go to a voting booth on a Saturday. But every state makes provisions for voting by absentee ballot. If someone knows in advance that the election will be held on a Saturday, there will be time to request and return a ballot before the election. Same-day voter registration, which is permitted in Maine, Minnesota, Wisconsin, and Wyoming would also increase turnout.

If a second constitutional convention wants to eliminate the Electoral College, it would have to decide which plan makes the most sense. But in a nation in which the people are supposed to be in charge, and in an era of modern communication technology, the time is long overdue for citizens to directly elect the president. The country should not wait until a president with fewer popular votes is elected, or the House selects the new president, and the nation is forced to endure all the problems those two situations would create.

CHAPTER TWELVE

Amendment "H": Protecting the Jurisdiction of the Federal Courts

The Petition

𝕿he legislature of the state of _____, being comprised of the duly elected representatives of the people thereof, formally request that the United States Congress call a constitutional convention under Article V of the United States Constitution so that the convention can consider, and in its discretion, propose an amendment or amendments addressing the subject of congressional authority to alter the appellate jurisdiction of the federal courts. This petition was approved by both houses of this legislature in accordance with its established rules and procedures.

Amendment "H": Power of Congress to Modify the Jurisdiction of the Federal Courts

Section 1. The Congress shall not have the power to alter, modify, restrict, or enhance the appellate jurisdiction of the federal courts.

Section 2. This amendment shall be in effect 30 days after its ratification.

Section 3. This amendment shall be inoperable unless ratified as an amendment to the United States Constitution within seven years from the date of its submission.

Section 4. Ratification of this amendment shall take place by conventions in each State whose delegates will be popularly elected.

Protecting The Federal Courts

Considering the importance of the judicial branch to the new nation, it is remarkable how little Article III of the Constitution says about the structure and powers of the federal court system. Article I, which establishes the Congress, and Article II, which creates the Executive Branch, provide fairly detailed requirements related to the selection of members of Congress and the president, respectively, and the scope of their powers. But when it came to the third branch of government, the Framers — either from fatigue or because they did not know how the judiciary should be organized — offered only the barest blueprint. They created a Supreme Court, designated a few types of cases that would go directly to it, and left almost everything else up to Congress.

Article III's opening sentence indicates how limited the Framers' plan for the judiciary was: "The judicial power of the United States shall be vested in one supreme court, and in such inferior courts as the Congress may, from time to time, ordain and establish." That line explains *who* is to exercise federal judicial power, but it does not define the *type* of power to be exercised. The Framers expected that the primary responsibility of the federal courts would be to decide "cases" and "controversies," as outlined in Section 2. But what is less clear is whether they realized that the Supreme Court would do much more than settle legal disputes between adverse parties. A few years after the Court met for the first time on February 2, 1790, it had assumed the authority to review the constitutionality of federal statutes. Not long afterward, it did so with respect to state laws. By exercising power through a combination of constitutional authority, legislative authorization, and judicial practice, the federal courts have been at the forefront of many of the nation's most contentious issues and have profoundly affected almost every aspect of the country's social and political life.

Because of the Court's seemingly awesome powers to interpret statutes, strike down laws passed by any legislative body, and develop constitutional principles, it is easy to overlook just how vulnerable the judicial system is to interference by the elected branches. The Constitution gave Congress near plenary power over the federal judicial system. There was little that Congress could *not* do to limit the scope of judicial authority as long as it had the cooperation of the president or enough votes to override a veto. Among its many powers was the authority to establish lower federal courts. If it wanted to, Congress could create only a limited federal court system, or later abolish lower federal courts, and thus severely hamper the ability of the Supreme Court to function by overwhelming it with cases. While Congress can only remove a sitting justice by impeachment and conviction, Congress can eliminate vacant positions or add additional justices — assuming the president appoints them — whenever it wants. Congress even has the authority to control the Court's calendar, and can thus prevent it from meeting — as it has done at least one time in our history — rather than let the Court decide a controversial case.

Of all the powers that the Framers gave Congress to develop and control the federal judiciary, the one that has the greatest potential to undermine its independence is congressional authority to remove cases from the appellate jurisdiction of the federal courts. Article III establishes the Supreme Court's original jurisdiction — those cases that come directly to it without being heard by lower courts. But there are few such cases and they are usually of minor importance. Of far more consequence is the second paragraph of Section 2 of Article III, which gives Congress the authority to remove cases it does not want the Court to decide: "The Supreme Court shall have appellate jurisdiction . . . with such exceptions, and under such regulations as the Congress shall make." If Article III gives Congress the authority to establish — and thus abolish — all federal courts except for the Supreme Court, it almost certainly gives Congress the lesser power of restricting the appellate jurisdiction of all federal courts.

Shortly after ratification of the Constitution, the Supreme Court had an opportunity to confront the issue of whether Congress could limit the Court's appellate jurisdiction. The Court could have argued that as with its original jurisdiction, the authority to hear cases on appeal emanates directly from the Constitution. But relying on long-settled principles of English common law related to jurisdiction, and Sections 21 and 22 of the Judiciary Act of 1789, the Supreme Court concluded in *Wiscart v. D'auchy* in 1796 that when Congress failed to provide a basis on which the Court could decide an appeal, the Court has no jurisdiction to hear the case.

Congress Removes a Case from the Supreme Court

Congress has restricted the Supreme Court's appellate jurisdiction on at least one occasion in the nation's history. During the Civil War era, Congress enacted laws imposing military rule on the South. In 1867, it authorized federal judges to grant a petition of habeas corpus to any person being held in violation of the U.S. Constitution or federal laws, and provided for appeal to the Supreme Court in such cases. The law was intended to protect the rights of newly freed slaves against oppressive actions by Southern states. But it was not a former slave whose case reached the Supreme Court and precipitated a constitutional crisis, but a white Mississippi newspaper editor.

A few years before the editor's case was heard, the Supreme Court in *Ex Parte Milligan* in 1866 overturned an important law Congress had passed allowing military commissions to try cases when civilian courts, especially those in Southern states, could not be trusted to do so fairly. U.S. Army officials — not in the South, but in Indiana — had arrested Lamdbin P. Milligan and several other prominent antiwar Democrats, charging them with conspiracy to seize munitions at federal arsenals and to liberate Confederate prisoners held in several northern prison camps. Army officials, worried that Indiana juries in civilian courts might not be willing to convict the defendants, chose to try them by military commission. Several of the defendants were convicted and sentenced to death. The Supreme Court unanimously reversed the convictions. Although not all justices agreed on the reasoning of the decision, their conclusion was primarily based on the argument that when civilian courts were available, the military tribunal lacked jurisdiction to try the defendants. The *Milligan* decision alarmed many Republicans in Congress who saw violence against newly freed slaves rising in the South and who did not trust Southern courts to bring the perpetrators of such acts to justice. They believed that military commissions must be available to try such cases.

Congress worried that when the Supreme Court next had the opportunity, it would declare unconstitutional the Reconstruction Act of 1867, which authorized military trials of civilians in the rebel states. That chance presented itself to the Court a short time later when William McCardle, a Vicksburg, Mississippi, newspaper editor, was arrested for publishing allegedly libelous editorials that incited insurrection. Federal authorities, invoking the Reconstruction Act, ordered McCardle tried by military commission. Citing *Ex Parte Milligan*, McCardle argued that he must be tried in civilian courts when they were available, and thus, under such circumstances, the Act was unconstitutional. He petitioned a federal court under the Habeas Corpus Act of 1867 to order his release from military custody. When his petition was denied, he appealed to the Supreme Court as was permitted under the law.

After seeing what the Supreme Court had done in *Milligan*, Republicans in Congress did not want to take the chance that the Court would use *Ex Parte McCardle* to invalidate the Act and possibly undermine the entire Reconstruction program. In March 1868, after the Court heard arguments in McCardle's case, but before it had handed down a decision, Congress removed — over President Johnson's veto — the section of the Habeas Corpus Act allowing appeals to the Supreme Court. In the new statute, Congress withdrew "any such jurisdiction by said Supreme Court, on appeals which have been, or may hereafter, be taken."

The Court, citing the words of Article III, Section 2, reluctantly concluded by an 8-0 decision that Congress had the authority to remove the case from the Court's appellate jurisdiction: "Without jurisdiction the court cannot proceed at all in any cause. Jurisdiction is power to declare the law, and when it ceases to exist, the only function remaining to the court is that of announcing the fact and dismissing the cause." Under the *McCardle* principle, it appears to be constitutional for Congress to limit or even abolish the appellate jurisdiction of the Supreme Court and the lower federal courts.

Congressional Threats

Over the last half-century, Congress has periodically considered bills that would remove certain types of cases from the Supreme Court's appellate jurisdiction. Although none has passed, their introduction in the House and Senate demonstrates how vulnerable the federal courts are to congressional tampering. The most active period during which Congress thought seriously about altering the appellate jurisdiction of the Supreme Court was during the "Red Scare" of the 1950s. After the Warren Court granted First Amendment protection to political dissidents and those accused of subversive activities, conservative members of Congress tried to persuade their colleagues to remove such cases from the Supreme Court. On July 26, 1957, Senator William E. Jenner of Indiana introduced a bill that would prevent the Supreme Court from considering cases dealing with those suspected of being disloyal. The five areas covered by the Jenner bill included prohibiting the Court from interfering with: state decisions that denied those suspected of being subversive from practicing law; congressional committees that exposed disloyal or subversive activity; the executive branch's use of loyalty-security programs; any state law or regulation seeking to control subversive activities within that state; and efforts of school boards to uncover subversive activities among teachers.

The Jenner bill was approved by a subcommittee, but then returned to the Senate Judiciary Committee for more hearings. After the new hearings and the addition of several amendments offered by Senator John

Butler of Maryland, the Senate Judiciary Committee gave its approval by a vote of 10 to 5 on April 30, 1958. Although the revised Jenner-Butler bill was substantially different from the original version, it nevertheless attempted to limit Supreme Court consideration of cases in two ways. First, when the disapproved decision was based on interpretation of a statute — and Congress did not like the Court's reading of the statute in a way that favored civil liberties — the Jenner-Butler bill would reverse the Court by revising the law. And second, when the Court's ruling was based on the Constitution, the bill would prevent the Court from further enlarging the rights at issue by denying it the authority to hear subsequent cases. Over on the House side, bills were introduced to limit the Supreme Court's appellate jurisdiction on subjects similar to those in the Senate, and four of the measures passed the full House.

During the last week of the 85th Congress, the Senate considered all the various bills. Although senators had been more restrained than their House colleagues and approved only one bill — which was limited to federal loyalty-security programs for employees in nonsensitive jobs — the Jenner-Butler bill, and several others, were still pending before the Senate and could be passed if there was time before adjournment.

Senate Majority Leader Lyndon Johnson (D-TX) had hoped that by bringing to the Senate floor some of the measures that were more limited in scope and thus less controversial, it would be unnecessary to consider bills that would remove from the Supreme Court a broad range of cases. But his plans went awry as liberal senators announced that they would fight all the bills on the floor of the Senate. With time running out before adjournment, and with debate on even the least contentious bills lasting for several days, there was a flurry of parliamentary activity. Amendments were introduced, then rejected or approved by the Senate, only to be revised later by other amendments. Finally, by a vote of 41 to 40, the Senate voted to recommit what had become the main bill back to committee, thus killing it and the efforts to rein in the Supreme Court. Congress had seriously considered tampering with the appellate jurisdiction of the Supreme Court, but ultimately failed to do so by a narrow margin.

The Court's Continued Vulnerability

It is difficult to predict whether Congress would seriously try again to remove a class of cases from the Supreme Court's appellate docket. Such an effort would probably alarm many Americans who generally recognize the indispensable role of the judiciary in our constitutional system, even while they disagree with particular decisions and believe that federal judges with lifetime tenure are unaccountable. In addition, congressional efforts to curtail the appellate docket may not go over well with some members of the Supreme Court. Some justices may find that the Court has inherent authority — perhaps based on the separation-of-powers doctrine — that justifies invalidating statutes that remove whole subject areas from the federal courts. But a judicially created principle that holds that Congress cannot remove cases from the federal judiciary is weak when confronted with the language of Article III, which gives Congress authority to create and control the federal courts. Although some justices would argue that the Constitution was never meant to give Congress such extensive control over the Court's docket, those who interpret constitutional clauses literally may conclude that the Constitution gives Congress that authority.

Whether it now seems likely that such an attempt would be successful, there is no explicit language in the Constitution that would prevent a determined Congress from removing issues from the federal courts that Congress would prefer to decide on its own. Assuming that the president agrees, or a veto could be overridden, Congress could, for example, remove the jurisdiction of the Supreme Court and lower federal courts to decide all cases dealing with abortion, affirmative action, and prayer in public schools.

The abortion example demonstrates that the situation is potentially more complicated than the language of Article III suggests. Congress could not, for example, simply overturn *Roe v. Wade* because the Court based its holding in the case on, among other grounds, the 14th Amendment and the "penumbra" of amendments in the Bill of Rights raising privacy issues that was first enunciated in *Griswold v. Connecticut* in 1965. A federal statute cannot override a constitutionally based right because the supremacy clause of Article VI means that the Constitution always takes precedence over a law enacted by a legislative body. But although Congress may be precluded from rolling back court decisions in some areas, it would be able to prevent the courts from extending such holdings in subsequent cases.

Ironically, if Congress took action in the abortion area and removed all cases related to that issue from the federal courts, it may find later that it acted precipitously. If Congress had only waited, it is possible that with a change in membership or attitude on the part of the justices, the Court may have reversed *Roe* or other previous decisions on its own if only given time to do so. Once Congress removes the authority of the courts to decide cases in a contentious area, it will not be able to restore that authority very easily.

The exercise of such power by Congress would severely harm the fragile legitimacy of the Supreme Court. It is difficult at the end of the 20th Century to conceive of the Supreme Court and lower federal courts as anything but powerful, co-equal branches of government. They have come a long way from the days when it took the political and judicial skills of Chief Justice John Marshall to help make the Court a powerful institution that could declare unconstitutional the actions of the elected branches of government. It has been quite a few years since public officials openly proclaimed either that they had a right to ignore a Supreme Court decision or would do so anyway.

But the Court's awesome powers rest largely on psychological grounds. It is true that the American people have come to accept the authority of the Court to decide difficult issues even when they dislike the conclusions reached in a particular case. Despite many unpopular rulings handed down by the federal courts, the nation recognizes that an independent judiciary is essential to check the excesses of the elected branches of government. Courts are especially needed to enforce the Bill of Rights and other sections of the Constitution on behalf of individuals who espouse dissenting views, who are subject to racial or gender discrimination, or who are accused of crimes. Americans believe that the Court is uniquely suited to be the final arbiter of the Constitution and that our system of government must have some finality.

Yet, all the respect the Court enjoys and the willingness on the part of citizens to comply with even unpopular decisions rests on a foundation far less firmly grounded than many people believe. The special place the Supreme Court has assumed in the national hierarchy is not due so much to specific language in the Constitution, but is based on the image we have of the way the Court does its job. The justices have all the outward trappings of divine beings: They meet in what could be, and has been described as, a marble temple. The huge columns inside their courtroom are draped with red velour that flow from the celestial ceilings. The justices, who wear black robes — suggesting solemn and wise authorities — sit above the lawyers and public spectators behind a large, imposing bench. They confer in secret in a room where no one but the justices themselves are allowed. They issue their opinions, but then refuse to elaborate on what those opinions mean either in their own writing or in press interviews; the opinions must speak for themselves. The language used in many opinions is legalistic, dense, and extremely difficult for a lay person to understand, thus adding to the perception that these great oracles of the law have special wisdom and insight, and their interpretation of statutes and the Constitution must be accepted. The faces of the nine justices may be unknown to most Americans — perhaps with the exception of those who appear on C-SPAN regularly — yet citizens assume that behind the closed doors of the Court, these great legal scholars are at work studying the Constitution and the nation's history. We are led to believe that they enjoy lifetime tenure so they can be insulated from the rough and tumble of politics and the passions of the moment.

Despite all the adornments that make the Supreme Court seem invincible to encroachments by the other branches of government, it has an Achilles' heel that if exploited, would result in the virtual evisceration of its prestige and legitimacy. Allowing Congress to remove — or even seriously threaten to remove — cases from the appellate jurisdiction of the federal courts would endanger the delicate balance among the three branches that evolved from the work of the Framers at the Constitutional Convention. It allows Congress to exercise powers over the Supreme Court that no institution should be able to exercise over an "equal" entity. Even if Congress had the support of the majority of Americans in removing only one subject area from the federal courts, it would set a precedent that could never be fully reversed and would irreparably harm their legitimacy. The Supreme Court especially would never be the same. Once the precedent is established, anytime the Court handed down an unpopular decision, there would be calls for Congress and the president to take away the Court's discretion to decide new cases involving the controversial subject.

If Congress tampered with the appellate jurisdiction of the federal courts, the principle that there should be some finality to decisions in our government and society, and that the Supreme Court must be the final interpreter of the Constitution, would be eroded. Everything would be open to further debate. Although theoretically no finality exists now because of the possibility of a constitutional amendment or reversal by the Court in a later decision, almost everyone accepts the Supreme Court's interpretation of the Constitution as conclusive. If even only a few members of Congress talked seriously about restricting the appellate jurisdiction of the Court, it would show the country that no matter how strong a force it has become, the Court is still vulnerable to congressional whim.

The New Amendment

The Constitution must be changed to prevent Congress from interfering with the appellate jurisdiction of the federal courts. There are, however, some risks in doing so. If, for example, the people persuaded Congress to approve campaign finance reform to limit campaign expenditures, and the Supreme Court continued to insist that such limits violate the First Amendment, Congress would be unable to remove that subject from court review if Amendment "H" had been approved. Thus, the country would be stuck with the principles of *Buckley v. Valeo* and would be unable to implement comprehensive campaign finance reform except through a constitutional amendment. If the nation came to a consensus that prayers in public school are needed — but the Supreme Court continued to hold to the principles of cases outlawing such practices — a change in Court membership or a constitutional amendment would have to occur to permit such activities in schools.

There is the possibility that at some point, the Supreme Court could become oppressive and it may be necessary to prevent the federal courts from hearing certain types of cases. Under Amendment "H," the justices could not be stopped from interpreting statutes or applying constitutional provisions in a way that is strongly opposed by the people and their elected officials. But in many respects, that is the situation now. When the Supreme Court rules in a way that appears to be contrary to majority sentiment and bases its decision on the Constitution — and declines to reconsider that interpretation — the only way the Court can be reversed is through a constitutional amendment. If Amendment "H" had already become part of the Constitution, either it would have to be repealed or a new amendment removing the issues from the federal courts would have to be approved.

Congress can now take cases away from the Supreme Court by a majority vote in both houses. If the president refuses to go along, Congress can still do it on its own with a two-thirds vote in each house. If Congress believes that voters are outraged enough about a Supreme Court decision that they will support members or candidates who favor a law removing that subject from the Court's appellate jurisdiction, Congress may act quickly without thinking much about the consequences.

Once Congress removes control over the appellate docket of the Court, only Congress can reverse that decision either by repealing the statute or by Congress or a second convention proposing a constitutional amendment. If Congress refused to restore the Supreme Court's authority in that area, there would be no way to reverse the decision until the public elected enough new members of Congress with differing views.

Amendment "H" preserves the status quo as long as Congress is content to leave the appellate jurisdiction of the federal courts intact. However, if there is no Amendment "H," and Congress reacts impulsively to an unpopular Supreme Court decision and takes advantage of the authority given to it in Article III, it will forever harm the stature of the federal judiciary.

CHAPTER THIRTEEN

Amendment "I":
Changing How the Constitution
is Amended

The Petition

𝕿he legislature of the state of_____, being comprised of the duly elected representatives of the people thereof, formally request that the United States Congress call a constitutional convention under Article V of the United States Constitution so that the convention can consider, and in its discretion, propose an amendment or amendments altering the process by which the United States Constitution is amended. This petition was approved by both houses of this legislature in accordance with its established rules and procedures.

Amendment "I": Amending Article V

Section 1. This Article of Amendment shall replace the sections of Article V related to amending the United States Constitution. There shall be three methods by which amendments can be proposed and ratified which shall be mutually exclusive.

Section 2. The Congress, whenever 60 percent of the members of both Houses who are present deem it necessary, shall propose amendments to this Constitution. The amendments shall be in effect when ratified by the legislatures or conventions of 60 percent of the states, with the mode of ratification to be decided by Congress.

Section 3. Upon receiving petitions from 50 percent of state legislatures requesting that Congress call a constitutional convention for the purpose of proposing amendments, Congress shall call such a convention within 90 days. The amendments proposed by such a convention shall be in effect when ratified by the legislatures or conventions of 60 percent of the states, with the mode of ratification within each state to be decided by that state's legislature.

Section 4. Upon receiving certification from 50 percent of the secretaries of state or other high level officials of the states that valid signatures on petitions have been obtained from the equivalent of 10 percent of those voting in the last general election within each state, Congress shall call a constitutional convention within 90 days for the purpose of proposing amendments. The amendments proposed by such a convention shall be in effect when ratified by conventions of 60 percent of the states.

Section 5. When the convention method of ratification is used, delegates to the conventions shall be elected by the people. States shall retain the authority to determine the qualifications of voters.

Section 6. Once a state legislature or state convention has ratified a constitutional amendment, such ratification cannot be rescinded. A state legislature that has failed to ratify or has rejected an amendment may ratify the amendment any time while it is pending. A state convention that has failed to ratify or has rejected an amendment may meet no more than once a year to consider ratification of the amendment during the time it is pending.

Section 7. No amendment shall be ratified more than seven years after it has been submitted for ratification to state legislatures or state conventions.

Section 8. This amendment shall be in effect 30 days after its ratification.

Section 9. This amendment shall be inoperable unless ratified as an amendment to the United States Constitution within seven years from the date of its submission.

Section 10. Ratification of this amendment shall take place by conventions in each state whose delegates will be popularly elected.

The Limits of Constitutional Interpretation

If a second constitutional convention is ever held, its most important challenge — and the one with the most potentially serious consequences for the nation — is the amending of Article V. The Framers struggled to find the right balance between creating a document that could be adapted to changing conditions and establishing a national charter that would embody the country's enduring values and its higher law. It is clear that they wanted to distinguish constitutional amendments from ordinary legislation, and thus they required supermajorities in Congress to propose amendments and again in state legislatures or conventions to ratify them.

The delegates to the Convention certainly succeeded in making it difficult to change the Constitution. Except for going to the extremes of the Articles of Confederation, which required unanimous approval of the states before an amendment could be adopted, it is hard to envision a process of changing the Constitution that is more arduous than the one established in Article V. The Framers may have worried that the American people would change the new Constitution so frequently it would become little more than a long list of legislative priorities and cease to be the nation's national charter establishing broad principles. That has often been the case with state constitutions, some of which have as many as 100 amendments. However, the analogy should be taken only so far because in many important respects, state constitutions do not serve the same purpose as the federal Constitution and are amended by a different process.

Whether through haste or distrust or a virtuous effort gone awry, the Framers failed to provide a process that permits the Constitution to be adapted to changing societal needs and conditions. The evidence is how few times such efforts to amend the Constitution have been successful even when there is overwhelming support for change among the people. Since 1791, when the first 10 amendments were added, the Constitution has been formally altered only 17 times. Hundreds of proposed amendments have been introduced in Congress without receiving two-thirds approval, while four have made it through the difficult congressional process only to fail to gain the support of three-quarters of the states. Among developed nations of the world, the U.S. Constitution is one of the most difficult to amend and compared to the constitutions of other democracies, has been changed relatively few times.

In the absence of the formal use of the amendment process, the Constitution has been "modified" through developments outside of Article V. When the procedure established under Article V is so difficult to implement even when there is widespread support for change, alternative methods for adapting the Constitution must be found. If no such alternatives were available, there would be a serious crisis in our political system.

The most common method of modifying the Constitution outside of the formal amendment process — through interpretation by the courts

— would be necessary even if Article V did not pose such formidable barriers. It would be impossible to amend the Constitution frequently enough and with enough specificity to keep up with the numerous issues faced by a complex society. Even trying to do so would diminish the legitimacy of the Constitution that should be a statement of the nation's fundamental law. Moreover, courts are needed to hand down decisions that help bring about fundamental change to the legal and political system, changes that elected branches of government would not enact. When the Supreme Court, for example, makes decisions of transcendent importance to the nation — which the Court has done perhaps a dozen times in our history — that action can forever change the nation's political and social system and how the Constitution itself is thereafter interpreted.

Conservative justices of the Supreme Court may argue that the Constitution should never be interpreted in a way that enhances or restricts the document itself; that should only be done through the formal amendment process. But despite such a philosophy — which has always been easier to proclaim than practice — the Court has been confined to such a limited role for only short time periods. The reasons are many. There is a natural tendency for justices to be activists on the Court, whether liberal or conservative. Few justices would consider a career on the Supreme Court to be fulfilling if they were remembered only for voting and writing opinions explaining why the Court should always refrain from deciding controversial issues. The temptation to leave one's mark on the American political system and the nation's history is irresistible for most justices.

Sometimes judicial "amendments" to the Constitution are the result of a single case, such as *Brown v. Board of Education* in 1954, which extensively modified and modernized the equal protection clause of the 14th Amendment. More commonly, the changing of the Constitution takes place over time through a series of decisions. The Warren Court's enhancement of procedural rights through interpretation of the Fourth, Fifth, and Sixth Amendments, and application of the Bill of Rights to the states through the 14th Amendment, are examples. It is important to keep in mind that most of the Supreme Court's work is the interpretation of statutes that is often done without invoking a specific section of the Constitution. The Court prefers to interpret statutes rather than the Constitution — and will go to sometimes extraordinary lengths to avoid a constitutional ruling — because an erroneous statutory interpretation can be corrected by Congress or another legislative body. A decision based on the Constitution can only be reversed, in a strict sense, by the Court itself or by a constitutional amendment. If a ruling is based on the Constitution, because of the principle that previous cases should be followed, and because another case may not present the opportunity for the Court to reconsider its judgment, the nation may be stuck with the unpopular and anachronistic decision for years.

The Role of the Elected Branches and the People

It has not only been the courts that have developed constitutional principles. From the nation's birth, the Constitution has also been transformed through the actions of the executive and legislative branches of government. From 1790 to 1801, many constitutional precedents were established not by the Supreme Court, but by the president or Congress. As Presidents Washington and Adams and the First through Sixth Congresses struggled to determine what the new document meant, the resolution of critical issues helped define the intent of the Framers and the text of the Constitution. Among the principles established largely outside of the Constitution was the precedent that the president would serve only two terms, which every subsequent president except one followed; the question of how much authority the president could delegate to subordinates; and interpretation of the "necessary and proper" clause defining the limits of congressional power. Congress's efforts to define its power outside of the Constitution included the deliberate effort to circumvent the First Amendment by punishing allegedly seditious speech.

Perhaps it would be expected that the new Congress, writing on a clean slate, would do so much to interpret and develop the new Constitution. The First Congress took specific action in a wide range of issues that implicated nonspecific provisions of the Constitution: Establishing Congress's procedures; creating executive departments; establishing the federal judiciary; enacting a system of taxation; arranging for payment of debts and creating a national bank; enacting laws respecting naturalization, patents, copyrights, and federal crimes; regulating relations among existing states and admitting new ones; and finally, proposing 12 amendments, ten of which became the Bill of Rights.

In the years since, the president and Congress have continued to modify and interpret the Constitution. Some scholars have argued that although the Constitution had been formally amended relatively few times, through the actions of the elected branches of government, the Constitution has been transformed and thus adapted to changing societal needs and conditions. Bruce Ackerman, a Yale professor of law and political science and well-known constitutional scholar, argues that periodically, the nation interrupts the flow of ordinary democratic politics and embarks upon intense periods of constitutional lawmaking that take place outside the Article V amending process. He believes the New Deal period in particular drastically changed the American political system and remade the Constitution, all without a single constitutional amendment. The Constitution, as originally conceived, did not authorize the elected branches to create a vast federal bureaucracy largely under the control of the executive branch with authorization and funding from the legislature. The separation-of-powers doctrine and other provisions of the Constitution would suggest that such a system would be contrary to at least the spirit of the document. Yet the constitutional precedents established during the New Deal period not only changed the country in the 1930s, Ackerman said, but they greatly enlarged the role that government plays in almost all aspects of American society.

Others, most notably Yale law professor Akhil Reed Amar, have written creatively on the subject of whether there are methods outside of Article V by which the American people can amend the Constitution. Amar bases his thesis on two arguments. First, the Constitution itself was adopted in an "extra-legal" manner when the Framers, ignoring the requirements in the Articles of Confederation that amendments be unanimously approved and the instructions from the Continental Congress that limited the task of the Framers to modifying the Articles, disobeyed the Articles and Congress and created a new Constitution. And second, Article V does not say it is the exclusive method by which the Constitution is to be amended. The Framers intended — or at least allowed for the possibility — that the people would be able to initiate constitutional amendments through some kind of referendum process. In Amar's view, because the Constitution is based on the notion of popular sovereignty, a majority of voters could petition Congress to call a constitutional convention or Congress could submit amendments to popular vote or referendum.

Although original and innovative, Amar's argument is flawed on several grounds. First, it has no basis in the text of the Constitution. Someone who reads Amar's description of Article V and wants to be involved in changing the Constitution, will have no idea where to begin. It is impractical to assume that Congress is suddenly going to recognize that the Constitution permits a process outside of Article V and encourage petitions submitted by citizens seeking the proposal of amendments. It is equally unrealistic to expect Congress to see a formal role for the people during the ratification process. The only way that the American people will get the opportunity to make significant changes to the Constitution — especially those opposed by Congress — is if enough states submit petitions to call a constitutional convention.

Second, Amar's argument fails because the Framers intended for most, if not all, of the provisions of the Constitution to be the sole method or principle establishing certain procedures, even though they did not say so explicitly. There would be a serious breakdown in constitutional order if every section of the Constitution that failed to state it was the exclusive method of doing something could be implemented through some other unspecified process. As cumbersome and difficult as Article V is to implement, the Framers intended for it to be *the* method by which the Constitution is to be changed. Even if an amendment made it all the way through some type of initiative and referendum process, the courts likely would invalidate it as contrary to Article V.

Whether constitutional change is considered to have occurred within or outside the formal process of Article V makes a difference. If true constitutional revision has been implemented only through the formal amendment process, then there is the legitimate question of whether Article V — because of the overwhelming consensus it requires — has prevented the country from responding to changing conditions and values. The evidence suggests that Article V has imposed overly restrictive limits on the country's ability to alter the Constitution during times when such change was needed. Despite all that the country has gone through over the last two centuries, we are still governed by a document written at the end of the 18th century that is still largely intact. If the Bill of Rights is considered part of the original Constitution, there have been even fewer significant changes to the document. No major amendment modifying key provisions — such as altering the structure of government — has ever been seriously considered for a possible amendment, at least by Congress or the states.

On the other hand, if because of Article V there has been a constant need to employ extra-constitutional procedures to avoid frequent constitutional crises that threaten the nation's political and social institutions, there is a stronger argument that the amendment process must be changed. Doing so would make altering the Constitution more predictable and more in keeping with the spirit of the document.

Although the Constitution may be changed formally by the method outlined in Article V, or — if Ackerman's thesis is accepted — by transformations of political and social institutions, as during the New Deal period, there is another way the Constitution can be modified without a word being added to the document or the country going through great political upheaval. This occurs when there is a change in the underlying perceptions of what the Constitution means and how it is supposed to work. Relatively few of sections of the Constitution have been altered by amendment. But while the phrases are the same as originally written, their meaning may not be. The American people and government officials come to see specific parts of the Constitution differently over time. Gradually, those perceptions are reflected in the appointment or election of judges who then generally implement those changing perceptions in their judicial decisions. The process is far from perfect. Judges may not reflect the prevailing view on important issues yet may still be elected or, in the case of federal judges, appointed by the president and approved by the Senate. With lifetime tenure, there is little direct incentive for them to modify their views. When the political process that selects judges fails to respond to changing conditions and expectations, a more drastic approach, such as a constitutional amendment, may be necessary.

The New Amendment

Even if there is general agreement that the Constitution should be easier to amend, there is likely to be debate over what amendment process is most appropriate for a large, complex society. If the process is too easy and amendments become routine, the Constitution will no longer be reserved for general principles that establish broad guidelines to be followed by the elected branches of government, the judiciary, and the people. Instead, it will become burdened with language that seems better suited to statutes and regulations.

Regardless of how difficult it will be to find the right formula for constitutional change, the amending process cannot stay the same. The overwhelming majorities in Congress required to propose amendments allow too few individuals in either house to block proposals supported by a large majority of the American people and many of their elected representatives. The ratification system is even more restrictive and gives states too much control over the process. Because only one house of 13 state legislatures needs to say no for an amendment to be rejected, it takes only a few legislators — a tiny fraction of the nation's population — to stop a constitutional amendment that enjoys widespread support.

Amendment "I" establishes three methods for changing the Constitution. The first keeps Congress largely in control of the method by which amendments are proposed and ratified. The second gives greater discretion to state legislatures. The third gives the people, for the first time, a direct role in the amendment process.

The first option is outlined in Section 2. It would lower from two-thirds to 60 percent the majorities required in each house of Congress to propose amendments. If all 100 senators were present and voting, 60 instead of 67 members would have to give their approval. In the House, with its 435 members, 261 votes would be required instead of the 290 now needed. As with Article V, Section 2 of the proposed amendment allows Congress to decide whether amendments that it proposes will be ratified by state legislatures or state conventions elected by the people.

In addition, Section 2 requires that 60 percent of state legislatures or state conventions approve an amendment for it to be ratified. Instead of the 38 states now required, 30 would have to give their approval.

Section 3, the second alternative, modifies the convention process for proposing amendments. Instead of petitions having to be sent from 34 states, 25 states need to forward petitions before Congress would be required to call a convention. As with Section 2, any amendments proposed by such a convention would become part of the Constitution only when ratified by 60 percent of the states. Unlike the current Constitution, however, which authorizes Congress to decide whether state legislatures or state conventions will ratify amendments, Section 3 gives that decision to state legislatures for amendments that were proposed by a national convention.

The last method of amending the Constitution, involving the people, is outlined in Section 4. Secretaries of state will receive signatures on petitions requesting that a constitutional convention be called. When officials from half the states certify that a sufficient number of signatures are valid, Congress must call a convention. The people will also play a direct role during the ratification process under this third option. If a convention is called through the petition process, proposed amendments must be approved by conventions elected by the people in 60 percent of the states.

Other sections of Amendment "I" clear up long-standing controversies and ambiguities. The amendment removes from states the discretion to rescind ratification once given, but offers a state the option of approving a previously rejected amendment — or where no formal vote has been taken — as long as the ratification period has not expired. It also establishes a time limit of seven years for ratification.

Difficult Issues

Amendment "I" obviously has potential problems. Legitimate questions can be raised over whether the lowering of the majorities required for proposing and ratifying amendments will result in too many amendments being added to the Constitution that look more like ordinary legislation or policy decisions than carefully considered changes to the nation's national charter.

The amendment also removes almost complete control over the amendment process from Congress and gives more of it to the states and the people. How they will use this power to initiate and ratify amendments would understandably make many people nervous.

Even the section of the amendment that appears to be the most democratic — the one giving the people the right to initiate and ratify amendments — is complicated. Among the major difficulties is how to coordinate the petitions that are used to gather signatures. To convene a second convention, this book recommends that the writing of petitions be done by the 100 delegates attending the national preconvention. The goal is for ten or 12 identical petitions to be taken to state legislatures in an effort to persuade them to approve and forward the petitions, unchanged, to Congress. If that happens, Article V requires Congress to call a convention.

Under Section 4 of Amendment "I," there would not likely be such a coordinated effort. If the secretaries of state forward petitions to Congress that ask for different amendments, or even use different wording in requesting the same amendment, Congress may argue that it does not have to call a convention.

Perhaps the only solution will be for people interested in the amendment process to gather at a national meeting and at least agree on the subjects to be considered — maybe along the lines of the petitions suggested in this book — and then gather signatures on the petitions. The problem is that citizens will be hesitant to sign petitions that say there should be a constitutional convention to discuss campaign finance reform or a new equal rights amendment, without knowing the specific language of the proposed amendments. They would have to be convinced that it is safe to sign a petition requesting a convention because the people they elect later to the ratifying conventions would still have to approve the specific language of the proposed amendments. But short of a nationwide coordinated campaign begun through the Internet, and culminating in a national convention, it is difficult to see how petitions from all over the country could be organized pursuant to Section 4.

The amendment process must require greater consensus than ordinary legislation, but it should not be as difficult as it is today to change the Constitution. Reducing the number of members of the House and Senate who must agree to propose amendments and the number of states that request a convention, and giving citizens a meaningful role for the first time, would probably lead to more amendments being considered. But even if more amendments are being reviewed for ratification — with 30 states as opposed to 38 required for approval — there will still be the opportunity for a serious discussion of amendments and their possible consequences. Because people know that proposed amendments have a much better chance of being ratified, they may pay closer attention and actively participate in the debate. Under Article V, the country has relatively little experience with constitutional amendments because so few of them are ever proposed by Congress. Amendment "I" has the potential to reinvigorate interest in the Constitution, politics, and government.

CHAPTER FOURTEEN

Amendment "J": Repealing the Second Amendment

The Petition

𝕿he legislature of the state of _____, being comprised of the duly elected representatives of the people thereof, formally request that the United States Congress call a constitutional convention under Article V of the United States Constitution so that the convention can consider, and in its discretion, propose an amendment or amendments relating to the Second Amendment of the United States Constitution. This petition was approved by both houses of this legislature in accordance with its established rules and procedures.

Amendment "J": Repealing the Second Amendment

Section 1. The Second Amendment of the United States Constitution is hereby repealed.

Section 2. This Amendment shall be in effect 30 days after its ratification.

Section 3. This Amendment shall be inoperable unless ratified as an amendment to the United States Constitution within seven years from the date of its submission.

Section 4. Ratification of this Amendment shall take place by conventions in each state whose delegates will be popularly elected.

The Troublesome Second Amendment

It would be difficult to find a section of the U.S. Constitution that is
more poorly worded and controversial than the Second Amendment. The
members of the First Congress assumed — wrongly as it turned out —
that in the decades after it was written and ratified, and now more than
two centuries later, we would understand what they meant by its awkward phrases. For reasons that are the subject of some disagreement, they
decided that the Second Amendment needed an introductory clause to
explain its purpose, the only amendment with such a clause. The result is
a muddle of words that condemns the country to an endless debate over
the constitutionality of laws regulating access to guns.

The Second Amendment provides that "A well regulated Militia, being necessary to the security of a free State, the right of the people to keep
and bear Arms, shall not be infringed." The main argument has been over
whether the introductory phrase means that only state militias — which
today would probably refer to the national guard — have a constitutional
right to possess weapons, or if individuals also enjoy that right. Every
word in the Amendment has been analyzed in recent years for its meaning
and context. For example, the word "bear" as in "bear arms" may mean
that only organized militias can constitutionally possess weapons because
"bear" suggests a military context. Others say that "keep" arms, which is
also in the Amendment, implies individual ownership unrelated to military service.

Some scholars who have studied the Second Amendment accept that
both state militias and individuals enjoy a constitutional right to possess
firearms. They realize that many people hate the idea that the Constitution gives individuals a right to have weapons, but they believe a careful
study of 18th Century American history and the record of the First Congress leads to such a conclusion. However, they also argue that reasonable
regulation is still permitted under the Second Amendment. Others insist
that if those who wrote the Bill of Rights intended to guarantee personal
ownership of guns, they would have said so explicitly.

When James Madison first introduced the proposed Bill of Rights in
June of 1789, what became the Second Amendment appeared to include
an individual right to bear arms. He recommended this language: "The
right of the people to keep and bear arms shall not be infringed; a well
armed and well regulated militia being the best security of a free country."

He then included a clause permitting those with religious objections to decline military service. The House committee to which the proposed amendments were assigned switched Madison's order of phrases and placed "a well regulated militia" at the beginning of the Amendment. The committee's language read thusly: "A well regulated militia composed of the body of the people, being the best security of a free State . . ."

That was confusing enough. But the Senate made it even more complicated. The phrase "the body of the people" was deleted, as was the clause about religious objection. Little is known about why the Senate changed the words in the proposed Amendment because it deliberated behind closed doors and its journal provided few details of the debate. The Senate may have been trying to shorten the language of proposed amendments, which it did with many of the articles in the Bill of Rights. Unfortunately, with the Second Amendment, that effort sacrificed clarity.

The Second Amendment uses the phrase "the right of the people," as do the First, Fourth, and Ninth Amendments. Those opposing gun regulation — and thus believing that government should impose nothing more than minimal controls, if any — argue that if the Second Amendment only authorized members of organized militias to possess weapons, it would have specifically protected the rights of the states, as does the Tenth Amendment. After all, it is argued, the same First Congress wrote both amendments and thus the failure to include explicit protection of the states in the Second Amendment proves it intended to give the people the right to have weapons. The opposite view — held by advocates of gun control — maintains that whatever the choice of words, the Second Amendment, as with many provisions of the Constitution that are not interpreted literally, should not prevent reasonable laws from being enacted to control access to guns.

The confusing language gives both sides of the dispute what they need to keep the argument going on forever. They have found little to agree on in recent years. Many opponents of gun control — several million of whom belong to the National Rifle Association, among the most well-financed and organized lobbying machines — fear that once government gets a foot in the door and regulates any aspect of gun use, it will move quickly to remove all guns from law-abiding citizens. This "slippery-slope" argument leads the NRA to fight almost every proposed gun law. It is difficult, for example, for many people to understand why the organization would oppose a short waiting period for the purchase of weapons; background checks on those buying guns from licensed dealers; requirements that unlicensed dealers also do such checks; and limitations on the importation and manufacture of assault weapons. More stringent measures such as registering every gun or gun owner with the government would be expected to generate strong resistance. But the NRA's opposition to reasonable measures is hard to justify, especially in an era in which so many adults and children are killed and injured by guns.

The NRA argues either that such laws will not work — in other words, will not cut down on gun violence — or they violate the Second Amendment, or that the government does not enforce existing laws. To many NRA members, and certainly its national leadership, such laws allow government to move toward what they believe to be its real goal: enslaving its citizens. They believe that as government disarms the people and embarks on a crusade to destroy democratic institutions, citizens will be left defenseless not only against the oppressive government, but against criminals who will be the only ones left with guns.

The allegation that a waiting period on the purchase of guns is part of a diabolical plan to take away our freedom and destroy the Constitution should be humorous. Sadly, it is anything but that because the NRA has convinced so many people that such a bleak outcome is inevitable unless they fight almost every limitation on gun ownership. Through campaign contributions and intimidation, the NRA has convinced legislators that there will be a heavy price to pay for failure to adhere to the organization's creed. Any state legislator or member of Congress who has deviated from the NRA's instructions on how to vote can tell horror stories of how quickly the group can flood legislative offices with mail and telephone calls from a district or state, and how long the NRA's institutional memory can be. Years after a legislator casts a single vote against the NRA — even if the law would create only a minor inconvenience for gun owners — the organization will pour money and resources into the opponent's campaign. Legislators soon get the message that whatever the majority of their constituents may want, it is the gun owners and their national organization that must not be disappointed.

The background checks that the NRA so vigorously opposed have had extraordinary results. In September 1999, the Justice Department reported that an estimated 100,000 convicted criminals, fugitives, and people with mental illness had been prevented from buying a gun in the first seven months of the program, beginning in November 1998. The report also found that for three-quarters of those who wanted to buy a gun, the instant check system gave a response in about 30 seconds even though law enforcement officials have three business days to complete the inquiry. Even for those situations where some questions were raised, the background check was finished quickly. For 95 percent of gun buyers, the check was done within two hours.

The Early Days

The history of the Second Amendment suggests its primary purpose was to give citizens of the new nation a way of protecting themselves if their government should become oppressive. They had just been through the ordeal of winning their freedom from British rule and were naturally hesitant to place all of their trust in the newly created national government. The Founders did not want citizens to be defenseless if that government was seized by those who ignored the democratic processes established in the new Constitution. The Declaration of Independence makes reference to the right of the people, as a last resort, to "alter" or "abolish" any government if it is tyrannical and unresponsive to democratic processes normally to be relied on for peaceful change. The Framers also expected that if local militias were armed, they would be available to fight lawless actions on the part of private individuals when national or local governments were unavailable to do so. That expectation was reasonable considering it would be almost a century before police forces were established, even within large cities.

The Founders were understandably worried about a standing army — such as the one maintained by the British during the Revolutionary War — which would keep an oppressive government in power. That is one reason the Constitution gave states the right to maintain armed militias that could be enlisted in the fight against a despotic regime. Armed militias could also be called on to help oppose a foreign power if the armed forces of the new federal government were unable to resist such threats on their own.

It is one thing, however, to have had a constitutionally protected right to serve in a militia and be armed in the early decades of the new nation, when a state or the federal government threatened individual liberty or was in turn threatened by a foreign power. It is something else to claim that individual possession of guns is necessary in the 21st Century to protect the people from their government or invading forces from other countries. State militias as they functioned during the nation's early history no longer exist. Undoubtedly, in a political sense, the Second Amendment is still important because arguments about its meaning will continue indefinitely; but in a literal sense, time has made the Second Amendment largely irrelevant. The closest entity we have today to an organized militia is the state national guards. Although the Second Amendment could be interpreted to mean that the federal government is prohibited from disarming the national guards, it cannot be used to oppose reasonable measures to control access to guns.

Even if individual ownership of guns were directly tied to protecting citizens from a standing army, there is the issue of whether even well-trained militias would have much success in opposing the better armed and organized government forces. If a president federalized the state militias, and ordered the armed forces of the United States to round up people for detention or attack groups considered to be dangerous — leaving aside for the moment the likelihood that such orders would not be carried out — there is little that the country's citizens would be able to do to successfully resist. There may be occasional victories as individuals fight approaching soldiers, but it would only be a matter of time before the government forces would win. The Second Amendment is not going to save citizens from oppressive actions of their government. People who want the right to buy guns from unlicensed individuals at gun shows because there are no background checks and waiting periods are not going to be fighting invading forces from across the ocean or whatever government at home they consider dangerous.

The belief that the Constitution gives citizens the right to keep guns has a patriotic ring to it. Whenever one speaks of the constitutional right to keep and bear arms, memories are stirred of the brave colonists in Concord and Lexington in 1775, fighting to win independence, and of the state militias that fought on their respective sides in the Civil War. There is also a long tradition of individualism in this country that stems from the settling of the frontier and the reliance on guns for hunting and protection.

Even if the Second Amendment were abolished, there would be nothing in the Constitution that prevents the enactment of a law permitting the keeping of guns in the home for protection. Having a firearm to defend the family, however, must be consistent with tough laws that regulate the ownership and use of guns. There must be serious penalties for parents who allow their children or visitors to the home to discover and discharge those weapons. When children take those guns to school to kill classmates and teachers, parents as well as their children must be held responsible. There must also be tough laws regulating the sale and purchase of guns in an effort to keep weapons out of the hands of dangerous and deranged individuals.

The great irony is that, for the most part, the Second Amendment has only symbolic value today. Its *legal* impact on the gun controversy has been limited. The Amendment has been interpreted by the Supreme Court on only a few occasions, and each time the Court held that the right to bear arms refers to organized militias and not to an individual right to keep weapons. But symbolism matters in the Constitution. The NRA and other organizations that energetically oppose gun regulations constantly cite the Second Amendment as the basis for opposing even modest restraints on the use of guns. Since there is a stalemate between groups for and against gun control over what the Second Amendment means that will likely never be resolved, the only solution is to remove the Amendment from the Constitution.

The Carnage of Recent Years

Because so much has changed in the 200-year history of the nation and the Constitution should reflect that evolution, something must be done with the Second Amendment. In the past few years, the country has been repeatedly horrified by young people killing classmates and teachers in school; by children being shot at day care centers; by people being slaughtered by gunmen at churches, office buildings, and other locations that would have been considered relatively safe in a different era. In at least some of those cases, stricter gun laws may have made a difference. During one eight-month period in 1999, the nation was repeatedly reminded of what dangerous people can do with guns:

• December 6, 1999: Seth Trickey, 13, allegedly shot and wounded five of his fellow students outside his middle school in Fort Gibson, Colorado. None of the wounds were life-threatening. He used a 9mm semiautomatic handgun that belonged to his father.

• November 2, 1999: Byran Uyesugi, 40, a Xerox employee, allegedly shot and killed seven co-workers at the company's Honolulu office. He used a 9mm pistol. Uyesugi was later apprehended after a stand-off with police.

• August 10, 1999: Buford O. Furrow, 37, a white supremacist, allegedly opened fire at a Jewish community center in Los Angeles, wounding five people including three children. The weapons used were a Uzi semi-automatic machine gun and a Glock 9mm handgun. He later killed a postal worker with the Glock handgun, which he apparently bought from a gun show or flea market where no background check was required.

• August 5, 1999: Alan Eugene Miller, 34, allegedly shot two co-workers to death at their office in Pelham, Alabama. He then allegedly killed a third man who worked at a company from which he had been fired. The weapon used was a .40-caliber Glock semi-automatic handgun.

• July 29, 1999: Mark Barton, 44, allegedly shot and killed nine and wounded 13 in Atlanta after bludgeoning his wife and two children to death. Among the many weapons used were a Glock 9mm pistol, Colt .45 pistol, and a .22-caliber Raven pistol.

• July 2–4, 1999: Benjamin Nathaniel Smith, 21, a white supremacist, allegedly killed two people and injured nine in a racially motivated three-day rampage in Illinois and Indiana before shooting himself. Among the weapons used were a Bryco .380 handgun and a .22-caliber Ruger pistol.

• May 29, 1999: T.J. Solomon, 15, allegedly shot and injured six students in Heritage High School in Conyers, Georgia. The weapons included a .22 caliber rifle and a .357-magnum revolver.

• April 20, 1999: Eric Harris, 18, and Dylan Klebold, 17, killed 12 students and a teacher and wounded 23 others before shooting themselves in the library at Columbine High School in Littleton, Colorado. Among the weapons used were a TEC-DC9 handgun, a sawed-off double-barreled shotgun, a pump-action shotgun, and a 9mm semi-automatic rifle.

• April 15, 1999: Sergei Babarin, 70, a schizophrenic, killed a woman and a guard and wounded four others at the Mormon Family History Library in Salt Lake City. He used a .22 caliber Ruger. He was fatally shot by police as they attempted to apprehend him.

In the previous year, there were other horrifying examples of what deranged adults and children can do with guns. On July 24, 1998, Russell Eugene Weston allegedly killed a policeman and federal guard and wounded a female visitor at the U.S. Capitol. On May 21 of that year, 15-year-old Kipland Kinkel killed two Thurston High School students in Springfield, Oregon. He was also charged with killing his parents the day before. On March 24, Mitchell Johnson, 13, and Andrew Golden, 11, allegedly killed a teacher and four students and wounded 10 others at a school in Jonesboro, Arkansas. In December 1997, Michael Carneal, a 14-year-old student, shot and killed three students and wounded five others at Heath High School in Paducah, Kentucky. On October 1, 1997, Luke Woodham, 16, stabbed his mother to death, then used a gun to kill two students and wound seven others at Pearl High School in Pearl, Mississippi.

The nation has been outraged over these and other incidents. While the killings continue, people still argue about what the Second Amendment means. Clearly, abolishing the Amendment will not on its own reduce gun-related violence. But it will remove from the national debate the argument that the Constitution prohibits reasonable regulation such as waiting periods, control over concealed weapons, importation of machine guns, and other measures. As long as the Second Amendment remains a part of the Constitution, it can always be used to justify opposition to gun control measures.

Limited Legal Impact

Because of how few times the courts have ruled in cases directly involving the Second Amendment, the nation knows little about the legal meaning of its words. The first time the Supreme Court dealt with the Second Amendment it was not deciding the specific question of whether the right to bear arms meant individuals could own guns. Instead, the Court had to determine whether the Second Amendment applied only to the federal government, or also restricted the power of the states. This is not a narrow legal question of interest only to lawyers. The Bill of Rights, as Chief Justice John Marshall confirmed in 1833, originally applied only to the federal government. That meant citizens for much of our nation's history could not use the Constitution to fight state abridgement of such protections as freedom of expression, the right not to incriminate oneself in a criminal prosecution, the right to an attorney, and other rights guaranteed by the first 10 amendments to the Constitution.

Many of the civil liberties we take for granted today were slow to develop. Until 1925, if state governments wanted to send people to prison for exercising First Amendment rights —and many of them did — there was nothing in the federal Constitution that could be used to stop that effort. State prosecutors could use evidence in court seized in violation of the Fourth Amendment to convict defendants until 1961. We are taught in school that one of the most precious values of this country is the right to an attorney. But until 1963, those who could not afford an attorney — even when accused of serious crimes resulting in long jail sentences — had to defend themselves in most state courts despite the language of the Sixth Amendment guaranteeing a "right to counsel." The reason was that the Sixth Amendment did not apply to the states. It was 1972 before the right to counsel was extended to individuals who could be imprisoned in cases involving nonfelonies.

Applying the protections of the Bill of Rights to the states was eventually accomplished through the language of the 14th Amendment. After the Civil War, Congress wanted to protect the rights of newly freed slaves, and thus specifically held that no "state shall deprive any person of life, liberty, or property, without due process of law." It was almost three decades before the Supreme Court took advantage of that language to extend one of the protections in the Bill of Rights to someone deprived of rights by a state or local government. But when the Court did so for the first time, it was not an ordinary citizen, but a corporation, that first enjoyed such protection. Beginning with *Chicago, Burlington & Quincy Railroad v. Chicago* in 1897, and continuing sporadically until 1972, the

Supreme Court applied many, but not all of the provisions of the Bill of Rights, to the states.

The first time the Court specifically considered the Second Amendment was in *United States v. Cruikshank* in 1875. The Court had to decide whether the Second Amendment placed limitations on the authority of the federal government alone. The Court concluded that the Amendment "means no more than that it shall not be infringed by Congress. This is one of the amendments that has no other effect than to restrict the powers of the national government." The Court confirmed this ruling 11 years later in *Presser v. Illinois* in 1886. In *Presser*, the Court decided that the Second Amendment permitted an Illinois law that prohibited "any body of men whatever, other than the regular organized volunteer militia of this State, and the troops of the United States . . . to drill or parade with arms in any city, or town, of this State, without the license of the Governor thereof." The law was intended to suppress labor unrest by making it illegal for workers to defend themselves against violent acts committed by the police and individuals hired by employers. *Cruikshank* and *Presser* thus established that the Second Amendment had not been incorporated into the 14th Amendment and made applicable to the states.

Whatever the Second Amendment means, it continues to apply only to the federal government. When the Supreme Court declined to hear the case *Quilici v. Village of Morton Grove* in 1983, it left unanswered the question of when, if ever, the Second Amendment would apply to the states. In that case, the U.S. Court of Appeals for the Seventh Circuit upheld a local ordinance in Morton Grove, Illinois, prohibiting the possession of handguns within its borders. *Morton Grove* has been the Supreme Court's only opportunity in recent years to interpret the Second Amendment. The Court could have used *Morton Grove* to determine what the language of the Second Amendment means and whether the Amendment would apply to both the federal government and the states.

Separate from the issue of whether the Second Amendment has been incorporated into the 14th Amendment is the question of whether it confers a right of ownership of weapons to individuals. Unfortunately, the Supreme Court has not been much help in clarifying that issue. *United States v. Miller*, decided in 1939, was the Court's only opportunity to consider whether the Second Amendment gave individuals the right to possess weapons, and the last time the Court has dealt with a Second Amendment case. Miller was charged with transporting a sawed-off shotgun in interstate commerce in violation of the National Firearms Act of 1934. He had not registered the gun as required by the law, among other alleged crimes. The trial court had dismissed the charge on the ground that the Act violated the Second Amendment. A unanimous Supreme

Court reversed the decision. The Court held that there was no evidence that Miller's possession of the shotgun showed a "reasonable relationship to the preservation or efficiency of a well regulated militia." The Court further noted that such a weapon "is not any part of the ordinary military equipment or that its use could contribute to the common defense."

It is easy to make too much of the *Miller* case. Although it can probably be read to either support an individual right to bear arms or as establishing the principle that only organized militias may possess such weapons, it dealt only indirectly with those issues. The Court's language suggested that if Miller had been charged with possession of a weapon used in warfare — an assault weapon, for example — the Court may have held that the Second Amendment protected his right to own it. The other side could argue that the Court concluded that only organized militia groups had such a right.

Miller was decided more than half a century ago, but it is only a matter of time before the right case gives the Supreme Court the opportunity to finally clarify the language of the Second Amendment. Such a case may have begun in April 1999, when a federal district court in Lubbock, Texas, issued a ruling that should alarm anyone supporting regulation of guns. The judge dismissed charges against a man arrested for owning a gun while under a restraining order. He had been charged the previous year with violating the restraining order after brandishing a pistol in front of his wife and her daughter. The judge accepted the defendant's argument that he had a right to own a gun under the Second Amendment and that any law infringing on that right was unconstitutional. Judge Sam Cummings held that the Second Amendment's right to bear arms is an individual right, and not just a right belonging to an organized militia. The court's decision is among the very few to ever hold that the Second Amendment protects individual rights to keep weapons. Federal prosecutors said they would appeal.

Preventing Reasonable Regulation: The NRA

Few organizations strike terror into the hearts and minds of state and federal legislators like the National Rifle Association. Through its ability to contact and mobilize its members, and with the millions of dollars the organization contributes to candidates, the NRA is among the most powerful lobbying groups on Capitol Hill and in state legislatures. Going up against the NRA requires courage by those in all but the safest districts. If a member of Congress dares to take a position that the NRA does not like, that member may find that within days, thousands of constituents have been mailed printed matter identifying — and sometimes distorting — the member's position and urging citizens to let their representative or senator know that such behavior will not be tolerated.

An example is former Senator David Pryor's experience with the NRA. Pryor was a Democrat from Arkansas who retired in 1997. He recalled the time when, as a state legislator in 1961, he proposed a bill that would have made it illegal to leave a loaded rifle or shotgun in an unattended, unlocked vehicle. The NRA killed the bill and then opposed him every time he ran for office over the next three decades.

The organization's commitment to defending the Second Amendment and resisting almost all restrictions on gun ownership is exemplified by a statement made by its then vice president, and now president, Charlton Heston, in September of 1997. The well-known actor, speaking to the National Press Club, said that the Second Amendment was the "most vital" of all the amendments and was "more essential" than the First Amendment. And, he added, "Among freedom of speech, of the press, of religion, of assembly, or redress of grievances, [the Second Amendment] is first among equals. . . . It alone offers the absolute capacity to live without fear. The right to keep and bear arms is the one right that allows rights to exist at all." A constitutional law expert, Christopher L. Eisgruber of New York University Law School, characterized as "bleak and unrealistic" and "outrageous" Heston's belief that "people having guns in their homes . . . is more central to maintaining American government than the free and independent discussion of ideas."

Heston's speech came during a time when the NRA had been sharply criticized for some of its lobbying positions and its alleged links with paramilitary organizations. Membership dropped by 700,000 members after the Oklahoma City bombing in 1995, and after a fundraising letter sent by the NRA compared some federal agents to "jackbooted government thugs." One month after the letter was sent to the members, former President George Bush, who had a lifetime membership, resigned from the organization.

The NRA was considered so powerful during much of the 1980s and 1990s, that if a candidate for public office whom it opposed won an election, speculation would soon follow that the organization was losing its grip on American politics. No single group should be so influential in the selection of elected officials that when a candidate it supports loses, the organization is blamed. To even discuss the NRA in those terms demonstrates how successful it has been in mobilizing its members and spending money to elect or defeat candidates.

In the November 1996 election, several NRA-supported House incumbents who had voted to repeal the Clinton Administration's 1994 ban on assault weapons were defeated for reelection. Those defeats seemed to tarnish the group's nearly unblemished record of keeping in office incumbents who have the organization's blessing. The NRA had required that any member of Congress who wanted its support had to vote for the repeal of the assault weapons ban. Out of the 23 incumbents in the House who lost their seats, all but four had voted in the spring of 1996 to repeal the ban. There was some speculation that the NRA was losing its clout in the national legislature.

But a closer look revealed that the organization had lost little ground, and may even have gained influence. The NRA increased the number of its defenders in the Senate, and even in the House, where NRA-supported incumbents lost, they were replaced with equally dedicated opponents of gun control. This suggested that in those races, the competency of the incumbent may have been more of a factor than positions on gun issues.

Even a net loss of 10 or 11 pro-NRA House members did not threaten the organization's majority. When the House voted to approve a repeal of the assault weapons ban in the spring of 1996, the vote was 239 to 173. A dozen votes would not have made a difference. The measure showed the NRA's strength in the House, although the bill was never brought to a vote in the Senate. Overall in 1996, the organization claimed it was successful in 84 percent of the 10,000 political races in which it participated.

A Memorable Vote

One of the House incumbents who was defeated in 1996, and who had voted to repeal the assault weapons ban, deserves special attention. There may not be a more appalling example in the 1990s of a member of Congress trying to please the NRA while demonstrating a shocking and callous indifference to the interests of his constituents. The roots of the controversy began in December 1993, when Colin Ferguson pulled out a 9-millimeter handgun on a Long Island Rail Road train and opened fire. Six people died, including Carolyn McCarthy's husband, Dennis. Her son Kevin was seriously wounded, among 19 injured in the shooting. In her grief and anger, McCarthy became an activist against gun violence.

Then came the vote in the House in March of 1996 to repeal President Clinton's ban on the importation of assault weapons. As expected, the NRA opposed the president's action as a violation of the Second Amendment and another step in the government's plan to control all ownership of guns. McCarthy was especially interested in how her congressman, Republican Dan Frisa, would vote. It was in his congressional district that the carnage had taken place. When it was time for Frisa to make a decision on whether to support a repeal of the ban, he apparently had no trouble choosing between the interests of the NRA or the citizens of his Long Island district. He chose the NRA.

The decision so disgusted McCarthy that she ran against Frisa as a Democrat. The retired nurse had been a registered Republican but she could not tolerate her party's stand on gun issues. At first, McCarthy had a difficult time raising money and getting people to take her seriously. But instead of the usual outcome where the incumbent wins, McCarthy was elected. The publicity generated after her husband's death made her much better known than most challengers and was undoubtedly an important factor in her victory. She also broadened her campaign beyond gun control so she would not be perceived as a single-issue candidate.

Still, Frisa might have won the election, or at least received significantly more votes, had he not run such an inept campaign against McCarthy. Ignoring Republican advisers in the district and avoiding reporters so frequently that he was rarely seen during the months before the election, Frisa relied almost entirely on a direct mail strategy. He may have thought that his vote for the NRA on the assault weapons issue was a mistake and rather than face tough questions from voters and the press, he decided to stay home and send out brochures. Not only was such a strategy considered ineffective, some of his mailings were denounced as misleading and not authorized by groups he claimed had given him their support. Had he voted against the repeal of the assault weapons ban, which was never approved by Congress, and accepted the NRA's punishment, he might still be in Congress today.

The NRA's Support for Assault Weapons

One of the positions that the NRA holds most dear — that baffles many who do not accept the argument that any regulation will lead to total confiscation of weapons — is its tireless fight against banning assault weapons. The organization strenuously opposed the Clinton Administration's efforts to impose a ban on 58 types of imported guns, including many assault weapons. Such assault weapons are not meant for sporting activities or the protection of one's home. They are designed to kill people as rapidly as possible and have been the weapon of choice of guerilla and terrorist organizations around the world for decades.

In April 1998, the White House announced the ban after the Bureau of Alcohol, Tobacco and Firearms concluded that 58 types of assault guns could not be classified as sporting weapons and thus could be banned under a 1968 gun control law. The president made the announcement shortly after four children and a teacher were killed at a Jonesboro, Arkansas, school. Among the weapons banned by the president were various models of assault weapons with large capacity magazines capable of loading and firing in quick succession. The Bush Administration had banned the assault weapons in 1989, and President Clinton extended that ban in 1994, but that did not stop the gun manufacturers from figuring out how to legally sell them in the United States. They simply modified the weapons slightly to avoid the ban. The Clinton Administration determined that despite the slight modification, the assault weapons were still covered by the law and thus could not be legally imported.

The NRA naturally opposed the administration's decision. Tanya Metaksa, the NRA's chief lobbyist, was quoted as saying, "We're not happy." An organization representing companies that import guns called it an "abuse of presidential authority." Both the NRA and other groups vowed to fight the president's action in Congress and the courts. Metaksa said that thousands of weapons had already been imported and paid for and had been stored in U.S. Customs' warehouses awaiting the Administration's ruling. Now, hundreds of importers will "be completely out of pocket," she said. And Metaksa added, "You can't return a firearm the way you can return a shirt to Macy's."

The gimmick of gun manufacturers making minor changes to weapons to get around the federal ban may not work as easily in the future. California is among the first states to outlaw guns based on their characteristics, not the model of the gun. Thus, a minor alteration that would have changed the gun from the proscribed model to something not covered by the ban will not work. California joined three other states — Maryland, Virginia, and South Carolina — in limiting handgun purchases to one a month. Under federal law, people who pass a background check can buy an unlimited number of guns at a single time and as often as they would like. Authorities believe that the new law will discourage buyers of large quantities of guns who sell them to criminals.

The NRA is not content to fight gun control laws within the United States. The group worries that whenever any country considers tougher laws related to ownership or access to guns, that sentiment might spread to this country. The organization gave $20,000 to an association in Australia to boost its lobbyists in their efforts to fight gun control measures and an undisclosed sum to a group in New Zealand. When Britain banned all guns except .22-caliber firearms in 1997, the NRA responded to what it considered growing efforts in countries to limit access to guns. The organization's chief lobbyist explained that "when guns are being confiscated in Australia and Britain . . . NRA members must stand shoulder to shoulder to defend the Second Amendment."

The NRA's opposition to regulation of assault weapons and other firearms has been widely publicized, often by the organization itself. What is less known is whether the NRA opposed efforts by Congress to ban ammunition that pierce the bullet-proof vests worn by police. There are many letters to the editor and newspaper commentaries that denounce the NRA for taking such an extreme position, but it is difficult to find any source that makes it clear that the NRA opposes such regulation.

In his 1996 book, *Inside the NRA: Armed and Dangerous*, veteran investigative reporter Jack Anderson explained that many police officers, while on duty, wear Kevlar vests made of several plastics that stop nearly all slugs. The vests are light enough to be worn while performing the duties of a police officer, and according to Anderson, they have saved thousands of police officers' lives.

In 1986, President Reagan signed a bill that banned metal bullets that pierce these vests. Some nine years later, police officials found that plastic bullets had been manufactured that could penetrate the vests. Rep. Charles Schumer (D-NY) introduced an amendment to President Clinton's anti-terrorism bill to ban the plastic bullets. On June 14, 1995, the House Judiciary Committee voted, 16 to 14, to ban any bullet, of whatever material, capable of penetrating the vests. Two freshmen Republicans joined Democrats in supporting the ban. According to Anderson, Neal Knox, an NRA board member and one of its more influential officials, said the two Republicans had voted that way because they "didn't know any better."

The next day, the vote was reconsidered and the two freshmen Republicans reversed themselves, and the broader ban on bullets that pierce police vests was dead. Although Anderson does not say that the NRA specifically told the two congressmen to change their votes, he quoted the NRA's executive vice president, Wayne LaPierre, as explaining it this way: "Bill Clinton wants the Treasury Department to ban any ammunition that will penetrate Kevlar, which includes virtually any hunter's ammunition. So it's basically an ammunition ban, in a back door way." President Clinton, speaking to a group of hunters, said, "I have never seen a deer, duck, or a wild turkey wearing a Kevlar vest. You don't need these bullets."

The American People Want Change

The FBI estimates there are 250 million firearms in the United States, one for nearly every man, woman, and child. More than a third of American households have a gun. Eighty-seven people a day are killed by firearms in this country. We lead the industrialized world in the rate at which children die from guns. The *Journal of American History* reported in 1997 that more people are killed with guns in the United States in a typical week than in all of Western Europe in a year. It is estimated that by 2002, gunfire may surpass cars to become the leading cause of nonnatural death in the United States.

Although there is disagreement about how well new laws will work, it is clear that the American people favor stricter measures. According to a *Newsweek* poll conducted in August 1999, 74 percent support registration of all handgun owners, and 93 percent favor a mandatory waiting period for people who want to buy handguns. Some gun owners also support gun laws. The *Newsweek* poll found that 81 percent of nongun owners want all handgun owners to register with the government, while 66 percent of gun owners do. When it comes to mandatory gun safety classes, nongun owners favor them by 88 percent, while 80 percent of gun owners do.

There is even support for more drastic measures. The poll found that 50 percent of the respondents who do not own firearms favor an outright ban on nonpolice handguns. Only 21 percent of gun owners favor such a ban. Sixty-eight percent say military-style assault guns should be outlawed, while 51 percent want to ban gun shows where weapons are bought and sold with little regulation.

The respondents in the poll were skeptical about whether stricter gun laws would have prevented the violence at schools and other places in 1999. Only 18 percent of respondents in the *Newsweek* poll said that gun control was the most effective deterrent to violent incidents, while 33 percent said that identifying those with antisocial behavior was the best answer. Twenty-three percent favored increasing security in schools and offices.

Although stricter gun laws may not be the whole answer, something must be done about a system that permits guns to be so easily available to violent individuals. *Newsweek* found through sources at the U.S. Bureau of Alcohol, Tobacco and Firearms that all of the guns that Buford Furrow allegedly used to shoot youngsters at the Jewish community center in Los Angeles, and the weapons used to kill a postal worker, were legally in circulation. According to *Newsweek*, they were all first sold by licensed dealers. Furrow bought two of the guns directly. The Glock pistol involved in the postal worker shooting was originally purchased in 1996 by the police department in a small town in Washington state. The department exchanged it at a firearms store in town. The store's owner sold it to a legal buyer, and that buyer gave it to a friend who sold it to Furrow at a gun show. Furrow bought four other guns in a similar way. According to the magazine, Furrow held a federal firearms license from 1992 to 1995, which allowed him to buy and sell guns across state lines. During that time he was eligible to apply for a permit to own fully automatic weapons such as machine guns.

The response to such stories from those opposed to restrictions on access to guns is that new laws are not needed, but existing ones must be more energetically enforced. But current laws protect gun dealers and make it very difficult for law enforcement officials to shut down gun operations even when they know that the guns being sold there are often used in crimes. A detailed report in the New York Times explained how difficult it is to go after gun dealers, and even if the prosecution is successful, many of the penalties are minor. For example, the Firearms Owners Protection Act of 1986 reduced the penalty for falsifying records from a felony to a misdemeanor. Unannounced inspections to review a dealer's records are limited to one a year. The standard to punish a gun dealer for selling a weapon to a "straw buyer" who they suspect will sell it to a criminal was increased, thus making prosecutions more difficult. The newspaper cited an example of a Baltimore gun shop that police believe sells 20 percent of the guns used in crimes in that city, but because of federal law, authorities have been unable to shut it down.

The American people, at least to the extent shown in the Newsweek poll, believe that other efforts must be made to cut down on violent crimes committed against children in schools, day care centers, and other places. The poll reported that 57 percent of respondents blamed poor parenting while 52 percent blamed the media for the increase in violence.

After the tragedy in Littleton, Colorado, which left 15 dead — including the two gunmen — on April 20, 1999, 95 students from the Denver area, including six from Columbine High School where the shooting took place, traveled to Washington to urge their members of Congress to consider new gun legislation. Several of the students who survived the shooting wondered whether their representatives had any sense of what they had been through and how urgently reform is needed. One student probably spoke for many people in asking, "What's more important: the right for people to bear arms, or the right of people not to be killed?" The group had meetings with President Clinton and Vice President Gore, who were supportive, but they will probably remember with frustration the meeting with the Republican House member, Scott McInnis, who represents the district that includes Columbine High School.

When two competing proposals to require mandatory background checks on all firearms buyers came before the House in June of 1999, two months after the killings, McInnis voted for the significantly more lenient one. The students knew that when they met with him. After listening politely on the steps of the Capitol while McInnis praised them for coming to Washington, several students asked tough questions about his vote. McInnis responded that lawmakers needed to make sure that they did not deprive law-abiding citizens of guns. The students insisted that stricter laws would help reduce the likelihood of violent acts being committed with guns. They reminded their congressman that all four guns used at Columbine were purchased without background checks at gun shows.

The NRA Responds

The NRA was quick to react to the shootings in Colorado. Two weeks after the last victim was buried, the organization sent letters to its 2.6 million members warning that President Clinton would "demand that you pay the price for the insanity of the killers" with new gun control measures. Checks began flowing into the NRA's headquarters. The organization said that after the Littleton shooting, its membership grew by tens of thousands. The new money helped create a $20 million lobbying and political fund to be used for campaign contributions for its supporters and to punish enemies in state and federal elections.

The executive vice president of the NRA, Wayne LaPierre, called the Columbine and day care shootings "horrible tragic situations," and said everyone shares the same emotion of wanting to stop such incidents. But he insisted that gun laws are not the way to do it. He argued that tougher enforcement of current laws — such as prosecuting criminals who are not supposed to have guns — is the best way to deal with the situation, and he accused the Clinton Administration of being more interested in playing politics than enforcing laws: "There's a deliberate effort by this administration and by the Department of Justice not to enforce the laws on the books and not to prosecute any of these cases. . . . Instead they're going to concentrate on cutting off guns at the source. Well, I mean, give me a break. They can try that for the next 50 years, and criminals that want guns are still going to get them." LaPierre called for more police officers and prosecutors and said that if violent offenders knew they were going to be sent to jail, they would be deterred from committing crimes.

When asked why the NRA vigorously opposes registration of guns, LaPierre said that people have a constitutional right to own guns, and they do not want their name on government lists because they own guns. And he added, "They know what the next step is. It's a knock on the door confiscating their guns." He believes the government wants to deprive people of their constitutional rights: "I think the real target is the Second Amendment. I don't think it has anything to do with crime. I don't think it has anything to do with stopping violence. I think the ultimate target is to take away the freedom and take away the Second Amendment."

Scholars have examined the issue of whether efforts to reduce the availability of guns will result in a reduction in crimes committed with firearms. Among the most controversial is John Lott, a fellow in law and economics at the University of Chicago. In his 1998 book, *More Guns, Less Crime*, he argued that in those states that require local officials to issue concealed weapons permits to qualified individuals, the incidents of violent crimes were reduced. The conclusion was that criminals will be hesitant to commit crimes when they suspect that the victim may be armed.

Lott examined 10 states that approved such laws from 1977 to 1992, and found that violent crimes had dropped significantly: murders by 8 percent; rapes by 5 percent; and aggravated assaults by 7 percent. Lott said that criminals stopped committing so many violent crimes and took up burglaries and other crimes where they do not have to confront a potentially armed victim. Not suprisingly, the book was applauded by the NRA. The organization sent 150,000 of its most loyal members a newsletter recommending it. *Gun Week* magazine endorsed it and G. Gordon Liddy, a radio talk show host who strongly promotes Second Amendment values on his show, enthusiastically plugged the book.

Not everyone applauded Lott's work. Some academics criticized his methods and conclusions. They argued that in those states that permit concealed weapons, only a tiny percentage of the population — about 1 to 2 percent — applied to carry a concealed weapon. Moreover, the statistics indicate that the people most likely to seek a concealed weapons permit are white males in suburban or rural settings, not the kind of people at high risk for being victims of homicide or robbery. The idea that criminals will be deterred from committing violent acts because of the possibility of encountering one of the few people who legally carry a concealed weapon cannot explain the reduction in crime, those scholars argue. Others re-examined Lott's data and found that they did not support his conclusions. They weighed Lott's numbers by looking at counties with populations of 100,000 or more, and found widely varying results. Murders climbed in one state by 105 percent after concealed weapons laws were passed, while declining 67 percent in other states. A statistician who looked at the numbers said that when a single state — Florida — was removed from Lott's data set, the positive effects of the law vanished.

Some Cities and States Fight Back

Some American cities have responded to the public outcry by filing lawsuits against gun manufacturers, arguing that they knew or should have known that the weapons they made would end up in the hands of criminals. About 30 cities had filed such lawsuits as of early fall 1999. But many of those cities may never get their day in court. As of September 1999, 13 states had approved laws prohibiting its cities from bringing such lawsuits. When Texas passed such a law, Governor George W. Bush not only signed it but also approved another law permitting Texans to carry concealed weapons. His support for those two measures may be an issue in the 2000 presidential election.

States are not the only impediment. Judges have dismissed several lawsuits brought by cities, on the grounds that gun manufacturers cannot be held liable for crimes committed with the weapons they make, or that cities lack standing to bring such legal action. On October 7, 1999, a state judge dismissed Cincinnati's lawsuit against gun manufacturers, a distributor, and three trade associations by holding that the claims were vague and not supported by law or prior court decisions. The lawsuit sought reimbursement for the costs of providing police, emergency, court, and prison services for shootings in the city, whether they were homicides or accidents. On October 14, 1999, by a 5-4 vote, the city council decided to appeal the judge's decision.

While Cincinnati is challenging the judge's dismissal of its lawsuit, California has won approval to sue a gun maker. On September 29, 1999, a California appellate court, in a 2-1 ruling, reinstated a lawsuit brought by the state against the manufacturer of semiautomatic pistols used to kill eight people in a law office in San Francisco in 1993. The ruling is the first by a state or federal appellate court anywhere in the nation to allow a lawsuit against a gun maker to go to trial. According to the First District Court of Appeal, the victims' families are entitled to a trial on their claims that the manufacturer marketed the guns to appeal to criminals and should have known that they would be used for criminal purposes.

The California court's decision, as well as increasing public pressure, may have persuaded gun manufacturers to agree to negotiations with cities in an effort to settle the lawsuits. The companies were also nervous about the first of the lawsuits moving into the discovery phase where damaging corporate documents could be made public. Such documents were essential in persuading tobacco companies to settle their lawsuits with the states. When the two sides met in early October 1999, the gun makers said they would quickly respond to some of the cities' demands, including mandatory safety devices on weapons and a crackdown on corrupt gun retailers.

They also said they would undertake other efforts to limit the flow of weapons to criminals. But those attending the talks between gun makers and government officials cautioned that the discussions were preliminary and that many obstacles to a settlement remained.

Some families have also sued gun makers, and in December 1999, an Illinois judge refused to dismiss such a suit. At the same time that the city of Chicago is suing gun manufacturers in a separate action, the families of three people killed by handguns accuse the gun industry of knowingly creating an underground market in handguns that they know poses a danger to the public. The judge declined to dismiss the lawsuit, holding that individuals and not just governments could bring a claim against the firearms industry.

Some gun makers are voluntarily deciding to curtail production of handguns. In October 1999, Colt said it would end much of its 144-year old retail gun business to limit its liability in lawsuits. The company said it would sell them mainly to law enforcement agencies and the military. It would stop selling them directly to civilians, except to gun collectors. One company executive expressed concern about the lawsuits that could be worth "zero, or a trillion dollars."

In what may be the legal action with the most far-reaching consequences, the White House and the Department of Housing and Urban Development prepared in early December 1999, to file a lawsuit on behalf of the three million people who live in public housing projects. The government spends $1 billion a year on security at the nation's public housing facilities. The Clinton Administration is hoping that the threat of legal action will intensify pressure on the gun industry to settle with the states, and now the federal government. HUD Secretary Andrew Cuomo said the administration wants to negotiate with gun manufacturers, but if no settlement is reached, the government would file the lawsuit in federal district court in Washington.

Some Governors Step In

Texas Governor George W. Bush surprised some Second Amendment supporters by endorsing two measures before Congress. One would outlaw imports of certain high-capacity ammunition clips. The other would raise the legal age from 18 to 21 for handgun purchases. "Those are reasonable measures" the governor was quoted as saying. But he added that his support for those bills did not mean he had changed his position on guns.

Some governors, including Republicans like Bush, have been push-ing for modest gun control measures, sometimes fighting their state legislatures and the gun lobbies in the process. In Illinois, first-term Re-publican Governor George Ryan signed a package of initiatives that in-cluded trigger locks to prevent child access, a gun storage law that holds parents accountable for acts of violence committed with a gun by their children, and new penalties for using guns in crimes. He said he would veto any bill that allowed Illinois residents to carry a concealed weapon. Other Republican governors — such as those in Colorado, Ohio, Utah, Kansas, and Connecticut — even though they had the support of the NRA, decided in the wake of the highly publicized shootings in 1998 and 1999, to endorse measures that range from the very modest to more comprehensive reform.

In his effort to convince the Illinois legislature to approve the new measures, Governor Ryan had the support of Handgun Control, an organization founded by Sarah Brady, the wife of presidential press secretary James Brady who was seriously wounded in the assassination attempt against President Reagan in March 1981. Based in Washington, D.C., Handgun Control speaks out on behalf of victims of gun violence and lobbies state and federal officials to enact new laws and regulations to limit the sale, distribution, and ownership of guns. Handgun Control was active in the campaign in Missouri to defeat a measure on the ballot to allow the carrying of concealed weapons. Although the NRA spent $3.7 million to convince voters to approve the measure, it was defeated on April 6, 1999, by 52 to 48 percent.

In October of 1999, New Jersey became the fourth state to prohibit the sale of any new handgun unless it came with a trigger lock. Republi-can Governor Christine Todd Whitman called it a major step to prevent gun violence. The legislature had seriously considered passing a law requiring "smart" gun technology on any handgun — which would per-mit only the owner to fire the weapon — but after intense lobbying, the opposition argued successfully that smart gun technology had not yet been fully developed and that such a law would be tantamount to a ban on handguns.

Stalemate in Congress

Despite strong public support for action in the wake of the 1999 car-nage, Congress seemed hopelessly divided about what new measures, if any, should be approved. No comprehensive gun legislation passed in 1999. One of the major sticking points was how extensively to regulate gun shows where, under current law, unlicensed dealers can sell guns to almost anyone without doing a background check. Only licensed dealers, who represent about 60 percent of the vendors at gun shows, must perform a check on customers. The Senate approved a measure that covered most gun shows and allowed up to three business days for vendors to get the results of a background check. House Republican leaders, however, wanted a narrower definition of gun shows and for the background check to be completed within 24 hours. Many believe that 24 hours is not enough time to uncover a buyer's criminal or mental illness record.

On June 18, 1999, the House rejected a gun control measure that was too restrictive for some representatives and not restrictive enough for others. The bill, which the House turned down by a vote of 280 to 147 — and which many considered significantly weaker than a bill approved by the Senate — would have provided only minimal changes to gun show background checks. The night before, the House defeated a bill sponsored by Carolyn McCarthy that would have required background checks on all buyers at gun shows, defined gun shows broadly, and would have given vendors up to three days to get the results of those checks.

After McCarthy's emotional speech on the House floor in which she referred to her murdered husband and her seriously wounded son, members of the House, including some Republicans and conservative Democrats, gave her a standing ovation. Moments later, however, the House defeated her proposal 253 to 193. The House then narrowly approved an amendment sponsored by John Dingell (D-MI) that would have made minimal changes to the current law. But it did not matter what happened to the Dingell amendment, or any others, because the final version of the bill before the House was defeated the next day. That was followed by the usual finger pointing with Republicans claiming that the Democrats missed an opportunity for real change, while Democrats charged that the Republicans were ignoring the pleas of the American people in the wake of recent gun violence.

The likelihood that the Second Amendment will ever be repealed is small. Supporters need only convince representatives or senators in one house in 13 state legislatures — whose members represent less than five percent of the country's population — to keep the Second Amendment as part of the Constitution and the unproductive debate about what it means going on forever. If a second constitutional convention is ever held, its first step should probably be approving Amendment "I" to make it easier to propose and ratify amendments, and more difficult for a small number of individuals to prevent change that may be favored by a large majority of the American people. Until then, the Second Amendment will remain a part of the Constitution.

Part IV

CHAPTER FIFTEEN

If A Second Convention Is Never Held

Almost from the day it was ratified in 1788, the Constitution has been viewed by many Americans as a sacred document that should only be discussed with reverence and devotion, and must not be sullied by the hands of those who think it is imperfect. It is more than a blueprint for establishing the branches of government, delineating their powers, and protecting individual liberty. Many believe the Constitution is the symbolic and literal soul of the nation and any tampering with it is a potential threat to the country's ongoing experiment in democracy. Even people who know little about specific provisions of the Constitution are likely to be suspicious of those wanting to change it.

To purists who argue that constitutional amendments should be avoided except in extraordinary and dire circumstances, any effort to make changes to the nation's founding document — even if done through the process that the Constitution provides — taints the work of the Philadelphia Framers. They would contend that even members of Congress defile the Constitution's legacy when they debate and vote on amendments, especially when those amendments are arguably policy-related rather than of constitutional dimension. Those who want to keep the Constitution under glass — available for viewing, but not for altering — must find disturbing the prospect of ordinary citizens discussing how to change the Constitution in the meetings described in this book.

Although there are a number of groups, former and current public officials, and legal scholars who passionately believe the Constitution should not be changed except for the most compelling of reasons, one

organization has attracted funding and has brought together distinguished individuals who oppose what they consider to be all too frequent
efforts in Congress to amend the Constitution. Citizens for the Constitution was formed in 1997, and was originally funded by the Century
Foundation. Now based at the Georgetown University Law Center in
Washington, D.C., the group has undertaken an initiative called "The
Constitution Project" that provides information about the constitutional amendment process through press announcements, the dissemination of documents to individuals on a mailing list, and through a Web
site. Most importantly, the organization denounces efforts in Congress
to solve problems through the introduction of constitutional amendments and it poses a series of questions, which it calls "Guidelines," that
should be asked before any amendment is considered.

On May 13, 1999, the group's co-chairs — former Rep. Mickey
Edwards (R-OK), former Rep. Abner Mikva (D-IL), who also served as
chief judge of the U.S. Court of Appeals for the District of Columbia,
and Professor Michael Seidman of Georgetown University Law Center,
the organization's legal advisor — briefed the national press about the
group's work and the guidelines that it had been preparing for more than
a year. After the briefing, the co-chairs met with Senator Orrin Hatch
(R-UT), the chair of the Senate Judiciary Committee, Rep. Henry Hyde
(R-IL), the chair of the House Judiciary Committee, and Rep. Charles
Canady (R-FL), the chair of the House Constitution Subcommittee. According to a letter from the Citizens group sent to those on its mailing
list, those three members of Congress expressed an interest in holding
hearings on how the Constitution should be amended.

Documents on the group's Web site reflect its passionate belief that
the nation's founders knew what they were doing when they made it extremely difficult for the Constitution to be amended: "They believed that
our nation had to be based on a stable constitutional structure that would
create respect for the rule of law, and thus foresaw a limited need for
amendments." The preface in the Web site documents offered Madison's
famous quote from *The Federalist* No. 49, arguing that the Constitution
should be amended only on "great and extraordinary occasions."

The organization warned that in recent years "there has been an
explosion in the number of proposed constitutional amendments on almost every conceivable topic. Amendment proposals now often seem to
be the favored first-step panacea for all societal ills." Among the group's
documents was a list of proposed amendments that were formally introduced or considered by the 105th Congress (1997–1998), that the organization believed dealt with matters of social policy or other issues not
worthy of constitutional consideration. The list included amendments

on flag desecration, a balanced budget, term limits, tax increases, victims' rights, religious equality, the Electoral College, and campaign finance. And, the group added, "The 106th Congress (1999–2000) promises more of the same."

According to the Citizens' literature, the Constitution is meant to establish broad principles that give the nation flexibility to decide policy issues through ordinary legislation and other processes that do not require changing the Constitution. The group believes that the Constitution has been an "effective constraint on the exercise of government power, enabling a wise people to pursue the wishes of the majority while still holding essential individual liberties sacred."

Getting a constitutional amendment approved through the processes established in Article V, even when there is widespread support, is difficult enough. If the questions posed by the Citizens for the Constitution had to be answered affirmatively, it would be even less likely that amendments would survive the proposal process and the state ratification requirement. Although Citizens for the Constitution would almost certainly think the ten amendments proposed in this book are not worthy of constitutional status, the questions posed by the guidelines raise important issues that should be considered any time there is debate over the nature of contemporary politics and whether the Constitution needs to be changed.

The Eight Guidelines

Citizens for the Constitution developed the guidelines over a period of several years after consulting with various individuals and organizations. The group recommends that eight questions be asked of any proposed constitutional amendment. Several of the guidelines have multiple questions, and there is some overlap among them that the organization acknowledges in the commentary accompanying the guidelines. The Web site includes discussion of each guideline and gives examples of amendments before Congress in recent years that should not be adopted. The group's commentary is well researched and interesting, but it is clear that few, if any, amendments would satisfy all of the criteria set forth in the guidelines.

1. Does the proposed amendment address matters that are of more than immediate concern that are likely to be recognized as of abiding importance by subsequent generations?

The organization believes that the Constitution should not be burdened with amendments that reflect short-term political considerations. It recommends that legislators avoid amendments "that are no more than part of a momentary political bargain, likely to become obsolete as the social and political premises underlying their passage wither or collapse." The commentary accompanying Guideline One argues that although the Constitution has some specific provisions — such as the day the president is inaugurated — it should remain a broad statement of principles that embodies the nation's enduring values and should not be burdened by specific policy statements. To support the contention that the Constitution should remain a statement of broad principles, the group cites the 50 state constitutions that have been amended some 6,000 times, as compared to 27 times for the U.S. Constitution. The implication is that state constitutions are less important in determining fundamental principles because they are overburdened by amendments better dealt with by legislation.

This argument fails to recognize some important differences between the U.S. Constitution and those of the states. State constitutions are significantly longer and contain detailed policy provisions that have to be amended more frequently to reflect changing conditions. While the U.S. Constitution has about 6,000 words, the average state constitution contains 26,000 and some run over 75,000. A state constitution with 100 amendments or more is likely not only to have provisions that are out of date, but provisions that inhibit the ability of government to implement necessary change. Moreover, state constitutions and state governments have to deal with a variety of matters with which the federal government does not have to bother.

It is also generally much easier to adopt amendments to state constitutions. Almost every state requires voters to approve changes, but there are four ways such amendments can be proposed: by legislatures, available in all states; by popular initiative, available in 17 states; by constitutional conventions, available in 41 states; and by constitutional commissions created by state legislatures that can recommend changes. States are also able to experiment more freely with changes in their constitutions because the U.S. Constitution provides a safety valve if the states make changes that interfere with fundamental rights. Because of the Supremacy Clause of Article VI of the U.S. Constitution — which says it is the "supreme law of the land" — the conflicting state constitutional provision must yield. No document provides such a safety valve for the U.S. Constitution, and thus it has to be changed more carefully.

All of the amendments proposed in this book appear to satisfy Guideline One. They address matters that are of more than immediate concern. For example, the way money is raised and spent in campaigns is of transcendent importance to the nation today and will be in the future.

Who wins elections, and whether those elected to public office serve the interests of voters or those who contribute money to the campaign, is an issue at the heart of a democratic system.

The Equal Rights Amendment, to the extent that it will change the political and social status of women, will be important to succeeding generations. A crime victims' bill of rights, if it has the effect of providing constitutional rights to crime victims and discouraging criminal activity, will be of "abiding" importance — to use the term in Guideline One — to subsequent generations.

The documents in the Citizens for the Constitution's Web site suggest that unless some proposed modification is of extraordinary dimensions, it should not be considered as a constitutional amendment. What the group largely fails to discuss is that many important changes can *only* be accomplished through constitutional amendments. The Supreme Court's *Buckley* decision in 1976 means there can be no limits on expenditures in campaigns unless the decision is reversed or the Constitution is changed. The Court's *Thornton* decision in 1995 requires a constitutional amendment for congressional term limits. Changing Senate terms or the majority needed to approve treaties cannot be accomplished by ordinary legislation because they are established by the Constitution. Even the Electoral College cannot be legislatively abolished because it is a feature of the Constitution.

If the Citizens for the Constitution were to ask if the country can survive with the Electoral College, or without a crime victims' bill of rights, the answer is yes. But if the American people want such changes, they are entitled to seek such amendments through the procedures provided in Article V.

Two of the proposed amendments in this book — protecting the jurisdiction of the federal courts, and repealing the Second Amendment — are less likely to be recognized as urgent by future generations. Congress has not shown much interest in recent years in tampering with the appellate jurisdiction of the federal courts, although as it will be recalled from Chapter 12, it has the power to do so. The Second Amendment has relatively little legal impact, although its symbolic importance is significant.

One constitutional amendment proposed in this book that clearly meets the first guideline, and which would especially concern the members of the Citizens for the Constitution, is the one proposing changes to Article V to make it easier to amend the Constitution. In an endnote in its introduction, the group says that it is not taking positions on the merits of proposed amendments. However, they added that "we have made a single exception in the case of an amendment that would itself make the amendment process less arduous. [Such a] proposal runs afoul of our core commitment to restraint, and we strongly oppose it." Clearly, the amendment discussed in Chapter 13 is of immediate and subsequent importance and could significantly alter the Constitution and the nation's political and social system, but would be vigorously opposed by the group.

2. Does the proposed amendment make our system more politically responsive or protect individual rights?

Many people believe that the Constitution should only be changed to enhance and not restrict civil liberties or other political rights. Another way of putting it is that the Constitution should be a "floor" below which any government entity — whether a state or local government, or the federal government — may not go, and thus the Constitution only permits the elevating of rights.

Among the proposed amendments in this book, the crime victims' bill of rights and the repeal of the Second Amendment have the potential to diminish the rights of individuals. In the former case, defendants who find victims of their crimes testifying at sentencing and parole hearings may see a diminution of their rights. To the extent the Second Amendment guarantees the right to bear arms to individuals, repeal of the amendment will restrict, not enhance rights.

The Citizens for the Constitution has an answer to whether a crime victims' bill of rights would be appropriate for a constitutional amendment. It says Congress should consider whether crime victims are a "discrete and insular minority" requiring constitutional protection against overreaching majorities, or whether they can be protected through ordinary political means. Although it draws no conclusion, because the group generally views proposed amendments with suspicion, it would probably like to see changes to the criminal process brought about through legislation and not constitutional change.

3. Are there significant practical or legal obstacles to the achievement of the objectives of the proposed amendment by other means?

The group argues that in order for the American people to maintain respect for the Constitution, it must not be burdened with amendments that are a "surrogate for ordinary legislation." One of the examples the group gives is the ERA. It believes that many of the objectives of the amendment have been achieved without having to change the Constitution. It believes that the victims' bill of rights is a more difficult question. Although Congress has considered enhancing the rights of crime victims through ordinary legislation, the group recognizes that there are constitutional protections given to criminal defendants that make extending protection to victims more difficult.

4. Is the proposed amendment consistent with related constitutional doctrine that the amendment leaves intact?

This is an important question that raises difficult issues any time a constitutional amendment is considered. Some amendments, such as the 16th Amendment permitting Congress to impose an income tax, was largely confined to the question of whether Congress had such authority and therefore, had little impact on other sections of the Constitution. But other amendments, such as the 14th, holding that states may not deprive its citizens of life, liberty or property without "due process of law," or equal protection of the law, raise many complicated constitutional issues.

The amendments proposed in this book would undoubtedly affect existing sections of the Constitution — and the cases that have interpreted those provisions — beyond the immediate subject of the proposed amendment. For example, reversing *Buckley* and making other changes in campaign finance would have serious implications for the First Amendment right to support or oppose candidates. Depending on how it is written and interpreted, a crime victims' amendment would affect many of the procedural rights enumerated in the Fourth, Fifth, and Sixth Amendments.

The difficult issues raised by Guideline Four is exemplified by an amendment considered by the 106th Congress to change the Constitution to punish desecration of the American flag. In *Texas v. Johnson* in 1989, and again in *United States v. Eichman* in 1990, the Supreme Court, divided 5-4 in both cases, held that laws punishing the burning of the flag violated the First Amendment. In June 1999, the House approved a flag burning amendment by the substantial margin of 305 to 124. As of early 2000, supporters in the Senate needed only a few more votes for the two-thirds approval in that body.

Many people believe that such an amendment would violate the First Amendment. The problem with such an assertion is that if a flag burning amendment became part of the Constitution, it would be as valid as any other section. Those who believe that the Constitution can be used only to enhance rights, and not restrict them, would argue that such an amendment itself would be unconstitutional because it has the effect of limiting free speech rights guaranteed by the First Amendment. The other side would maintain that if the people's representatives, using the process provided in Article V, believe that flag burning should not be considered protected speech, they should be able to make that change. Such a position would suggest that no section of the Constitution is unamendable.

Legal scholar Laurence Tribe of Harvard Law School believes that the Supreme Court would face a dilemma if a flag burning amendment were approved. If such an amendment became part of the Constitution, and Congress reenacted the flag desecration statute struck down in *Eichman*, the new law would be constitutional under the new amendment. But whether the law would be constitutional under the First Amendment — which would not have been repealed — is another matter. As Tribe put it, "Given the importance of the First Amendment to our constitutional scheme of individual liberty and self-government, might this entitle the justices to rule that since the First Amendment is still part of the Constitution it trumps the flag desecration amendment, and to hold therefore that flag-burning is still protected speech, notwithstanding the flag desecration amendment?" As difficult as this challenge might be, Tribe asserts that the Supreme Court would have to draw the line between protected expression and unprotected flag desecration in view of the conflicting constitutional amendments.

5. Does the proposed amendment embody enforceable, and not purely aspirational, standards?

Before any constitutional amendment is considered, there should be serious discussion about how it will be implemented. The amendment must be specific enough to provide guidance to courts and the elected branches of government that will interpret and carry out its provisions, and to the people who must know in advance what the rules are in society. If an amendment states only general, lofty principles, it may be mostly ignored by courts. That is largely the history of the Ninth and Tenth Amendments, although some Supreme Court justices and constitutional scholars have tried to breathe some life into those amendments that have been part of the Constitution since 1791. Despite efforts to revitalize amendments that state general, or aspirational goals, most are rarely applied to contemporary legal problems.

The commentary that accompanies Guideline Five emphasizes implementation of amendments, citing the difficulty of carrying out the fiscal responsibilities of the federal government if there were a balanced budget amendment. The commentary says that because Congress has been unable to balance the budget without the incentive of a constitutional amendment, such an amendment may be little more than a statement of principles that Congress will find easy to avoid. The commentary also notes that the balanced budget amendment that Congress considered during the late 1990s did not provide a plan for implementation.

Some amendments proposed in this book seek specific changes that can be easily implemented, while others will be more challenging.

For example, the amendment on campaign finance reform, discussed in Chapter Seven, has some sections that can be carried out with little dispute, while other elements will require extensive judicial interpretation. Among its provisions is the requirement that congressional candidates raise half the money for their campaigns from individuals or organizations based within their state or congressional district. Courts will have to decide such issues as whether an organization must have its headquarters in the state or district to qualify, or if an office is enough.

Other aspects of the campaign finance amendment will be more difficult to enforce. Section 1 states that regulation of contributions and expenditures shall not be interpreted as violating the First Amendment. Because political speech has historically been the form of speech most protected by the First Amendment, and considered the most essential to the functioning of a democratic society, courts would have to balance the language of the new campaign finance amendment with the First Amendment in a way that does not inhibit discussion of candidates and issues.

Citizens for the Constitution would probably also find the Equal Rights Amendment too vague and general, and thus unenforceable. It would add broad language prohibiting discrimination on the basis of gender, but would leave many questions unanswered. The amendment may possibly be interpreted in a way that restricts the rights of women. That was one reason opposition to the amendment grew quickly in the mid-1970s after it was initially ratified in several states. Despite such arguments, the discretion that courts would exercise in interpreting the ERA is not that different from the judgments that courts make in a wide range of constitutional cases. Many phrases in the Constitution require judges to consider the nation's political and social history, as well as legal precedents, in deciding how constitutional text will be applied. It is discretion that courts have long exercised and which is an indispensable characteristic of our constitutional system.

Other amendments proposed in this book would present significant implementation challenges. As discussed in Chapter Nine, among the most difficult to carry out would be the crime victims' bill of rights. The new amendment language would require judges and prosecutors to be sensitive to the rights of criminal defendants as guaranteed in other sections of the Constitution while allowing victims to participate in a meaningful way. Although the amendment proposed in this book outlines relatively specific procedures, ensuring that the new amendment does not interfere with rights under the Fourth, Fifth, and Sixth Amendments will be difficult.

The issue of implementation is, of course, different from the question of whether the amendment is a good idea. Many of the amendments proposed in this book can be implemented successfully and without much debate over *how* they are to be carried out. Congressional terms can be limited, Senate terms reduced, the majority needed for treaty approval changed, and the Second Amendment can be repealed. Putting those amendments into practice, which would be relatively straightforward, is a separate issue from whether we should have direct election of the president, whether members of Congress can serve only a fixed number of terms, and whether the Second Amendment should be repealed.

The Framers in Philadelphia were not writing a manual on how government should be structured, although the Constitution has many of those elements. They were trying to create a document that would embody general principles. The Citizens for the Constitution argues that the Framers were entitled to include broad statements in the original Constitution because they were starting a new nation. But once created, the Constitution became essentially a legal document, and thus the"addition of purely aspirational statements, designed solely for symbolic effect," would lead every segment of society to try to write its special concerns into the Constitution.

Just because various proposed amendments may require judicial interpretation does not mean that their effect on the Constitution is symbolic and potentially harmful. The Constitution can be both a working document laying out the specific duties of the branches of government and also embody the principles to which the nation has agreed to commit itself.

6. Have the proponents of the proposed amendment attempted to think through and articulate the consequences of their proposal, including the ways in which the amendment would interact with other constitutional provisions?

Guideline Six expresses the concern of Citizens for the Constitution that proposed amendments would have unanticipated and negative consequences for other sections of the Constitution. The group cites several examples, including the impact of campaign finance reform on the First Amendment. According to the commentary accompanying Guideline Six, once the government gets the approval to begin to regulate political speech, there would be no clearly defined limits. The government may be able to "ration core political speech" to serve a variety of legitimate government interests. If the amendment were broadly construed, the group argues, "not only could a legislature act to equalize participation in political debate by limiting spending, it could also curtail expenditures relevant to a particular issue in order to secure greater equality in the discussion of that issue."

The commentary with Guideline Six raises another significant issue. The group believes that the Framers drafted the Constitution "as a unified package." The organization notes that at the Philadelphia Convention, "much energy was directed to considering how the various parts of the Constitution would interact with each other and to the political philosophy expressed by the document as a whole." If that description is accurate, then amendments should be added to the Constitution only when they fit with the document's overall plan. As noted by the group, full discussion would be required to know whether an amendment would shift the balance of powers among the branches of government established by the Framers and developed over the nation's history.

As Laurence Tribe has argued, the Constitution should not be treated as a completely integrated document. However, he contends, it should also not be considered little more than a set of unrelated statements or principles. There must be a balance that permits sections of the Constitution to be interpreted without being overly burdened by their potential impact on other parts of the document. Tribe calls the two extremes "dis-integration" and "hyper-integration." The former means "approaching the Constitution in ways that ignore the salient fact that its parts are linked into a whole — that it is *a Constitution*, and not merely an unconnected bunch of separate clauses and provisions with separate histories, that must be interpreted." When Tribe refers to "hyper-integration," he means "approaching the Constitution in ways that ignore the no less important fact that the whole contains distinct parts — parts that were, in some instances, added at widely separated points in American history; parts that were favored or opposed by greatly disparate groups; parts that reflect quite distinct, and often radically incompatible, premises."

If such "hyper-integration" were to shape constitutional thinking, almost any amendment could be eliminated from consideration on the grounds that it does not fit into the Framers' grand design or conflicts with an existing section of the Constitution. That would greatly restrict — even more so than is already the case — the nation's ability to modify the Constitution to respond to changing values and conditions. On the other hand, the Constitution is not well served if it is viewed as individual parts that have little, if any, relationship to each other. If that theory governed constitutional evolution, then any change — whether policy oriented or constitutional in nature — could be added without regard to its effect on the delicate compromises and balance-of-power arrangements that the Framers agreed to, and which the country has either accepted or modified during its 200-year history.

7. Has there been full and fair debate on the merits of the proposed amendment?

Citizens for the Constitution divided consideration of any constitutional amendment into two phases: the policy question and the operational question. The first concerns whether the idea of the amendment is sound and whether the amendment is the type of change that belongs in the Constitution. The second question asks how well the amendment will work in practice. The group urges Congress and state legislatures to consider both elements before a constitutional amendment is approved. The organization believes that Congress gives too little consideration to the operational phase. The group offers the example of the balanced budget amendment and argues that there must be more discussion of the many implementation questions that will inevitably arise.

The process used to initiate and approve amendments to the Constitution requires an extraordinary level of consensus in Congress and among the states. By its nature, that process almost always leads to extensive debate in Congress — sometimes lasting many years — before sufficient support forms to get past the two-thirds threshold. Then, during the long ratification process — which may last seven years or longer — there will be consideration by every state legislature, with at least some holding hearings and looking carefully at the amendment.

If the process described in this book is followed, opportunity for even more extensive discussion of proposed amendments will exist. The process described here includes three levels of meetings — the congressional district/county gathering, the state convention, and the national preconvention — that are not included in Article V and have never been used before as part of the amendment process. Yet, they provide the opportunity for early and comprehensive discussion of amendments even before their wording is finalized. Then, when petitions written at the preconvention are presented to state legislatures and a campaign is undertaken to persuade state lawmakers to forward them to Congress, additional opportunities for debate over the amendments will be available. Finally, when the petitions are forwarded to Congress and a second convention is called, news coverage of the pending convention and possible amendments would probably exceed any level of debate of previous changes to the Constitution. Because amendments proposed by a constitutional convention would generate more interest and concern than those initiated by Congress, the media and the public would have greater incentive to follow the progress of the amendments as they are ratified or rejected by the states.

The second factor that all but guarantees full discussion of the amendments is that their consideration will coincide with the continued rapid development of Internet technology. Many more people will be able to access the Internet in the near future and they will find it easier to obtain relevant information. People who would not have been able to play a role in debating a proposed amendment in the past will be able to participate in a more meaningful way through the Internet.

Guideline Seven also asks whether there was a "fair" debate of the proposed amendments. Almost the entire commentary accompanying this guideline focuses on the procedures Congress should use in considering amendments to make certain that the process is fair. That is certainly a laudable goal. Whether a second convention process as outlined in this book would be "fair" will depend on what one means by that term. It depends to a large degree on those who are involved in the process of organizing a second convention. If the nation benefits when more citizens are able to meaningfully participate in important decisions — including whether to modify the Constitution — and involving more people adds to the fairness of the process, then the method of amending the Constitution described here would likely satisfy that part of Guideline Seven.

8. Has Congress provided for a nonextendable deadline for ratification by the states so as to ensure that there is a contemporaneous consensus by Congress and the states that the proposed amendment is desirable?

Citizens for the Constitution believes it was wrong for Congress to have extended the deadline for states to consider ratification of the ERA. The group argues in its commentary to Guideline Eight that if there were an extension, it must be approved by a two-thirds vote rather than a majority vote as was the case with the ERA. The group suggests that a seven-year deadline, which has been included in a number of amendments, is probably the appropriate amount of time. All of the amendments proposed in this book include a seven-year deadline. Considering the negative fallout as a result of the extension of the ERA deadline, Congress should only add additional time to the ratification period by a two-thirds vote. However, as noted in Chapter 13, states should not be able to rescind their ratification of an amendment, but may give their approval anytime during the ratification period.

Infrequent amendments

Professor Kathleen M. Sullivan of Stanford Law School wrote an essay that appeared in a 1997 book, *New Federalist Papers: Essays in Defense of the Constitution.* She argues that the Constitution should be "amended sparingly," and only when necessary to change fundamental legal principles. Citizens for the Constitution obviously approved of her thesis for it included her essay in its Web site. Sullivan maintains that inserting into the Constitution policy judgments better left to elected branches of government would injure the constitutional framework that was established for the long term.

She cites three reasons: 1) That it is "a bad idea to politicize the Constitution"; 2) Trying to place policy goals in the Constitution would "nearly always turn out to have bad and unintended structural consequences"; and 3) That "lurking in constitutional amendments" is a "mutiny against the authority of the Supreme Court." She cites, as do many people, the prohibition amendment — relating to the manufacture and distribution of alcohol — and its repeal as an example of why inserting a controversial social policy into the Constitution does not work. She also notes favorably how few times the U.S. Constitution has been amended as compared to those of the states, which she calls "typically voluminous tomes."

Sullivan also believes that using the amendment process to place policy preferences in the Constitution creates problems because it must be done piecemeal — as opposed to the work of the Framers that was considered as a whole document — and will thus almost always have negative and unanticipated results. She cites a term-limits amendment that would likely shift power from Congress to the permanent civil service, where, according to Sullivan, special interest influence would remain untouched. She also identifies a balanced budget amendment — which she believes would shift fiscal power from Congress to the president or the courts — as a proposal that would have unintended consequences. She notes that the Framers entrusted the "power of the purse" to the "most representative branch."

Lastly, she argues that constitutional amendments have the potential to undermine the authority of the Supreme Court. She maintains that the country has lasted two centuries with only 27 amendments because the Court has been given enough "interpretive latitude" to adapt the Constitution to changing times. The Court enjoys respect and legitimacy that would be diminished if amendments to overturn its decisions were enacted. Such an idea, according to Sullivan, creates the illusion that amendments would eliminate judicial discretion. Instead, such amendments would undermine the Court's authority and still require judicial interpretation of issues related to the subject of the amendment.

Professor Sullivan does not have to worry about the Constitution being amended too frequently. It has been almost 30 years since an amendment was ratified that was contemporaneously proposed by Congress. In 1971, the 26th Amendment giving the right to vote to 18-year olds in both state and federal elections was approved. In 1992, the original second amendment related to congressional salaries became the 27th Amendment. Rather than look at constitutional amendments as always looming on the horizon, one could consider the process to be so difficult to use that necessary amendments have not made it through even when substantial support for them exists. During some periods in our history, an individual could live an entire normal life span and never see an amendment to the Constitution being adopted.

It would be a different matter if Congress had not only tried but actually succeeded in constantly changing the Constitution for short-term policy reasons. If that were the case, the Citizens for the Constitution would be in a stronger position to argue, in the words of Professor Sullivan, that "recent Congresses have been stricken with constitutional amendment fever," and in the words of the preface of the group's Web site documents, that "amendment proposals now often seem to be the favored first-step panacea for all societal ills." Considering how few amendments have come close to gaining the two-thirds approval in Congress, such a "sky is falling" warning seems unnecessary. The Citizens for the Constitution identifies on its Web site how far each proposal has made it in Congress by listing whether a hearing has been held in a committee or a vote taken on the floor. The message appears to be that Congress is trying to steal our rights while no one is looking and that the American people should oppose congressional efforts to amend the Constitution.

Some of the amendments that recent Congresses have considered are inappropriate for inclusion in the Constitution and harmful to the long-term interests of the nation. Others, including the balanced budget amendment and the victims' rights amendment, may be of constitutional stature but would be difficult to implement. The flag desecration amendment and an amendment to make it easier for public bodies such as schools to support religious activities obviously challenge First Amendment principles.

It is important, however, to remember that Article V is still a part of the Constitution. It was not just intended to help with the ratification process in the months after the Philadelphia Convention; to be used to approve a few fundamental amendments such as those in the Bill of Rights and those considered after the Civil War; or for the purpose of approving a handful of "structural" amendments such as changing the date when the president takes office, when the new Congress begins, and other matters. The American people are no less entitled to use Article V than their ancestors. The argument that the Constitution would be diminished if frequently amended — especially if those amendments dealt with policy questions rather than fundamental principles — is persuasive. But when the elected branches of government and the courts are unwilling or unable to enact needed reform, the American people have no choice but to try to amend their nation's fundamental charter even if, in the view of some, they are not qualified to do so and their efforts would sully the great document.

Constitutional Defects

Some sections of the Constitution should be amended because the Framers overlooked or did not seriously consider the problems they could cause, or because modern times require a change. An example of the former is the apparent authority of the vice president to preside at his or her own impeachment trial. If Vice President Spiro Agnew — who resigned in 1973 after pleading no contest to income tax evasion and other crimes — had instead refused to leave office, Congress would have had no choice but to proceed with his impeachment.

Michael Stokes Paulsen, a professor of law at the University of Minnesota, wrote that the Constitution does not provide any alternative to the vice president presiding in such a situation. Under Article I, Section 3, Clause 4, the vice president is "President of the Senate." Clause 6 of the same section of Article I specifies that the Senate "shall have the sole power to try all impeachments." Thus the vice president is the presiding officer at the trial in the Senate. Paulsen believes there is no way around this. Nowhere does the Constitution say that the vice president loses the power to preside over the Senate when it considers his or her impeachment. The Senate pro tempore cannot serve that function because Article I, Section 3, Clause 5 states that the pro tempore serves in the *absence* of the vice president, or when the vice president is serving as president of the United States.

Unlike the House, which under the Constitution is given substantial latitude to develop its own rules, the Senate enjoys no such discretion when it comes to its presiding officer. According to Paulsen, if this power were not limited, the Senate would be able to restrict the vice president's rulings on procedural issues that come before the Senate. Nothing in the Constitution suggests that the powers to preside can be restricted because the matter before the Senate is impeachment of the vice president

Paulsen argues that this was not accidental. The Constitution specifically gives the Chief Justice of the United States the responsibility of presiding over an impeachment trial of the president. According to Paulsen, if the Framers intended to disqualify the vice president in the case of his or her own impeachment, they would have done so. Despite Paulsen's argument, the Framers do not appear to have given full consideration to the consequences of such a decision.

One can only imagine a defiant Agnew presiding over his own impeachment, ruling on motions, objections, evidence, and other important matters. He may have argued that because his offenses were not committed as vice president — he was accused of accepting bribes and kickbacks from building contractors while he was county executive of Baltimore County, Maryland, and later governor, and failing to report income — he should not be forced to leave office. Although he probably would have resigned before putting the country through an impeachment trial, it is impossible to know. In the future, if a vice president commits impeachable offenses and refuses to step down, an impeachment trial in the Senate may find the vice president presiding. If during the period of uncertainty the president were to die or become disabled, and the vice president became president, the country would face a political crisis. Had Agnew's criminal behavior in Maryland not been discovered prior to August of 1974, he would have become president when Nixon resigned.

If a Second Convention Is Never Held

No one can predict whether the method for amending the Constitution described in this book will be successfully used. As has been explained in Chapter Four and elsewhere, an extraordinary effort, probably lasting at least several years, would be required to organize the initial meetings and persuade state legislatures to forward petitions to Congress. It is also possible that many years from now — when the Internet and other forms of communication technology have become as easy to use as they are universal, and when frustration with government has reached a crisis level — people will read this book and consider the long road to a second convention to be the only opportunity to change the nature of politics in this country.

In the meantime, if there are no promising efforts to bring about a second convention, individuals and groups can do a few things to demonstrate their dissatisfaction with the current system and to bring about some change. The first suggestion is slow and cumbersome, and has not worked well so far: using available resources — especially the vast potential of the Internet — to support candidates for Congress who will push for campaign finance reform and other measures. But as explained in various sections of this book, even with a numerical majority in Congress supporting modest reforms such as Shays-Meehan or McCain-Feingold, a single senator or two using the threat of a filibuster can prevent the full Senate from voting on the measure. Congress would oppose most of the other amendments discussed in this book as well.

Over time, if a sufficient number of candidates favoring change are elected — and that is always a question — and those newly elected reform-minded members of Congress are able to resist the lure of special interests, there may be modest improvement. But comprehensive reform resulting in an overhaul of the system is not likely anytime during the next decade.

A second suggestion — a national boycott of a company that makes large soft money contributions — is more extreme and controversial, but may be worth the effort if for no other reason than its publicity value. In November 1999, Time Warner, one of the nation's largest corporations, announced that it would no longer make soft money contributions to the national political parties. In recent years, some businesses have resented what they consider to be "shakedowns" by politicians who suggest that if a business or industry wants a place at the table when policy decisions are made, they had to pay up. Time Warner may have adopted the new policy to save money because it assumes it has enough clout to still be a major player without buying access, or because it believes its action will help rein in a system that is out of control.

Building on the example set by Time Warner — and using the facilities of the Internet to spread the word — those who want to reform the system should choose a company that makes substantial soft money contributions to the national political parties and donations to independent groups, and begin a boycott of that company's products. A company that makes products that consumers use and where there are plenty of comparable and competing products to be substituted for those of the boycotted company must be chosen. A national effort — using both traditional media and Internet technology to generate publicity, which is always essential in a boycott — would have to be undertaken to both embarrass the company and, in order to get its attention, potentially affect its bottom line. Few giant corporations will be good citizens just because they are asked. If requested to curtail their contributions to parties, candidates and groups, most businesses would argue that such an action would be the equivalent of unilateral disarmament, and they would be at a disadvantage when compared with labor unions, their competitors, and others who continue to play the game as usual.

Part of the effort to pressure the company to stop making large soft money donations to parties and contributions to independent groups would be public exposure of examples when it appeared to have purchased special favors from elected officials. The press release sent to news organizations and posted on the Internet would need to state that company "A," its officers, and the officers' families — information that is available through the Federal Election Commission's Web site and from public interest organizations — donated X-amount of money to parties, candidates, and independent groups. The next sentence would explain what action Congress took or did not take in a specific policy area related to the interests of that company or industry. It is important, however, that the press release and any public statements be carefully worded so as not to say that "this is what the company or industry got for its money," because members of Congress will almost never admit that contributions had anything to do with their support or opposition to legislation. As the debate on McCain-Feingold demonstrated in the Senate in the fall of 1999, elected officials can disarm those favoring reform by demanding proof of a direct relationship between a contribution and an action taken or vote. Short of a confession by a member of Congress, no one can offer such proof and that encourages those opposed to reform to declare that such evidence does not exist.

Furthermore, the group sponsoring the boycott has to be careful not to accuse the business or industry of committing violations of law by suggesting they "bribed" public officials or "bought" their influence, or that they broke the law some other way. A group that makes such allegations, either in a written press release or orally at a press conference, runs the risk of being the target of a "SLAPP" suit — Strategic Lawsuits Against Public Participation — which are almost always intended to intimidate citizens who speak out on public issues. Rarely are such lawsuits filed so the plaintiff can be compensated for actual harm suffered. SLAPP suits are meant to inflict a heavy financial penalty on citizens who oppose actions taken by governmental or private entities — such as the construction of waste treatment plants or landfills near residential neighborhoods —and to put others on notice that although the First Amendment sounds great, exercising the rights granted by it can sometimes be emotionally draining and expensive.

Any company or industry subject to such a boycott would argue that labor unions also make unlimited contributions to parties, candidates, and organizations working in the background on behalf of candidates. The problem is that labor unions do not make a "product" that can be boycotted the way a business does. Although it is possible for the group advocating reform to urge people to refrain from purchasing products made by workers who belong to a labor union that makes such donations, the public would more easily understand a boycott if it is of a product made by a certain business.

If the boycott spreads and appears to impact the finances of the business — or causes sufficient embarrassment — that company may announce a reduction in soft money and independent contributions.

If that happens, other businesses or industries may follow. It is a long shot, but such a boycott could focus public attention on some of the problems of the campaign finance system.

An Appeal to Media Organizations

Every election night, TV anchors and reporters at stations around the country enthusiastically provide the public with the returns, and often use such expressions as "the voters have decided to give incumbent X another term in office." Even if the elected officials are members of the U.S. House or Senate — but especially if they are seeking reelection to state or local office — the mention of the incumbent on election night may be one of the few times during the incumbent's *entire* term that his or her name is ever spoken by a reporter for the electronic media. Broadcast journalists generally do a poor job of informing the public of the activities of local and statewide officials and even members of Congress, and sometimes barely mention local and federal legislators until it is time to air the election returns.

Many reasons exist for the lack of coverage of officeholders during their terms. First, in many TV markets, high turnover among news personnel is common as they look for jobs in larger stations with better equipment, higher salaries, and more interesting opportunities. A reporter is often at a TV station for only a year or so. Reporters often have neither the time nor much incentive to learn about how local elected and appointed officials are running the governments in the area served by the TV station. Second, not much of what public officials do is visual in nature, and thus stations are hesitant to cover their activities. If a city council meeting has an especially controversial issue on the agenda and a large and animated crowd will attend, TV stations will send a reporter. But for the routine story, where the day-to-day issues of government are decided, broadcast journalists are often not there.

Third, in many small and medium-sized TV markets, where the reporters and producers are likely to be young and inexperienced — either just out of college or with only a year or two in the business — news personnel who know appallingly little about politics and government will be in charge of news content. Without basic knowledge of how government works and little interest in finding out more, the news staff will be unable to provide substantive information to the audience on a regular basis. The reporters and producers may have taken one or more political science courses in college, but that does not mean they are well informed and interested in politics and are keeping up with how government is carrying out the people's business.

There may also be a geographical reason why members of state legislatures and the U.S. House are covered so infrequently by broadcast journalists. U.S. House members, for example, often get little attention because a media market will encompass several congressional districts and people represented by one member of the House may not be interested in the voting record of another from a neighboring district or a different part of the state. The print media generally do a better job of reporting regularly on the votes taken by all members of the state's congressional delegation.

The argument that print and broadcast media are different — that newspapers have more space to provide detailed information about bills pending before legislatures and how hometown representatives vote on them — only goes so far. If the nature of broadcasting itself were the limitation — that there is only a fixed amount of time to present news — then more TV stations would include detailed political information in their Web sites. Except when there is a scandal, broadcast journalists often seem content to cover staged events involving elected officials —ground-breaking and ribbon-cutting ceremonies — rather than report on their voting records and how they are fulfilling their responsibilities.

All media organizations — but especially broadcasters because most people say that TV is their primary source of news — owe it to their audience to do a better job of covering politics and government, and not just carry the results of the elections. The public should know much more than it does about how elected officials vote on important and mundane matters, and how appointed officials carry out the daily work of government. Those stories are not easy to cover, are often not very visual, and may sometimes bore the audience. But those reports can often be made compelling or interesting by journalists who are committed to showing viewers why they should care and pay attention.

To some extent at the presidential level and in races for the U.S. Senate, an effort on the part of media organizations to concentrate less on the "horse race" during the campaign, and more on the issues raised by the candidates, has been successful. But at the state and local level, relatively little information about the issues in a race, and even less about the voting record of incumbents, is available.

In short, media organizations need to make the public care more about politics and government. The response may be that news organizations give people what they want, and for the most part, they do not want to hear much about politicians unless there is a salacious scandal or a grotesque misuse of public money. In an ideal world, media organizations would provide more and better information about officials during their terms and not just mention them at election time; the public would be more interested in politics and would elect people who better represent their views; elected officials would make certain that the bureaucracy carried out the wishes of the people and did so in the most efficient manner; and the public, aware of how things are going, would be to able to make rational judgments about whether the same leaders should be returned to office.

Do People Care Enough?

Even if media organizations make a concerted effort to better inform the public and get them more interested in politics, there may still be declining voter turnout, low levels of political information, and increased cynicism about elected officials. In such a situation, it is unlikely that the Internet — even with every person in the country who is interested in politics exchanging e-mail, and visiting and creating Web sites and newsgroups — will overcome widespread discouragement about politics. It may take a major disruption to the political system, such as an economic crisis in the stock market or some other calamity, before people think more seriously about who represents them and how well they do it.

During times of prosperity, citizens have less incentive to undertake the effort required to arrange a second constitutional convention. But the good times are not going to last indefinitely. As the new century begins, the financial health of the nation cannot hide serious problems in our political system.

The American people have an opportunity through the method described in this book to try to organize a second convention. They should not feel self-conscious about doing so, as if they are unworthy of debating what is wrong with the Constitution, proposing amendments, and being involved in the effort to change the great document. They must learn to use the Internet and other new technology to communicate with their fellow citizens about how to improve the Constitution. They must be willing to commit themselves to a process that will be tremendously challenging. But their efforts will serve as an enduring reminder that the Constitution belongs not to the Framers who wrote it, or the elected officials who serve under it, but to the people.

Notes

Introduction

1 Probably at no: Democratic presidential candidate and former Senator Bill Bradley was quoted on the campaign trail as saying, "The level of cynicism about money and politics has never been higher." David M. Shribman, "Campaign 2000: Asleep At the Polls," *The Boston Globe* (January 16, 2000), p. C1. Almost three-quarters of the nation's population (71 percent) said in 1996 that they believed "government is run by a few big interests looking out for themselves," rather than "for the benefit of all the people." Adam Clymer, "College Students Not Drawn to Voting or Politics, Poll Shows," *New York Times* (January 12, 2000), p. A14. See also, Garry Wills, *A Necessary Evil: A History of American Distrust of Government* (New York: Simon & Schuster, 1999).

1 Even with the: Despite the nation's robust economy in 1998, 58 percent of respondents told the Roper Survey that it had been a "bad year" for national politics, while 11 percent said it was mixed. Only 20 percent said it had been a good year. Roper Center (December 13, 1998).

1 Voter turnout continues: Only 49 percent of voting-age Americans voted in 1996, the first time a majority did not vote in a presidential election since 1924. Only 36 percent voted in 1998. More than half the children in the United States live in households where neither parent votes. Adam Clymer, "Testing Politics: Does It Work? Should It Be Fixed?" *New York Times* (January 2, 2000), p. 1.

1 During the 1996: The scandals related to the 1996 campaign are discussed at length in Chapter One.

1 When he lied: See generally, Richard A. Posner, *An Affair of State: The Investigation, Impeachment, and Trial of President Clinton* (Cambridge, MA: Harvard University Press, 1999); and Michael Isikoff, *Uncovering Clinton: A Reporter's Story* (New York: Crown Publishers, 1999).

1 While the president: After 19 months of investigating, an independent counsel announced in October 1999, that no indictments would be sought in the case involving Interior Secretary Bruce Babbitt. The investigation centered on whether Babbitt lied in congressional testimony in 1997 about an Interior Department decision to deny an application by three Indian tribes to operate a casino in Wisconsin. David Johnston, "Prosecutor Clears Babbitt in Casino Inquiry," *New York Times* (October 14, 1999), p. A25; and David Johnston, "For Babbitt, a Wearying Exoneration," *New York Times* (October 15, 1999), p. A18. See also, "The Bruce Babbitt Case," (editorial) *New York Times* (August 13, 1999), p. A18. For a description of the independent counsel's investigation of Labor Secretary Alexis Herman, see John M. Broder, "Amid Political Cynicism, Standing Steadfast in Her Faith," *New York Times* (September 6, 1999), p. A8.

1 **At the same:** See Chapter One for a discussion of the president's friends and associates who faced criminal charges over the way they handled campaign money, and for other transgressions. In early 2000, potentially serious allegations arose about how criminal cases involving supporters of President Clinton were assigned by the chief judge of the U.S. Court of Appeals for the District of Columbia. Judge Norma Holloway Johnson allegedly assigned the six criminal cases on appeal to judges appointed by President Clinton instead of using the computer system normally used for randomly assigning cases. The Judicial Council, which oversees the conduct of federal judges, ordered an investigation. The Associated Press first reported the story in the summer of 1999 regarding the appeal of Webster Hubbell and presidential friend Charlie Trie. Pete Yost, "Complaint over judges resurfaces," (Associated Press) *Lexington (KY) Herald-Leader* (February 10, 2000), p. A15.

2 **In 2000, as:** Robin Toner, "Willing Contenders at a Premium In Fierce Fight to Rule Congress," *New York Times* (January 3, 2000), p. A1.

2 **Perhaps no more:** Ibid.

2 **No one should:** Curtis Gans, director of the Committee for the Study of the American Electorate, a Washington, D.C.-based research group, said that "interest in politics and the desire to participate are at an all-time low." Jeff Barker, "Supervoters Roar, Rest of People Whisper; Luring Citizens To Polls Goal For New Century," *The Arizona Republic* (September 11, 1999), p. A1. In November 1999, the Roper Center reported the results of a survey in which respondents were asked, "How interested are you in following news and information about politics and public policy?" Seventy-four percent said they were somewhat interested or not very interested. Only 26 percent said they were very interested. David M. Shribman, "Campaign 2000: Asleep At the Polls."

2 **Despite laws that:** The decline in turnout in the 1998 election came even though eight million more Americans were eligible to vote and four million more were registered, as compared with 1994's midterm election. Richard L. Berke, "The 1998 Elections: Democrats' Gains Dispel Notion That G.O.P. Benefits From Low Turnout," *New York Times* (November 6, 1998), p. A28.

2 **The future looks:** Richard L. Berke, "The 1998 Campaign: G.O.P. Given Ethics Edge in Poll, but Democrats Rate Higher on 3 Issues," *New York Times* (October 30, 1998), p. A30; Robert P. Sigman, "Kansans Who Hardly Vote," *Kansas City Star* (October 21, 1999), p. B7; and Adam Clymer, "College Students Not Drawn to Voting or Politics, Poll Shows," *New York Times* (January 12, 2000), p. A14. A Harvard poll conducted in January 2000 — just before the Iowa presidential caucuses and New Hampshire primary — showed that fewer than 10 percent of young people nationwide said they were paying any attention to politics. Shribman, "Campaign 2000: Asleep At the Polls."

2 **Without having learned:** In a November 1999, survey conducted by the Panetta Institute, headed by former White House chief of staff Leon Panetta, only 25 percent of college students said they would consider spending some time working

in politics. Many more students said they were interested in other types of volunteer activities. Adam Clymer, "College Students Not Drawn to Voting or Politics, Poll Shows." For an insightful discussion of why young people are generally uninterested in politics, see Ted Halstead, "A Politics For Generation X," *The Atlantic Monthly* (August, 1999), pp. 33–42.

2 The 2000 presidential: Presidential candidates who accept federal money for their campaigns must abide by limits on how much they can spend in each state based on population. Vice President Al Gore and Senator John McCain (R-AZ) said they would drastically overhaul campaign finance laws if elected president. However, in the New Hampshire primary and Iowa caucuses, both of their campaigns far exceeded the spending limits for those states. They used what the *New York Times* described as "loopholes, exemptions and accounting gimmickry" to do it. Both candidates said that their actions were legal. John M. Broder, "Stepping Through Loopholes in Spending Caps," *New York Times* (January 19, 2000), p. A17.

2 Months before the: By the end of October of 1999, Republican presidential candidates Elizabeth Dole, former Tennessee governor Lamar Alexander, and Rep. John Kasich (R-OH) had already dropped out of the race, citing the inability to raise enough money. Katharine Q. Seelye, "Low on Cash, Dole Withdraws From G.O.P. Race," *New York Times* (October 21, 1999), p. A1. See also, Richard L. Berke, "Wild Ride and a Wild Card In a Busy Campaign Week," *New York Times* (October 4, 1999), p. A22. Other experienced politicians declined to run for office because of the cost of campaigning. In September 1999, New Jersey Governor Christine Whitman said she would not seek the Senate seat being vacated by Democratic Senator Frank Lautenberg in 2000. She cited the amount of money that would need to be raised and how much time it would take to do it. Paul Zielbauer, "Citing Money, Whitman Decides She Won't Run for U.S. Senate," *New York Times* (September 8, 1999), p. A1.

3 Many Americans have: In a thoughtful commentary that discusses a Northwestern University study explaining why many people do not vote, syndicated columnist Clarence Page made this observation: "If you think your vote doesn't make a difference, you are kidding yourself. The lower the turnout, the easier it is for organized parties and other special interests to control the outcome." Clarence Page, "Apathy not only reason Americans aren't voting," *Lexington (KY) Herald-Leader* (January 13, 2000), p. A11. See also, Brian O'Connell, *Civil Society: The Underpinnings of American Democracy* (Hanover, MA: University Press of New England, 1999); Stephen L. Elkin and Karol Edward Solton, eds., *Citizen Competence and Democratic Institutions* (University Park, PA: Penn State University Press, 1999); Jedediah Purdy, *For Common Things: Irony, Trust, and Commitment in America Today* (New York: Alfred A. Knopf, 1999); Nat Hentoff, *Living the Bill of Rights: How to Be an Authentic American* (New York: HarperCollins, 1998); and Michael Schudson, *The Good Citizen: A History of American Civic Life* (New York: Free Press, 1998).

3 The way campaigns: In November of 1999, a nationwide Roper survey reported that 78 percent of respondents favored changing the campaign finance system to reduce how much money political parties can spend on candidates. Roper Center at University of Connecticut; Public Opinion Online (November 21, 1999). Another nationwide Roper survey conducted a few days earlier reported that only 10 percent of respondents thought the campaign finance system was essentially good, while 81 percent said it needed overhauling or improvements. Ibid. (November 18, 1999). The Roper Center reported in January 2000, that 61 percent in a nationwide survey believed that contributors to congressional campaigns get more than their money back in terms of favors and special interest legislation. Roper Center (January 14, 2000).

3 Contributors say they: For an example of how successful contributors and lobbyists can be in persuading Congress to enact their agenda, see Robert Pear, "Health Industry Sees Wish List Made Into Law," *New York Times* (December 6, 1999), p. A1.

4 With money pouring: Adam Clymer, "Standing Still on Campaign Finance," *New York Times* (October 9, 1999), p. A8. Many House members represent "safe" districts that have been drawn by state legislatures to favor one party, and they therefore rarely face a serious challenge in the general election. Because few incumbents ever face serious challenges in the primary, they are virtually assured of reelection.

4 Despite the loathing: Those members of Congress who care that citizens are fed up with the system promise periodically to try to change the way money is raised and spent in campaigns, but the votes are not there. In October 1999, the Senate again killed campaign finance reform. Alison Mitchell, "Vote on Campaign Finances is Blocked by Senate G.O.P. for Fourth Year in a Row," *New York Times* (October 20, 1999), p. A1. See also, "Campaign Reform's Moment," (editorial) *New York Times* (September 13, 1999), p. A22.

A majority of senators may have voted for a version of Shays-Meehan in the fall of 1999 — a bill approved by the House in September that would have taken modest steps toward reform — if they had the chance. The Senate sponsors, John McCain (R-AZ) and Russ Feingold (D-WI), had already agreed to remove from the Senate version the section of Shays-Meehan dealing with independent expenditures. The only restriction would have been on soft money contributions to political parties, a small first step. But because of a threatened filibuster by Senator Mitch McConnell (R-KY), who said he was defending freedom of speech, 60 votes were required to end debate. Reform proponents could get no more than 53.

When McCain dared to support campaign finance reform and denounce the system on the floor of the Senate, he was subjected to unusually harsh criticism from his Republican colleagues who do not want to see the system changed. See Eric Schmitt, "Campaign Bill Fuels Attack On McCain," *New York Times* (September 20, 1999), p. A12; "Bashing John McCain," (editorial) *New York Times* (September 23, 1999), p. A26; and Alison Mitchell, "Republicans Pillory McCain in Debate Over Soft Money," *New York Times* (October 15, 1999), p. A22.

4 As long as: Special interests have two ways of helping those they want to see in office. They give money to groups that are supposedly "independent" of the candidate. These groups, with names suggesting civic virtue, run advertisements criticizing, and often distorting, the record and character of the favored candidate's opponent. Such groups rarely have to defend the accuracy or fairness of their political commercials. When the candidate who benefits from the ads is asked about them, the response is that the group is independent of the campaign, as required by law, and the candidate has no control over their actions.

The other way huge sums are raised and spent on campaigns is through "soft money" contributions to the political parties. The parties claim the money is used for "party building" activities, and some of that is true. But millions of dollars are spent to support the party's candidates and attack their opponents. For both independent expenditures and soft money, there are no limits on the amount that can be raised and spent. The only rule, which is almost no impediment, is that independent groups or parties spending soft money cannot specifically say vote for or against candidate "X."

4 That is because: *Buckley v. Valeo*, 424 U.S. 1 (1976). The case and its consequences are discussed in Chapter Seven.

4 Even if idealistic: See Chapter One for a discussion of members of the U.S. House who were elected in 1994 in part because of their promise to serve only a fixed number of terms, but who have now decided to run for reelection; and a discussion of House freshmen who promised to support campaign finance reform when they were elected that year, but were quickly informed by senior members that if they pressed the issue, they would see few, if any, of their bills enacted.

5 The Constitution has: The Constitution was ratified in 1788 when New Hampshire became the ninth state to give its approval. Thus, the age of the Constitution is calculated here from 1788 to 2000.

5 As they did: These and related issues are discussed in Chapters Two and Three.

5 They wanted to: The Constitution establishes a two-stage process: the proposal of amendments and ratification by the states. Amendments have always been initiated by Congress with two-thirds approval in each house, then ratification by three-fourths (38) of state legislatures or state conventions. Under Article V, Congress decides which ratification method is to be used but has chosen state conventions on only one occasion, for the 21st Amendment to repeal prohibition. For that amendment, Congress required conventions in each state because it wanted to bypass conservative legislatures that might resist efforts to legalize the manufacture and distribution of alcohol.

The alternative method by which the Constitution can be changed, that is also provided for in Article V, has never been used. It requires Congress to call a constitutional convention if petitions are received from two-thirds (34) of state legislatures.

6 This book proposes: The use of the Internet in politics has come of age in the 1990s, and will be an important part of the 2000 presidential election and many campaigns for Congress and statewide office. The major presidential candidates all had elaborate Web sites through which they communicated with potential voters and raised money. Tina Kelley, "Candidate on the Stump Is Surely on the Web," *New York Times* (October 19, 1999), p. A1. By mid-October of 1999, Democratic presidential candidate Bill Bradley had raised almost $800,000 through his Internet site, four percent of his total contributions. Senator John McCain had raised $200,000 through his site as of September. Ibid., p. A15. By early February 2000, McCain had surged ahead, raising more than $2.5 million online since the start of the campaign, while Bradley had raised more than $1.6 million through the Internet, and Vice President Al Gore had raised about $1.1 million. Republican candidate George Bush had only raised $340,000 online, although he had taken in more than $68 million overall. "Bush in last place in Web fund raising," *Lexington (KY) Herald-Leader* (February 5, 2000), p. A3.

Other candidates, such as Republican Steve Forbes, had found innovative ways to use the Internet. His Web site helped find "e-precinct captains" who then used e-mail to recruit 10 supporters each who would travel to Ames, Iowa, to vote in that state's September straw poll where Forbes finished a respectable second. Howard Fineman, "Pressing the Flesh Online," *Newsweek* (September 20, 1999), p. 50. The Internet already helped some candidates win office. Minnesota Governor Jesse Ventura, who was elected in 1998 on the Reform Party ticket, acquired two-thirds of his contributions through his Web site. One of his aides said he could not have been elected without the site and an e-mail campaign. Ibid., pp. 50–51.

6 The petitions will: The petitions are discussed in detail in Chapter Four.

7 People who are: Individuals in various countries have tried to use the Internet to facilitate discussion of sensitive issues in a way that would not be permitted in traditional mass media. For efforts in China to use new communication technology, see Elisabeth Rosenthal, "Web Sites Bloom in China, and Are Weeded," *New York Times* (December 23, 1999), p. A1.

Chapter 1: Why A Second Constitutional Convention Is Needed

11 In the spring: Rhode Island was the only state that did not send a delegation to the Convention. For one of the best accounts of the Framers and the Constitutional Convention, see Clinton Rossiter: *1787: The Grand Convention* (New York: W.W. Norton & Co., 1987, originally published in 1966). For an explanation of why Rhode Island refused to send a delegation to the Convention and the view that its failure to participate was helpful to the delegates in Philadelphia, see Rossiter, pp. 87–89. Rossiter saw the Framers as mostly virtuous and visionary. His interpretation of the events of the summer of 1787 is at odds with other historians who believe the Framers created a Constitution that not only protected the interests of the affluent, but also showed a distrust of the American people.

11 The Framers were: James Wilson, a delegate from Pennsylvania whose brilliant mind and elegant prose contributed in many ways to the debate during the Convention and the final language of the Constitution, should also be listed among the most important members of the Convention. Unfortunately, Wilson is appreciated today mostly by historians; he is almost unknown to the American people. For a Web site that provides pictures and biographical information about the Framers, see *The Founding Fathers: A Brief Overview*, Founding Fathers Page, National Archives and Records Administration, <http://www.nara.gov/exhall/ charters/constitution/overview.html>. Thomas Jefferson and John Adams were not at the Convention. Jefferson was in Paris and Adams was in London representing the new nation's interests.

11 **On the best:** Christopher Collier and James Lincoln Collier, *Decision in Philadelphia: The Constitutional Convention of 1787* (New York: Random House, 1986), pp. 14–15.

12 **There were never:** *A More Perfect Union: The Creation of the U.S. Constitution*, Constitution Page, National Archives and Records Administration, <http://www. nara.gov/exhall/charters/constitution/conhist.html>.

12 **Making copies of:** The fact that presses were available to make printed copies of the completed Constitution probably had a significant positive effect on ratification. Newspapers throughout the country published the text of the Constitution, either all at once or in parts over several editions of the paper, and the public had a chance to read it before deciding whether to support or oppose the new Constitution in ratifying conventions. Because the Convention had kept its proceedings secret, there was much suspicion in the country that the Framers were creating a constitution that would favor affluent and propertied interests over the rights of ordinary citizens. That newspapers carried copies gave the public the chance to see the document and openly debate its merits and shortcomings. For a discussion of the effect that printing had on acceptance of the Constitution, see Daniel J. Boorstin, *Printing and the Constitution*, in *Constitution of the United States: Published for the Bicentennial of Its Adoption* (San Francisco: Arion Press, 1987).

12 **There is substantial:** See Charles Warren, *The Making of the Constitution* (1937), in Leonard W. Levy, ed., *Essays on the Making of the Constitution* (New York: Oxford University Press, 1987), pp. 33–43. For a discussion of whether the Constitutional Convention of 1787 was a "runaway" convention because it did not confine itself to amending the Articles of Confederation, see Paul J. Weber and Barbara A. Perry, *Unfounded Fears: Myths and Realities of a Constitutional Convention* (Westport, CT: Greenwood Press, 1989), pp. 13–30. See also, John R. Vile, *Contemporary Questions Surrounding the Constitutional Amending Process* (Westport, CT: Praeger, 1993), pp. 85, 102–103. For a look at how experience with the Articles of Confederation prepared the Framers for their work in Philadelphia, see Andrew C. McLaughlin, *A Constitutional History of the United States* (1935), in Levy, pp. 44–60.

12 **There had been:** Those states were Virginia, Pennsylvania, Delaware, New Jersey, and New York. The most important accomplishment of this brief meeting was the adoption of a report calling on the legislatures of the five states, and the others that had not sent representatives, to appoint delegates to "meet at Philadelphia on the second Monday in May next" to "devise . . . provisions as shall appear to them

necessary to render the constitution of the federal government adequate to the exigencies of the Union." Those provisions were to be submitted to the Congress and then, before they could be adopted, approved by the legislatures in every state. When Congress agreed to call the Philadelphia Convention on February 21, 1787, it used much of the language that James Madison and Alexander Hamilton had included in the Annapolis report. Rossiter, pp. 54–55.

13 One historian noted: Lance Banning, *The Sacred Fire of Liberty: James Madison and the Founding of the Federal Republic* (Ithaca: Cornell University Press, 1995), p. 113.

13 As presented by: Rossiter, p. 362.

13 He never claimed: Banning, p. 114.

14 Massachusetts' Elbridge Gerry: The Gerry, Morris, and Hamilton quotes are in Saul Padover (3d. ed. revised by Jacob W. Landynski), *The Living U.S. Constitution* (New York: Meridian, 1995), pp. 9–10. Charles Beard, among the best-known of the Progressive Era scholars who challenged conventional wisdom about the motives of the Framers, argued in a famous 1913 book that those who created the Constitution were much less concerned with establishing a democratic society than protecting their own economic interests. See Charles Beard, *An Economic Interpretation of the Constitution of the United States* (1913) in Levy, pp. 3–32. Beard's interpretation of the Convention has often been misunderstood because, according to Levy, subtle arguments that the Framers were not solely motivated by personal interest are overlooked in *An Economic Interpretation*, and because of neglect of Beard's lesser-known books.

14 Despite Morris's condescending: Rossiter, p. 199. For the Framers' discussion of whether the people should directly elect the president, see Max Farrand, editor, *The Records of the Federal Convention of 1787*, Vol. II. (Yale University Press, 1911), pp. 29–32. Only Pennsylvania supported Morris's proposal for direct election of the president.

14 Others, like George: *A More Perfect Union: The Creation of the U.S. Constitution*, Constitution Page, National Archives and Records Administration, <http://www.nara.gov/exhall/charters/constitution/conhist.html>. For a detailed statement by Mason outlining his objections to the Constitution, see Farrand, Vol. II, pp. 637–640, which is adapted from K.M. Rowland, *The Life of George Mason*, Vol. II, pp. 387–390.

14 They created a: For a critical look at whether the Framers were too concerned about dispersing power and thus created a system of government that lacks sufficient authority and direction, see Daniel Lazare, *The Frozen Republic: How The Constitution Is Paralyzing Democracy* (New York: Harcourt Brace & Co., 1996). See also, Thomas G. West, *Vindicating the Founders: Race, Sex, Class, and Justice in the Origins of America* (Lanham, MD: Rowman and Littlefield, 1997).

16 With a six-year: Some of the Framers, including Madison, were worried that the House of Representatives would act irresponsibly. As the only branch of government directly elected by the people, the lower house of Congress may show, in Madison's words, "the want" of "steadiness" and "wisdom." Banning, p. 134.

16 If the right: House Speaker Newt Gingrich spent $5 million in 1996 to keep his seat in suburban Atlanta, making it the most expensive House reelection campaign in the country. In the 1996 election, through personal appearances and the use of his name and image, Gingrich raised more than $100 million for the Republican Party. Leslie Wayne, "Gingrich in '98: Money Gushing Both In and Out," *New York Times* (August 12, 1997), p. A1.

17 The procedures the: Yale law scholar Akhil Reed Amar and co-author Alan Hirsch argue that because the Framers did not state in Article V that it provides the *exclusive* method of amending the Constitution, the American people — who as the sovereign retain the authority to alter their founding document — can change the Constitution through a national "referendum." The authors' thesis is creative but unrealistic. Akhil Reed Amar and Alan Hirsch, *For the People: What the Constitution Really Says About Your Rights* (The Free Press, 1998), pp. 3–33.

17 The Framers, exhausted: C. Herman Pritchett, *The American Constitution* (New York: McGraw-Hill Book Co., 1977), pp. 23–24. See also, Jack C. Rakove, *Original Meanings: Politics and Ideas in the Making of the Constitution* (New York: Alfred A. Knopf, 1996), pp. 91–92; and David E. Kyvig, *Explicit and Authentic Acts: Amending the U.S. Constitution, 1776–1995* (Lawrence: University Press of Kansas, 1996), pp. 42–86.

17 If there had: For a discussion of the ratifying efforts in each state, see Rakove, pp. 94–160; and Rossiter, pp. 274–298.

18 In July 1997: Richard L. Berke, "Hard of Hearing: A Scandal Falls Victim to Its Own Irrelevance," *New York Times* (July 13, 1997), Section 4, p. 1. In response to the question, "How likely do you think it is that President Clinton or Congress will change the way political campaigns are financed?" The responses were: Very likely, 8 percent; Fairly likely, 23 percent; Not too likely, 36 percent; Not likely at all, 31 percent; No opinion, 3 percent. Dan Balz and Ceci Connolly, "Voters Feeling Removed From Issues in Capital; Economic Contentment Gives Clinton a Boost," *The Washington Post* (July 10, 1997), p. A1.

18 the accusation that: Kathleen Willey told her story to a national audience on "60 Minutes" on March 15, 1998. For a detailed account and excerpts of her interview, see John M. Broder, "White House Volunteer, on TV, Details Encounter With President," *New York Times* (March 16, 1998), p. A1.

18 close friends and: For a list of those indicted or convicted in independent counsel Kenneth Starr's investigation, see "The Cast: A List Perhaps Most Noted for Those Who Failed to Make It," *New York Times* (May 6, 1998), p. A18.

18 cabinet members being: Former Secretary of Housing and Urban Development Henry Cisneros was indicted on 18 counts by a federal grand jury for lying in his confirmation proceedings to federal agents and Congress about payments he made to his longtime mistress. Stephen Labaton, "Ex-Housing Secretary Cisneros

Charged in 18-Count Indictment," *New York Times* (December 12, 1997), p. A1. In February 1997, Attorney General Janet Reno recommended the appointment of a special counsel to investigate Interior Secretary Bruce Babbitt. He was suspected of lying to Congress about whether the decision to reject a gambling casino on an Indian reservation was related to a large campaign contribution from a nearby reservation that had an existing casino and did not want competition. David Johnston, "Reno Asks Judges to Select Counsel in Babbitt Inquiry," *New York Times* (February 12, 1998), p. A1. Babbitt defended his actions before a House committee looking at campaign finance. Eric Schmitt, "Hostile Time For Babbitt At Hearing," *New York Times* (January 30, 1998), p. A10. The Attorney General requested an independent counsel in May 1998, for Labor Secretary Alexis Herman. She was suspected of being involved in a plan involving kickbacks and illegal campaign contributions when she worked as a presidential aide in the White House. David Johnston, "Reno Seeks Independent Counsel For Investigation of Labor Chief," *New York Times* (May 12, 1998), p. A1. In September 1997, former Secretary of Agriculture Mike Espy pleaded not guilty to charges that he accepted gifts from agricultural interests he was responsible for regulating in violation of federal law. Neil A. Lewis, "Ex-Agriculture Chief Pleads Not Guilty to Taking Gifts," *New York Times* (September 11, 1997), p. A12.

18 In February 1998: Terry M. Neal, "In Public Support for Clinton, An Apparent Contradiction; Many Voters Could Accept Adultery, but Not Lying About It," *The Washington Post* (February 24, 1998), p. A4.

18 Perhaps that ambivalence: Kathleen Hall Jamieson, "Facing Up to It: What Those Polls Are Telling Us," *The Washington Post* (March 22, 1998), p. C1. The *New York Times*/CBS poll was released on February 23, 1998.

19 In February 1998: Ibid. The Harris poll was published on February 25, 1998.

19 Although the American: Ibid. The CNN poll was broadcast on March 16, 1998.

19 When Washington Post: Balz and Connolly, "Voters Feeling Removed From Issues in Capital." The congressional districts were in Wisconsin, Missouri, and Washington. The quote is from Dennis Wight, an electrical engineer who lives in the Seattle suburbs. See generally, Haynes Johnson and David S. Broder, *The System: The American Way of Politics at the Breaking Point* (Boston: Little, Brown and Company, 1997); and E.J. Dionne, Jr., *Why Americans Hate Politics* (New York: Simon and Schuster, 1991).

20 Boren told the: Carey Goldberg, "Testing of a President: The Reaction; Nation Through a Looking Glass, Smudges, Cracks, Distortions and All," *New York Times* (February 3, 1998), p. A20.

20 And to me: Boren's characterization of his students' cynicism about government may be contradicted by the findings of a *New York Times*/CBS News poll that asked teenagers from the ages of 13–17 how they felt about various issues. Fifty percent of the teenagers said they trusted government, while only 26 percent of adults agreed with that statement a few months earlier. Laurie Goodstein,

"Teen-age Poll Finds a Turn to the Traditional," *New York Times* (April 30, 1998), p. A20.

21 But there has: An exit poll conducted during the 1998 congressional elections asked voters if they approved or disapproved of the way Congress is handling its job. Fifty-five percent said they disapproved, while 41 percent approved. "What Voters Said About..." *New York Times* (November 4, 1998), p. B1.

21 In April 1997: Adam Clymer, "Gingrich Will Get A Loan From Dole To Pay House Fine," *New York Times* (April 18, 1997), p. A1.

21 When there was: Sam Howe Verhovek, "To Jim Wright, What Goes Around ..." *New York Times* (January 5, 1997), Section 1, p. 12.

21 Gingrich's predecessor as: Gingrich had relentlessly pursued charges against Wright when the Texan accepted royalties from a book that some political associates bought in the thousands, and also over some business dealings. Wright insisted in 1989 when he resigned and years later that he had done nothing wrong. Ibid., p. 12.

21 In March 1998: Lizette Alvarez, "Lawmaker Votes in Congress After Conviction for a Crime," *New York Times* (March 11, 1998), p. A12.

22 The prosecutors themselves: Francis X. Clines, "Confined by Ankle Bracelet, In a Tight Race for Congress," *New York Times* (April 8, 1998), p. A1.

22 Although his campaign: Ibid.

22 In a four-person: Todd S. Purdum, "Primaries '98: The Overview," *New York Times* (June 4, 1998), p. A1.

23 It is becoming: See generally, Charles Lewis, *The Buying of the Congress: How Special Interests Have Stolen Your Right to Life, Liberty, and the Pursuit of Happiness* (New York: Avon Books, 1998); Larry J. Sabato and Glenn R. Simpson, *Dirty Little Secrets: The Persistence of Corruption in American Politics* (New York: Times Books, 1996); and Ralph Nader and Wesley J. Smith, *No Contest: Corporate Lawyers and the Perversion of Justice in America* (New York: Random House, 1996).

23 Beginning with the: For the seminal work on the Progressive Era, see Richard Hofstadter, *The Age of Reform* (New York: Vintage Books, 1955). See also, Grant McConnell, *Private Power and American Democracy* (New York: Vintage Books, 1966), pp. 30–50. For an excellent summary of the Progressive Era, see Page Smith, *America Enters The World: A People's History of the Progressive Era and World War I*, Vol. VII (New York: McGraw-Hill, 1985).

24 In recent years: For a thoughtful and disturbing commentary on what he calls the "grotesque" amounts of money pouring into the political system, see Richard N. Goodwin (assistant special counsel to President Kennedy and a special assistant to President Johnson), "The selling of the government," *Lexington (KY) Herald-Leader* (Los Angeles Times) (February 3, 1997), p. A9. See also, Suzanne Garment (resident scholar at the American Enterprise Institute), "Image and money: Politicians' obsession with appearances stoke the fire," *Lexington (KY) Herald-Leader* (Los Angeles Times) (March 18, 1997), p. 11. Former Republican representative and presidential candidate John Anderson has called on the parties to institute such reforms as limiting PAC contributions and spending in primaries. John B. Anderson, "A Quick Fix on Campaign Reform," *New York Times* (February 8, 1997), p. 17. James Glassman, a financial affairs reporter for the *Washington Post*, argued that no campaign finance reform will improve the electoral system. James K. Glassman, "Money will flow as long as government is all-powerful," *Lexington (KY) Herald Leader* (The Washington Post) (March 21, 1997), p. A11. Kevin Phillips, a respected conservative commentator, believes that in today's climate, there will be no reform such as term limits, serious election finance reform, and a "full-force" crackdown on lobbies and lobbyists. Kevin Phillips, "At the 'venal center,' money drives all politics," *Lexington (KY) Herald-Leader* (Los Angeles Times) (March 3, 1997), p. A9.

24 When people see: For an eloquent defense of the system whereby those making contributions are given access to elected officials, see Nelson Polsby, "Money Gains Access. So What?" *New York Times* (August 13, 1997), p. A19.

24 "Hard money donations: The 1974 amendments (Federal Election Campaign Act Amendments of 1974) are found at 88. Stat. 1263; The Election Campaign Act of 1971 is found at 86 Stat. 3.

25 Two years later: 424 U.S. 1 (1976). In April 1998, the U.S. Court of Appeals for the Sixth Circuit held unconstitutional a Cincinnati law limiting how much candidates could spend to get elected to the city council. It was the first time a federal court considered the issue since *Buckley*. The city ordinance limited spending on council races to $140,000. Citing *Buckley*, the court concluded that spending limits violated the First Amendment. *Kruse v. City of Cincinnati*, 142 F.3d 907 (6th Cir. 1998). See also, Bill Dedman, "Limits on Campaign Spending Are Invalid, Appeals Court Says," *New York Times* (April 28, 1998), p. A14.

25 The Court concluded: 424 U.S. at 20–21.

25 But the Court: 424 U.S. at 19.

25 As a result: See generally, Rodney M. Smolla, *Free Speech In An Open Society* (New York: Alfred A. Knopf, 1992), pp. 221–227.

25 Wealthy individuals have: Just spending millions of dollars on television advertising does not necessarily guarantee that the wealthy candidate will get elected. In the 1998 California gubernatorial primary, businessman Al Checchi spent $40 million of his own money, yet finished well behind the successful candidate, Lt. Governor Gray Davis. Also losing the race was Representative Jane Harmon, who spent $16 million of her family fortune on the race. Purdum, "Primaries '98: The Overview." See also, Todd S. Purdum, "Really Big Money Shouts in a California Contest," *New York Times* (May 20, 1998), p. A1; and Richard L. Berke, "Money and Polls Takes Center Stage in California Race," *New York Times* (June 1, 1998), p. A1.

25 Individuals contributing hard: Gary C. Jacobson, *The Politics of Congressional Elections* (New York: Longman, 1997), p. 80 n. 6.

26 According to Common: Amy Borrus and Mary Beth Regan, "The Backlash Against Soft Money," *Business Week* (March 31, 1997), p. 34.

26 Common cause reported: Don Van Natta Jr., "Republicans' Goal Is $1 Million Each From Top Donors," *New York Times* (August 9, 1999), p. A1.

26 The Republican and: Ibid.

26 In a survey: Borrus and Regan, "The Backlash Against Soft Money."

26 As one Republican: Ibid.

27 The *New York*: "Paying for One Big Party," *New York Times* (April 9, 1997), p. A20.

27 McConnell accused the: Don Van Natta Jr., "Defying Senator, Executives Press Donation Rules Change," *New York Times* (September, 1, 1999), p. A1. See also, Robin Toner, "The 'Designated Spear Catcher' on Campaign Finance," *New York Times* (October 18, 1999), p. A12.

27 On October 3: Don Van Natta Jr., "Executives Seeking Caps On Donations Stand Strong," *New York Times* (October 5, 1999), p. A18.

28 William Jordan, a: Leslie Wayne, "D'Amato Converted Donations To Help New York Candidates," *New York Times* (February 18, 1997), p. A1. A few months after press reports that D'Amato diverted funds, the DNC was found to have redirected at least $3.6 million to state parties. Charles R. Babcock and Ira Chinoy, "Democrats' Money Channeled Through State Organizations," *The Lexington (KY) Herald-Leader* (Washington Post) (April 13, 1997), p. A13.

28 Some months later: James Dao, "Soft Money Is Said to Help Finance Staten Island and New Jersey Races," *New York Times* (October 28, 1997), p. A14.

29 Senator D'Amato was: Ibid.

29 The day after: Leslie Wayne, "Shift of Money Was 'Proper,' D'Amato Says," *New York Times* (February 19, 1997), p. A14.

29 The amounts raised: Geraldine Ferraro, who ran for the Democratic Senate nomination, raised $1.35 million in the first three months she was in the race. Her main opponents for the nomination, Rep. Charles Schumer and Public Advocate Mark Green, had also raised substantial sums. Clifford J. Levy, "Ferraro Says Her Fund-Raising Shows Strength of Her Candidacy," *New York Times* (April 7, 1998), p. A22.

29 By February of: Leslie Wayne, "D'Amato Converted Donations To Help New York Candidates," p. A1 and p. A12.

29 Not surprisingly, much: The description of the committees comes from the *New York Times*. Ibid., p. A12.

29 By June 1998: Clifford J. Levy, "D'Amato's Campaign Awash in Donations By Hopeful Lobbies," *New York Times* (June 2, 1998), p. A1.

29 He told the: Ibid., p. A18. The list of corporations giving D'Amato money included many businesses under the jurisdiction of D'Amato's committees.

30 The financial services: Randy Kennedy, "A Political Peacekeeper Savors Victory in the Senate," *New York Times* (October 26, 1999), p. A25.

30 Schumer played a: Stephen Labaton, "Accord Reached on Lifting of Depression-Era Barriers Among Financial Industries," *New York Times* (October 23, 1999), p. A1.

30 But Governor Pataki: James Dao, "Ignoring Criticism, Pataki Gives Speech in Ohio for $15,000," *New York Times* (March 19, 1997), p. A16. In November 1999, the New York State Ethics Commission began an investigation into whether two trips by Governor Pataki to Hungary were illegally financed by companies with extensive interests before the governor, including tobacco giant Philip Morris. The company had previously said that its donations were not used to pay for the trip. Clifford J. Levy, "Albany Ethics Panel Investigating Whether Philip Morris Illegally Paid for Pataki Trips," *New York Times* (November 4, 1999), p. A25. Also in November, Philip Morris agreed to pay a fine of $75,000 — the largest ever imposed by regulators in New York state — for underreporting the amount of money it spent to lobby New York lawmakers on tobacco legislation. Raymond Hernandez, "Philip Morris to Pay Fine For Violating Lobby Law," *New York Times* (November 13, 1999), p. A11. See also, Clifford J. Levy, "Gift List Puts Focus on Legislators," *New York Times* (November 18, 1999), p. A23; and William K. Rashbaum, "Pataki Fund-Raiser Charged With Promising Parole Help," *New York Times* (December 16, 1999), p. C31.

31 Not surprisingly, voter: Jacobson, pp. 85–86. Jacobson defines turnout as a percentage of eligible voters. The percentage of registered voters going to the polls would be higher.

31 In 1998, 36: Richard L. Berke, "The 1998 Elections: Democrats' Gains Dispel Notion That the G.O.P. Benefits From Low Turnout," *New York Times* (November 6, 1998), p. A28; and Steven R. Weisman, "A Democratic 'Ground War' Slips by the Radar," (editorial) *New York Times* (November 16, 1998), p. A20. In New York state, the turnout was the lowest for a congressional election in more than 75 years. "Voter Turnout This Fall Was Lowest in 78 Years," (Associated Press) *New York Times* (December 2, 1998), p. B12.

31 The decline in: Eric Schmitt, "The 1996 Elections: The Presidency — The Voters: Half the Electorate, Perhaps Satisfied or Bored, Sat Out Voting," *New York Times* (November 7, 1996), p. B6.

32 For example, the: Jacobson, at 74–75. Senators often face more competitive elections because unlike House districts, whole states tend to have races where either party can potentially win. Ibid., p. 76. That often encourages senators to get a head start on raising money to discourage strong opponents from running.

32 Typically, since the: Jacobson, pp. 19–21.

32 Even as incumbents: Jacobson, p. 219, quoting a *New York Times*/CBS News poll. Jacobson discusses research suggesting that Congress is unpopular because of the complexity of the issues it must confront, and because the American people have unrealistic expectations of their national legislature. Ibid., pp. 218–219.

33 Term limits are: Although term limits have enjoyed widespread support on state ballots, supporters of term limits have had a much more difficult time defeating congressional incumbents who refuse to agree to a fixed number of terms in office. The organization "U.S. Term Limits" gave $300,000 to the challenger of Representative Bill Goodling (R-PA) in an effort to defeat the 70-year-old 12-term incumbent who had promised to step down but ran anyway for reelection in 1998. Goodling defeated his opponent in the primary by a margin of two-to-one. There may have been resentment on the part of the voters of an out-of-state organization pouring so much money into a campaign to defeat their congressman. Such an attitude makes it all the more difficult to defeat incumbents who break their pledge to only serve a limited number of terms. Katharine Q. Seelye, "Term-Limits Advocates Take a Bad Thrashing," *New York Times* (May 21, 1998), p. A12.

33 Congressional term limits: 514 U.S. 779 (1995).

33 Whatever one's opinion: David Broder, one of the nation's most astute political observers, is strongly opposed to term limits. In criticizing George Will's support for them, Broder wrote that to "advocate a scheme which would relieve people of the most basic duty of citizenship — the free choice of those who will represent us — is mindboggling." David Broder, "Term limits vote: Silly idea fell flat," *Lexington (KY) Herald-Leader* (February 19, 1997), p. 7. George Will wrote, "Term limits are a simple, surgical, Madisonian reform. By removing careerism — a relatively modern phenomenon — as a motive for entering politics and for behavior in office, term limits can produce deliberative bodies disposed to think of the next generation rather than the next election." George Will, "Save Us From The Purists," *Newsweek* (February 17, 1997), p. 78. Jacobson, in *The Politics of Congressional Elections*, makes the usual argument that because some members do not seek reelection, and others are defeated, there is sufficient turnover in Congress to make term limits unnecessary. He notes that more than half the House members of the 104th Congress (1995–1996) had served less than three terms, and more than half the senators were in their first or second term. Jacobson, p. 216. His argument is unconvincing, however, because incumbents who know they will almost certainly be reelected if they choose to run behave differently from those whose believe there is a genuine chance they will be defeated if they seek reelection.

33 Forty states impose: Jessica Lee, "Push for term limits still alive at state, local levels," *USA Today* (Oct. 15, 1997), p. 16A.

33 Arkansas' constitutional amendment: Linda Greenhouse, "Supreme Court Roundup: Term Limits," *New York Times* (February 25, 1997), p. A12. The other states are Alaska, Colorado, Idaho, Maine, Missouri, Nebraska, Nevada and South

Dakota. See also, Richard Carelli, "High court rejects term-limit provision," *Lexington (KY) Herald-Leader* (Associated Press) (February 25, 1997), p. A5.

33 Two weeks before: *Donovan v. Priest*, 931 S.W.2d 119 (Ark. 1996).

34 In February 1997: *Arkansas Term Limits v. Donovan, cert. denied sub nom*, 117 S. Ct. 1081 (1997).

34 Massachusetts citizens must: *League of Women Voters v. Massachusetts*, 681 N.E.2d 842 (1997). See also, Sara Rimer, "Top Massachusetts Court Overturns Term Limits," *New York Times* (July 12, 1997), p. 6.

34 The supporters of: *Legislature of the State of California v. March Fong Eu*, 816 P.2d 1309 (Cal. 1991).

34 California was the: For a description of the effect of term limits in California and other states, see B. Drummond Ayres, Jr., "Term Limit Laws Are Transforming More Legislatures," *New York Times* (April 28, 1997), p. A1.

34 In April 1997: *Bates v. Jones*, 958 F. Supp. 1446 (1997). See also, Todd S. Purdum, "Federal Judge Overturns Term Limits in California," *New York Times* (April 24, 1997), p. A19.

35 It was the: Ibid., p. A19.

35 Her ruling was: *Jones v. Bates, aff'd* 127 F.3d 839 (9th Cir. 1997), *rev'd* 131 F.3d 843 (9th Cir. 1997) (en banc).

35 In March of: *cert. den., Bates v. Jones*, 118 S. Ct. 1302 (1998). In January 1998, a federal district court in Sacramento struck down major parts of the campaign contribution limits that became law when California voters approved Proposition 208 in 1996. The initiative, which was approved by 61 percent of the voters, limited most contributions to state and local candidates to $500. Judge Lawrence Karlton ruled that the contribution limit was too low to pass constitutional muster. *California Prolife Council PAC v. Scully*, 989 F. Supp. 1282 (1998), *aff'd*, 164 F.3d 1189 (9th Cir. 1999). See also, "Political Gift Limits Struck Down in California," (Associated Press) *New York Times* (January 7, 1998), p. A14.

35 They knew that: Among the most interesting examples of a member of Congress deciding to stay despite a commitment to serve a fixed number of terms is George Nethercutt, a Republican from the Fifth District of Washington state. When he defeated then-Speaker of the House Tom Foley in 1994, he pledged to serve only six years. In 1998, Nethercutt said that because the issues before Congress are so complicated, six years "is probably not enough." Seelye, "Term-Limits Advocates Take a Bad Thrashing."

35 Speaker Newt Gingrich: See "Voters Be Ignored," editorial, *Wall Street Journal* (February 28, 1997), p. A14. For a commentary on campaign reform, see Garry Wills, "Politics By the Old Rules," *New York Times* (March 4, 1997), p. A15; David C. King (professor of public policy at Harvard), "It's up to the voters:

Campaign finance reform resides in the hinterlands," *Lexington (KY) Herald-Leader* (Newsday) (March 13, 1997), p. A15.

35 A constitutional amendment: Adam Clymer, "Term Limits Rejected by House, Bringing Campaign to Dead Halt, *New York Times* (February 13, 1997), p. A1. See also, Adam Clymer, "Measure on Term Limits Heads for House Vote," *New York Times* (February 5, 1997), p. A8; and Dane Strother, "Campaign Finance 'Reforms' Don't Work," *New York Times* (February 1, 1997), p. 17.

36 Congress may tinker: Senator Christopher Dodd (D-Connecticut) was general chairman of the DNC during the 1996 presidential campaign. While recognizing the need for the president and the Democratic Party to raise substantial sums, he was nevertheless disturbed by how money had "contaminated" the political process. He also said that campaign finance reform would not be passed by Congress because of insufficient public outrage. Francis X. Clines, "Democratic Fund-Raiser On Dollars and Darwin," *New York Times* (March 10, 1997), p. A11.

36 Although term limits: There has been substantial turnover in the state legislatures where term limits have been in effect. In California, for example, all 80 members of the state assembly have been elected since 1990. In Maine, many new legislators have been elected since a term limits law was passed in 1993. But the lack of experience on the part of the new legislators is creating some problems. In Maine, very little substantive legislation was enacted in the first few months of 1997. This may also be a problem in other states as new legislators address difficult problems. Once the existing term limits laws are fully phased in, they will cover a third of the nation's 7,424 state legislators. B. Drummond Ayres, Jr., "Term Limit Laws Are Transforming More Legislatures," *New York Times* (April 28, 1997), p. A1.

36 Term limits will: Economist Milton Friedman, in a speech to U.S. Term Limits Foundation donors in San Francisco on October 27, 1995, said, "What you have to do to have a change is not simply to elect the right people, but to change the institutional arrangement so the incentives which they have are different. If you're a member of Congress today, what's your main incentive? Your main incentive is to get reelected ... " <http://www.termlimits.org> downloaded February, 1997.

37 To further undermine: The Presidential Election Campaign Fund Act is found at 26 U.S.C. Section 9012(f).

37 In *Federal Election*: *Federal Election Commission (FEC) v. National Conservative Political Action Committee*, 470 U.S. 480 (1985).

37 In early 1997: For a detailed review of the fund-raising revelations up to that point, see David E. Rosenbaum, "Campaign Finance: Developments So Far," *New York Times* (April 3, 1997), p. A15; and Elizabeth Drew, "A Gourmet's Guide To the Campaign Finance Stew," *The Washington Post* (March 23, 1997), p. C1. Some potential contributors found the pressure to contribute to the DNC during visits to the White House to be unusually direct and heavy-handed. Don Van Natta Jr., "Democratic Math at a Coffee: 10 Texans and $500,000 Goal," *New York Times* (February 28, 1997), p. A1.

38 Almost no favor: Some contributors who paid a large amount of money for the privilege of a few minutes with the president saw little, if any, direct results. David E. Sanger, "Even a Big Donor Can Find Political Dividends Elusive," *New York Times* (March 15, 1997), p. 8.

38 This was not: David E. Sanger and Stephen Labaton, "Billions at Stake as Clinton and Bankers Met," *New York Times* (January 31, 1997), p. A1.

38 After news organizations: Alison Mitchell, "President Regrets Top U.S. Regulator Met With Bankers," *New York Times* (January 29, 1997), p. A1.

38 A few months: Robert D. Hershey, Jr., "Plan Is Offered To Reorganize Finance Sector," *New York Times* (May 22, 1997), p. C1.

39 In one of: Don Van Natta Jr., "A Fund-Raiser Tied Policy To Gifts, His Accusers Say," *New York Times* (March 1, 1997), p. 1. Brandt's tactics apparently did not trouble Hillary Rodham Clinton in her quest for a Senate seat from New York. In January 2000, he organized a fundraising event at his home in Florida, which the First Lady attended, where supporters paid $2,000 to eat light snacks and hear speeches. Mrs. Clinton's aides were quoted as saying Brandt had done nothing wrong and it was natural for people who supported the president to want to help Mrs. Clinton. Clifford J. Levy, "The First Lady Taps Donors Criticized for Assisting the President," *New York Times* (February 9, 2000), p. A24.

39 President Clinton personally: Don Van Natta Jr., "Clinton Sought Role as Fund-Raiser, Memo Says," *New York Times* (July 24, 1997), p. A1.

39 By February 1997: Alison Mitchell, "Clinton Pressed Plan to Reward Donors," *New York Times* (February 26, 1997), p. A1. For a list of the nearly 1000 guests who stayed overnight in the White House — many of whom were friends of the Clintons — see Mitchell, at A12. For an historical look at White House guests, see Julie V. Iovine, "At the White House, Everyone's a Guest," *New York Times* (March 6, 1997), p. B8. President Clinton probably spent significantly more money than his predecessors on entertaining at the White House. Eric Schmitt, "White House Documents Show Much Entertaining," *New York Times* (March 17, 1997), p. A10. For criticism of the President's denial that the Lincoln Bedroom had been for rent to large contributors, see "The File on President Clinton," (editorial) *New York Times* (February 27, 1997), p. A14. The President and his staff denied any wrongdoing in using the White House to reward contributors. James Bennet, "President Defends His Role In Raising Campaign Funds," *New York Times* (February 27, 1997), p. A1. There were also reports that the fund-raising controversy was interfering with the appointments of ambassadors and other officials. The White House was apparently worried about the reaction if contributors were appointed to such positions. Alison Mitchell, "Long Arm of the Financing Furor: Campaign Inquiries Tangle Administration on Many Fronts," *New York Times* (March 17, 1997), p. A10.

39 In his own: Mitchell, "Clinton Pressed Plan to Reward Donors."

39 He told a: Ibid.

39 He made phone: James Bennett, "Clinton Defends 1996 Fund-Raising But Hits System," *New York Times* (March 8, 1997), p. A1; and Don Van Natta Jr., "Note Suggests Clinton Made $50,000 White House Call," *New York Times* (September 23, 1997), p. A16.

40 Evelyn Lieberman, a: Mitchell, at A1.

40 A memo written: Stephen Labaton, "Democrats Say They'll Return About $1.5 Million More in Questionable Gifts," *New York Times* (March 1, 1997), p. 7 (The memo about privileges for donors, "Text of a Memo on Fund-Raising Plans," is on page 7).

40 For example, Jorge: Don Van Natta Jr., "An R.S.V.P. to the President: Deep Regrets. I'm in Custody," *New York Times* (March 22, 1997), p. 1.

40 Cabrera was first: Don Van Natta Jr., "A Felon's Donation to Democrats Was Sought in Cuba, Inquiry Says," *New York Times* (April 4, 1997), p. A1.

40 Another visitor to: Ronald Smothers, "Bail Revoked for Felon Who Visited White House," *New York Times* (February 28, 1997), p. 11.

41 Another frequent visitor: Don Van Natta Jr., "An R.S.V.P. to the President: Deep Regrets. I'm in Custody," *New York Times* (March 22, 1997), p. 1.

41 He told Congress: David E. Rosenbaum, "Oilman Says He Got 'Access' By Giving Democrats Money," *New York Times* (September 19, 1997), p. A1.

41 Russ Barakat, the: "What a Cast of Characters," *The Herald-Leader (KY)* (March 6, 1997), p. A12, reprinted from the *Washington Post*.

41 In December 1997: Noreen Marcus, "Barakat Could Escape Prison; Ex-Democratic Boss Now Faces Probation, *Sun-Sentinel* (Ft. Lauderdale) (December 19, 1997), p. 3B.

41 One creative White: Van Natta Jr., "An R.S.V.P. to the President: Deep Regrets. I'm in Custody."

41 Several visitors had: Tim Weiner, "Dubious Foreign Guests Visited White House After Screening System Ended," *New York Times* (February 3, 1997), p. A10.

42 China may have: Tim Weiner, "House Panel Opens Inquiry Into Possible Foreign Influence in '96 Elections," *New York Times* (March 6, 1997), p. A13. See also, Elaine Sciolino, "Campaign Finance Complicates China Policy," *New York Times* (March 10, 1997), p. A1.

42 Vice President Al: James Bennet, "Chinese Ask Gore About The Inquiry On Campaign Gifts," *New York Times* (March 26, 1997), p. A1.

42 In the spring: Eric Schmitt and Don Van Natta Jr., "Republicans Ask Clinton to Show Donations Didn't Breach Security," *New York Times* (May 16, 1998), p. A1. See also, Francis X. Clines, "U.S. Inquiry Opens Window On the Military Elite of China," *New York Times* (May 16, 1998), p. A1. See also, Jeff Gerth and John M. Broder, "Papers Show White House Staff Favored a China Satellite Permit," *New York Times* (May 23, 1998), p. A1.

42 Chinese officials also: Elisabeth Rosenthal, "Chinese Officials Denounce Reports of Gifts to Democrats," *New York Times* (May 20, 1998), p. A14.

42 The chairman of: Jeff Gerth and John M. Broder, "The White House Dismissed Warnings on China Satellite Deal," *New York Times* (June 1, 1998), p. A13.

42 The Republicans promised: Alison Mitchell, "Gingrich Announces Inquiry Into Clinton Moves on China," *New York Times* (May 20, 1998), p. A1. The *New York Times*, in an editorial, said the Chinese satellite issue "cannot be separated from fund-raising conducted by President Clinton and Vice President Gore," and it called on Speaker Gingrich to support legislation on campaign finance reform. "The Law and Mr. Clinton's Money," *New York Times* (May 21, 1998), p. A26.

43 Wang had been: In May 1999, Charlie Trie pleaded guilty in federal court in Arkansas to two charges related to his political fundraising, and agreed to cooperate with the Justice Department investigation into fund-raising in the 1996 presidential campaign. Trie, who owned a Little Rock restaurant, but eventually acquired an import-export business, had helped bring in $645,000 to the DNC and another $639,000 for the Clinton legal defense fund, both of which were eventually returned to donors. Trie pleaded guilty to a felony charge of causing false statements to be made and to a lesser misdemeanor charge. Among other acts, Trie was alleged to have ordered his office manager to dispose of documents sought by the Senate Government Affairs Committee. Also in May, a three-judge panel of the U.S. Court of Appeals for the District of Columbia reinstated five of six criminal charges against another Democratic fundraiser, Maria Hsia, which had been dismissed by a federal district court. David Johnston, "Friend of President Admits to Violating Fund-Raising Laws," *New York Times* (May 22, 1999), p. A1. Her trial began in February 2000. Neil A. Lewis, "Veteran Gore Fund-Raiser Goes on Trial," *New York Times* (February 8, 2000), p. A14.

43 The White House: Weiner, "Dubious Foreign Guests Visited White House After Screening System Ended."

43 One visitor with: Christopher Drew, "How Big Democratic Donor Weaved Access and Success," *New York Times* (February 22, 1997), p. 1.

43 A donor with: Stephen Labaton, "Aide To First Lady Was Given Check At White House," *New York Times* (March 6, 1997), p. A1; and Alison Mitchell, "First Lady's Aide Draws Criticism From Party Chief," *New York Times* (March 7, 1997), p. A1. When China's possible involvement in U.S. elections were reported in the press, the Democratic Party decided not to accept contributions from American subsidiaries of foreign companies and from their American employees.

The chairman of the Organization for International Investment thought that decision was unfair to the workers of such companies who are American citizens, voters, and taxpayers. Richard A. Goldstein, "Nothing 'Foreign' About Us," *New York Times* (March 11, 1997), p. A15. The Republicans, on the other hand, continued to accept such contributions. Don Van Natta Jr., "Subsidiaries of Foreign Companies Gave Heavily to G.O.P.," *New York Times* (February 21, 1997), p. A14.

43 The White House's: Weiner, at A10. See also, Mark Hosenball and Evan Thomas, "A China Connection? How charges of Clinton campaign sleaze could turn into a spy scandal," *Newsweek* (February 24, 1997), p. 34.

44 The largest of: Jeff Gerth and Stephen Labaton, "2 Advisers Knew of Hubbell Plight," *New York Times* (May 5, 1997), p. A1. There were also reports that Hubbell received money from the organizers of a multibillion dollar development in China that received the endorsement of the Clinton Administration. Jeff Gerth and Stephen Labaton, "Payment to an Ex-Clinton Aide Is Linked to Big Chinese Project," *New York Times* (March 6, 1997), p. A1.

44 In December 1994: Ibid.

44 While the reports: Ibid.

44 The aides involved: Jeff Gerth, "White House Aides Helped Job Hunt of Clinton Friend," *New York Times* (April 2, 1997), p. A1.

44 The *New York*: Ibid.

44 The *Los Angeles*: Todd S. Purdum, "Report Says Hubbell Defrauded Los Angeles by Taking Fees for Work He Never Did," *New York Times* (June 24, 1997), p. A12.

45 In April 1998: Stephen Labaton, "Friend of Clinton Indicted a 2d Time; Tax Scheme Cited," *New York Times* (May 1, 1998), p. A1. On July 1, 1998, a federal district judge in Washington, D.C. dismissed the indictment against Hubbell and his co-defendants on the grounds that the independent counsel, Kenneth Starr, had exceeded his authority in investigating Hubbell's financial dealings, and that the prosecutor had violated Hubbell's right against self-incrimination. Starr promised an appeal of the decision. Stephen Labaton, "In Slap At Starr, A Judge Dismisses Hubbell Tax Case," *New York Times* (July 2, 1998), p. A1.

45 In June 1999: Neil A. Lewis, "For Starr and Hubbell, an Accord of Sorts," *New York Times* (July 1, 1999), p. A14; and Linda Greenhouse, "Justices Agree to Hear Starr's Appeal in Hubbell Immunity Case," *New York Times* (October 13, 1999), p. A18.

45 In the meantime: Ibid. Hubbell was given a $400,000 advance for a book, *Friends in High Places*, published by William Morrow in 1997. The book received tepid reviews in part because there were no major disclosures and not much inside information on the Clintons. Several sources in the publishing industry told the *New York Times* that the publisher failed to recover the advance. Hubbell's effort to interest a movie producer in *Friends*, and to sell two new book proposals, were put on hold after his latest indictment.

46 A White House: Todd S. Purdum, "New Fund-Raising Cloud: List of Visitors," *New York Times* (March 31, 1997), p. A14. For criticism of the First Lady's involvement with the computer list, see William Safire, "Clintons' Data Base," *New York Times* (February 24, 1997), p. A15.

46 It was also: David Stout, "White House to Remove Aides from Party Payroll," *New York Times* (February 21, 1997), p. A14. See also, Christopher Drew, "Questions Over a Blend Of White House Duties," *New York Times* (March 3, 1997), p. A12. For a look at how White House staff tried to separate official business from politics, see Alison Mitchell, "White House Political Tightrope: Separating Business From Politics," *New York Times* (March 5, 1997), p. A1. President Clinton asked former Senator Nancy Kassebaum Baker and former Vice President and Senator Walter Mondale to lead an effort to promote campaign finance reform. They were optimistic that legislation would pass that would change the campaign finance system. They wrote in a *New York Times* commentary that it is "easy to be cynical, to assume that this year, as before, there will be no reform. But Americans have a chance to beat the cycle of fund-raising that demeans our politicians and our political system." "The Money Pit," *New York Times* (March 25, 1997), p. A19. The public, however, continued to be cynical about the prospects of real campaign finance reform. Only 3 in 10 believed the president really wanted change, while only 23 percent were convinced that Congress actually wanted to change the current laws. Francis X. Clines, "Most Doubt a Resolve to Change Campaign Financing, Poll Finds," *New York Times* (April 8, 1997), p. A1.

46 Vice President Gore: Alison Mitchell, "Gore's Fund-Raising Casts a Political Shadow," *New York Times* (March 3, 1997), p. A1; and Alison Mitchell, "Acknowledging Calls to Donors, Gore Says He Did Nothing Illegal," *New York Times* (March 4, 1997), p. A1. In an editorial, a former Gore chief of staff and White House counsel defended the vice president's actions as legal. Jack Quinn, "The Law and Mr. Gore," *New York Times* (March 10, 1997), p. A15. At the same time that fund-raising activities had been criticized, the former chairman of the Clinton/Gore reelection campaign solicited tax-free donations to refurbish the vice president's residence. Leslie Wayne, "A New Request for Donations Is Raising Democratic Eyebrows," *New York Times* (March 7, 1997), p. A11.

47 The public eventually: Leslie Wayne, "Number of Calls by Gore To Donors Is Now Put at 86," *New York Times* (August 27, 1997), p. A10.

47 In denying that: Ibid. *New York Times* columnist Anthony Lewis believed that the law did not cover such activities as a vice president making telephone calls to donors from the White House. He wrote that the intent of the law was to prevent the soliciting of one federal employee by another in person in federal buildings. Anthony Lewis, "Whose Ox Is Gored," *New York Times* (September 15, 1997), p. A15. For a searing commentary about Clinton and Gore's handling of the campaign finance allegations, see Maureen Dowd, "Lonely At the Top," *New York Times* (March 8, 1997), p. 21.

47 Vice President Gore: David Johnston, "Reno Rejects Call To Name A Counsel Over Fund-Raising," *New York Times* (April 15, 1997), p. A1; and David Johnston, "Reno Rejects A Prosecutor On Clinton And Gore Calls; Bitter, G.O.P. Vows to Fight," *New York Times* (Dec. 3, 1997), p. A1. See also, David Johnston, "Reno is Expanding Inquiry Into Calls By Gore For Cash," *New York Times* (Oct. 3, 1997), p. A1.

47 But the vice: In 1996, the vice president appeared at a fund-raising event at a Buddhist temple in Los Angeles. Several nuns associated with the temple, who had taken a vow of poverty, made sizable contributions to the DNC after the vice president's visit. The event was organized by John Huang who raised hundreds of thousands of dollars for the 1996 campaign. Eric Schmitt, "In a Rebuff to Justice Dept., Panel Immunizes 5 Witnesses," *New York Times* (July 24, 1997), p. A1.

47 A *Wall Street*: John Harwood, "Gore's Image Takes a Beating From Fund Controversy," *Wall Street Journal* (September 18 1997), p. A16.

47 Republicans criticized the: Eric Schmitt, "G.O.P. Steps Up Attack on Gore's Fund-Raising," *New York Times* (September 11, 1997), p. A1.

47 In his first: Richard L. Berke, "Gore Insists G.O.P. Is at Fault for Fund-Raising 'Adversity,'" *New York Times* (Dec. 5, 1997), p. A1. For an editorial critical of Gore and how he handled fund-raising chores, see "More About Mr. Gore," *New York Times* (September 5, 1997), p. A20. See also, Richard L. Berke, "Gore Is Facing Toughest Point Of His Career," *New York Times* (September 13, 1997), p. 1. In December 1999, Democratic donors contributed $1 million to refurbish the vice president's residence which had been in need of repair for some time. Businesses giving money to renovate the 33-room mansion included Bell Atlantic, Coca-Cola and General Motors. Microsoft's Bill Gates, who was fighting an antitrust suit against the Justice Department, donated a $30,000 cobalt-blue glass sculpture, but according to the *New York Times*, it was put in a closet because it clashed with the Victorian interiors. Howard Glicken, a Florida businessman and Democratic donor who pleaded guilty to campaign finance violations in 1998, donated a $6,000 billiard table. Mark Jimenez gave $20,000 while under indictment in 1998 on campaign finance violations. In December, he was negotiating his extradition from the Philippines. Peter Eisner, the managing director of the Center for Public Integrity, criticized the donations as an effort by a "small group of people making an investment in the vice president's residence for access and influence and it's largely out of public view."

47 It was estimated: Richard L. Berke, "Democratic Party Is Unable To Pay '96 Election Bills," *New York Times* (March 27, 1997), p. A1.

47 In the months: Stephen Labaton, "Democrats Say They'll Return About $1.5 million More in Questionable Gifts," *New York Times* (March 1, 1997), p. 7. The Justice Department also subpoenaed the records of Johnny Chung, the California businessman who gave the Democratic Party $391,000. Christopher Drew, "Inquiry Widens Into Gifts By Big Democratic Donors," *New York Times* (February 25, 1997), p. A10. See also, Melinda Liu, "The Portrait of a Hustler," *Newsweek* (March 31, 1997), p. 36.

47 Among contributions returned: Neil A. Lewis, "U.S. Agents Seize Documents from Group Tied to Democratic Fund-Raising," *New York Times* (February 28, 1997), p. A12.

47 Dozens of members: Leslie Wayne, "Gephardt to Return $22,000 in Questionable Contributions," *New York Times* (March 19, 1997), p. A14. The national DNC and members of Congress were not alone in having problems with handling contributions. The Kentucky Democratic Party agreed to pay a fine of $75,000 imposed by the Federal Election Commission for improperly reporting disbursements of money, "fictitious" transfers of $450,000, and for accepting $11,000 in impermissible contributions. The fine was reported to be among the largest imposed on a state party by the FEC. Bill Estep, "Kentucky Democrats agree to $75,000 fine," *Lexington (KY) Herald-Leader* (March 1, 1997), p. A1.

48 By giving at: Katharine Q. Seelye, "G.O.P.'s Reward for Top Donors: 3 Days With Party Leaders," *New York Times* (Feb. 20, 1997), p. A15.

48 The Republicans' Team: Ibid.

48 In May 1997: Leslie Wayne, "G.O.P., for First Time, Admits It Accepted Foreign Donations," *New York Times* (May 9, 1997), p. A1.

48 Press reports indicated: Leslie Wayne, "Papers Detail G.O.P. Ties To Tax Group," *New York Times* (November 10, 1997), p. A18.

49 The Republicans were: Leslie Wayne and Christopher Drew," G.O.P. Tool to Revive Party Instead Results in Scrutiny," *New York Times* (June 2, 1997), p. A10.

49 The Forum, which: Barbour insisted that he had done nothing wrong. David E. Rosenbaum, "Ex-G.O.P. Chairman Strongly Defends His Fund-Raising," *New York Times* (July 25, 1997), p. A1.

49 An official with: Ibid.

49 The Republicans also: Adam Clymer, "G.O.P. Freshmen Abandon Plan to Curb 'Soft' Money," *New York Times* (June 30, 1997), p. A9.

49 In August 1999: Don Van Natta Jr., "Republicans' Goal Is $1 Million Each From Top Donors."

49 The National Governor's: John H. Cushman Jr., "Corporate Gifts Open Door To Governors' Inner Sanctum," *New York Times* (May 17, 1997), p. 1.

50 *The New York*: Ibid.

50 Chaired by Republican: For a report on the difficult job that Thompson faced in chairing the hearings, see Adam Clymer, "A Senator Finds Himself In Conflicting Roles Again," *New York Times* (July 15, 1998), p. A11.

50 By the end: Francis X. Clines, "Subjects of Hearings on Campaign Finance Speak, but Not at the Hearings," *New York Times* (July 28, 1997), p. A9.

51 More than two: Neil A. Lewis, "Nonprofit Groups to Defy Subpoenas in Senate Inquiry," *New York Times* (September 4, 1997), p. A9.

51 The committee did: David E. Rosenbaum, "Panel Is Told Huang Kept Close Ties to Ex-Employer," *New York Times* (July 16,1997), p. A1.

51 But the number: Francis X. Clines, "Map of Campaign Finance Trail Leads to Labyrinth," *New York Times* (July 16, 1997), p. A11.

51 At the beginning: According to the Center for Media and Public Affairs, between July 8 and July 31, CBS did 22 stories totaling 43 minutes of air time; NBC ran 15 stories for 31 minutes; and ABC had 14 stories and 24 minutes devoted to the hearings. David Lightman, "High-Profile Hearings, Low-Profile Coverage," *American Journalism Review* (November 1997), p. 14.

51 Before long only: Walter Goodman, "Campaign Finance Hearings, the Great Snooze," *New York Times* (July 16, 1997), p. B3.

51 As the New: "Campaign Disarmament," *New York Times* (July 10, 1997), p. A20.

51 Democrats were outraged: Eric Schmitt, "Subpoena Power Granted as Democrats Cry 'Witch Hunt,'" *New York Times* (June 21, 1997), p. 7.

52 In October, a: Tom Squitieri, "Thompson challenges president," *USA Today* (October 8, 1997), p. 6A.

52 The Burton committee: On October 31, 1999, Burton's committee said it will release FBI notes of its interrogation of John Huang, a Democratic Party fundraiser, because it believed the federal agency was not vigorously investigating illegality related to the 1996 campaign. Rep. Burton said that the notes raise serious questions about the failure of the Justice Department to investigate accusations of wrongdoing such as violation of the Hatch Act, which prohibits supervisors in government from pressuring subordinates to be involved in political activities. Neil A. Lewis, "House Panel Says It Will Release F.B.I. Notes in Fund-Raising Case," *New York Times* (November 1, 1999), p. A19.

52 As the Thompson: Francis X. Clines, "F.E.C. Budget Is No Match For Its Task, Panel Is Told," *New York Times* (September 26, 1997), p. A12. In June 1998, the Supreme Court allowed voters to sue the FEC for not adequately enforcing the disclosure requirements imposed by federal law on certain political groups. Although the decision somewhat liberalized "standing" rules to permit voters to bring actions against federal agencies, the FEC decision may have limited impact because the Commission is changing the definition of certain political groups to allow them to keep the names of donors confidential, and the Supreme Court indicated a willingness to defer to the Commission. *FEC v. Akins*, 524 U.S. 11 (1998). See also, Linda Greenhouse, "High Court Lowers Shield of Election Panel," *New York Times* (June 2, 1998), p. A16.

52 In October 1997: David Stout, "Company Agrees to Pay Highest Penalty for Campaign-Finance Violation," *New York Times* (October 10, 1997), p. A16.

52 In March 1998: Lisa Wiehl, "Guilty Plea in a Campaign Finance Case," *New York Times* (March 19, 1998), p. A18.

52 In the same: Don Terry, "Democratic Fund-Raiser Pleads Guilty to Fraud and Conspiracy," *New York Times* (March 17, 1998), p. A18.

53 Johnny Chung faced: Jeff Gerth, "Under Scrutiny: Citibank's Handling of High-Profile Foreigners' Accounts," *New York Times* (July 27, 1999), p. A6.

53 A national poll: Carey Goldberg, "Sleepovers Elicit No Ire In a Capital," *New York Times* (February 28, 1997), p. A11. See also, R.W. Apple, Jr., "Why a Capital Uproar Is a Hinterland Beep," *New York Times* (March 13, 1997), p. A12.

53 A Gallup Poll: Michael Golay, *Where America Stands on Today's Most Critical Issues* (New York: John Wiley & Sons, 1997), p 222.

53 In 1972, all: Ibid, p. 224.

53 In the 1996: Ibid.

53 Only 20 percent: Ibid., p. 235.

Chapter 2: The Birth of Article V

A note about the notes

From the time the Supreme Court first handed down decisions in the early 1790s, until 1875, citations for Court decisions in the United States Reports included the name of the Court reporter. For example, the citation for *Chisholm v. Georgia*, could appear in several different forms: 2 Dall. (2 U.S.) 419 (1793) or more commonly, 2 Dall. 419 (1793). In this book, the names of the Court reporters are omitted. For readers who want to find cases under the formal name, here is a list of Court reporters and the years they served:

- Dallas (Dall.) 1789–1800
- Cranch (Cranch or Cr.) 1801–1815
- Wheaton (Wheat.) 1816–1827
- Peters (Pet.) 1828–1842
- Howard (How.) 1843–1860
- Black (Black) 1861–1862
- Wallace (Wall.) 1863–1874

From Ellen Greenberg, *The Supreme Court Explained* (New York: W.W. Norton & Co., 1997), p. 88.

57 It is difficult: See generally, Stanley Elkins and Eric McKitrick, *The Age of Federalism: The Early American Republic, 1788–1800* (New York: Oxford University Press, 1993); Mortimer J. Adler, *We Hold These Truths: Understanding the Ideas* *and Ideals of the Constitution* (New York: Macmillan, 1987); and Forrest McDonald, *Novus Ordo Seclorum: The Intellectual Origins of the Constitution* (Lawrence, KS: University Press of Kansas, 1985).

57 The delegates decided: Max Farrand, *The Records of the Federal Convention of 1787* (New Haven, CT: Yale University Press, 1911), Vol. 1, p. xi.

58 In 1818, President: Ibid., p. xii.

58 According to Adams: Ibid.

58 Jackson "looked over: Ibid.

58 By supplementing the: The volume was published in Boston in 1819 under the title of *Journal, Acts and Proceedings of the Convention . . . which formed the Constitution of the United States.* Farrand, Vol. 1, p. xii. It was an octavo-sized volume of some 500 pages. Farrand warned that with "the notes so carelessly kept, as were evidently those of the secretary, the Journal cannot be relied upon absolutely." Ibid., p. xiii.

58 In his will: Herbert R. Collins and David V. Weaver, *Wills of the U.S. Presidents* (New York: Communication Channels, Inc., 1976), p. 45.

59 In March 1837: Ibid., p. 48.

59 He sat at: Clinton Rossiter, *1787: The Grand Convention* (New York: W.W. Norton & Co., 1987, originally published in 1966), p. 162.

59 Robert Yates of: Once the Journal was published in 1819, other records were published. The notes of the late Robert Yates were published in 1921 under the title of *Secret Proceedings and Debates of the Convention Assembled at Philadelphia, in the year 1787, for the purpose of forming the Constitution of the United States of America, From Notes taken by the late Robert Yates, Esq. Chief Justice of New York, and copied by John Lansing.* Yates and Lansing left the Convention early because they believed their instructions did not permit them to participate — or even be present — at a Convention that created a national government at the expense of the states. Yates's notes end on July 5, 1787. Farrand, Vol. 1, p. xiv.

59 Rufus King of: King took notes on what Farrand describes as "odds and ends of paper," but he carefully dated most of the pages so historians have been able to piece together a record that some consider second only to Madison's notes in importance. King tried to organize his notes in 1818, but made relatively minor changes. They were published in 1894 as an appendix to Vol. I of the *Life and Correspondence of Rufus King.*

59 James McHenry of: McHenry's notes provided important information about the early days of the Convention. He took detailed notes about Randolph's speech presenting the Virginia Resolutions on May 29. Due to his brother's illness, however, he left Philadelphia on June 1 and was gone during June and July. Upon returning in August, he continued his energetic note taking and his records provide valuable insights into the latter part of the Convention's work. Farrand,

Vol. 1, p. xxi. William Pierce of Georgia, William Paterson of New Jersey, Alexander Hamilton of New York, and George Mason of Virginia also took some notes, but they have been of limited value to historians. Ibid., pp. xxi–xxii. The source of statements from the records of the Convention is indicated below in parentheses.

59 For reasons that: Ibid., pp. xv–xix. Because of the different fading of inks used by Madison in 1787 and years later while making the corrections, and because Madison referred to himself as "M" or "Mr. M." in the original notes, but by his full name in the revisions, historians have been able to tell in many cases which statements were original and which were corrected years later.

60 Of the original: John R. Vile, *The Constitutional Amendment Process in American Political Thought* (New York: Praeger Publishers, 1992), p. 25.

60 The remaining states: Ibid.

60 One of the: Article XIII required that any alterations to the Articles be "agreed to in a congress of the United States, and be afterwards confirmed by the legislatures of every state."

60 All states approved: C. Herman Pritchett, *The American Constitution* (New York: McGraw-Hill, 1977), p. 6.

60 Four years later: Ibid.

60 The first time: Farrand, Vol. I, p. 22 (Madison).

60 The delegates decided: Ibid., p. 117 (Journal).

60 According to Madison's: Ibid., p. 121 (Madison).

60 On the other: Ibid., p. 122 (Madison).

61 According to Madison's: Ibid., p. 202 (Madison).

61 However, George Mason: Ibid., p. 202 (Madison). Mason and other delegates believed that an orderly process of amendment was much preferred over the more chaotic and dangerous alternative of changing the founding document by abolishing the government and creating a new Constitution. The Declaration of Independence recognized that the people were endowed with certain rights such as life, liberty, and the pursuit of happiness, and "that whenever any Form of Government becomes destructive of those Ends, it is the Right of the People to alter or abolish it, and to institute new Government." But the Declaration cautions that, "Prudence, indeed, will dictate that Governments long established should not be changed for light and transient Causes."

61 He suggested that: Ibid., pp. 202–203 (Madison).

61 Mason was especially: Ibid., p. 203 (Madison).

61 The delegates unanimously: Ibid. (Madison).

61 The delegates had: For a discussion of the Committee's work, see Rossiter, *The Grand Convention*, pp. 200–205.

62 "Resolved That Provision: Farrand, Vol. II, p. 133 (Madison).

62 The Committee later: Ibid., p. 148. The odd use of parentheses and other symbols is taken from Farrand.

62 In a later: Ibid., p. 159 (Madison).

62 The Committee kept: Ibid., p. 174 (Madison).

62 According to Madison's: Ibid., p. 188 (Madison).

62 The one comment: Ibid., p. 468 (Madison).

63 He feared the: Ibid., p. 557–558 (Madison).

63 The brilliant New: Rossiter said Hamilton was "far and away the most disappointing man" at the Convention. Rossiter, *The Grand Convention*, p. 252.

63 Hamilton reminded the: Farrand, Vol. II, p. 558 (Madison).

64 Madison's notes say: Ibid. (Madison).

64 In addition to: Ibid. (Madison).

65 James Wilson recommended: Ibid. (Madison).

65 Madison did not: Ibid. (Madison).

65 Wilson moved to: Ibid., p. 559 (Madison).

65 After Wilson's motion: Ibid, p. 559. Madison's proposal read as follows: "The Legislature of the U-S — whenever two thirds of both Houses shall deem necessary, or on the application of two thirds of the Legislatures of the several states, shall propose amendments to this Constitution, which shall be valid to all intents and purposes as part thereof, when the same shall have been ratified by three fourths at least of the Legislatures of the several states, or by Conventions in three fourths thereof, as one or the other mode of ratification may be proposed by the Legislature of the U.S:" (punctuation in original).

66 To appease Rutledge: Ibid., p. 559 (Madison).

66 According to Madison's: Ibid., p. 629 (Madison).

67 He thought the: Ibid. (Madison).

67 In the margin: Ibid. (Madison).

67 Roger Sherman tried: Ibid., p. 630 (Madison).

67 Madison argued against: Ibid. (Madison).

68 Madison noted "this: Ibid., p. 631 (Madison).

68 On September 15: The final version of Article V reads: "The Congress, whenever two thirds of both Houses shall deem it necessary, shall propose Amendments to this Constitution, or, on the Application of the Legislatures of two thirds of the several States, shall call a Convention for proposing Amendments,

which, in either Case, shall be valid to all Intents and Purposes, as Part of this Constitution, when ratified by the Legislatures of three fourths of the several states, or by Conventions in three fourths thereof, as the one or the other Mode of Ratification may be proposed by the Congress; Provided that no Amendment which may be made prior to the Year One thousand eight hundred and eight shall in any Manner affect the first [importation of slaves] and fourth [levying taxes on slaves other than the three-fifths rule] clauses in the Ninth Section of the first Article; and that no State, without its Consent, shall be deprived of its equal suffrage in the Senate."

70 **Article I, Section:** The one exception that Article I, Section 7 makes is for adjournment of Congress. No presidential action is required.

70 **The Court's eventual:** *Chisholm v. Georgia*, 2 U.S. 419 (1793).

71 **In 1798 in:** 3 U.S. 378 (1798).

71 **And interestingly, on:** President James Buchanan signed the Corwin amendment, which would have protected slavery in the states where it existed and required the return of escaped slaves, and which was proposed by the lame-duck Congress in early 1861. It became one of the six amendments in the nation's history approved by Congress but not ratified by the states. In 1865, President Abraham Lincoln signed the 13th Amendment abolishing slavery. John R. Vile, *Encyclopedia of Constitutional Amendments, Proposed Amendments, and Amending Issues, 1789–1995* (Santa Barbara: ABC-CLIO, 1996), p. 244.

72 **The vice president:** See the discussion of proposed revisions of the Constitution later in this chapter.

72 **Except for being:** Article I, Section 3, Clause 4 of the Constitution provides that the vice president shall be president of the Senate, "but shall have no Vote, unless they be equally divided." Clause 5 of the same section requires the Senate to choose a "President pro tempore" who presides in the absence of the vice president. That person is third in line in presidential succession after the vice president and Speaker of the House. The figure on how many times vice presidents have broken ties comes from Blake Eskin, *The Book of Political Lists* (New York: Villard, 1998), p. 86–87.

72 **But Roger Sherman:** Farrand, Vol. II, p. 537 (September 7, 1787) (Madison).

73 **There are a:** The Constitution, in Article II, Section 2, Clause 2, provides that the Senate approve treaties by a two-thirds vote. The Framers apparently envisioned the Senate working closely with the President as treaties were negotiated. President George Washington went to the Senate to seek "advice and consent" as he was negotiating a treaty with Southern Indians in August 1789. Washington hoped that the president and Senate could work together to settle treaties so as to avoid the problem, frequently encountered in our history, of having the Senate insist on modifying or adding amendments to treaties already approved by other nations. The Senate, however, declined to discuss the treaty in the presence of Washington, much to his disappointment. Pritchett, p. 259. The Senate's author-

ity to confirm many presidential appointees is found in Article II, Section 2, Clause 2. Its power to try impeachments is described in Article I, Section 3, Clause 6.

74 At least four: *Chisholm v. Georgia,* 2 U.S. 419 (1793); *Dred Scott v. Sanford,* 60 U.S. 393 (1857); *Pollock v. Farmers Loan & Trust Co.,* 158 U.S. 601 (1895); and *Oregon v. Mitchell,* 400 U.S. 112 (1970).

75 Even during the: David E. Kyvig, *Explicit and Authentic Acts: Amending the U.S. Constitution, 1776–1995* (Lawrence, Kansas: University Press of Kansas, 1996), pp. 292–294. The Court struck down the National Recovery Administration in *Schechter Poultry Corp. v. United States,* 295 U.S. 495 (1935); portions of the National Industrial Recovery Act of 1933 in *Panama Refining Co. v. Ryan,* 293 U.S. 388 (1935); and the coal industry codes set up under the Bituminous Coal Conservation Act in *Carter v. Carter Coal Co.,* 298 U.S. 238 (1936).

75 FDR considered whether: Stephen M. Griffin, "Constitutionalism in the United States: From Theory to Politics," in Sanford Levinson, ed., *Responding to Imperfection: The Theory and Practice of Constitutional Amendment* (Princeton, NJ: Princeton University Press, 1995), pp. 51–52. Yale legal scholar Bruce Ackerman maintained that by 1937, when the Supreme Court began upholding New Deal legislation and state wage and hour laws, and FDR finally got the opportunity to appoint the first of nine justices he would eventually name to the Court, the Constitution had undergone significant changes without using the amendment process of Article V. See Bruce Ackerman, *We The People: Foundations* (Cambridge, Mass: Belknap Press of Harvard University Press, 1991). See also, Bruce Ackerman, "Higher Lawmaking," in Levinson, pp. 80–82. For criticism of the Ackerman theory, see David R. Dow, "The Plain Meaning of Article V," in Levinson, pp. 117–144.

75 There is some: Laurence Tribe, "A Constitution We Are Amending: In Defense of a Restrained Judicial Role," 97 *Harvard Law Review* (December 1983), p. 433. Tribe was responding to a detailed article by Walter Dellinger in the same volume of the law review, in which Dellinger advocated a strong role for the judicial branch in deciding cases relating to the proposing and ratification of constitutional amendments. Walter Dellinger, "The Legitimacy of Constitutional Change: Rethinking the Amendment Process," 97 *Harvard Law Review* (December 1983), p. 386. Dellinger's brief rejoinder to Tribe's article is found at page 446.

76 For example, in: B. Drummond Ayres, Jr., "Women in Washington Statehouse Lead U.S. Tide," *New York Times* (April 14, 1997), p. A1.

76 In Kentucky, the: Hermione Malone, "Female leaders from South plan Lexington meeting," *Lexington (KY) Herald-Leader* (May 31, 1997), p. C1.

76 The national average: In 1997, women held 4 out of every 10 seats in the Washington legislature. In the U.S. Congress, women hold about 10 percent of the 535 seats. B. Drummond Ayres, Jr., "Women in Washington Statehouse Lead U.S. Tide," p. A12.

76 **The 424 state:** Thomas Dye, *Politics in States and Communities* (Prentice Hall: Upper Saddle River, NJ., 1997), p. 169.

76 **Their California counterparts:** Ibid., p. 168.

77 **In only one:** Paul J. Weber and Barbara A. Perry, *Unfounded Fears: Myths and Realities of a Constitutional Convention* (New York: Greenwood Press, 1989), p. 55.

77 **Congress was concerned:** Kyvig, pp. 280–288.

78 **In *Hawke v. Smith*:** 253 U.S. 221 (1920). In November 1918, Ohio voters amended the state constitution to require their approval of federal constitutional amendments: "The people also reserve to themselves the legislative power of the referendum on the action of the general assembly ratifying any proposed amendment to the constitution of the United States." The Court held Article V "is a grant of authority by the people to Congress," and the determination of the method of ratification is the exercise of national power specifically granted by the Constitution. The Court noted in *Hawke* that the Framers could have chosen a different method of ratification, but it is "not the function of courts or legislative bodies, national or state, to alter the method which the Constitution has fixed." At 227.

78 **Akhil Reed Amar:** Akhil Reed Amar, "Philadelphia Revisited: Amending the Constitution Outside Article V," 55 *University of Chicago Law Review* (Fall 1988), p. 1043.

79 **He restated this:** Akhil Reed Amar and Alan Hirsch, *For the People: What the Constitution Really Says About Your Rights* (New York: The Free Press, 1998), pp. 3–33.

79 **Therefore, even though:** Amar, "Philadelphia Revisited: Amending the Constitution Outside Article V," p. 1055.

79 **However, on eight:** Eskin, *The Book of Political Lists*, p. 205. Roger MacBride, an elector from Virginia in 1972, made history when he refused to give his vote to Richard Nixon who had won the state, and instead cast his ballot for John Hospers, the Libertarian Party candidate. Hospers's vice presidential running mate was Theodora Nathan. Thus, she became the first woman to ever receive an electoral vote.

80 **Madison strongly opposed:** Weber and Perry, pp. 31–54.

80 **He wrote to:** Edward P. Smith, "The Movement Toward a Second Constitutional Convention," in J. Franklin Jameson, ed., *Essays in the Constitutional History of the United States in the Formative Period, 1775–1789* (New York: Da Capo Press, 1970) (reprint of the 1889 edition), p. 95. The Smith essay is still considered to be one of the most comprehensive pieces on efforts to organize a second constitutional convention before the Constitution was ratified.

80 In *The Federalist*: Clinton Rossiter, *The Federalist Papers* (New York: Penguin Books, 1961), p. 314. See also, Kyvig, pp. 129–130.

81 "Having witnessed the: Weber and Perry, p. 47.

81 But the lack: See Lance Banning, *The Sacred Fire of Liberty: James Madison and the Founding of the Federal Republic* (Ithaca, NY: Cornell University Press, 1995), pp. 281–290.

81 George Mason, among: Kyvig, pp. 90–92.

81 Mason said he: Adrienne Koch, *Notes of Debates in the Federal Convention of 1787 Reported by James Madison* (Athens, Ohio: Ohio University Press, 1966), p. 630.

82 Considering that Rhode: For an explanation of why Rhode Island did not send delegates to the Convention, see John P. Kaminiski, "'Outcast' Rhode Island — The Absent State," in *This Constitution: From Ratification to the Bill of Rights* (Wash., D.C.: Congressional Quarterly, Inc., 1988), pp. 49–54. For a discussion of the referendum that Rhode Island conducted as part of the ratification process, see James S. Fishkin, *The Voice of the People: Public Opinion and Democracy* (New Haven, CT: Yale University Press, 1995).

82 Progressive-era historian: Levy, pp. 27–30.

83 Nevertheless, they mounted: For a detailed account of the effort of the Anti-Federalists to defeat the Constitution, see Ralph Ketchum, *The Anti-Federalist Papers and the Constitutional Convention Debates* (New York: Penguin Books, 1986).

83 Patrick Henry of: Vile, p. 32. Among the most eloquent of statements opposing the need for a new central government were Henry's speeches to the Virginia ratifying convention on June 5 and 7, 1788. See Ketchum, pp. 199–216. Virginia narrowly voted to ratify the Constitution 89–79 on June 25, 1788, primarily because the convention had learned that New Hampshire had just become the ninth state to approve the Constitution and thus Virginia's vote against ratification would not have prevented the Constitution from taking legal effect, but would have kept Virginia out of the Union.

83 Speaking of the: Ketchum, p. 204.

83 That would have: For a discussion of Madison's indispensable role in persuading the First Congress to propose the Bill of Rights, see Leonard W. Levy, *The Emergence of a Free Press* (New York: Oxford University Press, 1985), pp. 257–263. See also, Helen E. Veit, et. al., *Creating The Bill of Rights: The Documentary Record from the First Federal Congress* (Baltimore: Johns Hopkins University Press, 1991).

83 When Virginia's legislature: Weber and Perry, pp. 45–48.

83 By campaigning energetically: Jack N. Rakove, "James Madison and the Bill of Rights," in *This Constitution: From Ratification to the Bill of Rights* (Wash., D.C.:

Congressional Quarterly, Inc., 1988), p. 173. For a description of the campaign, see Banning, pp. 270–273.

84 They have been: For a detailed look at how *The Federalist Papers* have been used in Supreme Court decisions, see Buckner F. Melton, Jr., "The Supreme Court and the Federalist: A Citation List and Analysis, 1789–1996," 85 *Kentucky Law Review* No. 2 (1996–1997), p. 243.

84 The amending mechanism: Vile, pp. 34–42.

85 Although there have: For a list of the number of proposals by year, see Vile, *Encyclopedia of Constitutional Amendments*, pp. 363–380. For a discussion of the opposition to the Equal Rights Amendment, see Chapter Eight.

85 At least four: Weber and Perry, pp. 55–80.

85 At first it: Ibid., pp. 55–56.

85 In the first: Ibid., p. 56.

85 It would be: Ibid., p. 58–59.

85 On the eve: Ibid., p. 59.

86 From 1861 to: Ibid., p. 60.

86 Between 1893 and: Ibid., p. 61.

86 Between 1906 and: Ibid., pp. 61–62.

86 Several petitions were: Ibid., p. 62.

86 Despite the substantial: Ibid., p. 63.

86 Others issues that: Ibid.

87 States submitted petitions: Ibid., p. 64–68. *Brown v. Board of Education*, 347 U.S. 483 (1954); *Baker v. Carr*, 369 U.S. 186 (1962); *Reynolds v. Sims*, 377 U.S. 533 (1964).

87 Several states also: *Engel v. Vitale*, 370 U.S. 421 (1962); *Abington School District v. Schempp*, 374 U.S. 203 (1963).

87 In the years: Weber and Perry, pp. 68–75. *Roe v. Wade*, 410 U.S. 113 (1973).

87 By 1983, 32: Ibid., p. 74.

87 The amendment was: *Hammer v. Dagenhart*, 247 U.S. 251 (1918).

88 In order to: *McCullough v. Maryland*, 4 U.S. 316 (1819).

88 The intentional misinterpretation: *United States v. Darby Lumber Co.*, 312 U.S. 100 (1941).

88 On February 6, 1788: Veit, p. 14.

89 They did not: Ibid.

89 **The South Carolina:** Ibid., p. x.

89 **The proposed amendments:** Ibid., p. x.

89 **The 15th amendment:** Ibid., p. 18.

89 **Virginia had also:** The Virginia convention's application for a second convention stated in part: "We do, therefore, in behalf of our constituents, in the most earnest and solemn manner, make this application to Congress, that a Convention be immediately called of deputies from the several states, with full power to take into their consideration the defects of this Constitution that have been suggested by the state Conventions, and report such amendments thereto, as they shall find best suited to promote our common interests, and secure to ourselves and our latest posterity, the great and unalienable rights of mankind." Veit, p. 235–237.

90 **Although he was:** On December 20, 1787, a few months after the Convention in Philadelphia ended, Jefferson wrote to Madison: "I will now add what I do not like [about the proposed Constitution]. First, the omission of a bill of rights providing clearly . . . for freedom of religion, freedom of the press, protecting against standing armies, restriction against monopolies, the eternal and unremitting force of the habeas corpus laws, and trials by jury in all matters of fact triable by the laws of the land. . . . Let me add that a bill of rights is what the people are entitled to against every government on Earth, general or particular, and what no just government should refuse, or rest on inference." In a letter to Jefferson on October 17, 1788, Madison wrote: "My own opinion has always been in favor of a bill of rights, provided it be so framed as not to imply powers not meant to be included. . . . At the same time I have never thought the omission a material defect, nor been anxious to supply it even by subsequent amendment, for any other reason than that it is anxiously desired by others. I have favored it because I supposed it might be of use, and if properly executed could not be of disservice. I have not viewed it in an important light." Linda R. Monk, *The Bill of Rights: A User's Guide* (Washington, D.C.: Close Up Publishing, 1995), p. 32.

91 **Among the most:** Leonard W. Levy, *The Emergence of a Free Press*, p. 262.

91 **It took Roger:** As reported by the *Daily Advertiser*, on August 13, 1789, Sherman told the House that the amendments should be "supplemental" to the Constitution and should "not be incorporated in the body of the instrument which was made by authority of the people." He added that "any alterations of the individual articles of the constitution was a repeal of the constitution; that the house had no possible power of repealing. . . . The original form of the constitution ought to remain inviolate and all amendments which the Congress were authorized to make were only legislative acts which ought to be detached from the constitution and be supplementary to it." Veit p. 105.

93 **The Supreme Court:** *Barron v. Baltimore*, 7 U.S. 243 (1833).

93 **That meant that:** In an almost offhand and unexpected remark, Justice Edward Sanford surprised the country by agreeing in *Gitlow v. New York*, 268 U.S. 652 (1925), that freedom of speech, protected by the First Amendment from

encroachment by the federal government, would also apply to the states through the due process clause of the 14th Amendment.

93 It took until: The Supreme Court first applied the "exclusionary rule" to the states by which prosecutors were prohibited from using illegally seized evidence in court in *Mapp v. Ohio*, 367 U.S. 643 (1961). The rule had applied to the federal courts for many years. See *Weeks v. United States*, 232 U.S. 383 (1914).

93 Today, there are: They include the Second Amendment's right to bear arms, the Third Amendment's guarantee on quartering troops, the Fifth Amendment's guarantee of a grand jury indictment, the Seventh Amendment's right to a jury trial in a civil case, and the Eighth Amendment's guarantee against excessive fines and bail. Vile, *Encyclopedia of Constitutional Amendments*, p. 164.

93 A private entity: For a discussion of the extent to which the "state action" doctrine should apply in First Amendment cases, see Matthew D. Bunker, "Constitutional Baselines: First Amendment Theory, State Action and the "New Realism," *Communication Law and Policy*, Vol. 5 (Winter 2000), pp. 1–32.

93 In the famous: *Civil Rights Cases*, 109 U.S. 3 (1883).

94 The 11th Amendment: *Chisholm v. Georgia*, 2 U.S. 419 (1793).

94 Congress overlooked numerous: Farber and Sherry, pp. 322–323.

94 Finally, the 16th: *Pollock v. Farmers Loan & Trust Co.*, 157 U.S. 429 and 158 U.S. 601 (1895).

94 The statute at: Pritchett, pp. 168–169. See also, Kyvig, pp. 194–201.

95 State legislatures often: Kyvig, pp. 209–210.

95 Because of the: Kyvig, pp. 268–275.

96 It partially overturned: *Oregon v. Mitchell*, 400 U.S. 112 (1970).

96 Political scientist and: Vile is professor and chair of the Political Science Department at Middle Tennessee State University. See generally, John R. Vile, *Rewriting the United States Constitution: An Examination of Proposals from Reconstruction to the Present* (New York: Praeger, 1991); *The Constitutional Amending Process in American Political Thought* (New York: Praeger, 1992); *Contemporary Questions Surrounding the Constitutional Amending Process* (New York: Praeger, 1993). See also *Encyclopedia of Constitutional Amendments, Proposed Amendments, and Amending Issues, 1789–1995* (Santa Barbara, CA: ABC-CLIO, 1996).

98 Charles O'Conor: Charles O'Conor, "The President and Party Responsibility," *The Nation*, Vol. 24 (May 17, 1877), pp. 288–289.

99 For a brief: Eskin, *The Book of Political Lists*, p. 253.

99 Cambridge, Massachusetts, may: Ibid.

99 Albert Stickney (1839–1908): Albert Stickney, *A True Republic* (New York: Harper & Brothers, 1879).

100 Among his best-known: Woodrow Wilson, *Congressional Government: A Study in American Politics* (Boston: Houghton Mifflin, 1885).

100 Others supporting the: Henry Lockwood, *The Abolition of the Presidency* (New York: R. Worthington, 1884; reprint, (Farmingdale, NY: Darbor Social Science Publications, 1978).

100 Lockwood also argued: Vile, *Encyclopedia of Constitutional Amendments*, p. 192.

100 In 1884, he: Isaac Rice, "Work for a Constitutional Convention," *The Century Magazine*, Vol. 28 (August 1884), pp. 534–540.

100 Rice also did: Vile, *Encyclopedia of Constitutional Amendments*, p. 258.

101 Caspar Hopkins (1826–1893): Caspar Hopkins, "Thoughts Toward Revising the Federal Constitution," *Overland Monthly*, Vol. 6 (October 1885), pp. 388–398.

101 Hopkins said he: Vile, *Encyclopedia of Constitutional Amendments*, p. 160.

101 Judge Walter Clark: Walter Clark, "The Constitutional Changes Demanded to Bulwark Democratic Government," *Arena* (February 1907), pp. 141–154.

101 Henderson, a professor: Yandell Henderson, "The Progressive Movement and Constitutional Reform," 3 *Yale Review* (October 1913), pp. 78–90.

102 Shortly after World: William MacDonald, *A New Constitution for a New America* (New York: B.W. Heubsch, 1922).

102 He would also: Vile, *Encyclopedia of Constitutional Amendments*, p. 197.

103 Charles Merriam (1874–1953): Charles Merriam, *The Written Constitution and the Unwritten Attitude* (New York: Richard R. Smith, 1931).

103 Even though such: Vile, *Encyclopedia of Constitutional Amendments*, p. 204.

103 William Yandell Elliott: William Y. Elliott, *The Need for Constitutional Reform: A Program for National Security* (New York: Whittlesey House, 1935).

103 Although Elliott did: Vile, *Encyclopedia of Constitutional Amendments*, p. 114.

104 Writing during World: Henry Hazlitt, *A New Constitution Now* (New York: McGraw-Hill, 1942), later revised and published by Arlington House Publishers in New Rochelle, New York, in 1974 under the same title.

104 The group's report: Committee on Federal-State Relations, "Amending the Constitution to Strengthen the States in the Federal System," *State Government*, Vol. 10 (Winter 1963), p. 10.

104 A second proposal: *Baker v. Carr*, 369 U.S. 186 (1962).

105 Ten years later: Leland Baldwin, *Reframing the Constitution: An Imperative for Modern America* (Santa Barbara, CA: ABC-CLIO, 1972).

105 **In his first:** Vile, *Encyclopedia of Constitutional Amendments*, p. 310.

105 **In his 1974:** Rexford Tugwell, *The Emerging Constitution* (New York: Harper & Row, 1974).

106 **Despite Tugwell's diligent:** Vile, *Encyclopedia of Constitutional Amendments*, p. 312.

106 **Political scientist Charles:** Charles Hardin, *Presidential Power & Accountability: Toward a New Constitution* (Chicago: University of Chicago Press, 1974).

107 **Henry Reuss, a:** Henry S. Reuss, "An Introduction to the Vote of No Confidence," 43 *George Washington Law Review* (January 1974), pp. 333–335. Published as part of a *Symposium on the Reuss Resolution: A Vote of No Confidence in the President*.

107 **Donald Robinson, a:** Donald L. Robinson, *Reforming American Government: The Bicentennial Papers of the Committee on the Constitutional System* (Boulder, CO: Westview Press, 1985).

107 **James Sundquist, who:** James L. Sundquist, *Constitutional Reform and Effective Government* (Washington, D.C.: Brookings Institution, 1986).

107 **He recommended that:** Vile, *Encyclopedia of Constitutional Amendments*, p. 295.

109 **After reviewing the:** Ibid., pp. 164–166.

Chapter 3: The Role of Courts in "Amending" the Constitution

111 **For more than:** Legal scholar Sanford Levinson makes a distinction between constitutional "interpretation," which he says is, almost by definition, "unexceptional" — what courts routinely do when they decide constitutional cases — as opposed to the formal "amendment" of the Constitution, which he says is "extraordinary" and "something truly *new.*" (Emphasis in original). Sanford Levinson, "How Many Times Has the Constitution Been Amended?" in Sanford Levinson, ed., *Responding to Imperfection: The Theory and Practice of Constitutional Amendment* (Princeton, NJ: Princeton University Press, 1995), pp. 14–15.

111 **Judges cannot, however:** For a thoughtful and provocative argument that citizens should take more responsibility for protection of their rights, see Mark Tushnet, *Taking the Constitution Away From the Courts* (Princeton, NJ: Princeton University Press, 1999).

111 **But judges cannot:** Benjamin Cardozo, a Supreme Court justice from 1932–1938, but whose primary influence over the law may have emanated from his years before he served on the Court, described how slowly the common law develops: "This work of modification is gradual. It goes on inch by inch. Its effects must be measured by decades and even centuries. Thus measured, they are seen to have behind them the power and the pressure of the moving glacier." Cardozo,

p. 25. To Cardozo, this gradual development of the common law does not mean that judges can ignore previous cases: "Adherence to precedent must then be the rule rather than the exception if litigants are to have faith in the even-handed administration of justice in the courts." Ibid., p. 34.

114 It may take: An example of how a single case can establish a precedent that lasts for many years was the Supreme Court's decision that major league baseball was a "club" and not a business, thus providing the league with an invaluable exemption to the antitrust laws, which continues to this day. *Federal Baseball Club of Baltimore v. National League of Professional Baseball Clubs*, 295 U.S. 200 (1922). Some members of Congress have tried to reverse that decision by passing a law requiring baseball to be covered by the antitrust laws, but no one has been able to get such a bill through Congress and another case challenging baseball's status has not come before the Supreme Court.

117 The Constitution prohibited: Article III, Section 1 states in part that "judges ... shall at stated Times, receive for their Services, a Compensation, which shall not be diminished during their Continuance in Office."

117 Besides the nine: Robert Carp and Ronald Stidham, *Judicial Process in America* (Washington, D.C.: CQ Press, 1996), p. 39 (court of appeals judges), and p. 46 (district court judges).

117 Non-Article III: See 5 U.S.C. Section 3105, 7521.

117 Their decisions can: See generally William F. Fox, Jr., *Understanding Administrative Law*, 2nd ed. (New York: Matthew Bender & Co., 1992), pp. 218–232.

118 For example, on: Tim Golden, "U.S. Judge Blocks Enforcing of Law Over Preferences," *New York Times* (December 24, 1996), p. A1.

118 The U.S. Court: *Coalition For Economic Equity v. Wilson*, 110 F.3d 1431, 1437 (9th Cir. 1997). See also, Tim Golden, "Federal Appeals Court Upholds California's Ban on Preferences," *New York Times* (April 9, 1997), p. A1.

119 Federal judges have: In *Swann v. Charlotte-Mecklenburg Board of Education*, 402 U.S. 1 (1971), the Supreme Court upheld a judge's order requiring that a North Carolina school district integrate its schools when there has been a history of discrimination in the district. In *Hutto v. Finney*, 437 U.S. 678 (1978), the Court granted broad powers to a federal district court judge to remedy barbaric conditions in the Arkansas prison system. The Court upheld a lower court's order requiring the Department of Housing and Urban Development to remedy past discrimination by implementing a plan that went beyond the Chicago city limits in *Hills v. Gautreaux*, 425 U.S. 284 (1976). For a forceful and thoughtful statement on why federal courts must act to preserve constitutional rights when states refuse to carry out their required duties, see Frank Johnson, "The Constitution and the Federal District Judge," 54 *Texas Law Review* (1976), p. 903. Johnson was a U.S. District Court judge in Alabama from 1956 to 1979, and he issued and supervised many orders against Alabama officials. In 1979, President Carter appointed Johnson to the Court of Appeals. Those opposed to Johnson's desegregation orders

THE SECOND CONSTITUTIONAL CONVENTION

threatened him and his family, and his home was bombed. Johnson himself was ostracized in the community where he lived. In 1995, President Clinton awarded Johnson a Presidential Medal of Freedom to honor his more than 40 years on the federal bench. "Judge Johnson's Medal," *The New York Times* (July 10, 1995), p. A12. For an excellent biography of Johnson, which demonstrates why federal judges must have lifetime tenure, see Robert F. Kennedy, *Judge Frank A. Johnson: A Biography* (New York: Putnam Publishing Group, 1978).

119 Although democratically elected: Cardozo, quoting a Supreme Court decision, commented on the role of the elected branches in protecting rights: "It must be remembered that legislatures are ultimate guardians of the liberties and welfare of the people in quite as great a degree as courts." Benjamin Cardozo, *The Nature of the Judicial Process* (New Haven, Ct.: Yale University Press, 1921), p. 90, quoting *Missouri, Kansas and Texas Railway Co. v. May*, 194 U.S. 267, 270 (1904).

120 Alexander Hamilton, in: Clinton Rossiter, ed., *The Federalist Papers* (New York: Penguin Books, 1961), p. 466.

120 In a letter: Linda R. Monk, *The Bill of Rights: A User's Guide* (Alexandria, VA: Close Up Publishing, 1995), p. 32.

120 The original justices: C. Herman Pritchett, *The American Constitution* (New York: McGraw-Hill, 1977), p. 37.

121 The dual service: Gordon S. Wood, "Comment," in Antonin Scalia, *A Matter of Interpretation: Federal Courts and the Law* (Princeton, N.J.: Princeton University Press, 1997), pp. 54–56.

121 Chase's acquittal has: See generally, Robert G. McCloskey, *The American Supreme Court* (Chicago: University of Chicago Press, 1994), pp. 28–30. McCloskey wrote that the "failure of the Chase impeachment is one of the signal events in the history of the federal judiciary, because it set a precedent against loose construction of the impeachment power and thus supported the doctrine of judicial independence." Ibid., p. 30.

121 The Supreme Court: Pritchett, pp. 89–91.

121 Franklin Roosevelt, having: Roosevelt won every state except Maine and Vermont, gaining 523 electoral votes to Alfred Landon's 8. Roosevelt received 11 million more popular votes than Landon, a huge margin. Paul F. Boller, Jr., *Presidential Campaigns* (New York: Oxford University Press, 1984), p. 244.

121 Despite FDR's popularity: For a description of the court-packing plan, see McCloskey, pp. 117–120.

122 During the 12-year: Pritchett, p. 89.

122 He is often: Bernard Schwartz, *A Book of Legal Lists* (New York: Oxford University Press, 1997), pp. 5–7. See also, Darien A. McWhirter, *The Legal 100: A Ranking of the Individuals Who Have Most Influenced the Law* (Secaucus, NJ: Carol Publishing/Citadel Press, 1998).

122 Schwartz quoted Oliver: Ibid., p. 5.

122 Justice Benjamin Cardozo: Cardozo, pp. 169–170.

123 Thus even if: Pritchett, pp. 95–96.

123 Congress did so: The Judiciary Act of 1789, I Stat. 73. For an excellent discussion of the Judiciary Act, see Wilfred J. Ritz, *Rewriting the History of the Judiciary Act of 1789* (Norman, OK: University of Oklahoma Press, 1990).

123 Congress is considering: Carp and Stidham, p. 152, n. 2.

124 In *Ex Parte McCardle*: *Ex Parte McCardle*, 74 U.S. 506, 514 (1869). See also, *Ex Parte Milligan*, 4 U.S. 2 (1866), in which the Court declared President Lincoln's military commissions unconstitutional.

124 However, once it: *Wiscart v. D'Auchy*, 3 U.S. 321 (1796).

124 While it is: Carp and Stidham note the congressional power over federal court jurisdiction exercised in *McCardle* shows the "awesome nature of this legislative prerogative" that "haunts the judiciary to this day." p. 136.

125 Justices would spend: Mary Ann Harrell, *Equal Justice Under Law: The Supreme Court in American Life* (Washington, D.C.: The Supreme Court Historical Society, 1994), p. 15.

126 The lame-duck: For a discussion of the various judiciary acts, see Carp and Stidham, pp. 21–67.

126 The justices were: Pritchett, p. 90.

127 Judges also have: In *Youngstown Sheet & Tube Co. v. Sawyer*, 343 U.S. 579 (1952), the Supreme Court held that President Truman's seizure of the steel mills to prevent a strike that would interfere with the flow of munitions to American troops in Korea was unauthorized by statute and unjustified by inherent presidential powers. In *Hague v. CIO*, 307 U.S. 496 (1939), the Supreme Court determined that the mayor of Jersey City, New Jersey, could not deny a labor union the use of public buildings on the ground that it was a Communist organization.

127 The delegates considered: Max Farrand, *The Records of the Federal Convention of 1787* (New Haven, CT: Yale University Press, 1911), Vol. 1, pp. 138–140 (Madison).

128 It would also: Ibid., p. 138.

128 The delegates rejected: Ibid., p. 140.

128 Charles Pinckney of: Ibid., Vol. II, p. 298.

128 The delegates defeated: Ibid.

128 No additional effort: Pritchett, p. 125.

128 In describing the: Clinton Rossiter, ed., *The Federalist Papers*, p. 466.

128 And he added: Ibid., p. 467–468.

129 In a 1989: William H. Rehnquist, *The Supreme Court: How It Was, How It Is* (New York: Wm. Morrow & Co., 1989), p. 306.

129 Although the Supreme: The Supreme Court examined whether a state law was contrary to the state's constitution in *Cooper v. Telfair*, 4 U.S. 14 (1800), struck down a state law based on the supremacy clause of the U.S. Constitution in *Ware v. Hylton*, 3 U.S. 199 (1796), and reviewed the constitutionality of a federal statute in *Hylton v. United States*, 3 U.S. 171 (1796). Justice James Iredell had explicitly asserted the power of judicial review in both *Chisholm v. Georgia*, 2 U.S. 419 (1793) and *Calder v. Bull*, 3 U.S. 386 (1798). Former judge and unsuccessful Supreme Court nominee Robert Bork identified *Hayburn's Case*, 2 U.S. 409 (1792) as the first one clearly asserting the Court's right to review the constitutionality of legislation. Robert Bork, *The Tempting of America: The Political Seduction of the Law* (New York: Free Press, 1989), p. 24.

130 At this early: The Supreme Court's reliance on the elected branches of government to help enforce its orders was obvious during the Jackson administration. When the Court ordered the state of Georgia in *Worcester v. Georgia*, 6 U.S. 515 (1832), to release two missionaries convicted of violating a state law requiring those living in Cherokee country to swear allegiance to the state, Georgia refused. At first it appeared that President Jackson would not intervene to force Georgia to release the missionaries. He was quoted as saying, "John Marshall has made his decision, now let him enforce it." But the showdown was eventually averted when Georgia granted pardons to the missionaries. Archibald Cox, *The Court and the Constitution* (Boston: Houghton Mifflin Co., 1987), p. 14. Other scholars believe it is unlikely that Jackson made the statement. Robert Scigliano, *The Supreme Court and the Presidency* (New York: The Free Press, 1971), p. 36–37.

130 Writing for a: 5 U.S. 137 (1803).

130 The law that: Pritchett, p. 126.

131 Marshall left no: 5 U.S. at 177.

131 Section 13, it: Pritchett, p. 127.

131 After *Marbury*, no: *Dred Scott v. Sandford*, 19 U.S. 393 (1857).

131 The Court did: *Fletcher v. Peck*, 10 U.S. 87 (1810); *Martin v. Hunter's Lessee*, 14 U.S. 304 (1816); and *Cohens v. Virginia*, 19 U.S. 264 (1821).

132 During the New: Pritchett, p. 128.

132 By 1994, the: Elder Witt, *The Supreme Court A to Z* (Washington, D.C.: Congressional Quarterly, 1994), p. 433.

133 It is the: Identifying the principle, or *ratio decidendi*, of a case, is no simple task. A legal scholar once wrote that "[w]ith the possible exception of the legal term 'malice,' [*ratio decidendi*] is the most misleading expression in English law, for the reason which the judge gives for his decision is never the binding part of the precedent." Arthur L. Goodhart, "Determining the *Ratio Decidendi* of a Case," 40 *Yale Law Journal* (1930), pp. 161–162.

133 As Cardozo observed: Cardozo, p. 14.

134 Cardozo observed many: Ibid., pp. 135–136. (Emphasis in original).

136 Such was the: *Brown v. Board of Education*, 347 U.S. 483 (1954); and 349 U.S. 294 (1955).

138 In one of: Oliver Wendell Holmes, *The Common Law* (Boston: Little Brown, 1881), p. 1. See also, Holmes, "The Path of the Law," 10 *Harvard Law Review* (1897), p. 457. Other influential members of the movement included Roscoe Pound (1870–1964), who was to become dean of the Harvard Law School. See Roscoe Pound, *An Introduction to the Philosophy of Law* (New Haven, CT: Yale University Press, 1922).

138 He recognized that: Cardozo, p. 112.

139 The "realists," who: Among the groups' most prominent works were Karl Llewellyn's *The Bramble Bush* (New York: Oceana Publications, 1951); and Jerome Frank's *Law and the Modern Mind* (New York: Brentano's, 1930). Frank later became a court of appeals judge. See also, Walter Murphy and C. Herman Pritchett, *Courts, Judges, and Politics: An Introduction to the Judicial Process* (New York: Random House, 1979), p. 6.

139 The Constitution is: Article VI states in part: "This Constitution, and the Laws of the United States which shall be made in Pursuance thereof . . . shall be the Supreme Law of the Land; and the Judges in every State shall be bound thereby, any Thing in the Constitution or Laws of any State to the Contrary notwithstanding."

141 Furthermore, Charles Beard: Charles Beard, *An Economic Interpretation of the Constitution*, in Leonard W. Levy, ed., *Essays on the Making of the Constitution* (New York: Oxford University Press, 1987), pp. 27–30.

141 The conventions not: David E. Kyvig, *Explicit and Authentic Acts: Amending the U.S. Constitution, 1776–1995* (Lawrence, KS: University Press of Kansas, 1996), pp. 66–86.

142 Chief Justice Charles: See generally, *West Coast Hotel v. Parrish*, 300 U.S. 379 (1937).

143 In one of: Schwartz, p. 34.

143 Scalia voted with: *Texas v. Johnson*, 491 U.S. 397 (1989); and *United States v. Eichman*, 496 U.S. 310 (1990).

143 In the 1992: *Hudson v. McMillian*, 503 U.S. 1 (1992).

144 In *Harmelin v. Michigan*: *Harmelin v. Michigan*, 501 U.S. 957 (1992).

144 "Yes, Judge Scalia: Anthony Lewis, "The Court: Scalia," *New York Times* (June 26, 1986), p. A23.

144 "No one is: Anthony Lewis, "Reading the Text," *New York Times* (August 3, 1990), p. A27.

144 Among Scalia's many: Antonin Scalia, *A Matter of Interpretation: Federal Courts and the Law* (Princeton, N.J.: Princeton University Press, 1997).

144 He argues that: Ibid., p. 39.

144 Scalia describes himself: Ibid., p. 23–25.

145 In the Supreme: Ibid., p. 13.

145 To Scalia, the: Ibid., pp. 40–41.

145 He rejects the: Ibid., pp. 38–47.

146 He instead argues: Ibid., p. 38.

146 The Eighth Amendment: Scalia, p. 46, cites these cases where three of his brethren announced their opposition to the death penalty: *Gregg v. Georgia*, 428 U.S. 153, 227 (1976) (Brennan, J., dissenting); *id.* at 231 (Marshall, J., dissenting); *Callins v. Collins*, 510 U.S. 1141 (1994) (Blackmun, J., dissenting from denial of certiorari).

146 Therefore, in Scalia's: Ibid., p. 46.

147 He noted that: Ibid., p. 47.

147 He observed that: Ibid., p. 45.

147 Justice William J. Brennan Jr.: Linda Greenhouse, "William Brennan, 91, Dies; Gave Court Liberal Vision," *New York Times* (July 25, 1997), p. A1. See also, Anthony Lewis, "Our Better Angels," *New York Times* (August 1, 1997), p. A19; and Stephen J. Wermeil, "Justice on a Grand Scale," *Newsweek* (August 4, 1997), p. 72.

147 Among Brennan's most: *New York Times v. Sullivan*, 376 U.S. 254 (1964). For an excellent and thorough discussion of the case, see Anthony Lewis, *Make No Law: The Sullivan Case and the First Amendment* (New York: Random House, 1991).

148 Brennan's exceptional opinion: Among the case's most famous phrases is this: "Thus we consider this case against the background of a profound national commitment to the principle that debate on public issues should be uninhibited, robust and wide-open, and that debate on public issues may well include vehement, caustic, and sometimes unpleasantly sharp attacks on government and public officials." 276 U.S. at 270–271.

148 The most forceful: Scalia, pp. 65–94.

149 He cites Brown: *Brown v. Board of Education*, 347 U.S. 483 (1954); and 349 U.S. 294 (1955).

149 In fact, Congress: David E. Kyvig, *Explicit and Authentic Acts: Amending the U.S. Constitution, 1776–1995* (Lawrence, KS: University Press of Kansas, 1996), pp. 154–187.

149 To Tribe, the: Scalia, p. 68. (Emphasis in original).

149 Tribe noted that: Ibid., p. 81. (Emphasis in original).

149 Scalia argues that: Ibid., p. 134

150 Instead, Scalia argued: Ibid., p. 135.

150 The Supreme Court: *City of Boerne v. Flores*, 521 U.S. 507 (1997). See also, Linda Greenhouse, "High Court Voids A Law Expanding Religious Rights," *New York Times* (June 26, 1997), p. A1.

151 The Constitution says: Article II, Section 2 states in part: "And he shall nominate . . . by and with the Advice and Consent of the Senate . . . Judges of the Supreme Court, and all other officers of the United States . . . which shall be established by Law."

151 One former assistant: Carp and Stidham, p. 247.

151 In October of: B. Drummond Ayres Jr., "Missouri Senate Race Hits All the Hot Issues," *New York Times* (October 17, 1999), p. 26. For a scathing commentary on the Senate's action, see Anthony Lewis, "Hypocrites in Power," *New York Times* (November 9, 1999), p. A25.

152 President Eisenhower, for: For an excellent biography of Brennan with a detailed discussion of the process that led to his appointment, see Kim Isaac Eisler, *A Justice For All: William J. Brennan, Jr., And The Decisions That Transformed America* (New York: Simon & Schuster, 1993). See also, Robert D. Richards, *Uninhibited, Robust, and Wide Open: Mr. Justice Brennan's Legacy to the First Amendment* (Boone, NC: Parkway Publishers, 1994); and Hunter R. Clark, *Justice Brennan: The Great Conciliator* (New York: Birch Lane Press, 1995).

152 Eisenhower told his: Ibid., p. 84. For a summary of Brennan's career upon his death in 1997, see Linda Greenhouse, "William Brennan, 91, Dies; Gave Court Liberal Vision," *New York Times* (July 25, 1997), p. A1. See also, Katharine Q. Seelye, "With Gentle Humor, Brennan Is Buried," *New York Times* (July 30, 1997), p. A11; and Anthony Lewis, "Our Better Angels," *New York Times* (August 1, 1997), p. A19;

153 Senator Edward Kennedy: Philip Shenon, "Senate, Ending Judicial Fight, Gives Manion Final Approval," *New York Times* (July 24, 1986), p. A1.

153 Illustrating the political: Timothy Eagan, "Judge in Seattle Finally Sworn In," *New York Times* (December 3, 1987), p. A36.

153 **Apparently, he helped:** Neil A. Lewis, "Clinton Agrees to G.O.P. Deal On Judgeships," *New York Times* (May 5, 1998), p. A1.

153 **In striking the:** Ibid., p. 20.

153 **In recent years:** See generally, Stephen L. Carter, *The Confirmation Mess: Cleaning Up the Federal Appointments Process* (New York: Basic Books, 1994).

153 **With the Senate:** In November 1999, the White House and Senate leaders reached an agreement that would allow a vote on a few of the Clinton nominees to the federal bench. Neil A. Lewis, "Senate Leaders Move to Bring Judicial Nominees to a Vote," *New York Times* (November 11, 1999), p. A16. However, a month later, Senator James Inhofe (R-OK), who was angry about the administration's appointing of senior officials while Congress was in recess, threatened to block every judicial nominee until the end of the Clinton Administration. "Block Promised On Nominees Clinton Offers," (Associated Press) *New York Times* (December 21, 1999), p. A22.

153 **As of August:** Angie Cannon and Ron Hutcheson, "Federal judge vacancies delay, deny justice," *Lexington (KY) Herald-Leader* (Knight-Ridder News Service) (August 8, 1997), p. A1.

154 **In January 1998:** "Senate Confirms 3 Judges in Nominee Backlog," (Associated Press) *New York Times* (January 29, 1998), p. A12.

154 **In his end-of-the-year:** John H. Cushman, Jr., "Senate Imperiling Judicial System, Rehnquist Says," *New York Times* (January 1, 1998), p. A1.

154 **In response, the:** Neil A. Lewis, "Senator Responds To Sharp Attack By Chief Justice," *New York Times* (January 2, 1998), p. A1.

154 **They considered, but:** Neil A. Lewis, "Move to Limit Clinton's Judicial Choices Fails," *New York Times* (April 30, 1997), p. A15.

155 **He said he:** Neil A. Lewis, "Head of Senate's Judiciary Committee Reconsiders Advisory Role of A.B.A.," *New York Times* (February 19, 1997), p. A11.

155 **Meanwhile, a group:** Katherine Q. Seelye, "Conservatives in House Are Preparing an Impeachment List of Federal Judges," *New York Times* (March 14, 1997), p. A13. For commentary critical of the plan by both liberals and conservatives, see Anthony Lewis, "Menacing The Courts," *New York Times* (March 28, 1997), p. A19; and Bruce Fein, "Judge Not," *New York Times* (May 8, 1997), p. A23.

155 **Ironically, President Clinton's:** Carp and Stidham, 247, 267–274. See also, C.K. Rowland and Robert A. Carp, *Politics and Judgment in Federal District Courts* (Lawrence, KS: The University Press of KS, 1996).

155 **For instance, Republicans:** Neil A. Lewis, "Attack on Clinton Nominee May Backfire on the G.O.P.," *New York Times* (February 10, 1998), p. A12.

155 **It was a:** Ibid.

156 Nancy Gertner was: Margaret A. Jacobs, "Federal Judge With a Radical Past Hands Down Mainstream Rulings," *Wall Street Journal* (November 20, 1997), p. B2.

156 There is no: See generally, Stephen L. Carter, *The Confirmation Mess: Cleaning Up the Federal Appointment Process* (New York: Basic Books, 1994).

156 With increasing life: There have been notorious cases of federal judges who are mentally ill or senile, yet remain on the bench for years. See Carp and Stidham, *Judicial Process in America*, pp. 279–283.

156 Two weeks after: For a discussion of federal judges who have been impeached and convicted, see Max Boot, *Out of Order: Arrogance, Corruption and Incompetence on the Bench* (New York: Basic Books, 1998). See also, Carp and Stidham, p. 279–281.

157 In 1980, a: Ibid., p. 281.

157 For selection of: Thomas R. Dye, *Politics in States and Communities* (Upper Saddle River, NJ: Prentice Hall, 1997), p. 224.

157 State judges do: For a discussion of the selection and tenure of state trial and appellate judges, see Carp and Stidham, pp. 256–262.

159 Offering advisory opinions: In 1902, Congress passed a law that appeared to require the federal courts, including the Supreme Court, to issue advisory opinions in disputes related to land allocated to the Cherokee Indians. The Supreme Court held the law to be unconstitutional, arguing that it would be "required to give opinions in the nature of advice concerning legislative action — a function never conferred upon it by the Constitution." *Muskrat v. United States*, 219 U.S. 346 (1911).

159 Despite this principle: *Pollock v. Farmers' Loan and Trust Co.*, 157 U.S. 429; 158 U.S. 601 (1895).

159 Although both plaintiffs: Kyvig, p. 196–198. Kyvig said the lack of a legitimate basis for the suit remained "concealed" from the Court. Ibid., p. 196.

159 The legal rules: The issue of standing to sue in the federal courts has been developed unevenly in a substantial number of cases. Among the most important standing cases are *Allen v. Wright*, 468 U.S. 737 (1984), in which the Supreme Court denied standing to black parents suing the Internal Revenue Service for failing to deny tax-exempt status to private schools that discriminate on the basis of race; *Association of Data Processing Services Organizations v. Camp*, 397 U.S. 150 (1970), requiring that a plaintiff show "injury in fact" and not just a legal interest to gain standing; *Sierra Club v. Morton*, 405 U.S. 727 (1972), where the Court denied standing to plaintiffs who were not directly affected by plans to construct a recreation area in a national forest; and *United States v. Student Challenging Regulatory Agency Procedures (SCRAP)*, 412 U.S. 669 (1973), where the Court surprisingly found that environmental groups could challenge the Interstate Commerce Commission's failure to suspend surcharges on railroad freight rates when recyclable materials were being shipped. The Supreme Court has rarely granted standing to taxpayers on the ground that the alleged injury is too general and applies to too many people. The Court did grant standing to taxpayers to challenge aid to religious schools in *Flast v. Cohen*, 392 U.S. 83 (1968), but denied taxpayer standing in *Valley Forge Christian College v. Americans United*, 454 U.S. 464 (1982), *United States v. Richardson*, 418 U.S. 166 (1974), and *Frothingham v. Mellon*, 262 U.S. 447 (1923).

160 As the Supreme: *Frothingham v. Mellon*, 262 U.S. 447, 488 (1923).

160 More than 250,000: Carp and Stidham, p. 16.

160 For the 12-month: Ibid., p. 126

160 In 1993, almost: Ibid., p. 127.

161 More than 7,000: Ibid., p. 132.

161 In the term: Linda Greenhouse, "Supreme Court Roundup; Justices Get Early Start, Adding Several Cases," *New York Times* (September 11, 1999), p. A8.

161 It is not: The Supreme Court in *United States v. Providence Journal Co.*, 485 U.S. 693 (1988), had the opportunity to settle an important issue related to the power of judges to issue restraining orders against the press, and then hold journalists in contempt for violating those orders even if they were later determined to be unconstitutional. The U.S. Court of Appeals for the First Circuit concluded in *In re Providence Journal Co.*, 820 F.2d 1342 (1st Cir. 1986), *modified en banc*, 820 F.2d 1354 (1st Cir. 1987), that journalists could not be punished for disobeying unconstitutional orders. The U.S. Court of Appeals for the Fifth Circuit, however, came to the opposite conclusion. It upheld the power of judges to punish defiance of their orders, even when they are later invalidated on appeal, in *United States v. Dickinson*, 465 F.2d 496 (5th Cir. 1972). The Supreme Court could not settle the issue because it learned that the attorney representing the federal judge in the *Providence* case had failed to obtain permission from the Attorney General or the Solicitor General to represent the federal government before the Supreme Court, as required by 28 U.S.C. Section 518(a). The Supreme Court had to dismiss the writ of certiorari and thus could not decide the merits of the case. See Richard Labunski, "A First Amendment Exception to the 'Collateral Bar' Rule: Protecting Freedom of Expression and the Legitimacy of Courts," 22 *Pepperdine Law Review* No. 2 (1995), p. 405.

161 The Supreme Court: In a concurring opinion in *Ashwander v. Tennessee Valley Authority*, 297 U.S. 288, 347 (1936), Justice Louis Brandeis reviewed the standards the Court had developed to avoid passing on constitutional questions, and stated that the Court "will not 'formulate a rule of constitutional law broader than is required by the precise facts to which it is to be applied.'" (quoting *Liverpool, N.Y. & Phil. S.S. Co. v. Commissioners of Emigration*, 113 U.S. 33, 39 (1885)).

162 The First Congress: For an excellent discussion of the ratification of the 27th Amendment, see Kyvig, pp. 461–487.

163 **But because there:** A 20-year-old University of Texas student, Gregory Watson, learned about the unratified second amendment while writing a paper on the equal rights amendment. After Watson sent letters to state legislatures informing them that the pay raise had no time limit on ratification, they quickly began to ratify the amendment. On May 7, 1992, Michigan approved the 27th Amendment, becoming the 38th state to do so. Kyvig, pp. 465–467.

163 **Although the Supreme:** The Supreme Court initially determined that Congress could fix a period for ratification within "reasonable limits," and in *Dillon v. Gloss*, 256 U.S. 368 (1921), the Court found that seven years was reasonable. The Court later held in *Coleman v. Miller*, 307 U.S. 433 (1939), that Congress, not the Court, should determine what is a reasonable period for ratification.

163 **Nevertheless, the Court:** *Coleman*, 307 U.S. at 453.

163 **If the 27th:** Those amendments that were approved by both houses of Congress but never ratified include the 1810 amendment banning citizens from accepting foreign titles of nobility, the 1861 amendment guaranteeing the continuation of slavery in states where it then existed, and the 1924 amendment banning child labor. Kyvig, p. 469.

163 **The House by:** Kyvig, p. 469.

163 **Because only members:** In 1993, then-Speaker of the House Thomas Foley (D-WA) filed suit in federal district court in Seattle seeking to overturn the term limits initiative for members of Congress passed in 1992 by Washington voters. Foley was eventually successful when the Supreme Court invalidated federal term limits in *U.S. Term Limits v. Thornton*, 514 U.S. 779 (1995). The U.S. Court of Appeals for the Ninth Circuit followed *Thornton* in *Thorsted v. Munro*, 75 F.3d 454 (9th Cir. 1996). But although Foley won the lawsuit, it was at great personal cost. His involvement in the litigation was probably a significant factor in his defeat for reelection in 1994 after 30 years in the House.

165 **In an important:** *Branzburg v. Hayes*, 408 U.S. 655 (1972).

165 **Although the practice:** For a scathing criticism of the way reporters used confidential sources while covering the story about President Clinton and Monica Lewinsky, see Bill Kovach and Tom Rosenstiel, *Warp Speed: America in the Age of Mixed Media* (New York: The Century Foundation Press, 1999).

165 **A North Carolina:** Barry Meier, "Jury Says ABC Owes Damages of $5.5 Million," *New York Times* (January 23, 1997), p. A1. In October 1999, the U.S. Court of Appeals for the Fourth Circuit reversed the trial court's award, calling the lower court's judgment "an end-run" around First Amendment protections for journalists. Felicity Barringer, "Appeals Court Rejects Damages Against ABC in Food Lion Case," *New York Times* (October 21, 1999), p. A1.

166 **Justices of the:** See generally, Richard Labunski, "Judicial Discretion and the First Amendment: Extending the Holding Beyond the Facts Through 'Contiguous Decision-Making,'" 13 *Comm/Ent - A Journal of Communications and Enter-*

tainment Law No. 1, Hastings College of the Law, University of California, San Francisco (Fall 1990).

166 Some lower courts: The Supreme Court was divided 5–4 in *Branzburg*, but one of the justices in the majority, Justice Lewis Powell, wrote a short concurring opinion suggesting there are circumstances under which the First Amendment does protect the right of reporters to keep sources confidential. Because of Powell's concurrence and the unrepresentative circumstances presented in the case, some lower courts believe *Branzburg* was really a 4-1-4 decision. As a result, those courts that want to extend a First Amendment privilege have adopted the test included in Justice Potter Stewart's dissent, which makes forced disclosure of confidential sources very difficult to obtain.

167 For example, the: *Hopwood v. Texas*, 78 F.3d 932 (5th Cir. 1996), *cert. denied sub nom, Thurgood Marshall Legal Society v. Hopwood*, 116 S. Ct. 2580 (1996). See generally, Ellis Close, "The Color Bind," *Newsweek* (May 12, 1997), p. 58. There has been a decrease in minority enrollment at some universities in recent years. See Karen W. Arenson, "College Minority Enrollment Slowed in 1995," *New York Times* (May 19, 1997), p. A11. See also, Douglas Lederman, "Backers of Affirmative Action Struggle to Find Research That Will Help in Court, *Chronicle of Higher Education* (May 23, 1997), p. A28.

167 It also held: Anthony Lewis, "Down the River," *New York Times* (July 5, 1996), p. A23.

167 Justice Ruth Bader: Linda Greenhouse, "Justices Deny Affirmative-Action Case," *New York Times* (July 2, 1996), p. A12.

168 Generally by the: An exception to the general principle that an appellate court hears an appeal from a lower trial court would be in administrative law. Appeals from federal administrative agencies go to one of the U.S. courts of appeals rather than to a U.S. district court. See Fox, pp. 241–309.

168 Except for certain: Because of the importance of free expression in a democratic society, the Supreme Court has required appellate courts to closely scrutinize the decisions of trial courts where libel judgments have been issued against news organizations. In those cases, the appellate court will conduct a *de novo* review, which requires the appellate court to consider whether there was sufficient evidence to support the verdict. See *Bose Corp. v. Consumers Union*, 446 U.S. 485 (1984).

168 A famous example: *Near v. Minnesota*, 283 U.S. 697 (1931).

168 The Saturday Press: For a lively account of the newspaper and the case, see Fred W. Friendly, *Minnesota Rag: The Dramatic Story of the Landmark Supreme Court Case That Gave New Meaning to Freedom of the Press* (New York: Vintage Books, 1982).

169 But by providing: Listing the exceptions to the prior restraint standard may have had a practical basis, for Hughes may have needed to include them to secure the fifth vote from one of his staunchly conservative colleagues.

169 He cited as: 283 U.S. at 716.

169 Four decades after: *New York Times v. United States*, 403 U.S. 713 (1971).

169 Justice William Brennan: Ibid., p. 726.

170 In *United States v. Progressive*: *United States v. Progressive*, 467 F. Supp. 990 (W.D. Wis. 1979).

170 In "*Near v. Minnesota*: Ibid., p. 992.

170 "This Court concludes: Ibid., p. 996.

170 The judge understood: Ibid.

171 *Cantrell v. Forest City Publishing Co.*: *Cantrell v. Forest City Publishing Co.*, 419 U.S. 245 (1974).

172 Yet the article: Ibid. at 248, quoting Joe Eszterhas, "Legacy of the Silver Bridge," *Plain Dealer* (August 4, 1968), p. 32.

172 False light generally: William Prosser, "Privacy," 48 *California Law Review* (1960), p. 398. Prosser noted that the material need not be defamatory in false-light privacy, which is required in libel, but might well be. Ibid., p. 400. The most typical instances of false light are coincidental uses of names, fictionalization, distortion, embellishment, and misuse of names and pictures through unfortunate juxtapositions in otherwise legitimate news stories. Donald Gillmor, et. al., *Mass Communication Law* (St. Paul: West Publishing Co., 5th ed., 1990), p. 314. For an excellent discussion of other privacy issues, see Ellen Alderman and Caroline Kennedy, *The Right To Privacy* (New York: Alfred A. Knopf, 1995).

172 The jury awarded: Warren Weaver, Jr., *New York Times* Abstracts (December 19, 1974), p. 39.

172 The newspaper appealed: *Forest City Publishing Co. v. Cantrell*, 484 F.2d 150 (6th Cir. 1973). The court of appeals appeared to be overly forgiving of the transgressions of the newspaper reporter:

> Although Mrs. Cantrell and her son were displeased with the article published by the *Plain Dealer* and the article was not as carefully written as it should have been, nevertheless there was no proof that the [newspaper] printed and distributed the article with any knowledge of the falsities contained in it or in reckless disregard of whether or not it was true. . . . The failure of the defendant . . . to verify the factual assertions in the story is not condoned, but there was no evidence of calculated falsehood. 484 F.2d at 157.

173 Juries in these: Libel is among the most complicated areas of First Amendment law and for news organizations, presents the constant threat of huge legal bills and enormous judgments. Recent examples include: The *Philadelphia In-quirer*, one of the nation's best newspapers, defended a libel suit against a for-mer assistant district attorney over the course of 23 years. The jury had awarded the prosecutor, Richard Sprague, $34 million (later reduced by a court to $24 million) after the newspaper published an article suggesting that he was "partly responsible for deciding not to prosecute" the son of a former state police com-missioner who had been connected with a 1963 homicide. In April 1996, after the newspaper had exhausted all appeals, it settled with Sprague for an undisclosed sum that was probably close to what the jury awarded. Iver Peterson, "Media Chain Agrees to Pay in Libel Case," *New York Times* (April 2, 1996), p. A12. The settlement reached between Sprague and Knight-Ridder, the *Philadelphia Inquirer's* parent company, may not have set the record for the largest libel settle-ment. After a jury awarded a former Waco, Texas, district attorney $58 million against WFAA-TV in Dallas, the company that owned the station paid him a reported $20 million to settle the case rather than pay interest on the award dur-ing the lengthy appeals process. Kim Cobb, "Attorney Considered by Turner Gains Prestige in Libel Lawsuits," *Houston Chronicle* (February 10, 1992), p. A11. In December 1996, ABC lost a $8.75 million libel judgment to the chairman of a Miami bank. The jury also awarded $1.25 million to the bank. Barry Meier, "Banker Wins A Libel Suit Against ABC Over '20/20'," *New York Times* (Decem-ber 19, 1996), p. A18. In May 1997, a federal judge in Houston reduced a record jury award of $222.7 million by $200 million in a lawsuit brought by a brokerage firm against the *Wall Street Journal*. Edwin McDowell, "Award Is Cut In Dow Jones Libel Case," *New York Times* (May 24, 1997), p. 21. In October 1996, an un-successful mayoral candidate in Houston won a $5.5 million judgment against KTRK-TV, the ABC affiliate in Houston. Sam Howe Verhovek, "Houston May-oral Candidate Gets $5.5 Million Libel Award," *New York Times* (October 15, 1996), p. C20. There is also the serious problem of developers, government offi-cials, and others who file libel suits against citizens who dare to oppose major projects or other actions that affect their interests. See generally, George W. Pring and Penelope Canan, *SLAPPS: Getting Sued for Speaking Out* (Philadelphia, PA: Temple University Press, 1996).

174 The trial judge: *Time, Inc. v. Hill*, 385 U.S. 374 (1967).

174 To win an: The actual malice test was developed in *New York Times v. Sullivan*, 376 U.S. 254 (1964), among the most important First Amendment cases ever decided. In adopting the actual malice standard, the Court required that a plaintiff in a libel suit prove reckless disregard for the truth with "convincing clarity," a higher standard than the usual level of proof required in a civil suit. A plaintiff normally must show a "preponderance of the evidence," to win a law-suit. But in an effort to further protect news organizations from libel suits, the Court required that evidence be presented with convincing clarity. Only "beyond a reasonable doubt," the standard for criminal cases, is more difficult to prove. Ibid., at 285–286. See generally, Richard Labunski, *Libel and the First Amend-ment: Legal History and Practice in Print and Broadcasting* (New Brunswick, N.J.: Transaction Publishers, 1989).

174 **Under those circumstances:** An important Supreme Court decision that refined the actual malice standard, and from which the "purposeful avoidance of the truth" quote is taken is *Harte-Hanks Communications v. Connaughton*, 491 U.S. 657, 692 (1989).

174 **The Supreme Court:** The landmark decisions giving media defendants substantial protection against libel suits include *New York Times v. Sullivan*, 376 U.S. 254 (1964) (requiring that public officials prove actual malice); and *Curtis Publishing Co. v. Butts and Associated Press v. Walker*, 388 U.S. 130 (1967) (decided together) (requiring that public figures prove actual malice).

174 **It tentatively came:** *Rosenbloom v. Metromedia*, 403 U.S. 29 (1971).

174 **But a few:** *Gertz v. Welch*, 418 U.S. 323 (1974) (creating the category of "private persons" and holding that states may determine what standard such plaintiffs have to prove to win a libel suit as long as there is some level of fault on the part of the news organization). See also, *Time, Inc. v. Firestone*, 424 U.S. 448 (1976) (reinforcing the holding from *Gertz* that individuals must voluntarily inject themselves into a public controversy before they are considered to be public figures who must prove actual malice).

175 **Thus, the key:** *Cantrell v. Forest City Publishing Co.*, 419 U.S. 245, 253 (1974).

176 **They maintain that:** The phrase "consciously abstained" is from *Dodrill v. Arkansas Democrat Co.*, 590 S.W.2d 840 (1979). The court in *Dodrill* stated that it is "the duty of this court to follow the mandate of [*Hill*] until the rule announced therein has been modified or overruled." 590 S.W.2d at 845 n.9. The Kentucky Supreme Court similarly held in *McCall v. Courier-Journal and Louisville Times*, 623 S.W.2d 882 (Ky. 1981) that "[u]ntil the Supreme Court has spoken, we must comply with the ruling in *Hill*." 623 S.W.2d at 888.

176 **A private person:** *Fellows v. National Inquirer*, 721 P.2d 97 (Cal. 1986); *McCammon & Assoc. v. McGraw-Hill Broadcasting Co.*, 716 P.2d 490 (Colo. Ct. App. 1986); *Colbert v. World Publishing Co.*, 747 P.2d 286 (Okla. 1987); *Lorentz v. Westinghouse Elec. Corp.*, 472 F. Supp. 946 (W.D. Pa 1979).

176 **If, on the:** *Braun v. Flynt*, 726 F.2d 245 (5th Cir. 1984); *Wood v. Hustler Magazine, Inc.*, 736 F.2d 1084 (5th Cir. 1984); *Dresbach v. Doubleday*, 518 F. Supp. 1285 (D.D.C. 1981); *Rinsley v. Brandt*, 446 F. Supp. 850 (D. Kan. 1977), *aff'd*, 700 F.2d 1304 (10th Cir. 1983); *Deitz v. Wometco West Michigan TV*, 407 N.W.2d 649 (1987); *Fils-Aime v. Enlightenment Press, Inc.*, 507 N.Y.S. 947 (N.Y. Sup. Ct. 1986); and *Crump v. Beckley Newspapers, Inc.*, 320 S.E.2d 70 (W. Va. 1984). A typical approach of those courts that refuse to apply the *Hill* standard was exemplified by Judge Green in *Dresbach*:

> Although the Supreme Court has had no occasion to decide the matter, no reason appears to distinguish false light invasion of privacy actions from defamation actions in this regard. Since the District of Columbia applies a negligence standard to defamation actions involving private individuals,

that standard should also be applied to a false light action. 518 F. Supp. at 1288.

176 The Supreme Court: *See Keeton v. Hustler*, 465 U.S. 770 (1984) and *Calder v. Jones*, 465 U.S. 783 (1984).

177 Instead, it concluded: 419 U.S. at 250–251.

Chapter 4: The Road to Amending the Constitution

180 "Citizens for the: In October 1999, the organization sent a letter that included an appeal for financial help and a series of questions that should be asked before constitutional amendments are considered. The guidelines strongly suggest that the Constitution be amended for only the most urgent and appropriate reasons. The group also established an elaborate and informative Web site at <www. citcon.org>. Citizens for the Constitution, along with Citizens for Independent Courts <www.faircourts.org> — a group dedicated to protecting the independence of the judicial branch — are part of an umbrella organization called The Constitution Project. It is now located at the Georgetown University Law Center in Washington, D.C.

181 Kentucky, New Jersey: Donald E. Kyvig, *Explicit and Authentic Acts: Amending the U.S. Constitution, 1776–1995* (Lawrence, KS: University Press of Kansas, 1996), p. 150.

182 The proposed amendments: Ibid.

182 A joint resolution: Jesse L. Keene, *The Peace Convention of 1861* (Tuscaloosa, AL: Confederate Publishing Co., 1961), p. 49.

182 Some peace conference: Robert Gray Gunderson, *Old Gentlemen's Convention: The Washington Peace Conference of 1861* (Madison: The University of Wisconsin Press, 1961), p. 10.

182 Several state legislatures: Ibid., p. 58.

185 A distinguished political: See James S. Fishkin, *The Voice of the People: Public Opinion & Democracy*, (New Haven, CT: Yale University Press, 1997).

185 For example, the: Ibid., pp. 181–182.

186 Not only did: Ibid., p, 187.

190 When James Fishkin: Ibid., pp. 171–172.

194 Although the Internet: See generally, Gary W. Selnow, *Electronic Whistle-Stops: The Impact of the Internet on American Politics* (Westport, CT: Praeger Publishers, 1998); Graeme Browning, *Electronic Democracy: Using The Internet To Influence American Politics* (Wilton, CT: Pemberton Press, 1996); Ed Schwartz, *Net Activism: How Citizens Use the Internet* (Sebastopol, CA: Songline Studios, 1996); Morley Winograd and Dudley Buffa, *Taking Control: Politics in the Information Age* (New York: Henry Holt, 1996); and Barry Krusch, *The*

21st Century Constitution (New York: Stanhope Press, 1992). For the view that new technology can interfere with politics, see Lawrence K. Grossman, *The Electronic Republic: Reshaping Democracy in the Information Age* (New York: Viking, 1995).

196 One author described: Robert Allen Rutland, *James Madison: The Founding Father* (Columbia, MO: University of Missouri Press, 1987), p. 245.

198 Those selecting delegates: When Congress proposed the 21st Amendment repealing prohibition, it required for the first time that the states hold conventions to ratify an amendment. Congress let each state decide how the delegates to the conventions would be selected. Edward S. Corwin and Jack W. Peltason, *Understanding the Constitution* (New York: William Sloane Assoc., 1949), p. 75.

201 They are *The*: Angela Roddey Holder and John Thomas Roddey Holder, *The Meaning of the Constitution* (Hauppauge, NY: Barron's, 1997); John R. Vile, *A Companion to the United States Constitution and Its Amendments*, 2d ed., (Westport, CT: Praeger, 1997).

201 Nevertheless, some issues: See generally, *Griswold v. Connecticut*, 381 U.S. 479 (1965); *Roe v. Wade*, 410 U.S. 113 (1973); *Maher v. Roe*, 423 U.S. 464 (1977); *Harris v. McRae*, 448 U.S. 297 (1980); and *Webster v. Reproductive Health Services*, 492 U.S. 490 (1989).

215 Beginning with *Baker v. Carr*: *Baker v. Carr*, 369 U.S. 186 (1962); *Wesberry v. Sanders*, 376 U.S. 1 (1964); *Reynolds v. Sims*, 377 U.S. 533 (1964). The Court first used the term "one person, one vote" in *Gray v. Sanders*, 372 U.S. 368 (1963), in which it invalidated an unusual system in Georgia for conducting statewide primary elections. The "county-unit" system gave rural counties an unfair advantage over urban areas.

216 After the reapportionment: Kyvig, p. 376.

216 Over the next: Ibid.

216 Senator William Proxmire: Ibid., p. 377.

216 They did not: For a discussion on how similar the petitions need to be, see Russell L. Caplan, *Constitutional Brinkmanship: Amending the Constitution by National Convention* (New York: Oxford University Press, 1988), pp. 105–108.

217 In August 1967: Ibid., p. 378.

217 Although he introduced: Ibid., p. 440.

217 In 1985, Senators: "Constitutional Convention Implementation Act of 1985," 99th Cong., 1st sess. (January 3, 1985).

217 Although approved by: Kyvig, p. 441.

218 The committee stated: "Amendment of the Constitution by the Convention Method Under Article V," American Bar Association Special Constitutional Convention Study Committee (Chicago: ABA, 1974), pp. 18–19.

218 On the question: Ibid., p. 30.

218 The ABA committee: The Supreme Court in *Hawke v. Smith* (No. 1) stated that whether Congress requires that amendments are to be ratified by state legislatures or conventions, both methods are a "call for action by deliberative assemblages representative of the people, which it was assumed would voice the will of the people." 253 U.S. at 226–27.

218 Although the ABA: "Amendment of the Constitution by the Convention Method Under Article V," pp. 30–31.

219 More than half: Lester Bernhardt Orfield, *The Amending of the Federal Constitution* (Chicago: Callaghan & Co., 1942), pp. 40–43.

219 Rather than be: Ibid., p. 42. Other scholars do not share Orfield's view that Congress would have to call a convention. Corwin and Peltason argued that although the word "shall" is used in Article V in connection with calling a convention, there would be "no way to compel Congress to do so. . . . the Constitution relies for its observance on the good faith of Congress." Corwin and Peltason, pp. 74–75.

219 Orfield suggested that: Ibid.

224 Even when states: For a list of Article V petitions from 1789 to 1989, see Paul J. Weber and Barbara A. Perry, *Unfounded Fears: Myths and Realities of a Constitutional Convention* (New York: Greenwood Press, 1989), pp. 168–69.

224 Its report stated: Common Cause, "Constitutional Convention is 'Great Unknown,'" *In Common* (Winter 1979), pp. 3–6, cited in Wilbur Edel, *A Constitutional Convention: Threat or Challenge?* (New York: Praeger Publishers, 1981), p. 84.

224 It further noted: Ibid.

224 In the state: Ibid., p. 85.

225 Governor Jerry Brown: Caplan, p. 80.

225 The state legislature's: Ibid.

225 After testimony from: Ibid., p. 81. See Laurence H. Tribe, "Issues Raised by Requesting Congress to Call a Constitutional Convention to Propose a Balanced Budget Amendment," 10 *Pacific Law Journal* No. 2 (July, 1979) in which he strongly argued against holding a convention.

225 President Jimmy Carter: Ibid., p. 82. According to Caplan, Vice President Walter Mondale called the convention "the worst idea he had ever heard."

225 But even that: Ibid., pp. 82–89.

226 The number of: Harold A. Hovey and Kendra A. Hovey, *CQ's State Fact Finder, 1997: Rankings Across America* (Washington, D.C.: Congressional Quarterly Inc., 1997), p. 96.

226 **The overall numbers:** After the 1990 census, Montana lost one congressional seat and ended up with the largest district in the nation with 803,655 residents. Wyoming's single district is the least populous with 455,975 people. *Congressional Districts in the 1990s: A Portrait of America* (Washington, D.C.: Congressional Quarterly Inc., 1993), p. 8.

226 **These figures contrast:** Roger H. Davidson and Walter J. Oleszek, *Congress and Its Members* (Washington, D.C.: CQ Press, 1998), p. 25.

226 *Congressional Quarterly* **analyzed:** *Congressional Districts in the 1990s: A Portrait of America,* p. 100.

Chapter 5: The Internet, Politics, and the Constitution

229 **Someone sitting down:** There is a growing market for refurbished computers costing as little as $500, which until recently would have been thrown away. Anne Eisenberg, "Used-PC Bargains Add Appeal to Life in the Slow Lane," *New York Times* (March 4, 1999), p. D11.

229 **Online sales have:** "Optimism Over the Internet's Growth Leads Shares Higher," *New York Times* (April 2, 1999), p. C4. See generally, Saul Hansell, "America Online's Profits Increase Sharply as Sales Near $1 Billion," *New York Times* (January 28, 1999), p. C2. For a discussion of some of the many potential problems created by online commerce, see Steve Lohr, "Internet Companies Set Policies to Help Protect Consumer Privacy," *New York Times* (November 5, 1999), p. C1; Bob Tedeschi, "E-Commerce Report: Far too many Internet Retailers hide the true costs of purchases," *New York Times* (April 5, 1999), p. C4; Denise Caruso, "Digital Commerce: In a society dependent on technology, reliability is paramount. Problem is, today's technology isn't reliable," *New York Times* (November 2, 1998), p. C5; Saul Hansell and Amy Harmon, "Caveat Emptor on the Web: Ad and Editorial Lines Blur," *New York Times* (February 26, 1999); Pamela LiCalzi O'Connell, "We Got Your E-Mail; Just Don't Expect a Reply," *New York Times* (July 6, 1998), p. C3; and Saul Hansell, "News-Ad Issues Arise in New Media," *New York Times* (December 8, 1997), p. C10.

229 **Many businesses sell:** See generally, Tina Kelley, "Internet Shopping: A Mixed Bag," *New York Times* (July 30, 1998), p. D1; and Saul Hansell, "Hackers' Bazaar: On-Line Auction Services Put Haggling Back Into Sales," *New York Times* (April 2, 1998), p. C1. See generally, Leslie Kaufman and Saul Hansell, "Initial Data Show On-Line Retailers Top Expectations," *New York Times* (December 29, 1998), p. A1. For difficulties that many Internet-based companies faced, see Don Clark, "Facing Early Losses, Some Web Publishers Begin to Pull the Plug," *Wall Street Journal* (January 14, 1997), p. A1. One of the most successful online ventures has been newsletters, some of which are free and some of which require subscription fees. See Sreenath Sreenivasan, "Newsletters Find Haven on-line," *New York Times* (July 7, 1997), p. C7.

229 Computer users will: "E-mail and the Internet Brighten Nursing Homes (Associated Press) *New York Times* (November 23, 1999), p. D6. See also, Esther Dyson, *Release 2.0: A Design For Living in the Digital Age* (New York: Broadway Books, 1997).

230 In addition, e-mail: For what can go wrong when an e-mail message is read by the wrong people, see Susan Stellin, "Increasingly, E-Mail Users Find They Have Something to Hide," *New York Times* (February 10, 2000), p. D8.

230 The estimated 15,000: Alan M. Schlein, *Find It Online: The Complete Guide to Online Research* (Tempe, AZ: Facts on Demand Press, 1999), pp. 78–80.

230 Although there are: Mike Wendland, *Wired Journalist: Newsroom Guide to the Internet* (Washington, D.C.: Radio and Television News Directors Foundation, 1999), p. 19.

230 When those lists: The First Amendment does not protect expression abridged by private entities. The Supreme Court has long held that there must be "state action" before constitutional guarantees can be invoked. In early 1995, a history professor wrote a first-person account of how he had been excluded from various lists because of what the system operator considered to be controversial views. When the professor wanted to post a message explaining to the list's subscribers that he was prevented from posting additional messages, the system operator refused to forward the message. Jesse Lemisch, "The First Amendment is Under Attack in Cyberspace," *The Chronicle of Higher Education* (January 20, 1995), p. A56. See also, "Judge Upholds Restrictions on Access to Internet Forums at U. of Oklahoma," *Chronicle of Higher Education* (January 29, 1997); Jeffrey R. Young, "U. of Okla. Sued for Blocking Sexually Explicit Material," *Chronicle of Higher Education* (May 10, 1996), p. A28; Jeffrey R. Young, "U. of Oklahoma Revises Policy on Access to Newsgroups," *Chronicle of Higher Education* (November 29, 1996), p. A27. In 1997, Virginia Tech University became the first American college to require graduate students to post their master's theses and doctoral dissertations on the Internet so scholars and the public around the world could study them. "University Establishes Policy To Post Work on the Internet," *New York Times* (July 28, 1997), p. A9.

231 There are more: Wendland, p. 14.

231 In the old: For a detailed and insightful book on how concentration of media ownership will affect democratic institutions and diversity of viewpoints, see Robert W. McChesney, *Rich Media, Poor Democracy: Communication Politics in Dubious Times* (Urbana, IL: University of Illinois Press, 1999).

231 Today's cyberspace-era: Video is already available through the Web, but the images often have poor sound and picture quality, primarily because telephone lines have limited bandwidth. In as little as a few years, there will be significant breakthroughs that will vastly improve the picture quality. See generally, Vincent Kiernan, "Project to Improve Internet Video Could Make Possible Webcasts of TV Quality," *Chronicle of Higher Education* (November 6, 1998), p. A36.

232 Although the invention: For a thoughtful comment on how great works of literature were created before computers, see Theodore Roszak, "Shakespeare Never Lost a Manuscript to a Computer Crash," *New York Times* (March 11, 1999), p. D8.

232 In 1981, the: Some of the description of the Internet included here comes from the excellent historical and contemporary summary in the district court's opinion in *American Civil Liberties Union v Reno*, 929 F. Supp. 824, 831 (E.D. Pa. 1996). The summary was compiled from stipulations made by the parties in the case.

232 It is estimated: These figures come from Wendland, pp. iv, 2–3.

232 The U.S. Commerce: Ibid. There is increasing concern about the widening gap between those who have computers and access to the Internet and those who do not. A federal study released in September 1999, showed that black and Hispanic families are less than half as likely as white families to have access to the Internet from home, work or school. At the lowest income levels, the gap is substantial where a low-income white family is much more likely to have access than a low-income black or Hispanic family. Pam Belluck, "What Price Will Be Paid By Those Not on the Net?" *New York Times* (September 22, 1999), p. 12.

232 No government or: See generally, Jeri Clausing, "'Cybersquatting' Measure Attached to Satellite-TV Bill," *New York Times* (November 11, 1999), p. C2; and Jeri Clausing, "A Challenge to Domain-Name Speculators," *New York Times* (April 5, 1999), p. C4. For issues related to government regulation, see Jeri Clausing, "Internet Makes an Easy Target For Lobbyists and Lawmakers," *New York Times* (November 22, 1999), p. C1; Seth Schiesel, "The F.C.C. Faces Internet Regulation," *New York Times* (November 2, 1998), p. C5; and John M. Broder, "Let It Be: Ira Magaziner Argues for Minimal Internet Regulation," *New York Times* (June 30, 1997), p. C1.

232 The lack of: In February 2000, an attack over several days upon some of the most popular Internet sites such as Yahoo!, CNN and eBay caused major disruptions in access to those sites and led to an investigation by the FBI. Matt Richtel and Joel Brinkley, "Spread of Attacks on Web Sites Is Slowing Traffic on the Internet," *New York Times* (February 10, 2000), p. A2. Other attacks have also created instances of widespread disruptions of Internet service. See John Markoff, "Network Problem Disrupts Internet: Chaos Prevails for Hours After Lapse by Systems Worker," *New York Times* (July 18, 1997), p. A1; and Matt Richtel, "Super-Fast Computer Virus Heads Into the Workweek," *New York Times* (March 29, 1999), p. A14.

233 Besides textual messages: As telephone, cable and satellite companies provide high-speed access to the Internet, the quality of video will improve significantly and will be similar to what is seen on a television screen. Seth Schiesel, "A Rush to Provide High-Speed Internet Access," *New York Times* (January 12, 2000), p. C1. See generally, Bruce M. Owen, *The Internet Challenge to Television* (Cambridge, MA: Harvard University Press, 1999).

234 The impact of: Several non-profit organizations have developed sophisticated Web sites to provide interested citizens with a medium for discussing politics, candidates, elected officials, and for trying to influence the decisions of government. One of the most interesting is MoveOn.org <www.moveon.org>, started by two software developers to protest the impeachment of the president. The site encourages citizens to become actively involved in politics through petition drives and by donating money to five challengers who have a chance of beating congressional incumbents who supported impeachment. Other sites, such as Democracy Network <www.dnet.org>, which is co-sponsored by the League of Women Voters and the Center for Governmental Studies, provides voters with detailed information about issues and candidates in the 2000 election.

235 A University of: Rebecca Fairley Raney, "Politicians Woo Voters On the Web," *New York Times* (July 30, 1998), p. D1. See also, Edmund L. Andrews, "'Euroskeptics' Offer a Lesson On the Web as Political Arena," *New York Times* (July 28, 1997), p. C1. In January 2000, Time/CNN conducted a nationwide poll asking whether the respondents used the Internet to access information about politics, candidates or political campaigns. Thirty-two percent said yes, while 68 percent said no. Roper Center at the University of Connecticut, Public Opinion Online, January 14, 2000. A poll conducted by the Democracy Online Project at George Washington University found that likely voters who use the Internet at least once a week are more likely to be independents rather than belong to one of the major political parties. Of the 1,205 respondents who said they paid close attention to government, 37 percent of Independents had used the Internet for political information, compared with 31 percent of Republicans and 22 percent of Democrats. Interestingly, 75 percent of those polled believed candidate information on the Internet was very or somewhat accurate, and 64 percent trusted the information they found. Mike Allen, "Netting the Independent Vote; Uncommitted More Likely to Surf for Candidates, Poll Finds," *Washington Post* (December 7, 1999), p. A5.

235 One political consultant: The quote was from Washington-based consultant Mark Mellman, whose clients included Senators Tom Daschle (D-SD) and Barbara Boxer (D-CA). Rebecca Fairley Raney, "Politicians Woo Voters On the Web," *New York Times* (July 30, 1998), p. D1. See also, Sandy Nelson, "It May Be 1997, But Election 2000 Has Already Started on the Web," *Wall Street Journal* (November 13, 1997), p. B1.

235 In 1996, both: Edmund L. Andrews, "The '96 Race on the Internet: Surfer Beware," *New York Times* (October 23, 1995), p. A1.

236 But a growing: When businessman and publisher Steve Forbes revealed that he was running again for president in March 1999, he announced his "information campaign" on the Internet as well as at a traditional press conference. While all major presidential candidates had Web sites and said they would make greater use of the Internet during the campaign, Forbes promised — in the words of the *New York Times* — "bells and whistles," including making live photographs of his campaign appearances available through the Internet. Richard L. Berke,

"Forbes Declares Candidacy On Internet and the Stump," *New York Times* (March 17, 1999), p. A19.

236 **For example, in:** Rebecca Fairley Raney, "Online Campaign Contributions Still a Promising Experiment," *New York Times* (November 22, 1998). See also, Matt Richtel, "On-Line Polling Is More Business Than Science," *New York Times* (July 9, 1998), p. D3.

236 **A survey done:** Ibid.

236 **Ventura's campaign site:** Bill McAuliffe, "Ventura Riding the Web," *Star Tribune* (March 1, 1999).

237 **In Philadelphia, two:** "Philadelphia campaign Web sited pulled," *USA Today* (March 1, 1999).

237 **One White adviser:** William Bunch, "High-tech dirty tricks," *Philadelphia Daily News* (February 26, 1999).

237 **With an estimated:** Tina Kelley, "Candidate on the Stump Is Surely on the Web," *New York Times* (October 19, 1999), p. A1.

238 **During the seven:** Ibid., p. A1.

238 **Businessman Steve Forbes:** Ibid., p. A15.

238 **One study indicated:** Ibid.

238 **Some analysts predict:** Ibid.

238 **The Federal Election:** "Opinion Calls Independent Web Sites Volunteer," *New York Times* (November 12, 1999), p. A23.

239 **In November 1999:** Rebecca Fairley Raney, "Republicans Plan to Offer A Party Line To the Internet," *New York Times* (November 8, 1999), p. C1.

239 **A lobbyist for:** Rebecca Fairley Raney, "Lobbyist Turns to Internet To Influence Policy Makers," *New York Times* (November 15, 1999), p. C5.

240 **Former presidential adviser:** Rebecca Fairley Raney, "In E-Politics, Clinton's Ex-Adviser Still Plays by His Rules," *New York Times* (November 12, 1999), p. A16.

240 **Researcher Elaine Ciulla:** Elaine Ciulla Kamarck, "Campaigning on the Internet in the Off Year Elections of 1998," John F. Kennedy School of Government, Harvard University, downloaded March 1999 from: <http://www.ksg.harvard.edu/visions/kamarck.htm>.

242 **Such a citizen:** Cliff Edwards, "PCs losing ground to hand-held gizmos or Web access," *Lexington (KY) Herald-Leader* (Associated Press) (November 17, 1999), p. C1.

243 Only occasionally does: For a scathing indictment of the court system, see Max Boot, *Out of Order: Arrogance, Corruption and Incompetence on the Bench* (New York: Basic Books, 1998).

245 The Court did: *New York Times v. Sullivan,* 376 U.S. 254 (1964). For the establishment of the category of "public figure" libel plaintiffs, see *Curtis Publishing Co. v. Butts and Associated Press v. Walker* (decided together), 388 U.S. 130 (1967); for development of "private person" plaintiffs, see *Gertz v. Welch,* 418 U.S. 323 (1974); and *Time, Inc. v. Firestone,* 424 U.S. 448 (1976). See generally, Anthony Lewis: *Make No Law: The Sullivan Case and the First Amendment* (New York: Random House, 1991); and Bruce W. Sanford, *Don't Shoot the Messenger: How Our Growing Hatred of the Media Threatens Free Speech For All of Us* (New York: Free Press, 1999).

245 By the 1980s: See generally, *Hutchinson v. Proxmire,* 443 U.S. 111 (1979); *Wolston v. Readers Digest,* 443 U.S. 157 (1979); *Philadelphia Newspapers v. Hepps,* 475 U.S. 767 (1986); *Harte-Hanks Communications v. Connaughton,* 491 U.S. 657 (1989); *Masson v. New Yorker,* 501 U.S. 496 (1991); and *Milkovich v. Lorain-Journal,* 497 U.S. 1 (1990).

245 As if that: For a thoughtful argument that the First Amendment should apply to the Internet as it does to more traditional technologies, see Laurence H. Tribe, "The Internet vs. the First Amendment," (commentary) *New York Times* (April 28, 1999), p. A27.

246 But journalists have: 376 U.S. at 272.

246 If, however, courts: In *Smith v. California,* 361 U.S. 147 (1959), the Supreme Court held that a bookstore owner could not be convicted of possessing obscene material unless he knew the contents of the books he was selling. The Court required that prosecutors demonstrate scienter, or guilty knowledge, on the part of the bookseller or vendor. Justice Brennan, writing the majority opinion, was concerned that if a conviction were upheld against a bookstore owner or vendor without prosecutors showing specific knowledge of the obscene content, book sellers would be forced to limit their inventory to materials they had personally inspected. A federal district court applied the *Smith* standard in *Cubby, Inc. v. Compuserve,* 776 F. Supp. 135 (S.D.N.Y. 1991), in holding that Compuserve could not be held responsible for allegedly defamatory statements made by a company with a contract with Compuserve to provide a bulletin board about the broadcasting industry. The court said Compuserve could not review messages in advance and is the "functional equivalent of a more traditional news vendor." *Id.* at 140. Under the Telecommunications Act of 1996, those who provide access or connection to a computer network, but do not create their own content, cannot be prosecuted if minors get access to indecent material over their facilities. 47 U.S.C. Section 223(e)(1). For examples of other issues that courts must face related to the Internet, see Amy Harmon, "The Law Where There Is No Land: A Legal System Built on Precedents Has Few of Them in the Digital World," *New*

York Times (March 16, 1998), p. C1; and Geanne Rosenberg, "Trying to Resolve Jurisdictional Rules on the Internet," *New York Times* (April 14, 1997), p. C1.

246 Section 230 of: This section is often referred to as part of the "Communications Decency Act," originally introduced by Senator James Exon (R-NE). The Act was intended to punish Internet companies that failed to prevent the dissemination of indecent communication to minors when they had the opportunity. The Act was incorporated into Title V of the Telecommunications Act of 1996 and is not a separate law. It is especially misleading to refer to Section 230 as part of the CDA because the immunity that Section 230 grants has little to do with indecency.

246 In *Zeran v. America Online:* 129 F.3d 327 (4th Cir. 1997), *cert. den.*, 524 U.S. 937 (1998).

247 The company may: Fred Vogelstein, "Computer bulletin-board libel suit is settled, but free speech is not," *Seattle Times* (Newsday news service), December 28, 1993, p. D3.

247 In October 1994: Peter H. Lewis, "Prodigy Seeks to Reargue Its Defense in Libel Lawsuit," *New York Times* (July 25, 1995), p. C2.

247 When the firm: *Stratton Oakmont, Inc., v. Prodigy Servs. Co.,* 1995 N.Y. Misc. Lexis 229 (N.Y. Sup. Ct. 1995).

247 In May 1995: In New York, trial courts of general jurisdiction are called "supreme courts" and thus the judges who preside are "justices."

248 In its defense: *Cubby, Inc. v. Compuserve,* 776 F. Supp. 135 (S.D.N.Y., 1991).

248 The court held: Ibid., p. 140.

248 In October 1995: Peter H. Lewis, "For an Apology, Firm Drops Suit Against Prodigy," *New York Times* (October 25, 1995) p. C1. Under terms of the settlement, Prodigy did not pay any money to the company or its president. The apology stated: "Prodigy is sorry if the offensive statements concerning Stratton and Mr. Porush [the company and its president], which were posted on Prodigy's Money Talk bulletin board by an unauthorized and unidentified individual, in any way caused injury to their reputation." Ibid., p. C5.

248 In December 1995: *The News Media and the Law* (The Reporters Committee for Freedom of the Press), Winter 1996, p. 18.

249 Under Supreme Court: Justice Lewis Powell wrote in *Gertz* that: "We hold that, so long as they do not impose liability without fault, the States may define for themselves the appropriate standard of liability for a publisher or broadcaster of a defamatory falsehood injurious to a private individual. This approach provides a more equitable boundary between the competing interests involved here. It recognizes the legitimate state interest in compensating private individuals for wrongful injury to reputation, yet shields the press and broadcast media from the rigors of strict liability for defamation. 418 U.S. at 347–348.

249 The owner of: Brian Bergstein, "Case Seeks to Lift Anonymity of Computer Network Subscriber," *Lexington Herald-Leader (KY)* (Associated Press), September 16, 1995, p. A3.

249 The writer did: The petition included "Jenny's" statement: "My husband and I visited the Carib Inn last month. Since I'm a little new at diving needless to say diving with a stoned instructor was a little scary. We left after three days and went to the Sand Dollar. I won't mention his name but he's the only white instructor there. Sand Dollar was super nice." *Bowker v. America Online*, No. 95L013509 (Cir. Ct. Cook County, Ill., filed September 12, 1995). One employer obtained subpoenas requiring Yahoo! to reveal the identities of those suspected by the company of sharing company secrets on the Internet. When Raytheon obtained the names, several employees resigned. Tom Kirchofer, "Raytheon busts online chatter," *Lexington Herald-Leader (KY)* (Associated Press) (April 6, 1999), p. C2. Public officials at all levels of government are also coping with the difficult issue of when journalists and the public are entitled to see their e-mail messages. Tina Kelley, "Behind Closed E-Mail: Politicians Grapple With Public Scrutiny Of Their Electronic Communications," *New York Times* (April 1, 1999), p. D1.

249 When she did: In the petition for discovery, the plaintiffs explained that they filed in Chicago because the Carib Inn "attracts hundreds of guests and divers from the Midwest." The plaintiffs sought "complete copies or printouts of computer screens and other documents revealing subscriber information" that would enable the petitioners to identify and locate the individuals "responsible for the posting of the defamatory material and other messages on AOL's bulletin boards or in electronic mail." After the judge issued a subpoena, AOL complied by providing Carib's attorney with Jenny's real name and address. "Legal uncertainties abound online," *Tampa Tribune* (February 17, 1996), p. 19.

250 Bowker listed other: Bruce Bowker, "Carib Inn Cleared — There Never Was A Jenny TRR," *Dive Industry News* (July 5, 1996), <http://www.empg.com/news/carib.htm>.

250 Those "reporters," who: Traditional journalists have found their way to the cyberspace world. Michael Kinsley, the former editor of the *New Republic* and for six years a co-host of CNN's "Crossfire," announced in November 1995, that he would head Microsoft's online magazine to be distributed over the Internet on Microsoft's Web page and on the Microsoft Network. "Slate" features commentary on news, politics, and culture. Steve Lohr, "Kinsley Hired for New Microsoft Magazine," *New York Times* (November 7, 1995) p. C5; and Timothy Egan, "In the Capital Of Cyberspace, But Far From Capital Politics," *New York Times* (April 29, 1996), p. C1. See also, Alex Kuczynski, "Slate Drops Its On-Line Subscription Fee: Microsoft's Electronic Magazine Gives Up on a 10-Month Experiment," *New York Times* (February 15, 1999), p. C11. There have been many instances of information being provided through the Internet that has turned out to be a hoax. Among the best known involved the writer, Kurt Vonnegut, who was credited with making a commencement speech at MIT that he never gave. Ian Fisher, "What Vonnegut Never Said Is All the Talk on the Internet Now," *New York*

Times (August 6, 1997), p. A16. See also, Jeffrey R. Young and David L. Wilson, "Researchers Warn of the Ease With Which Fake Web Pages Can Fool Internet Users," *Chronicle of Higher Education* (January 10, 1997), p. A25.

251 He was also: In November 1999, Drudge and Fox parted company when the network would not allow him to show certain pictures on his program. James Barron, "Public Lives: No Picture, And No TV Show," *New York Times* (November 16, 1999), p. B4. See also, Jared Sandberg, "Call It the Drudgegate Affair," *Newsweek* (November 29, 1999), p. 50.

251 Drudge was one: Janny Scott, "Impeachment: The Media; In Scandal Coverage, Risky Era for News Business," *New York Times* (December 24, 1998), p. A16.

251 On that day: *Blumenthal v. Drudge*, 922 F. Supp. 44 (D.D.C., 1998). This is what appeared in his column on AOL: "The DRUDGE REPORT has learned that top GOP operatives who feel there is a double-standard of only reporting republican shame believe they are holding an ace card: New White House recruit Sidney Blumenthal has a spousal abuse past that has been effectively covered up. The accusations are explosive. There are court records of Blumenthal's violence against his wife, one influential republican, who demanded anonymity, tells the DRUDGE REPORT. If they begin to use [Don] Sipple and his problems against us, against the Republican Party . . . to show hypocrisy, Blumenthal would become fair game. Wasn't it Clinton who signed the Violence Against Women Act? There goes the budget deal honeymoon. One White House source, also requesting anonymity, says the Blumenthal wife-beating allegation is a pure fiction that has been created by Clinton enemies. [The First Lady] would not have brought him in if he had this in his background, assures the well-placed staffer. This story about Blumenthal has been in circulation for years. Last month President Clinton named Sidney Blumenthal an Assistant to the President as part of the Communications Team. He's brought in to work on communications strategy, special projects themeing — a newly created position. Every attempt to reach Blumenthal proved unsuccessful." Ibid., p 46.

251 Drudge is emblematic: See generally, Frank Rich, "The Strange Legacy of Matt Drudge," *New York Times* (commentary) (December 4, 1999), p. A29.

252 By March 1995: Ibid., p. 47.

252 Drudge later admitted: Howard Kurtz, "Cyber-Libel and the Web Gossip-Monger: Matt Drudge's Internet Rumors Spark Suit by White House Aide," *Washington Post* (August 15, 1997), p. G1. Drudge insisted, however, that the fact that Republican "operatives" were discussing Blumenthal's alleged abusive behavior was newsworthy, and therefore needed to be reported.

253 They filed a: Robert M. O'Neil, "The Drudge Case: A Look at Issues in Cyberspace Defamation," 73 *Washington Law Review* (July 1998), at p. 624. See also, Michael Hadley, "The Gertz Doctrine and Internet Defamation," 84 *Virginia Law Review* (April 1998), pp. 477–508; Sarah B. Boehm, Note, "A Brave New World of Free Speech: Should Interactive Computer Service Providers Be

Held Liable for the Material They Disseminate," 5 *Richmond Journal of Law and Technology* (Winter 1998). See also, *Ben Ezra, Weinstein, and Company, Inc. v. America Online, Inc.*, No. CIV 97-485 (D.C. N.M.); *Jane Doe v. America Online*, Case No. 97-25 87 (Fla. Dist. Ct. App. October 14, 1998); *Lumney v. Prodigy Services Company*, (N.Y. App. Div. September 24, 1998).

253 Congress thus established: 47 U.S.C. Section 230(c)(1).

253 As the U.S.: *Zeran v. American Online, Inc.*, 129 F.3d 327, 333 (4th Cir. 1997), quoted in *Blumenthal v. Drudge* at 52. See generally, David R. Sheridan, *"Zeran v. AOL* and the Effect of Section 230 of the Communications Decency Act Upon Liability for Defamation on the Internet," 61 *Albany Law Review* (1997).

253 Congress apparently believed: 129 F.3d at 333.

253 The statute goes: 47 U.S.C. Section 230(e)(3).

253 The court noted: 922 F. Supp. at 49.

254 Zeran had nothing: See Sheridan, at 162.

254 The court held: 129 F.3d at 333.

254 The court concluded: 922 F. Supp. at 56. See also, Robert M. O'Neil, "The Drudge Case: A Look at Issues in Cyberspace Defamation," 73 *Washington Law Review* (July 1998).

254 The court must: See generally, *International Shoe Co. v. Washington*, 326 U.S. 310 (1945); *World-Wide Volkswagen Corp. v. Woodson*, 444 U.S. 286 (1980); *Burger King Corp. v. Rudzewicz*, 471 U.S. 462 (1985); and *Asahi Metal Industry Co. v. Superior Court*, 480 U.S. 102 (1987).

254 In deciding whether: 922 F. Supp. at 54.

255 Drudge argued that: Ibid.

255 The court concluded: See generally, *Zippo Mfg. Co. v. Zipp Dot Comm. Inc.*, 952 F. Supp. 1119, 1124 (W.D. Pa. 1997); *Heroes, Inc. v. Heroes Foundation*, 958 F. Supp. 1, 4–5 (D.D.C. 1996); *Telco Communications v. An Apple A Day*, 977 F. Supp. 404, 407 (E.D. Va. 1997); *Digital Equipment Corp. v. Altavista Technology, Inc.*, 960 F. Supp. at 467 (D. Mass., 1997).

255 To the court: 992 F. Supp. at 56.

256 The Blumenthals vowed: See Bill Miller, "AOL Off the Hook in Drudge Case," *Washington Post* (April 23, 1998), p. B1; David Stout, "America Online Libel Suit Dismissed," *New York Times* (April 23, 1998), p. A21.

257 When an executive: Jan Crawford Greenburg, "'Deleted' company e-mail being used as evidence in lawsuits against firms," *Lexington (KY) Herald-Leader* (Chicago Tribune), (September 25, 1995), p. A3.

257 She hired a: The newspaper quoted the message as saying, "Get that b---- out of here as fast as you can . . . I don't care what it takes. Just do it."

257 **According to news:** For other lawsuits over computer communication, see "A Computer User, Offended by Slurs, Wants $40 Million," *New York Times* (March 9, 1995), p. A8; "Scientist sues over computer billboard notice," *Seattle Times* (Associated Press), (March 7, 1995), p. A11. See also, Peter Katel, "Cybercrooks, Beware: Here Come the Cybercops; Anything on your hard disk can be used against you," *Newsweek* (June 9, 1997), p. 86; Matthew Hawn, "Easy Now to Keep Tabs on Users' Internet Postings," *New York Times* (January 6, 1997), p. C5; and Geanne Rosenberg, "Electronic Discovery Proves an Effective Legal Weapon: Looking for Evidence in Discarded E-Mail," *New York Times* (March 31, 1997), p. C5.

257 **Because they use:** In November 1999, teachers in the New York City schools complained to the New York Civil Liberties Union about filtering software that blocked access to news and sex education topics, including those of major news organizations, policy groups and scientific and medical organizations. For example, when the teachers tried to access Internet sites about breast cancer, anorexia, child labor, and AIDS, they contained censored words and access was denied. Anemona Hartocollis, "Board Blocks Student Access at School Computers to Some Web Sites," *New York Times* (November 10, 1999), p. A22. Officials of the school district defended the filtering software and said that the teachers' complaints were exaggerated. Anemona Hartocollis, "School Officials Defend Filtering of Web Sites," *New York Times* (November 11, 1999), p. C29.

258 **In November 1998:** Amy Harmon, "Library Suit Becomes Key Test of Freedom to Use the Internet," *New York Times* (March 2, 1998), p. C1. See also, Katie Hafner, "Library Grapples With Internet Freedom: In Austin, Almost Everyone Has Doubts About How Best to Protect Children and Free Speech," *New York Times* (October 15, 1998), p. D1. See also, Denise Caruso, "Digital Commerce: It seems there's no fail-safe way of protecting children on the Internet," *New York Times* (February 16, 1998), p. C3; Amy Harmon, "To Screen or Not to Screen: Libraries Confront Internet Access," *New York Times* (June 23, 1997), p. C1. In April 1999, the Loudoun County Library System Board voted 7-2 not to appeal the judge's decision. *Freedom to Read Foundation News* (November, 1999), p. 5.

258 **Parents are sometimes:** Parents also have to worry about whether companies trying to sell products to children are learning too much personal information about them. One company had a Web site where children could play a trivia game about investing, learn how to open a savings account, and participate in a contest where prizes included a digital video camera. But in order to be eligible for the prizes, the children must complete a survey asking their age, sex, and whether they have received savings bonds, stocks, mutual funds or gold coins as gifts. Parents often do not know their children are providing such information. Pamela Mendels, "Internet Sites for Children Raise Concerns on Privacy: Offering to Trade Fun for Personal Details," *New York Times* (July 4, 1998), p. B3. Some companies have responded by requiring that a consent form be downloaded and printed, signed by a parent, and mailed to the company before children are allowed access to certain sites that request personal information or

may not be appropriate for children. Pamela Mendels, "New Serious Side to Child's Play on Web: Privacy Protection Law is Likely to Make Access More Difficult," *New York Times* (November 27, 1998), p. A20.

259 The Supreme Court: *Reno v. ACLU,* 521 U.S. 844 (1997).

259 Two provisions of: 47 U.S.C. Section 223(a)(1)(B)(ii).

259 Another section of the: 47 U.S.C. Section 223(d).

259 Those responsible for: 47 U.S.C. Section 223(e)(5)(A).

260 However, the First: *Miller v. California,* 413 U.S. 15 (1973).

260 The First Amendment: *Texas v. Johnson,* 491 U.S. 397 (1989) and *U.S. v. Eichman,* 496 U.S. 310 (1990).

260 Today, there are: Michael Janofsky, "Anti-Defamation League Tells of Rise in Web Hate Sites," *New York Times* (October 22, 1997), p. A17; and Elizabeth G. Olson, "As Hate Spills Onto the Web, a Struggle Over Whether, and How, to Control It," *New York Times* (November 24, 1997), p. C11. In 1998, the Anti-Defamation League developed software that blocked access to several hundred Web sites that the organization said advocated bigotry. Pamela Mendels, "Filter Blocks Access to Hate Speech on Internet," *New York Times* (November 12, 1998), p. A25.

260 On February 2, 1999: Sam Howe Verhovek, "Creators of Anti-Abortion Web Site Told to Pay Millions," *New York Times* (February 3, 1999). See also, "When Speech Becomes a Threat," (editorial) *New York Times* (February 6, 1999), p. A28.

261 The Court created: *Schenck v. United States,* 249 U.S. 47 (1919).

261 The clear and: *Frohwerk v. United States,* 249 U.S. 204 (1919); *Debs v. United States,* 249 U.S. 211 (1919); and *Abrams v. United States,* 250 U.S. 616 (1919). For an excellent discussion of the *Abrams* case and government efforts to suppress speech during the World War I era, see Richard Polenberg, *Fighting Faiths: The Abrams Case, the Supreme Court, and Free Speech* (New York: Viking Penguin, 1987).

261 The clear and: *Dennis v. United States,* 341 U.S. 494 (1951).

261 It was not: *Yates v. United States,* 354 U.S. 298 (1957).

261 Finally, in 1969: *Brandenburg v. Ohio,* 395 U.S. 444 (1969).

262 The Pew Research: Felicity Barringer, "Media: The Internet news audience is young, male and hungry for facts. And it's checking in from work," *New York Times* (July 27, 1998), p. C9.

262 Among the most: Larry Williams, "Weather is now most popular online news draw, study says," *Lexington (KY) Herald-Leader* (January 15, 1999), p. A14.

263 **It is estimated:** John V. Pavlik, *New Media Technology: Cultural and Commercial Perspectives* (Boston: Allyn and Bacon, 1998), p. 21.

263 **A study conducted:** Denise Caruso, "Technology: Critics are picking apart a professor's study that linked Internet use to loneliness and depression," *New York Times* (September 14, 1998), p. C5.

263 **Computer companies contributed:** Jerry Adler, "Online and Bummed Out: One study says the Internet can be alienating," *Newsweek* (September 14, 1998), p. 84.

263 **Family members were:** Ibid.

263 **An executive with:** Ibid. AOL has many times that number of subscribers today.

264 **Compared to just:** For a comprehensive explanation of Internet technology and how people get access to the Internet, see Peter Wayner, "Plugging in to the Internet: Many Paths, Many Speeds," *New York Times* (July 2, 1998), p. D11.

265 **If someone uses:** On November 5, 1999, Judge Thomas Penfield Jackson issued his "findings of fact" in the antitrust case against Microsoft. The judge found that the company has used its monopoly power to stifle innovation, reduce competition and hurt customers. His "conclusions of law," the next phase in the process, was expected by spring of 2000, unless there was a settlement between Microsoft and the Justice Department. Joel Brinkley, "U.S. Judge Declares Microsoft A Monopoly Stifling A Market; Gates Dissents, Favoring Talks," *New York Times* (November 6, 1999), p. A1.

265 **Some strongly argue:** For a discussion of universal telephone service and the role it plays in forming telecommunications policy, see Patricia Aufderheide, *Communications Policy and the Public Interest: The Telecommunications Act of 1996* (New York: The Guilford Press, 1999).

266 **Even if a:** In February 2000, President Clinton announced a $2.3 billion initiative to encourage companies through tax incentives to donate computers and sponsor technology centers in poor neighborhoods in an effort to bring more people to the Internet. The plan would require congressional approval. Marc Lacey, "Clinton Enlists Help for Plan To Increase Computer Use," *New York Times* (February 3, 2000), p. A23.

266 **Something is fundamentally:** Despite the potential of the Internet to link people from all over the world, some countries, such as China, want to control use of communication technology to make sure its citizens do not challenge the government's authority. Elisabeth Rosenthal, "China Lists Controls To Restrict the Use Of E-Mail and Web," *New York Times* (January 27, 2000), p. A1.

267 **There is also:** For an interesting discussion of this issue, see Taegan D. Goddard and Christopher Riback, *You Won — Now What?: How Americans Can Make Democracy Work from City Hall to the White House* (New York: Scribner, 1998).

268 Larry Grossman, a: Larry K. Grossman, *The Electronic Republic: Reshaping Democracy in the Information Age* (New York: Viking, 1995).

268 Grossman wrote his: See generally, Katharine Q. Seelye, "Impeachment: The National Debate; Public is Flooding Capitol with Impeachment Views," *New York Times* (December 15, 1998), p. A24.

270 One survey revealed: Roger H. Davidson and Walter J. Oleszek, *Congress and Its Members* (Washington, D.C.: CQ Press, 6th ed., 1998), p. 106.

270 Mark Edmundson, a: Mark Edmundson, "Creating a True Democracy — on-line," *Chronicle of Higher Education* (May 2, 1997), p. A60. See also, Howard Fineman, "The Brave New World of Cybertribes," *Newsweek* (February 27, 1995), p. 30.

Chapter 6: The Legal Consequences of a Second Convention

275 The first time: *Hollingsworth v. Virginia*, 3 U.S. 378 (1798).

276 In *Hawke v. Smith*: *Hawke v. Smith*, 253 U.S. 221 (1920).

276 In November 1918: The amendment of 1918 provided that "the people also reserve to themselves the legislative power of the referendum on the action of the general assembly ratifying any proposed amendment to the constitution of the United States." Ibid., p. 225.

276 The Framers could: Ibid., p. 227.

276 The Court noted: Ibid., p. 230. In *Smith v. Hawke* (II), 253 U.S. 231 (1920), the Court in a short opinion said that the same principle that applied to the 18th Amendment in *Smith v. Hawke* (I) would apply to the proposed 19th Amendment.

276 Later in the: *National Prohibition Cases*, 253 U.S. 350 (1920).

277 In *Dillon v. Gloss*: *Dillon v. Gloss*, 256 U.S. 368 (1921).

277 The Court, recognizing: Ibid., p. 374–375.

277 Although ratification must: Ibid., p. 375.

277 The Court noted: Ibid., p. 376.

277 The Court in: The four amendments referred to by the Court were: the original first amendment dealing with the size of the House of Representatives; the original second amendment related to congressional pay raises, which was eventually ratified in 1992; an amendment proposed in 1810 relating to acceptance by citizens of the United States of titles of nobility from any foreign government; and an amendment proposed in 1861 to prevent amendments that would abolish slavery in the states or jurisdictions where it existed. Three other amendments have since been proposed but never ratified. They were the Child Labor Amendment proposed in 1926, the Equal Rights Amendment proposed in 1972, and a 1978 amendment to give the District of Columbia full representation in Congress. Thus, a total of six amendments have won two-thirds approval from both houses of Congress but were not approved by the states.

277 **The justices apparently:** *Coleman v. Miller*, 307 U.S. 433 (1939).

277 **In *Leser v. Garnett*:** *Leser v. Garnett*, 258 U.S. 130, 135–136 (1922).

277 **Referring to *Hawke v. Smith*:** Ibid., p. 137.

278 **The Court concluded:** Ibid.

278 **Finally, in *U.S. v. Sprague*:** *U.S. v. Sprague*, 282 U.S. 716 (1931).

278 **The Court held:** Ibid., p. 730.

278 **In *Coleman v. Miller*:** *Coleman v. Miller*, 307 U.S. 433 (1939).

279 **The Supreme Court:** Ibid., p. 447.

279 **When new legislatures:** David E. Kyvig, *Explicit and Authentic Acts: Amending the U.S. Constitution, 1776–1995* (Lawrence, KS: University Press of Kansas, 1996), pp. 181–182.

279 **On July 9, 1868:** 307 U.S. at 448.

280 **The next day:** Ibid., p. 449.

280 **This was the:** Walter Dellinger, "The Legitimacy of Constitutional Change: Rethinking the Amendment Process," 97 *Harvard Law Review* (December 1983), p. 399.

280 **The resolution proclaiming:** Ibid., p. 400.

280 **Instead, the Court:** 307 U.S. at 450.

280 **Later in the:** Ibid., p. 454.

280 **Three members of:** Ibid., p. 459 (Black, J., concurring).

280 **Walter Dellinger, a:** Dellinger, p. 387.

280 **Grover Rees III:** Grover Rees III, "Throwing Away the Key: The Unconstitutionality of the Equal Rights Amendment Extension," 58 *Texas Law Review* (1980), p. 875.

281 **As noted by:** Dellinger, p. 398.

281 **The convention process:** See Dellinger, "The Recurring Question of the 'Limited' Constitutional Convention," 88 *Yale Law Journal* (1979), at pp. 1625–1626.

282 **At least four:** See Dellinger, "The Legitimacy of Constitutional Change," p. 414–415.

282 **Justice Lewis Powell:** *Goldwater v. Carter*, 444 U.S. 996 (1979) (Powell, J., concurring in the judgment). Noting that the Child Labor Amendment would have sought to overturn the Supreme Court's disastrous decision in *Hammer v.*

Dagenhart, 247 U.S. 251 (1918), Powell wrote: "The proposed constitutional amendment at issue in *Coleman* would have overruled decisions of this Court . . . Thus, judicial review of the legitimacy of a State's ratification would have compelled this Court to oversee the very constitutional process used to reverse Supreme Court decisions. In such circumstances, it may be entirely appropriate for the Judicial Branch of Government to step aside." Ibid., p. 1001 n.2.

283 Professor Laurence H. Tribe: Laurence H. Tribe, "Comment: A Constitution We Are Amending: In Defense of a Restrained Judicial Role," 97 *Harvard Law Review* (December 1983), p. 433.

283 Tribe recognizes that: Ibid.

283 He is especially: Ibid., pp. 435–436.

283 Tribe admits that: Ibid., p. 436.

283 If states petition: Ibid.

283 But Tribe also: Laurence H. Tribe, "Issues Raised by Requesting Congress to Call a Constitutional Convention to Propose a Balanced Budget Amendment," 10 *Pacific Law Journal* (July 1979), p. 627.

283 Testifying before a: Tribe, "A Constitution We Are Amending," p. 442.

283 In his brief: "Constitutional Politics: A Rejoinder," 97 *Harvard Law Review* (December 1983), p. 446.

283 In rejecting the: Ibid., p. 450.

283 In *Dyer v. Blair* in: *Dyer v. Blair*, 390 F. Supp. 1291 (N.D. Ill. 1975).

284 Judge John Paul: Ibid., pp. 1300–1302.

284 Stevens concluded that: Ibid., pp. 1305–1307.

284 In *Idaho v. Freeman*: *Idaho v. Freeman*, 529 F. Supp. 1107 (D. Idaho 1981).

284 After reviewing the: Ibid., p. 1140. See *Baker v. Carr*, 369 U.S. 186 (1962) and *Reynolds v. Sims*, 377 U.S. 533 (1963).

284 He also found: Ibid., pp. 1144–1150.

284 The judge further: Ibid., p. 1152.

284 His ruling was: Vacated as moot *sub nom. National Organization for Women v. Idaho*, 459 U.S. 809 (1982).

285 If, for example: *Buckley v. Valeo*, 424 U.S. 1 (1976).

286 The Ervin bill: John R. Vile, *Encyclopedia of Constitutional Amendments, Proposed Amendments, and Amending Issues, 1789–1995* (Santa Barbara: ABC-CLIO, 1996), p. 187.

286 Hatch's bill, S. 40: Paul J. Weber and Barbara A. Perry, *Unfounded Fears: Myths and Realities of a Constitutional Convention* (Westport, CT: Greenwood Press, 1989), p. 111.

287 The Ervin bill: Vile, p. 187.

287 S. 40 authorized: Section 2(a).

287 A revised version: Vile, pp. 187–188.

287 S. 40 required: Section 7(a).

288 Once three-fourths: Section 14.

288 Finally, S. 40 permitted: Section 15(a).

Chapter 7: Campaign Finance Reform Amendment

295 Every year millions: See generally, James W. Loewen, *Lies My Teacher Told Me* (New York: Touchstone Books, 1995).

295 We learn that: The Declaration of Independence says that governments derive their power "from the consent of the governed."

295 We are taught: On June 2, 1999, citizens of all races in South Africa had the opportunity to vote for only the second time in the nation's history. A photograph was taken from overhead by a helicopter or plane, and which was published in newspapers all over the United States, that showed thousands of people in a long line that snaked from one end of a huge open area to the other. People waited for hours in the hot sun to be able to cast a ballot for president and other offices. See front page photo, *New York Times* (June 3, 1999), p. A1.

296 A depressingly small: The turnout for voters in a primary election in Kentucky in May 1999 was a record low 6 percent of registered voters. If the measure was eligible voters — citizens 18 and over who have not lost the voting privilege because of a criminal conviction — no more than 1 or 2 percent voted. Jack Brammer, "Voter turnout a record low 6%," *Lexington (KY) Herald-Leader* (May 26, 1999), p. B5.

297 Campaign finance laws: The *New York Times* reported in December 1999, just how easy it is to circumvent finance limits. The Democratic Party established a half-dozen committees — so-called "victory funds" — to channel what the newspaper called "large, unregulated" contributions to Senate races. Millions of dollars of what was really soft money was given to committees whose donations to candidates was coordinated by the party's national headquarters. The Democrats claimed that because the money was not raised for individual candidates, the contributions were legal. John M. Broder, "Democrats Try to Circumvent Donation Limit," *New York Times* (December 22, 1999), p. A1.

298 Protection of political: For an eloquent statement of this principle, see Justice William Brennan's opinion for the Court in *New York Times v. Sullivan*, 376 U.S. 254 (1964).

298 The Nixon campaign: E. Joshua Rosenkranz, *Buckley Stops Here* (New York: The Century Foundation Press, 1998), p. 23.

298 There was also: See generally, Carl Bernstein and Bob Woodward, *All the President's Men* (New York: Simon and Schuster, 1974).

299 Several important changes: Federal Election Campaign Act Amendments of 1974, Pub. L. No. 93-443, 88 Stat. 1263 (1974) (codified as amended at 2 U.S.C. Section 431 *et seq.* and 26 U.S.C. Section 9001 *et seq.*).

299 In the 1974: This summary of the 1974 amendments was adapted from Rosenkranz, *Buckley Stops Here*, pp. 24–25.

300 Congress rushed to: Ibid., p. 25.

300 Take a very: Ibid., pp. 25–26.

300 The case raced: Ibid., p. 26.

301 The Supreme Court: Ibid.

301 Justice Marshall later: In *FEC v. National Conservative Political Action Committee*, 470 U.S. 480, 521 (1985) (Marshall, J., dissenting), Marshall wrote that he was "now unpersuaded by the distinction established in *Buckley*."

301 If this soft-money: Texas Governor George W. Bush, whose campaign raised more than $60 million dollars by the fall of 1999, announced that his campaign would not accept public financing. Alison Mitchell, "House Passes Bill With New Limits on Campaign Gifts," *New York Times* (September 15, 1999), p. A1.

302 In *Colorado Republican*: *Colorado Republican Federal Campaign Committee v. FEC*, 518 U.S. 604 (1996). In June 1998, the Supreme Court surprisingly decided that voters could bring a lawsuit against the Federal Election Commission claiming that the commission has not adequately enforced the disclosure requirements imposed by federal law on certain political groups. The 6-3 decision in *F.E.C. v. Akins*, 524 U.S. 11 (1998), was unexpected because the Court has often protected federal agencies from lawsuits brought by individuals on the ground that they lacked legal "standing" to pursue a claim. Linda Greenhouse, "High Court Lowers Shield of Election Panel," *New York Times* (June 2, 1998), p. A16.

303 In November 1998: *cert. denied*, 119 S. Ct. 511 (1998).

303 The U.S. District: *Kruse v. City of Cincinnati*, 142 F.3d 907 (6th Cir. 1998). See also, Bill Dedman, "Limits on Campaign Spending Are Invalid, Appeals Court Says," *New York Times* (April 28, 1998), p. A14.

303 The National Voting: Linda Greenhouse, "Justices Reject Appeals in Two Cases Involving Limits on Political Money," *New York Times* (November 17, 1998), p. A18.

303 The attorneys general: Ibid.

303 The law provided: Ibid. See also, "Time to Rethink *Buckley v. Valeo*," (editorial) *New York Times* (November 12, 1998), p. A30.

303 The U.S. Court: *Russell v. Burris*, 146 F.3d 563, 570 (8th Cir. 1998)

304 The Supreme Court: *Nixon v. Shrink Missouri Government PAC*, 2000 U.S. LEXIS 826 (2000). See also, Joel M. Gora (counsel for ACLU in *Buckley*), "Even With Limits, Politics as Usual," *New York Times* (January 26, 2000), p. A29; and "The Law on Campaign Money," (editorial) *New York Times* (January 26, 2000), p. A28.

304 Thirty-five states: Linda Greenhouse, "Justices Uphold $1,000 Limit On Contributions to Campaigns," *New York Times* (January 25, 2000), p. A1.

304 In the *Nixon*: *Shrink Missouri Government PAC v. Adams*, 161 F.3d 519 (8th Cir. 1998).

304 Justice David Souter: 2000 U.S. LEXIS 826, at 36.

305 A concurring opinion: Ibid., p. 40.

305 Antonin Scalia and: Ibid., p. 58. For a commentary generally supportive of the *Nixon* case, see Anthony Lewis, "The Court Sees Reality," *New York Times* (January 29, 2000), p. A29. For a more critical comment on the decision, see "The Flaw in *Buckley v. Valeo*," (editorial) *New York Times* (February 8, 2000), p. A30. For criticism of efforts to curtail campaign spending, see George Will, "A 100 Percent Tax On Speech," *Newsweek* (October 11, 1999), p. 96.

305 The Court may: *Kentucky Right to Life v. Terry*, 108 F.3d 637 (6th Cir. 1997).

305 *Bray v. Shrink Missouri*: Linda Greenhouse, "After 23 Years, Justices Will Revisit Campaign Limits," *New York Times* (January 26, 1999), p. A13.

305 The Supreme Court: *Buckley v. American Constitutional Law Foundation*, 525 U.S. 182 (1999).

305 The law required: Linda Greenhouse, "Court Turns Back An Effort To Limit Ballot Initiatives," *New York Times* (January 13, 1999), p. A1.

305 She said the: In a previous decision, *Meyer v. Grant*, 486 U.S. 414 (1988), the Court ruled that Colorado's prohibition on paid circulators violated the First Amendment by curbing "interactive communication concerning political change."

306 As Senator Mitch: David E. Rosenbaum, "Once-Obscure Lawmaker Battles Campaign-Law Status Quo," *New York Times* (July 2, 1998), p. A17. See also, Francis X. Clines, "A Senator Fights Limits on Donations," *New York Times* (August 21, 1997), p. A14. McConnell had the support of various groups that do not normally work together on issues including the ACLU, the National Education Association, various unions, and such groups as the NRA, the National Right-to-Life Committee, the Christian Coalition, the National Association of Broadcasters, the National Association of Realtors and the Direct Marketing Association, all of which say they are concerned about the impact of reform on freedom of expression. Katharine Q. Seelye, "Army of Strange Bedfellows Battles Spending Limits," *New York Times* (March 15, 1997), p. 8.

306 Because Smith supported: Jill Abramson, "Tally is Mixed for Foe of Revising Campaign Finances," *New York Times* (November 6, 1998), p. A23. See also, "The Soft-Money Dodge in 1998," (editorial) *New York Times* (October 28, 1998), p. A26.

306 Feingold, who imposed: Feingold and his opponent, Rep. Mark Neumann (R-WI) promised to limit donations from political action groups to 10 percent of the total money raised; vowed that less than 25 percent of the money raised from individual contributions would come from out of state; imposed a spending limit of $2,000 of the candidate's own money; and limited overall spending to $1 per registered voter. Feingold pledged to spend no more than $3.8 million, less than half of what Paul Wellstone spent on his successful 1996 Senate race in neighboring Minnesota, a state with fewer people. Dirk Johnson, "In Wisconsin Race for Senate, 2 Opponents Put Limits on Campaign Coffers," *New York Times* (September. 23, 1998), p. A14.

306 Baesler had also: David E. Rosenbaum, "Once-Obscure Lawmaker Battles Campaign-Law Status Quo," *New York Times* (July 2, 1998), p. A17.

307 He took that: Ibid.

307 Eighty-two percent: Rosenkranz, *Buckley Stops Here*, p. 70.

307 In 1998, in: Larry Makinson, "The Fat Cats Keep on Purring," (commentary) *New York Times* (November 3, 1998), p. A31. Makinson is executive director of the Center for Responsive Politics, a nonpartisan research organization that studies money in politics.

307 In the 21: Ibid.

307 In 94 percent: Leslie Wayne, "If No Guarantee of Victory, Money Sure Makes It Easier," *New York Times* (November 6, 1998), p. A23.

307 In more than: Ibid.

308 Overcoming strong opposition: Alison Mitchell, "House Endorses Financial Limit On Campaigns," *New York Times* (August 4, 1998), p. A1.

308 A second vote: Under a bizarre procedure used by the Republican leadership to stop the bill, the House had to vote a second time on Shays-Meehan after 11 different bills seeking to weaken reform efforts were defeated. Ibid., p. A10. Some liberal Democrats opposed the bill because soft-money contributions have often paid for get-out-the-vote drives. One member of the Congressional Black Caucus, Rep. Albert R. Wynn (D-MD), said, "I think that's a legitimate source of money for party-building activities such as voter registration, which are particularly important to minority communities." Alison Mitchell, "Fund-Raising Overhaul in Tight Spot," *New York Times* (June 8, 1998), p. A14.

308 The bill would: See generally, Jill Abramson, "Political Parties Channel Millions To Attack Issues," *New York Times* (October 26, 1998), p. A1; and Jill Abramson, "Well-Fed Loath to Upset A Capitol Money Trough," *New York Times* (June 15, 1998), p. A1.

308 After trying to: Alison Mitchell, "House Votes to Consider 258 Amendments to Campaign Bill," *New York Times* (June 19, 1998), p. A17.

308 The decision to: David E. Rosenbaum, "Campaign Finance Legislation Set for New Push," *New York Times* (Jan. 14, 1999), p. A17.

308 When Democratic supporters: Ibid.

308 The *New York*: "G.O.P. Trickery in the House," (editorial) *New York Times* (June 8, 1998), p. A22.

308 Although Republican leaders: Alison Mitchell, "Campaign Finance Bill Is Approved by House, but Faces Heavy Opposition in Senate," *New York Times* (August 7, 1998), p. A15.

308 Despite the urging: See "Campaign Reform's Next Hurdle," (editorial) *New York Times* (August 31, 1998), p. A18.

308 When it returned: Eric Schmitt, "Senate Effectively Kills Finance Overhaul," *New York Times* (September 11, 1998), p. A14. See also, "A Fund-Raising Frankenstein," (editorial) *New York Times* (October 8, 1998), p. A30; and "Illegal Use of Soft Money," (editorial) *New York Times* (December 2, 1998), p. A30.

309 Those senators who: Ibid. The *New York Times* described Senator McCain as "visibly dejected" after the vote. See also, John McCain, "The Scandal In Our Midst," *Newsweek* (August 17, 1998), p. 13.

309 Even Rep. Shays: Frank Bruni, "Tightrope for Republicans on Campaign Finance," *New York Times* (April 23, 1999), p. A20. Eventually six Republican House members defied the House leadership and signed the discharge petition. Alison Mitchell, "6 Republicans Break Ranks On Campaign Finance Issue," *New York Times* (May 27, 1999), p. A1. Shays accused House Republican Whip Tom DeLay of threatening to donate money to a primary challenger against him if he signed the petition.

310 Although 30 Republicans: Ibid.

310 Even after House: Alison Mitchell, "Speaker Is Pressed on Campaign Finance Bill," *New York Times* (May 6, 1999), p. A25. See also, Richard L. Berke, "Bradley and McCain Feed from Bitten Hands," *New York Times* (April 6, 1999), p. A1.

310 In a statement: Ibid. See also, "A New Speaker Errs on Reform," (editorial) *New York Times* (March 8, 1999), p. A18; "Reform Test in the House," (editorial) *New York Times* (April 12, 1999), p. A26; and "Campaign Reform, Again," (editorial) *New York Times* (April 19, 1999), p. A26.

310 About two-thirds: Michael J. Malbin and Thomas L. Gais, *The Day After Reform: Sobering Campaign Finance Lessons from the American States* (Albany, NY: The Rockefeller Institute Press, 1998), p. 13. Much of the discussion about state campaign finance reform is adapted from this book.

310 For example, after: Ibid., p. 15.

311 Those states that: Ibid., p. 21.

311 Other states in: Ibid., pp. 134–145.

311 The number of: Ibid., p. 22.

311 In addition, the: Ibid., pp. 24–30.

311 If the goals: Ibid., p. 163.

311 Efforts at the: For a discussion of potential reforms, see Frank J. Sorauf, *Inside Campaign Finance* (New Haven, CT: Yale University Press, 1992) pp. 191–246. Silicon Valley millionaire Ron K. Unz began an initiative drive in early 1999 to get a campaign reform measure on the California ballot. The proposal, known as the California Voters Bill of Rights, would: require all contributions of $1,000 or more to be disclosed electronically within 24 hours of their receipt by a campaign committee; bar candidates for statewide office from raising money except in the 12 months before their primary elections; impose a contribution limit of $5,000 per election to candidates for statewide office; and ban corporate contributions outright. The measure would also create a system of public matching funds for gubernatorial candidates who agree to limit their spending. His organization needs to gather 670,000 signatures for the initiative to get on the ballot. Todd S. Purdum, "California Republican Tries Altering Campaign Finance," *New York Times* (March 25, 1999), p. A18.

312 Shortly after they: Adam Clymer, "G.O.P. Freshmen Abandon Plan to Curb 'Soft' Money," *New York Times* (June 30, 1997), p. A9.

312 The leaders told: Ibid.

Chapter 8: The Equal Rights Amendment

316 Such restrictions were: For evidence that women are still subject to discrimination by private entities, see Marcia Chambers, "Steep Sex-Bias Penalties for Golf Club," *New York Times* (November 30, 1999), p. A27. In November 1999, a Massachusetts jury awarded nine women golfers $1.9 million because of systematic discrimination on the part of the Haverhill Golf and Country Club, located just north of Boston. The women, nearly all of them spouses of members, were denied full membership in the club, convenient tee-off times, and were subject to other discriminatory actions. Not only did the jury find that the private club's membership and business practices qualified it as a "public accommodation," and thus subject to the state's antidiscrimination laws, the attorney general asked the judge to appoint a monitor to take over the club. The plaintiffs had been subject to a variety of forms of retaliation after they filed the lawsuit against the club, and the attorney general believed such retaliation would continue without court supervision.

316 **What is perhaps:** The expression "civilly dead" comes from the Seneca Falls Declaration of Rights and Sentiments, July 19, 1948. Sandra F. VanBurkleo, "No Rights But Human Rights: The Emancipation of American Women," *Constitution* (Spring/Summer, 1990), p. 7.

316 **Married women were:** Ibid., p. 6.

316 **As English legal:** Ibid, pp. 6–8.

317 **In *Bradwell v. Illinois*:** 83 U.S. 130 (1873).

318 **Justice Joseph Bradley:** *Slaughterhouse Cases*, 83 U.S. 36 (1873).

318 **The natural and proper:** 83 U.S. 130, 141 (1873). See also, *In re Lockwood*, 154 U.S. 116 (1894).

318 **Two years later:** *Minor v. Happersett*, 88 U.S. 162 (1875).

319 **In the garment:** VanBurkleo, p. 12.

319 **The membership of:** Ibid., p. 13.

319 **Wyoming was admitted:** Ibid., p. 14. See also, David E. Kyvig, *Explicit & Authentic Acts: Amending the U.S. Constitution 1776–1995* (Lawrence, KS: University Press of Kansas, 1996), p. 227. Kyvig argued that, at least in the case of Wyoming and Utah, their admission to the Union with the provisions in the territorial charters granting the vote to women was less a commitment to women's rights than a strategy to keep political power in the hands of settled families in the face of an influx of largely male miners and drifters.

319 **In 1915, states:** Kyvig, p. 229.

320 **In May of:** Ibid., p. 233.

320 **He issued a:** Ibid.

320 **On February 10, 1919:** Ibid., p. 235.

321 **At the urging:** Ibid., p. 238.

321 **Many women in:** VanBurkleo, p. 16.

321 **But others thought:** Kyvig, p. 397.

321 **In 1961, President:** Ibid., p. 401.

322 **Despite division over:** For a discussion of efforts between 1923 and 1972 to win congressional approval of the ERA, see Kyvig, pp. 397–407.

322 **The amendment was:** Ibid., pp. 406–407.

322 **The opposition organization:** Ibid., p. 410.

322 **It had enjoyed:** Ibid., p. 417.

323 Women not only: In *Sugarman v. Dougall*, 413 U.S. 634 (1973), the Court invalidated a law excluding noncitizens from any civil service positions filled by competitive examination by applying a "strict scrutiny" standard. In *Graham v. Richardson*, 403 U.S. 365, 372 (1971), the Court invalidated a state statute disqualifying aliens from receiving various forms of welfare assistance. Justice Harry Blackmun wrote for the Court that "classification based on alienage, like those based on nationality or race, are inherently suspect." Children born out of wedlock, who are deprived of rights that marital children otherwise enjoy, also enjoy heightened status. See also, *Pickett v. Brown*, 462 U.S. 1 (1983).

324 Justice Felix Frankfurter: *Goesaert v. Cleary*, 335 U.S. 464, 466 (1948).

324 Justice John Harlan: *Hoyt v. Florida*, 368 U.S. 57, 61 (1961).

324 In *Reed v. Reed*: *Reed v. Reed*, 404 U.S. 71 (1971).

325 In *Frontiero v. Richardson*: *Frontiero v. Richardson*, 411 U.S. 677 (1973).

325 Eight members of: Since this case involved a federal statute, and the 14th Amendment applies only to the states, the Court used the "equal protection" component of the Fifth Amendment's due process clause to invalidate the legislation. Of course, the Fifth Amendment says nothing about equal protection, but the Court had to find a way to apply such principles to the federal government.

325 Writing for the: 411 U.S. 677 at 684.

325 And Justice Brennan: Ibid., p. 685.

326 But he cautioned: Ibid., p. 692.

326 The Court outlined: *Craig v. Boren*, 429 U.S. 190 (1976).

327 Similarly, in *Mississippi*: 458 U.S. 718 (1982). See also, *Stanley v. Illinois*, 405 U.S. 645 (1972), in which the Court struck down an Illinois statute that automatically made children of unwed fathers wards of the state on the death of their mothers, but in contrast, unwed mothers could be deprived of their children only upon a showing that they were unfit parents; *Taylor v Louisiana*, 419 U.S. 522 (1975), in which the Court held that the exclusion of women from jury service deprived the defendant of a Sixth Amendment right to a fair trial; *Weinberger v. Wiesenfeld*, 420 U.S. 636 (1975), where the Court used equal protection analysis to strike down a section of the Social Security Act entitling a widowed mother, but not a widowed father, to benefits based on the earnings of the deceased spouse; and *Stanton v. Stanton*, 421 U.S. 7 (1975), in which the Court rejected a Utah statute that required parents to support male children until age 21, while requiring support of female children only until age 18.

327 In *Kahn v. Shevin*: *Kahn v. Shevin*, 416 U.S. 351 (1974).

327 In *Schlesinger v. Ballard*: *Schlesinger v. Ballard*, 419 U.S. 498 (1975).

328 In *Rostker v. Goldberg*: *Rostker v. Goldberg*, 453 U.S. 57 (1981).

328 In *Michael M. v. Sonoma*: *Michael M. v. Sonoma County Superior Court*, 450 U.S. 464 (1981).

329 The Court concluded: See also, *Parham v. Hughes*, 441 U.S. 347 (1979), permitting the mother, but not the father of an illegitimate child, to sue for the wrongful death of the child; *Kirchberg v. Feenstra*, 450 U.S. 455 (1981), striking down a Louisiana statute giving a husband the unilateral right to dispose of property jointly owned by his wife without her permission; and *Caban v. Mohammed*, 441 U.S. 380 (1979), striking down a New York law requiring consent of the mother, but not the father, for adoption of a child born out of wedlock. But see also, *Lehr v. Robertson*, 463 U.S. 248 (1983), where the Court upheld a New York statute permitting the mother to veto adoption of nonmarital children. Under the law, the father was not even entitled to notice of the proceedings unless he had registered his intent to claim paternity with the state.

329 Women still earn: See generally, Alice Kessler-Harris, *A Woman's Wage: Historical Meanings & Social Consequences* (Lexington, KY: University Press of Kentucky, 1990).

331 In explaining why: Margo E. Ely, "Federal law protecting women begets a house divided," *Chicago Daily Law Bulletin* (April 12, 1999), p. 6.

331 Chief Justice William: Ibid.

331 However, five years: Ibid.

332 An example of: *United States v. Lopez*, 514 U.S. 549 (1995).

332 Rehnquist held that: Ibid., p. 564. The dissenters vigorously argued that the buying, selling, and possessing of guns implicated interstate commercial activity. Justice Stephen Breyer said in dissent that he could not understand why the majority would accept that Congress had the power to regulate the school environment by keeping it free from controlled substances, asbestos, and alcohol, but not guns.

332 In March 1999: *Brzonkala v. Virginia Polytechnic Institute and State University*, 169 F.3d 820 (4th Cir. 1999), *cert. granted*, 120 S. Ct. 11 (1999). When the Supreme Court heard oral argument in the Brzonkala case in January 2000, the justices appeared ready to strike down the Violence Against Women Act. Linda Greenhouse, "Justices Cool to Law Protecting Women," *New York Times* (January 12, 2000), p. A15.

332 The Fourth Circuit: Ibid., p. 834.

333 Such an amendment: *Cert. granted, sub. nom.*, *Brzonkala v. Morrison*, 1999 U.S. Lexis 4745. In February 2000, a bill was introduced in the Illinois legislature permitting victims of violence based on gender or sexual orientation to sue their attackers. Robyn Meredith, "Illinois Mulls New Tactic Over Violence Based on Sex," *New York Times* (February 9, 2000), p. A12.

333 In a report: Elizabeth Fox-Genovese, "Women's Status: A Century of Enormous Change," *The Public Perspective* (Roper Center for Public Opinion Research) (April 1999). In December 1999, CBS News asked nearly 1,600 respondents nationwide what the main achievement was of the women's movement that made their lives better. Twenty-eight percent said better jobs, while 15 percent answered better or equal pay. [Roper Center, December 20, 1999.]

334 The lower house: Ed Vogel, "Change in Clout," *Las Vegas Review-Journal* (May 17, 1999), p. 1B.

334 Because only five: See generally, B. Drummond Ayres Jr., "Women in Washington Statehouse Lead U.S. Tide," *New York Times* (April 14, 1997), p. A1. See also, Sheryl Gay Stolberg, "Women's Issues and Wariness in Congress," *New York Times* (May 26, 1997), p. A7.

334 The authors wrote: "... To Form A More Perfect Union ..." Report of the National Commission on the Observance of International Women's Year (1976), pp. 374–375.

Chapter 9: A Crime Victims' Bill of Rights Amendment

338 It took until: *Brown v. Mississippi*, 297 U.S. 278 (1936). In *Ashcroft v. Tennessee*, 322 U.S. 143 (1944), the Court overturned the conviction of a defendant who had been "mentally" coerced into confession. Ashcroft had been convicted of murder. His "confession" came after 36 hours of questioning under electric lights by officers, investigators, and lawyers. The Court found that such a situation was "so inherently coercive that its very existence is irreconcilable with the possession of mental freedom by a lone suspect against whom the full coercive force is brought to bear." See also, *Fikes v. Alabama*, 352 U.S. 191 (1957).

339 The country would: *Malloy v. Hogan*, 378 U.S. 1 (1964). *Malloy*, a 5-4 decision, overturned *Twining v. New Jersey*, 211 U.S. 78 (1908) and *Adamson v California*, 332 U.S. 46 (1947), and held that the Fifth Amendment privilege against self-incrimination applied to state prosecutions. See also, *Hurtado v. California*, 110 U.S. 516 (1884).

339 Two of the: *Powell v. Alabama*, 287 U.S. 45 (1932). The dissenting justices were James McReynolds, whose dissent in *Powell* should have come as no surprise, and Pierce Butler who, although a member of the Court's conservative wing, had occasionally shown a willingness to be more open-minded in his interpretation of the Constitution. For example, Butler was the only justice to dissent in *Palko v. Connecticut*, discussed below, although he did so without comment. Three years after *Powell*, in *Norris v. Alabama*, 294 U.S. 587 (1935), the convictions of the same defendants were again reversed by the Supreme Court, this time on the grounds that the exclusion of blacks from grand juries and trial juries in Alabama deprived the defendants of their equal protection rights under the 14th Amendment. See generally, Dan T. Carter, *Scottsboro: A Tragedy of the American South* (Baton Rouge, LA: Louisiana State University Press, 1979).

339 It would take: *Gideon v. Wainright*, 372 U.S. 335 (1963). See generally, Anthony Lewis, *Gideon's Trumpet* (New York: Random House, 1964).

340 The federal government: *Weeks v. United States*, 232 U.S. 383 (1914). See also, *Boyd v. United States*, 116 U.S. 616 (1886).

340 But it was: *Mapp v. Ohio*, 367 U.S. 643 (1961). See also, *Wolf v. Colorado*, 338 U.S. 25 (1949).

340 He appealed his: The Fifth Amendment reads in part ". . . nor shall any person be subject for the same offense to be twice put in jeopardy of life or limb."

340 In 1937, the: *Palko v. Connecticut*, 302 U.S. 319 (1937).

340 Justice Benjamin Cardozo: Ibid., p. 325.

340 In 1969, the: *Benton v. Maryland*, 395 U.S. 784 (1969).

340 The Warren Court: See generally, Morton J. Horowitz, *The Warren Court and the Pursuit of Justice* (New York: Hill and Wang, 1998).

340 Many police officers: See, for example, *Terry v. Ohio*, 392 U.S. 1 (1968), limiting the circumstances under which police officers can stop and search suspects; and *Miranda v. Arizona*, 384 U.S. 436 (1966), requiring police officers to inform suspects of their right to an attorney and protection against self-incrimination.

340 In *Brewer v. Williams*: *Brewer v. Williams*, 430 U.S. 387 (1977). See also, Linda R. Monk, *The Bill of Rights: A User's Guide* (Alexandria, VA: Close Up Publishing, 1995), p. 126.

341 The debate still: In December 1999, the Supreme Court said that it would hear a case that gives the justices the opportunity to substantially modify or even overrule *Miranda v. Arizona*, 384 U.S. 436 (1966), the famous decision in which the Court required that suspects be told of the right against self-incrimination and to the assistance of an attorney. The latest case involves a man charged with robbing a bank who allegedly confessed before being given his Miranda rights. The Court will decide whether *Miranda* established a rule of constitutional law or whether it merely expressed the Court's preferred method of enforcing the constitutional right against compelled self-incrimination. Linda Greenhouse, "Justices To Hear Case That Tests Miranda Decision," *New York Times* (December 7, 1999), p. A1.

341 As Attorney General: *A Proposed Constitutional Amendment to Protect Victims of Crime: Hearing Before the Senate Judiciary Committee*, 105th Congress, 1st Session 41 (April. 16, 1997), cited by Paul G. Cassell, professor of law at University of Utah, in his testimony before the Senate Judiciary Committee on March 24, 1999.

341 Ellen Greenlee, president: *Proposals for a Constitutional Amendment to Provide Rights for Victims of Crime: Hearings Before the House Judiciary Committee*, 104th Congress, 2d Session, 143 (1996), cited in Cassell's testimony.

342 A 1998 report: Cited in Cassell.

343 Its literature suggests: NOVA's Web site is at <http://www.try-nova.org>.

343 By 1998, almost: Ibid.

343 Another large and: NCVC's Web site is at <http://www.ncvc.org>. There is also an organization of attorneys which represents crime victims. See the National Crime Victims Bar Association at <http://www.ncvc.org/victimbar/main.htm>.

343 The National Victims': NVCAN's Web site is at <http://www.nvcan.org>.

344 The Kyl amendment: S.J. Res. 44, 105th Congress, 2d Session, United States Senate, April 1, 1998. The amendment can be found at <http://www.nvcan.org/sjr44.htm>.

345 During the current: In September 1999, the Senate Judiciary Committee again considered a crime victims' amendment, which the *New York Times* in an editorial said "trifles" with the Constitution, and is "unnecessary." "Victims and the Constitution," *New York Times* (September 30, 1999), p. A28.

347 He cited the: *A Proposed Constitutional Amendment to Protect Victims of Crime: Hearing Before the Senate Judiciary Committee,* 104th Congress, 2d Session, 143 (1996).

348 The appeals court: *United States v. McVeigh,* 106 F.3d 325 (10th Cir. 1997).

349 The Victims' Rights: 142 Cong. Rec. H1068 (daily ed. Mar. 19, 1997), codified as 18 U.S.C. Section 3510.

349 Currently, states enjoy: The 11th Amendment was proposed by Congress in 1794 and ratified in 1798. It is perhaps best known as the first amendment to overturn a Supreme Court decision. In *Chisholm v. Georgia,* 2 U.S. 419 (1793), the Court decided that a state could be sued by a citizen of another state who claimed that he had never been paid for debts from the Revolutionary War era. The states strongly objected to such suits, claiming they would cause a financial hardship. In addition, states argued that Federalists had assured them in the state ratifying conventions that they would enjoy sovereign immunity and could not be sued without their consent. The Supreme Court later misinterpreted the 11th Amendment by extending protection from such lawsuits to states when sued by their own citizens in *Hans v. Louisiana,* 134 U.S. 1 (1890). In a more recent case, *Seminole Tribe of Florida v. Florida,* 517 U.S. 44 (1996), the Court appeared to confirm the ruling in *Hans* by holding that the 11th Amendment barred Indian tribes from suing a state over what they alleged to be a failure of the state to negotiate in good faith over establishing casinos on Indian lands. The lawsuit was based on the Gaming Regulatory Act of 1988 in which Congress required states to negotiate with tribes, and allowed tribes to file lawsuits in federal courts when they alleged states failed to negotiate fairly. The Court was divided 5-4 on the difficult issues raised by the case. Justice David Souter took the unusual step of reading his entire dissent aloud to the full Court. Souter and three other justices insisted that Congress had always intended for the states to be subject to the jurisdiction of federal courts and that the Gaming Act was constitutional: "The court today holds for the first time since the founding of the republic . . . that Congress has no authority to subject a state to the jurisdiction of a federal court at the behest of an individual asserting a federal right." Ibid., p. 100.

350 In addition, judges: See generally, *Stump v. Sparkman*, 435 U.S. 349 (1978); *Malina v. Gonzales*, 994 F.2d 1121 (5th Cir. 1993); and *Harper v. Merckle*, 638 F.2d 848 (5th Cir. 1981). For one of the few cases in which judicial immunity was not upheld, see *Zarcone v. Perry*, 572 F.2d 52 (2nd Cir. 1978).

Chapter 10: Congressional Term Limits; Reducing Senate Terms; Changing the Majority Required for Approval of Treaties

353 That voters do: Alison Mitchell and Janet Elder, "Congress's Rating Continue To Slip In Inquiry's Wake," *New York Times* (October 15, 1998), p. A1.

353 In the 20: In Washington state, voters turned down a term limits initiative in 1991, but passed one by a margin of 52-48 percent in 1992. Utah voters rejected a term limits measure that would have covered congressional and all state and local offices by a substantial margin in 1994. Thomas R. Dye, *Politics in States and Communities* (Upper Saddle River, NJ: Prentice Hall, 1997), p. 48.

353 In Florida and: Ibid.

354 In 1995, the: *U.S. Term Limits v. Thornton*, 514 U.S. 779 (1995).

354 According to the: The relevant sections are Article I, section 2, clause 3 for the House of Representatives, and Article I, section 3, clause 3 for the Senate.

354 Stevens noted that: Article V of the Articles of Confederation states in part: "No person shall be capable of being a delegate for more than three years in any term of six years."

354 Even James Madison: Jack N. Rakove, *Original Meanings: Politics and Ideas in the Making of the Constitution* (New York: Alfred A. Knopf, 1996), p. 37. Upon leaving the Continental Congress, Madison began service in the Virginia Assembly as a delegate from Orange County until he was eligible to return to Congress in the winter of 1787.

354 Stevens concluded that: 514 U.S. at 850.

355 Those who support: See Chapter 1 and accompanying notes for reference to David Broder's opposition to term limits and George Wills's support for them.

356 Even those members: The Republican Party promised the country in the "Contract with America" in 1994 that when it became the majority party in Congress, it would seriously consider imposing term limits. See Chapter 1 for a discussion of how they tried to convince the public they were serious about term limits when they had no intention of approving them. See also, David E. Kyvig, *Explicit & Authentic Acts: Amending the U.S. Constitution 1776–1995* (Lawrence, KS: The University Press of Kansas), pp. 454–455.

356 Nethercutt told voters: Sam Howe Verhovek, "Some Backtracking on Term Limits," *New York Times* (April 12, 1999), p. A20.

356 Fifty-eight members: Ibid.

356 He said he: Ibid.

356 In an editorial: "Do-It-Yourself Term Limits," *New York Times* (April 13, 1999), p. A28. Former congressman Timothy Penny (D-MN), who served 12 years and voluntarily left office, urged voters to support candidates willing to impose their own term limits: "I'm not sure if term limits would be good public policy. I know voters strongly favor them, but that is not enough for me to endorse them. . . . What I am far more comfortable with is creating a dialogue between voters and lawmakers about the time someone should spend in Congress. I think it's important for voters to ask candidates and current office holders just how long they intend to stay in Congress." Timothy J. Penny and Major Garrett, *Common Cents: A Retiring Six-Term Congressman Reveals How Congress Really Works and What We Must Do to Fix It* (New York: Avon Books, 1996), pp. 229–230.

357 In those states: See generally, Todd S. Purdam, "Term Limits Give Rise To a Comeback Kid, 65," *New York Times* (February 6, 1998), p. A10; and B. Drummond Ayres, Jr., "Term Limit Laws Are Transforming More Legislatures," *New York Times* (April 28, 1997), p. A1.

358 The amendment would: Among the individuals who have had a distinguished career in the House after a Senate career was Claude Pepper, a Democrat from Florida. Elected to the Senate in 1936, Pepper served until 1951. He was probably defeated for reelection because he was too progressive on civil rights. He was elected to the House in 1962. As the oldest member of Congress, he became the nation's most powerful advocate of legislation and programs to benefit the elderly. He died in 1989. John Quincy Adams was the only former president to serve in the House. After leaving the presidency in 1829, he was elected to the House to represent Quincy, Massachusetts, and its surrounding areas in 1831, and served until his death in 1848.

359 Some of those: Catherine Drinker Bowen, *Miracle at Philadelphia* (New York: The American Past, 1986), p. 122. The Framers discussed the length of Senate terms in detail on June 26, 1787. Madison supported Read of Delaware's amendment that Senate terms be nine years. Read wanted to make sure that small states would be represented in the Senate by members with experience. After considering the relative merits of a six- or nine-year term, the delegates rejected the longer term by a vote of 8-3, then approved six years by 7-4. Max Farrand, *The Records of the Federal Convention of 1787* (New Haven, CT: Yale University Press, 1911), Vol. I., (Madison), pp. 421–426.

360 There was also: See Chapter 2 for a discussion of some writers who believed that members of Congress should enjoy far greater independence from the people than the current system affords them.

361 Over the years: John R. Vile, *Encyclopedia of Constitutional Amendments, Proposed Amendments, and Amending Issues, 1789–1995* (Santa Barbara, CA: ABC-CLIO, 1996), p. 73–73, citing Sula Richardson, *Congressional Terms of Office and Tenure: Historical Background and Contemporary Issues* (Washington, D.C.: Congressional Research Service, Library of Congress, 1991).

363 The House threatened: David P. Currie, *The Constitution in Congress: The Federalist Period 1789–1801* (Chicago: University of Chicago Press, 1997), pp. 211–217.

363 President Washington sent: Ibid.

363 Some commentators suggested: Vile, p. 309. See Chapter 2 for some proposals to change the Senate treaty approval process.

363 The Senate, however: In the 1950s, the Senate came within one vote of approving a constitutional amendment that would have repealed the supremacy clause in Article VI of the Constitution and substituted a phrase more clearly indicating that treaties had to be made "in pursuance" of the Constitution and not simply under its authority. The reason for concern was that Article VI held that all treaties, as with the Constitution itself, would be the "supreme" law of the nation, and there was the possibility that a treaty could be used to restrict domestic individual rights. Support for such an amendment, which was never approved by Congress, can be traced in part to several Supreme Court decisions suggesting that Congress could exercise powers under the authority of treaties that it did not have under the Constitution. See *Missouri v. Holland*, 252 U.S. 416 (1920); *United States v. Pink*, 315 U.S. 204 (1942); *Rice v. Sioux City Memorial Park*, 348 U.S. 880, 349 U.S. 70 (1955); and *Reid v. Covert*, 354 U.S. 1 (1957).

364 It has done: Roger H. Davidson and Walter J. Oleszek, *Congress and Its Members* (Washington, D.C.: CQ Press, 1998), p. 385.

364 Of the approximately: Ibid.

364 This agreement, and: Ibid., p. 310, citing Bruce Ackerman and David Golove, "Is NAFTA Constitutional?" *Harvard Law Review* (February 1995), pp. 799–929.

Chapter 11: Abolition of the Electoral College

367 Next to the: Cleveland, who was the incumbent, received about 100,000 more popular votes than Harrison. (Cleveland: 5,540,329; Harrison: 5,439,853). But Harrison received 233 electoral votes to Cleveland's 168. Although the 1888 election was the only time in the nation's history when no other factor besides the mathematics of the Electoral College resulted in a president with fewer popular votes being elected, it almost happened again in 1976. The switch of a few thousand votes in a handful of states would have given the election to Gerald Ford despite Jimmy Carter having received 1.7 million more votes.

367 The Electoral College: Akhil Reed Amar, "A Constitutional Accident Waiting to Happen," in *Constitutional Stupidities, Constitutional Tragedies*, William N.

Eskridge, Jr. and Sanford Levinson, eds. (New York: New York University Press, 1998), p. 15.

367 A Green Party: Audie Bock shocked the political establishment when she won a special election in 1999 to the California State Assembly, defeating former Oakland Mayor Elihu Harris. She became the first minor-party candidate to win a California legislative seat in eight decades and the first Green Party member to win a major political campaign anywhere in the country. Not suprisingly, Democratic leaders in the State Assembly, who were embarrassed by her victory, have done everything they could to keep her from successfully representing her district. They want to minimize her reelection chances by not considering any of her proposed bills and are taking other action to keep her from being able to tell her constituents about any accomplishments. Democrats say they would accept her if she renounced the Green Party and ran as a Democrat in the next election. The Democratic leadership apparently cannot tolerate someone other than a Democrat holding the Oakland seat, and over a year before the election, they were already looking for candidates to run against her in 2000. Dan Walters, "Green Party legislator won't give up the fight," *Fresno Bee* (August 2, 1999), p. A11.

368 Running as a: Thurmond won 1,760,125 popular votes and the states of South Carolina, Mississippi, Alabama, and Louisiana.

368 With Thurmond's success: If the House had decided the 1948 election, it would have been a political nightmare. The House on January 3, 1949, had 21 state delegations with a Democratic majority, 20 with a Republican majority, three were evenly divided, and four represented states carried by the States' Rights party. It would have been incredibly difficult to get 25 of these delegations to choose among Harry Truman, Thomas Dewey, or Strom Thurmond in the 17 days between January 3 and January 20. C. Herman Pritchett, *The American Constitution* (New York: McGraw-Hill, 1977), pp. 223–224.

368 Again in 1960: Ibid., p. 224.

368 In 1968, George: One of Wallace's electoral votes came from Lloyd Bailey of North Carolina who was pledged to give his vote to Richard Nixon, the winner of the state. Blaine Eskin, *The Book of Political Lists* (New York: Villard, 1998), p. 205.

369 But sometimes electors: Known as "faithless electors," seven have refused to give their vote to the presidential candidate who won the state and to which they were pledged in presidential elections. Six states — Alabama, California, Idaho, Massachusetts, Mississippi, and Oregon — have passed laws requiring presidential electors to vote for the candidate of their political party to whom they were pledged. The first state to require electors to cast their ballot for presidential and vice presidential candidates who won their state was Maine on March 25, 1969. Joseph Nathan Kane, *Presidential Fact Book* (New York: Random House, 1998), p. 373.

369 **Perhaps more troubling:** Ibid., p. 223.

369 **In 1876, there:** For a recounting of this episode, see Paul F. Boller, Jr., *Presidential Campaigns* (New York: Oxford University Press, 1984), pp. 133–141.

370 **If a state:** Pritchett, pp. 220–221.

370 **The allocation of:** To get to 270 electoral votes out of 538, which constitutes a majority, a candidate could win these 11 states and be elected: California (54 electoral votes); New York (33); Texas (32); Florida (25); Pennsylvania (23); Illinois (22); Ohio (21); Michigan (18); New Jersey (15); North Carolina (14); and either Georgia (13) or Virginia (13). If the candidate lost the other 39 states by a large margin, the difference between the popular vote total and that of the Electoral College could be huge. Eskin, *The Book of Political Lists*, p. 204.

371 **The delegates ultimately:** See generally, Jack C. Rakove, *Original Meanings: Politics and Ideas in the Making of the Constitution* (New York: Alfred A. Knopf, 1996), pp. 256–261; and Clinton Rossiter, *1787: The Grand Convention* (New York: W.W. Norton & Co., 1987, originally published in 1966), pp. 198–205.

373 **At least 850:** John R. Vile, *Encyclopedia of Constitutional Amendments, Proposed Amendments, and Amending Issues, 1789–1995* (Santa Barbara: ABC-CLIO, 1996), p. 109.

373 **Most of the:** Ibid.

374 **Although there have:** Roosevelt received 27.4 percent of the popular vote, finishing ahead of incumbent William Howard Taft who won 23.1 percent. Democrat Woodrow Wilson was elected president with 41.8 percent.

376 **Same-day voter:** North Dakota is the only state that does not require registration at all. Thomas R. Dye, *Politics in States and Communities* (Upper Saddle River, NJ: Prentice Hall, 1997), p. 96.

Chapter 12: Protecting the Jurisdiction of the Federal Courts

378 **The Framers expected:** For a discussion of the experience of the colonists with the Royal Courts, and why the Framers wanted a different judicial system, see Jack N. Rakove, Original Meanings: *Politics and Ideas in the Making of the Constitution* (New York: Knopf, 1996), pp. 297–302.

378 **A few years:** Scholars disagree over when the Supreme Court first exercised the power of judicial review. Former judge and unsuccessful Supreme Court nominee Robert Bork identified *Hayburn's Case*, 2 U.S. 409 (1792), as the first one clearly asserting the right to review the constitutionality of legislation. Robert Bork, *The Tempting of America: The Political Seduction of the Law* (New York: Free Press, 1989), p. 24. Justice James Iredell had explicitly asserted the power of judicial review in both *Chisholm v. Georgia*, 2 U.S. 419 (1793) and in *Calder v. Bull*, 3 U.S. 386 (1798). The Court reviewed the constitutionality of a federal statute in *Hylton v. United States*, 3 U.S. 171 (1796) and examined whether a state law was contrary to the state's constitution in *Cooper v. Telfair*, 4 U.S. 14 (1800).

The most famous early effort to review the constitutionality of a federal law was in *Marbury v. Madison*, 5 U.S. 137 (1803).

378 Not long afterward: Section 25 of the Judiciary Act of 1789 gave the Supreme Court authority to review state laws and the decisions of state courts that conflict with a federal statute or the federal Constitution. See *Fairfax's Devisee v. Hunter's Lessee*, 7 U.S. 603 (1813); *Martin v. Hunter's Lessee*, 14 U.S. 304 (1816); and *Cohens v. Virginia*, 19 U.S. 264 (1821).

379 Congress even has: See Chapter 3 for a discussion of how Congress prevented the Supreme Court from meeting for 14 months so it could not consider *Marbury* until 1803.

379 Article III establishes: Cases coming to the Court in its original jurisdiction include those in which a state is a party, and cases involving ambassadors, public ministers, and consuls. The Court hears few such cases. Almost all cases come as appeals from other courts.

379 But relying on: *Wiscart v. D'Auchy*, 3 U.S. 321 (1796). See also, *Durousseau v. United States*, 6 U.S. 307 (1810).

380 In *Ex Parte Milligan*: *Ex Parte Milligan*, 71 U.S. 2 (1866).

381 "Without jurisdiction the: *Ex Parte McCardle*, 74 U.S. 506, 514 (1869).

381 Under the *McCardle*: C. Herman Pritchett: *The American Constitution* (New York: McGraw-Hill, 1977), p. 96–97. See also, *Ex Parte Yerger*, 75 U.S. 85 (1869), and *United States v. Klein*, 80 U.S. 128 (1872).

381 After the Warren: Among the cases that most incensed conservatives were *Yates v. United States*, 354 U.S. 298 (1957), and *Watkins v. United States*, 354 U.S. 178 (1957). The effort to restrict the Court's jurisdiction was also based on strong disapproval of *Brown v. Board of Education*, 347 U.S. 483 (1954), by southern members of Congress.

381 On July 26, 1957: C. Herman Pritchett, *Congress Versus the Supreme Court* (Minneapolis: University of Minnesota Press, 1961), p. 31. For a discussion of the debate over the various bills, see pp. 31–40.

381 The five areas: Ibid, p. 31.

382 Over on the: Ibid., p. 33.

383 Assuming that the: For an excellent discussion of some of the most controversial issues decided by the Court, and how the news media portray them, see Elliot E. Slotnick and Jennifer A. Segal, *Television News and the Supreme Court* (New York: Cambridge University Press, 1998).

383 Congress could not: *Roe v. Wade*, 410 U.S. 113 (1973); *Griswold v. Connecticut*, 381 U.S. 479 (1965).

384 They have come: Many legal scholars believe that Marshall was not only the Court's greatest justice, but credit him with making the Court into a co-equal and independent branch of government. See generally, Bernard Schwartz, *A Book of Legal Lists: The Best and Worst in American Law* (New York: Oxford University Press, 1997), pp. 5–7.

384 It has been: Among the many examples is *Jaffree v. Board of School Commissioners*, 554 F. Supp. 1104, 1128 (S.D. Ala. 1983), in which an Alabama federal judge decided that the Supreme Court had "erred in its reading of history" when it held that prayers in public schools violated the Constitution's prohibition against establishment of religion. He refused to force the Board to comply with the Court's decision.

384 Despite many unpopular: Almost everyone agrees that the Supreme Court's worst decision was *Dred Scott v. Sandford*, 60 U.S. 393 (1857), which held that slaves were not citizens and they could not sue in federal court. The decision helped ignite the Civil War. Other "unpopular" decisions such as *Brown v. Board of Education* in 1954 are now recognized as among the Court's greatest achievements. See generally, Bernard Schwartz, *A Book of Legal Lists: The Best and Worst in American Law.*

834 They confer in: Legal scholar Bernard Schwartz was able to obtain notes from and interviews with several justices and clerks about the way the Court decides cases. He convincingly demonstrates that the decision-making process is often anything but majestic. Bernard Schwartz, *Decision: How the Supreme Court Decides Cases* (New York: Oxford University Press, 1996). See also, Edward Lazarus, *Closed Chambers: The First Eyewitness Account of the Epic Struggles Inside the Supreme Court* (New York: Times Books, 1998).

386 Thus, the country: *Buckley v. Valeo*, 424 U.S. 1 (1976).

386 If the nation: See *Engel v. Vitale*, 370 U.S. 421 (1962) and *School District of Abington Township v. Schempp*, 374 U.S. 203 (1963).

Chapter 13: Changing How the Constitution is Amended

388 The Framers struggled: In *Federalist* No. 49, James Madison wrote that the frequent recourse to the amending process would undermine the stability of government because it would suggest that the Constitution was seriously defective. He noted that the Constitution would benefit from "that veneration which time bestows on everything." See Stephen M. Griffin, "Constitutionalism in the United States: From Theory to Politics," in Sanford Levinson, editor, *Responding to Imperfection: The Theory and Practice of Constitutional Amendment* (Princeton, NJ: Princeton University Press, 1995), pp. 37–61.

389 That has often: See Donald S. Lutz, "Toward a Theory of Constitutional Amendment," in Levinson, pp. 246–260.

389 Since 1791, when: See generally, Sanford Levinson, "How Many Times Has the United States Constitution Been Amended?" in Sanford Levinson, editor, *Responding to Imperfection: The Theory and Practice of Constitutional Amendment*, pp. 13–36.

536   THE SECOND CONSTITUTIONAL CONVENTION

389 Hundreds of proposed: For a comprehensive description of proposed amendments, see John R. Vile, *Encyclopedia of Constitutional Amendments, Proposed Amendments, and Amending Issues, 1789–1995* (Santa Barbara, CA: ABC-CLIO, 1996), pp. 363–380.

389 Among developed nations: Lutz, in Levinson, pp. 260–274.

390 When the Supreme: Among the cases that have created fundamental changes are: *Marbury v. Madison*, 5 U.S. 137 (1803), firmly establishing the Supreme Court's power to review and invalidate congressional legislation; *McCullough v. Maryland*, 17 U.S. 316 (1819), upholding the establishment of a national bank and supporting a broad construction of Congress's power under the "necessary and proper" clause; *Gibbons v. Ogden*, 22 U.S. 1 (1824), upholding Congress's power to regulate interstate commerce; *Dred Scott v. Sandford*, 60 U.S. 393 (1857), holding that Congress cannot bar slavery from the territories and that slaves are not citizens of the United States; *Plessy v. Ferguson*, 163 U.S. 537 (1896), upholding legally mandated racial segregation in public transportation and establishing the principle of "separate but equal"; *Brown v. Board of Education*, 347 U.S. 483 (1954) declaring racial segregation in elementary and secondary schools to be unconstitutional; *Baker v. Carr*, 369 U.S. 186 (1962), permitting the federal courts to require reapportionment and redistricting of state legislatures; and *New York Times v. Sullivan*, 376 U.S. 254 (1964), extending substantial First Amendment protection to media defendants in libel suits and thus establishing the right to discuss public officials and public issues as a core value of the First Amendment.

390 Conservative justices of: Justice Felix Frankfurter insisted that "nothing new can be put into the Constitution except through the amendatory process. Nothing old can be taken out without the same process." *Ullmann v. United States*, 350 U.S. 422, 428 (1956). See Sanford Levinson, "How Many Times Has the United States Constitution Been Amended?" in Levinson, editor, *Responding to Imperfection: The Theory and Practice of Constitutional Amendment*, pp. 13–36.

390 Few justices would: Some, but not all, of the justices considered to be among the worst to serve on the Supreme Court exemplified this philosophy. See generally, Bernard Schwartz, *A Book of Legal Lists*, pp. 28–46.

390 Sometimes judicial "amendments": *Brown v. Board of Education*, 347 U.S. 483 (1954).

390 The Warren Court's: See generally, C. Herman Pritchett, *The American Constitution* (New York: McGraw-Hill, 1977), pp. 422–482; and Morton J. Horwitz, *The Warren Court and the Pursuit of Justice* (New York: Hill and Wang, 1998).

390 It is important: Antonin Scalia, *A Matter of Interpretation: Federal Courts and the Law* (Princeton, N.J.: Princeton University Press, 1997, p. 13.

390 The Court prefers: See, for example, Justice Louis Brandeis's concurring opinion in *Ashwander v. Tennessee Valley Authority*, 297 U.S. 288, 347 (1936).

390 If a ruling: The principle of *stare decisis* is not inflexible, and courts do reverse themselves. But because of the need for stability and consistency in the development of the law, courts generally try to follow the principles of previous cases. Even if a change in membership or attitude would permit a reversal or modification of a precedent, the case with the right set of facts may not present itself for a long time. See generally, Richard Labunski, "Judicial Discretion and the First Amendment: Extending the Holding Beyond Facts Through 'Contiguous Decision-Making,'" *Comm/Ent* (Hastings Communication and Entertainment Law Journal), University of California, San Francisco, (Fall 1990), pp. 15–56.

391 Among the principles: David P. Currie, *The Constitution in Congress: The Federalist Period 1789–1801* (Chicago: University of Chicago Press, 1997), pp. 3–5.

391 Congress's efforts to: For a discussion of the Alien and Sedition Acts of 1798, see Leonard W. Levy, *The Emergence of a Free Press* (New York: Oxford University Press, 1985), pp. 220–281.

391 Bruce Ackerman, a: His works on this subject include, *We The People: Transformations* (Cambridge, MA: Harvard University Press, 1998); *We The People: Foundations* (Cambridge, MA: Harvard University Press, 1991); "Constitutional Politics/Constitutional Law," *Yale Law Journal* (December 1989); and "Transformative Appointments," *Harvard Law Review* (1988). See also, Griffin in Levinson, pp. 49–58.

392 He believes the: During the early stages of the New Deal period, one amendment was ratified — the 21st Amendment repealing prohibition — in December 1933.

392 Yet the constitutional: The second great era of constitutional transformation, according to Ackerman, was during the 1860s, the period during and after the Civil War. Although there were amendments approved during this time, most notably the 14th Amendment, Ackerman argues that the relationship between the national government and the states was changed largely outside of the Constitution. See Ackerman in Levinson, p. 67. He cites as an example the assertion by Congress that the states were not equal partners with Congress when it came to modifying the Constitution. The first sentence of the 14th Amendment proclaims the primacy of federal over state citizenship. Ibid., p. 77. To Ackerman, both the substance of the 14th Amendment and the process by which it was enacted are grounded in the principle that Congress, not the states, will have primary responsibility for amending the Constitution.

392 Others, most notably: Among Amar's work is "The Consent of the Governed: The Constitutional Amendment Outside Article V," *Columbia Law Review* (March 1994); "The Bill of Rights as a Constitution," *Yale Law Journal* (Winter 1992); and "Philadelphia Revisited: Amending the Constitution Outside Article V," *University of Chicago Law Review* (Fall 1988).

392 Someone who reads: Akhil Reed Amar and Alan Hirsch, *For the People: What the Constitution Really Says About Your Rights* (Free Press, 1998).

393 This occurs when: Frederick Schauer, "Amending the Presuppositions of a Constitution," in Levinson, pp. 145–161.

396 Because people know: Justice Oliver Wendell Holmes wrote this about suggesting changes in the Constitution: "Surely, it cannot show a lack of attachment to the principles of the Constitution that [a person] thinks it can be improved. I suppose that the most intelligent people think that it can be." *United States v. Schwimmer*, 279 U.S. 644, 654 (1929) (Holmes, J., dissenting).

Chapter 14: Repealing the Second Amendment

400 It would be: Legal scholar Sanford Levinson wrote that "no one has ever described the Constitution as a marvel of clarity, and the Second Amendment is perhaps one of the worst drafted of all its provisions." Sanford Levinson, "The Embarrassing Second Amendment," 99 *Yale Law Journal* (December 1989), pp. 643–644. Levinson argues that the Second Amendment should be taken seriously by legal scholars and is still relevant to today's society. See also, Dennis Henigan, "Arms, Anarchy, and the Second Amendment," 26 *Valparaiso University Law Review* (1991) p. 107.

400 For reasons that: Some sections of the original Constitution include similar phrases. An example is the patents and copyright clause that sets out the power of Congress "to promote the Progress of Science and useful Arts, by securing respective Writings and Discoveries." U.S. Constitution, Article I, Section 8.

400 The result is: For an excellent analysis of the language of the Second Amendment, see Akhil Reed Amar, *The Bill of Rights: Creation and Reconstruction* (New Haven, CT: Yale University Press, 1998), pp. 46–59.

400 For example, the: Akhil Reed Amar and Alan Hirsch, *For The People: What The Constitution Really Says About Your Rights* (New York: Free Press, 1998), p. 170.

400 Some scholars who: For a thoughtful discussion of the Second Amendment, see Daniel Lazare, "Your Constitution Is Killing You," *Harper's* (October 1999), p. 57.

400 When James Madison: Helen E. Veit, Kenneth R. Bowling, and Charlene Bangs Bickford, editors, *Creating the Bill of Rights: The Documentary Record from the First Federal Congress* (Baltimore: Johns Hopkins University Press, 1992), p. 12.

401 The confusing language: *New York Times* columnist William Safire recommended that a constitutional amendment be introduced in Congress to repeal the "ambiguous preamble" of the Second Amendment. Then the country, in his view, could have a serious debate and decide once and for all whether the Amendment gives the right to possess weapons only to organized militias or to individuals. He argues that the Amendment cannot do both. William Safire, "An Appeal for Repeal," *New York Times* (June 10, 1999), p. A31.

402 The background checks: Fox Butterfield, "Instant Checks on Gun Buyers Has Halted 100,000 of Them," *New York Times* (September 9, 1999), p. A19. It was important that a computerized national system of background checks be in place because in June of 1997, the Supreme Court, in a 5-4 decision, overturned the portion of the 1993 Brady law that required state officials to conduct background checks on prospective handgun purchasers. The Court found that the law violated "the very principle of separate state sovereignty." Linda Greenhouse, "Justices Limit Brady Gun Law as Intrusion on States' Rights," *New York Times* (June 28, 1997), p. A1. The potential negative impact of the Court's Brady decision was limited because as of November 30, 1998, gun dealers were required to check the names of prospective gun buyers through a computerized list of names provided by the FBI. Lizette Alvarez, "Lawmakers See Minor Defeat Over Checks of Gun Buyers," *New York Times* (June 28, 1997), p. A1.

403 Although the Second: Reed and Hirsch, p. 170.

404 There may be: See Levinson, p. 657.

404 There is also: Robert Jay Lifton, "The Psyche of a 'Gunocracy,'" *Newsweek* (August 23, 1999), p. 49. Lifton is Distinguished Professor of Psychiatry and Psychology at John Jay College of the City University of New York. Historian Michael Bellesiles has done research showing that from the Revolution to about 1850, no more than a tenth of the population owned guns. *Newsweek* editorial, p. 24. See also, Tamar Lewin, "Experts Note Access to Guns and Lack of Ties to Adults," *New York Times* (March 26, 1998), p. A21.

405 December 6, 1999: Jim Yardley, "Boy Shoots 5 Schoolmates in Oklahoma," *New York Times* (December 7, 1999), p. A15. See also, "Watching for Warning Signs," *Newsweek* (December 20, 1999), p. 39.

405 November 2, 1999: "Seven People Killed In a Honolulu Office," *New York Times* (November 3, 1999), p. A1.

405 August 10, 1999: The remainder of this list comes from a special report in *Newsweek*. See "In the Line of Fire," *Newsweek* (August 23, 1999), p. 18.

405 He later killed: Ibid., p. 25.

406 Among the weapons: See generally, Sam Howe Verhover, "2 Youths Wanted to 'Destroy the School,'" Sheriff Says," *New York Times* (April 23, 1999), p. A1. In December 1999, the sheriff's department released a videotape made by Harris and Klebold in which they said they hoped to kill 250 people, yet were sympathetic to their parents for what they would endure as result of their actions. Michael Janofsky, "Student Killers' Tapes Filled With Rage," *New York Times* (December 14, 1999), p. A19.

406 But it will: Amar and Hirsch argue that reasonable gun regulations are permissible. Allowing anyone to purchase any kind of weapon — such as a machine gun or a handgun that can be concealed — would, in their view, itself threaten the "security of a free state." But they argue that confiscating all guns from the people would clearly violate the Constitution, pp. 178–179.

407 The Bill of: *Barron v. Baltimore*, 32 U.S. 243 (1833).

407 Until 1925, if: *Gitlow v. New York*, 268 U.S. 652 (1925).

407 State prosecutors could: *Mapp v. Ohio*, 367 U.S. 643 (1961).

407 But until 1963: *Gideon v. Wainwright*, 372 U.S. 335 (1963).

407 It was 1972: *Argersinger v. Hamlin*, 407 U.S. 25 (1972).

407 Beginning with *Chicago*: *Chicago, Burlington & Quincy Railroad v. Chicago*, 166 U.S. 226 (1897).

408 The first time: *United States v. Cruikshank*, 92 U.S. 542 (1875).

408 The Court confirmed: *Presser v. Illinois*, 116 U.S. 252, 267 (1886).

408 The law was: A group of Chicago socialists had formed an armed club to protect workers against police and military assaults, as well as against physical intimidation at the polls. There was frequent violence against workers trying to form unions. Socialist leaders were arrested. Workers were determined not to be subject to such violence without resistance. Levinson, p. 652, note 78.

408 When the Supreme: *Quilici v. Village of Morton Grove*, cert. denied, 464 U.S. 863 (1983).

408 In that case: *Quilici v. Village of Morton Grove*, 695 F.2d 261 (7th Cir. 1982).

408 *United States v. Miller*: *United States v. Miller*, 307 U.S. 174 (1939).

409 The Court held: Ibid., p. 178.

409 The Court's language: See Levinson, p. 654.

409 The judge dismissed: *U.S. v. Emerson*, 46 F. Supp.2d 598 (N.D.Tex.). See also, "Judge's Decision Sets Precedent That May Imperil Curb on Guns," *New York Times* (April 3, 1999), p. A10.

409 Few organizations strike: Other groups are equally aggressive about opposing gun measures, but they lack the NRA's huge membership and financial resources. See Frank Bruni, "Speaking Up for Guns, Lots of Them, for Nearly Anyone," *New York Times* (April 26, 1999), p. A14. Larry Pratt, executive director of the Gun Owners of America, believes there should be no regulations governing the sale or purchase of handguns, including no waiting period, no background checks, and no trigger locks. According to Pratt, automatic weapons should be as available as hunting rifles. Pratt maintains that if the teachers or the principal at Columbine had quick access to guns, some lives might have been saved. See also, Michael Janofsky, "Shooting-Sports Group Is Thrust Into an N.R.A. Realm," *New York Times* (January 22, 2000), p. A7. See also, Michael Janofsky, "Gun Producers, Under Assault, Turn to Politics," *New York Times* (January 19, 2000), p. A1.

410 He recalled the: James Dao and Don Van Natta Jr., "N.R.A., Thriving Under Attacks, Mobilizes to Fight New Gun Curbs," *New York Times* (June 12, 1999), p. A10. In criticizing the NRA's efforts to punish Pryor, author and columnist Anna Quindlen called his bill a "clear violation of the constitutional right to be unbelievably stupid." Anna Quindlen, "The Widows and the Wounded: Americans believe in gun control. It's time for them to act as if they do," *Newsweek* (November 1, 1999), p. 98.

410 The well-known actor: Katharine Q. Seelye, "Heston Asserts Gun Ownership Is Nation's Highest Right," *New York Times* (September 12, 1997), p. A12.

410 A constitutional law: Ibid.

410 One month after: Ibid. Although the NRA admitted that it had lost members during this period, it claimed that its membership was returning to its 1993 peak of 3 million.

410 In the November: Michael Wines, "As Key Allies of Gun Lobby Lose, Questions Arise About Its Power," *New York Times* (Dec. 24, 1996), p. A1.

411 The NRA increased: Ibid.

411 When the House: Ibid.

412 But instead of: Dan Barry, "Widow of Rail Shooting Victim Defeats Incumbent in Emotional Contest on L.I.," *New York Times* (November 6, 1996), p. B15. See also, Dan Barry, "In a Blaze of Attention, McCarthy Joins Congress," *New York Times* (January 8, 1997), p. B6.

412 She also broadened: John Rather, "Clinton Tide on L.I. Misses Incumbents," *New York Times* (November 10, 1996), p. 1.

412 Ignoring Republican advisers: Barry, November 6, 1996.

412 In April 1998: John M. Broder, "Clinton to Impose a Ban on 58 Types of Imported Guns," *New York Times* (April 6, 1998), p. A1.

412 The president made: In the Jonesboro shooting, the assailants used handguns and hunting rifles that would not be subject to the ban on assault weapons.

413 The Bush Administration: John M. Broder, "Clinton to Impose a Ban on 58 Types of Imported Guns," p. A17. For a thoughtful discussion of the proposed ban, see Lucian K. Truscott 4th, "A 'Right' to Bear 50 Assault Weapons," *New York Times* (commentary) (April 7, 1998), p. A27. In December 1999, the Clinton Administration announced that it was increasing the budget for the development of a national database of shell casings and bullets. The database would contain the unique "fingerprint" that a bullet or casing leaves when fired. That would help law enforcement officials to solve crimes when the only evidence are shell casings left at a crime scene. Fox Butterfield, "U.S. to Develop a System For "Fingerprinting Guns," *New York Times* (December 20, 1999), p. A17.

413 Tanya Metaksa, the: John M. Broder, "Clinton to Impose a Ban on 58 Types of Imported Guns."

413 And Metaksa added: Ibid.

413 California is among: Todd S. Purdum, "California Enacts The Toughest Ban On Assault Guns," *New York Times* (July 20, 1999), p. A1.

413 California joined three: Barry Meier, "California Measure Would Limit Handgun Buyers to One a Month," *New York Times* (July 2, 1999), p. A1.

413 The organization gave: Katharine Q. Seelye, "National Rifle Association Is Turning to World Stage to Fight Gun Control," *New York Times* (April 2, 1997), p. A12. See also, James Brooke, "Canada Split As Gun Laws Are Tightened," *New York Times* (December 7, 1999), p. A9.

414 In his 1996: Jack Anderson, *Inside the NRA: Armed and Dangerous* (Beverly Hills, CA: Dove Books, 1996), p. 101–102.

414 President Clinton, speaking: The NRA provides money for the states to sponsor such events as "Take a Kid Pheasant Hunting Day" in New Jersey. The state supplied the game wardens and the land, while the NRA provided the birds and the shotgun shells. Andrew C. Revkin, "Gun Lobby Helps States Train Young Hunters," *New York Times* (November 17, 1999), p. A1.

414 The FBI estimates: Seelye, p. A12.

414 More than a: "Guns in America: What Must Be Done," *Newsweek* (editorial) (August 23, 1999), p. 24.

415 The *Journal of*: Seelye, p. A12.

415 It is estimated: Ibid.

415 According to a: The poll was conducted by Princeton Research Associates, who queried 753 adults by telephone August 12–13, 1999. The margin of error was plus or minus four percentage points. *Newsweek*'s editors recommend the following measures in their August 23, 1999, issue on guns: 1) require background checks on all sales and transfers; 2) enforce what is on the books; 3) ban assault weapons for real; and 4) license owners and register all guns. Ibid., p. 25.

415 There is even: *Newsweek* (August 23, 1999), p. 31.

415 Sixty-eight percent: Ibid., p. 33.

415 Only 18 percent: Ibid., p. 28.

415 *Newsweek* found through: Ibid.

416 A detailed report: Fox Butterfield, "Limits on Power and Zeal Hamper Firearms Agency," *New York Times* (July 22, 1999), p. A1. See also, Fox Butterfield, "Firearms Agency Intensifies Scrutiny of Suspect Dealers: Rifle Association Dismisses Effort as a Stunt," *New York Times* (February 4, 2000), p. A12.

416 After the tragedy: Frank Bruni, "Littleton Students Listen to Gun Debate, Wondering if They Have Been Heard," *New York Times* (July 15, 1999), p. A16. Just finding out what a representative's position is on gun control is difficult. Some cast yes votes for different measures that are clearly contradictory. Such a strategy provides a member of Congress with the chance to talk about different bills to different groups within the district or state. See James Dao, "Congressman's Gun Votes: Consistency or Calculation?" *New York Times* (June 21, 1999), p. A15.

417 They reminded their: In a tragic footnote to the Columbine shooting, the mother of a 17-year old student who had been shot and partially paralyzed in the rampage at the school walked into a pawn shop, asked to see a gun, loaded it with bullets she had brought with her, and killed herself. "Mother of Injured Columbine Students Kills Herself," *New York Times* (Associated Press) (October 23, 1999), p. A11. For a report on how the Columbine shooting has created hostility among some of the victims' families, see Michael Janofsky, "Far Beyond Columbine, Rancor and Tension," *New York Times* (October 4, 1999), p. A12. See also, Michael Janofsky, "A Columbine Student Is Seized in a Threat to 'Finish the Job,'" *New York Times* (October 22, 1999), p. A20. Some members of Congress, such as Senator Gordon Smith (R-Oregon), who have received the financial support of the NRA, were reconsidering their opposition to gun control measures in the wake of the killings. See Robin Toner, "Earlier School Shooting Makes Senator Rethink Guns," *New York Times* (May 17, 1999), p. A12.

417 Checks began flowing: James Dao and Don Van Natta Jr., "N.R.A., Thriving Under Attacks, Mobilizes to Fight New Gun Curbs," *New York Times* (June 12, 1999), p. A1.

417 The executive vice: *Newsweek* (August 23, 1999), p. 30.

417 He believes the: Ibid., p. 31.

418 In his 1998: John R. Lott, Jr., *More Guns, Less Crime* (Chicago: University of Chicago Press, 1998).

418 Not suprisingly, the: Christopher Shea, "'More Guns, Less Crime,': A Scholar's Thesis Inflames Debate Over Weapons Control," *The Chronicle of Higher Education* (June 5, 1998), p. A14.

418 They argued that: Ibid.

418 A statistician who: Ibid.

419 Some American cities: For a comprehensive look at how cities are trying to prove that gun manufacturers are liable for the costs related to crimes committed with the weapons they make, see Barry Meier, "Cities Turn to U.S. Gun-Tracing Data for Legal Assault on Industry," *New York Times* (July 23, 1999), p. A12. New York Attorney General Eliot Spitzer also threatened to sue the industry if he could not reach an agreement with them on the way they trace distribution of their guns. Barry Meier, "A Gun Accord in New York Could Set U.S. Standard," *New York Times* (July 22, 1999), p. A17. See also, Elizabeth Mehren, "Conn.

Police get broader power to take guns; critics decry law," *Lexington (KY) Herald-Leader* (Los Angeles Times) (October 2, 1999), p. A8; and Michael Janofsky, "Philadelphia Takes Action Against Gun Violence," *New York Times* (May 20, 1998), p. A12.

419 As of September: Newsletter of Handgun Control (a public interest organization in Washington, D.C.) (Fall 1999), p. 6.

419 When Texas passed: "Bush Signs Bill Banning Anti-Gun Lawsuits," *New York Times* (June 19, 1999), p. A11.

419 On October 7: "Cincinnati to appeal dismissal of suit against firearms-makers," *Lexington (KY) Herald Leader* (Associated Press) (October 15, 1999), p. B7. See also, Fox Butterfield, "Judge Dismisses Cincinnati's Suit on Firearms," *New York Times* (October 8, 1999), p. A12.

419 On September 29: "California Appellate Court Allows Gun Maker to Be Sued," *New York Times* (Associated Press) (September 30, 1999), p. A22.

419 The ruling is: Ibid.

419 The California court's: Fox Butterfield, "Major Gun Makers Talk With Cities On Settling Suits," *New York Times* (October 2, 1999), p. A1.

420 Some families have: Fox Butterfield, "Judges Allows 3 Families To Sue Firearms Industry," *New York Times* (December 6, 1999), p. A16.

420 In October 1999: Mike Allen, "Colt's to Curtail Sale of Handguns," *New York Times* (October 11, 1999), p. A1.

420 In what may: David Stout and Richard Perez-Pena, "U.S. Uses Threat of a Lawsuit As a Lever for a Deal on Guns," *New York Times* (December 8, 1999), p. A1. See also, "New Pressure on Gun Makers," (editorial) *New York Times* (December 8, 1999), p. A30.

420 The Clinton Administration: Matt Bai, "The Feds Fire a Round," *Newsweek* (December 20, 1999), p. 38.

420 Texas Governor George: David Stout, "Bush, Usually Opponent of Gun Control, Backs 2 Restrictions Proposed in Congress," *New York Times* (August 28, 1999), p. A8.

421 In Illinois, first-term: Michael Janofsky, "Many G.O.P. Governors Now Pushing for Greater Gun Control," *New York Times* (September 4, 1999), p. A7. After the Illinois Supreme Court struck down the law making it a felony to carry a concealed weapon, Governor Ryan called the legislature into special session to fix the problems in the law identified by the court. However, Republican leaders in the Senate were fighting the enactment of a revised law. Dirk Johnson, "Republicans in Illinois Feud Over Gun Control," *New York Times* (December 29, 1999), p. A14. As state legislatures convened in January 2000, many bills related to gun ownership and registration were introduced. In some states, such as California, Democrats who control both houses of the legislature want to add to the tough restrictions they passed the year before. Michael Janofsky, "Concerns About Guns Put Pressure on State Legislators," *New York Times* (January 5, 2000), p. A12.

421 Although the NRA: James Dao and Don Van Natta Jr., "N.R.A., Thriving Under Attacks, Mobilizes to Fight New Gun Curbs," *New York Times* (June 12, 1999), p. A1. See also, Andrew Bluth, "Missouri Voters Reject Plan to Permit Concealed Weapons," *New York Times* (April 8, 1999), p. A20. The proposal to allow concealed weapons was approved in all but 12 of the state's 116 counties, but voters in St. Louis and Kansas City overwhelmingly defeated it.

421 In October of: David Kocieniewski, "Whitman Signs Bills Requiring Trigger Locks on Handguns," *New York Times* (October 13, 1999), p. A22.

421 Despite strong public: Frank Bruni, "Stalemate on Gun Shows Makes New Law Unlikely Before Recess, Armey Says," *New York Times* (August 4, 1999), p. A10.

422 On June 18, 1999: Frank Bruni and James Dao, "Gun-Control Bill Rejected in House in Bipartisan Vote," *New York Times* (June 19, 1999), p. A1.

422 The House then: Ibid., p. A11. See also, James Dao, "Michigan Lawmaker's Agenda Highlights a Split," *New York Times* (June 18, 1999), p. A24.

Chapter 15: If A Second Convention Is Never Held

423 Almost from the: Thomas Jefferson said in 1816 that we should not treat the Constitution "like the ark of the covenant, too sacred to be touched." Kathleen M. Sullivan, "What's Wrong With Constitutional Amendments," in Alan Brinkley, Nelson W. Polsby, and Kathleen M. Sullivan, *New Federalist Papers: Essays in Defense of the Constitution* (New York: W.W. Norton, 1997), p. 63.

424 Now based at: The group's Web site is found at: <www.citcon.org>.

424 On May 13, 1999: Letter dated October 29, 1999, from Virginia E. Sloan, the executive director of Citizens for the Constitution. At the end of 1999, Edwards was the John Quincy Adams Lecturer in Legislative Politics at the John F. Kennedy School of Government at Harvard University. Mikva was a Distinguished Visiting Professor of Law at the University of Illinois College of Law. Citizens for the Constitution has an affiliated group, Citizens for Independent Courts, that argues for protecting judicial autonomy from interference by the elected branches of government. The Web site is: <www.faircourts.org>.

424 "They believed that: From the preface of "Great and Extraordinary Occasions" Web page, <www.citcon.org>, Citizens for the Constitution.

424 The preface in: The Madison quote was in reference to Jefferson's suggestion that whenever two of the three branches of government believe it to be necessary, a constitutional convention should be called. Jefferson worried about one of the branches becoming weaker in the face of "invasion" by one of the others. He argued that only the people are able to decide, through a convention to alter the Constitution, what the relative powers of the branches should be. This was

Madison's response: "There is certainly great force in this reasoning, and it must be allowed to prove that a constitutional road to the decision of the people ought to be marked out and kept open, for certain great and extraordinary occasions." But Madison was not arguing that the Constitution should not be amended, and the way the Citizens for the Constitution uses the Madison quote from *Federalist* No. 49 is somewhat out of context.

424 The organization warned: From Preface, Citizens for the Constitution Web site. See also, Richard B. Bernstein, *Amending America: If We Love the Constitution So Much, Why Do We Keep Trying to Change It?"* (Lawrence, KS: University Press of Kansas, 1993).

424 Among the group's: Ibid., Appendix B.

426 To support the: Quoting, Council of State Governments, *The Book of the States, 1998–1999* (Lexington, KY: Council of State Governments, 1998).

426 While the U.S.: Thomas Dye, *Politics in States and Communities* (Upper Saddle River, NJ: Prentice Hall, 1997), p. 29.

426 Almost every state: Ibid., p. 36. There have been over 230 state constitutional conventions. They are generally proposed by state legislatures, and the question of whether to hold one is often submitted to voters. The legislature usually decides how convention delegates are to be selected, how the convention is organized, and whether the convention will be limited to specific proposals or will even write a new constitution. Although voters almost always have the option of later voting to approve or reject the proposals from a convention, they are often hesitant to allow one to be called. The last state constitutional convention was in Georgia in 1982. Ibid., p. 37–38.

427 However, they added: Introduction, Citizens for the Constitution Web site, note 5.

428 Another way of: See generally, *Pruneyard Shopping Center v. Robins*, 447 U.S. 74 (1980).

429 Some amendments, such: The Amendment was enacted to overturn *Pollock v. Farmers Loan & Trust Co.*, 157 U.S. 429 (1895), which had invalidated a federal income tax.

429 In *Texas v. Johnson*: *Texas v. Johnson*, 491 U.S. 397 (1989), and *United States v. Eichman*, 496 U.S. 310 (1990).

430 Legal scholar Laurence: Laurence H. Tribe and Michael C. Dorf, *On Reading The Constitution* (Cambridge, MA: Harvard University Press, 1991), p. 26.

430 As Tribe put: Ibid.

430 That is largely: See generally John R. Vile, *A Companion to the United States Constitution and Its Amendments* (Westport, CT: Praeger, 1997), pp. 167–172.

431 Courts will have: Courts have long experience in deciding jurisdictional issues related to how much contact individuals or organizations must have with a state. See Chapter 3.

431 Because political speech: For an eloquent statement of this principle, see Justice Brennan's opinion for the Court in *New York Times v. Sullivan*, 376 U.S. 254 (1964).

432 The government may: Guideline Six, Citizens for the Constitution Web site.

433 The group believes: Ibid.

433 As Laurence Tribe: Tribe and Dorf, pp. 19–30.

433 The former means: Ibid., p. 20. (Emphasis in original.)

434 The first concerns: Guideline Seven, Citizens for the Constitution Web site.

435 Professor Kathleen M. Sullivan: Sullivan, in Brinkley, Polsby and Sullivan, p. 62.

437 Rather than look: See Chapter Eight for a discussion of the ERA.

437 During some periods: After the 12th Amendment providing for separate voting in the Electoral College for president and vice president was ratified in 1804, another amendment was not added until 61 years later when the 13th Amendment prohibiting slavery became part of the Constitution after the Civil War. A period of 43 years passed between the 15th Amendment prohibiting abridgment of the right to vote based on race in 1870, and the 16th Amendment in 1913 allowing the federal government to collect taxes on income.

438 If Vice President: For a discussion of the Agnew case, see Elizabeth Drew, *Washington Journal: The Events of 1974–1974* (New York: Random House, 1974).

438 Michael Stokes Paulsen: Michael Stokes Paulsen, "Someone Should Have Told Spiro Agnew," in William N. Eskridge, Jr., and Sanford Levinson, *Constitutional Stupidities, Constitutional Tragedies* (New York: New York University Press, 1998), p. 75. "Stupidities" listed by other authors include the decision to give each senator one vote; the Electoral College, including how deadlocks are resolved in the House; the time lag between a president's election and inauguration; the difficulty of adopting legislation; the difficulty of amending the Constitution; the assignment of voting rules to the states instead of Congress; the requirement that the president be a "natural born" citizen at least 35-years-old; the assurance of lifetime tenure for federal judges; and the housekeeping provisions of the Constitution which trivialize the document itself. Ibid., pp. 3–4.

438 Under Article I, Section: As discussed in Chapter Two, the Framers recognized that allowing the vice president to preside over the Senate violated the principle of separation of powers, but as Roger Sherman of Connecticut observed, if not given that responsibility, there would be nothing for the vice president to do.

439 He may have: Drew, p. 6.

440 In November 1999: John M. Broder, "Time Warner Says It Is Ending 'Soft Money' Gifts to Parties," *New York Times* (November 18, 1999), p. A21. For a commentary from a business executive who says corporate gifts to politicians are not voluntary, see Edward A. Kangas, "Soft Money and Hard Bargains," *New York Times* (October 22, 1999), p. A29.

441 A group that: For an excellent discussion of SLAPP suits, see Robert D. Richards, *Freedom's Voice: The Perilous Present and Uncertain Future of the First Amendment* (Washington, D. C: Brassey's, 1998), pp. 7–26; and George W. Pring and Penelope Canan, *SLAPPs: Getting Sued For Speaking Out* (Philadelphia, PA: Temple University Press, 1996).

443 All media organizations: In 1999, Walter Cronkite, the former CBS anchorman, called on every broadcaster to offer five minutes of substantive campaign coverage on each of 30 nights leading up to an election. As honorary co-chair of the Alliance for Better Campaigns, Cronkite said that broadcasters made a commitment to provide such coverage when Congress decided to give them, for free, spectrum space for digital television. He said "we simply have to take American democracy off the auction block, and this is a way of getting it done." Paige Albiniak, "Alliance pushes for airtime," *Broadcasting & Cable* (December 13, 1999), p. 20. See also, Larry J. Sabato, *Feeding Frenzy: How Attack Journalism Has Transformed American Politics* (New York: Free Press, 1991).

444 But their efforts: One person who did care enough was a remarkable woman whose commitment to campaign finance reform made headlines in 1999. At the age of 89, Doris Haddock, known as "Granny D," a great-grandmother of 11 children, walked across the United States to highlight her concern about the effect of money on politics and her desire for reform. She enjoyed enthusiastic support from people along the way who provided shelter and other amenities, and encouraged her to continue. Granny D received substantial news coverage, from both newspapers and broadcasters, as she continued her long journey. Despite her valiant efforts to call attention to her cause, there was no indication that her pilgrimage had any effect on either members of Congress who opposed reform, or the special interests that keep them in office. Frank Bruni, "89, and 2,000 Miles to Go for 'Democracy,'" *New York Times* (April 27, 1999), p. A16. By early January she had made it to West Virginia, and planned to arrive in Washington, D.C. on February 29.

Appendix

THE CONSTITUTION OF THE UNITED STATES

PREAMBLE

WE THE PEOPLE of the United States, in Order to form a more perfect Union, establish Justice, insure domestic Tranquility, provide for the common defence, promote the general Welfare, and secure the Blessings of Liberty to ourselves and our Posterity, do ordain and establish this Constitution for the United States of America.

Articles

ARTICLE ONE

Section 1. All legislative powers herein granted shall be vested in a Congress of the United States, which shall consist of a Senate and House of Representatives.

Section 2. The House of Representatives shall be composed of members chosen every second year by the people of the several States, and the electors in each State shall have the qualifications requisite for electors of the most numerous branch of the State legislature.

No Person shall be a Representative who shall not have attained to the age of twenty five years, and been seven years a citizen of the United States, and who shall not, when elected, be an inhabitant of that State in which he shall be chosen.

Representatives and direct taxes shall be apportioned among the several States which may be included within this Union, according to their respective numbers, which shall be determined by adding to the whole number of free persons, including those bound to service for a term of years, and excluding Indians not taxed, three fifths of all other persons. The actual enumeration shall be made within three years after the first meeting of the Congress of the United States, and within every subsequent term of ten years, in such manner as they shall by law direct. The number of Representatives shall not exceed one for every thirty thousand, but each State shall have at least one Representative; and until such enumeration shall be made, the State of New Hampshire shall be entitled to choose three, Massachusetts eight, Rhode Island and Providence Plantations one, Connecticut five, New York six, New Jersey four, Pennsylvania eight, Delaware one, Maryland six, Virginia ten, North Carolina five, South Carolina five and Georgia three.

When vacancies happen in the Representation from any State, the executive authority thereof shall issue writs of election to fill such vacancies.

The House of Representatives shall choose their Speaker and other officers; and shall have the sole power of Impeachment.

Section 3. The Senate of the United States shall be composed of two Senators from each State, chosen by the legislature thereof, for six years; and each Senator shall have one Vote.

Immediately after they shall be assembled in consequence of the first election, they shall be divided as equally as may be into three classes. The seats of the Senators of the first class shall be vacated at the expiration of the second year, of the second class at the expiration of the fourth year, and of the third class at the expiration of the sixth year, so that one third may be chosen every second year; and if vacancies happen by resignation, or otherwise, during the recess of the legislature of any State, the executive thereof may make temporary appointments until the next meeting of the legislature, which shall then fill such vacancies.

No person shall be a Senator who shall not have attained to the age of thirty years, and been nine years a citizen of the United States, and who shall not, when elected, be an inhabitant of that State for which he shall be chosen.

The Vice-President of the United States shall be President of the Senate, but shall have no vote, unless they be equally divided.

The Senate shall choose their other officers, and also a President pro tempore, in the absence of the Vice-President, or when he shall exercise the office of President of the United States.

The Senate shall have the sole power to try all impeachments. When sitting for that purpose, they shall be on oath or affirmation. When the President of the United States is tried, the Chief Justice shall preside: And no Person shall be convicted without the concurrence of two thirds of the members present.

Judgment in cases of impeachment shall not extend further than to removal from office, and disqualification to hold and enjoy any office of honor, trust or profit under the United States: but the party convicted shall nevertheless be liable and subject to indictment, trial, judgment and punishment, according to law.

Section 4. The times, places and manner of holding elections for Senators and Representatives, shall be prescribed in each State by the legislature thereof; but the Congress may at any time by law make or alter such regulations, except as to the places of choosing Senators.

The Congress shall assemble at least once in every year, and such meeting shall be on the first Monday in December, unless they shall by law appoint a different day.

Section 5. Each house shall be the judge of the elections, returns and qualifications of its own members, and a majority of each shall constitute a quorum to do business; but a smaller number may adjourn from day to day, and may be authorized to compel the attendance of absent members, in such manner, and under such penalties as each house may provide.

Each house may determine the rules of its proceedings, punish its members for disorderly behavior, and, with the concurrence of two-thirds, expel a member.

Each house shall keep a journal of its proceedings, and from time to time publish the same, excepting such parts as may in their judgment require secrecy; and the yeas and nays of the members of either house on any question shall, at the desire of one fifth of those present, be entered on the journal.

Neither house, during the session of Congress, shall, without the consent of the other, adjourn for more than three days, nor to any other place than that in which the two Houses shall be sitting.

Section 6. The Senators and Representatives shall receive a compensation for their services, to be ascertained by law, and paid out of the Treasury of the United States. They shall in all cases, except treason, felony and breach of the peace, be privileged from arrest during their attendance at the session of their respective houses, and in going to and returning from the same; and for any speech or debate in either house, they shall not be questioned in any other place.

No Senator or Representative shall, during the time for which he was elected, be appointed to any civil office under the authority of the United States which shall have been created, or the emoluments whereof shall have been increased during such time; and no person holding any office under the United States, shall be a member of either house during his continuance in office.

Section 7. All bills for raising revenue shall originate in the House of Representatives; but the Senate may propose or concur with amendments as on other bills.

Every bill which shall have passed the House of Representatives and the Senate, shall, before it become a law, be presented to the President of the United States; If he approve he shall sign it, but if not he shall return it, with his objections to that house in which it shall have originated, who shall enter the objections at large on their journal, and proceed to reconsider it. If after such reconsideration two thirds of that house shall agree to pass the bill, it shall be sent, together with the objections, to the other house, by which it shall likewise be reconsidered, and if approved by two thirds of that house, it shall become a law. But in all such cases the votes of both houses shall be determined by yeas and nays, and the names of the persons voting for and against the bill shall be entered on the journal of each house respectively. If any bill shall not be returned by the President within ten days (Sundays excepted) after it shall have been presented to him, the same shall be a law, in like manner as if he had signed it, unless the Congress by their adjournment prevent its return, in which case it shall not be a law.

Every order, resolution, or vote to which the concurrence of the Senate and House of Representatives may be necessary (except on a question of adjournment) shall be presented to the President of the United States; and before the same shall take effect, shall be approved by him, or being disapproved by him, shall be repassed by two thirds of the Senate and House of Representatives, according to the rules and limitations prescribed in the case of a bill.

Section 8. The Congress shall have power to lay and collect taxes, duties, imposts and excises, to pay the debts and provide for the common defence and general welfare of the United States; but all duties, imposts and excises shall be uniform throughout the United States;

To borrow money on the credit of the United States;

To regulate commerce with foreign nations, and among the several States, and with the Indian tribes;

To establish an uniform rule of naturalization, and uniform Laws on the subject of bankruptcies throughout the United States;

To coin money, regulate the value thereof, and of foreign coin, and fix the standard of weights and measures;

To provide for the punishment of counterfeiting the securities and current Coin of the United States;

To establish post-offices and post-roads;

To promote the progress of science and useful arts, by securing for limited times to authors and inventors the exclusive right to their respective writings and discoveries;

To constitute tribunals inferior to the Supreme Court;

To define and punish piracies and felonies committed on the high seas, and offenses against the law of nations;

To declare war, grant letters of marque and reprisal, and make rules concerning captures on land and water;

To raise and support armies, but no appropriation of money to that use shall be for a longer term than two years;

To provide and maintain a navy;

To make rules for the government and regulation of the land and naval forces;

To provide for calling forth the militia to execute the laws of the union, suppress insurrections and repel invasions;

To provide for organizing, arming, and disciplining, the militia, and for governing such part of them as may be employed in the service of the United States, reserving to the States respectively, the appointment of the officers, and the authority of training the militia according to the discipline prescribed by Congress;

To exercise exclusive legislation in all cases whatsoever, over such district (not exceeding ten miles square) as may, by cession of particular States, and the acceptance of Congress, become the seat of the Government of the United States, and to exercise like authority over all places purchased by the consent of the legislature of the State in which the same shall be, for the erection of forts, magazines, arsenals, dockyards, and other needful Buildings; and

To make all laws which shall be necessary and proper for carrying into execution the foregoing powers, and all other powers vested by this Constitution in the Government of the United States, or in any department or officer thereof.

Section 9. The migration or importation of such persons as any of the States now existing shall think proper to admit, shall not be prohibited by the Congress prior to the Year one thousand eight hundred and eight, but a tax or duty may be imposed on such importation, not exceeding ten dollars for each person.

The privilege of the writ of habeas corpus shall not be suspended, unless when in cases of rebellion or invasion the public safety may require it.

No bill of attainder or ex post facto law shall be passed.

No capitation, or other direct tax shall be laid, unless in proportion to the census or enumeration herein before directed to be taken.

No tax or duty shall be laid on articles exported from any State.

No preference shall be given by any regulation of commerce or revenue to the ports of one State over those of another: nor shall vessels bound to, or from, one State, be obliged to enter, clear, or pay duties in another.

No money shall be drawn from the Treasury, but in consequence of appropriations made by law; and a regular statement and account of the receipts and expenditures of all public money shall be published from time to time.

No title of nobility shall be granted by the United States; and no person holding any office of profit or trust under them, shall, without the consent of the Congress, accept of any present, emolument, office, or title, of any kind whatever, from any king, prince or foreign State.

Section 10. No State shall enter into any treaty, alliance, or confederation; grant letters of marque and reprisal; coin money; emit bills of credit; make anything but gold and silver coin a tender in payment of debts; pass any bill of attainder, ex post facto law, or law impairing the obligation of contracts, or grant any title of nobility.

No State shall, without the consent of the Congress, lay any imposts or duties on imports or exports, except what may be absolutely necessary for executing it's inspection laws: and the net produce of all duties and imposts, laid by any State on imports or exports, shall be for the use of the Treasury of the United States; and all such laws shall be subject to the revision and control of the Congress.

No State shall, without the consent of Congress, lay any duty of tonnage, keep troops, or ships of war in time of peace, enter into any agreement or compact with another State, or with a foreign power, or engage in war, unless actually invaded, or in such imminent danger as will not admit of delay.

ARTICLE TWO

Section 1. The executive power shall be vested in a President of the United States of America. He shall hold his office during the term of four years, and, together with the Vice-President chosen for the same term, be elected, as follows:

Each State shall appoint, in such manner as the legislature thereof may direct, a number of electors, equal to the whole number of Senators and Representatives to which the State may be entitled in the Congress: but no Senator or Representative, or person holding an office of trust or profit under the United States, shall be appointed an elector.

The electors shall meet in their respective States, and vote by ballot for two persons, of whom one at least shall not lie an inhabitant of the same State with themselves. And they shall make a list of all the persons voted for, and of the number of votes for each; which list they shall sign and certify, and transmit sealed to the seat of the government of the United States, directed to the President of the Senate. The President of the Senate shall, in the presence of the Senate and House of Representatives, open all the certificates, and the votes shall then be counted. The person having the greatest number of votes shall be the President, if such number be a majority of the whole number of electors appointed; and if there be more than one who have such majority, and have an equal number of votes, then the House of Representatives shall immediately choose by ballot one of them for President; and if no person have a majority, then from the five highest on the list the said House shall in like manner choose the President. But in choosing the President, the votes shall be taken by States, the representation from each State having one vote; a quorum for this purpose shall consist of a member or members from two thirds of the States, and a majority of all the States shall be necessary to a choice. In every case, after the choice of the President, the person having the greatest number of votes of the electors shall be the Vice-President. But if there should remain two or more who have equal votes, the Senate shall choose from them by ballot the Vice-President.

The Congress may determine the time of choosing the electors, and the day on which they shall give their votes; which day shall be the same throughout the United States.

No person except a natural born citizen, or a citizen of the United States, at the time of the adoption of this Constitution, shall be eligible to the office of President; neither shall any person be eligible to that office who shall not have attained to the age of thirty five years, and been fourteen years a resident within the United States.

In case of the removal of the President from office, or of his death, resignation, or inability to discharge the powers and duties of the said office, the same shall devolve on the Vice-President, and the Congress may by law provide for the case of removal, death, resignation or inability, both of the President and Vice-President, declaring what officer shall then act as President, and such officer shall act accordingly, until the disability be removed, or a President shall be elected.

The President shall, at stated times, receive for his services, a compensation, which shall neither be increased nor diminished during the period for which he shall have been elected, and he shall not receive within that period any other emolument from the United States, or any of them.

Before he enter on the execution of his office, he shall take the following oath or affirmation:

"I do solemnly swear (or affirm) that I will faithfully execute the office of President of the United States, and will to the best of my ability, preserve, protect and defend the Constitution of the United States."

Section 2. The President shall be Commander-in-Chief of the Army and Navy of the United States, and of the militia of the several States, when called into the actual service of the United States; he may require the opinion, in writing, of the principal officer in each of the executive departments, upon any subject relating to the duties of their respective offices, and he shall have power to grant reprieves and pardons for offenses against the United States, except in cases of impeachment.

He shall have power, by and with the advice and consent of the Senate, to make treaties, provided two thirds of the Senators present concur; and he shall nominate, and by and with the advice and consent of the Senate, shall appoint ambassadors, other public ministers and consuls, judges of the Supreme Court, and all other officers of the United States, whose appointments are not herein otherwise provided for, and which shall be established by law: but the Congress may by law vest the appointment of such inferior officers, as they think proper, in the President alone, in the courts of law, or in the heads of departments.

The President shall have power to fill up all vacancies that may happen during the recess of the Senate, by granting commissions which shall expire at the end of their next session.

Section 3. He shall from time to time give to the Congress information of the State of the Union, and recommend to their consideration such measures as he shall judge necessary and expedient; he may, on extraordinary occasions, convene both houses, or either of them, and in case of disagreement between them, with respect to the time of adjournment, he may adjourn them to such time as he shall think proper; he shall receive ambassadors and other public ministers; he shall take care that the laws be faithfully executed, and shall commission all the officers of the United States.

Section 4. The President, Vice-President and all civil officers of the United States, shall be removed from office on impeachment for, and conviction of, treason, bribery, or other high crimes and misdemeanors.

ARTICLE THREE

Section 1. The judicial power of the United States, shall be vested in one Supreme Court, and in such inferior courts as the Congress may from time to time ordain and establish. The judges, both of the supreme and inferior courts, shall hold their offices during good behavior, and shall, at stated times, receive for their services, a compensation, which shall not be diminished during their continuance in office.

Section 2. The judicial power shall extend to all cases, in law and equity, arising under this Constitution, the laws of the United States, and treaties made, or which shall be made, under their authority; to all cases affecting ambassadors, other public ministers and consuls; to all cases of admiralty and maritime jurisdiction; to controversies to which the United States shall be a party; to controversies between two or more States; between a State and citizens of another State; between citizens of different States; between citizens of the same State claiming lands under grants of different States, and between a State, or the citizens thereof, and foreign States, citizens or subjects.

In all cases affecting ambassadors, other public ministers and consuls, and those in which a State shall be party, the Supreme Court shall have original jurisdiction. In all the other cases before mentioned, the Supreme Court shall have appellate jurisdiction, both as to law and fact, with such exceptions, and under such regulations as the Congress shall make.

Trial of all crimes, except in cases of impeachment, shall be by jury; and such trial shall be held in the State where the said crimes shall have been committed; but when not committed within any State, the trial shall be at such place or places as the Congress may by law have directed.

Section 3. Treason against the United States, shall consist only in levying war against them, or in adhering to their enemies, giving them aid and comfort. No person shall be convicted of treason unless on the testimony of two witnesses to the same overt act, or on confession in open court.

The Congress shall have power to declare the punishment of treason, but no attainder of treason shall work corruption of blood, or forfeiture except during the life of the person attainted.

ARTICLE FOUR

Section 1. Full faith and credit shall be given in each State to the public acts, records, and judicial proceedings of every other State. And the Congress may by general laws prescribe the manner in which such acts, records and proceedings shall be proved, and the effect thereof.

Section 2. The citizens of each State shall be entitled to all privileges and immunities of citizens in the several States.

A person charged in any State with treason, felony, or other crime, who shall flee from justice, and be found in another State, shall on demand of the executive authority of the State from which he fled, be delivered up, to be removed to the State having jurisdiction of the crime.

No person held to service or labor in one State, under the laws thereof, escaping into another, shall, in consequence of any law or regulation therein, be discharged from such service or labor, But shall be delivered up on claim of the party to whom such service or labor may be due.

Section 3. New States may be admitted by the Congress into this Union; but no new States shall be formed or erected within the jurisdiction of any other State; nor any State be formed by the junction of two or more States, or parts of States, without the consent of the legislatures of the States concerned as well as of the Congress.

The Congress shall have power to dispose of and make all needful rules and regulations respecting the territory or other property belonging to the United States; and nothing in this Constitution shall be so construed as to prejudice any claims of the United States, or of any particular State.

Section 4. The United States shall guarantee to every State in this Union a republican form of government, and shall protect each of them against invasion; and on application of the legislature, or of the executive (when the legislature cannot be convened) against domestic violence.

ARTICLE FIVE

The Congress, whenever two thirds of both houses shall deem it necessary, shall propose amendments to this Constitution, or, on the application of the Legislatures of two thirds of the several States, shall call a convention for proposing amendments, which, in either case, shall be valid to all intents and purposes, as part of this Constitution, when ratified by the Legislatures of three fourths of the several States, or by conventions in three fourths thereof, as the one or the other mode of ratification may be proposed by the Congress; provided that no amendment which may be made prior to the Year One thousand eight hundred and eight shall in any manner affect the first and fourth Clauses in the Ninth Section of the first Article; and that no State, without its consent, shall be deprived of it's equal suffrage in the Senate.

ARTICLE SIX

All debts contracted and engagements entered into, before the adoption of this Constitution, shall be as valid against the United States under this Constitution, as under the Confederation.

This Constitution, and the laws of the United States which shall be made in pursuance thereof; and all treaties made, or which shall be made, under the authority of the United States, shall be the supreme law of the land; and the judges in every State shall be bound thereby, anything in the Constitution or laws of any State to the contrary notwithstanding.

The Senators and Representatives before mentioned, and the members of the several State Legislatures, and all executive and judicial officers, both of the United States and of the several States, shall be bound by oath or affirmation, to support this Constitution; but no religious test shall ever be required as a qualification to any office or public trust under the United States

ARTICLE SEVEN

The ratification of the Conventions of nine States, shall be sufficient for the establishment of this Constitution between the States so ratifying the same.

AMENDMENTS

AMENDMENT ONE

Congress shall make no law respecting an establishment of religion, or prohibiting the free exercise thereof; or abridging the freedom of speech, or of the press; or the right of the people peaceably to assemble, and to petition the government for a redress of grievances.

AMENDMENT TWO

A well regulated militia, being necessary to the security of a free State, the right of the people to keep and bear arms, shall not be infringed.

AMENDMENT THREE

No soldier shall, in time of peace be quartered in any house, without the consent of the owner, nor in time of war, but in a manner to be prescribed by law.

AMENDMENT FOUR

The right of the people to be secure in their persons, houses, papers, and effects, against unreasonable searches and seizures, shall not be violated, and no warrants shall issue, but upon probable cause, supported by Oath or affirmation, and particularly describing the place to be searched, and the persons or things to be seized.

AMENDMENT FIVE

No person shall be held to answer for a capital, or otherwise infamous crime, unless on a presentment or indictment of a Grand Jury, except in cases arising in the land or naval forces, or in the militia, when in actual service in time of war or public danger; nor shall any person be subject for the same offence to be twice put in jeopardy of life or limb; nor shall be compelled in any criminal case to be a witness against himself, nor be deprived of life, liberty, or property, without due process of law; nor shall private property be taken for public use, without just compensation.

AMENDMENT SIX

In all criminal prosecutions, the accused shall enjoy the right to a speedy and public trial, by an impartial jury of the State and district wherein the crime shall have been committed, which district shall have been previously ascertained by law, and to be informed of the nature and cause of the accusation; to be confronted with the witnesses against him; to have compulsory process for obtaining witnesses in his favor, and to have the assistance of counsel for his defence.

AMENDMENT SEVEN

In suits at common law, where the value in controversy shall exceed twenty dollars, the right of trial by jury shall be preserved, and no fact tried by a jury, shall be otherwise re-examined in any court of the United States, than according to the rules of the common law.

AMENDMENT EIGHT

Excessive bail shall not lie required, nor excessive fines imposed, nor cruel and unusual punishments inflicted.

AMENDMENT NINE

The enumeration in the Constitution, of certain rights, shall not be construed to deny or disparage others retained by the people.

AMENDMENT TEN

The powers not delegated to the United States by the Constitution, nor prohibited by it to the States, are reserved to the States respectively, or to the people.

AMENDMENT ELEVEN

January 8, 1798
The judicial power of the United States shall not be construed to extend to any suit in law or equity, commenced or prosecuted against one of the United States by Citizens of another State, or by citizens or subjects of any foreign State.

AMENDMENT TWELVE

September 25, 1804
The electors shall meet in their respective States, and vote by ballot for President and Vice-President, one of whom, at least, shall not be an inhabitant of the same State with themselves; they shall name in their ballots the person voted for as President, and in distinct ballots the person voted for as Vice-President, and they shall make distinct lists of all persons voted for as President, and of all persons voted for as Vice-President and of the number of votes for each, which lists they shall sign and certify, and transmit sealed to the seat of the Government of the United States, directed to the President of the Senate; The President of the Senate shall, in the presence of the Senate and House of Representatives, open all the certificates and the votes shall then be counted; the person having the greatest number of votes for President, shall be the President, if such number be a majority of the whole number of Electors appointed; and if no person have such majority, then from the persons having the highest numbers not exceeding three on the list of those voted for as President, the House of Representatives shall choose immediately, by ballot, the President. But in choosing the President, the votes shall be taken by States, the representation from each State having one vote; a quorum for this purpose shall consist of a member or members from two-thirds of the States, and a majority of all the States shall be necessary to a choice. And if the House of Representatives shall not choose a President whenever the right of choice shall devolve upon them, before the fourth day of March next following, then the Vice-President shall act as President, as in the case of the death or other

constitutional disability of the President. The person having the greatest number of votes as Vice-President, shall be the Vice-President, if such number be a majority of the whole number of Electors appointed, and if no person have a majority, then from the two highest numbers on the list, the Senate shall choose the Vice-President; a quorum for the purpose shall consist of two-thirds of the whole number of Senators, and a majority of the whole number shall be necessary to a choice. But no person constitutionally ineligible to the office of President shall be eligible to that of Vice-President of the United States.

AMENDMENT THIRTEEN

December 18, 1865

Section 1. Neither slavery nor involuntary servitude, except as a punishment for crime whereof the party shall have been duly convicted, shall exist within the United States, or any place subject to their jurisdiction.

Section 2. Congress shall have power to enforce this AMENDMENT by appropriate legislation.

AMENDMENT FOURTEEN

July 28, 1868

Section 1. All persons born or naturalized in the United States, and subject to the jurisdiction thereof, are citizens of the United States and of the State wherein they reside. No State shall make or enforce any law which shall abridge the privileges or immunities of citizens of the United States; nor shall any State deprive any person of life, liberty, or property, without due process of law; nor deny to any person within its jurisdiction the equal protection of the laws.

Section 2. Representatives shall be apportioned among the several States according to their respective numbers, counting the whole number of persons in each State, excluding Indians not taxed. But when the right to vote at any election for the choice of Electors for President and Vice-President of the United States, Representatives in Congress, the executive and judicial officers of a State, or the members of the Legislature thereof, is denied to any of the male inhabitants of such State, being twenty-one years of age, and citizens of the United States, or in any way abridged, except for participation in rebellion, or other crime, the basis of representation therein shall be reduced in the proportion which the number of such male citizens shall bear to the whole number of male citizens twenty-one years of age in such State.

Section 3. No person shall be a Senator or Representative in Congress, or elector of President and Vice-President, or hold any office, civil or military, under the United States, or under any State, who, having previously taken an oath, as a member of Congress, or as an officer of the United States, or as a member of any State legislature, or as an executive or judicial officer of any State, to support the Constitution of the United States, shall have engaged in insurrection or rebellion against the same, or given aid or comfort to the enemies thereof. But Congress may by a vote of two-thirds of each House, remove such disability.

Section 4. The validity of the public debt of the United States, authorized by law, including debts incurred for payment of pensions and bounties for services in suppressing insurrection or rebellion, shall not be questioned. But neither the United States nor any State shall assume or pay any debt or obligation incurred in aid of insurrection or rebellion against the United States, or any claim for the loss or emancipation of any slave; but all such debts, obligations and claims shall be held illegal and void.

Section 5. The Congress shall have power to enforce, by appropriate legislation, the provisions of this AMENDMENT.

AMENDMENT FIFTEEN

March 30, 1870

Section 1. The right of citizens of the United States to vote shall not be denied or abridged by the United States or by any State on account of race, color, or previous condition of servitude.

Section 2. The Congress shall have power to enforce this AMENDMENT by appropriate legislation.

AMENDMENT SIXTEEN

February 25, 1913

The Congress shall have power to lay and collect taxes on incomes, from whatever source derived, without apportionment among the several States and without regard to any census or enumeration.

AMENDMENT SEVENTEEN

May 31, 1913

The Senate of the United States shall be composed of two senators from each State, elected by the people thereof, for six years; and each Senator shall have one vote. The electors in each State shall have the qualifications requisite for electors of the most numerous branch of the State legislature.

When vacancies happen in the representation of any State in the Senate, the executive authority of such State shall issue writs of election to fill such vacancies: Provided, That the legislature of any State may empower the executive thereof to make temporary appointments until the people fill the vacancies by election as the legislature may direct.

This amendment shall not be so construed as to affect the election or term of any senator chosen before it becomes valid as part of the Constitution.

AMENDMENT EIGHTEEN

January 29, 1919

Section 1. After one year from the ratification of this AMENDMENT, the manufacture, sale, or transportation of intoxicating liquors within, the importation thereof into, or the exportation thereof from the United States and all territory subject to the jurisdiction thereof for beverage purposes is hereby prohibited.

Section 2. The Congress and the several States shall have concurrent power to enforce this AMENDMENT by appropriate legislation.

Section 3. This AMENDMENT shall be inoperative unless it shall have been ratified as an amendment to the Constitution by the legislatures of the several States, as provided in the Constitution, within seven years from the date of the submission hereof to the States by Congress.

AMENDMENT NINETEEN

August 26, 1920

The right of citizens of the United States to vote shall not be denied or abridged by the United States or by any States on account of sex.

The Congress shall have power by appropriate legislation to enforce the provisions of this AMENDMENT.

AMENDMENT TWENTY

February 6, 1933

Section 1. The terms of the President and Vice-President shall end at noon on the twentieth day of January, and the terms of Senators and Representatives at noon on the third day of January, of the years in which such terms would have ended if this AMENDMENT had not been ratified; and the terms of their successors shall then begin.

Section 2. The Congress shall assemble at least once in every year, and such meeting shall begin at noon on the third day of January, unless they shall by law appoint a different day.

Section 3. If, at the time fixed for the beginning of the term of the President, the President-elect shall have died, the Vice-President-elect shall become President. If a President shall not have been chosen before the time fixed for the beginning of his term, or if the President-elect shall have failed to qualify, then the Vice-President-elect shall act as President until a President shall have qualified; and the Congress may by law provide for the case wherein neither a President-elect nor a Vice-President-elect shall have qualified, declaring who shall then act as President, or the manner in which one who is to act shall be selected, and such person shall act accordingly until a President or Vice-President shall have qualified.

Section 4. The Congress may by law provide for the case of the death of any of the persons from whom the House of Representatives may choose a President whenever the right of choice shall have devolved upon them, and for the case of the death of any of the persons from whom the Senate may choose a Vice-President whenever the right of choice shall have devolved upon them.

Section 5. Sections 1 and 2 shall take effect on the 15th day of October following the ratification of this AMENDMENT.

Section 6. This AMENDMENT shall be inoperative unless it shall have been ratified as an amendment to the Constitution by the legislatures of three-fourths of the several States within seven years from the date of its submission.

AMENDMENT TWENTY-ONE

December 5, 1933

Section 1. The eighteenth AMENDMENT of amendment to the Constitution of the United States is hereby repealed.

Section 2. The transportation or importation into any State, Territory, or possession of the United States for delivery or use therein of intoxicating liquors, in violation of the laws thereof, is hereby prohibited.

Section 3. The AMENDMENT shall be inoperative unless it shall have been ratified as an amendment to the Constitution by conventions in the several States, as provided in the Constitution, within seven years from the date of the submission hereof to the States by the Congress.

AMENDMENT TWENTY-TWO

February 26, 1951

Section 1. No person shall be elected to the office of the President more than twice, and no person who has held the office of President, or acted as President for more than two years of a term to which some other person was elected President shall be elected to the office of the President more than once. But this AMENDMENT shall not apply to any person holding the office of President when this AMENDMENT was proposed by the Congress, and shall not prevent any person who May be holding the office of President, or acting as President, during the term within which this AMENDMENT becomes operative from holding the office of President or acting as President during the remainder of such term.

Section 2. This AMENDMENT shall be inoperative unless it shall have been ratified as an amendment to the Constitution by the legislatures of three-fourths of the several States within seven years from the date of its submission to the States by the Congress.

AMENDMENT TWENTY-THREE

June 16, 1960

Section 1. The District constituting the seat of government of the United States shall appoint in such manner as the Congress may direct:

A number of electors of President and Vice-President equal to the whole number of Senators and Representatives in Congress to which the District would be entitled if it were a State, but in no event more than the least populous State; they shall be in addition to those appointed by the States, but they shall be considered, for the purposes of the election of President and Vice-President, to be electors appointed by a State; and they shall meet in the district and perform such duties as provided by the twelfth AMENDMENT of amendment.

Section 2. The Congress shall have power to enforce this AMENDMENT by appropriate legislation.

AMENDMENT TWENTY-FOUR

February 4, 1964

Section 1. The right of citizens of the United States to vote in any primary or other election for President or Vice-President, for electors for President or Vice-President, or for Senator or Representative in Congress, shall not be denied or abridged by the United States or any State by reason of failure to pay any poll tax or other tax.

Section 2. The Congress shall have power to enforce this AMENDMENT by appropriate legislation.

AMENDMENT TWENTY-FIVE

February 10, 1967

Section 1. In case of the removal of the President from office or of his death or resignation, the Vice-President shall become President.

Section 2. Whenever there is a vacancy in the office of the Vice-President, the President shall nominate a Vice-President who shall take office upon confirmation by a majority vote of both Houses of Congress.

Section 3. Whenever the President transmits to the President pro tempore of the Senate and the Speaker of the House of Representatives his written declaration that he is unable to discharge the powers and duties of his office, and until he transmits to them a written declaration to the contrary, such powers and duties shall be discharged by the Vice-President as Acting President.

Section 4. Whenever the Vice-President and a majority of either the principal officers of the executive departments or of such other body as Congress may by law provide, transmit to the President pro tempore of the Senate and the Speaker of the House of Representatives their written declaration that the President is unable to discharge the powers and duties of his office, the Vice-President shall immediately assume the powers and duties of the office as Acting President.

Thereafter, when the President transmits to the President pro tempore of the Senate and the Speaker of the House of Representatives his written declaration that no inability exists, he shall resume the powers and duties of his office unless the Vice-President and a majority of either the principal officers of the executive department or of such other body as Congress may by law provide, transmit within four day to the President pro tempore of the Senate and the Speaker of the House of Representatives their written declaration that the President is unable to discharge the powers and duties of his office. Thereupon Congress shall decide the issue, assembling within forty-eight hours for that purpose if not in session. If the Congress, within twenty-one days after receipt of the latter written declaration, or, if Congress is not in session, within twenty-one days after Congress is required to assemble, determines by two-thirds vote of both Houses that the President is unable to discharge the powers and duties of his office, the Vice-President shall continue to discharge the same as Acting President; otherwise, the President shall resume the powers and duties of his office.

AMENDMENT TWENTY-SIX

July 1, 1971

Section 1. The right of citizens of the United States, who are eighteen years of age or older, to vote shall not be denied or abridged by the United States or by any State on account of age.

Section 2. The Congress shall have power to enforce this AMENDMENT by appropriate legislation.

AMENDMENT TWENTY-SEVEN

May 8, 1992

No law, varying the compensation for the services of the Senators and Representatives, shall take effect, until an election of Representatives shall have intervened.

Index

About the Author

Richard Labunski is an associate professor in the School of Journalism and Telecommunications at the University of Kentucky where he teaches media law, the First Amendment and new technology, and broadcast journalism. He has a B.A. in political science from the University of California, Berkeley, and an M.A. and Ph.D. in political science from the University of California, Santa Barbara. His J.D. is from Seattle University School of Law. He is the author of two previous books, law review articles, and newspaper commentaries. He worked for ten years in radio and TV news and has been an expert witness in First Amendment cases.